# The Netherlands

written and researched by

## Martin Dunford, Jack Holland and Phil Lee

with additional contributions by
### Cass Gilbert and Laura Stone

ROUGH
GUIDES

www.roughguides.com

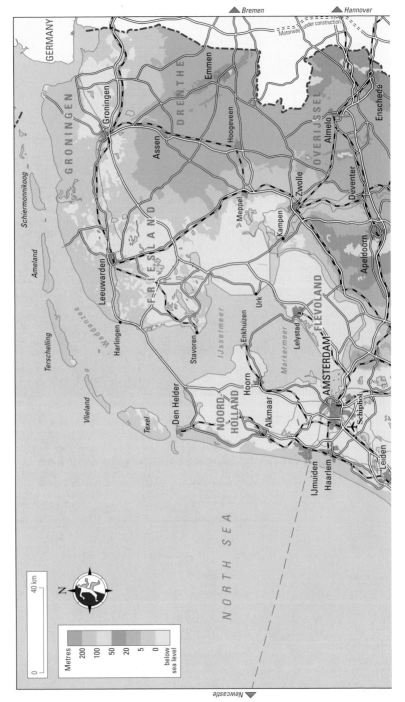

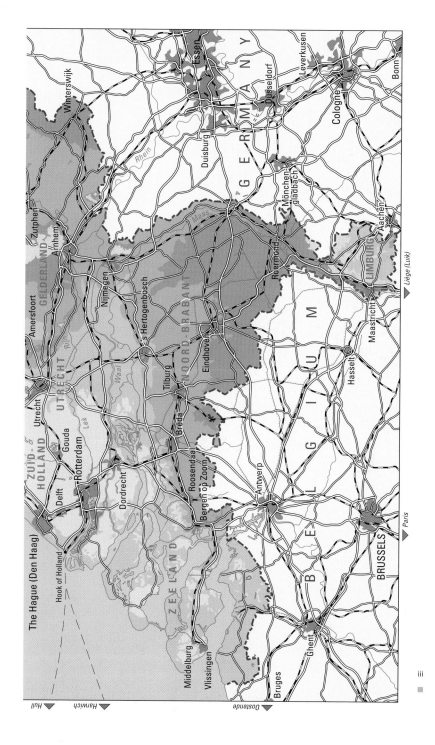

Introduction to

# The
# Netherlands

**To a large extent, the Netherlands is a country reclaimed from the blue-black waters of the North Sea, an artificially created land, around half of which lies at or below sea level. Land reclamation has been the dominant motif of Dutch history, the result being a country of unique and resonant images, the fertile, pancake-flat landscapes gridded with canals and interrupted by windmills and church spires, all beneath huge, open skies.**

Perhaps as a consequence, the country's merchants were keen on the vertical, building ornately gabled town houses in every city in the country – to greatest and most noble effect in Amsterdam – while the bulbfields provide bold splashes of colour in springtime and, in the west, the long coastline is marked by mile upon mile of protective dune, backing onto wide stretches of pristine, sandy beach.

A major colonial power, the Dutch mercantile fleet once challenged the English for world naval supremacy, and throughout its seventeenth-century Golden Age, the standard of living (for the majority at least) was second to none. There have been a few economic ups and downs since then, but today the Netherlands is one of the most developed countries in the world, small and urban, with the highest population density in Europe, its sixteen million inhabitants

## Fact file

● The Netherlands has a **population** just short of 16 million. Of these, some 730,000 live in the capital Amsterdam, 600,000 in Rotterdam and 450,000 Den Haag (The Hague). "**Holland**" comprises just two of the twelve Dutch provinces: Noord-Holland around Amsterdam, and Zuid-Holland around Rotterdam and Den Haag.

● The country is a constitutional **monarchy**; the present queen, Beatrix, was crowned in 1980. She presides – in a titular sense – over the country's bicameral **parliament**, named the States-General, which comprises an Upper House or First Chamber and a Lower House or Second Chamber. Parliament sits in Den Haag. The Lower House is directly elected; the Upper comprises representatives of the country's twelve provinces.

● Every Dutch city has a municipal **council** with delegated powers over a wide range of social issues, from public order and safety, drugs and housing through to economic development and culture. Currently, the two largest national political parties are the left-of-centre PvdA and the right-of-centre CDA. The green-left Groenlinks also make a significant showing in the big cities.

● Almost half the population declare no **religious** affiliation. The three largest churches are the Catholics, the Dutch Reformed and its nineteenth-century breakaway, the Reformed; there is also a sizeable Muslim minority.

▽ Carnival at Bergen-op-Zoom (see p.319)

concentrated into an area about the size of the US state of Maine. It's an international, well-integrated place too: many people speak English, at least in the heavily populated west of the country; communications and infrastructure are efficient; and its companies are generally reckoned to be dynamic and enterprising.

Successive Dutch governments have steered towards political consensus – indeed, this has been the drift since the Reformation, when the competing pillars of Dutch society (originally the Calvinists and the Catholics) learnt to live with – or ignore – each other, aided by the fact that trading wealth was lubricating the whole social structure. Almost by accident, therefore,

Dutch society became tolerant and, in its enthusiasm to blunt conflict, progressive. These days, many insiders opine that the motive force behind liberal Dutch attitudes towards drug use and prostitution isn't freewheeling permissiveness so much as apathy.

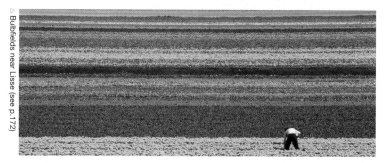

△ Bulbfields near Lisse (see p.172)

# Where to go

Say you're going to the Netherlands and everyone will immediately assume you're going to **Amsterdam**. Indeed for such a small and accessible country, the Netherlands is, apart from Amsterdam, relatively unknown territory. Some people may confess to a brief visit to Rotterdam or Den Haag (The Hague), but for most

## Dutch herring

The Dutch love their herring, eaten every which way, but usually raw, on a bread roll and garnished with onions. Best of all, however, is to catch sight of occasional intrepid herring-eaters, tilting their head back and lowering a whole fish into their mouth from on high with considerable skill. The herring season starts in late May and there's a fair old frenzy to get hold of the new season's fish. The Dutch herring fleet is a shadow of its former self, numbering just 25 large ships, but the first vessel back to port with the May catch gives a barrel of herring to Queen Beatrix and receives a prize of €1500 – which the captain donates to Greenpeace.

## Jan Vermeer

Little is known for certain about the artist Jan Vermeer (1632–75), though it is likely he lived all his life in Delft, where he was a prominent member of the painters' guild. Neither is it clear quite why his surviving oeuvre is so limited – only around 35 paintings are now attributed to him – though it's likely his paintings proved hard to sell and that he therefore had to work as an innkeeper and picture dealer to feed his large family (he had eleven children). Vermeer's painting career divides into three distinct phases and it's from the middle period that his most celebrated works come, when he adopted the compositional simplicity that was to prove so extraordinarily popular a couple of hundred years or more after his death, smooth and finely detailed canvases on which the predominant colours are yellow, blue and grey. Look out for examples of his work at the Rijksmuseum in Amsterdam (see p.99) and the Mauritshuis in Den Haag (see p.177).

visitors Amsterdam *is* the Netherlands, the assumption being that there's nothing remotely worth seeing elsewhere – a prejudice shared, incidentally, by many Amsterdammers. To accept this is to miss much, but there's no doubt that Amsterdam has more cosmopolitan dash than any other Dutch city, both in its restaurant and bar scene and in the pre-eminence of its three great attractions. These are the Anne Frank House, where the young Jewish diarist hid away during the World War II Nazi occupation; the Rijksmuseum, with its wonderful collection of Dutch paintings, including several of Rembrandt's finest works; and the peerless Vincent van Gogh Museum, with the world's largest collection of the artist's work.

In the west of the country, beyond Amsterdam, the provinces of **Noord-** and **Zuid-Holland** are for the most part unrelentingly flat, reflecting centuries of careful reclamation work as the Dutch have slowly pushed back the sea. These provinces are intensively urban, especially Zuid-Holland, and home to a grouping of towns known collectively as the Randstad (literally "rim town"), an urban sprawl which holds all the country's largest cities and the majority of its population. Travelling in this part of the country is easy, with trains and buses that are fast, inexpensive and efficient; highlights include amenable **Haarlem**, with its fine Frans Hals Museum; the old university town of **Leiden**; and **Delft**, with its fine medieval buildings and diminutive, canal-girded centre. The gritty port city of **Rotterdam**, reborn, revitalized and festooned with prestigious modern architecture, is worth a visit too, as is **Den Haag (The Hague)**, one of the most laid-back and relaxing capitals in Europe, with several fine museums, most memorably the Mauritshuis with its wonderful collection of Golden Age paintings. Neither should you miss the **Keukenhof gardens**, with the finest and most extensive bulbfields in the country, and the old Zuider Zee ports and small villages to the north of Amsterdam, particularly **Edam** and **Enkhuizen**.

△ Amsterdam

## Wadlopen

Twice daily, the sea pulls back from the northern coast of the provinces of Groningen and Friesland to reveal a vast, treacle-like expanse of mud that squeaks and pops as millions of tiny creatures dig and feed. Enticing to some, vaguely appalling to others, this phenomenon has spawned the hobby-cum-sport of **wadlopen**, or mudflat-walking, a strenuous activity that can only be done safely with a guide as the tides swill inconsistently and the mud is of variable depth. Needless to say, you have to wear the right gear. See p.251 for more.

Beyond lies a quieter, more rural country, especially in the far north where a chain of low-lying islands separates the open North Sea from the coast-hugging Waddenzee. Prime resort territory, the islands possess a blustery, bucolic charm all of their own and thousands of Dutch families come here every summer for their holidays. Most of the islands lie offshore from the coast of the province of **Friesland**, named after the Germanic Frisians who first settled the region and whose language – Frysk – is still spoken by some of the locals. Friesland's capital, **Leeuwarden**, is a likeable, eminently visitable city, and neighbouring **Groningen** is one of the country's busiest cultural centres, given verve by its large student population. To the south, the provinces of Overijssel and Gelderland are dotted with charming old towns, most notably **Deventer** and **Zutphen**, whilst their eastern portions herald the Netherlands' first few geophysical bumps as

▽ Ball-houses, Den Bosch

x

■

the landscape rolls up towards the German frontier. Here also are two lively and diverting towns – **Arnhem**, a hop and a skip from the open heaths of the Hoge Veluwe National Park, and the lively college town of **Nijmegen**. Further south still are the predominantly Catholic provinces of Limburg, Noord-Brabant and Zeeland. The last of these is well named (literally "Sealand"), made up of a series of low-lying islands connected by road and protected from the encroaching waters of the North Sea by one of the country's most ambitious engineering plans, the **Delta Project**. Heading east from here, you reach Noord-Brabant, gently rolling scrub and farmland which centres on the historic cities of **Breda** and **'s Hertogenbosch**, and, not least, the modern manufacturing hub of **Eindhoven**, home to the electronics giant Philips. The province of Limburg occupies the slim scythe of land that reaches down between the Belgian and German borders, its landscape, in the south at least, truly hilly, and with a charming, cosmopolitan capital in **Maastricht**.

Even better, everywhere is easy to reach on a public transport system of trains and buses, whose efficiency may make British and American visitors want to weep with envy.

△ Nieuwe Kerk, Delft

# When to go

The Netherlands enjoys a temperate **climate**, with fairly mild summers and moderately cold winters. Generally speaking, temperatures rise the further south you go, with the south of the country perhaps a couple of degrees warmer than the north and east for much of the year. This is offset by the prevailing westerlies that

sweep in from the North Sea, making the wetter coastal provinces both warmer in winter and colder in summer than the eastern provinces, where the more severe climate of continental Europe begins to dominate. As far as showers go, be prepared for them at any time: rain is a strong possibility all year round.

| | Jan | Feb | Mar | Apr | May | Jun | Jul | Aug | Sep | Oct | Nov | Dec |
|---|---|---|---|---|---|---|---|---|---|---|---|---|
| **Amsterdam** | | | | | | | | | | | | |
| Av min °C | 1 | 0 | 2 | 4 | 8 | 10 | 13 | 12 | 10 | 7 | 4 | 2 |
| Av max °C | 5 | 6 | 9 | 12 | 17 | 19 | 21 | 22 | 18 | 14 | 9 | 7 |
| Rainfall, mm | 62 | 43 | 59 | 41 | 48 | 68 | 66 | 61 | 82 | 85 | 89 | 75 |
| Sun, hrs/day | 2 | 3 | 4 | 6 | 7 | 7 | 7 | 7 | 4 | 3 | 2 | 1 |
| **Enschede** | | | | | | | | | | | | |
| Av min °C | -1 | -1 | 2 | 3 | 7 | 10 | 12 | 11 | 9 | 6 | 3 | 1 |
| Av max °C | 4 | 5 | 9 | 13 | 17 | 20 | 22 | 22 | 18 | 14 | 8 | 6 |
| Rainfall, mm | 71 | 43 | 66 | 46 | 56 | 74 | 69 | 60 | 66 | 64 | 67 | 77 |
| Sun, hrs/day | 2 | 3 | 3 | 5 | 6 | 6 | 6 | 6 | 4 | 3 | 2 | 1 |
| **Leeuwarden** | | | | | | | | | | | | |
| Av min °C | 0 | 0 | 2 | 3 | 7 | 10 | 12 | 12 | 10 | 7 | 3 | 1 |
| Av max °C | 5 | 5 | 8 | 11 | 16 | 18 | 20 | 21 | 18 | 13 | 9 | 6 |
| Rainfall, mm | 66 | 42 | 59 | 39 | 51 | 69 | 64 | 60 | 82 | 78 | 84 | 73 |
| Sun, hrs/day | 2 | 3 | 4 | 6 | 7 | 7 | 7 | 6 | 4 | 3 | 2 | 1 |
| **Maastricht** | | | | | | | | | | | | |
| Av min °C | 0 | 0 | 2 | 4 | 8 | 11 | 13 | 13 | 10 | 7 | 3 | 1 |
| Av max °C | 5 | 6 | 10 | 13 | 18 | 20 | 23 | 23 | 19 | 14 | 9 | 6 |
| Rainfall, mm | 61 | 51 | 61 | 46 | 64 | 74 | 67 | 58 | 60 | 63 | 66 | 70 |
| Sun, hrs/day | 2 | 3 | 4 | 5 | 6 | 6 | 6 | 6 | 4 | 4 | 2 | 1 |
| **Rotterdam** | | | | | | | | | | | | |
| Av min °C | 1 | 0 | 2 | 4 | 7 | 10 | 13 | 12 | 10 | 7 | 4 | 2 |
| Av max °C | 6 | 6 | 10 | 13 | 17 | 19 | 22 | 22 | 19 | 14 | 9 | 7 |
| Rainfall, mm | 67 | 47 | 65 | 41 | 52 | 72 | 68 | 66 | 82 | 90 | 86 | 80 |
| Sun, hrs/day | 2 | 3 | 4 | 5 | 7 | 6 | 7 | 6 | 4 | 3 | 2 | 1 |

# 27

## things not to miss

*It's not possible to see everything that the Netherlands has to offer in one trip – and we don't suggest you try. What follows is a selective and subjective taste of the country's highlights: cosmopolitan cities, peaceful villages, memorable landscapes and outstanding museums. They're arranged in five colour-coded categories to help you find the very best things to see, do and experience. All entries have a page reference to take you straight into the guide, where you can find out more.*

**01 Queen's Day** Page **42** • Every April 30, the whole country goes nuts, ostensibly to celebrate the birthday of Queen Juliana, the current monarch's mother: there's live music, street-partying, parades and unregulated trading, as everyone empties out their attic to sell their accumulated junk on the streets.

## 02

### The Biesbosch

Page **206** • As an escape from Dutch urban life, the reedy marshes and lagoons of the Biesbosch are hard to beat.

## 03

**Cycling** Page **30** • No country in Europe is so kindly disposed towards the bicycle than the pancake-flat Netherlands: you'll find bike paths in and around all towns, plus long-distance touring routes taking you into the deep countryside.

## 04

### Anne Frank House, Amsterdam

Page **84** • A poignant and personal evocation of the Nazi persecution of the Jews. The photo shows the bookcase behind which the Frank family hid for two years.

**06 Delft** Page **186** • Eulogized by Vermeer, Delft's centre is particularly handsome, and its market square is one of the country's best.

**05 Dutch cheeses** Page **35** • Balls of Edam and huge wheels of Gouda are the mainstays of the Dutch cheese industry, on sale everywhere at different grades of maturity and quite unlike the bland, rubbery creations sold abroad.

**07 Maastricht** Page **335** • This atmospheric, laid-back city in the far south, squeezed between the porous Belgian and German borders, offers a worldly outlook and a superb old quarter.

**08** **The Elfstedentocht** Page 236 • Watch, or even better join in with, the speed-skaters of Friesland as they tear round the province's canals in this infrequently staged open-air race.

**09** **Hoge Veluwe National Park** Page 294 • A richly forested swathe of dunes and woodland in the middle of the country. Cycle your way around thanks to a fleet of free-to-use white bicycles.

**10 Delta Expo**
Page **315** • A series of huge dykes and flood-barriers in the far-flung western province of Zeeland that bear witness to the country's long battle to hold the sea at bay, celebrated in an adjacent exhibition hall.

**11 Coastal dunes**
Page **155** • The Dutch have protected long stretches of their coast from the developers, one result being great tracts of pris-tine dune, ideal for a day's stroll and picnic.

**12 St Janskerk, Gouda** Page **199** • Archetypal country town of canals and fancy gables, plus a church with a wonderful set of stained-glass windows.

**13** **Den Haag/The Hague** Page **173** • Den Haag has a reputation for dourness that is completely undeserved, boasting a first-rate restaurant scene, smart hotels and enough prime museums to exhaust the most energetic sightseer.

**14**

**Van Gogh Museum, Amsterdam**
Page **101** • Quite simply the best and most comprehensive collection of Van Gogh's work anywhere.

**15 Brown cafés** Page **36** • Cosy and relaxing brown cafés – so named for their tobacco-stained walls – are the epitome of the Dutch drinking scene.

**16 Groningen** Page **242** • Bustling, cosmopolitan university town in the far north that boasts a uniquely bike-focused ambience and an eye-poppingly avant-garde art museum.

**17** **Edam** Page **140** • Perhaps the prettiest village in the country, its huddle of fine old houses flanking sleepy canals.

**18** **Kröller-Müller Museum** Page **295** • Superb art museum and sculpture garden set in the heart of the Hoge Veluwe National Park.

## 19 Cannabis coffeeshops

Page **37** • Every Dutch city – and a fair few smaller towns as well – has a choice of "coffeeshops", where you can buy and smoke marijuana and hash. Many are tourist-oriented dives, but there are plenty of congenial, attractive places to sit back and enjoy a spliff or two.

## 20 Indonesian food Page **36** •

Thanks to the Netherlands' colonial adventures in Southeast Asia, restaurants around the country prepare some of the finest Indonesian cuisine on offer outside Indonesia.

## 21 Keukenhof gardens

Page **172** • Some seven million flowers are on show here in these extensive gardens, which specialize in daffodils, narcissi, hyacinths and – of course – tulips.

## 22 Frans Hals Museum, Haarlem

Page **134** • Often neglected, Hals was one of the finest of the Golden Age painters, his later canvases acutely dark and broody.

**23 Amsterdam canals** Page **83** • Amsterdam's canals – often frozen solid in winter – girdle the city, offering some of its most beguiling moments.

**24 's Hertogenbosch** Page **324** • This lively market town features an intricate old quarter of canals and picturesque bridges, plus a stunning cathedral.

**25 Rijksmuseum, Amsterdam** Page **99** • Grand museum with a superb collection of seventeenth-century Dutch paintings, including several of Rembrandt's key works.

**26**
**Enkhuizen**
Page **145** •
One-time
Zuider Zee port
and now a
charming holi-
day resort, with
old barges
stacked up in
the harbour and
antique houses
flanking its
canals.

**27**
**Frisian
Islands**
Page **229** • Of
the string of
wild and
windswept
holiday islands
off the northern
Dutch coast,
Terschelling is
the most
popular, a fine
spot for walks
and bike-rides
amidst the
dunes.

# Contents

# Using this Rough Guide

We've tried to make this Rough Guide a good read and easy to use. The book is divided into six main sections, and you should be able to find whatever you want in one of them.

## Colour section

The front colour section offers a quick tour of the Netherlands. The **introduction** aims to give you a feel for the country, with suggestions on where to go. We also tell you what the weather is like and include a basic fact file.

Next, our authors round up their favourite aspects of the country in the **things not to miss** section – whether it's great food, amazing sights or a special event. Right after this comes a full **contents** list.

## Basics

The Basics section covers all the **pre-departure** nitty-gritty to help you plan your trip. This is where to find out which airlines fly to your destination, what paperwork you'll need, what to do about money and insurance, about Internet access, food, public transport, car rental – in fact just about every piece of **general practical information** you might need.

## Guide

This is the heart of the Rough Guide, divided into user-friendly chapters, each of which covers a specific area. Every chapter starts with a list of **highlights** and an **introduction** that helps you to decide where to go, depending on your time and budget. Likewise, introductions to the various towns and smaller regions within each chapter should help you plan your itinerary. We start most town accounts with information on arrival and accommodation, followed by a tour of the sights, and finally reviews of places to eat and drink, and details of nightlife. Longer accounts also have a directory of practical listings. Each chapter concludes with **public transport details** for that region.

## Contexts

Read Contexts to get a deeper understanding of what makes the Netherlands tick. We include articles about **history** and **Dutch art**, and a detailed further reading section that reviews dozens of **books**.

## Language

The **language** section gives useful guidance for speaking Dutch and pulls together all the vocabulary you might need on your trip, including a comprehensive **menu reader**. Here you'll also find a **glossary** of Dutch terms.

## Index + small print

Apart from a **full index**, which includes maps as well as places, this section covers publishing information, credits and acknowledgements, and also has our contact details in case you want to send in updates and corrections to the book – or suggestions as to how we might improve it.

# Chapter list

# Contents

## Colour section                                    i–xxiv

## Basics                                            7–49

## Guide                                             51–347

# Contexts

## 349–380

# Language

## 381–392

# Index and small print

## 393–401

# Map symbols

maps are listed in the full index using coloured text

| | | | |
|---|---|---|---|
| --- | Chapter division boundary | ⊥ | Gardens |
| --- | International boundary | ▬▬▬ | Wall |
| --·· | Provincial boundary | ⚊ | Campsite |
| ═══ | Motorway | △ | Hostel |
| ══ | Main road | ✈ | Airport |
| ── | Minor road | Ⓜ | Metro station |
| ----- | Tunnel | ✡ | Synagogue |
| | Pedestrianized street | ♱ | Cemetery |
| ----- | Footpath | ⊠ | Post office |
| ━━━ | Railway | ⓘ | Tourist information (VVV) |
| | River/canal | ⊞ | Hospital |
| — — | Ferry route | | Building |
| )( | Bridge | ⊞ | Church |
| ♦ | Point of interest | | Park |
| ♠ | Museum | | Beach/dune |
| ⊙ | Statue | | |

# Basics

# Basics

# Getting there

The easiest way to reach the Netherlands is to fly: Amsterdam is a major international hub, served by dozens of short- and long-haul airlines, and there are smaller airports at Maastricht, Eindhoven and Rotterdam. Another option from the UK is travelling by train through the Channel Tunnel, little cheaper than a flight, but with the advantage of taking you direct to smaller towns around the country. Long-distance bus travel, and deals for drivers on ferry routes into Dutch and Belgian ports, are particularly competitive.

Airfares always depend on the **season**, with the highest being around June to August, when the weather is best; fares drop during the "shoulder" seasons – April to May and September to October – and you'll get the best prices during the low season, November to March (excluding Christmas and New Year when prices are hiked up and seats are at a premium). Note also that flying on weekends ordinarily adds considerably to the round-trip fare; price ranges quoted below assume midweek travel.

You can often cut costs by going through a **specialist flight agent** – either a consolidator, who buys up blocks of tickets from the airlines and sells them at a discount, or a **discount agent**, who in addition to dealing with discounted flights may also offer special student and youth fares and a range of other travel-related services such as travel insurance, rail passes, car rentals, tours and the like. Some agents specialize in **charter flights**, which may be cheaper than anything available on a scheduled flight, but again departure dates are fixed and withdrawal penalties are high. For the Netherlands, you may even find it cheaper to pick up a bargain **package deal** from one of the tour operators listed below and then find your own accommodation when you get there. A further possibility is to see if you can arrange a courier flight, although you'll need a flexible schedule, and preferably be travelling alone with very little luggage. In return for shepherding a parcel through customs, you can expect to get a deeply discounted ticket. You'll probably also be restricted in the duration of your stay.

Many airlines and discount travel websites offer you the opportunity to book your tick-ets **online**, cutting out the costs of agents and middlemen. Good deals can often be found through discount or auction sites, as well as through the airlines' own websites.

## Flights from the UK

**Flying** to any of the major airports in the Netherlands – Amsterdam Schiphol (pronounced *skip-oll*), Rotterdam, Eindhoven or Maastricht – saves a lot of time over the ferry or train connections: Schiphol, for example, is just an hour's flying time from London, or ninety minutes from Scotland and the north of England. Amsterdam is one of the UK's most popular short-haul destinations, and you'll find loads of choice in carriers, flight times and departure airports. Aside from the major **full-service** carriers (KLM and British Airways), there are plenty of **no-frills** airlines operating to Amsterdam, including easyJet, BMIbaby and MyTravelLite, as well as a few business-oriented small carriers such as VLM. Bear in mind that competition in the no-frills sector is hotting up: new routings often open up and existing ones are abandoned, as these tightly run operations struggle to secure a market share.

### Routings and fares

To get to **Amsterdam**, there's a choice of dozens of flights from a fistful of UK airports. Full-service carriers include KLM, British Airways and British Midland (plus tiny Scotairways), while no-frills airlines such as easyJet, BMIbaby and Ryanair jostle for supremacy to this popular destination. You'll find plenty of choice of daily flights out of London – Heathrow, Gatwick, Stansted, Luton and City – plus nonstop flights from loads of other airports, including Birmingham, East Midlands, Cardiff, Southampton, Norwich, Liverpool, Manchester, Leeds-Bradford, Humberside, Newcastle, Teesside, Edinburgh, Glasgow and Aberdeen. **Fares** with a no-frills airline such as easyJet range from £35 return to £100 or more, with the cheapest tickets needing to be booked weeks in advance, entailing midweek travel at unsociable hours, and being non-exchangeable and/or non-refundable. Booking at the last minute can mean shelling out £300–400. For weekend travel and more reasonable departure and arrival times, no-frills flights can often be matched by the full-service airlines, with KLM's prices starting at £59, and rising, with improved flexibility, to around £280. For BA, fares start around £79 (including taxes) for a non-flexible, non-refundable return economy flight, and rise to almost £400, without the restrictions and closer to the date of departure. All carriers offer their lowest prices online, rather than with phone booking.

To **Rotterdam**, you've a choice of KLM from Heathrow, the Belgian airline VLM from Jersey (via London City) and Manchester, and the Dutch carrier Trans Travel Airlines (TTA) from Gatwick or Birmingham. A typical KLM non-refundable fare is around £110. **Eindhoven** is well connected, with flights from Birmingham (on TTA via Rotterdam), Heathrow (on KLM, via Amsterdam) and Stansted (on KLM and Ryanair); a midweek flight on Ryanair can cost a very reasonable £50 return, on KLM around £160. **Maastricht** is served daily from Stansted by TTA, KLM and Ryanair. Again, Ryanair offers the best value at £42 return, while an equivalent KLM flight costs from £125. Since these flights to Eindhoven, Rotterdam and Maastricht are targeted at business travellers, expect early-morning departure times and higher flight frequency during the week.

## Airlines in the UK

**BMI British Midland** ☎0870/607 0555, ⓦwww.flybmi.com.
**BMIbaby** ☎0870/264 2229, ⓦwww.bmibaby.com.
**British Airways** ☎0845/773 3377, ⓦwww.ba.com.
**easyJet** ☎0870/600 0000, ⓦwww.easyjet.com.
**KLM** ☎0870/507 4074, ⓦwww.klmuk.com.
**MyTravelLite** ☎0870/156 4564,

ⓦwww.mytravellite.com.
**Ryanair** ☎0871/246 0000, ⓦwww.ryanair.com.
**Scotairways** ☎0870/606 0707, ⓦwww.scotairways.co.uk.
**Trans Travel** ☎0870/872 0996, ⓦwww.tta.nl.
**VLM London** ☎020/7476 6677, Manchester ☎0161/493 3232, Jersey ☎01534/783 283, ⓦwww.vlm-airlines.com.

## Flight and travel agents in the UK

**Bridge the World** ☎0870/444 7474, ⓦwww.bridgetheworld.com. Good deals aimed at the backpacker market.
ⓦ**www.cheapflights.co.uk** Flight deals, travel agents, plus links to other travel sites.
**Destination Group** ☎020/7400 7045, ⓦwww.destination-group.com. Good discount flights to Amsterdam, part of the lastminute.com online booking service.
ⓦ**www.expedia.co.uk** Discount airfares, all-airline search engine and daily deals.
**Flightbookers** ☎0870/010 7000, ⓦwww.ebookers.com. Low fares on an extensive selection of scheduled flights.
**Flight Centre** ☎0870/890 8099, ⓦwww.flightcentre.co.uk. Good discounts on scheduled flights.
**Flynow** ☎0870/444 0045, ⓦwww.flynow.com. Large range of discounted tickets.
ⓦ**www.lastminute.com** Offers good last-minute holiday package and flight-only deals.
**North South Travel** ☎01245/608 291, ⓦwww.northsouthtravel.co.uk. Friendly, competitive travel agency offering discounted fares worldwide – profits are used to support projects in the developing world, especially the promotion of sustainable tourism.
ⓦ**www.priceline.co.uk** Name-your-own-price website that has deals at around forty percent off standard fares. You cannot specify flight times (although you do specify dates) and the tickets are non-refundable, non-transferable and non-changeable.
**STA Travel** ☎0870/160 0599, ⓦwww.statravel.co.uk. Worldwide specialists in low-cost flights and tours for students and under-26s, though other customers welcome.
**Top Deck** ☎020/7244 8000, ⓦwww.topdecktravel.co.uk. Long-established agent dealing in discount flights.
**Trailfinders** ☎020/7628 7628, ⓦwww.trailfinders.co.uk. One of the best-informed and most efficient agents for independent travellers.
**Travel Cuts** ☎020/7255 2082, ⓦwww.travelcuts.co.uk. Specialists in budget, student and youth travel.

## Tour operators in the UK

**Airtours** ☎0870/238 7788, ⊛www.uk.mytravel
.com. Large tour company offering trips worldwide.
**AngloDutch** ☎020/8511 1551,
⊛www.anglodutchsports.co.uk. Eight different
tours: cycling, river-cruising, sailing or a combination
of all three.
**Bridge Travel** ☎0870/191 7117, ⊛www.bridge-
travel.co.uk. Tour operator offering city breaks to
Amsterdam, The Hague, Rotterdam and Maastricht
as well as smaller towns such as Arnhem and Delft.
Will also tailor-make packages for cycling holidays
and excursions to the bulbfields.
**Brightwater Holidays** ☎01334/657 155,
⊛www.brightwaterholidays.com. Fife-based tour
operator running trips to the Dutch bulbfields,
departing from London and Dover.
**Cresta Holidays** ☎0870/238 7711,
⊛www.crestaholidays.co.uk. Part of the Mytravel
Group, offering city breaks to Amsterdam.
**Martin Randall Travel** ☎020/8742 3355,
⊛www.martinrandall.com. Small-group, 5-day
"Dutch Painting" tour, led by expert on seventeenth-
century Dutch art.
**Prospect Music and Art Tours** ☎020/7486
5704, ⊛www.prospecttours.com. Springtime river
cruises through the bulbfields, exploring towns on
foot with a local guide.
**Thomas Cook Holidays** ☎01733/563 200,
⊛www.thomascook.com. City breaks in
Amsterdam, The Hague and Rotterdam, with good
deals on flights and accommodation.
**Travelscene** ☎0870/777 9987,
⊛www.travelscene.co.uk. City breaks to
Amsterdam, The Hague, Maastricht and Rotterdam.
**Travelscope** ☎01453/821 210,
⊛www.travelscope.co.uk. Tour operator offering a
variety of family-friendly packages to the Netherlands
including city-breaks, cycling holidays, river cruises
and trips to the flower festivals.

## By train from the UK

The simplest and quickest way to go **by
train** is to take the Eurostar service from
London nonstop to Brussels, from where
there are numerous services to many points
in the Netherlands. All the alternatives
involve using the more time-consuming ferries, the fastest route being from Harwich to
the Hook of Holland. The encyclopedic
Dutch Railways website ⊛www.ns.nl has
full timetable details (in English) of trains from
any station in the UK to any station in the
Netherlands, including tube journeys across

London and – if you deselect the High-
Speed Train ("HSP") option – ferry times.

There are normally 7 or 8 **Eurostar** departures a day from London Waterloo and
Ashford (Kent) to Brussels via the Channel
Tunnel (2hr 40min). Trains arrive at Bruxelles-
Midi station (Brussel-Zuid in Dutch), from
where plenty of fast trains – including **Thalys**
high-speed services (⊛www.thalys.com) –
head on to Rotterdam (1hr 45min), The
Hague (2hr) and Amsterdam (around 2hr
45min). The total journey time from London
is **six hours**, give or take fifteen minutes.
With a week's notice, Eurostar can through-
ticket your journey from any point in the UK
to any point in the Netherlands. The cheapest fare from London, a Leisure Apex 14, is
£90 to Amsterdam; this requires booking at
least 14 days in advance, and staying for at
least two nights. Typical add-on prices are
around £30 from Edinburgh or Glasgow, £20
from Manchester and £14 from Birmingham.
Special deals and bargains are commonplace, especially in the low season; you can
also reduce costs by accepting certain ticketing restrictions. A standard return fare to
Amsterdam, with more flexibility, is £125,
while a fully-flexible and refundable ticket for
travel any day of the week will set you back
a ridiculous £310. Inter-Rail holders are not
entitled to a discount, but there is a youth
discount for the under-26s.

A longer, cheaper **rail-and-ferry** route is
available through Stena Line in conjunction
with several train operators – Scotrail, Anglia,
First North Western, First Great Western and
Virgin. The journey operates twice daily
(morning and late afternoon) from London's
Liverpool Street station to Harwich (1hr
40min) and connects with the rapid ferry
crossing to the Hook of Holland, or Hoek
van Holland (3hr 40min), from where fast
trains head on to Rotterdam (35min), The
Hague (50min) and Amsterdam (1hr 35min).
Total journey time from London is around
**eight hours**; the afternoon departure doesn't
get in until after 2am. Prices from London
start at £60 return for an Apex fare, which
must be booked at least a week in advance,
with the return journey being made within
one month. A standard open return costs
£79, or £52.50 with a young person's rail-
card. Tickets are available from Anglia
Railways and larger mainline stations.

See p.27 for details of Dutch and international train passes.

## Rail contacts

**Anglia Railways** ☎0870/040 9090,
Ⓦ www.angliarailways.co.uk.
**Eurostar** ☎0870/160 6600,
Ⓦ www.eurostar.com.
**International Rail** (formerly Holland Rail)
☎0870/120 1606, Ⓦ www.international-rail.com.
**Rail Europe** ☎0870/584 8848,
Ⓦ www.raileurope.co.uk.
**Trainseurope** ☎0900/195 0101,
Ⓦ www.trainseurope.co.uk.

# Driving from the UK

To reach the Netherlands by **car** or **motorbike**, you can either use the ferries or – preferable for its simplicity and hassle-free crossing – Eurotunnel's shuttle-train through the Channel Tunnel. Note that Eurotunnel only carries cars (including occupants) and motorbikes; cyclists and foot passengers must travel by ferry instead.

## Eurotunnel

The easiest way to take a car or motorbike to the Netherlands is to drive to Folkestone, drive on to **Eurotunnel**'s shuttle trains, and drive off at Calais for the straightforward run through Belgium: Amsterdam is roughly 370km from the tunnel exit, Rotterdam 200km, Arnhem 260km. There are up to four shuttle trains per hour (only 1 per hour midnight–6am), taking 35min (45min for some night departure times); you must check-in at least 30min before departure. It's possible to turn up and buy your ticket at the toll booths (exit the M20 at junction 11a), though at busy times booking is advisable. **Fares** depend on the time of year, time of day and length of stay (the cheapest ticket is for a day-trip, followed by a five-day return); it's cheaper to travel between 10pm and 6am, while the highest fares are reserved for weekend departures and returns in July and August. Prices are charged **per vehicle**, with no additions for passengers. Return trips made within five days entitle you to short-stay savers which, for a car, start from £107 (booked 7 days in advance). If you wish to stay more than 5 days, a long-stay saver costs from £197 (booked 14 days in advance), soaring up to £327 for travelling on weekends in July. To take a **motorbike** costs from £73, a cara-

van from £82. Before going ahead and booking, ask about special offers, since there are usually some available. Call ☎0870/535 3535, or, for the lowest rates, book at Ⓦ **www.eurotunnel.com**.

## Ferries

The alternative is to take the **ferry**, an especially attractive option if you're starting from Scotland or the north of England. Three operators run ferries from the UK direct to ports in the Netherlands, and all offer year-round services. Tariffs vary enormously, depending on when you leave, how long you stay, if you're taking a car, what size it is and how many passengers are in it. There are discounts for students and under-26s, though these will involve some travel restrictions. Speediest of all is Stena Line on the route from Harwich in Essex to the **Hook of Holland** (daytime 3hr 40min; overnight 6hr 15min): a weekend fare in high season costs from £233 for a car with four passengers on a daytime crossing, or £426 travelling overnight with basic cabin accommodation. P&O North Sea Ferries operate from Hull to **Rotterdam** (11hr); booking well in advance, a car plus four people, with a basic cabin and meals included, costs around £600. DFDS Seaways sails from Newcastle (North Shields) to IJmuiden near **Amsterdam** (14hr); booking 21 days ahead nets a Seapex fare from £64 per person return.

Aside from these options direct to Dutch ports, you might want to consider the ferry routes to Belgium and France. P&O sail once a day from Hull to **Zeebrugge** in Belgium (14hr 30min), while Norfolkline operates a year-round service from Dover to the French border town of **Dunkerque** (2hr). If you don't mind a detour driving on the scenic roads through northern France and Belgium to reach the Netherlands, the Dover–**Calais** route can be particularly good value: operators include Hoverspeed (55min), P&O Ferries (from 75min on their "superferry") and SeaFrance (1hr 30min). Prices are keen, with some very competitive special offers that can drop as low as £19 return.

**DFDS Seaways** ☎0870/533 3000,
Ⓦ www.dfdsseaways.co.uk. Newcastle to Amsterdam.
**Hoverspeed** ☎0870/240 8070,
Ⓦ www.hoverspeed.co.uk. Dover to Calais.
**Norfolkline** ☎0870/870 1020,

Tram outside Amsterdam Centraal Station △

Ⓦwww.norfolkline.com. Dover to Dunkerque.
P&O North Sea Ferries ⓉO870/129 6002,
Ⓦwww.ponsf.com. Hull to Rotterdam or
Zeebrugge.
P&O Stena Line ⓉO870/600 0600,
Ⓦwww.posl.com. Dover to Calais.
Sea France ⓉO870/571 1711,
Ⓦwww.seafrance.com. Dover to Calais.
Stena Line ⓉO870/570 70 70,
Ⓦwww.stenaline.co.uk. Harwich to Hook of
Holland.

## By coach from the UK

Travelling by long-distance **coach** is generally the cheapest way of reaching the
Netherlands from the UK, but it is very time-
consuming: the main route, London to
Amsterdam, takes ten hours or more.
Eurolines operates three services daily
(8.30am, 8pm & 10.30pm) from London's
Victoria Coach Station to Amsterdam's
Amstel Station, southeast of the city centre,
all using Eurotunnel. A standard fare is £49
return (under-26s and over-60s pay £46),
though promotional return fares can be
snapped up for just £19. National Express
has connections into London from all round
the UK. The lesser-known Anglia Lines operates a coach service between London
Victoria and central Amsterdam, which
leaves twice daily and costs £35 return if
booked seven days in advance.

**Busabout** is a private bus service aimed
primarily at backpackers in Europe. It runs
every 2–3 days (April–Oct) on 5 circuits taking in 70 European cities, with add-on connections to 5 more, plus a link to London
and through-ticketing from elsewhere in
Britain and Ireland. You can get tickets for
15 or 21 consecutive days, or 1, 2 or 3
months, or flexipasses for 10 or 15 days'
travel within 2 months, 21 days' travel within
3 months, or 30 days out of 4 months;
there are also special deals on set itineraries. The passes are also available from
STA Travel in the US. For an idea of prices,
a 1-month pass costs £359 (under-26s
£319), while a Flexipass giving 12 days travel
in 2 months costs £349 (£309).

As well as ordinary tickets on its scheduled
coach services to an extensive list of over
460 European cities, **Eurolines** offers a pass
for Europe-wide travel, for either 15, 30, or
60 days between 46 European cities, including London, Amsterdam, Barcelona, Berlin,
Budapest, Copenhagen, Florence, Madrid,
Paris, Prague, Rome, Tallinn, Vienna etc. A
15-day pass costs €117 (under-26s €99), a
30-day pass €167 (€136), a 60-day pass
€211 (€167).
Anglia Lines ⓉO870/608 8806, Ⓦwww.anglia-
lines.co.uk.
Busabout ⓉO20/7950 1661,
Ⓦwww.busabout.com.
Eurolines ⓉO870/514 3219,
Ⓦwww.gobycoach.com. You can also buy tickets
from National Express ⓉO870/580 8080.

## From Ireland

**Flying** to the Netherlands from Northern
Ireland, the easiest option is with easyJet
out of Belfast International to Amsterdam;
see p.10 for fare advice. From the Republic,
Aer Lingus flies six times daily to
Amsterdam out of Dublin and twice daily
from Cork, for a minimum €175–200 return,
depending on the season, up to €450 or
more. Skynet flies from Shannon six times a
week, from €195 (requiring 2 days minimum stay) to €445. The upper-end tickets
are fully flexible and fully refundable within a
12-month period.

If you're **driving**, you have two choices:
cross the Irish Sea and sail from an English
port, or sail directly to France and travel
onwards overland. Options across the
English Channel are outlined on p.12; for
getting to the French coast, Irish Ferries
sail from Cork to Roscoff (spring and summer; 16hr), as do Brittany Ferries
(March–Oct; 14hr). Irish Ferries also sail
Rosslare–Cherbourg (spring and summer;
17hr) and Rosslare–Roscoff (summer;
14hr 30min). Prices vary tremendously
according to the day of travel; as an example, booking well ahead for a car plus
two adults and two kids, with a cabin,
costs in the order of €1000–1300 in the
summer peak.

**Coach** was once the cheapest way to
reach the Netherlands from Ireland, but now
you should check out budget flights first:
they might save you a long chinwag with
your knees. Eurolines has twice-daily services to Amsterdam from Dublin, taking around
25 hours. Beginning at the Dublin Busáras,
the route runs by ferry to Holyhead, then
London, the Eurotunnel, Antwerp,
Rotterdam and The Hague before reaching
Amsterdam. A standard return costs €120

(€135 high season); under-26s pay €110 (€125); book through Bus Éireann (☎01/836 6111, ⓦwww.buseireann.ie).

## Airlines in Ireland

**Aer Lingus** ☎0818/365 000, ⓦwww.aerlingus.ie.
**BMI British Midland** ☎01/407 3036, ⓦwww.flybmi.com.
**British Airways** ☎1800/626 747, ⓦwww.ba.com.
**easyJet** UK ☎0870/600 0000, ⓦwww.easyjet.com.
**KLM** UK ☎0870/507 4074, ⓦwww.klmuk.com.
**Ryanair** ☎0818/303 030, ⓦwww.ryanair.com.
**Skynet** ☎061/234 455, ⓦwww.skynetair.net.

## Flight and travel agents in Ireland

**Aran Travel International** ☎091/562 595, ⓦhomepages.iol.ie/~arantvl/aranmain.htm. Good-value flights.
**CIE Tours** ☎01/703 1888, ⓦwww.cietours.ie. General flight and tour agent.
**Co-op Travel Care** Belfast ☎0870/112 0099, ⓦwww.travelcareonline.com. Flights and holidays to Amsterdam.
**Go Holidays** ☎01/874 4126, ⓦwww.goholidays.ie. Offers package tours, especially city-breaks.
**Joe Walsh Tours** ☎01/676 0991, ⓦwww.joewalshtours.ie. General budget fares agent.
**Lee Travel** ☎021/427 7111, ⓦwww.leetravel.ie. Flights and holidays worldwide.
**McCarthy's Travel** ☎021/427 0127, ⓦwww.mccarthystravel.ie. General flight agent.
**Neenan Travel** ☎01/607 9900, ⓦwww.neenantrav.ie. Specialists in European city breaks.
**Rosetta Travel** Belfast ☎028/9064 4996, ⓦwww.rosettatravel.com. Flight and holiday agent.
**Student & Group Travel** ☎01/677 7834. Student and group specialists.
**Trailfinders** ☎01/677 7888, ⓦwww.trailfinders.ie. One of the best-informed and most efficient agents for independent travellers.

## Ferry operators in Ireland

**Brittany Ferries** ☎021/427 7801, ⓦwww.brittanyferries.ie. Cork to Roscoff.
**Irish Ferries** ☎1890/313 131,

ⓦwww.irishferries.com. Dublin to Holyhead; Rosslare to Pembroke; Rosslare to Cherbourg or Roscoff (March–Sept only).
**Norse Merchant Ferries** UK ☎0870/600 4321, Republic of Ireland ☎01/819 2999, ⓦwww.norsemerchant.com. Dublin or Belfast to Liverpool.
**P&O Irish Sea** UK ☎0870/242 4777, Republic of Ireland ☎1800/409 049, ⓦwww.poirishsea.com. Larne to Fleetwood; Dublin to Liverpool.
**Sea Cat** UK ☎0870/552 3523, ⓦwww.seacat.co.uk, Republic of Ireland ☎1800/805 055, ⓦwww.seacat.ie. Belfast to Heysham; Dublin to Liverpool.
**Stena Line** ☎01/204 7777, ⓦwww.stenaline.ie. Dun Laoghaire and Dublin to Holyhead; Rosslare to Fishguard.
**Swansea Cork Ferries** ☎021/427 1166, ⓦwww.swansea-cork.ie. Cork to Swansea (March–Oct only).

## From North America

Amsterdam's Schiphol airport is among the most popular and least expensive gateways to Europe **from North America**, and getting a convenient and good-value flight is rarely a problem. Virtually every region of the US and Canada is well served by the major airlines: KLM/Northwest, Continental, Singapore Airways and Delta all offer nonstop flights. Many more fly via London and other European centres – and are nearly always cheaper because of it.

KLM and Northwest, which operate a joint service, offer the widest range of flights, with direct or one-stop flights to Amsterdam from eleven US cities, and connections from dozens more. An average high-season round-trip fare from New York (flight time 8hr 10min) comes in at $585; from Chicago $750 (11hr 15min); and from Los Angeles $755 (10hr 30min).

Of the other carriers, Singapore Airlines offer the cheapest fares from New York at $600 for a high-season return, followed by United Airlines, Continental and topped off by Delta at a pricey $840. From elsewhere in the US, the Dutch charter firm Martinair flies year round from Miami and Orlando direct to Amsterdam, with fares from both cities averaging $600. Singapore Airlines and United also fly direct to Amsterdam from Chicago, while Delta operates from Atlanta (direct) and Salt Lake City (with one stop); Continental flies non-stop from Houston for around $790.

From Canada, KLM flies year-round direct to Amsterdam from Vancouver (9hr 45min) with a round-trip fare for roughly C$1600, and from Toronto (7hr 30min) for C$1310. Flying from Montréal involves a stop-over, and costs about C$1360. In summer (April–Oct), Martinair flies from Toronto, Vancouver, Edmonton and Calgary; sample fares for a high-season round-trip are C$1015 from Toronto, and C$1170 from Vancouver.

As with any long-distance flight, it is nearly always cheaper to fly non-direct. Many European carriers fly from major US and Canadian cities to Amsterdam Schiphol via their own capitals, for example Air France from New York and Los Angeles via Paris, from $640 return fare.

## Airlines in North America

**Air Canada** ☎ 1-888/247-2262, ⓦ www.aircanada.ca.
**Air France US** ☎ 1-800/237-2747, ⓦ www.airfrance.com, Canada ☎ 1-800/667-2747, ⓦ www.airfrance.ca.
**American Airlines** ☎ 1-800/433-7300, ⓦ www.aa.com.
**British Airways** ☎ 1-800/247-9297, ⓦ www.ba.com.
**Continental Airlines** ☎ 1-800/231-0856, ⓦ www.continental.com.
**Delta** ☎ 1-800/241-4141, ⓦ www.delta.com.
**Martinair Holland** ☎ 1-800/627-8462, ⓦ www.martinairusa.com.
**Northwest/KLM** ☎ 1-800/447-4747, ⓦ www.nwa.com.
**Singapore Airlines** ☎ 1-800/742-3333, ⓦ www.singaporeair.com.
**United** ☎ 1-800/538-2929, ⓦ www.ual.com.

## Courier flights from North America

**Air Courier Association** ☎ 1-800/282-1202, ⓦ www.aircourier.org. Courier flight broker. Membership ($29/yr) also entitles you to twenty percent discount on travel insurance and name-your-own-price non-courier flights.
**International Association of Air Travel Couriers** ☎ 308/632-3273, ⓦ www.courier.org. Courier flight broker with membership fee of $45/yr.

## Discount travel companies in North America

**Air Brokers International** ☎ 1-800/883-3273,

ⓦ www.airbrokers.com. Consolidator and specialist in round-the-world tickets.
**Airtech** ☎ 212/219-7000, ⓦ www.airtech.com. Standby seat broker; also deals in consolidator fares and courier flights.
**Airtreks.com** ☎ 1-877-AIRTREKS or 415/912-5600, ⓦ www.airtreks.com. Round-the-world tickets. The website lets you build and price your own RTW itinerary.
ⓦ www.cheapflight.com & ⓦ www.cheapflights.ca Flight deals, travel agents, plus links to other travel sites.
ⓦ www.cheaptickets.com Discount flight specialists.
**Council Travel** ☎ 1-800/2COUNCIL, ⓦ www.counciltravel.com. Mostly specializes in student/budget travel.
**Educational Travel Center** ☎ 1-800/747-5551 or 608/256-5551, ⓦ www.edtrav.com. Student/youth discount agent.
ⓦ www.expedia.com & ⓦ www.expedia.ca Discount airfares, all-airline search engine and daily deals.
ⓦ www.flyaow.com Online air travel info and reservations site.
ⓦ www.hotwire.com Last-minute savings of up to forty percent on regular published fares. Travellers must be at least 18 and there are no refunds, transfers or changes allowed.
**New Frontiers** ☎ 1-800/677-0720 or 310/670-7318, ⓦ www.newfrontiers.com. Discount travel firm.
ⓦ www.priceline.com Name-your-own-price website that has deals at around forty percent off standard fares. You cannot specify flight times (although you do specify dates) and the tickets are non-refundable, non-transferable and non-changeable.
ⓦ www.skyauction.com Auctions tickets and travel packages using a "second bid" scheme.
**SkyLink US** ☎ 1-800/AIR-ONLY or 212/573-8980, Canada ☎ 1-800/SKY-LINK, ⓦ www.skylinkus.com. Consolidator.
**STA Travel US** ☎ 1-800/781-4040, Canada 1-888/427-5639, ⓦ www.sta-travel.com. Worldwide specialists in independent travel; also student IDs, travel insurance, car rental, rail passes, etc.
**Student Flights** ☎ 1-800/255-8000 or 480/951-1177, ⓦ www.isecard.com. Student/youth fares, student IDs.
**TFI Tours** ☎ 1-800/745-8000 or 212/736-1140, ⓦ www.lowestairprice.com. Consolidator.
**Travac** ☎ 1-800/TRAV-800, ⓦ www.thetravelsite.com. Consolidator and charter broker.

**Travel Avenue** ☎1-800/333-3335,
Ⓦwww.travelavenue.com. Full-service travel agent
that offers discounts in the form of rebates.
**Travel Cuts** Canada ☎1-800/667-2887, US ☎1-
866/246-9762, Ⓦwww.travelcuts.com. Student
travel organization.
**Travelers Advantage** ☎1-877/259-2691,
Ⓦwww.travelersadvantage.com. Discount travel
club, with membership fee.
Ⓦwww.travelocity.com Destination guides, hot
web fares and best deals for car rental,
accommodation and lodging as well as fares.
**Worldtek Travel** ☎1-800/243-1723,
Ⓦwww.worldtek.com. Discount travel agency for
worldwide travel.

## Tour operators in North America

**Abercrombie & Kent** ☎1-800/323-7308 or
630/954-2944, Ⓦwww.abercrombiekent.com.
Upmarket tours taking in Amsterdam and its
surroundings.
**Backroads** ☎1-800/GO-ACTIVE or 510/527-
1555, Ⓦwww.backroads.com. Easy cycling tours
for families, from Arnhem to Kinderdijk.
**CBT Tours** ☎1-800/736-2453 or 312/475-0625,
Ⓦwww.cbttours.com. Bicycle tours from
Amsterdam to Brussels following the North Sea
Coast. Springtime tours to the bulbfields and
Keukenhof Gardens.
**Contiki Tours** ☎1-888/CONTIKI, Ⓦwww
.contiki.com. The Netherlands features briefly on the
European whistle-stop tours for 18- to 35-year-olds.
Choice of camping or hotel-based accommodation.
**Cosmos** ☎1-800/276-1241,
Ⓦwww.cosmosvacations.com. Will plan vacation
packages in Amsterdam with an independent focus.
**Euro-Bike & Walking Tours** ☎1-800/321-6060,
Ⓦwww.eurobike.com. One to two week cycling
tours of the Netherlands, can also include Belgium
and Germany. Luxury accommodation.
**Globus** ☎1-866/755-8581,
Ⓦwww.globusjourneys.com. Planned vacation
packages, including one week tour of the
Netherlands by coach.
**Holland Bicycling Tours** ☎1-714/593-1710,
Ⓦwww.hollandbicyclingtours.com. Group and
customized tours through the backroads, from
Friesland and Drenthe to Noord-Brabant and
Limburg, as well as a popular tulip tour.
**Pack and Pedal Europe** ☎1-570/965-2064,
Ⓦwww.tripsite.com. Offer eleven guided and
self-guided cycling tours of the Netherlands
and Belgium, accommodation usually in 2- or
3-star hotels.
**REI Adventures** ☎1-800/622-2236,

Ⓦwww.rei.com/travel. Small group cycling tours of
up to 10 days, with town walks along the way.
Accommodation in small hotels.
**Venture Out** ☎1-888/431-6789, Ⓦwww.venture-
out.com. Cycling and cultural small-group tours for gay
travellers; optional add-on for Amsterdam's Gay Pride.

## From Australia and New Zealand

There's no shortage of flights to the
Netherlands **from Australia and New
Zealand**, though all of them involve at least
one stop. Singapore Airways and Malaysian
offer the most direct routes out of Sydney
(stopping in Singapore and Kuala Lumpur
respectively). Thai, Austrian and Qantas all
have two stops (Bangkok/Frankfurt, Kuala
Lumpur/Vienna and Singapore/Frankfurt).
One further option is to pick up a cheap ticket
to London, and then continue your journey
to Amsterdam with one of the no-frills budget airlines (see p.10).

Tickets purchased direct from the airlines
tend to be expensive, with published fares
ranging from A\$2000/NZ\$2500 in low season to A\$2500–3000/NZ\$3000–3600 in
high season. Travel agents can offer better
deals, and have the latest information on
special promotions, such as free stopovers
en route and fly-drive-accommodation packages. Flight Centre and STA generally offer
the best discounts, especially for students
and those under 26. For a discounted
ticket from Sydney, Melbourne or Auckland,
expect to pay A\$1600–2500/NZ\$
2000– 2700.

For extended trips, a **round-the-world**
(RTW) ticket, valid for up to a year, can be
good value. Fares are based either on the
number of continents you visit, or the number of miles you travel, and tickets are usu-
ally cheapest through travel agents. The
lowest-priced tickets usually involve three to
four stopovers, with prices rising the further
you travel or the more stops you add.
Those that take in Amsterdam include the
"Star Alliance" (Air Canada, Air NZ,
Lufthansa, SAS, Singapore, Thai and
United) which starts at A\$2800/NZ\$3350,
and the One World Alliance "Global
Explorer" (American, British Airways,
Canadian, Cathay, Finnair, Iberia and
Qantas) which starts at A\$2400–2900/
NZ\$2900–3400.

## Airlines in Australia & NZ

**Air New Zealand** Australia ☎13 24 76, ⓦwww.airnz.com.au, NZ ☎0800/737 000, ⓦwww.airnz.co.nz.

**British Airways** Australia ☎1300/767 177, NZ ☎0800/274 847, ⓦwww.ba.com.

**Cathay Pacific** Australia ☎13 17 47, NZ ☎09/379 0861, ⓦwww.cathaypacific.com.

**KLM/Northwest** Australia ☎1300/303 747, NZ ☎09/309 1782, ⓦwww.klm.com.

**Malaysia Airlines** Australia ☎13 26 27, NZ ☎0800/777 747, ⓦwww.malaysiaairlines.com.my.

**Qantas** Australia ☎13 13 13, ⓦwww.qantas.com.au, NZ ☎0800/808 767, ⓦwww.qantas.co.nz.

**Singapore Airlines** Australia ☎13 10 11, NZ ☎0800/808 909, ⓦwww.singaporeair.com.

**Thai Airways** Australia ☎1300/651 960, NZ ☎09/377 0268, ⓦwww.thaiair.com.

## Travel agents in Australia & NZ

ⓦwww.cheapflights.com.au Flight deals, travel agents, plus links to other travel sites.

**Flight Centre** Australia ☎13 31 33 or 02/9235 3522, ⓦwww.flightcentre.com.au, NZ ☎0800/243 544 or 09/358 4310, ⓦwww.flightcentre.co.nz.

**Harvey World Travel** ⓦwww.harveyworld .com.au Online flight bookings and package deals; local agents in Australia and NZ.

**Holiday Shoppe** NZ ☎0800/808 480, ⓦwww.holidayshoppe.co.nz.

ⓦwww.lastminute.com.au Good last-minute holiday package and flight-only deals.

**New Zealand Destinations Unlimited** NZ ☎09/414 1685 ⓦwww.holiday.co.nz.

**Northern Gateway** Australia ☎1800/174 800, ⓦwww.northerngateway.com.au.

**STA Travel** Australia ☎1300/733 035, ⓦwww.statravel.com.au, NZ ☎0508/782 872, ⓦwww.statravel.co.nz.

**Student Uni Travel** Australia ☎02/9232 8444, ⓦwww.sut.com.au, NZ ☎09/379 4224, ⓦwww.sut.co.nz.

**Trailfinders** Australia ☎02/9247 7666, ⓦwww.trailfinders.com.au.

**travel.com.au & travel.co.nz** Australia ☎1300/130 482, NZ ☎0800/468 332. Comprehensive online travel company.

ⓦwww.travelshop.com.au Discounted flights, packages, insurance, and online bookings.

## Tour operators in Australia & NZ

**Abercrombie and Kent** Australia ☎03/9536 1800 or 1300/851 800, NZ ☎0800/441 638, ⓦwww.abercrombiekent.com.au. Upmarket river-cruise tour of the Netherlands, starting in Amsterdam.

**Contiki** Australia ☎02/9511 2200, NZ ☎09/309 8824, ⓦwww.contiki.com. Includes Amsterdam on its European camping country-hopping tours, aimed at 18- to 35-year-old party animals.

**Explore Holidays** Australia ☎02/9857 6200 or 1300/731 000, ⓦwww.exploreholidays.com.au. Accommodation and sight-seeing tours packages in and around Amsterdam.

**Kumuka Expeditions** Australia ☎1800/804 277 or 02/9279 0491, ⓦwww.kumuka.com.au. Independent tour operator, covers the Netherlands as part of western and central European overland trip.

**Viator** Australia ☎02/8219 5400, ⓦwww.viator.com. Fly-drive packages in the Netherlands, plus city tours in Amsterdam and Maastricht, bookable on-line.

# Red tape and visas

Citizens of the UK, Ireland, Australia, New Zealand, Canada and the US do not need a visa to enter the Netherlands if you're staying for three months or less. However, you do need a passport valid for at least six months after your arrival, a return airline ticket and/or funds deemed to be sufficient for your stay.

If you intend to stay beyond three months, you must apply for a **temporary residence permit** (a "VTV") within three days of your arrival in the Netherlands. Go to your local Aliens Police office (Vreemdelingenpolitie) armed with your birth certificate and proof that you have the funds to finance your stay in the Netherlands, a fixed address, and health insurance. For further information, visit the Ministry of Foreign Affairs website ⓦwww.minbuza.nl.

If you intend to work, you will need a **work permit**, for which your employer must apply on your behalf. The exceptions to this rule are the work schemes set up for Australian, New Zealand and Canadian citizens aged 18–30, who can stay for up to 12 months in the Netherlands on a "Working Holiday Scheme", provided you can convince the authorities that your main priority is holidaying, not working. For further information, contact the Dutch embassies in Canberra, Wellington, Ottawa or London.

## Dutch embassies abroad

**Australia** 120 Empire Circuit, Yarralumla, ACT 2600 ☎02/6220 9400, ⓦwww.netherlands.org.au.
**Canada** 350 Albert St #2020, Ottawa, ON, K1R 1A4 ☎613/237 5030, ⓦwww.netherlandsembassy.ca.
**Ireland** 160 Merrion Rd, Dublin 4 ☎01/269 3444, ⓦwww.netherlandsembassy.ie.
**New Zealand** Investment House, Ballance/Featherston St, Wellington ☎04/471 6390 ⓦwww.netherlandsembassy.co.nz.
**UK** 38 Hyde Park Gate, London, SW7 5DP ☎020/7590 3200, ⓦwww.netherlands-embassy.org.uk.
**USA** 4200 Linnean Ave NW, Washington, DC 20008 ☎202/244 5300, ⓦwww.netherlands-embassy.org.

## Embassies and consulates in the Netherlands

**Australia** Carnegielaan 4, 2517 KH Den Haag ☎070/310 8200, ⓦwww.australian-embassy.nl.
**Canada** Sophialaan 7, 2514 JP Den Haag ☎070/311 1600, ⓦwww.canada.nl.
**Ireland** Dr Kuijperstraat 9, 2514 BA Den Haag ☎070/363 0993, ⓦwww.irishembassy.nl.
**New Zealand** Carnegielaan 10, 2517 KH Den Haag ☎070/346 9324, ⓦwww.nzembassy.com.
**UK** Lange Voorhout 10, 2514 EG Den Haag ☎070/427 0427, ⓦwww.britain.nl. Consulate-General: Koningslaan 44, PO Box 75488, 1070 AL Amsterdam ☎020/676 4343.
**USA** Lange Voorhout 102, 2514 EJ Den Haag ☎070/310 9209, ⓦwww.usemb.nl. Consulate General: Museumplein 19, 1071 DJ Amsterdam ☎020/575 5309.

## Customs restrictions

There are **no restrictions** on importing goods (except tobacco) from another EU country, as long as they are not duty-free and you can prove that the goods are for personal use. If you are arriving in the Netherlands from a non-EU country, the following import limits apply: 200g cigarettes or 250g tobacco, 1 litre spirits or 2 litres of wine, 50g perfume. Coffee and tea are also subject to restrictions. If you're caught with more than these amounts, you'll have to pay tax on them, and possibly import duties as well. When you leave the Netherlands, there are no export restrictions on goods if you're travelling on to a EU country, but if you're travelling to a non-EU destination, you will be subject to the import regulations of your destination country. There are no restrictions on the import and export of currency.

# Information, websites and maps

For pre-departure planning, there is plenty of information available on the Internet, and from the Netherlands Board of Tourism. Nearly everybody in the Dutch tourist business has a website – from the largest hotel to the tiniest campsite. Most towns and provinces also maintain websites, often in English, with links to local attractions.

The Netherland's Board of Tourism's all-encompassing website Ⓦ**www.holland.com** highlights upcoming events, and is particularly strong on practical information. They also publish a wide range of brochures and guides.

## VVVs

Once in the Netherlands, almost every place you visit will have a **tourist office**, universally known as a **VVV** (pronounced *fay-fay-fay*), with a distinctive triangular logo. In towns, the VVV is usually either in the centre, often on the Grote Markt (the main square), or by the train station. Staff are nearly always enthusiastic and helpful, and speak excellent English. In addition to handing out basic maps (often for free) and English information on the main sights, many VVVs also keep lists of nearby accommodation, which they can book for you at a small fee (say €2.50). Quite often, these lists include lodgings in private houses (see p.32), which are accessible only through the VVV. Many VVV offices also keep information on neighbouring towns, which can be a great help for forward planning, particularly if the VVV in question has a counter of the Dutch motoring organization ANWB, where you'll find plenty of maps and touring information.

If you're roaming around a small area, the VVVs' chunky **province guides** can be useful, as they list every sort of accommodation from plush hotels to minicampings, albeit in Dutch. However, establishments must pay for inclusion, so there are many small hotels, pensions and campsites that are of perfectly good quality but which choose not to be represented in the official bumf.

## Useful websites

Ⓦ**www.ajax.nl** Virtual home of the world-famous Ajax Amsterdam football team – but doesn't sell match tickets.

Ⓦ**www.amsterdam.nl** Excellent site maintained by the municipality, with a useful facility enabling you to print a map for any address in the city.

Ⓦ**www.amsterdamhotspots.nl** City guide emphasizing music and club listings. Also good for the gay scene, coffeeshops and the Red Light District.

---

### Main city and regional VVVs

**Amsterdam** Ⓦ www.visitamsterdam.nl
**Flevoland** Ⓦ www.vvvflevoland.nl
**Friesland & Groningen area** Ⓦ www.beleefnoordnederland.nl
**Gelderland & Overijssel** Ⓦ www.overijsseltoerisme.nl
**Haarlem area** Ⓦ www.vvvzk.nl
**The Hague** Ⓦ www.denhaag.com
**Limburg** Ⓦ www.lb-toerisme.nl & Ⓦ www.vvvzuidlimburg.nl
**Maastricht** Ⓦ www.vvvmaastricht.nl
**Noord-Brabant** Ⓦ www.toerismebrabant.nl
**Noord-Holland** Ⓦ www.noord-holland-tourist.nl
**Rotterdam** Ⓦ www.rotterdam.info
**Utrecht** Ⓦ www.utrechtstad.com
**Zeeland** Ⓦ www.vvvzeeland.nl
**Zuid-Holland** Ⓦ www.zuid-hollandinfo.nl

Ⓦ **www.bbh.nl** The Flower Council of Holland, with listings of flower-related events.

Ⓦ **www.detelefoongids.nl** Search the Dutch phone directory (in Dutch).

Ⓦ **www.hollandmuseums.nl** Slick site with information on museums in the Netherlands and links to further information.

Ⓦ **www.hsa.lr.tudelft.nl/~bvo/fiets/nlbybike .htm** Informative site on cycling, with sound detail on bike culture, road rules and useful links.

Ⓦ **www.koninklijkhuis.nl** The Dutch royal family.

Ⓦ **www.learndutch.org** Good resource for getting to grips with the Dutch language.

Ⓦ **www.nl-menu.nl** Encyclopedic site crammed with links ranging from province websites to art, computers and philosophy.

Ⓦ **www.rnw.nl** Radio Netherlands, broadcasting Dutch news in English, with articles on current affairs, lifestyle issues, science, health and social issues.

Ⓦ **www.sievers.nl** Private site with atmospheric photographs of the Netherlands, especially landscapes.

Ⓦ **www.thehollandring.com** Over 300 pages of information on all things Dutch, aimed at the Dutch expat community.

Ⓦ **www.vangoghmuseum.nl** Online guide to the Amsterdam gallery, including essays by experts on some of Van Gogh's major works.

Ⓦ **www.woodenshoes.nl** Provides the (surely unique?) "clog-o-paedia", as well as history and online shopping for the famous wooden shoes.

## Maps

Several road **maps** of the Netherlands are widely available abroad and in the country. The Hallwag offering is particularly good: it's also the most detailed, at 1:200,000, a feat it accomplishes by being double-sided. Motorways and main roads are particularly lurid, but minor roads and villages are represented in considerable detail, and it includes an index. Kümmerly & Frey's country map (1:300,000) uses the excellent ANWB (Royal Dutch Touring Club) cartography, giving good road coverage with detailed insets for The Hague, Amsterdam, Rotterdam and Utrecht. With Michelin, you can either go for the annually updated 1:400,000 red-covered

*Benelux*, complete with index, or the two 1:200,000 yellow-covered indexed sheets covering the Netherlands only (Amsterdam–Groningen and Amsterdam–Maastricht). The ANWB publishes a broad variety of maps covering the country, ranging from three sectional maps (north, middle & south), to individual province maps and waterproof 1:100K sets specifically for cyclists (see p.30). Of the city maps, Falk publish the best; others are the Cito series and Geocart.

### Map outlets

#### UK & Ireland

**Blackwell's** UK ☎ 01865/793 550, Ⓦ www.blackwell.co.uk.
**Easons** Dublin ☎ 01/858 3881, Ⓦ www.eason.ie.
**Hodges Figgis** Dublin ☎ 01/677 4754, Ⓦ www.hodgesfiggis.com.
**Map Shop** UK ☎ 0116/247 1400, Ⓦ www.mapshopleicester.co.uk.
**Stanfords** UK ☎ 020/7836 1321, Ⓦ www.stanfords.co.uk.

#### US & Canada

**Adventurous Traveler** US ☎ 1-800/282-3963, Ⓦ www.adventuroustraveler.com.
**Elliot Bay Book Co.** US ☎ 1-800/962-5311, Ⓦ www.elliotbaybook.com.
**Globe Corner** US ☎ 1-800/358-6013, Ⓦ www.globecorner.com.
**Rand McNally** US ☎ 1-800/333-0136, Ⓦ www.randmcnally.com.
**World of Maps** Canada ☎ 1-800/214-8524, Ⓦ www.worldofmaps.com.

#### Australia & NZ

**Map Shop** Australia ☎ 08/8231 2033, Ⓦ www.mapshop.net.au.
**Mapland** Australia ☎ 03/9670 4383, Ⓦ www.mapland.com.au.
**Perth Map Centre** Australia ☎ 08/9322 5733, Ⓦ www.perthmap.com.au.
**Specialty Maps** NZ ☎ 09/307 2217, Ⓦ www.ubdonline.co.nz/maps.

### Museumjaarkaart

If you're planning to visit even a handful of museums around the Netherlands, you'll save money with a **Museumjaarkaart** (Museum Year-Card), which gives free entry to over 400 attractions nationwide. It costs €25 for a year (€12.50 if you're 24 or under), plus a one-off fee of €4.95. Full details, including online ordering, are at Ⓦ www.museumjaarkaart.nl.

# Insurance and health

Even though EU health care privileges apply in the Netherlands, you'd do well to take out an insurance policy before travelling to cover against theft, loss and illness or injury. No vaccinations are required.

Before paying for a new insurance policy, it's worth checking whether you're already covered: some all-risks home insurance policies may cover your possessions when overseas, and many private medical schemes include cover when abroad. In Canada, provincial health plans usually provide partial cover for medical mishaps overseas, while holders of official student/teacher/youth cards in Canada and the US are entitled to meagre accident coverage and hospital in-patient benefits. Students will often find that their student health coverage extends during the vacations and for one term beyond the date of last enrollment.

After exhausting these possibilities, you might want to contact a specialist travel insurance company, or consider the travel insurance deal offered by Rough Guides (see box). A typical policy usually provides cover for the loss of baggage, tickets and – up to a certain limit – cash or cheques, as well as cancellation or curtailment of your journey. Many policies can be chopped and changed to exclude coverage you don't need: sickness and accident benefits can often be

excluded or included at will. If you do take medical coverage, ascertain whether benefits will be paid as treatment proceeds or only after your return home, and whether there's a 24-hour medical emergency number. When securing baggage cover, make sure that the per-article limit – typically under £500/$750 – will cover your most valuable possession. If you need to make a claim, you should keep all receipts, and in the event you have anything stolen, you must obtain an official statement from the police.

## Health

As a member of the European Union, the Netherlands has free reciprocal health agreements with other member states. EU citizens are entitled to free treatment within the Netherlands' public health-care system on production of a stamped **Form E111** ("one-eleven"), available in Britain from post offices and online at ⊛ www.doh.gov.uk/traveladvice. It's a good idea to always keep your original E111 and several photocopies to hand, to show to doctors or ambulance crews in case of emergency. Australians are able to receive

---

### Rough Guides travel insurance

**Rough Guides** offers its own travel insurance, customized for our readers by a leading UK broker and backed by a Lloyd's underwriter. It's available for anyone, of any nationality and any age, travelling anywhere in the world. There are two main Rough Guide insurance plans: **Essential**, for basic, no-frills cover; and **Premier**, with more generous and extensive benefits. Alternatively, you can take out **annual multi-trip insurance**, which covers you for any number of trips throughout the year (with a maximum of 60 days for any one trip). Unlike many policies, the Rough Guides schemes are calculated by the day, so if you're travelling for 27 days rather than a month, that's all you pay for. If you intend to be away for the whole year, the **Adventurer** policy will cover you for 365 days. Each plan can be supplemented with a "Hazardous Activities Premium" if you plan to indulge in sports considered dangerous, such as skiing or trekking. For a policy quote or purchase, check out ⊛ **www.roughguidesinsurance.com** or call UK freephone ☎ 0800/015 0906, US toll-free ☎ 1-866/220 5588, or ☎ +441243/621046.

treatment through a reciprocal arrangement with Medicare (check with your local office for details). Anyone planning to stay for three months or more is required by Dutch law to have **private health insurance**. Taking out private insurance means the cost of items not within the purview of the EU scheme, such as dental treatment and repatriation on medical grounds, will be covered. **Non-EU residents**, apart from Australians, will need to insure themselves against all eventualities, including medical costs. In the case of major expense, the more worthwhile policies promise to sort matters out before you pay rather than after, but if you do have to pay upfront, make very sure that you always keep full doctors' reports, signed prescription details and all receipts.

## Medical treatment

Minor ailments can be remedied at a **drugstore** (*drogist*). These sell non-prescription drugs as well as toiletries, tampons, condoms and the like. A **pharmacy** (*apotheek*) – generally open Mon–Fri 9.30am–6pm, but often closed Monday mornings – is where you go to get a prescription filled. There aren't many 24-hour pharmacies, but the local VVV (see p.20), as well as most of the better hotels, will supply addresses of ones that stay open till late.

In more serious cases, you can get the address of an English-speaking **doctor** from your local pharmacy, tourist office or hotel. The 24-hour medical **helpline** Centrale Doktorsdienst (℡0900/503 2042) can give general advice about medical symptoms and let you know the details of duty doctors. If you're entitled to free treatment under EU health agreements, double-check that the doctor is both working within, and regarding you as a patient of, the public health care system. Bear in mind though, that even within the EU agreement you may still have to pay a significant portion of the prescription

charges (although senior citizens and children are exempt). Most private health insurance policies don't help cover prescription charges either, and although the "excesses" are usually greater than the cost of the medicines, it's worth keeping receipts just in case.

Minor accidents can be treated at the outpatients department of a **hospital** (*ziekenhuis*), but in **emergencies** phone ℡112. Again if you're reliant on free treatment within the EU health scheme, try to make this clear to the ambulance staff, and, if you're whisked off to hospital, to the medic you subsequently encounter. If possible, it's a good idea to hand over a photocopy of your E111 on arrival in the hospital to ensure your non-private status is clearly understood. In terms of describing symptoms, you can be pretty sure that someone will speak English. Without an E111 you won't be turned away from a hospital, but you will have to pay for any treatment you receive and should therefore get an official receipt, a necessary preamble to the long-winded process of trying to get at least some of the money back.

**Dental treatment** is not within the scope of the EU health agreement: again, enquire at the local tourist office or your hotel reception for an English-speaking dentist.

### Medical resources for travellers

ⓦ **health.yahoo.com** Information on specific diseases and conditions, drugs and herbal remedies, as well as advice from health experts.

ⓦ **www.fitfortravel.scot.nhs.uk** UK NHS website carrying information about travel-related diseases and how to avoid them.

ⓦ **www.istm.org** The website of the International Society for Travel Medicine, with a full list of clinics specializing in international travel health.

ⓦ **www.tripprep.com** Travel Health Online provides an online-only comprehensive database of necessary vaccinations for most countries, as well as destination and medical service provider information.

# Costs, money and banks

Accommodation in the Netherlands is moderately expensive by western European standards, and will probably prove to be the biggest drain on your budget. On the upside, public transport and food are reasonably priced. If you're planning to spend most of your time in Amsterdam you'll pay for the privilege, as hotel prices are around thirty percent more than in the rest of the country.

## Daily costs

For an idea of **daily costs**, the cheapest and easiest way to see the Netherlands is to travel by bicycle, eating picnics bought from supermarkets and cooking your own food at campsites. Doing this, it's quite possible to keep costs down to £10–15/US$15–20 a day per person. If you don't want to lug camping equipment with you, cycling also entitles you to the creature comforts of the excellent Vrienden op de Fiets (see p.32) – you'll need to factor in another £9.50/$15 to the daily budget. £20/$30 will cover the costs of using public transport to get around, enjoying a café lunch and camping at nights. Moving up a notch, if you picnic at lunch, stick to less expensive bars and restaurants, and stay in hostels you could get by on around £25/$40 a day. Staying in two-star hotels, eating out in medium-range restaurants and going to bars, you should reckon on at least £70/$115 a day, the main variable being the cost of your room – plus the higher prices in Amsterdam. On £100/$160 a day and upwards, you'll be limited only by your energy reserves, though if you're planning to stay in a five-star hotel anywhere in the country and have a big night out, this still won't be enough.

**Restaurants** don't come cheap, but costs remain manageable if you avoid the extras and concentrate on the main courses, for which around £10/$16 will normally suffice – twice that with a drink, starter and dessert. You can, of course, pay a lot more: a top restaurant can be £40/$60 a head, and then some. As always, if you're travelling alone you'll spend much more on accommodation than you would in a group of two or more: most hotels do have single rooms, but they're fixed at about 75 percent of the price of a double.

As for **incidental expenses**, a cup of coffee, a small glass of beer or a wedge of apple

cake cost less than £1/$1.60; today's English newspaper is about £3.30/$5; and developing a roll of film an amazing £13/$20. Museum admission prices hover around the £1–4/$2–6 mark. Current prices per gram of hash and marijuana range from £4.50/$7 for low-grade stuff up to £15/$25 for top-quality hash and as high as £23/$36 for really strong grass.

## Currency

The currency of the Netherlands – like much of the rest of the EU – is the **euro** (€), divided into 100 **cents**. There are notes of €500, €200, €100, €50, €20, €10 and €5, and coins of €2, €1, 50c, 20c, 10c, 5c, 2c and 1c. Euro coins feature a common EU design on one face, but different country-specific designs on the other, but no matter what the design, all euro coins and notes are legal tender in all of the following countries as well as the Netherlands: Austria, Belgium, Finland, France, Germany, Greece, Ireland, Italy, Luxembourg, Portugal and Spain.

## Carrying and changing money

The Netherlands is a cash society; as a general rule, people prefer to pay for most things with notes and coins. However, debit cards are becoming increasingly popular, and most shops and restaurants accept these and credit cards.

Dutch banks and post offices usually offer the best deals on **changing money**. Hours are Monday to Friday 9am to 4pm, with a few big-city banks also open Thursday until 9pm or on Saturday morning; all are closed on public holidays (see p.41). Outside these times, changing money is rarely a problem: there's a nationwide network of **GWK** exchange offices, usually at train stations, which are open late every day – sometimes, as at Amsterdam Centraal Station and Schiphol Airport, even 24 hours. GWK offers competitive rates and charges reasonable commissions, but some other agencies do not, so be cautious. VVV tourist offices also change money, as do most hotels and campsites and some hostels, but their rates are generally poor.

## Travellers' cheques

The safest way to carry your funds is in **travellers' cheques**; the usual fee for their purchase is one to two percent of face value, though this fee may be waived if you buy the cheques through a bank where you have an account. It pays to get a selection of denominations. Make sure you keep the purchase agreement and a record of cheque serial numbers safe and separate from the cheques themselves. In the event that cheques are lost or stolen, the issuing company will expect you to report the loss immediately; consequently, when you buy your cheques, ensure you have details of the company's emergency contact numbers or the addresses of their local offices. Most companies claim to replace lost or stolen cheques within 24 hours. When you cash your cheques, you'll find that almost all banks make a percentage charge per transaction on top of a basic minimum charge. American Express cheques are sold through most North American, Australasian and European banks, and are the most widely accepted cheques in the Netherlands; there's no charge for cashing American Express cheques at any of Amex's Dutch offices.

## Credit and debit cards

**Credit cards** are a very handy backup source of funds, and can be used either in ATMs or over the counter: Visa and Mastercard are widely accepted. When making a card purchase in a shop, you may be prompted to punch in your PIN code, one of the measures being taken in the Netherlands to combat credit (and debit) card fraud. You can use many Visa, Mastercard and UK debit cards (within the Cirrus, Plus or Maestro systems) to withdraw cash from ATMs – often the quickest and easiest way of obtaining money. There are dozens dotted across every major city and a reasonable number in smaller places too. They usually give instructions in a variety of languages. Check with your bank to find out about reciprocal arrangements.

**Visa TravelMoney** (ⓦ www.visa.com) combines the security of travellers' cheques with the convenience of plastic. It's a disposable debit card, charged up before you leave home with whatever amount you like, separate from your normal banking or credit accounts. You can then access these dedicated travel funds from any ATM that accepts Visa worldwide, with a PIN that you select yourself. Travelex/ Interpayment outlets sell the card worldwide (see ⓦ www.travelex.com for locations). When your money runs out, you just throw the card away. Since you can buy up to nine cards to access the same funds – useful for families travelling together – it's recommended that you buy at least one extra card as a back-up in case your first is lost or stolen. The 24-hour Visa customer service line from the Netherlands is ☏ 0800/022 3110.

### Lost and stolen

**American Express** cards ☏ 020/504 8000; travellers' cheques ☏ 0800/022 0100.
**Diners Club** ☏ 020/654 5511.
**Mastercard** ☏ 0800/022 5821.
**Visa** cards ☏ 0800/022 3110; travellers' cheques ☏ 0800/022 5484.

# Getting around

Getting around is never a problem in the Netherlands: it's a small country, and the longest journey you'll ever make – say from Amsterdam to Maastricht – takes under three hours by train or car. Furthermore, the public transport system is exemplary, a fully integrated network of trains and buses that brings even the smallest of villages within easy reach, and at very reasonable prices. Train and bus stations are almost always next door to each other, and several of the larger cities have a tram network.

## By train

The best way of travelling around the Netherlands is to take the **train**. The system, run by Nederlandse Spoorwegen or NS (Dutch Railways), is one of the best in Europe: trains are fast, modern, frequent and very punctual, fares are relatively low, and the network of lines comprehensive. Domestic services come in three types: the speedy **Intercity** for city-to-city connections, the normal **Sneltrein** which stops at main towns, and the snail-like **Stoptrein** which stops at every station. Ordinary fares are calculated by the kilometre, diminishing proportionately the further you travel: reckon on spending about €7 to travel 50km or so. Same-day return tickets (*dagretour*) knock about ten percent off the price of one-way tickets for the same journey, but otherwise returns are simply double the price of singles. First-class fares cost about fifty percent on top of the regular fare. With any ticket, you're free to stop off anywhere en route and continue your journey later that day, but you're not allowed to backtrack. For a one-way ticket, ask for an *enkele reis*; a return trip is a *retour*. See opposite for details of passes.

NS publishes mounds of information on its various services, passes and fares. Full information is at ⓦwww.ns.nl and ☎0900 9292. Their comprehensive and easy-to-use timetable (*spoorboekje*) is available inexpensively at major stations and in advance from the Netherlands Board of Tourism.

Before you start queueing with only a minute or two until your train, it's useful to know that you cannot **pay** for a train ticket with a credit card or a foreign debit card. Train station ticket desks accept only cash or the Dutch "PIN" pass debit card. This goes for the automatic ticket machines too – and these take coins only, not banknotes. Train stations in main towns all have a GWK change office with an ATM, which means you can withdraw the necessary cash before facing the queues.

### Treintaxis

In NS's **treintaxi** scheme, rail passengers can be assured of a taxi to or from most major stations. At the start of your journey, to get to the station call the local *treintaxi*

---

### Planning a journey

For pre-departure information on your train journey, the **"Planner Plus"** feature on the Dutch railways website ⓦ**www.ns.nl** is hard to beat. Type in your departure and arrival points (train station, street address or even just the name of a museum or concert hall), and it will not only give you a street map to get to the nearest station, but will also tell you what platform your train leaves from, how many changes to make (and where, with platform numbers), and how much your ticket will cost. It even tells you how long your journey will take, factoring in how you get to and from the train station at either end – on foot, by bike, driving or on the bus.

## MAJOR RAIL ROUTES

number or ☎0900/873 4682, at least half an hour in advance; within the city limits, the fare is a flat-rate €3.50. On arrival at the local station, you can either book a *treintaxi* for your destination station when you buy your ticket (€3.80), or wait till you get there and pay the driver (€4.80). Most major stations have *treintaxi* buttons at the entrance, which you press to summon a *treintaxi* for your onward journey (within the city limits). Note that *treintaxis* are not the same as regular taxis – you may well, for instance, have to share with other people taking a similar route. The cabs are identifiable by a "*treintaxi*" sign on the roof and they have a separate rank outside train stations.

### Rail passes

NS offers several discount tickets, including a **Day Pass** for unlimited travel on any train (first-class €55; second-class €36), and the

OV-Day Pass (€59; €40), which includes all trams and buses. The **Railrunner** ticket means up to three children aged 4–11 can travel with an adult for just €1 per journey. A particularly good deal in July and August is the **Zomertoer** (Summer Trip) ticket, which for €59 enables two people to travel anywhere in the Netherlands by public transport over three days; these days don't have to be consecutive, but must be within ten days of the first time you use the ticket.

If you intend to use the trains at all frequently and are travelling in a group, then it's worth considering the **Vordeel-urenkaart** (Off-peak Discount Pass). For €45, you get a discount of forty percent off all off-peak journeys (ie after 9am), and so do up to three people travelling with you.

In addition to these, there's a host of pan-European rail passes. Some have to be bought before leaving home while others can be bought only in specific countries. Rail Europe is the umbrella company for all national and international rail purchases, and its comprehensive website (@www .raileurope.com) is the most useful source of information on which rail passes are available; it also gives current prices.

### Inter-Rail and Eurail

An **Inter-Rail pass** (@www.inter-rail.co.uk) is only available to European residents, and comes in under-26 and over-26 versions. The pass covers 28 European countries (including Turkey and Morocco) grouped together in zones; the Netherlands falls in Zone E, along with France, Belgium and Luxembourg. It's available for 22 days (one zone only) or a month (one or more zones). A 12-day pass for one zone costs £119/169 for under/over 26s. Online purchase is discounted, as are trains within the UK (including London–Paris by Eurostar) and cross-Channel ferries. If you're coming from Ireland, you must buy a pass for two zones (under/over 26s pay €285/402) in order to cover travel across the UK (Zone A) before you reach Zone E; this also gives reductions on the ferries.

A **Eurailpass** (@www.raileurope.com) – for non-EU residents only – allows first-class train travel in 17 countries, including the Netherlands; it's only an economical option if you're planning to venture further afield. The pass, only buyable outside Europe, is available for 15 days (US$588), 21 days (US$762), or 1, 2 or 3 months. A **Eurailpass**

**Youth** is valid for second-class travel for under-26s; 2–5 people travelling together can get a joint **Eurail Saverpass**. A **Eurailpass Flexi** is good for 10 days' (US$694) or 15 days' (US$914) first-class travel within a two-month period, and has under-26 (**Eurailpass Youth Flexi**) and group (**Eurailpass Saver Flexi**) versions. Finally, the **Eurail Selectpass** lets you travel in 3, 4 or 5 adjoining countries for either 5, 6, 8, 10 or 15 days within a two-month period; for this plan, Belgium, Luxembourg and the Netherlands count as one country. A 5-day pass over 3 countries costs US$356. It also comes in under-26 (**Eurail Selectpass Youth**) and group (**Eurail Selectpass Saver**) versions.

A **Euro-Domino** pass – for those who've lived in the EU for at least six months (@www.raileurope.co.uk) – is valid on Dutch trains for between 3 and 8 days' travel within a one-month period; to get a 5-day pass, under/over-26s pay £64/84. Euro Domino pass-holders pay half-price on the ferries between Ireland and the UK, and between the UK and the Netherlands, and also get a 25-percent discount on the train journey across the UK to Harwich.

## By bus, tram and metro

Supplementing the extensive train network are **buses** – run by local companies but again amazingly efficient, spreading out to span the local surroundings from ranks of bus stops almost always located bang next to the train station. Ticketing is straightforward, using *strippenkaarts* (see box). However, some long-distance routes, covered by fast and reliable Interliner coaches (@www.interliner.nl), don't accept *strippenkaarts* – on these buses, you must pay the driver for your journey.

Bear in mind that in more rural areas, some bus services only operate when passengers have made advance bookings. Local timetables indicate where this applies.

Within major towns, urban public transport systems are extensive, cheap and frequent, which make getting around straightforward and hassle-free; they generally run from 6am until about midnight. **Trams** coast the streets of The Hague, Amsterdam and Rotterdam, while Amsterdam and Rotterdam also have **metro** systems. *Strippenkaarts* can be used on all public transport (including the trams and metros), except night buses, where you must purchase a ticket from the driver.

## Travelling on a strippenkaart

Ticketing for all kinds of buses in the Netherlands, plus city metros and trams, is simple, organized on a universal, nationwide system. You need to buy just one kind of ticket wherever you are: a **strippenkaart** – a piece of card made out of strips. The whole country is divided up into zones; you need to cancel one strip on your *strippenkaart* for yourself plus one for each of the zones you travel through. On city trams and metro systems you cancel the *strippenkaart* yourself by folding it over to the right place and inserting it into the date-stamping machines provided; you only need to stamp the last of however many strips you need, not every single strip. On buses, generally you hand the *strippenkaart* to the driver, who will do the stamping for you. In larger towns and cities, two strips is enough to take you anywhere in the centre.

You can buy 2- and 3-strip *strippenkaarts* at a premium from bus drivers, or pick up the better-value 15-strip (€6.20) or 45-strip (€18.30) *strippenkaarts* in advance from train stations, tobacconists and local public transport offices.

One *strippenkaart* can be used by any number of people, provided that the requisite number of strips is cancelled for each person's journey. Similarly, strips can be carried over from one *strippenkaart* to another: if you've used up, say, 14 of your 15 strips, you can stamp the 15th strip on one card and the first strip on another, new card in order to travel.

Such a well-integrated transport system makes travelling within cities by car rather redundant – indeed, plenty of "Park and Ride" or Transferium schemes encourage drivers to leave their vehicle in designated car parks on the outskirts and catch the bus into town. It makes sense to take advantage of these, as most towns have a deliberate policy of making parking for non-residents awkward and often expensive.

## By car

**Driving** around the Netherlands is pretty much what you would expect: smooth, easy and quick. The country has a uniformly good road network, with most of the major towns linked by some kind of motorway or dual carriageway; traffic gets congested only on the outskirts of the major cities. Rules of the road are straightforward: you drive on the right, and **speed limits** are 50kph in built-up areas, 80kph outside, 120kph on motorways – though some motorways have a speed limit of 100kph, indicated by small yellow signs on the side of the road. Drivers and front-seat passengers are required by law to wear seatbelts, and penalties for drunk driving are severe. There are no toll roads, and although petrol isn't particularly cheap, at around €1.10 per litre, the short distances mean this isn't much of a factor.

All EU driving licences are valid in the Netherlands, but other nationals will need an International Driver's Licence (available at minimal cost from your home motoring organization). Any sort of provisional licence is, however, not acceptable. If you're bringing your own car, you must have vehicle registration papers, adequate insurance, a first-aid kit, a warning triangle and a green card (available from your insurers or motoring organization). Extra insurance coverage for unforeseen legal costs is also well worth having, as is an appropriate breakdown policy from a motoring organization back home.

### Motoring organizations

**Australia** AAA ☎ 02/6247 7311, ⓦ www.aaa.asn.au.
**Canada** CAA ☎ 613/247-0117, ⓦ www.caa.ca.
**Ireland** AA ☎ 01/617 9988, ⓦ www.aaireland.ie.
**Netherlands** ANWB ☎ 0800 0503, ⓦ www.anwb.nl.
**New Zealand** AA ☎ 09/377 4660, ⓦ www.nzaa.co.nz.
**UK** AA ☎ 0800/444 500, ⓦ www.theaa.co.uk; RAC ☎ 0800/550 055, ⓦ www.rac.co.uk.
**US** AAA ☎ 1-800/222-4357, ⓦ www.aaa.com.

### Renting a car

All the major international **car rental** agencies are represented in the Netherlands;

contact details are given in the "Listings" section at the end of the guide accounts of major towns. To rent a car, you'll have to be 21 or over (and have been driving for at least a year), and you'll need a credit card – though some local agencies will accept a hefty cash deposit instead. Rental charges are fairly high, beginning around €300 per week for unlimited mileage in the smallest vehicle, but include collision damage waiver and vehicle (but not personal) insurance. To cut costs, watch for special deals offered by the bigger companies. If you go to a smaller, local company (of which there are many), you should proceed with care: in particular, check the policy for the excess applied to claims and ensure that it includes a collision damage waiver (applicable if an accident is your fault) as well as adequate levels of financial cover. Bear in mind, too, that it's almost always less expensive to rent your car before you leave home and pick it up at the airport on arrival.

If you break down in a rented car, you'll get roadside assistance from the particular repair company the rental firm has contracted. The same principle works with your own vehicle's breakdown policy.

**Avis** UK ☏0870/606 0100, ⓦwww.avis.co.uk; Ireland ☏01/605 7500, ⓦwww.avis.ie; US ☏1-800/331-1084, Canada ☏1-800/272-5871, ⓦwww.avis.com; Australia ☏13 63 33, ⓦwww.avis.com.au; NZ ☏09/526 2847, ⓦwww.avis.co.nz.

**Budget** UK ☏0800/181 181, ⓦwww.budget.co.uk; Ireland ☏0903/27711, ⓦwww.budget.ie; US ☏1-800/527-0700, ⓦwww.budget.com; Australia ☏1300/362 848, ⓦwww.budget.com.au; NZ ☏09/976 2222, ⓦwww.budget.co.nz.

**Europcar** UK ☏0870/607 5000, ⓦwww.europcar.co.uk; Ireland ☏01/614 2800, ⓦwww.europcar.ie; US & Canada ☏1-877/940 6900, ⓦwww.europcar.com.

**Hertz** UK ☏0870/848 4848, ⓦwww.hertz.co.uk; Ireland ☏01/676 7476, ⓦwww.hertz.ie; US ☏1-800/654-3001, Canada ☏1-800/263-0600, ⓦwww.hertz.com; Australia ☏13 30 39; NZ ☏0800/654 321.

**Holiday Autos** UK ☏0870/400 0099, Ireland ☏01/872 9366, US ☏1-800/422-7737, Australia ☏1300/554 432, NZ ☏0800/144 040, ⓦwww.holidayautos.com.

**National** UK ☏0870/536 5365, ⓦwww.nationalcar.co.uk; US ☏1-800/227-7368, ⓦwww.nationalcar.com; Australia ☏13 10 45,

ⓦwww.nationalcar.com.au; NZ ☏0800/800 115, ⓦwww.nationalcar.co.nz.

**Thrifty** UK ☏01494/751 600, ⓦwww.thrifty.co.uk; Ireland ☏1800/515 800, ⓦwww.thrifty.ie; US ☏1-800/367-2277, ⓦwww.thrifty.com; Australia ☏1300/367 227, ⓦwww.thrifty.com.au, NZ ☏09/309 0111, ⓦwww.thrifty.co.nz.

## Cycling

By far the best way to see the Netherlands, whether you're a cyclist or not, is to travel **by bike** (*fiets*). **Cycle-touring** is a short-cut into Dutch culture and offers insights that will pass you by in a blur from the train or car – from a bike, you can peer into homes, be bemused by garden knick-knacks or just watch the cows chewing the cud. Kilometres of beaches, forests and heather are accessible to you if you have a bike; you can find yourself battling against a head-wind powering a wind farm, or swallowed up in a shoal of cyclists commuting to work.

To the Dutch, the bicycle is both a utility and recreational mode of transport, and there are thousands of kilometres of quiet cycleways. The mostly flat landscape makes travelling by bike an almost effortless pursuit (until the wind starts blowing) and the short distances involved make it possible to see most of the country with relative ease, using the nationwide system of well-marked cycle paths. A circular blue sign with a white bicycle on it indicates an obligatory cycle lane, separate from car traffic. Red lettering on signposts give distances for fairly direct routes, lettering in green denote a more scenic (and lengthy) mosey. Long-distance (LF) routes weave through the cities and countryside, often linking up to local historic loops and scenic trails.

The Dutch as a nation are celebrated touring cyclists, and bookshops are packed with cycling books; however, for all but the longest trips the maps and route advice provided by most VVVs are fine.

After a day in the saddle, the best advice is to visit a member of the *Vrienden op de Fiets* (see p.32), who for €14 will put you up for the night in their home and feed you a princely breakfast the next morning. Many hosts are wonderfully warm and hospitable, as well as experts on cycling in their own country (and often many others).

Most visitors to the Netherlands either bring their own bike or **rent** one. You can rent a bike from all main train stations for around €5.20 a day or €18 per week, plus a €50 deposit (€100 in larger centres). Most bikes are single-speed, though there are some 3-speeds to be had, and even mountain bikes in the hillier south. You'll also need some form of ID. The snag is that cycles must be returned to the station from which they were rented, making onward hops by rented bike impossible. Most bike shops rent bicycles out for around the same amount, and they may be more flexible on deposits – some may accept a passport in lieu of cash. Wherever you're intending to rent your bike from, in summer it's a good idea to reserve one in advance. It is possible to take your bike on **trains**, and the bike carriages have a clear cycle symbol on the exterior. You'll need to buy a flat-rate €6 ticket (*dagkaart fiets*) for your bike, which is valid for the whole day. Space can be limited,

despite the variety of ingeniously folding bikes favoured by locals, and because of this you won't be allowed on at all during the morning and evening rush hours (6.30–9am and 5.30–6pm), except in July and August.

Note that in the larger cities in particular, but really anywhere around the country, you should never, ever, leave your bike **unlocked**, even for a few minutes. In central Amsterdam and elsewhere, thieves armed with bolt-cutters and sophisticated lock-picking equipment tour the streets day and night: used bikes are big business for individuals within the Netherlands and organized gangs shipping stolen bikes around Europe. You should always bring your bike in off the street at night, if you can. Almost all train stations have somewhere you can store your bike safely for less than a euro.

# Accommodation

With prices comparable to those of most of western Europe, few would claim that hotel accommodation is much of a bargain in the Netherlands, though a wide network of inexpensive hostels and well-equipped campsites can, if needs must, keep costs down. Wherever you stay, you should book ahead of time during the summer and over holiday periods like Easter, when rooms can run short. In Amsterdam, room shortages are commonplace throughout the year, so advance booking is always required, and note also that Amsterdam hotel prices are on average about thirty percent higher than elsewhere in the country.

## Hotels

All **hotels** in the Netherlands are graded on a star system. One-star and no-star hotels are rare, and prices for two-star establishments start at around €50 for a double room without private bath or shower; count on paying at least €75 if you want ensuite facilities. Three-star hotels cost upwards of about €75; for four- and five-star places you'll pay €125-plus. Generally, the stated price includes breakfast – except in the most expensive and the very cheapest of hotels.

During the summer in all parts of the country – but especially in Amsterdam and the major tourist centres – it's pretty much essential to reserve a room in advance, if you are to avoid spending above your budget. You can do this most easily by calling the hotel direct; English is almost always spoken so there should be no language problem. You can also contact the Netherlands Reservations Centre, or NRC (☎0299/689 114, ✉info@hotelres.nl), which coordinates the website ⊛www.hotelres.nl, where you can view availability and prices and make

## Accommodation price codes

All the hotels listed in this guide have been graded according to the following **price codes**, which indicate the price for the cheapest double room available during high season. In the case of hostels we've given the code if they have double rooms; otherwise, we've stated the price per dorm bed in euros. Single rooms generally cost between sixty and eighty percent of the double-room rate. These codes are above all a guide to price, and aren't intended to indicate the level of facilities available. You'll also find that many bottom-end hotels have a mixture of rooms, some with ensuite facilities, some without; an establishment graded, for example, as a ❸ may also have plenty of more comfortable rooms at ❹ prices.

| | | |
|---|---|---|
| ❶ up to €50 | ❹ €90–120 | ❼ €180–230 |
| ❷ €50–70 | ❺ €120–150 | ❽ €230–300 |
| ❸ €70–90 | ❻ €150–180 | ❾ over €300 |

hotel and apartment bookings online. You'll find a similar service at not-so-slick ⓦ www.hotels-holland.com and other sites. In The Netherlands itself, you can make advance bookings in person through any VVV office for a nominal fee.

### Private rooms

One way of cutting costs is, wherever possible, to use **private** accommodation – rooms in private homes that are let out to visitors on a bed and breakfast basis; they're sometimes known in the Netherlands as pensions. Prices are usually quoted per person and are normally around €20; breakfast is usually included, but if not will cost about €3.50 on top. You have to go through local VVVs to find private rooms: they will either give you a list to follow up independently or will insist that they book the accommodation themselves and levy a minimal booking fee. Bear in mind, also, that not all VVVs are able to offer private accommodation; generally you'll find it only in the larger towns and tourist centres.

### Vrienden op de Fiets

If you're cycling or walking around the Netherlands, the organization **Vrienden op de Fiets** (Friends of the Bicycle; ⓦ www .vriendenopdefiets.nl) is an absolute bargain. For a €6 joining fee, you'll be sent a book of almost two thousand addresses in the Netherlands where you can stay the night in somebody's home for a maximum of €14 per person; all you have to do is phone 24 hours in advance. Accommodation can range from stylish townhouses to suburban semis to centuries-old farmhouses – you don't know until you turn up – and staying in somebody's home can give a great insight into Dutch life. Hosts are usually very friendly, can offer local information about the area and will provide a breakfast of often mammoth proportions the next morning to send you on your way.

### Hostels

If you're travelling on a budget, a **hostel** is likely to be your accommodation of choice, whether you're youthful or not. They can often be extremely good value, and offer clean and comfortable dorms as well as a choice of rooms (doubles and sometimes singles) that can often undercut normal hotel prices. Both city and country locations can get very full between June and September, when you should book in advance. If you're planning on spending some nights in hostels, it makes sense to join your home HI organization (see opposite) before you leave in order to avoid paying surcharges.

Stayokay (ⓦ www.stayokay.com) – formerly the Dutch Youth Hostel Association (NJHC) – runs thirty **hostels** in the Netherlands, all affiliated to Hostelling International (HI). Dorm beds cost between €15–25 per person per night including breakfast, depending on the season and the hostel's facilities; there are no age restrictions. Accommodation is usually in small dormitories, though most hostels have single- and double-bedded rooms. Meals are often available – about €8 for a filling dinner – and in some hostels there are kitchens where you can cook your own food. If you're not already an HI member, you normally have to pay a small surcharge of €2.50. Most Stayokay hostels accept online bookings. In addition to Stayokay HI hostels, the larger cities – particularly Amsterdam – have a number of other hostels offering dormitory accommodation (and invariably double- and triple-bedded rooms, too) at broadly similar prices, though standards are frequently not as high as the official HI places, and are sometimes extremely poor; we've given detailed reviews in the guide.

In some cities you may also come across something known as a **Sleep-in**: dormitory accommodation established and run by the local council, and normally only open during the summer. This often turns out to be cheaper than staying in a hostel. Locations vary from year to year; for the most up-to-date information on local sleep-ins, contact the VVV. The same goes for student accommodation, which is sporadically open to travellers during the summer holidays in some university towns.

## HI hostel associations

**Australia** ☎02/9261 1111, ⊛www.yha.org.au.
**Canada** ☎800/663-5777, ⊛www.hihostels.ca.
**England & Wales** ☎0870/770 8868,
⊛www.yha.org.uk.
**Netherlands** ☎010/264 6064,
⊛www.stayokay.com.
**New Zealand** ☎03/379 9970,
⊛www.yha.org.nz.
**Northern Ireland** ☎028/9032 4733,
⊛www.hini.org.uk.
**Republic of Ireland** ☎01/830 4555,
⊛www.anoige.ie.
**Scotland** ☎0870/155 3255, ⊛www.syha.org.uk.
**USA** ☎202/783-6161, ⊛www.hiayh.org.

# Camping and trekkers' huts

**Camping** is a viable proposition in the Netherlands: there are plenty of sites, most are very well equipped, and they represent a good saving on other forms of accommodation. Prices vary greatly, mainly depending on the facilities available, but you can generally expect to pay around €2.50–5 per person, plus the same again for a tent, and another €2.50–5 or so if you have a car or motorbike. All VVVs have details of their nearest sites, and we've mentioned campsites throughout the guide. A list of selected sites is available from the Dutch camping association, Stichting Vrije Recreatie, Broekseweg 75–77, 4231 VD Meerkerk (☎0183/352 741). If you don't mind your facilities basic then look out for **mini-campings** that are generally signed off the roads. These are often family-run – you may end up pitched next to their house – and are informal, cheap and friendly. Details of VVV-affiliated minicampings can be found in the accommodation sections of the province guides, available in every VVV. Campsites run by Staatsbosbeheer (the National Forestry Commission) are scenically located on nature reserves; they are basic, but the surroundings make up for it. Bookshops carry a variety of publications on the country's campsites.

Some campsites also offer **trekkers' huts** – frugally furnished wooden affairs that can house a maximum of four people for €30 a night (excluding nominal tourist tax). You can get details of the national network, with good information in English, and a list of sites province-by-province, at ⊛www.trekkershutten.nl.

# Eating and drinking

Quite rightly, the Netherlands is not renowned for its cuisine, but although much of Dutch fare is unimaginative, prices won't break the bank. Where the Netherlands scores is in its array of ethnic restaurants, especially Indonesian and Chinese; you can get some of Europe's best Southeast Asian food in Amsterdam and the other big cities. Drinking, too, is easily affordable – indeed, downing a Dutch beer at one of the country's many good bars is one of the real pleasures of a visit.

## Food

Dutch **food** tends to be higher in protein content than variety: steak, chicken and fish, along with filling soups and stews, are staple fare, usually served up in enormous quantities. It can, however, at its best, be excellent, some restaurants – and even bars and *eet-cafés* – offering increasingly adventurous crossovers with French cuisine at good-value prices. However, it has to be said that Dutch service is not known for its speed, and isn't always the friendliest, either.

### Breakfast

In all but the cheapest and most expensive of hotels, **breakfast** (*ontbijt*) will be included in the price of the room. Though usually nothing fancy, it's always substantial: rolls, cheese, ham, hard-boiled eggs, jam and honey or peanut butter are the principal ingredients. Many bars and cafés serve rolls and sandwiches in similar mode, although few open much before 8 or 8.30am.

Dutch **coffee** is normally good and strong, served with a little tub of *koffiemelk* (evaporated milk); ordinary milk is rarely used. If you want coffee with warm milk, ask for a *koffie verkeerd*. Tea generally comes with lemon if anything – if you want milk you have to ask for it. Chocolate (*chocomel*) is also popular, hot or cold: for a real treat, drink it hot with a layer of fresh whipped cream (*slagroom*) on top. Some coffeeshops also sell aniseed-flavoured warm milk (*anijsmelk*).

### Snacks, sandwiches and cakes

Beyond breakfast, eating cheaply, particularly on your feet, is no real problem, although those on the tightest of budgets may find themselves dependent on the dubious delights of Dutch **fast food**. This has its own peculiarities. Chips/fries (*frites* or *patat*) are the most common standby – *vlaamse* or "Flemish" style are the best – sprinkled with salt and smothered with huge gobs of mayonnaise (*fritesaus*) or, alternatively, curry, sateh, goulash, or tomato sauce. If you just want salt, ask for "*patat zonder*"; fries with salt and mayonnaise are "*patat met*". You'll also come across *kroketten* – spiced minced meat (usually either veal or beef), covered with breadcrumbs and deep fried – or *fricandel*, a frankfurter-like sausage. All these are available over the counter at evil-smelling fast-food places, or, for a euro or so, from coin-op heated glass compartments on the street and in train stations.

Tastier are the **fish** specialities sold by street vendors, which are good as a snack or a full lunch: salted raw herring, rollmops, smoked eel (*gerookte paling*), mackerel in a roll (*broodje makreel*), mussels, and various kinds of deep-fried fish are all delicious. Look out, too, for "green" or *maatje* herring, eaten raw with onions in early summer: hold the fish by the tail, tip your head back and dangle it into your mouth, Dutch-style.

Another snack you'll see everywhere is *shoarma* or *shwarma* – another name for a doner kebab, shavings of lamb pressed into a flat pitta bread – sold in numerous Middle Eastern restaurants and takeaways for about €3. Other, less common, street foods include pancakes (*pannekoeken*), sweet or spicy, also widely available at sit-down restaurants; waffles (*stroopwafels*), doused with syrup; and, in November and December, *oliebollen*, greasy doughnuts sometimes filled with fruit (often apple) or custard as a *berliner* and traditionally eaten on New Year's Eve.

## Dutch cheese

The Netherlands' **cheeses** have an unjustified reputation abroad for being bland – the Dutch tend to export the lower-quality stuff and keep the best for themselves. On home turf, Dutch cheese can be delicious, although there isn't the variety on show in, say, France or Switzerland. Most Dutch cheeses vary little from the familiar pale yellow, semi-soft **Gouda**, within which differences in taste come with the varying stages of maturity: *jong* cheese has a mild flavour, *belegen* is much tastier, while *oud* can be pungent and strong, with a grainy, flaky texture. The best way to eat it is as the Dutch do, in thin slices (cut with a cheese slice, or *kaasschaaf*) rather than large hunks. Among other names to look out for, best known is **Edam**, also semi-soft in texture but slightly drier than Gouda; it's usually shaped into balls and coated in red wax ready for export – it's not eaten much in the Netherlands. **Leidse** is simply a bland Gouda laced with cumin or caraway seeds; most of its flavour comes from the seeds. **Maasdam** is a Dutch version of Emmental or Jarlsberg, strong, creamy and full of holes, sold under brand names such as Leerdammer and Maasdammer. You'll also find Dutch-made Emmental and Gruyère.

Bars often serve sandwiches and rolls (*boterham* and *broodjes*) – often open, and varying from a slice of tired cheese on old bread to something so embellished it's almost a complete meal – as well as different kinds of more substantial fare. A sandwich made with French bread is known as a *stokbrood*. In the winter, *erwtensoep* (or *snert*) – thick pea soup with smoked sausage, served with smoked bacon on pumpernickel – is available in many bars, and at about €4 a bowl makes a great buy for lunch. Or there's an *uitsmijter* (a "kicker-out", derived from the practice of serving it at dawn after an all-night party to prompt guests to depart): widely available at all times of day, it comprises one, two, or three fried eggs on buttered bread, topped with a choice of ham, cheese, or roast beef – at about €5, another good budget lunch.

### Cakes and cookies

Dutch **cakes** and cookies are always good, best eaten in a *banketbakkerij* (patisserie) with a small serving area; or buy a bag and munch them on the hoof. Top of the list is the ubiquitous Dutch speciality *appelgebak* – chunky, memorably fragrant apple-and-cinnamon pie, served hot in huge wedges, often with whipped cream (*met slagroom*). Other nibbles include *speculaas*, a crunchy cinnamon cookie with gingerbread texture; *stroopwafels*, butter wafers sandwiched together with runny syrup; and *amandelkoek*, cakes with a crisp cookie outside and melt-in-the-mouth almond paste inside. In and around Maastricht, don't miss *Limburgse Vlaai*, a pie with various fruit fillings.

### Sit-down eating

You'll find that the majority of **bars** serve food, everything from sandwiches to a full menu – in which case they may be known instead as an **eetcafé**. This type of place tends to be open all day, serving both lunch and an evening meal. Full-blown **restaurants**, on the other hand, tend to open in the evening only, usually from around 5.30pm or 6pm until around 11pm. Bear in mind that everywhere, especially in the smaller provincial towns, the Dutch tend to eat early, usually around 7.30 or 8pm: after about 10pm you'll find many restaurant kitchens closed.

If you're on a budget, stick to the *dagschotel* (dish of the day) wherever possible, for which you pay around €10 for a meat or fish dish, heavily garnished with potatoes and other vegetables and salad; note, though, that it's often only served at lunchtime or between 6 and 8pm. Otherwise, you can pay up to €15 for a meat course in an average restaurant; fish is generally high quality but rarely cheap at €12–17. A three-course *tourist menu*, which you'll see displayed at some mainstream restaurants, is – at €14 or so – reasonable value, but the food is often dull.

Surprisingly enough, train station restaurants are a good standby: every station has one serving full meals, in huge portions, for €5–7.50. Consider also the Netherlands' cheapest option for eating out, the university mensa restaurants in larger towns, where – with international student ID – you can get a filling, if not especially exciting, meal for under €6.

**Vegetarian** dining isn't a problem. Many eetcafés and restaurants have at least one meat-free menu item, and you'll find a few veggie restaurants in most of the larger towns, offering full-course set meals for €5–7.50 – although bear in mind that they often close earlier than normal.

Of foreign cuisines, Italian food is ubiquitous: pizzas and pasta dishes start at a fairly uniform €8 or so in all but the ritziest places. To eat Spanish and Tex-Mex costs a little more. **Surinamese** restaurants are a good bet for eating on a budget: try roti, flat pancake-like bread served with a spicy curry, hardboiled egg, and vegetables. **Chinese** and **Indonesian** restaurants, too, are widespread, and are normally well worth checking out. Nasi goreng and bami goreng (rice or noodles with meat) are good basic dishes, though there are normally more exciting items on the menu, some very spicy; chicken or beef in peanut sauce (sateh) is always available. Or you could try a rijsttafel – a sampler meal, comprising boiled rice and/or noodles served with perhaps ten or twelve small, often spicy dishes and hot sambal sauce on the side. Eaten with the spoon in the right hand, fork in the left, and washed down with a beer or dry white or rosé wine, this doesn't come cheap, but it's delicious and is normally more than enough for two; indeed that's the usual way to order it – reckon on paying around €45 for two people.

## Drinking

Most **drinking** is done either in the cosy surroundings of a brown café (bruin kroeg) – so named because of the colour of the walls, often stained by years of tobacco smoke – or in more modern-looking places, everything from slick designer bars, minimally furnished and usually catering for a younger crowd, to cosy neighbourhood bars. Most bars stay open until around 1am during the week and 2am at weekends, though some don't bother to open until lunchtime, a few not until 4 or 5pm. There is another drinking establishment that you may come across, though they're no longer common – proeflokaalen or tasting houses, originally the sampling premises of small distillers, now small, old-fashioned bars that only serve spirits (and maybe a few beers) and sometimes close early at around 8pm.

**Beer**

The most commonly consumed beverage countrywide is **beer**, pilsener-type lager usually served in a relatively small measure (just under a half-pint, with a foaming head on top) – ask for een pils. Prices are fairly standard: you don't pay much over the odds for sitting outside or drinking in a swanky bar or club. Reckon on paying about €1.50 pretty much everywhere. Some bars, particularly those popular with the local English community, serve beer in larger measures, close to a pint, for which you can expect to pay €3–4. Beer is much cheaper from a supermarket, most brands retailing at just under €1 for a half-litre bottle.

The most common Dutch brands are Heineken, Amstel, Oranjeboom and Grolsch, all of which you can find more or less nationwide. Expect them to be stronger and more distinctive than the watery approximations brewed abroad under licence. In the south of the country, you'll also find a number of locally brewed beers which are worth sampling – Bavaria from Noord-Brabant, De Ridder, Leeuw, Gulpen and Brand (the country's oldest brewer) from Limburg. For something a little less strong, look out for donkenbier, which is about half the strength of an ordinary pilsener beer. There are also a number of seasonal beers: rich, fruity bokbier is widespread in autumn, while in summer (and year-round in some places) you'll see witbier (white beer) such as Hoegaarden, Dentergems or Raaf – refreshing and potent in equal measure, and often served with a slice of a lemon or lime.

Around the country, you'll also spot plenty of the better-known Belgian brands available on tap, like Stella Artois and the darker De Koninck, as well as bottled beers like Duvel, Chimay and various brands of the cherry-flavoured Kriek.

## Cannabis coffeeshops

Art, architecture and cycling aside, a fair proportion of visitors to the Netherlands – and to Amsterdam in particular – have come for one thing: the **drugs**. Dutch cities remain just about the only ones in the world where you can stand in a public place and announce in a loud, clear voice that you intend to buy and smoke a large, well-packed joint, and then do just that in front of the watching police. In theory, purchases of up to 5g of cannabis, and possession of up to 30g (the legal limit) are tolerated; in practice, many coffeeshops offer discounted bulk purchases of 50g with impunity (though bear in mind that if the police do search you, they're entitled to confiscate any amount they find). No one will ever call the police on you in the major cities for discreet, personal dope-smoking, but if in doubt about whether smoking is OK in a given situation, ask somebody – the worst you'll get will be a "no".

The first thing you should know about Dutch **coffeeshops** is that locals use them too. The second thing you should know is that the only ones locals use are outside touristed areas (such as Amsterdam's Red Light District). Practically all the coffeeshops you'll run into in city centres are worth avoiding, either for their decor, their deals or their clientele. Plasticky, neon-lit dives abound, pumping out mainstream varieties of rock, reggae or house at ear-splitting levels. The dope on offer is usually limited and of poor quality – and, since they're mostly serving tourists, they can rig the deals without fear of comeback. A short time exploring quieter, more residential districts will turn up plenty of congenial, high-quality outlets for buying and enjoying cannabis.

When you first walk into a coffeeshop, how you buy the stuff isn't immediately apparent – it's illegal to advertise cannabis in any way, which includes calling attention to the fact that it's available at all. What you have to do is ask to see the **menu**, which is normally kept behind the counter. This will list all the different hashes and grasses on offer, along with (if it's a reputable place) exactly how many grammes you get for your money. The in-house dealer will be able to help you out with queries.

**The hash** you come across originates in various countries and is pretty self-explanatory, apart from *Pollem*, which is compressed resin and stronger than normal. **Marijuana** is a different story, and the old days of imported Colombian, Thai and sensimelia are fading away; taking their place are limitless varieties of "Nederwiet", Dutch-grown under UV lights and more potent than anything you're likely to have come across. Skunk, Haze and Northern Lights are all popular types of Dutch weed, and should be treated with caution – a smoker of low-grade British draw will be laid low (or high) for hours by a single spliff of Skunk. You would be equally well advised to take care with **spacecakes** (cakes or biscuits baked with hash), which are widely available: you can never be sure exactly what's in them; they tend to have a delayed reaction (up to two hours before you notice anything strange – don't get impatient and gobble down another one!); and once they kick in, they can bring on an extremely intense, bewildering high – 10–12 hours is common. You may also come across cannabis seeds for growing your own: while locals are permitted to grow a small amount of marijuana for personal use, the import of cannabis seeds is illegal in any country, so don't even think about trying to take some home.

And a word of warning: since all kinds of cannabis are so widely available over-the-counter in coffeeshops, there's no need to buy any on the street. If you do, you're simply asking for trouble.

## Wine and spirits

**Wine** is reasonably priced – expect to pay around €4 or so for an average bottle of French white or red, though it will cost you €15 in a restaurant. As for spirits, the indigenous drink is **jenever**, or Dutch gin – not unlike British gin, but a bit weaker and oilier, made from molasses and flavoured with juniper berries: it's served in a small glass (for around €1.50) and is traditionally drunk straight, often knocked back in one gulp with much hearty back-slapping. There are a number of varieties: *Oud* (old) is smooth and mellow, *Jong* (young) packs more of a punch – though neither is extremely alcoholic. The older *jenevers* (including *zeer oude*, very old) are a little more expensive but are stronger and less

oily. In a bar, ask for a *borreltje* (straight *jenever*) or a *bittertje* (with angostura); if you've a sweet tooth, try a *bessenjenever* (flavoured with blackcurrant). A glass of beer with a *jenever* chaser is a *kopstoot*. Imported spirits are considerably more expensive, and it is worth noting that you can't buy spirits in supermarkets.

Other drinks you'll see include numerous Dutch liqueurs, notably *advocaat* or eggnog; sweet, blue *curaçao*; and luminous green *pisang ambon*; as well as an assortment of luridly coloured fruit brandies best left for experimentation at the end of an evening. There's also a Dutch-produced brandy, *Vieux*, which tastes as if it's made from prunes but is in fact grape-based, and various regional firewaters, such as *elske* from Maastricht – made from the leaves, berries and bark of alder bushes.

# Communications

As you'd expect, the Netherlands has an efficient postal system and a first-rate phone network. The flat landscape means that most mobile phone networks have excellent coverage too.

Dutch **post offices** are plentiful and mostly open Monday to Friday 8.30am to 5pm, though some big-city branches also open on Saturday from 8.30am to noon. Postal charges are €0.50 for a postcard or airmail letter (up to 20g) within the EU; €0.65 airmail to the rest of the world. Stamps are sold at a wide range of outlets including many shops and hotels. Postboxes are everywhere, but be sure to use the correct slot – the one labelled *overige* is for post going outside the immediate locality. All major post offices offer a poste restante service; to collect items, you need your passport.

### Phones

**Public phones** are a dying breed in the Netherlands: many campsites, for instance, don't have one. Although there are still some coin-operated examples surviving, the vast

majority of public phones take only phonecards (and often credit cards too). They're easy to use: most are multilingual, switching between different languages, including English, when you press the appropriately labelled button. International direct dialling is straightforward. It is worth bearing in mind, however, that phone boxes are provided by different companies and their respective phonecards aren't mutually compatible, so when you buy your card check which phones you'll have access to (KPN is the most common). Many outlets sell €5 and €10 phonecards, including post offices, tobacconists and VVVs. The cheap-rate period for international calls is between 8pm and 8am during the week and all day at weekends. Numbers prefixed ☏0800 are free, while those prefixed ☏0900 are generally premium-rated; a message before you're connected tells you how much you will be paying for the call.

## Useful numbers

**All emergencies** (police, fire service, ambulance) ☎112
**Operator** (domestic and international) ☎0800 0410
**Directory enquiries**
  – domestic ☎0900 8008 (€0.90 per call)
  – international ☎0900 8418 (€1.15 per call)

Alternatively, you might consider a **phone charge card** from your phone company back home; most providers in Europe, North America, Australia and New Zealand have their own versions. Using a PIN number, they let you make calls from most hotels, public and private phones – via a toll-free Swiss number – that are charged to your home account. Most are free to obtain.

To use your **mobile phone**, check with your provider whether it will work in the Netherlands and what the charges will be; you may have to get "international roaming" switched on. In the Netherlands, mobile technology is GSM (@www.gsmworld. com), and coverage is excellent. Unless you have a triband phone, it's unlikely that a mobile bought for use in North America will work elsewhere. Most mobiles in Australia and New Zealand are GSM, but it pays to check before you leave home.

### Phoning home

**To the UK** ☎0044 + area code without zero + number.
**To the Republic of Ireland** ☎00353 + area code without zero + number.
**To the US or Canada** ☎001 + area code + number.
**To Australia** ☎0061 + area code without zero + number.

**To New Zealand** ☎0064 + area code without zero + number.

### Calling from abroad

First dial your **international access code** (00 from the UK, Ireland and New Zealand; 011 from the US and Canada; 0011 from Australia), followed by **31** for the Netherlands, followed by the local number **excluding the initial zero**.

### Email

The Netherlands, and particularly Amsterdam, is well-geared up for **Internet** access. In most large cities you'll find Internet cafés, which charge around €0.20 for every twenty minutes spent online, but you'll often find that the local town library offers free access. Occasionally, you may also come across *internetzuilen* – "Internet poles" – fixed pillars in the street with a screen and keyboard, which you access by using a card (available from VVVs); the minimum-value card is €5 and every twenty minutes spent online costs around €2.50.

The useful website @www.kropla.com gives details of how to plug your lap-top in when abroad, phone country codes around the world, and information about electrical systems in different countries.

# The media

English-speakers will find themselves quite at home in the Netherlands, as Dutch TV broadcasts a wide range of British programmes, and English-language newspapers from around the world are readily available.

## The press

There's no difficulty in finding British **newspapers** – they're on sale in every major city on the day of publication, for around €4. Newsagents located at train stations will almost always have copies if no one else does. Current issues of UK and US **magazines** are widely available too, as is the *International Herald Tribune*.

Of the Dutch newspapers, *NRC Handelsblad* is a right-of-centre paper that has perhaps the best news coverage and a liberal stance on the arts; *De Volkskrant* is a progressive, leftish daily; the popular right-wing *De Telegraaf* boasts the highest circulation figures in the country and has a well-regarded financial section; *Algemeen Dagblad* is a right-wing broadsheet; while the middle-of-the-road *Het Parool* ("The Password") and the news magazine *Vrij Nederland* ("Free Netherlands") are the successors of underground Resistance newspapers printed during wartime occupation. The Protestant *Trouw* ("Trust"), another former underground paper, is centre-left in orientation with a focus on religion.

Bundled in with the weekend edition of the *International Herald Tribune* is *The Netherlander*, a small but useful business-oriented review of Dutch affairs in English.

## TV and radio

Dutch **TV** isn't up to much, although the quantity of English-language programmes broadcast is high. If you're staying somewhere with cable TV (which covers over ninety percent of Dutch households), it's also possible to find many foreign TV channels: Britain's BBC1 and BBC2 are available everywhere. Popular cable offerings include the National Geographic channel, Eurosport and Discovery. There's also a host of German, French, Spanish, Italian, Turkish and Arabic stations, some of which occasionally show undubbed British and US movies. Other Dutch and Belgian TV channels, cable and non-cable, regularly run English-language movies with Dutch subtitles.

As for Dutch **radio**, Radio Honderd – only available in and around Amsterdam, at 99.3FM – was a stalwart of the squat movement until commercialization in summer 2002, with a wide-ranging playlist from world dance to electronica. Jazz Radio, at 99.8FM, speaks for itself. The Dutch Classic FM, at 101.2FM, like the British version, plays bits of well-known classical music, with jazz after 10pm. There's next to no English-language programming, but the **BBC World Service** broadcasts pretty much all day in English on 648kHz (medium wave); between 2am and 7am it also occupies 198kHz (long wave). Thousands of radio stations, including all BBC output (ⓦwww.bbc.co.uk), Voice of America (ⓦwww.voa.gov), Radio Canada (ⓦwww.rcinet.ca) and Radio Australia (ⓦwww.abc.net.au), broadcast online.

# Opening hours, public holidays and festivals

Although there's recently been some movement towards greater flexibility, opening hours for shops, businesses and tourist attractions – including museums – remain a little restrictive. Travel plans can be disrupted on public holidays, when most things close down, apart from restaurants, bars and hotels, and public transport is reduced to a Sunday timetable. At a local level, the same applies during festivals and major events.

## Opening hours

The Dutch weekend fades painlessly into the working week, with many smaller shops and businesses staying closed on Monday mornings until noon. Normal **opening hours** are, however, Monday to Friday 8.30/9am to 5.30/6pm and – for shops, not businesses – Saturday 8.30/9am to 4/5pm. That said, shops are permitted to stay open seven days a week from 9am to 10pm, and an increasing number are doing so; where this isn't the case, many open late on Thursday or Friday evenings for *koopavond* (evening shopping). In the cities, a handful of night shops – *avondwinkels* – stay open into the small hours or round the clock. Most towns have a market day, usually midweek (and sometimes Saturday morning), and this is often the liveliest day to visit, particularly when the stalls fill the central square, the *markt*. Note that most supermarkets are shut on Sundays, so some advance shopping might be required.

**Museums**, especially those that are state-run (a *rijksmuseum*), tend to follow a pattern: closed on Monday, open Tuesday to Saturday from 10am to 5pm, and on Sundays from 1 to 5pm, although things are slowly changing in favour of seven-day opening. Though closed for Christmas and New Year, the state-run museums adopt Sunday hours on the remaining public holidays, when most shops and banks are closed. Galleries tend to be open from Tuesday to Sunday noon to 5pm. We've quoted precise opening hours throughout the guide.

Most **restaurants** are open in the evening from about 5 or 6pm, and though many close as early as 9pm, a few stay open past 11pm. **Bars**, **cafés** and **coffeeshops** are either open all day from around 10am or don't open until about 5pm; both varieties close at 1am during the week and 2am at weekends. **Clubs** generally function from 11pm to 4am during the week, staying open until 5am at weekends.

## Public holidays

**Public holidays** (*Nationale feestdagen*) provide the perfect excuse to shut up shop and take to the streets. The most celebrated of the lot is **Queen's Day** on April 30, when the Dutch indulge in the equivalent of a national flea market: tradition dictates that each household sells all the junk it has accumulated over the past year on the streets. In Amsterdam at any rate, the gay community party so hard you would be forgiven for wondering which queen they are celebrating.

Jan 1, New Year's Day
Good Friday (many shops open)
Easter Sunday and Monday
April 30, Queen's Day
May 5, Liberation Day
Ascension Day
Whit Sunday and Monday
Dec 25, Christmas Day
Dec 26

## Festivals and events

The Netherlands has few national annual **festivals**, and aside from the carnivals that are celebrated in the southern part of the country and a sprinkling of religious-oriented celebrations, most annual festivities are arts- or music-based affairs, confined to a particular town or city. In addition there are also markets and folkloric events; traditionally, locals turned out in peasant costume on market day and in remoter towns and villages this practice still survives, though some are rather bogusly sustained for tourists – the Alkmaar cheese market (see p.153) being a prime example.

Most festivals take place during the summer. Contact the local VVV for up-to-date details – and remember that wherever you might be staying, large swathes of the country are no more than a short train ride away.

Of the country's annual cultural events, the **Holland Festival**, held in June in Amsterdam, Rotterdam and The Hague, is probably the most diverse, with most performing arts represented and an increasingly international feel. The country's keen interest in jazz is reflected in the large number of regional jazz festivals, of which The Hague's **North Sea Jazz Festival** in July is the most prestigious, attracting all the big names. Check out also the renowned **Pink Pop Festival**, held in Landgraaf near Maastricht early the same month: this three-day event also attracts top-level performers.

Outside summer, other annual events include viewing the **bulbfields** – at their best between March and May (tulips from mid-April to mid-May). If you're visiting the country in February or March, look out for the number of towns in the southern provinces that host Mardi Gras **carnivals**, notably Maastricht; while an event to look out for in January (or when the weather is cold enough) is the **Elfstedentocht** (see p.236), Friesland's uniquely exciting, and gruelling, canal skating race between the province's eleven towns – though it's only been held once in the last twenty years so don't plan your trip around it.

## Events diary

### January

**Mid-Jan** Leiden – Jazz Week, featuring mainly Dutch performers ⓦ www.leiden.nl.

### February

**Mid- to late Feb** Bovenkarspel – Holland Flowers Festival: the world's largest covered flower show held over ten days ⓦ www.hollandflowersfestival.nl.
**Late Feb to early March** Carnivals at the beginning of Lent in Breda, 's Hertogenbosch, Maastricht (ⓦ www.cybercomm.nl/~karneval) and other southern towns.

### March

**Sunday closest to March 15** Amsterdam – Stille Ommegang procession through the city streets to the Oude Kerk.
**Late March to late May** Keukenhof Gardens,

Lisse: world renowned floral displays in the bulbfields and hothouses of this 23-hectare park ⓦ www.keukenhof.nl.

### April

**April–Sept** Alkmaar – "traditional" cheese market on Friday mornings ⓦ www.vvvalkmaar.nl.
**2nd week** Nationaal Museumweekend – free entrance to all of the country's museums for a weekend ⓦ www.museumweekend.nl.
**Penultimate weekend** North Holland – flower Parade from Noordwijk to Haarlem.
**Last Sunday** Rotterdam Marathon ⓦ www.rotterdammarathon.nl.
**April 30** All round the country – Koninginnedag (Queen's Day), celebrated by street markets, partying and fireworks. One site is ⓦ www.koninginnedag.nl, but most regions have their own websites.

### May

**May 5** Bevrijdingfestival – outdoor festivals around the country celebrating liberation at the end of World War II.
**Early May** Amersfoort Jazz – featuring mainly national talent ⓦ www.keistadjazz.nl.
**Mid-May** Amsterdam – Drum Rhythm Festival, two-day outdoor rhythm and roots music festival ⓦ www.drumrhythm.com.
**End May** Breda Jazz Festival – with open-air concerts and street parades ⓦ www.bredajazzfestival.nl.
**Mid-May to early June** Scheveningen – Sand Sculpture Festival, with hard-working teams descending on the resort from all over Europe to create amazing sand sculptures, which are left for three weeks for visitors to admire ⓦ www.scheveningenbeach.nl.
**May 30** Scheveningen – Vlaggetjesdag ("Flag Day"), where the town's boats are decorated with flags at a gala held to celebrate the commencement of the Dutch herring season ⓦ www.vlaggetjesdag.com.

### June

**Throughout June** Amsterdam, Rotterdam and The Hague – Holland Festival, a month-long arts festival covering all aspects of both national and international music, theatre, dance and the contemporary arts ⓦ www.hollandfestival.nl.
**June–Sept** Maastricht – European Summer Cultural Programme, with music, theatre, and more ⓦ www.vvvmaastricht.nl.
**Early June** Landgraaf – Pink Pop festival, a top-notch, three-day open-air rock festival ⓦ www.pinkpop.nl.

**Early June** Bolsward – Frisian "eleven cities" cycle race, using bicycles instead of the ice skates used in the traditional Elfstedentocht.

**Mid-June** Scheveningen – Internationaal Vliegerfeest, with stunt kite tournaments held on the beach.

**Mid-June** Terschelling – Oerol Festival, a ten-day event featuring location theatre and stand-up comedy Ⓦ www.oerol.nl.

**Mid-June to mid-July** Middelburg – International festival of new avant-garde music Ⓦ www.nieuwe-muziek.nl.

## July

**July–Aug** Bloemendaal – "Woodstock69" festival held on Bloemendaal beach and featuring live percussion, dance acts and plenty of revelry Ⓦ www.woodstock69.nl.

**July–Sept** The Hague – International Rose Exhibition, with participants competing for the prestigious "Golden Rose".

**Early July** The Hague – North Sea Jazz Festival, outstanding three-day jazz festival showcasing international names as well as local talent. Thirteen stages and a thousand musicians Ⓦ www.northseajazz.nl.

**Mid-July** Drentse Fiets 4Daagse – four-day cycling event, with routes ranging from 30km to 150km, and departure points at Assen, Emmen, Hoogeveen and Meppel Ⓦ www.fiets4daagse.nl.

**Late July** Nijmegen – Internationale Vierdaagse Afstandmarsen, one of the world's largest walking events, with over 30,000 participants walking 30–50km per day over four days Ⓦ www.4daagse.nl.

## August

**Early Aug** Sneek Week – international sailing event at Sneek, with around 1000 boats competing in over thirty classes Ⓦ www.sneekweek.nl.

**1st or 2nd weekend** Amsterdam Pride – the city's gay community celebrates, with street parties and performances, as well as a "Canal Pride" flotilla of boats parading along the Prinsengracht Ⓦ www.amsterdampride.nl.

**Mid-Aug** Scheveningen – International Firework Festival, with two displays each evening.

**Last week** Amsterdam Grachtenfestival – international musicians perform classical music at twenty historical locations in the city. Includes the Prinsengrachtconcert, one of the world's most prestigious open-air concerts, featuring a stage over the canal and a promenading audience.

## September

**Early Sept** Aalsmeer – Bloemencorso, a flower parade to Amsterdam Ⓦ www.bloemencorsoaalsmeer.nl.

**Mid-Sept** Brabantse Fietsdag – for one day, 100 cycle routes are laid out in Noord-Brabant, ranging in length from 15km to 50km.

## October

**Early/mid-Oct** Amsterdam city marathon Ⓦ www.amsterdammarathon.nl.

## November

**Mid-Nov** Parades throughout the country celebrating the arrival of St Nicholas.

## December

**Dec 5** Pakjesavond, celebrated nationwide – though it tends to be a private affair, this is the day Dutch kids receive their Christmas presents. If you have Dutch friends, it's worth knowing that it's traditional to give a present together with a satirical poem you have written caricaturing the recipient.

# Crime and personal safety

By comparison with other parts of Europe, the Netherlands is relatively free of crime, so there's little reason why you should ever come into contact with the Dutch police force. Bar-room brawls are highly unusual, muggings uncommon, and street crime much less conspicuous than in many other countries.

Even in Amsterdam and the larger cities you shouldn't have problems, though it's advisable to be on your guard against petty theft: secure your things in a locker when staying in hostel accommodation, and never leave any valuables in a tent or car. If you're on a bike, make sure it is well locked up: bike theft and resale is a major industry here.

Almost all the problems tourists encounter are to do with **petty crime** – pickpocketing and bag-snatching – rather than more serious physical confrontations, so it's as well to be on your guard and know where your possessions are at all times. Thieves often work in pairs and, although theft is far from rife, you should be aware of certain ploys, such as: the "helpful" person pointing out "birdshit" (actually shaving cream or similar) on your coat, while someone else relieves you of your money; being invited to read a card or paper on the street to distract your attention; someone in a café moving for your drink with one hand while the other is in your bag as you react; and if you're in a crowd of tourists, watch out for people moving in unusually close.

If you are robbed, you'll need to go to a police station to report it, not least because your insurance company will require a police report; remember to make a note of the report number – or, better still, ask for a copy of the statement itself. Don't expect a great deal of concern if your loss is relatively small – and don't be surprised if the process of completing forms and formalities takes ages.

## Personal safety

Although it's generally possible to walk around without fear of harassment or assault, certain parts of all the big cities – especially Rotterdam and Amsterdam – are decidedly dodgy, and wherever you go at night it's always better to err on the side of caution. In particular, Amsterdam's Red Light District can have an unpleasant, threatening undertow (although the crowds of people act as a deterrent), whilst Rotterdam's docklands are similarly grim. Using public transport, even late at night, isn't usually a problem, but if in doubt take a taxi. In the unlikely event that you are mugged, or otherwise threatened, never resist, and try to reduce your contact with the robber to a minimum; either just hand over what's wanted, or throw money in one direction and take off in the other. Afterwards go straight to the police, who are likely to be sympathetic and helpful on these occasions. Most police officers speak at least some English.

## Drugs

Thousands of visitors come to the Netherlands in general, and Amsterdam in particular, just to get stoned. This is the one Western country where the purchase of **cannabis** is entirely legal, and the influx of people drawn to the country by this fact creates problems: many Amsterdammers, for instance, get mightily hacked off with "drug tourism", as do folk in border towns, who have to deal with tides of people popping over the international frontier to the first "coffeeshop" they see (for more on coffeeshops, see p.37). The Dutch government's attitude to soft drugs is more complex than you might think: the use of cannabis is tolerated but not condoned, with the result being a rather complicated set of rules and regulations that can be safely ignored as long as you buy very small amounts for personal use only (see p.37 for details). Buy in bulk, or sell to other people, and you become liable under Dutch criminal law. Needless to say, the one thing you shouldn't attempt to do is take any form of cannabis out of the country. A surprising number of people think (or claim to think) that if it's bought in the Netherlands it can be taken back home legally; this story won't wash with customs officials and drug enforcement officers, who will happily add your stash to the statistics of national drug seizures, and arrest you into the bargain. Sniffer dogs invariably meet all flights arriving from Dutch airports.

As far as other drugs go, the Dutch law surrounding **magic mushrooms** is that you can legally buy and possess any amount so long as they are fresh, but as soon as you tamper with them in any way (dry or process them, boil or cook them), they become as illegal as **crack**. Despite the existence of a lively and growing trade in **cocaine** and **heroin**, possession of either could mean a

stay in one of the Netherlands' lively and growing jails. **Ecstasy**, **acid** and **speed** are as illegal in the Netherlands as they are anywhere else.

## Being arrested

If you're detained by the police, you don't automatically have the right to a phone call, although in practice they'll probably phone your consulate for you – not that consular officials have a reputation for excessive helpfulness (particularly in drug cases). If your alleged offence is a minor matter, you can be held for up to six hours without questioning; if it is more serious, you can be detained for up to 24 hours.

 # Travellers with disabilities

**Despite its general social progressiveness, the Netherlands is only just getting to grips with the particular requirements of people with mobility problems.**

In Amsterdam and most of the other major cities the most obvious difficulty you'll face is in negotiating the cobbled streets and narrow, often broken pavements of the older districts, where the key sights are usually located. Similarly, provision for people with disabilities on the country's urban public transport is only average, although improving – many new buses, for instance, are now wheelchair-accessible. And yet, while it can be difficult simply to get around, practically all public buildings, including museums, theatres, cinemas, concert halls and hotels, are obliged to provide access, and do. Places that have been certified wheelchair-accessible now bear an International Accessibility Symbol (IAS). Bear in mind, however, that a lot of the older, narrower hotels are not allowed to install lifts, so check first. The national tourist office website Ⓦ www.visitholland .com has an online search facility within its Services menu, where you can find attractions and accommodation that have a wheelchair available and/or bear an

IAS symbol. The tourist board also provides access information and local contact numbers.

If you're planning to use the Dutch train network during your stay and would appreciate assistance on the platform, phone the Bureau Assistentieverlening Gehandicapten (Disabled Assistance Office) on ☏ 030/235 7822 (Ⓕ 235 3033) at least three hours before your train departs, and there will be someone to meet and help you at the station. NS publishes information about train travel for people with disabilities online at Ⓦ www.ns.nl and in various leaflets, stocked at main stations.

### Contacts for travellers with disabilities

#### UK & Ireland

**Access Travel** ☏ 01942/888 844, Ⓦ www .access-travel.co.uk. Small, personal-service tour operator that can arrange flights, transfer and accommodation for Amsterdam city breaks.
**Holiday Care** ☏ 0845/124 9971, Minicom

☎ 0845/124 9976, 🖥 www.holidaycare.org.uk.
Provides an information pack for £2.50 which
details transport options, accommodation, special
services, tour operators and useful contacts for
travelling around the Netherlands, Belgium and
Luxembourg.
**Irish Wheelchair Association** ☎ 01/833 8241,
🖥 www.iwa.ie. Useful information about travel
abroad.
**RADAR (Royal Association for Disability and
Rehabilitation)** ☎ 020/7250 3222, Minicom
☎ 020/7250 4119, 🖥 www.radar.org.uk. A good
source of advice, with a useful website.
**Tripscope** ☎ 0845/758 5641,
🖥 www.justmobility.co.uk/tripscope. Registered
charity providing free advice on international
transport.

## US & Canada

**Access-Able** 🖥 www.access-able.com. Online
resource for travellers with disabilities.
**Directions Unlimited** ☎ 1-800/533-5343 or
914/241-1700. Tour operator.
**Mobility International USA** ☎ 541/343-1284,
🖥 www.miusa.org. Information and referral
services, access guides, tours and exchange
programmes.
**Society for the Advancement of Travelers
with Handicaps (SATH)** ☎ 212/447-7284,
🖥 www.sath.org. Non-profit educational
organization.
**Travel Information Service** ☎ 215/456-9600.
Information and referral service.
**Twin Peaks Press** ☎ 1-800/637-2256 or
360/694-2462,
🖥 disabilitybookshop.virtualave.net. Disability-
oriented publisher.
**Wheels Up!** ☎ 1-888/389-4335,

🖥 www.wheelsup.com. Provides discounted airfare
and tour prices and a free monthly newsletter.
Comprehensive website.

## Australia & NZ

**ACROD (Australian Council for Rehabilitation
of the Disabled)** ☎ 02/6282 4333. Provides lists
of travel agencies and tour operators.
**Disabled Persons Assembly (NZ)** ☎ 04/801
9100. Resource centre with lists of travel agencies
and tour operators.

## The Netherlands

**Landelijk Bureau Toegankelijkheid** National
Bureau for Accessibility, Utrecht ☎ 030/276 9970,
📧 sdg@wxs.nl. Part of the Stichting
Dienstverleners Gehandicapten (Foundation for
Rehabilitation), which promotes accessibility,
mobility and technology.
**Mobility International Nederland** Heidestein 7,
3971 ND Driebergen ☎ 0343/521795,
📧 bijning@worldonline.nl. Largest Dutch
information and advice service for people with
disabilities.
**Stadsmobiel** Postbus 2131, 1000 CC Amsterdam
☎ & 📠 020/613 4769, 🖥 www.stadsmobiel.nl.
Provides an accessible shuttle service in and
around Amsterdam (including the airport) for
members.
**Stichting Informatie Gehandicapten (SIG)**
Zakkedragershof 34–44, Postbus 70, 3500 AB
Utrecht ☎ 030/234 5611. General disability
information.
**Stichting Recreatie Gehandicapten** Postbus
4140, 2003 EC Haarlem ☎ 023/536 8409,
🖥 www.srg-vakanties.nl. Organizes tours around
Amsterdam and Europe.

# Gay and lesbian travellers

The Netherlands ranks as one of the top gay-friendly countries in Europe. The superstar of the country's gay and lesbian scene is of course Amsterdam, where attitudes are tolerant, bars are excellent and plentiful, and support groups and facilities are unequalled.

In the other major cities of the Netherlands, while the scene isn't anywhere near as extensive, it's well organized: Rotterdam, The Hague, Nijmegen and Groningen each has a visible and enjoyable gay nightlife. The native lesbian scene is smaller and more subdued: many politically active lesbians move in close-knit communities, and it takes time for foreign visitors to find out what's happening.

The **COC** (Ⓦwww.coc.nl), the national organization for gay men and women, dates from the 1940s and is actively involved in gaining equal rights for gays and lesbians, as well as informing society's perceptions of homosexuality. The national HQ is at Rozenstraat 14 in Amsterdam (Mon–Fri 9am–5pm; ☏020/626 8300), and all cities of any size have a branch office which can offer help, information on events and promotions – and usually a sociable coffee bar. For more help and advice contact Amsterdam's Gay and Lesbian Switchboard on ☏020/623 6565. Gay legislation in the Netherlands is streets ahead of the rest of the world; same-sex marriage and adoption by same-sex partners were legalized in 2001, and within six months over two thousand couples had tied the knot. The age of consent is 16.

Consider timing your visit to coincide with Amsterdam's **Gay Pride** (Ⓦwww.amsterdampride.nl) on the first weekend in August. Celebrations are unabashed, with music, theatre, street parties and floats parading through the canals. Other events of interest might include the Fetish Fantasy Weekend (end of March), Queen's Day (not that sort of queen, but with lots of gay parties anyway, on April 30) and Amsterdam's Leather Pride in late October. Contact the Tourism Board or COC for more details.

## Contacts for gay and lesbian travellers

### UK

Ⓦww.gaytravel.co.uk Online gay and lesbian travel agent, offering good deals on all types of holiday. Also lists gay- and lesbian-friendly hotels around the world.
**Dreamwaves Holidays** ☏0870/042 2475, Ⓦwww.gayholidaysdirect.com. Specializes in exclusively gay holidays, including skiing trips and summer sun packages.
**Madison Travel** ☏01273/202 532, Ⓦwww.madisontravel.co.uk. Established travel agents specializing in packages to gay- and lesbian-friendly mainstream destinations, and also to gay/lesbian destinations.
**Respect Holidays** ☏0870/770 0169, Ⓦwww.respect-holidays.co.uk. Offers exclusively gay packages to all popular European resorts.

### US & Canada

**Damron** ☏1-800/462-6654 or 415/255-0404, Ⓦwww.damron.com. Publisher of the *Men's Travel Guide*, a pocket-sized yearbook full of listings of hotels, bars, clubs and resources for gay men; the *Women's Traveler*, which provides similar listings for lesbians; and *Damron Accommodations*, which provides detailed listings of over 1000 accommodations for gays and lesbians worldwide. All of these titles are offered at a discount on the website. No specific city guides – everything is incorporated in the yearbooks.
**gaytravel.com** ☏1-800/GAY-TRAVEL, Ⓦwww.gaytravel.com. The premier site for trip planning, bookings, and general information about international gay and lesbian travel.
**International Gay & Lesbian Travel Association** ☏1-800/448-8550 or 954/776-2626, Ⓦwww.iglta.org. Trade group that can provide a list of gay- and lesbian-owned or -friendly travel agents, accommodation and other travel businesses.

### Australia & NZ

**Gay and Lesbian Tourism Australia**
Ⓦ www.galta.com.au. Directory and links for gay
and lesbian travel in Australia and worldwide.
**Parkside Travel** ☎ 08/8274 1222,
Ⓔ parkside@herveyworld.com.au. Gay travel agent
associated with local branch of Hervey World Travel; all
aspects of gay and lesbian travel worldwide.

**Silke's Travel** ☎ 1800/807 860 or 02/8347 2000,
Ⓦ www.silkes.com.au. Long-established gay and
lesbian specialist, with the emphasis on women's
travel.
**Tearaway Travel** ☎ 1800/664 440 or 03/9510
6644, Ⓦ www.tearaway.com. Gay-specific
business dealing with international and domestic
travel.

# Directory

**Addresses** These are written, for example,
as Haarlemmerstraat 15 III, meaning the
third-floor (US fourth-floor) apartment at no.
15 Haarlemmerstraat. The ground floor is
indicated by hs (*huis*, "house") after the
number; the basement is sous (*sousterrain*).
The figures 1e, 2e, 3e and 4e before a street
name are an abbreviation for Eerste,
Tweede, Derde and Vierde, respectively –
the first, second, third and fourth streets of
the same name. Some sidestreets, rather
than have their own name, take the name of
the street which they run off, but with the
addition of the word *dwars*, meaning crossing – so Palmdwarsstraat is a sidestreet off
Palmstraat. T/O (*tegenover*, or "opposite") in
an address shows that the address is a
boat: hence "Prinsengracht T/O 26" would
indicate a boat to be found opposite building no. 26 on Prinsengracht. Dutch post
codes – made up of four figures and two letters – can be found in the directory kept at
post offices.

**Clogs** You'll see these on sale in all the main
tourist centres, usually brightly painted and
not really designed for wearing. It's estimated
that about three million clogs are still made
annually in the Netherlands; interestingly,
only about half are for the tourist market, the
rest being worn mainly by industrial workers
as foot protection.

**Electric current** 220v AC. British equipment
needs only a plug adaptor; American apparatus requires a transformer and an adaptor.

**Flowers** It doesn't take long to notice the
Dutch enthusiasm for flowers and plants of
all kinds: windows are often festooned with
blooms and greenery, and shops and markets sell sprays and bunches for next to
nothing. Flowers are grown year-round,
though spring is the best time to come if this
is your interest, when the bulbfields (and
glasshouses) of Noord- and Zuid-Holland
are dense with colour – tulips, hyacinths,
and narcisi are the main blooms. Later in
the year there are rhododendrons and, in
Friesland and Groningen, fields of yellow
rapeseed; in summer roses appear, while the
autumn sees late chrysanthemums.

**ISIC cards** Student ID is useful for mensas
(university canteens), but won't help you
gain reduced admission to very much, and
certainly not museums or mainstream tourist
attractions.

**Left luggage** At all train stations. Where
there is no actual office, there will always be
coin-operated lockers.

**Long-stay visitors** For those planning a
long-term stay in the Netherlands, a good
source of information is a non-profit organization called Access, Societeit de Witte,
Plein 24, 2511 CS Den Haag (☎ 070/346
2525, Ⓦ www.access-nl.org). They operate a
very useful English-language information line
on everything from domestic services to
legal matters, as well as running courses on
various aspects of Dutch administration and
culture.

**Mosquitoes** These pesky blighters thrive in
the Netherlands' watery environment and
can be particularly bad at campsites. An anti-
histamine cream such as Phenergan is the

best antidote, although this can be difficult to find – in which case preventative sticks like Autan or Citronella are the best idea.

**Public toilets** Arm yourself with plenty of small change as there's no such thing as a free Dutch public toilet. Expect to pay between €0.10–€0.50; train stations, libraries and *McDonalds* often charge the same.

**Time** The whole country is on Central European Time (CET) – one hour ahead of London, six hours ahead of New York, and eight hours behind Sydney.

**Tipping** Appreciated (at around 10–15 percent), but not essential since restaurants, hotels, taxis, etc, must include a fifteen percent service charge by law. In public toilets, it's normal to leave about €0.25.

**War cemeteries** There was fierce fighting in parts of the Netherlands during World War II, notably at Arnhem (see p.288), where several thousand British and Polish servicemen are remembered at the Oosterbeek cemetery. There are other military cemeteries in the east and south of the country, not least at Margraten, where around eight thousand US soldiers lie buried.

**Windmills** The best place to see windmills is at Kinderdijk near Dordrecht (see p.207); they're also still very much part of the landscape in the polderlands north of Amsterdam. Some, too, have been moved and reassembled out of harm's way in the open-air museums at Zaanse Schans (see p.151) and the Open-Air Museum just outside Arnhem (see p.293).

# Guide

# Guide

# Amsterdam

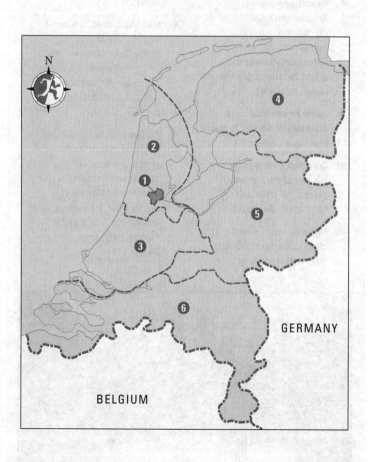

# CHAPTER 1 Highlights

✳ **Bloemenmarkt**
Legendary floating
flower market – a riot of
colour, texture and fra-
grance. See p.81

✳ **Grachtengordel**
Amsterdam's "girdle" of
canals lattice the city
centre – spend a snoozy
afternoon viewing the
grand facades from the
water. See p.83

✳ **Anne Frank House** A
poignant memorial to the
Holocaust. See p.84

✳ **Jordaan** Picturesque
quarter of tree-shaded
canals, an ideal setting
for a stroll. See p.90

✳ **Rijksmuseum** World-
class collection of Dutch
paintings, including

Rembrandt's *Nightwatch*.
See p.99

✳ **Van Gogh Museum** The
world's finest collection
of the master's paintings.
See p.101

✳ **Het Molenpad** The most
alluring of Amsterdam's
many "brown" cafés, its
dim, smoke-stained inte-
rior extending back from
a beautiful canal. See
p.111

✳ **Coffeeshops** Not all the
city's cannabis "coffee-
shops" feature shifty
characters nodding
along to Bob Marley;
plenty offer a pleasant
environment to sample
high-quality dope.
See p.111

# Amsterdam

**A** **MSTERDAM** is a compact, instantly likeable city. It's appealing to
look at and pleasant to walk around, an intriguing mix of the parochial
and the international; it also has a welcoming attitude towards visitors
and a uniquely youthful orientation, shaped by the liberal counter-cul-
ture that took hold in the 1960s. Also engaging are the buzz of open-air summer events and the intimacy of its clubs and bars, not to mention the Dutch
facility with languages: just about everyone you meet in Amsterdam will be
able to speak near-perfect English, on top of their own native Dutch and often
French and German too.

The city's layout is determined by a web of **canals**. The historical centre,
which dates from the thirteenth century, is girdled by five concentric canals
– the **Grachtengordel** – dug in the seventeenth century as part of a
planned expansion to create a uniquely elegant urban environment. It is
here that the city's merchant class built their grand mansions, typified by tall,
gracefully decorated gables, whose fine proportions are reflected in the still,
olive-green waters below. The city council exercised strict control over this
expansion – proscribing, for example, the width and length of every building lot – resulting in the homogeneous architecture that survives today. With
its antique houses, cobbled streets, humpback bridges and tree-lined canals,
Amsterdam is – at its best – acutely beautiful.

The conventional sights are for the most part low-key, the most promoted
being the **Anne Frank House**. What sways the balance, however, is Amsterdam's
world-class group of museums and galleries. For many, the **Van Gogh Museum**
alone is reason enough to visit the city, but add to this the **Rijksmuseum**, with
its collections of medieval and seventeenth-century Dutch paintings, and the
contemporary and experimental art of the **Stedelijk Museum**, and the international quality of the art on display in the city is self-evident.

But it's Amsterdam's **population and politics** that constitute its most
enduring characteristics. Notorious during the 1960s and 1970s as the zenith
– or nadir – of radical permissiveness, the city mellowed only marginally during the Eighties, and, despite the gentrification of the last ten years or so, retains
a uniquely laid-back feel, with much to it that is both innovative and comfortably familiar. Indeed, Amsterdammers make much of their city and its
attractions being *gezellig*, a rather over-used Dutch word roughly corresponding to "cosy", "appealingly lived-in" and "warmly convivial" all at the same
time. The city's unparalleled selection of *gezellig* drinking-places is a delight,
whether you choose to visit a traditional, bare-floored **brown café** or one
of the many designer bars and grand cafés. Furthermore, Amsterdam's
unique approach to combating hard-drug abuse – embodied in the effective

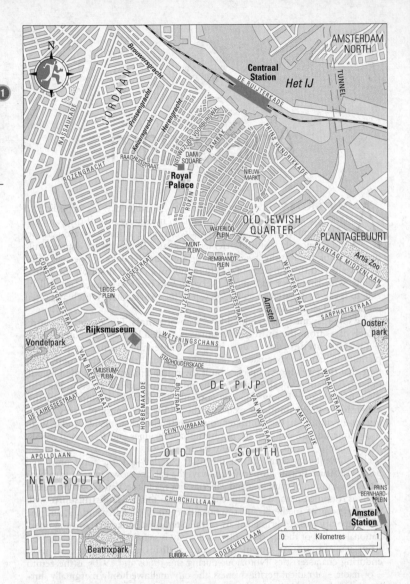

decriminalization of cannabis – has led to a proliferation of **coffeeshops** that sell high-quality marijuana and hashish. Entertainment has a similarly innovative edge, exemplified by **multimedia complexes**, whose offerings are at the forefront of contemporary European film, dance, drama and music. There is any amount of affordable **live music** from all genres – although the Dutch have a particular soft spot for jazz – and Amsterdam has one of the world's leading classical **orchestras**, with generously subsidized ticket prices. The **club** scene is by contrast relatively subdued, even modest by the standards of other capital cities, though **gay** men will find that Amsterdam has one of Europe's more active and convivial nightlife network, at least partly justifying its claim to be the "Gay Capital of Europe". Gay women, on the other hand, with far fewer options, may feel the tag to be unwarranted.

# Arrival

**Arriving** in Amsterdam by train and plane could hardly be easier. Schiphol, Amsterdam's international airport, is a quick and convenient train ride away from Centraal Station, the city's international train station. Long-distance and international buses terminate at Amstel Station, a ten-minute metro ride south of Centraal Station. Centraal Station is also the hub of an excellent public transport network, whose trams, buses and metro combine to delve into every corner of the city and its suburbs.

### By air

Amsterdam's international airport, **Schiphol**, is located about 18km southwest of the city centre. Arriving passengers are funnelled into a large plaza, which has all the standard facilities, including bureaux de change, car rental outlets, left luggage lockers and ATMs. In addition, there's a Dutch Railways (NS) ticket office and a **Holland Tourist Office** (daily 7am–10pm), though this has surprisingly little free English-language information; the compensation is that they will book accommodation anywhere in the country on your behalf at no extra cost.

From the airport, **trains** run direct to Centraal Station (Amsterdam C.S.) – a fast service leaving every fifteen minutes during the day, and every hour at night (12.30–6am). The journey takes between fifteen and twenty minutes and costs €3.10. There are also trains from Schiphol to most of the suburban stations around Amsterdam as well as direct express services to many other Dutch cities.

The main alternative to the train is the **Airport Hotel Shuttle bus** (☎020/653 4975), which departs from the designated bus stop outside the Arrivals hall, though note that the buses themselves bear several different liveries, with the newest being marked "Connexxion." Departures are every fifteen minutes or so during peak times (7am–2pm) and every half-hour at other times (5–7am & 2–8pm); fares are €10.50 one-way, €19 return, and journey time is about half-an-hour into the city centre. The route followed by the bus can vary with the needs of the passengers it picks up, providing the required destination is one of the fifty hotels on the shuttle list; however, passengers don't have to be hotel guests to use the bus. Bear in mind that the bus follows a set route on its return journey back to the airport.

The **taxi** fare from Schiphol to the Old Centre is around €35–40.

### By train and bus

Amsterdam's **Centraal Station** (C.S.) has regular train connections with key cities in Germany, Belgium and France, as well as all the larger towns and cities of the Netherlands. As you would expect, Centraal Station has a good spread of facilities, including ATMs, a bureau de change and both coin-operated luggage lockers and a staffed left-luggage office (both daily 7am–11pm). Small coin-operated lockers cost €2.70, the larger ones €4.20 per 24 hours; left luggage costs €5.70 per item. In addition, there's a VVV tourist office (see p.20 for more details) on platform 2 and another directly across from the main station entrance on Stationsplein. If you arrive late at night, it's best to take a taxi to your hotel or hostel – and you should certainly avoid wandering aimlessly around the station: it's not a dangerous place by any means, but there are too many shifty characters to make hanging around advisable. Centraal Station is also the hub of the city's excellent public transport system: trams and buses depart from outside on Stationsplein, which is also the location of a metro station and a GVB public transport information office (for more, see p.61). There's a taxi rank on Stationsplein too. On the train lines either side of Centraal Station are several suburban stations (including Muiderpoort and Sloterdijk), but these are principally for the convenience of commuters.

Eurolines long-distance international buses arrive at **Amstel Station**, about 3.5km to the southeast of Centraal Station. The metro journey to Centraal Station takes about ten minutes.

### By car

Arriving **by car** on either the A4 (E19) from The Hague or the A2 (E35) from Utrecht, you should experience few traffic problems, and the city centre is clearly signposted as soon as you approach Amsterdam's southern reaches. Both roads feed onto the A10 (E22) ring road; on its west side, leave the A10 at either the Osdorp or Geuzenveld exits for the city centre. However, be warned that driving in central Amsterdam – never mind parking – is extremely difficult; see p.62 for further details.

# Information and tours

The Amsterdam Tourist Board runs three **tourist offices** in the city centre: on platform 2 of Centraal Station (Mon–Sat 8am–8pm, Sun 9am–5pm); on Stationsplein, across from the entrance to Centraal Station (daily 9am–5pm); and on Leidsestraat, just off the main Leidseplein square (daily 9am–5pm). These three offices share one premium-rate **information line** on ☎0900/400 4040 (calls cost €0.55 per minute). The official tourist board website is ⓦ**www.visitamsterdam.nl**. These offices, known here as elsewhere in the Netherlands as the **VVV** (pronounced "fay-fay-fay"; see p.20), offer a wide range of services and sell a competent range of maps and guide-books as well as tickets and passes for public transport. They are extremely popular, so come early if you want to beat the queues, especially in the summer; note also that the office on Centraal Station's platform 2 is often less busy than its counterparts.

In addition, the VVV takes in-person bookings for **canal cruises** and other organized excursions. Its extremely efficient **accommodation reservation** service is especially useful in the height of the season, when accommodation gets mighty tight; the service costs just €3 plus a refundable deposit which is subtracted from your final hotel bill, but bear in mind that during peak periods the wait can be exhausting.

As for cultural **events**, the VVV sells a comprehensive, but largely uncritical monthly listings magazine, *Day by Day – What's On in Amsterdam* (€1.50), which details everything from theatre and ballet through to rock concerts. They also sell **tickets** for most forthcoming performances, from rock and classical concerts through to theatre, as does the Amsterdam Uitburo, or **AUB**, operated by the city council, which has a walk-in booking centre tucked away in a corner of the Stadsschouwburg theatre on Leidseplein (daily 10am–6pm, Thurs until 9pm; ☎0900/0191).

## Some Internet cafés

**Conscious Dreams Kokopelli**
Warmoesstraat 12 ☏020/421 7000,
⊛www.consciousdreams.nl. Everything
you could ever want to know about
stimulating products, from books
through to aphrodisiacs, plus net
access and DJs on the weekend.
Located in the Red Light district. Daily
11am–10pm; €1 per 30min.

**Dreamlounge** Kerkstraat 93 ☏020/ 626
6907, ⊛www.consciousdreams.nl. A
small shop in the Grachtengordel with
net access. Mon–Wed 11am–7pm,
Thurs–Sat 11am–8pm, Sun noon–5pm;
€1 per 30min.

**easyInternetcafé** ⊛www.easyevery-
thing.com. This international chain has
two outlets in Amsterdam – one near
Centraal station at Damrak 33 (daily
7.30am–11.30pm), the other at
Reguliersbreestraat 22, near
Rembrandtplein (daily 24hr). Minimum
purchase €0.05.

**Het Internetcafe** Martelaarsgracht 11
☏020/627 1052,
⊛www.internetcafe.nl. Straightforward
cybercafé just 100m from Centraal
Station. Sun–Thurs 9am–1am, Fri & Sat
9am–3am; €1 per 30min.

## Tourist passes

The VVV's much-touted **Amsterdam Pass** provides free and unlimited use of
the city's public transport network, plus a canal cruise and free admission to the
bulk of the city's museums and attractions. It costs €26 for one day, €36 for two
consecutive days and €46 for three consecutive days. Altogether it's not a bad deal,
but you have to work fairly hard to make it worthwhile. A much more tempting
proposition, especially if you're staying for more than a couple of days, is the
**Museumjaarkaart** (Museum Year-Card; see also p.21). This pass gives free entry to
most museums in the whole of the Netherlands for a year; it costs €25 (or €12.50
for those 24 years old and under), and you need a passport-sized photo to get one.

## Organized tours

Although for many visitors a **canal trip** is delightful, for others the running
commentary is purgatorial and the views disappointing, though it's certainly
true that Amsterdam can look enchanting at night when the bridges are illuminated. No one could say the city's tourist industry doesn't make the most of
the canals: a veritable armada of glass-topped **cruise boats** shuttles daily along
the city's inner waterways, offering everything from a quick hour-long excursion to a fully-fledged dinner cruise.

There are several major operators occupying the jetties near Centraal Station
– on Stationsplein, beside the Damrak, and on Prins Hendrikkade. Despite the
competition, prices are fairly uniform: the one-hour tour costs around €8 per
adult, €5.50 per child (4–12 years old), €23 (€15) for a two-hour candlelit
cruise. The big companies also offer more specialized boat trips, from the once-
weekly Architecture Cruise run by the Lovers company (☏020/530 1090,
⊛www.lovers.nl) through to the Red Light District Cruises operated by just
about everyone.

All these – and especially the shorter and less expensive cruises – are extremely
popular and long **queues** are commonplace throughout the summer. One way
to avoid much of the crush is to walk down from Centraal Station to the quieter jetty at the near end of the Rokin, where the first-rate company Rederij
P. Kooij (☏020/623 3810) offers all the basic options – from one-hour jaunts
to candlelit cruises – at very competitive prices.

## Selected tour companies

**Holland International** Prins Hendrikkade 33 ⓣ020/625 3035, ⓦwww.thatsholland.com. Large tour operator running an extensive range of bus trips, from city sightseeing tours (1 daily; 3hr 30min; €26) to a gallop through the whole country on their "Grand Holland Tour" (1 daily except Sat; 8hr 30min; €40). Also does canal cruises, beginning with the basic one-hour sightseeing trip round the city centre (€8.50): boats depart (every 15min 9am–6pm, every 30min 6–10pm) from the jetty facing Centraal Station on Prins Hendrikkade.

**Let's Go** ⓦwww.letsgo-amsterdam. com. Various well-organized bike tours around Amsterdam and its environs, including a twice-weekly one to Edam and Volendam (see p.140; May–Sept only; 4hr 30min; €22). Also has a twice-weekly "Mystery Walking Tour"

around the city centre (May–Sept; 1hr 30min; €10). You can book either direct or at the VVV; tours leave from the VVV office on Stationsplein.

**Mee in Mokum** Hartenstraat 18 ⓣ020/625 1390. Two-hour guided walking tours of the older parts of the city provided by long-time, older (50+) Amsterdam residents. Tours once daily on Sat & Sun only; €2.50 per person. Advance reservations required.

**Yellow Bike Tours** Nieuwezijds Kolk 29, off Nieuwezijds Voorburgwal ⓣ020/620 6940, ⓦwww.yellowbike.nl. This efficient company organizes a lively programme of three-hour guided cycling tours around the city and its environs (April to mid-Oct 1 or 2 daily). Tours cost €17 per person, including the bike. Advance reservations are required.

Amsterdam's tour operators also offer a wide range of non-nautical excursions, everything from guided cycle rides to a quick zip round the city by bus. A selection is given in the box, but if you have a specific interest – Dutch art for example – it's well worth asking at the VVV to see what's on offer.

# City transport

Almost all of Amsterdam's leading attractions are clustered in or near the city centre, within easy walking distance of each other. For longer jaunts, the city has a first-rate **public transport system**, comprising trams, buses, a pint-sized metro and four passenger ferries across the River IJ to the northern suburbs. Centraal Station is the hub of this transit system, which is run by GVB (ⓦwww.gvb.nl).

GVB's remit does not extend to the city's **canals**, which are mainly the haunt of cruise boats, but there are one or two interesting and reasonably economic options for getting round the city by boat. Amsterdam is also ideal for **cycling**, but **driving** – never mind parking – is a pain. **Taxis** are plentiful and there are ranks liberally distributed across the city centre; taxis can also be hailed on the street, though some taxi drivers aren't too keen. If all else fails, call the city's central, 24hr taxi number on ⓣ020/677 7777. Fares are metered and pricey, but there again distances are small: the trip from Centraal Station to the Leidseplein, for example, costs just €8 (a bit more late at night).

## Trams, buses and the metro

The city centre is criss-crossed by **trams**, which operate on about fifteen different routes and are the mainstay of the system. One of the most useful is tram #20 (daily 9am–6pm; every 10min), which threads a circuitous route through the centre passing by most of the leading attractions. For the most part, you enter at the rear doors (push the button); if the doors start to close before you've got on, put your foot on the bottom step to keep them open. **Buses**, which are always entered at the front, are mainly useful for going to the outskirts, and the same applies to the **metro**, which is clean, modern and punctual but at night attracts too many shifty characters for its own good – there are just two useful downtown metro stations, Nieuwmarkt and Waterlooplein.

The bulk of the transport system operates daily from 6am to midnight, and is supplemented by a limited number of nightbuses (*nachtbussen*). All tram and bus stops display a detailed map of the network. For further details on all services, head for the main **GVB information office** (Mon–Fri 7am–9pm, Sat & Sun 8am–9pm; ℡0900/9292, ⊛www.gvb.nl) on Stationsplein, in front of Centraal Station. Their free, English-language *Tourist Guide to Public Transport* is very helpful.

Amsterdam's public transport system is divided into fifteen **zones**. The "Centre" zone covers the city centre and its immediate surroundings (well beyond Singelgracht). The most common type of ticket, used on all forms of GVB transport, is the **strippenkaart** – a piece of card divided into strips (see p.29 for more). On the city's trams, unless there's a conductor, you insert your *strippenkaart* into the on-board franking machine: fold it over to expose only the last of the strips required for your journey before doing so (a journey in the central zone requires two strips for each person travelling). On the metro, the franking machines are on the station concourse, but on the buses the driver does the job. A stamped *strippenkaart* is valid for travel – with unlimited changes between trams, buses and the metro – for up to an hour. Currently, a two-strip *strippenkaart* **costs** €1.60, three-strip €2.40, fifteen-strip €6.20 and a 45-strip €18.30. The 45-strip is available at a wide variety of outlets including tobacconists, the GVB, the VVV and metro stations. The 15-strip is available at the same locations and from some bus drivers, primarily on routes that go beyond the city limits. However, most bus and tram drivers will only issue the two- or three-strip *strippenkaart,* which are also available at metro stations, but not from tobacconists and the VVV.

To avoid all this stamping, you can instead opt for a **dagkaart** (day ticket), which gives unlimited access to the GVB system for as many days as you need, up to a maximum of seven. Prices start at €5.50 for one day and €8.80 for two, with seven days costing €21.30; concessions apply to the over-65s and youngsters from 4 to 11 years old. In all cases, children up to four travel free. For long-term stays, you might consider a season ticket, valid for a month or a year. For further details and advice visit the GVB office, whose operatives usually speak English.

## Canal transport

One good way to get around Amsterdam's waterways is to take the **Canal Bus** (℡020/623 9886, ⊛www.canal.nl). This operates on three circular routes, which meet once, at the jetty opposite Centraal Station beside Prins Hendrikkade. Two of the three routes also meet on the Singelgracht (opposite the Rijksmuseum), behind the Leidseplein and beside the Town Hall on Waterlooplein. There are eleven stops in all and together they give easy access to all the major sights. Boats leave from opposite Centraal Station (every 10–20min 10am–5pm) and at least every half-hour from any other jetty. A day ticket for all three routes, allowing you to hop on and off as many times as you like, costs €14 per adult, €10 for children (4–12 years old); it's valid until noon the following day and entitles the bearer to minor discounts at several museums.

A similar boat service, the **Museumboot** (☎020/530 1090, ⓦwww.lovers.nl) calls at seven jetties located at or near many of the city's major attractions. It departs from opposite Centraal Station (every 30–45min 9.30am–5.30pm); a hop-on-hop-off day ticket costs €14.25.

### Cycling

One of the most agreeable ways to explore pancake-flat Amsterdam is by **bicycle**. The city has an excellent network of designated bicycle lanes (*fietspaden*) and for once cycling isn't a fringe activity – there are cyclists everywhere. Much to the chagrin of the city's taxi drivers, the needs of the cyclist often take precedence over those of the motorist and by law if there's a collision it's always the driver's fault. There's a high incidence of **bike theft** in the city (see p.31) – this is a real problem, and you should be sure to lock up your bike whenever it's not in use.

Bike **rental** is straightforward. There are lots of rental companies (*fietsenverhuur*) but **MacBike** (☎020/620 0985, ⓦwww.macbike.nl) sets the benchmark, charging €6.50 per day, €16.50 for three days and €30 for the week for a standard bicycle; 21-speed machines cost exactly twice as much. MacBike has three rental outlets in central Amsterdam, one at the west end of Centraal Station, a second beside Waterlooplein at Mr Visserplein 2, and a third near Leidseplein at Weteringschans 2. For a list of other rental companies, see the Directory on p.125. Before renting, make sure you check the return time and the bike's age and condition. All firms, including MacBike, ask for some type of security, usually in the form of a cash deposit (some will take credit card imprints) and/or passport. Remember that you are legally obliged to have reflector bands on both wheels.

### Driving

The centre of Amsterdam is geared up for trams and bicycles rather than **cars**, as a matter of municipal policy. Pedestrianized zones as such are not extensive, but motorists still have to negotiate a convoluted one-way system, avoid getting boxed onto tram lines and steer round herds of cyclists. **On-street parking** is also very limited – with far too many cars chasing too few spaces – and quite expensive. Every city-centre street where parking is permitted is **metered** (Mon–Sat 9am–midnight, Sun noon–midnight), with a standard cost of €2.80 for one hour, €16.80 for a day (9am–5pm), €11.20 for the evening (7pm–midnight), or €25.20 for the full period. If you overrun your ticket, you can expect your vehicle to be clamped by eager-beaver traffic wardens; thereafter, if you don't follow the instructions posted on your windscreen promptly, your vehicle will be removed to the municipal pound. The good news is that signs on all the main approach roads to Amsterdam indicate which of the city's **car parks** have spaces and will, in the near future, also detail relative costs. Car parks in the centre charge comparable rates to the metered street spaces, but those on the outskirts are a good deal less expensive and are invariably but a short journey from the centre by public transport. Note, too, that some of the better hotels either have their own parking spaces or offer special deals with nearby car parks.

# Accommodation

**Accommodation** in Amsterdam can be extremely difficult to find, and is characteristically expensive: even hostels are pricey for what you get, and hotels are among the most costly in Europe. What's more, if you arrive without a reservation, you'll need to search hard to find a decent place to stay, though at least the city's compactness means that you're pretty much bound to end up somewhere within easy reach of the centre. At peak periods throughout the year – July and August, Easter, Christmas – you're strongly advised to **book well ahead**; hotel rooms and even hostel beds can be swallowed up remarkably quickly, and if you leave finding a room to chance, you may well be disappointed (and/or out of pocket). The VVV will make advance bookings, and book rooms on the spot for a €3 fee, or sell you a comprehensive leaflet on hotels in the city (€3.50). You can also reserve rooms in advance by contacting the **Netherlands Reservation Centre** (☎0299/689 144, @www.hotelres.nl), or via websites such as @www.bookings.nl or @www.hotels-holland.com, all of which allow you to view availability and prices before making a booking. Something to bear in mind when choosing a hotel is the fact that many of Amsterdam's buildings have narrow, very steep staircases, and not all hotels have installed lifts. If this is a consideration for you, check before you book.

If you arrive at Centraal Station, you'll probably be approached by **touts** offering rooms or beds in hostels and cheap hotels. Despite the fact that most of them are genuine enough, our advice is to steer clear. If the place they're offering is in our listings you can phone it directly yourself, and if it isn't, it's been left out for a reason.

All the places reviewed here are located on a map: the most central ones on p.73, the remainder on p.64–65.

## Hotels

In the main, Amsterdam's hotel prices start at around €60 for a double, and although some form of **breakfast** – "Dutch" (bread and jam) or "English" (eggs) – is normally included at all but the cheapest and the most expensive hotels, some places can give the barest value for money. A number of hotels in Amsterdam also have large three- or four-bed family rooms available for around €150. The establishments listed below have something particular to recommend them over the rest – location, value for money or ambience. Don't be afraid to ask to see the room first, and to refuse it if you don't like it.

### The Old Centre

#### Inexpensive

**Amsterdam House (Eureka)** 's-Gravelandseveer 3 ☎020/624 6607, @www.amsterdamhouse .com. Considering it's just across the Amstel from Rembrandtplein, this delightful hotel is located in a surprisingly quiet part of town. Rooms are small but clean and pleasant, the staff are friendly, and you're perfectly positioned for the nightlife. Tram #4, #9, #16, #24 or #25 to Muntplein. ❸
**Rokin** Rokin 73 ☎020/626 7456, @www .rokinhotel.com. Three-star family hotel in a new building with a lift; it's also recently undergone major expansion. Doubles from €75, including breakfast. Private car park. Tram #4, #9, #16, #24 or #25 to Dam or Spui. ❸
**Tourist Inn** Spuistraat 52 ☎020/421 5841, @www.tourist-inn.nl. Popular budget hotel,

with clean and comfortable rooms and friendly staff. Six-person dorms with TV cost €25 per person, doubles without shower from €80. Triples and quads also available. Higher weekend rates. Lift access. 5min from Centraal Station. ❸
**Utopia** Nieuwezijds Voorburgwal 132 ☎020/626 1295, @www.hotelutopia.nl. Self-confessed "smokers' hotel" above a coffeeshop – tiny, musty rooms over the street, reached by a near-vertical staircase. Basic, and generally welcoming, though we've had complaints about unhelpful staff during peak season. 10min from Centraal Station. ❷
**Winston** Warmoesstraat 123 ☎020/623 1380, @www.winston.nl. Hotel designed for an arty crowd – safe, but popular and noisy. Rooms are

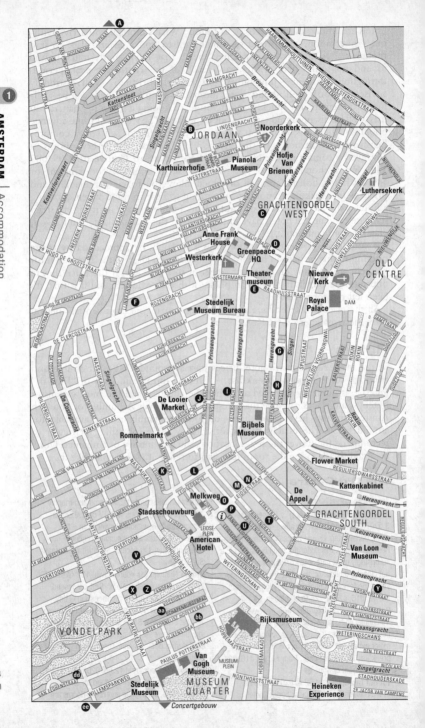

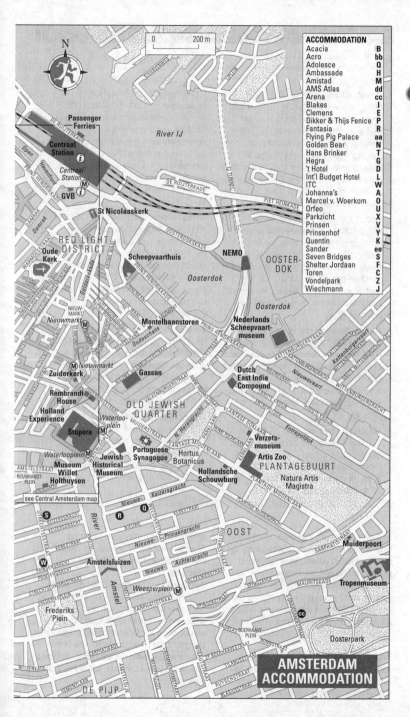

**ACCOMMODATION**

| | |
|---|---|
| Acacia | B |
| Acro | bb |
| Adolesce | Q |
| Ambassade | H |
| Amistad | M |
| AMS Atlas | dd |
| Arena | cc |
| Blakes | I |
| Clemens | E |
| Dikker & Thijs Fenice | P |
| Fantasia | R |
| Flying Pig Palace | aa |
| Golden Bear | N |
| Hans Brinker | T |
| Hegra | G |
| 't Hotel | D |
| Int'l Budget Hotel | L |
| ITC | W |
| Johanna's | A |
| Marcel v. Woerkom | O |
| Orfeo | U |
| Parkzicht | X |
| Prinsen | V |
| Prinsenhof | Y |
| Quentin | K |
| Sander | ee |
| Seven Bridges | S |
| Shelter Jordaan | F |
| Toren | C |
| Vondelpark | Z |
| Wiechmann | J |

## Gay hotels

All the hotels listed in this box cater specifically to gay men (and, rarely, lesbians). For more on Amsterdam's gay life, see p.118.

**Amistad** Kerkstraat 42 ☎020/624 8074, ⓦwww.amistad.nl. Stylish hotel conveniently located on Kerkstraat that's recently gone through a total revamp. Each room equipped with soft lighting, cosy duvets, TV, fridge and a safe. Rooms vary from standard without shower to deluxe with shower (and in some cases bathtub). Late breakfast 10am–2pm. ②–⑤

**Anco** Oudezijds Voorburgwal 55 ☎020/624 1126, ⓦwww.ancohotel.nl. Small and friendly hotel in the Red Light District, with private bar catering exclusively to leather-wearing gay men. Three and four-person dorms are €37 per bed, also studios available with private bathroom and kitchenette. Booking advised. ③–⑤

**Centre Apartments** Heintje Hoeksteeg 27 ☎020/627 2503, ⓦwww.amsterdam-gay-accommodation.nl. Studios and apartments for rent in the middle of the Old Centre. The same people also run a small, less expensive guesthouse out in the Jordaan, with singles and doubles. ④

**Golden Bear** Kerkstraat 37 ☎020/624 4785, ⓦwww.goldenbear.nl. Solid budget option, with a good range of clean, comfortable rooms, some en suite. Booking essential. Tram #1, #2 or #5 to Prinsengracht. ②–④

**ITC (International Travel Club)** Prinsengracht 1051 ☎020/623 0230, ⓦwww.itc-hotel.com. A little way away from the major gay areas, close to the Amstelveld on a tranquil section of canal, and perhaps the least expensive gay hotel of this quality. Five percent discount on cash payments. Women welcome. Tram #4 to Prinsengracht. ②–⑤

**Orfeo** Leidsekruisstraat 14 ☎020/623 1347, ⓦwww.hotelorfeo.com. Very pleasant gay and lesbian hotel round the back of Leidseplein. Decent breakfasts served until midday. Rooms with shared shower starting from €75, some triples and quads available, with more rooms planned. Tram #1, #2 or #5 to Prinsengracht. ②

**Sander** Jacob Obrechtstraat 69 ☎020/662 7574, Ⓔhtlsandr@xs4all.nl. Right behind the Concertgebouw, a spacious, pleasant hotel, especially welcoming to gay men and women – though heteros are welcome too. Tram #16 to Jacob Obrechtstraat. ④

**Waterfront** Singel 458 ☎020/421 6621, ⓦwww.waterfront.demon.nl. Smart, good-value hotel on a major canal, close to shops and nightlife, with decent rooms and service. Tram #1, #2 or #5 to Koningsplein. ④

---

light and airy (sleeping from one to six), some en suite, some with a communal balcony; many of them are specially commissioned "art" rooms, including the Durex Room, Heineken Room and Schiffmacher Room (the management plans to refurbish all the rooms in this way over the next few years). Lift and full disabled access. A basic hotel underneath all the trimmings. 10min from Centraal Station. ③

### Mid-range

**AMS City Centre** Nieuwezijds Voorburgwal 50 ☎020/422 0011, ⓦwww.ams.nl. A three-star hotel which is sparkling clean and decked out with attractive Art Deco fittings and furnishings. En-suite rooms with TV and tea- and coffee-making facilities. 10min from Centraal Station. ⑥

**De Gerstekorrel** Damstraat 22–24 ☎020/624 1367, Ⓔgersteko@euronet.nl. Small, simple hotel, steps away from the Dam, with large, brightly decorated and well-lit rooms, but located on a noisy, bustling street (ask for a back room). Pleasant staff and good buffet breakfast (€9.50). One of the cheaper options within this price range. No ground floor rooms. Tram #4, #9, #16, #24 or #25 to Dam square. ⑤

**Nes** Kloveniersburgwal 137–139 ⓣ020/624
4773, ⓦwww.hotelnes.nl. Extremely pleasant and
quiet, with a lift; well-positioned away from noise
but close to shops and nightlife. Helpful staff.
Prices vary, depending on the view. Tram #4, #9,
#16, #24 or #25 to Muntplein. ❻
**Rho** Nes 5 ⓣ020/620 7371,
ⓦwww.rhohotel.com. A very comfortable hotel in
a quiet alley off the Dam, with an extraordinary
high-ceilinged lounge, originally built as a theatre
in 1908. The place looks a bit run-down from the
outside, but it's still a fine city-centre option, with
helpful and welcoming staff. Towards the top end
of its price bracket. Tram #4, #9, #16, #24 or #25
to Dam square. ❺

## The Grachtengordel

### Inexpensive

**Brian** Singel 69 ⓣ020/624 4661,
ⓔhotelbrian@hotmail.com. A cheap and friendly
hotel in a good spot; €54 for a very basic, but
clean, double, including breakfast and free tea and
coffee throughout the day. Its compact rooms and
narrow stairways do, however, mean that it suffers
from "slamming door syndrome" late at night; not
the best place if you're looking for somewhere
peaceful. 10min from Centraal Station. ❷
**Clemens** Raadhuisstraat 39 ⓣ020/624 6089,
ⓦwww.clemenshotel.nl. Friendly, well-run budget
hotel, close to the Anne Frank House and museums. One of the better options along this busy
main road. Individually decorated doubles without
shower from €70, with shower €110. Breakfast
extra. All rooms offer free Internet connection, and
you can rent a laptop for €8. Recommended. Tram
#13, #14 or #17 to Westermarkt. ❸–❹
**Hegra** Herengracht 269 ⓣ020/623 7877, ⓕ623
8159. Welcoming atmosphere and relatively cheap
for the location, on a beautiful stretch of the canal.
Rooms are small but comfortable; a few have a
private bath instead of a shower. Tram #1, #2 or
#5 to Spui. ❷–❸
**Orfeo** Leidsekruisstraat 14 ⓣ020/623 1347,
ⓦwww.hotelorfeo.com. Very pleasant gay and lesbian hotel round the back of Leidseplein, with
decent breakfasts served until midday. Rooms with
shared shower starting from €75, some triples
and quads available with more rooms planned for
future. Popular with gay visitors. Tram #1, #2 or #5
to Prinsengracht. ❸
**Prinsenhof** Prinsengracht 810 ⓣ020/623 1772,
ⓦwww.hotelprinsenhof.com. Tastefully decorated,
this is one of the city's best budget options; the best
rooms are at the back. €60 without shower.

## Expensive

**Grand** Oudezijds Voorburgwal 197 ⓣ020/555
3111, ⓦwww.thegrand.nl. Originally a Royal Inn
dating from 1578, and after that the Amsterdam
Town Hall, this extraordinary building is a centrepiece of the city's medieval district. It claims to
offer "a sublime combination of luxury, warm hospitality and unrivalled grandeur" – overblown, but
not by much. €420 or so for a double. Tram #4,
#9, #16, #24 or #25 to Dam square. ❾
**Victoria** Damrak 1–5 ⓣ020/623 4255, ⓔvi-
cres@parkplazahotels.nl. The *Victoria* is one of the
landmarks of the city – a tall, elegant building,
wonderfully decorated throughout – and one of the
classiest hotels, with every possible amenity.
Opposite Centraal Station. ❾

Booking essential. Tram #4 to Prinsengracht. ❷–❸
**Quentin** Leidsekade 89 ⓣ020/626 2187, ⓕ622
0121. Very friendly small hotel, often a stopover for
artists performing at the Melkweg. Welcoming to
all, and especially well-regarded among gay and
lesbian visitors; families with children might feel
out of place. Tram #1, #2 or #5 to Leidseplein. ❸

### Mid-range

**Agora** Singel 462 ⓣ020/627 2200,
ⓔagora@worldonline.nl. Nicely located, small and
amiable hotel right near the flower market; doubles cost upwards of €110, three- and four-bed
rooms proportionately less. You'll pay more for a
canal view. Tram #1, #2 or #5 to Koningsplein. ❹
**Hoksbergen** Singel 301 ⓣ020/626 6043,
ⓔhotelhoksbergen@wxs.nl. Friendly, standard
hotel, with a light and open breakfast room overlooking the canal. Basic en-suite rooms, all with
telephone and TV. Self-catering apartments also
available. Tram #1, #2 or #5 to Spui. ❹
**'t Hotel** Leliegracht 18 ⓣ020/422 2741,
ⓔth.broekema@hetnet.nl. Extremely pleasant
hotel located along a quiet canal. Owned by the
proprietor of an antique shop, who believes in
making people feel at home. Eight spacious
rooms, large bed, TV, fridge and either bath or
shower. No groups. Minimum three-night stay
weekends. Tram #13, #14 or #17 to Westermarkt.
❺
**Marcel van Woerkom** Leidsestraat 87
ⓣ020/622 9834, ⓦwww.marcelamsterdam.com.
Well-known, popular B&B-cum-hotel run by an
English-speaking graphic designer and artist, who
attracts like-minded people to this stylish restored
house. Four en-suite doubles available for two,
three or four people sharing. Quiet and peaceful,

but in a very handy location. Regulars return year after year, so you'll need to ring well in advance in high season. Breakfast not included, but there are tea- and coffee-making facilities. Tram #1, #2 or #5 to Prinsengracht. **④**

**Seven Bridges** Reguliersgracht 31 ⊤020/623 1329, no fax. Perhaps the city's most charming hotel – and certainly one of its better-value ones. Takes its name from its canalside location with views over seven little humpback bridges. Beautifully decorated, spotless rooms, which are regularly upgraded. Small and popular, so often booked solid. Breakfast is served in your room. Highly recommended. Room price depends on the view. Tram #4 or #9 to Prinsengracht. **④–⑥**

**Toren** Keizersgracht 164 ⊤020/622 6033, ⓔ hotel.toren@tip.nl. Fine example of a seventeenth-century canal house, once the home of a Dutch prime minister, now popular with American visitors. Opulently designed en-suite doubles from €130. Some deluxe rooms have Jacuzzi. Friendly and efficient staff ensure the hotel retains a good deal of grace. Well-priced option within this band. Tram #13, #14 or #17 to Westermarkt. **⑤**

**Wiechmann** Prinsengracht 328–332 ⊤020/626 3321, ⓦ www.hotelwiechmann.nl. Another canal-house restoration project, family-run for fifty years, with dark wooden beams and restrained style throughout. Large, bright rooms with TV and shower, kept in perfect condition. Close to the Anne Frank House. Doubles from €125. Tram #13, #14 or #17 to Westermarkt. **⑤**

### Expensive

**Ambassade** Herengracht 341 ⊤020/555 0222, ⓦ www.ambassade-hotel.nl. Elegant canalside hotel made up of ten seventeenth-century houses, with elegant furnished lounges, an enviably stocked library and comfortable en-suite rooms. Breakfast is an extra €14, but well worth it. Tram #1, #2 or #5 to Spui. **⑦**

**Blakes** Keizersgracht 384 ⊤020/530 2010, ⓦ www.blakes-amsterdam.com. The latest Anouska Hempel hotel (there are already two in London), housed in a seventeenth-century building, centred on a beautiful courtyard and terrace. Both the decor and the restaurant menu combine Oriental and European styles. Hip without being (overly) pretentious. Richly decorated doubles from €370. Tram #1, #2 or #5 to Keizersgracht. **⑨**

**Dikker & Thijs Fenice** Prinsengracht 444 ⊤020/620 1212, ⓦ www.dtfh.nl. Small and stylish hotel on a beautiful canal close to all the shops. Rooms vary in decor but all include a minibar, telephone and TV; those on the top floor give a good view of the city (there's a lift, but it's small and old-fashioned). Tram #1, #2 or #5 to Prinsengracht. **⑦–⑧**

## The Jordaan and the west

**Acacia** Lindengracht 251 ⊤020/622 1460, ⓔ acacia .nl@wxs.nl. Well-kept hotel, which was one of the filming locations for the *Heimat* TV series. Situated right on a corner, so some of the rooms have a great panoramic view. They also let self-catering apartments. Doubles from €80, as well as 3, 4 and 5-bed rooms available. 15min from Centraal Station. **③**

**Johanna's** Van Hogendorpplein 62 ⊤020/684 8596, ⓦ www.johannasbnb.com. A privately-run B&B, which is very friendly and helpful to newcomers. A little difficult to get to, situated out near the Westergasfabriek, but with excellent prices. Two double rooms only, so reserve in advance. Tram #10 from Leidseplein to Van Limburg Stirumplein. **③**

## The Old Jewish Quarter and the east

**Adolesce** Nieuwe Keizersgracht 26 ⊤020/626 3959, ⓔ adolesce@xs4all.nl. Large, popular and welcoming hotel, with neat if unspectacular rooms and a large dining room and bar. Tram #9 or #14 to Waterlooplein. **③**

**Fantasia** Nieuwe Keizersgracht 16 ⊤020/623 8259, ⓦ www.fantasia-hotel.com. Nicely situated family-run hotel on a broad, quiet canal just off the Amstel; the rooms are well maintained, connected by quaint, narrow corridors, and there are also some very attractive attic rooms for €75. Triples and quads also available. Tram #9 or #14 to Waterlooplein. **③**

**Hotel Arena** 's-Gravesandestraat 51 ⊤020/850 2410, ⓦ www.hotelarena.nl. A little way out of the centre to the east, in a renovated old convent on the edge of the Oosterpark, this place has recently been revamped from a popular hostel into a hip 3-star hotel complete with split level rooms and minimalist decor. However, despite its apparent move into lofty pretentiousness it still manages to retain a relaxed vibe, attracting both business people and travellers alike. Lively bar, intimate restaurant and late-night club (Fri & Sat) are located within the former chapel. Doubles start from €125. Metro Weesperplein then walk, or tram #6 from Leidseplein to Korte 's-Gravesandestraat. **⑤**

## The Museum Quarter and the Vondelpark

**Acro** Jan Luyckenstraat 44 ☎020/662 5538, ⓦwww.acro-hotel.nl. Excellent, modern hotel with stylish rooms, a plush bar and self-service restaurant (breakfast only). Well worth the money, reserve at least 2 months in advance. Tram #2 or #5 to Van Baerlestraat. ❹

**AMS Atlas** Van Eeghenstraat 64 ☎020/676 6336, ⓦwww.ams.nl. Situated just to one side of the Vondelpark, this Art Nouveau building houses a personable modern hotel with every convenience and comfort, plus an à la carte restaurant. Small, tranquil and very welcoming. Tram #2 to Jacob Obrechtstraat. ❺

**Parkzicht** Roemer Visscherstraat 33 ☎020/618 1954, ⓕ618 0897. Quiet unassuming little hotel on a pretty backstreet near the Vondelpark and museums, with pleasant enough staff and an appealingly lived-in look – clean and characterful. Basic doubles. Tram #1 to 1e Constantijn Huygensstraat. Closed Dec–March. ❸

**Prinsen** Vondelstraat 38 ☎020/616 2323, ⓦwww.prinsenhotel.demon.nl. Family-style hotel on the edge of the Vondelpark; quiet and with a large, secluded garden at the back. Higher weekend rates. Tram #1 to 1e Constantijn Huygensstraat. ❺

**Sander** Jacob Obrechtstraat 69 ☎020/662 7574, ⓦwww.xs4all.nl/~htlsandr. Right behind the Concertgebouw, a spacious, pleasant hotel, welcoming to gay men and women, and everyone else too. Tram #16 to Jacob Obrechtstraat. ❺

# Hostels

The bottom line for most travellers is taking a dormitory bed in a **hostel**, and there are plenty to choose from: official HI places (dubbed "Stayokay"), unofficial private hostels, even Christian hostels – new arrivals are often accosted outside the train station with numerous offers of beds (which you'd do best to resist). Most hostels will either provide (relatively) clean bed linen or charge a few euros for it – so your own sleeping bag may be a better option. Many hostels also lock guests out for a short period each day to clean the place and some set a nightly curfew, though these are usually late enough not to cause too much of a problem. Many hostels don't accept reservations from June to August.

The cheapest dorms you'll find are the Christian hostels, at around €15.50 per person per night, with the average elsewhere being closer to €20. Much more and you might as well be in a hotel room. Note that any place that won't allow you to see the dorm before you pay is worth avoiding. If you want a little extra privacy, many hostels also offer triples, doubles and singles for much less than you'd pay in a regular hotel, though the quality and size of rooms can leave a lot to be desired.

## The Old Centre

**Bob's Youth Hostel** Nieuwezijds Voorburgwal 92 ☎020/623 0063, ⓕ675 6446. An old favourite of backpackers and a grungy crowd, Bob's is lively and smoky. Small dorms at €17 per person, including breakfast in the coffeeshop on the ground floor (which also does cheap dinners). They also let four apartments (€70 for two people, €80 for three). However, they kick everyone out at 10am to clean – not so good if you fancy a lie in. 10min from Centraal Station.

**Bulldog Low-Budget Hotel** Oudezijds Voorburgwal 220 ☎020/620 3822, ⓦwww .bulldog.nl. Part of the Bulldog coffeeshop chain, and recently renovated into "a five-star hotel for backpackers". Bar and DVD lounge downstairs complete with leather couches and soft lighting. Dorms with TV and shower start at €26, including breakfast, linen and wake-up service, if you need it. Doubles (❸) and fully equipped luxury apartments (from €130) available. Tram #4, #9, #16 or #24 to Dam, then a 3min walk.

**Durty Nelly's** Warmoesstraat 115–117 ☎020/638 0125, ⓔnellys@xs4all.nl. Good-quality partitioned dorms above a packed Irish pub, with a cooked breakfast, sheets and lockers included. €22 per person, €25 weekends. Street-side dorms are lighter and airier. 5min from Centraal Station.

**Flying Pig Downtown** Nieuwendijk 100 ☎020/420 6822, ⓦwww.flyingpig.nl. Clean, large and well-run by ex-travellers who are familiar with the needs of backpackers. Free use of kitchen facilities, no curfew, and there's a late-night coffee shop next door. Hostel bar open all night. Justifiably popular, and a very good deal, with a dorm bed priced between €19 and €25 depending on the size of the dorm; queensize bunks sleeping two also available. €10 deposit for sheets and keys. During the peak season you'll need to book well in advance. See also the *Flying Pig Palace*, below. 5min from Centraal Station.

**The Shelter City** Barndesteeg 21 ⊕020/625 3230, ⊛www.shelter.nl. A non-evangelical Christian youth hostel smack in the middle of the Red Light District. At €15.50, these are some of the best-value beds in Amsterdam, with bed linen, shower and sizeable breakfast included. Dorms are single-sex, lockers require a €5 deposit and there's a midnight curfew (1am at weekends). You might be handed a booklet on Jesus when you check in, but you'll get a quiet night's sleep and the sheets are clean. Metro Nieuwmarkt.

**Stadsdoelen** Kloveniersburgwal 97 ⊕020/624 6832, ⊛www.stayokay.com. The closer to the station of the city's two official HI hostels, with clean, semi-private dorms at €17.50 for members, who get priority in high season; non-members pay €20.65. Includes linen, breakfast and locker, plus use of communal kitchen. Guests get a range of discounts on activities in the city. The bar overlooks the canal and serves good-value if basic food, and there's a 2am curfew (though the door opens for three 15min intervals between 2am and 7am). The other HI hostel is the Vondelpark, which is better equipped for large groups (see opposite). Metro Nieuwmarkt, or tram #4, #9, #16, #20, #24 or #25 to Muntplein.

## The Grachtengordel

**Hans Brinker** Kerkstraat 136 ⊕020/622 0687, ⊛www.brinker.nl. Well-established and raucously popular Amsterdam cheapie, which has over 500 beds. Dorm beds go for around €21 including breakfast. Singles and doubles (❷) also available. The facilities are good: there's free Internet after 10pm, a disco every night, and dorms are basic and clean, plus it's very close to the Leidseplein buzz. One to head for if you're out for a good time and not too bothered about getting a good night's sleep, though be prepared to change dorms several times during your stay. Walk-in policy only. Tram

#1, #2 or #5 to Prinsengracht.

**International Budget Hotel** Leidsegracht 76 ⊕020/624 2784, ⊜info @internationalbudgethotel.com. An excellent budget option on a peaceful little canal in the heart of the Grachtengordel. Small, simple rooms sleeping up to four (from €30 per person), with singles and doubles (❸) available. Young, friendly staff. Tram #1, #2 or #5 to Prinsengracht.

## The Jordaan and the west

**The Shelter Jordaan** Bloemstraat 179 ⊕020/624 4717, ⊛www.shelter.nl. The second of Amsterdam's two Christian youth hostels, again great value at €15.50 per bed, with breakfast and bed linen included. Dorms are single-sex, lockers require a €5 deposit and there's a 2am curfew. Friendly and helpful staff, plus a decent café. Sited in a particularly attractive part of the Jordaan. Tram #13, #14 or #17 to Marnixstraat.

## The Museum Quarter and the Vondelpark

**Flying Pig Palace** Vossiusstraat 46 ⊕020/400 4187, ⊛www.flyingpig.nl. The better of the two Flying Pig hostels, facing the Vondelpark and close to the most important museums. Immaculately clean and well-maintained by a staff of travellers, who well understand their backpacking guests. Free use of kitchen facilities, no curfew and good tourist information. Ten-bed dorms start at €18 per person, 2-person queensize bunks at €27 and double rooms (❶–❷) are available too. Great value. Tram #1, #2 or #5 to Leidseplein, then walk.

**Vondelpark** Zandpad 5 ⊕020/589 8993, ⊛www.stayokay.com. Well located and, for facilities, the better of the two HI hostels, with a bar, restaurant, TV lounge, free Internet access and bicycle shed, plus various discount facilities for tours and museums. HI members have priority in high season and receive a €2.50 discount. Standard rates are €21 per person in the dorms, including use of all facilities, shower, sheets and breakfast. Singles, doubles (❷) and rooms sleeping up to six are available. Secure lockers; lift; no curfew. To be sure of a place in high season you'll need to book at least two months ahead. Tram #1, #2 or #5 to Leidseplein, then walk.

# Campsites

There are several **campsites** in and around Amsterdam, most of them easily accessible by car or public transport. The three listed below are recommended by the VVV, divided into "youth campsites", which are self-explanatory, and family campsites", which are more suitable for those seeking some quiet, or touring with a caravan or camper. For information on city campsites throughout the Netherlands, take a look at Ⓦwww.stadscampings.nl.

## "Youth" sites

**Vliegenbos** Meeuwenlaan 138 ☎020/636 8855, Ⓦwww.vliegenbos.com. A relaxed and friendly site, just a 10min bus ride into Amsterdam North from the station. Facilities include a general shop, bar and restaurant. Rates are €7.25 per night per person, hot showers included. There are also huts with bunk beds and basic cooking facilities, for €45.30 per night for four people; phone ahead to check availability. Under-16s need to be accompanied by an adult; no pets. Bus #32 or #36 (nightbus #73) from Centraal Station. Exit S116 off the A10 motorway. April–Sept.

**Zeeburg** Zuiderzeeweg 20 ☎020/694 4430, Ⓦwww.campingzeeburg.nl. Slightly better equipped than the Vliegenbos, but more difficult to get to. Rates are €2–4 per person, plus €3.50 for a tent, €2.50 for a motorbike and €4 for a car. Hot showers are an extra €0.80. Cabins sleeping two to six are €16.25 per person per night, including bed linen. Bus #22 to Kramatweg; also served by tram #14 from Dam Square. Exit S114 off the A10. Open all year.

## "Family" site

**Amsterdamse Bos** Kleine Noorddijk 1, Aalsmeer ☎020/641 6868, Ⓔcamping@dab.amsterdam.nl. Facilities include a bar, shop and restaurant, but this campsite is a long way out, on the southern reaches of the lush and well-kept Amsterdamse Bos (forest). Rates are €4.45 per person per night (children under 3 are free), hot showers included, plus €2.35 for a car, €5.60 for a camper and €3.30 for a caravan. Huts sleeping up to four cost €38.60 a night, which includes a gas stove. Take yellow NZH bus #171 from Centraal Station. Exit 6 off the A9 towards Aalsmeer. April to mid-Oct.

# The City

Confined by the circuitous sweep of the Singelgracht canal, Amsterdam's compact centre contains most of the city's leading attractions but it takes only about forty minutes to stroll from one end to the other. **Centraal Station**, where you're most likely to arrive, lies on the centre's northern edge, its back to the River IJ, and from here the city fans south in a web of concentric canals, surrounded by expanding suburbs. The city centre readily divides into a network of distinct neighbourhoods and the description below hops from one area to another following Amsterdam's historic development, beginning with the oldest part of the city, the Old Centre. Bear in mind, however, that just wandering around to get the flavour of the place is often the most enjoyable way to proceed.

At the heart of the city is Amsterdam's most vivacious district, the **Old Centre**, an oval-shaped area featuring a jumble of antique streets and beautiful, narrow little canals. This is the unlikely setting for the sleazy, infamous Red Light District.

Forming a ring around it is the first of the major canals, the Singel, followed closely by the Herengracht, Keizersgracht and Prinsengracht – collectively known as the **Grachtengordel**, or "Girdle of Canals". These were part of a major seventeenth-century urban extension and, with the interconnecting radial streets, form the city's distinctive web shape. This is the Amsterdam you see in the brochures: still, dreamy canals, crisp reflections of seventeenth-century town houses, cobbled streets, railings with chained bicycles – an image which, although perhaps a little too familiar, is still utterly authentic.

Beyond the Grachtengordel, the **Jordaan** to the west grew up as a slum and immigrant quarter and remains the traditional heart of working-class Amsterdam, though in recent years it has experienced a measure of gentrification.

Its mazy streets and narrow canals make it a pleasant area to wander. On the east side of the centre is the **Old Jewish Quarter**; since the Nazi occupation during World War II, this area has changed more than any other – its population gone and landscape altered – but there are several poignant reminders of earlier times, most notably the first-rate Jewish Historical Museum.

Amsterdam's three leading museums are clustered together just beyond the southern boundary of the Grachtengordel, in what is sometimes known as the **Museum Quarter**, on the edge of Museumplein. The world-class trio – the **Rijksmuseum**, the **Van Gogh Museum** and the **Stedelijk Museum** – between them possess an outstanding assortment of paintings, and they also form a cultural prelude to the sprawling greenery of the nearby **Vondelpark**, Amsterdam's loveliest park.

## The Old Centre

The **Old Centre** was where Amsterdam began, starting out as a fishing village at the mouth of the River Amstel and then, when the river was dammed in 1270, flourishing as a trading centre and receiving its municipal charter from a new feudal overlord, the Count of Holland, in about 1300. Thereafter, the city developed in stages, each of which was marked by the digging of new canals and, after a particularly severe fire in 1452, by the abandonment of timber for stone and brick as the main building materials. Today, it's the handsome stone and brick buildings of subsequent centuries, especially the seventeenth, which provide the old centre with most of its architectural highlights.

Strolling across the bridge from Centraal Station brings you onto the **Damrak**, the spine of the Old Centre and the thoroughfare that once divided the **Oude Zijde** (Old Side) of the medieval city to the east from the smaller **Nieuwe Zijde** (New Side) to the west. The Damrak culminates in **Dam square**, flanked by two of the city's most impressive buildings, the Koninklijk Paleis (Royal Palace) and the Nieuwe Kerk.

To the east of Damrak is the **Red Light District**, which stretches up to Nieuwmarkt. It's here you'll find many of the city's finest buildings, though the seediness of the tentacular red-light zone dulls many charms. That said, be sure to spare time for the district's two delightful churches – the Amstelkring and the Oude Kerk.

Just beyond the reach of the Red Light District is careworn **Nieuwmarkt**, an unappetizing start to the **Kloveniersburgwal**, which forms one of the most beguiling parts of the Old Centre, with a medley of handsome old houses lining the prettiest of canals. From here, it's a short walk west to the **Rokin**, a shopping boulevard running south from the Dam to **Muntplein**, a busy square where you'll find the floating flower market.

### Junkies in the Old Centre

The hang-around **junkies** of the Old Centre are not generally dangerous, but they are certainly disconcerting wherever and whenever they gather in groups – especially if the streets happen to be quiet. The edgiest area is generally regarded as being just to the east of the Oude Kerk on O.Z. Voorburgwal and O.Z. Achterburgwal, with the Nieuwmarkt square periodically becoming enmeshed too. It almost goes without saying that cutting any kind of drug deal with a street dealer is both illegal and highly ill-advised.

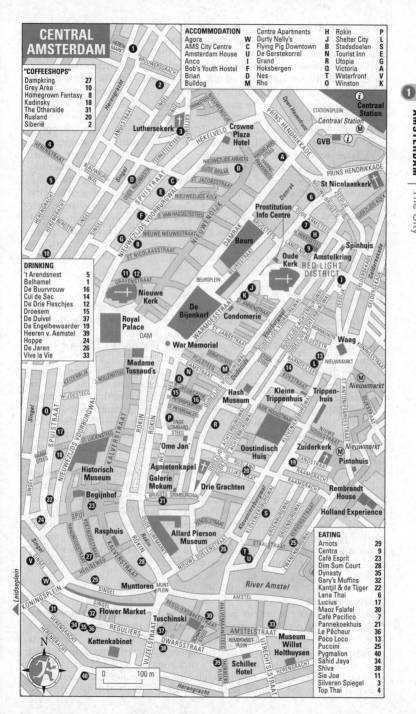

# CENTRAL AMSTERDAM

**ACCOMMODATION**

| | | | |
|---|---|---|---|
| Agora | W | Centre Apartments | H | Rokin | P |
| AMS City Centre | C | Durty Nelly's | J | Shelter City | L |
| Amsterdam House | U | Flying Pig Downtown | B | Stadsdoelen | S |
| Anco | I | De Gerstekorrel | N | Tourist Inn | E |
| Bob's Youth Hostel | F | Grand | R | Utopia | G |
| Brian | D | Hoksbergen | Q | Victoria | A |
| Bulldog | M | Nes | T | Waterfront | V |
| | | Rho | O | Winston | K |

**"COFFEESHOPS"**

| | |
|---|---|
| Dampkring | 27 |
| Grey Area | 10 |
| Homegrown Fantasy | 8 |
| Kadinsky | 18 |
| The Otherside | 31 |
| Rusland | 20 |
| Siberië | 2 |

**DRINKING**

| | |
|---|---|
| 't Arendsnest | 5 |
| Belhamel | 1 |
| De Buurvrouw | 16 |
| Cul de Sac | 14 |
| De Drie Fleschjes | 12 |
| Droesem | 15 |
| De Duivel | 37 |
| De Engelbewaarder | 19 |
| Heeren v. Aemstel | 39 |
| Hoppe | 24 |
| De Jaren | 26 |
| Vive la Vie | 33 |

**EATING**

| | |
|---|---|
| Arnots | 29 |
| Centra | 9 |
| Café Esprit | 23 |
| Dim Sum Court | 28 |
| Dynasty | 35 |
| Gary's Muffins | 32 |
| Kantjil & de Tijger | 22 |
| Lana Thai | 6 |
| Lucius | 17 |
| Maoz Falafel | 30 |
| Café Pacifico | 7 |
| Pannekoekhuis | 21 |
| Le Pêcheur | 36 |
| Poco Loco | 13 |
| Puccini | 25 |
| Pygmalion | 40 |
| Sahid Jaya | 34 |
| Shiva | 38 |
| Sie Joe | 11 |
| Silveren Spiegel | 3 |
| Top Thai | 4 |

0 — 100 m

N

## Centraal Station and around

With its high gables and cheerful brickwork, the neo-Renaissance **Centraal Station** is an imposing prelude to the city. At the time of its construction in the 1880s, it aroused much controversy because it effectively separated the centre from the River IJ, source of the city's wealth, for the first time in Amsterdam's long history. Outside, **Stationsplein** is a messy open space, edged by ovals of water, packed with trams and dotted with barrel organs and chip stands – in the summer street performers complete the picture.

Across the water, to the southeast on Prins Hendrikkade, rise the whopping twin towers and dome of **St Nicolaaskerk** (Mon–Sat noon–3pm; free), the city's foremost Catholic church. Dating back to the 1880s, the cavernous interior holds some pretty dire religious murals, mawkish concoctions only partly relieved by swathes of coloured brickwork. Above the high altar is the crown of the Habsburg emperor Maximilian, very much a symbol of the city and one you'll see again and again. Amsterdam had close ties with Maximilian: in the late fifteenth century he came here as a pilgrim and stayed on to recover from an illness. The burghers funded many of his military expeditions and, in return, he let the city use his crown in its coat of arms – a practice which, rather surprisingly, survived the seventeenth-century revolt against Spain.

## Along Damrak

From Stationsplein, **Damrak**, a wide but unenticing avenue lined with tacky restaurants, bars and bureaux de change, slices south into the heart of the city, first passing an inner harbour crammed with the bobbing canal boats of Amsterdam's considerable tourist industry. Just beyond the harbour is the imposing bulk of the **Beurs**, the old Stock Exchange (Tues–Sun 11am–5pm; admission depends on exhibition; Ⓦwww.beursvanberlage.nl) – known as the "Beurs van Berlage" – a seminal work designed at the turn of the century by the leading light of the Dutch Modern movement, Hendrik Petrus Berlage (1856–1934). The Beurs has long since lost its commercial function and nowadays holds a modest exhibition on the history of the exchange, but the building is the main event, from the graceful exposed ironwork and shallow-arched arcades of the main hall through to a fanciful frieze celebrating the stockbroker's trade.

Just along from the Beurs, the enormous and long-established **De Bijenkorf** – literally "beehive" – department store extends south along the Damrak. Amsterdam's most upmarket store, De Bijenkorf posed all sorts of problems for the Germans when they first occupied the city in World War II. It was a Jewish concern, so the Nazis didn't really want their troops shopping here, but it was just too popular to implement a total ban; the bizarre solution was to prohibit German soldiers from shopping on the ground floor, where the store's Jewish employees were concentrated, as they always had been, in the luxury goods section.

## Dam square

Situated at the heart of the city just beyond De Bijenkorf, **Dam square** gave Amsterdam its name: in the thirteenth century the River Amstel was dammed here, and the fishing village that grew around it became known as "Amstelredam". Boats could sail into the square down the Damrak and unload right in the middle of the settlement, which soon prospered by trading herrings for Baltic grain. In the early fifteenth century, the building of Amsterdam's principal church, the Nieuwe Kerk, and thereafter the town hall (now the

Royal Palace), formally marked the Dam as Amsterdam's centre, but since World War II it has lost much of its dignity. Today it's open and airy but somehow rather desultory, despite – or perhaps partly because of – the presence of the main municipal **war memorial**, a prominent stone tusk adorned by bleak, suffering figures and decorated with the coats of arms of each of the Netherlands' provinces (plus the ex-colony of Indonesia). The local branch of **Madame Tussaud's** waxworks is at no. 20 (daily: mid-July to Aug 9.30am–7.30pm; rest of year 10am–5.30pm; €17.50, Ⓦwww.madame-tussauds.com).

Dominating the Dam is the **Koninklijk Paleis** (Royal Palace; open for guided tours & exhibitions; check hours & admission on Ⓣ020/620 4060, Ⓦwww.koninklijkhuis.nl). The title is deceptive, given that this vast sandstone structure started out as the city's Stadhuis (town hall) in the mid-seventeenth century, and only had its first royal occupant when Louis Bonaparte moved in during the French occupation (1795–1813). At the time of the building's construction, Amsterdam was at the height of its powers. The city was pre-eminent amongst Dutch towns, and had just resisted William of Orange's attempts to bring it to heel; predictably, the council craved a residence that was a declaration of the city's municipal power and opted for a startlingly progressive design by **Jacob van Campen**, who proposed a Dutch rendering of the classical principles revived in Renaissance Italy. Initially, there was opposition to the plan from the council's Calvinist minority, who pointed out that the proposed Stadhuis would dwarf the neighbouring Nieuwe Kerk (see below), an entirely inappropriate ordering, so they suggested, of earthly and spiritual values. However, when the Calvinists were promised a new church spire (it was never built) they promptly fell in line and in 1648 work started on what was then the largest town hall in Europe, supported by no less than 13,659 wooden piles driven into the Dam's sandy soil – a number every Dutch schoolchild remembers by adding a "1" and a "9" to the number of days in the year. The poet Constantijn Huygens called the new building "The world's Eighth Wonder / With so much stone raised high and so much timber under".

The Stadhuis received its royal designation in 1808, when Napoleon's brother Louis, who had recently been installed as king, commandeered it as his residence. Lonely and isolated, Louis abdicated in 1810 and high-tailed it out of the country, leaving behind a large quantity of Empire furniture, most of which is exhibited in the rooms he converted. Possession of the palace subsequently reverted to the city, who sold it to the state in 1935, since when it has been used by royalty on very rare occasions.

## The Nieuwe Kerk

Vying for importance with the Royal Palace is the adjacent **Nieuwe Kerk** (open for exhibitions; check hours and admission on Ⓣ020/638 6909, Ⓦwww.nieuwekerk.nl). Despite its name ("New Church"), it's an early fifteenth-century structure built in a late flourish of the Gothic style, with a forest of pinnacles and high, slender gables. Badly damaged by fire on several occasions and

While the Rijksmuseum (see p.99) is undergoing long-term renovation work – starting in December 2003 and due to last for five years – some works from the museum collection will be shown in the Nieuwe Kerk on a rotational basis. Similarly, until the Stedelijk Museum (see p.102) reopens in 2005, some of its artworks will also be on display in the church. Check with the VVV for the latest information.

unceremoniously stripped of most of its fittings by the Calvinists, the interior is a hangar-like affair of sombre demeanour, whose sturdy compound pillars soar up to support the wooden vaulting of the ceiling. Amongst a scattering of decorative highlights, look out for an extravagant, finely-carved mahogany **pulpit** that was fifteen years in the making, a cleverly worked copper **chancel screen** long and illustrious naval career Ruyter trounced in succession the Spaniards, the Swedes, the English and the French, and his rise from deck-hand to Admiral-in-Chief is the stuff of national legend. His most famous exploit was a raid up the River Thames to Medway in 1667 and the seizure of the Royal Navy's flagship, The Royal Charles; the subsequent Dutch crowing almost drove Charles II to distraction.

After the church, pop into the adjoining 't Nieuwe Kafé, which occupies one of the old ecclesiastical buildings and serves up excellent coffee and delicious lunches and snacks.

To the east of Dam square stretches the Red Light District. South via trafficky Nieuwezijds Voorburgwal, or the pedestrianized shopping street Kalverstraat, are Spui (see p.81) and the Flower Market.

## The Red Light District

The whole area to the east of Damrak, between Warmoesstraat, Nieuwmarkt and Damstraat, is the **Red Light District**, known locally as "De Walletjes" (small walls) – since this was where the old city walls ran. It stretches across the two canals that marked the eastern edge of medieval Amsterdam, **Oudezijds Voorburgwal** and **Oudezijds Achterburgwal**, both of which are now seedy and seamy: the legalized prostitution here is world-renowned and has long been one of the city's most distinctive and popular draws. The two canals, with their narrow connecting passages, are thronged with "window brothels" and, at busy times, the crass onstreet haggling over the price of various sex acts is drowned out by a surprisingly festive atmosphere – entire families grinning more or less amiably at the women in the windows or discussing the specifications (and feasibility) of the sex toys in the shops. Groups of men line the streets hawking the peep shows and "live sex" within – and, unlike in London or New York, there actually is live sex within. There's a nasty undertow to the district too, oddly enough sharper during the daytime, when the pimps hang out in shifty gangs and drug addicts wait anxiously, assessing the chances of scoring their next hit. Dodging the dealers, the district also contains two prime attractions, the medieval Oude Kerk and the clandestine Amstelkring Catholic church.

Soliciting hasn't always been the principal activity on sleazy **Warmoesstraat**. It was once one of the city's most fashionable streets, home to Holland's foremost poet, **Joost van den Vondel** (1587–1679), who ran his hosiery business from no. 110 in between writing and hobnobbing with the Amsterdam elite. Vondel is a kind of Dutch Shakespeare: his Gijsbrecht van Amstel, a celebration of Amsterdam during its Golden Age, is one of the classics of Dutch literature, and he wrote regular, if ponderous, official verses, including well over a thousand lines on the inauguration of the new town hall. He had more than his share of hard luck too. His son frittered away the modest family fortune and Vondel lived out his last few years as doorkeeper of the pawn shop on Oudezijds Voorburgwal (see p.78), dying of hypothermia at what was then the remarkable age of 92. Witty to the end, his own suggested epitaph ran:

Here lies Vondel, still and old
Who died – because he was cold.

## Commercial sex in Amsterdam

Developed in the 1960s, Amsterdam's liberal approach to social policy has had several unforeseen consequences, the most dramatic being its international reputation as a centre for both drugs (see p.80) and **prostitution**. However, the tackiness of the Red Light District is just the surface sheen on what is a serious attempt to address the reality of sex-for-sale, and to integrate this within a normal, ordered society. In Dutch law, prostituting oneself has long been legal, but the state has always drawn the line at brothels. The difficulties this created for the police were legion, and so finally, in 1999, brothels were legalized in the hope that it would bring a degree of stability to the sex industry. The authorities were particularly keen to get a grip on the use of illegal immigrants as prostitutes, but in doing so they limited the number of "window brothels" – now, a significant group of women have begun to ply their trade illicitly in bars and hotels. The new legislation was partly the result of a long and determined campaign by the prostitutes' trade union, **De Rode Draad** ("The Red Thread"), which has improved the lot of its members by setting up nascent health insurance and pension schemes.

One of the strongest features of the Dutch approach to commercial sex is its lack of prudery. The **Prostitution Information Centre**, at Enge Kerksteeg 3, in between Warmoesstraat and the Oude Kerk (Tues, Wed, Fri & Sat 11.30am–7.30pm), is a legally recognized *stichting*, or charitable foundation, set up to provide prostitutes, their clients and general visitors with clear, dispassionate information about prostitution. In addition to selling books and pamphlets, the PIC publishes the *Pleasure Guide* in Dutch and English, which bills itself as "an informative magazine about having a paid love-life". By positioning itself on the commercial interface between the Red Light District and the rest of the city – and devoting itself to aiding communication between the two – the PIC has done much to subvert the old exploitative dominance of underworld pimps.

The city government website @www.amsterdam.nl has more about regulations and official attitudes towards prostitution.

Vondel's Warmoesstraat house was knocked down decades ago, and aside from the Prostitution Information Centre (see box), the street holds few attractions. The **Condomerie Het Gulden Vlies**, at no. 141, is worth a look: it specializes in every imaginable design and make of condom, in sizes ranging from the small to the remarkable.

### The Oude Kerk

Just to the east of Warmoesstraat is the city's most appealing church, the **Oude Kerk** (Mon–Sat 11am–5pm, Sun 1–5pm; €4; @www.oudekerk.nl), an attractive Gothic structure with high-pitched gables and finely worked lancet windows. There's been a church on this site since the middle of the thirteenth century, but most of the present building dates from a century later, funded by the pilgrims who came here in their hundreds following a widely publicized miracle. The story goes that, in 1345, a dying man regurgitated the Host he had received at Communion, which, when it was then thrown on the fire, did not burn. The unburnable Host was placed in a chest (now in the Amsterdam Historical Museum) and installed in a long-lost chapel somewhere off Nieuwezijds Voorburgwal, before finally being transferred to the Oude Kerk a few years later. It disappeared during the Reformation, but to this day thousands of the faithful still come to take part in the annual Stille Omgang, a silent nocturnal procession held in mid-March that terminates at the Oude Kerk. The church is regularly used for art displays and concerts.

The Protestants cleared the church of almost all of its ecclesiastical tackle during the Reformation, but its largely bare interior does hold several interesting features. These include some fruity and folksy misericords, a few faded vault paintings recovered from beneath layers of whitewash in the 1950s and the unadorned memorial tablet of Rembrandt's first wife, Saskia van Uylenburg; it's near the choir organ – pick up a free plan of the church at reception. Much more diverting, however, are the three beautifully coloured **stained-glass windows** beside the ambulatory in what was once the Chapel of Our Lady. Dating from the 1550s, all three depict religious scenes, from left to right the Annunciation, the Adoration of the Shepherds and the Dormition of the Virgin, and each is set above its respective donors. The characters are shown in classical gear with togas and sandals and the buildings in the background are firmly classical too, reflecting both artistic fashion and a belief that Greco-Roman detail was historically accurate.

## The Amstelkring

The front of the Oude Kerk overlooks the northern reaches of **Oudezijds Voorburgwal**, whose handsome facades recall ritzier days before the prostitutes took up residence, when this was one of the wealthiest parts of the city, richly earning its nickname the "Velvet Canal". A few metres north of the church, at no. 40, is the clandestine **Amstelkring** (Mon–Sat 10am–5pm, Sun 1–5pm; €6; ⓦ www.museumamstelkring.nl), which was once the city's principal Catholic place of worship and is now one of Amsterdam's most enjoyable museums. In 1578, the city forsook the Catholic Habsburgs and declared for the Protestant rebels in what was known as the Alteratie (Alteration). Broadly speaking, the new regime treated its Catholics well – commercial pragmatism has always outweighed religious zeal here – but there was a degree of discrimination; Catholic churches were recycled for Protestant use and their members no longer allowed to practise openly. The result was an eccentric compromise: Catholics were allowed to hold services in any private building provided that the exterior revealed no sign of their activities – hence the development of the city's clandestine churches (*schuilkerken*), amongst which the Amstelkring is the only one to have survived intact.

The church, entitled *Ons' Lieve Heer op Solder* ("Our Dear Lord in the Attic"), occupies the loft of a wealthy merchant's house and is perfectly delightful, with a narrow nave skilfully shoehorned into the available space. Flanked by elegant balconies, the nave has an ornately carved organ at one end and a mock-marble high altar, decorated with Jacob de Wit's mawkish *Baptism of Christ*, at the other. Even the patron of the church, one Jan Hartman, clearly had doubts about de Wit's efforts: the two spares he procured just in case are now displayed behind the altar. The rest of the house has been left untouched, its original furnishings reminiscent of interiors by Vermeer or De Hooch. Amstelkring, meaning "Amstel Circle", is the name of the group of nineteenth-century historians who saved the building from demolition.

From the Amstelkring, it's the briefest of walks south to the Nieuwmarkt at the northern end of Kloveniersburgwal.

## Nieuwmarkt and Kloveniersburgwal

**Nieuwmarkt** was long one of the city's most important market squares and the place where gentiles and Jews from the nearby Jewish Quarter – just southeast along St Antoniebreestraat – traded. All that came to a traumatic end during World War II, when the Nazis cordoned off the Nieuwmarkt with barbed wire and turned it into a holding pen. After the war, the square's old exuberance never returned and these days its focus is the sprawling multi-turreted **Waag**, dating from the 1480s and with a chequered history. Built as one of Amsterdam's fortified gates, the city's expansion soon made it obsolete and the ground floor was turned into a municipal weighing-house (*waag*), with the rooms upstairs taken over by the surgeons' guild. It was here that the surgeons held lectures on anatomy and public dissections, the inspiration for Rembrandt's *Anatomy Lesson of Dr Tulp*, displayed in the Mauritshuis Collection in The Hague. Abandoned by the surgeons and the weigh-masters in the nineteenth century, the building served as a furniture store and fire station before falling into disuse, though it has recently been renovated to house a good café-bar and restaurant, *In de Waag*.

Nieuwmarkt sits at the head of the **Kloveniersburgwal**, a long, dead-straight waterway that was the outermost of the three eastern canals of the medieval city. The canal is framed by a string of old and dignified facades, one of which, the **Trippenhuis**, at no. 29, is a huge overblown mansion complete with Corinthian pilasters and a grand frieze built for the Trip family in 1662. One of the richest families in Amsterdam, the Trips were a powerful force among the Magnificat, a clique of families (Six, Trip, Hooft and Pauw) who shared power during the Golden Age. One part of the Trip family dealt with the Baltic trade, another with the manufacture of munitions (in which they had the municipal monopoly), but in addition to this they also had trade interests in Russia and the Middle East, much like the multinationals of today. Almost directly opposite, on the west bank of the canal, the **Kleine Trippenhuis**, at no. 26, is, by contrast, one of the narrowest houses in Amsterdam, albeit with a warmly carved facade. Legend asserts that Mr Trip's coachman was so taken aback by the size of the new family mansion that he exclaimed he would be happy with a home no wider than the Trips' front door – which is exactly what he got. His reaction to his new lodgings is not recorded.

Further along the canal, on the corner of Oude Hoogstraat, is the former headquarters of the Dutch East India Company, the **Oostindisch Huis**, a monumental red-brick structure built in 1605 shortly after the founding of the company. It was from here that the Company organized and regulated its immensely lucrative trading interests in the Far East, importing shiploads of spices, perfumes and exotic woods. This trade underpinned Amsterdam's Golden Age, but predictably the people of what is now Indonesia, the source of most of the raw materials, received little in return. Nevertheless, despite the building's historic significance, the interior is of no interest today, being occupied by university classrooms and offices.

From the Oostindisch Huis, you can either proceed along Oude Hoogstraat to the Hash Museum (see below) or keep to Kloveniersburgwal, whose southern reaches are flanked by a comely collection of old canal houses interrupted by the occasional nineteenth-century extravagance. In particular, turn east across the canal along Staalstraat and stop at the second of the two little drawbridges for one of the finest views in the city down the slender **Groenburgwal**, with the Zuiderkerk (see p.94) looming beyond.

## Hash Marihuana Hemp Museum and around

From the Oostindisch Huis (see above), it's a couple of minutes walk west to the **Hash Marihuana Hemp Museum**, Oudezijds Achterburgwal 148 (daily 11am–10pm; €5.70), which is still going strong despite intermittent battles with the police. As well as featuring displays on the various types of dope and numerous ways to smoke it, the museum has a live indoor marijuana garden, samples of textiles and paper made with hemp, and pamphlets explaining the medicinal properties of cannabis. There's also a shop selling pipes, books, videos and plenty of souvenirs. Amsterdam's reliance on imported dope ended in the late 1980s when it was discovered that a reddish weed

## Drugs in Amsterdam

Amsterdam's liberal policies on commercial sex (see p.77) are similarly extended to **soft drugs**, and the city has an international reputation as a haven for the dope-smoker, though, in fact, this confuses toleration with approval, decriminalization with legality. Many visitors are surprised to find that all drugs, hard and soft, are technically illegal in Amsterdam, the caveat being that since 1976 the possession of small amounts of cannabis (up to 30g/1oz) has been ignored by the police. This pragmatic approach has led to the rise of "smoking" **coffeeshops**, selling bags of dope much in the same way as bars sell glasses of beer.

From its inception, there have been problems with this policy. In part, this is because the Dutch have never legalized the cannabis supply chain – or more specifically that section of it within their national borders – and partly because the 30g-rule has proved difficult to enforce. Other complications have arisen because of the difference between the Netherlands' policy and that of its European neighbours. Inevitably, the relative laxity of the Dutch has made the country in general, and Amsterdam in particular, attractive to soft (and, arguably, hard) **drug dealers**. The Dutch authorities have tried to keep organized crime out of the soft drug market, but drug dealing and drug tourism – of which there is an awful lot – irritate many Amsterdammers no end.

In recent years, the French and German governments have put pressure on the Dutch to bring their drug policy into line with the rest of the EU – one recent concession obliged coffeeshops to choose between selling dope or alcohol, and many chose the latter. Overall however, while the Dutch have found it prudent to keep a rigorous eye on the coffeeshops and emphasize their credentials in the fight against hard drugs, they have stuck to their liberal guns on cannabis. As justification, they cite the lack of evidence to link soft- and hard-drug use; indeed, the country's figures for hard-drug addiction are actually among the lowest in Europe.

Furthermore, by treating drugs as a **medical** rather than criminal problem, Amsterdam's authorities have been able to pioneer positive responses to drugs' issues. The city council runs a wide range of rehabilitation programmes and recently decided to overhaul the methadone programme it introduced for heroin addicts in 1979. Here as elsewhere, methadone is now largely discredited as a means of weaning addicts off heroin and as a result the Dutch began issuing free heroin in tightly controlled quantities to users in 1998, a nationwide trial whose success is still being evaluated.

Nevertheless, for the casual visitor the main blot on the Amsterdam landscape is the groups of **hang-around junkies** who gather in and near the Red Light District, especially amongst the narrow streets and canals immediately to the east of the Oude Kerk (see p.77). The police estimate that there are around a thousand hard-drug users who, as they put it, "cause nuisance," and although the addicts are unlikely to molest strangers, they are a threatening presence, especially if you're travelling alone. In fairness, however, the police have done their best to clean things up, dramatically improving the situation on the Zeedijk and Nieuwmarkt, which were once notorious for hard drugs, and at the canal bridge on Oude Hoogstraat, formerly nicknamed the "Pillenbrug" ("Pill Bridge"). The website ⓦwww.thc.nl has more about the city government's regulations and attitude towards cannabis.

bred in America – "skunk" – was able to flourish under artificial lights; nowadays over half the dope sold in the coffeeshops is grown in the Netherlands.

The triangular parcel of land at the southern end of **Oudezijds Achterburgwal** is packed with university buildings, mostly modern or nineteenth-century structures built in a vernacular Dutch style. Together they form a pleasant urban ensemble, but the red-shuttered, mullion-windowed seventeenth-century **Huis op de Drie Grachten**, the "House on the Three Canals", stands out, sitting prettily on the corner of Oudezijds Achterburgwal and Oudezijds Voorburgwal. From here, it's the briefest of walks west to the Rokin.

## The Rokin, Muntplein and the flower market

The main street **Rokin** picks up where the Damrak (see p.74) leaves off, cutting south in a wide sweep that follows the former course of the River Amstel. This boulevard was the business centre of the nineteenth-century city, but today it's too jammed with traffic to be much fun. The Rokin hits the city's canal system footsteps from the **Allard Pierson Museum**, at Oude Turfmarkt 127 (Tues–Fri 10am–5pm, Sat & Sun 1–5pm; €4.30; Ⓦ www.uba.uva.nl/apm) – a good, old-fashioned archeological museum in a solid Neoclassical building. The collection is spread over two floors and has a wide-ranging, if fairly small, assortment of finds. The particular highlight is the museum's Greek pottery, with fine examples of both the black- and red-figured wares produced in the sixth and fifth centuries BC. Look out also for the Roman sarcophagi, especially a marble whopper decorated with Dionysian scenes and a very unusual wooden coffin from around 150 AD, which is partly carved in the shape of the man held within.

Past the museum, it's a brief stroll to the **Muntplein**, a dishevelled square where the **Munttoren** of 1480 was originally part of the old city wall. Later, it was adopted as the municipal mint – hence its name – a plain brick structure to which Hendrik de Keyser, in one of his last commissions, added a flashy spire in 1620. A few metres away, the floating **Bloemenmarkt** (Flower Market; daily 9am–5pm, though some stalls close on Sun; see also p.123), extends along the southern bank of the Singel west as far as Koningsplein. Popular with locals and tourists alike, the market is one of the main supplier of flowers to central Amsterdam; its blooms and bulbs now share stall space with souvenir clogs, garden gnomes and Delftware.

From Muntplein, seedy Reguliersbreestraat leads east to the bars and restaurants of Rembrandtplein (see p.87), while the flower market trails along the Singel as far as Koningsplein, near the Spui.

## Spui and the Begijnhof

The west end of the **Spui** (rhymes with "cow") opens out into a wide, tram-clanking square flanked by bookshops and popular café-bars. In the middle is a cloying statue of a young boy, known as **'t Lieverdje** ("Little Darling" or "Loveable Scamp"), a gift to the city from a cigarette company in 1960. It was here in the mid-1960s, with the statue seen as a symbol of the addicted consumer, that the playful **Provos** (see box on p.361) organized some of their most successful *ludiek* ("pranks").

A fancy little gateway on the north side of the Spui leads into the **Begijnhof** (daily 10am–5pm; free), where a huddle of immaculately maintained old houses looks onto a central green, their backs to the outside world; if this door is locked, try the main entrance, just a couple of hundred metres north of Spui on Gedempte Begijnensloot. The Begijnhof was founded in the fourteenth-

## The beguinages

One corollary of the urbanization of the Low Countries from the twelfth century onwards was the establishment of **beguinages** (*begijnhoven* in Dutch, *béguinages* in French) in almost every city and town. These were semi-secluded communities, where widows and unmarried women – the **beguines** (*begijns*) – lived together, the better to do pious acts, especially caring for the sick. In construction, beguinages follow the same general plan with several streets of whitewashed, brick terraced cottages hidden away behind walls and gates and surrounding a central garden and chapel.

The origins of the beguine movement are somewhat obscure, but it would seem that the initial impetus came from a twelfth-century Liège priest, a certain Lambert Le Bègue (the Stammerer). The main period of growth came later with the establishment of dozens of new beguinages, like the ones in Ghent and Bruges in Belgium and Breda and Amsterdam in the Netherlands. All were sponsored by the nobility and the later foundations – like the one here in Amsterdam – were established despite the opposition of the Papacy, which had declared against them as a potential source of heresy at the Council of Vienna in 1311.

Beguine communities were different from convents in so far as the inhabitants did not have to take vows and had the right to return to the secular world if they chose. At a time when hundreds of women were forcibly shut away in convents for all sorts of reasons (primarily financial), this element of choice was crucial.

century as a home for the *beguines* – members of a Catholic sisterhood living as nuns, but without vows and with the right of return to the secular world. The original medieval complex comprised a series of humble brick cottages, but these were mostly replaced by the larger, grander houses of today shortly after the Reformation, though the secretive, enclosed design survived. A couple of pre-Reformation buildings do remain, including the **Houten Huys**, at no. 34, whose wooden facade dates from 1477, the oldest in Amsterdam and erected before the city forbade the construction of timber houses as an essential precaution against fire. The **Engelse Kerk** (English Reformed Church), which takes up one side of the Begijnhof, is of medieval construction too, but it was taken from the *beguines* and given to Amsterdam's English community during the Reformation. Plain and unadorned, the church is of interest for its carefully worked pulpit panels, several of which were designed by a youthful Piet Mondriaan (1872–1944), the leading De Stijl artist. After they had lost their church, and in keeping with the terms of the Alteratie (see p.78), the *beguines* were allowed to celebrate Mass inconspicuously in the clandestine Catholic **chapel** (Mon 1–6pm, Tues–Sun 9am–6pm; free), which they established in the house opposite their old church. It's still used today, a cosy little place with some terribly sentimental religious paintings, one of which – to the left of the high altar – depicts the miracle of the unburnable Host (see p.77).

### Amsterdams Historisch Museum

Emerging from the east side of the Begijnhof, turn left onto narrow Gedempte Begijnensloot and it's 100m or so to the **Schuttersgalerij** – the Civic Guard Gallery. Here, an assortment of huge group portraits of the Amsterdam militia, ranging from serious-minded paintings of the 1540s through to lighter affairs from the seventeenth century, is displayed for free in a glassed-in passageway. They are interesting paintings, no doubt, and the pick are those by Nicolaes Pickenoy (1588–1650), but the finest militia painting by a long chalk – Rembrandt's *The Nightwatch* – is exhibited in the Rijksmuseum (see p.99).

The Schuttersgalerij is part of the **Amsterdams Historisch Museum** (Mon–Fri 10am–5pm, Sat & Sun 11am–5pm; €6; <sup>ⓦ</sup>www.ahm.nl), which occupies the smartly restored but rambling seventeenth-century buildings of the municipal orphanage. The museum attempts to survey the city's development with a scattering of artefacts and lots of paintings from the thirteenth century onwards. It's a garbled collection, lacking continuity, but there are several worthwhile highlights, beginning with the paintings illustrating the country's former maritime prowess in Room 5, titled "Rulers of the Seas". Room 10, "Social Care & Stern Discipline" examines the harsh paternalism of the city's merchant oligarchy, with paintings depicting the regents of several orphanages, self-contented bourgeoisie in the company of the grateful poor. Nearby, Room 11, "The Art of the Golden Age", is distinguished by three paintings of the surgeons' guild at work – look out for Rembrandt's wonderful *Anatomy Lesson of Dr Jan Deijman* – while the orphanage's own Regentenkamer (Regents' Room; Room C), dating from the seventeenth century, has survived in excellent repair.

The museum is footsteps from **Kalverstraat**, a pedestrianized shopping strip that runs north to Dam square. The street has been a commercial centre since medieval times, when it was used as a calf market.

## The Grachtengordel

Medieval Amsterdam was enclosed by the Singel, part of the city's protective moat, but this is now just the first of five canals that reach right around the city centre, extending anti-clockwise from Brouwersgracht to the River Amstel in a "girdle of canals" or **Grachtengordel**. The Grachtengordel is the most charming part of Amsterdam, its lattice of olive-green waterways and small humpback bridges overlooked by street upon street of handsome seventeenth- and eighteenth-century houses. It's a subtle cityscape too – full of surprises, with an unusual facade stone here, a bizarre carving there – and one whose overall atmosphere appeals rather than any specific sight (with the notable exception of the **Anne Frank House**).

The canals were dug in the early years of the seventeenth century as part of a comprehensive plan to extend the boundaries of a city no longer able to accommodate its burgeoning population. Increasing the area of the city from 450 to 1800 acres was a monumental task, and the conditions imposed by the council were strict. The three main waterways, Herengracht, Keizersgracht and Prinsengracht, were set aside for the residences and businesses of Amsterdam merchants, while the radial canals were reserved for more modest artisans' homes. Everyone, even the wealthiest merchant, had to comply with a set of planning rules. In particular, the council prescribed the size of each building plot – the frontage was set at thirty feet, the depth two hundred – and although there was a degree of tinkering, the end result was the loose conformity you can see today: tall, narrow residences, whose individualism is mainly restricted to decorative gables and the occasional facade stone to denote name and occupation. It was almost the end of the century before the scheme was finished – a time when, ironically, Amsterdam's decline had already begun – but it remains to the council's credit that it was executed with such success.

Of the three main canals, **Herengracht**, the "Gentlemen's Canal", was the first to be dug, followed by the **Keizersgracht**, the "Emperor's Canal" named after the Holy Roman Emperor and fifteenth-century patron of the city, Maximilian. Further out still, the **Prinsengracht**, the "Princes' Canal", was named in honour of the princes of the House of Orange. The merchants who dominated Amsterdam soon lined the three with their mansions, the grandest concentrated on Herengracht, where the stretch of water between Leidsegracht and the Amstel was soon nicknamed the "**Golden Bend**" (De Gouden Bocht).

Our account follows a long, circuitous walking route right around the Grachtengordel to the River Amstel, then doubling back to end at the main Leidseplein square, within spitting distance of the main art museums. However, you can, of course, cut corners wherever you fancy: picking any of the three main canals to head down means missing out on the beauty of the other two.

## Brouwersgracht to Leliegracht

Running west to east along the northern edge of the three main canals is leafy **Brouwersgracht**, one of the most peaceful and picturesque waterways in the city. In the seventeenth century, Brouwersgracht lay at the edge of Amsterdam's great harbour. This was where many of the ships returning from the East unloaded their silks and spices, and as one of the major arteries linking the open sea with the city centre, it was lined with storage depots and warehouses. Breweries flourished here too, capitalizing on their ready access to shipments of fresh water. Today, the harbour bustle has moved elsewhere, and the warehouses have been converted into apartments, their functional architecture interrupted by residential facades. Look down any of the major canals from here and you'll see why visitors admire the city for its gentle interplay of water, brick, and stone.

Strolling south along **Prinsengracht** from Brouwersgracht, past handsome canal houses and tumbledown houseboats, it only takes a minute or two to reach the **Hofje Van Brienen**, at Prinsengracht 85–133, which you can walk around for free. This is one of the prettiest of the city's *hofjes*, or courtyard almshouses, built in 1804, according to the entrance tablet, "for the relief and shelter of those in need." Continue walking for a few metres more and you'll come to the first cross-street connecting the main canals, **Prinsenstraat**, which quickly runs into **Herenstraat**, an appealing little street of flower shops and cafés, greengroceries and secondhand clothes shops. At the east end of Herenstraat, turn right onto Herengracht and it's a short walk to the **Leliegracht**, one of the tiny radial canals that cut across the Grachtengordel, and home to a number of bookshops and canal-side bars. Though there are precious few extant examples of Art Nouveau and Art Deco architecture in Amsterdam, one of the finest is the tall and striking building at the Leliegracht–Keizersgracht junction. The building was designed by Gerrit van Arkel in 1905, and is now the world headquarters of Greenpeace.

## The Anne Frank House

In 1957, the Anne Frank Foundation set up the **Anne Frank House** (daily: April–Aug 9am–9pm; Sept–March 9am–7pm; closed Yom Kippur; €6.50; Ⓦwww.annefrank.nl) in the house at Prinsengracht 267, close to the Leliegracht, where the young diarist used to listen to the Westerkerk bells until they were taken away to be melted down for the Nazi war effort. Since the posthumous publication of her diaries, Anne Frank has become extraordinarily famous, in the first instance for recording the iniquities of the Holocaust, and latterly as a symbol of the fight against oppression and, in particular, racism. The house is now one of the most popular attractions in town, so try to go early (or late) to avoid the crowds.

The story of Anne, her family and friends, is well known. Anne's father, **Otto Frank**, was a well-to-do Jewish businessman who ran a successful spice-trading business and lived in the southern part of Amsterdam. After the Nazi occupation of the Netherlands, he felt – along with many other Jews – that he could avoid trouble by keeping his head down. However, by 1942, it was clear that this was not going to be possible: Amsterdam's Jews were isolated and conspicuous, being confined to certain parts of the city and forced to wear a yellow star. Roundups, too, were becoming increasingly commonplace. In desperation, Otto Frank decided – on the advice of two Dutch friends, Mr Koophuis and Mr Kraler – to move the family into the unused back of his company's warehouse on the Prinsengracht. The Franks went into hiding in July 1942, along with a Jewish business partner and his family, the Van Daans. They were separated from the eyes of the outside world by a bookcase that doubled as a door. As far as everyone else was concerned, they had fled to Switzerland.

So began the two-year occupation of the *achterhuis*, or back annexe. The two families were joined in November 1942 by a Mr Dussel, a dentist friend. Koophuis and Kraler, who continued working in the front office, regularly brought supplies and news of the outside world. In her diary Anne Frank describes the day-to-day lives of the inhabitants of the annexe: the quarrels, frequent in such a claustrophobic environment; celebrations of birthdays, or of a piece of good news from the Allied Front; and her own, slightly unreal, growing-up (much of Anne's description of which, it's been claimed, was later deleted by her father).

Two years later, the atmosphere was optimistic: the Allies were clearly winning the war and liberation seemed within reach. It wasn't to be. One day in the summer of 1944 the Franks were betrayed by a Dutch collaborator and the Gestapo arrived and forced Mr Kraler to open up the bookcase. Thereafter, the occupants of the annexe were all arrested and quickly sent to Westerbork (see p.254) – the transit camp in the north of the country where all Dutch Jews were processed before being moved to Belsen or Auschwitz. Of the eight from the annexe, only Otto Frank survived; Anne and her sister died of typhus within a short time of each other in Belsen, just one week before the German surrender.

Anne Frank's **diary** was among the few things left behind in the annexe. It was retrieved by one of the people who had helped the Franks and handed to Anne's father on his return from Auschwitz; he later decided to publish it. Since its appearance in 1947, the diary has been constantly in print, translated into over sixty languages, and has sold millions of copies worldwide. The rooms the Franks lived in for two years are left much the same as they were during the war, even down to the movie star pin-ups in Anne's bedroom and the marks on the wall recording the children's heights. Remarkably, despite the number of visitors, there is a real sense of intimacy here and only the coldest of hearts could fail to be moved. Apposite video clips on the family in particular and the Holocaust in general give the background. Anne Frank was only one of about 100,000 Dutch Jews who died during World War II, but this, her final home, provides one of the most enduring testaments to its horrors. Her diary has been a source of inspiration to many, including Nelson Mandela.

### The Westerkerk, Westermarkt and around
Immediately to the south of the Anne Frank House, the **Westerkerk** (Mon–Fri 10am–4pm, Sat 10am–1pm; free) dominates the district, its 85-metre tower (April–Sept Mon–Sat 10am–4pm; €3) – without question Amsterdam's finest – soaring imperiously above the gables of Westermarkt. On its top perches the crown of the Habsburg Emperor Maximilian, a constantly recurring symbol of Amsterdam and the finishing touch to what was only the city's second

place of worship built expressly for Protestants. The church was designed by Hendrik de Keyser and completed in 1631 as part of the general enlargement of the city, but whereas the exterior is all studied elegance, the interior – as required by the Calvinist congregation – is bare and plain. The church is also the reputed resting place of **Rembrandt**, though the location of his pauper's tomb is not known. Instead, the painter is commemorated by a small memorial in the north aisle, close to which his son Titus is buried. Rembrandt adored his son – as evinced by numerous portraits – and the boy's death dealt a final crushing blow to the ageing and embittered artist, who died just over a year later.

**Westermarkt**, an open square in the shadow of the Westerkerk, possesses two evocative statues. At the back of the church, beside Keizersgracht, are the three pink granite triangles (one each for the past, present and future) of the **Homo-Monument**. The world's first memorial to persecuted gays and lesbians, commemorating all those who died at the hands of the Nazis, it was designed by Karin Daan and recalls the pink triangles that homosexuals were forced to sew into and display on their clothes during the occupation. The monument's inscription, by the Dutch writer Jacob Israel de Haan, translates as "Such an infinite desire for friendship". Nearby, on the south side of the church by Prinsengracht, is a small but beautifully crafted **statue of Anne Frank** by the gifted Dutch sculptor Mari Andriessen (1897–1979), who is also the creator of the dockworker statue outside Amsterdam's Portuguese Synagogue (see p.95).

A few metres away at Herengracht 168, the **Theatermuseum** (Tues–Fri 11am–5pm, Sat & Sun 1–5pm; €3.85) holds an enjoyable collection of theatrical bygones, from props through to stage sets, with a particularly good selection of costumes and posters. Occupying a pair of fine old mansions – the restrained Neoclassicism of no. 168 contrasting with the ostentatious neo-Renaissance facade of the Hendrik de Keyser-designed house next door – the museum runs a lively programme of temporary exhibitions. At times however, the sumptuousness of the interior almost overwhelms the displays, not least with the eighteenth-century ceiling paintings by Jacob de Wit, the extravagant stucco work and, most dramatic of all, the slender and ornate spiral staircase.

### Raadhuisstraat to Leidsegracht

Westermarkt flows into **Raadhuisstraat**, the principal thoroughfare into the Old Centre, running east to Dam square (see p.74). South of here the main canals are less appealing than the narrow cross-streets, many of which are named after animals whose pelts were used in the local tanning industry – Reestraat ("Deer Street"), Hartenstraat (Hart) and Berenstraat (Bear), to name but three. The tanners are thankfully long gone, but they've been replaced by some of the most pleasant shopping streets in the city, selling everything from carpets and handmade chocolates to designer toothbrushes and beeswax candles. The area's southern boundary is marked by **Leidsegracht**, a mostly residential canal, lined with chic town houses and a medley of handsome gables.

This section of the Grachtengordel offers one notable attraction, the idiosyncratic **Bijbels Museum** (Biblical Museum; Mon–Sat 10am–5pm, Sun 1–5pm; €5; Ⓦwww.bijbelsmuseum.nl), which occupies a splendid seventeenth-century stone mansion frilled with tendrils, carved fruit and scrollwork at Herengracht 366, just north of Leidsegracht. Built for one of Amsterdam's wealthy merchant families, the Cromhouts, the house, along with adjacent nos. 364, 368 and 370, was designed by Philips Vingboons (1607–78), arguably the most inventive of the architects who worked on the Grachtengordel. The interior is comparatively plain, but the main salon does sport an extravagant painted ceiling portraying classical gods and goddesses – the work of Jacob de Wit. In these proud premises are exhibited a series of models of the temples of Solomon and Herod as well as the Tabernacle made by a Protestant vicar, one Leendert Schouten (1828–1905). Attempts to reconstruct these biblical temples were something of a cottage industry in the Netherlands in the late nineteenth century, with scores of Dutch antiquarians beavering away, bible in one hand and modelling equipment in the other, but Schouten went one step further and made it his lifetime's work. Nowadays, it all seems rather strange, but the museum also contains a few old bibles, including the first Dutch-language bible ever printed, dating from 1477, and a scattering of archeological finds from Palestine and Egypt.

A little beyond the Leidsegracht and the Bijbels Museum, all three main canals are crossed by the hectic **Leidsestraat**, a tram-packed and pedestrian-heavy artery cutting a swathe between the Old Centre and the main **Leidseplein** square (see p.89) on the outer ring of the Grachtengordel.

## The Golden Bend

Strolling southeast from Leidsegracht, the elegant sweep of the main **Herengracht** canal unravels in the so-called "**Golden Bend**" (De Gouden Bocht), where the canal is overlooked by a long sequence of double-fronted mansions, some of the most opulent dwellings in the city. Most of the houses here date from the eighteenth century, with double stairways leading to the entrance, underneath which the small door was for the servants. Classical references are common, both in form – pediments, columns and pilasters – and decoration, from scrolls and vases through to geometric patterns inspired by ancient Greece. One of the first buildings to look out for on the north side of the canal is **no. 475**, an extravagant edifice surmounted by a slender French-style balustrade and decorated with twin caryatids. It was completed in 1672, whereas the comparable residence at **no. 493**, complete with its good-looking balcony, was finished in the 1730s. In a rather more modest mansion a couple of doors down, at no. 497, is the peculiar **Kattenkabinet** (Cats' Cabinet; Mon–Fri 9am–2pm, Sat & Sun 1–5pm; €4.50; ⓦwww.kattenkabinet.nl), an enormous collection of art and artefacts relating to cats installed by a Dutch financier, whose own cherished moggy, John Pierpont Morgan, died in 1984; feline fanatics will be delighted. Metres away, at the corner of Vijzelstraat, **no. 507** is an imposing building too, all Neoclassical pilasters and slender windows; it was once the home of Jacob Boreel, the one-time major whose attempt to impose a burial tax prompted a riot during which the mob ransacked his house. Opposite, across the canal, is the mammoth lumpiness of the ABN-AMRO bank, a broadly Expressionist structure dating to 1923.

## Rembrandtplein and beyond

Pushing on along the north side of Herengracht, it takes a couple of minutes to reach pedestrianized **Thorbeckeplein**, a scrawny adjunct to **Rembrandtplein**, itself a dishevelled bit of greenery that was formerly Amsterdam's butter market, renamed after the artist in 1876. Rembrandtplein is one of the city's nightlife centres, though the crowded restaurants are firmly tourist-targeted. The great man's statue stands in the middle, his back wisely turned against the square's worst excesses, which include live (but deadly) outdoor muzak. Of the prodigious number of cafés and bars here, only the bar of the Schiller Hotel at no. 26 stands out, with an original Art Deco interior reminiscent of an ocean liner.

Tacky Reguliersbreestraat, leading off the northwest corner of

Rembrandtplein, is notable only for the city's most extraordinary cinema, the **Tuschinski**, at nos. 26–28, which boasts a marvellously well-preserved Art Deco interior. Opened in 1921 by a Polish Jew, Abram Tuschinski, the cinema boasts Expressionist paintings, coloured marbles and a wonderful carpet, hand-woven in Marrakesh to an original design.

Back on the Herengracht, near the River Amstel, the **Museum Willet-Holthuysen** (Mon–Fri 10am–5pm, Sat & Sun 11am–5pm; €4; ⓦwww .willetholthuysen.nl), at no. 605, is billed as "a peep behind the curtains into an historic Amsterdam canal house" which just about sums it up. The house itself dates from 1685, but the interior was remodelled by successive members of the coal-trading Holthuysen family until the last of the line, Sandra Willet-Holthuysen, gifted her home and its contents to the city in 1895. Renovated a number of years ago, most of the public rooms, notably the Blue Room and the Dining Room, have now been returned to their original eighteenth-century Rococo appearance – a flashy and ornate style copied from France, which the Dutch merchants held to be the epitome of refinement and good taste. The chandeliers are gilded, heavy affairs, the plasterwork neat and fancy, and graceful drapes hang to either side of long and slender windows. The museum's collection of fine and applied arts belongs to Sandra's husband, Abraham Willet; its forte is glass, silver and ceramics, including a charming selection of Chinese porcelain exhibited in the Blue Room.

## The River Amstel

Herengracht and the other main canals come to an abrupt halt beside the wide and windy **River Amstel**, which was long the main route into the interior, with goods arriving by barge and boat to be traded for the imported materials held in Amsterdam's many warehouses. Turning left here takes you to the **Blauwbrug** ("Blue Bridge") and the Old Jewish Quarter (see p.92), whilst in the opposite direction the **Magere Brug** ("Skinny Bridge") is arguably the cutest of the city's many swing bridges. From here, it's a few metres further to the **Amstelsluizen**, the Amstel Locks. Every night, the municipal water department closes these locks to begin the process of sluicing out the canals. A huge pumping station on an island out to the east of the city then starts to pump fresh water into the canal system from the IJsselmeer (see p.138); similar locks on the west side of the city are left open for the surplus to flow into the IJ and, from there, out to sea via the North Sea Canal. The watery contents of the canals is thus refreshed every three nights – though, what with three centuries of algae, prams, shopping trolleys and a few hundred rusty bikes, the water is appealing just as long as you're not in it.

## To the Van Loon Museum

Doubling back along the Amstel, turn down **Keizersgracht** and you'll soon reach **Reguliersgracht** at a point where its humpback bridges are overlooked by several fine facades: nos. 37 and 39 have the classic neck gables popular with the merchants of the day, as do the slightly more ornate nos. 17–21. Numbers 11 and 13 are different again, these two buildings possessed of the plain spout gables, external pulleys and shuttered windows used in the construction of the city's seventeenth-century warehouses.

From the junction, it's just a few metres more to the **Van Loon Museum** at no. 672 (Fri–Mon 11am–5pm; €4.50; ⓦwww.musvloon.box.nl), which has perhaps the finest accessible canal house interior in Amsterdam. Built in 1672, the first tenant of the property was the artist Ferdinand Bol, who seems to have been one of the few occupants to have avoided some sort of scandal. The Van

Loons, who bought the house in 1884 and stayed until 1945, are a case in point. The last member of the family to live here was Willem van Loon, a banker whose wife, Thora van Loon-Egidius, was *dame du paleis* to Queen Wilhelmina. Of German extraction, Thora was proud of her roots and allegedly entertained high-ranking Nazi officials here during the occupation – a charge of collaboration that led to the Van Loons being shunned by polite society. Recently renovated, the interior of the house has been returned to its eighteenth-century appearance, a bright and breezy Rococo style of stucco, colourful wallpaper and rich wood panelling. The top-floor landing has several pleasant Grisaille paintings sporting Roman figures and one of the bedrooms – the "painted room" – is decorated with a Romantic painting of Italy, depicting the overgrown classical ruins and diligent peasants that were a favourite theme in Amsterdam from around 1750 to 1820. The oddest items are the fake bedroom doors: the eighteenth-century owners were so keen to avoid any lack of symmetry that they camouflaged the real bedroom doors and created imitation, decorative doors in the "correct" position instead.

### Vijzelstraat and the Heineken Brewery

A short walk west along Keizersgracht from the Van Loon Museum brings you to **Vijzelstraat**, a busy, trafficky street that cuts across the Grachtengordel. Ten minutes' walk south is the **Heineken Experience** (Tues–Sun 10am-6pm; €7.50; Ⓦ www.heinekenexperience.nl), in the old Heineken brewery on the far side of the Singelgracht canal at Stadhouderskade 78. The brewery was Heineken's headquarters from 1864 to 1988, at which point the company was restructured and brewing was moved to a more efficient location out of town. Since then, Heineken has developed the site as a tourist attraction with displays on the history of beer-making in general and Heineken in particular. The old brewing facilities are included on the tour, but for many the main draw is the **free beer**, though the days when you could quaff unlimited quantities are long gone.

To get to Leidseplein from the brewery you can either take a pleasant route by doubling back along Vijzelgracht and heading west along Prinsengracht, or the direct route along busy and unappealing Weteringschans.

## Leidseplein

**Leidseplein** is the bustling hub of Amsterdam's nightlife, a cluttered and disorderly open space criss-crossed by tram lines. The square once marked the end of the road in from Leiden and, as horse-drawn traffic was banned from the centre long ago, it was here that the Dutch left their horses and carts – a sort of equine car park. Today, it's quite the opposite: continual traffic gives the place a frenetic feel and the square and its surroundings are flanked by dozens of bars, restaurants and clubs, a bright jumble of jutting signs and neon lights.

Leidseplein also contains two buildings of some architectural note. The first is the grandiose **Stadsschouwburg**, a neo-Renaissance edifice dating from 1894 which was so widely criticized for its clumsy vulgarity that the city council of the day withheld the money for decorating the exterior. Home to the National Ballet and Opera until the Muziektheater (see p.95) was completed on Waterlooplein in 1986 it is now used for theatre, dance and music performances. However, its most popular function is as the place where the Ajax football team gather on the balcony to wave to the crowds whenever they win anything – as they often do.

Close by, just beside the square at Leidsekade 97, is the four-star **American**

**Hotel**. One of the city's oddest buildings, it's a monumental and slightly disconcerting rendering of Art Nouveau, with angular turrets, chunky dormer windows and fancy brickwork. Completed in 1902, the present structure takes its name from its demolished predecessor, which was – at the whim of its architect, a certain W. Steinigeweg – decorated with statues and murals of North American scenes. Inside the present hotel is the *Café Americain*, once the fashionable haunt of Amsterdam's literati, but now more a mainstream location for drinks and lunches. The Art Nouveau decor is well worth a look – an array of stained glass, shallow brick arches and heavy-duty chandeliers.

From Leidseplein, it's a short walk west across the Singelgracht to Amsterdam's main green space, the Vondelpark (see p.103), and not much further to the city's premier art galleries, the Rijksmuseum (see p.99) and the Van Gogh Musem (see p.101).

## The Jordaan

Lying to the west of the city centre and the Grachtengordel, its boundaries clearly defined by the Prinsengracht and the Lijnbaansgracht, the **Jordaan** is a likeable and easily explored area of slender canals and narrow streets flanked by an agreeable mix of architectural styles, from modern terraces to handsome seventeenth-century canal houses. In all probability the district takes its name from the French word *jardin* ("garden"), since the area's earliest settlers were Protestant Huguenots, who fled here to escape persecution in the sixteenth and seventeenth centuries. Another possibility is that it's a corruption of the Dutch word for Jews, *joden*. Whatever the truth, the Jordaan developed from open country – hence the number of streets and canals named after flowers and plants – into a refugee enclave, a teeming, cosmopolitan quarter beyond the pale of bourgeois respectability. Indeed, when the city fathers planned the expansion of the city in 1610, they made sure the Jordaan was kept outside the city boundaries. Consequently, the Jordaan was not subject to the rigorous planning restrictions of the Grachtengordel, and its lattice of narrow streets followed the lines of the original polder drainage ditches rather than any municipal outline. This gives the district its distinctive, mazy layout, and much of its present appeal.

Traditionally the home of Amsterdam's working class, the Jordaan has in recent years been transformed by a middle class influx, with the district now one of the city's most sought-after residential neighbourhoods. Before then, and until the late 1970s, the Jordaan's inhabitants were primarily stevedores and factory workers, earning a crust amongst the docks, warehouses, factories and boatyards that extended north beyond Brouwersgracht (see p.84), the Jordaan's northern boundary and nowadays one of Amsterdam's prettiest canals. Specific sights are, however, few and far between – the best you'll do is probably the **Noorderkerk** – but nonetheless it's still a pleasant area to wander.

### The Jordaan's hofjes

One feature of the Jordaan's low-key architectural pleasures is its **hofjes** – almshouses built around a central courtyard and originally occupied by the city's elderly and needy. There were – and are – *hofjes* all over the city (most famously the Begijnhof – see p.81), but there's a concentration here in the Jordaan. Most date back to the seventeenth or eighteenth century, but the majority have been rebuilt or at least revamped, and all are still lived in. The Jordaan's most diverting example is the Karthuizerhofje, on Karthuizersstraat (see p.91).

## Rozengracht to Westerstraat

The streets and canals extending north from **Rozengracht** to **Westerstraat** form the heart of the Jordaan and hold the district's prettiest moments. Beyond Rozengracht, the first canal is the **Bloemgracht** (Flower Canal), a leafy water-way dotted with houseboats and arched by little bridges, its network of cross streets sprinkled with cafés, bars and idiosyncratic shops. There's a warm, relaxed community atmosphere here which is really rather beguiling, not to mention a clutch of old and handsome canal houses. Pride of architectural place goes to nos. 89–91, a sterling Renaissance building of 1642 complete with mullion win-dows, crowstep gable, brightly painted shutters and distinctive facade stones, rep-resenting a *steeman* (city-dweller), *landman* (farmer) and a *seeman* (sailor). Next door, nos. 85–87 were built a few decades later, two immaculately maintained canal houses adorned by the bottleneck gables typical of the period.

From Bloemgracht, it's a few metres north to **Egelantiersgracht** (Rose-Hip Canal), where, at no. 12, *Café 't Smalle* is one of Amsterdam's oldest cafés, opened in 1786 as a *proeflokaal* - a tasting house for the (long-gone) gin dis-tillery next door. In the eighteenth century, when quality control was inter-mittent, each batch of *jenever* (Dutch gin) could turn out very differently, so customers insisted on a taster before they splashed out. As a result, each distill-ery ran a *proeflokaal* offering free samples and this is a rare survivor. The café's waterside terrace remains an especially pleasant spot to take a tipple.

A narrow cross-street – Tweede Egelantiersdwarsstraat and its continuation Tweede Tuindwarsstraat and Tweede Anjeliersdwarsstraat – runs north from Bloemgracht flanked by many of the Jordaan's more fashionable stores and clothing shops as well as some of its liveliest bars and cafés. At the end is worka-day **Westerstraat**, a busy thoroughfare, which is home to the small but fasci-nating **Pianola Museum** (Sun 11.30am–5.30pm; €3.75), at no. 106, whose collection of pianolas and automatic music-machines dates from the beginning of the twentieth century. Fifteen have been restored to working order. These machines, which work on rolls of perforated paper, were the jukeboxes of their day, and the museum has a vast collection of 14,000 rolls of music, some of which were "recorded" by famous pianists and composers – Gershwin, Debussy, Scott Joplin, Art Tatum and others. Nearby, and also of some interest, is the largest of the Jordaan's hofjes, the **Karthuizerhofje**, Karthuizersstraat 89–171, a substantial courtyard complex established as a widows' hospice in the middle of the seventeenth century, though the present buildings are much later.

## The Noorderkerk and around

At the east end of Westerstraat, overlooking the Prinsengracht, is Hendrik de Keyser's **Noorderkerk** (March–Nov Sat 11am–1pm; free), the architect's last creation and probably his least successful, finished two years after his death in 1623. A bulky, overbearing brick building, it represented a radical departure from the conventional church designs of the time, having a symmetrical Greek-cross floor plan, with four equally proportioned arms radiating out from a steepled centre. Uncompromisingly dour, it proclaimed the serious intent of the Calvinists who worshipped here in so far as the pulpit – and therefore the preacher proclaiming the Word of God – was at the centre and not at the front of the church, a symbolic break with the Catholic past. Nevertheless, it's still hard to understand quite how Keyser, who designed such elegant structures as the Westerkerk (see p.85), could have ended up designing this.

The **Noordermarkt**, the somewhat inconclusive square outside the church, holds a statue of three figures bound to each other, a poignant tribute to the bloody Jordaanoproer riot of 1934, part of a successful campaign to stop the government cutting unemployment benefit during the Depression. The inscription reads: "The strongest chains are those of unity". The square also hosts two of Amsterdam's best open-air **markets**. There's an antiques and general household goods market on Monday mornings (9am–1pm) plus a popular Saturday farmers' market, the Boerenmarkt (9am–3pm), a lively affair selling organic fruit and vegetables, freshly-baked breads and a plethora of oils and spices. Cross an unmarked border though and you'll find yourself in the middle of a Saturday bird market, which operates on an adjacent patch at much the same time, and, if you're at all squeamish, is best avoided – brightly coloured birds squeezed into tiny cages are not for everyone. Incidentally, the *Lunchcafé Winkel*, beside the Noordermarkt at the corner with Westerstraat, sells huge wedges of homemade apple pie, which Jordaaners (and others) swear is the best in town.

Just to the north of the Noorderkerk, the **Lindengracht** ("Canal of Limes") lost its waterway decades ago, but has had a prominent role in local folklore since the day in 1886 when a policeman made an ill-advised attempt to stop an eel-pulling contest. Horrible as it sounds, eel-pulling was a popular pastime hereabouts with tug-o'-war teams holding tight to either end of the poor creature, which was smeared with soap to make the entertainment last a little longer. The crowd unceremoniously bundled the policeman away, but when reinforcements arrived, the whole thing got out of hand and there was a full-scale **riot** – the Paling-Oproer - which lasted for three days and cost 26 lives.

The east end of the Lindengracht intersects with leafy Brouwersgracht (see p.84), which marks the northerly limit of both the Jordaan and the Grachtengordel.

## The Old Jewish Quarter and the East

Originally one of the marshiest parts of Amsterdam, prone to regular flooding, the narrow slice of land sandwiched between the curve of the Amstel, Kloveniersburgwal and the Nieuwe Herengracht was the home of Amsterdam's Jews from the sixteenth century up until World War II. By the 1920s, this **Old Jewish Quarter**, aka the Jodenhoek ("Jews' Corner"), was crowded with tenement buildings and smoking factories, but in 1945 it lay derelict – and neither has postwar redevelopment treated it kindly. Its focal point, **Waterlooplein**, has been overwhelmed by a whopping town hall and concert hall complex, which caused much controversy at the time of its construction, and the once-bustling Jodenbreestraat is now bleak and very ordinary, with Mr Visserplein, at its east end, one of the city's busiest traffic junctions. Picking your way round these obstacles is not much fun, but you should persevere – amongst all the cars and concrete are several moving reminders of the Jewish community that perished in the war.

Immediately to the east of the Old Jewish Quarter lies the **Plantagebuurt**, a trim district spined by the **Plantage Middenlaan**, a wide boulevard that was constructed in the mid-nineteenth century as the first part of the creation of this leafy suburb – one of Amsterdam's earliest. The avenue borders the city's largest botanical gardens, the **Hortus Botanicus**, and runs close to both the **Artis Zoo** and the first-rate **Verzetsmuseum** (Dutch Resistance Museum). Just slightly to the north of here are the artificial islands that comprise the **Oosterdok** (East Dock) quarter, dredged out of the River IJ to accommodate warehouses and docks in the seventeenth century. These islands once formed part of a vast maritime complex that spread right along the River IJ. Industrial decline set in during the 1880s, but the area is currently being redefined as a residential district, whilst its nautical heyday is recalled by the **Nederlands Scheepvaartmuseum** (Netherlands Maritime Museum).

## The Jews in Amsterdam

From the late sixteenth century onwards, Amsterdam was the refuge of **Jews** escaping persecution throughout the rest of Europe. The **Union of Utrecht**, ratified in 1579, signalled the start of the influx. Drawn up by the largely Protestant northern Dutch provinces in response to the invading Spanish army, the treaty combined the United Provinces (later to become the Netherlands) in a loose federation, whose wheels could only be greased by a degree of religious toleration then unknown elsewhere across the continent. Whatever the Protestants may have wanted, they knew that the Catholic minority (around 35 percent) would only continue to support the rebellion against the Spanish Habsburgs if they were treated well – the Jews benefited by osmosis and consequently immigrated here in their hundreds.

The toleration did, however, have its limits: Jewish immigrants were forced to buy citizenship, Christian-Jewish marriages were illegal, and, as with the Catholics, Jews were only allowed to practise their religion discreetly behind closed doors. A proclamation in 1632 also excluded them from most guilds – effectively withdrawing their right to own and run businesses. This forced them to either excel in those trades not governed by the guilds or introduce new non-guild trades into the city. Nonetheless, by the middle of the eighteenth century the city's Jewish community was active in almost every aspect of the economy, with particular strongholds in bookselling, tobacco, banking and commodity futures.

The first major Jewish influx was of **Sephardic** Jews from Spain and Portugal, where persecution had begun in earnest in 1492 and continued throughout the sixteenth century. In the 1630s, the Sephardim were joined in Amsterdam by hundreds of (much poorer) **Ashkenazi** Jews from German-speaking central Europe. The two groups established separate synagogues and, although there was no ghetto as such, the vast majority settled on and around what is now Waterlooplein, then a distinctly unhealthy tract of marshland subject to regular flooding by the River Amstel. Initially known as **Vlooyenburg**, this district was usually referred to as the **Jodenhoek**, or "Jews' Corner", though this was not, generally speaking, a pejorative term and neither did the Dutch eschew living here: Rembrandt, for instance, was quite happy to take up residence and frequently painted his Jewish neighbours. Indeed, given the time, the most extraordinary feature of Jewish settlement in Amsterdam was that it occasioned mild curiosity rather than outright hate, as evinced by contemporary prints of Jewish religious customs, where there is neither any hint of stereotype nor discernible demonization.

The restrictions affecting both Jews and Catholics were removed during **Napoleon**'s occupation of the United Provinces, when the country was temporarily renamed the Batavian Republic (1795–1806). Freed from official discrimination, Amsterdam's Jewish community flourished and the Jewish Quarter expanded, nudging northwest towards Nieuwmarkt and east across Nieuwe Herengracht, though this was just the focus of a community whose members lived in every part of the city. In 1882, the dilapidated houses of the Jodenhoek were razed and several minor canals filled in to make way for **Waterlooplein**, which became a largely Jewish marketplace, a bustling affair that sprawled out along St Antoniesbreestraat and Jodenbreestraat.

At the turn of the twentieth century, there were around 60,000 Jews living in Amsterdam, but refugees from Hitler's Germany swelled this figure to around 120,000 in the 1930s. The disaster that befell this community during the Nazi occupation is hard to conceive, but the bald facts speak for themselves: when Amsterdam was liberated, there were only 5000 Jews left and the Jodenhoek was, to all intents and purposes, a ghost town. At present, there are about 25,000 Jews resident in the city, but while Jewish life in Amsterdam has survived, its heyday has passed.

## St Antoniesbreestraat and the Zuiderkerk

Stretching south from Nieuwmarkt (see p.78), **St Antoniesbreestraat** once linked the city centre with the Jewish quarter, but its huddle of shops and houses was mostly demolished in the 1980s to make way for a main road. The plan was subsequently abandoned, but the modern buildings that now line most of the street hardly fire the soul, even if the modern symmetries – and cubist coloured panels – of the apartment blocks that spill along part of the street are at least visually arresting. One of the few survivors of all these munic-ipal shenanigans is the **Pintohuis** (Pinto House; Mon & Wed 2–8pm, Fri 2–5pm, Sat 11am–4pm; free), at no. 69, which is now a public library. Easily spotted by its off-white Italianate facade, the mansion is named after Isaac De Pinto, a Jew who fled Portugal to escape the Inquisition and subsequently became a founder of the East India Company. Pinto bought this property in 1651 and promptly had it remodelled in grand style, the facade interrupted by six lofty pilasters, which lead the eye up to the blind balustrade. The mansion was the talk of the town, even more so when Pinto had the interior painted in a similar style to the front – pop in to look at the birds and cherubs of the orig-inal painted ceiling.

Across the street, through an old archway, the **Zuiderkerk** (Mon 11am-4pm, Tues–Wed & Fri 9am–4pm, Thurs 9am–8pm; free), dating from 1611, was the first Amsterdam church built specifically for the Protestants. It was designed by the prolific architect and sculptor, Hendrick de Keyser (1565–1621), whose distinctive – and very popular – style extrapolated elements of traditional Flemish design, with fanciful detail and frilly towers added wherever possible. The basic design of the Zuiderkerk is firmly Gothic, but the soaring tower is typical of his work, complete with balconies and balustrades, arches and columns. Now deconsecrated, the church has itself been turned into a munic-ipal information centre, with displays on housing and the environment, plus temporary exhibitions revealing the city council's future plans. The **tower**, which has a separate entrance, can be climbed during the summer (June–Sept Wed–Sat 2–4pm; €3).

## Jodenbreestraat and the Rembrandt House

St Antoniesbreestraat runs into **Jodenbreestraat**, the "Broad Street of the Jews", at one time the main centre of Jewish activity. Badly served by postwar development, this ancient thoroughfare is now short on charm, but in these unlikely surroundings, at no. 6, stands **Het Rembrandthuis** (Rembrandt House; Mon–Sat 10am–5pm, Sun 1–5pm; €7; ⓦwww.rembrandthuis.nl), whose intricate facade is decorated by pretty wooden shutters and a small ped-iment. Rembrandt bought this house at the height of his fame and popularity, living here for over twenty years and spending a fortune on furnishings – an expense that ultimately contributed to his bankruptcy. An inventory made at the time details the huge collection of paintings, sculptures and art treasures he'd amassed, almost all of which was confiscated after he was declared insol-vent and forced to move to a more modest house on Rozengracht in the Jordaan in 1658. The city council bought the Jodenbreestraat house in 1907 and has subsequently revamped the premises on several occasions, most recent-ly in 1999. A string of period rooms now gives a clear impression of Rembrandt's life and times, while the adjoining modern wing displays an extensive collection of Rembrandt's etchings as well as several of the original copper plates on which he worked. The biblical illustrations attract the most attention, though the studies of tramps and vagabonds are equally appealing. An accompanying exhibit explains Rembrandt's engraving techniques and there are also regular temporary exhibitions on Rembrandt and his contemporaries; to see his paintings, however – and superb they are too – you'll have to go to the Rijksmuseum (see p.79).

Next door, the multimedia **Holland Experience** (daily 10am–6pm; €8; Ⓦwww.holland-experience.nl) is a kind of sensory-bombardment movie about Amsterdam and the Netherlands, with synchronized smells and a moving floor – not to mention special 3D effects.

## Waterlooplein

Jodenbreestraat runs parallel to the Stadhuis en Muziektheater (Town Hall and Concert Hall), a sprawling complex whose indeterminate modernity dominates **Waterlooplein**, a rectangular parcel of land that was originally swampy marsh. This was the site of the first Jewish Quarter, but by the late nineteenth century it had become an insanitary slum, home to the poorest of the Ashkenazi Jews. The slums were cleared in the 1880s and thereafter the open spaces of the Waterlooplein hosted the largest and liveliest marketplace in the city, the place where Jews and Gentiles met to trade. In World War II, the Nazis used the square to round up their victims, but despite these ugly connotations the Waterlooplein was revived in the 1950s as the site of the city's main **flea market** and remains so to this day (Mon–Sat 9am–5pm; see also p.123). The market is, however, nowhere as large as it once was thanks to the town hall and concert hall development.

## Mr Visserplein and the Portuguese Synagogue

Just behind the Muziektheater, **Mr Visserplein** is a busy junction for traffic speeding towards the IJ tunnel. It takes its name from Mr Visser, President of the Supreme Court of the Netherlands in 1939. He was dismissed the following year when the Germans occupied the country, and became an active member of the Jewish resistance, working for the illegal underground newspaper *Het Parool* ("The Password") and refusing to wear the yellow Star of David. He died in 1942, a few days after publicly – and famously – denouncing all forms of collaboration.

Unmissable on the corner of Mr Visserplein is the brown and bulky brickwork of the **Esnoga** or **Portugees synagoge** (Portuguese Synagogue; Sun–Fri 10am–4pm; closed Yom Kippur; €3.50), completed in 1675 for the city's Sephardic Jews. One of Amsterdam's most imposing buildings, the central structure, with its grand pilasters and blind balustrade, was built in the broadly Neoclassical style that was then fashionable in Holland. It is surrounded by a courtyard complex of small outhouses, where the city's Sephardim have fraternized for centuries. Barely altered since its construction, the synagogue's lofty interior follows the Sephardic tradition in having the Hechal (the Ark of the Covenant) and *tebah* (from where services are led) at opposite ends. Also traditional is the seating, with two sets of wooden benches (for the men) facing each other across the central aisle – the women have separate galleries up above. A set of superb brass chandeliers holds the candles that remain the only source of artificial light. When it was completed, the synagogue was one of the largest in the world, its congregation almost certainly the richest; today, the Sephardic community has dwindled to just sixty-odd members, most of whom live outside the city centre. In one of the outhouses, a video sheds light on the history of the synagogue and Amsterdam's Sephardim; the mystery is why the Nazis left it alone. No one knows for sure, but it seems likely that they intended to turn it into a museum once all the Jews had been polished off.

Next to the synagogue, on the south side of its retaining wall, is **Jonas Daniel Meijerplein**, a scrawny triangle of gravel named after the eponymous lawyer, who in 1796, at the age of just sixteen, was the first Jew to be admitted to the Amsterdam Bar. It was here in February 1941 that around 400 Jewish men were forcibly loaded up on trucks and taken to their deaths at Mauthausen concentration camp, in reprisal for the killing of a Dutch Nazi during a street fight. The arrests sparked off the February Strike (Februaristaking), a general strike in protest against the Germans' treatment of the Jews. It was organized by the outlawed Communist Party and spearheaded by Amsterdam's transport workers and dockers – a rare demonstration of solidarity with the Jews whose fate was usually accepted without visible protest in all of occupied Europe. The strike was quickly suppressed, but is still commemorated by an annual wreath-laying ceremony on February 25, as well as by Mari Andriessen's **statue** of the Dokwerker (Dockworker) here on the square.

### Jewish Historical Museum

Across J.D. Meijerplein, on the far side of the main road, the **Joods Historisch Museum** (Jewish Historical Museum; daily 11am–5pm; closed Yom Kippur; €5; ⓦ www.jhm.nl) is cleverly shoehorned into four Ashkenazi synagogues dating from the late seventeenth century. For years after World War II these buildings lay abandoned, but they were finally refurbished – and connected by walkways – in the 1980s to accommodate a Jewish resource centre and exhibition area. The latter is located in the handsome Grote Synagoge of 1671 and features a fairly small but wide-ranging collection covering most aspects of Dutch Jewish life. Downstairs, in the main body of the synagogue, is a fine collection of religious silverware as well as a handful of paintings and all manner of antique artefacts illustrating religious customs and practises. The gallery above holds a finely judged social history of the city's Jews, tracing their prominent role in a wide variety of industries, both as employers and employees and examining, in brief, the trauma of World War II, complete with several especially moving photographs.

### East into the Plantagebuurt

From Mr Visserplein, it's a short walk east along Muiderstraat to the lush **Hortus Botanicus** (April–Sept Mon–Fri 9am–5pm, Sat & Sun 11am–5pm, €5; Oct–March Mon–Fri 9am–4pm, Sat & Sun 11am–4pm, €3.40; ⓦ www.hortus-botanicus.nl), a pleasant botanical garden at the corner of Plantage Middenlaan and Plantage Parklaan. Founded in 1682, the gardens contain around six thousand plant species (including various carnivorous varieties) on display both outside and in a series of hothouses, including a Three-Climates Glasshouse, where the plants are arranged according to their geographical origins. The garden makes a relaxing break on any tour of central Amsterdam and you can stop off for coffee and cakes in the orangery.

Continue down the right-hand side of Plantage Middenlaan to reach another sad relic of the war, **De Hollandsche Schouwburg**, at no. 24 (daily 11am–4pm; closed Yom Kippur; free). Formerly a Jewish theatre, the building became the main assembly point for Amsterdam Jews prior to their deportation. Inside, there was no daylight and families were interned in conditions that foreshadowed those of the camps they would soon be taken to. The building has been refurbished to house a small exhibition on the plight of the city's Jews, but the old auditorium out at the back has been left as an empty, roofless shell. A memorial column of basalt on a Star of David base stands where the stage once was, an intensely mournful monument to suffering of unfathomable proportions.

A brief walk northeast along Plantage Kerklaan is the **Artis Zoo** (April–Oct daily 9am–6pm; Oct–March daily 9am–5pm; €13.50; Ⓦwww.artis.nl). Opened in 1838, the zoo has long been one of the city's top tourist attractions and thankfully its layout and lack of bars and cages mean that it never feels overcrowded. Aside from the usual beasts and creepy-crawlies, the huge aquariums are one of its main features as is the Children's Farm, where kids can come nose-to-nose with sheep, calves, goats, etc. Feeding times – always popular – are as follows: 11am birds of prey; 11.30am and 3.45pm seals and sea-lions; 2pm pelicans; 2.30pm crocodiles (Sun only); 3pm lions and tigers (not Fri); 3.30pm penguins. The on-site **Planetarium** has five or six shows daily, all in Dutch; you can pick up a leaflet with an English translation from the desk.

Near the zoo, at Plantage Kerklaan 61, is the excellent **Verzetsmuseum** (Dutch Resistance Museum; Tues–Fri 10am–5pm, Sat, Sun & Mon noon–5pm; €4.50; Ⓦwww.verzetsmuseum.org). The museum outlines the development of the Dutch Resistance from the Nazi invasion of the Netherlands in May 1940 to the country's liberation in 1945. Thoughtfully presented, the main gangway examines the experience of the majority of the population, dealing honestly with the fine balance between co-operation and collaboration. Side rooms are devoted to different aspects of the resistance, from the brave determination of the Communist Party, who went underground as soon as the Germans arrived, to more ad hoc responses like the so-called Milk Strike of 1943, when hundreds of milk producers refused to deliver. Interestingly, the Dutch Resistance proved especially adept at forgery, forcing the Nazis to make the identity cards they issued more and more complicated – but without much success. Fascinating old photographs illustrate the (English and Dutch) text along with a host of original artefacts, from examples of illegal newsletters to signed German death warrants. Apart from their treatment of the Jews, which is detailed here, perhaps the most chilling feature of the occupation was the use of indiscriminate reprisals to terrify the population. For the most part it worked, though there were always a minority courageous enough to resist. The museum has dozens of little metal sheets providing biographical sketches of the members of the Resistance – and it's this mixture of the general and the personal that is its real strength.

## Entrepotdok

At the northern end of Plantage Kerklaan, just beyond the Dutch Resistance Museum, a footbridge leads over to **Entrepotdok**, on the nearest, and most interesting, of the Oosterdok islands. On the far side of the bridge, old brick warehouses stretch right along the quayside, distinguished by their spout gables, multiple doorways and overhead pulleys. Built by the Dutch East India Company in the eighteenth century, they were once part of the largest warehouse complex in continental Europe, a gigantic customs-free zone established for goods in transit. On the ground floor, above the main entrance, each warehouse sports the name of a town or island; goods for onward transportation were stored in the appropriate warehouse until there was enough to fill a boat or barge. The warehouses have been tastefully converted into offices and apartments, a fate that must surely befall the central East India Company compound, whose chunky Neoclassical entrance is at the west end of Entrepotdok on Kadijksplein, from where it's a couple of minutes' walk to the Maritime Museum.

## The Dutch East India Company

Founded in 1602, the **Dutch East India Company** was the chief pillar of Amsterdam's wealth for nearly two hundred years. Its high-percentage profits came from importing spices into Europe, and to secure them the company's ships ventured far and wide, establishing trading links with India, Sri Lanka, Indo-China, Malaya, China and Japan, though modern-day Indonesia was always the main event. Predictably, the company had a cosy relationship with the merchants who steered the Dutch government: the company was granted a trading monopoly in all the lands east of the Cape of Good Hope and could rely on the warships of the powerful Dutch navy if they got into difficulty. Neither was their business purely mercantile: the East India Company exercised unlimited military, judicial and political powers in those trading posts it established, the first of which was Batavia in Java in 1619. In the 1750s, the Dutch East India Company went into decline, partly because the British expelled them from most of the best trading stations, but mainly because the company over-borrowed. The Dutch government took it over in 1795.

## Dutch Maritime Museum and around

The **Nederlands Scheepvaartmuseum** (Dutch Maritime Museum; Tues–Sun 10am–5pm; mid-June to mid-Sept also Mon 10am–5pm; €7; ⓦ www.generali .nl/scheepvaartmuseum) occupies the old arsenal of the Dutch navy, a vast sandstone structure built in the Oosterdok on Kattenburgerplein. It's underpinned by no less than 18,000 wooden piles driven deep into the riverbed at enormous expense in the 1650s. The building's four symmetrical facades are dour and imposing despite the odd stylistic flourish, principally some small dormer windows and Neoclassical pediments, and they surround a central, cobbled courtyard. It's the perfect location for a maritime museum – or at least it would be if the museum's collection, spread over three floors, was larger; in the event the collection seems a little forlorn, rattling around a building that's just too big.

The ground floor displays a flashy gilded barge built for King William I in 1818 and is used to host temporary exhibitions. The next floor up, devoted to shipping in the seventeenth and eighteenth centuries, is the most diverting. It includes garish ships' figureheads, examples of early atlases and navigational equipment, and finely detailed models of the clippers of the East India Company, then the fastest ships in the world. Contemporary shipbuilders tried hard to make the officers' quarters as domestic as possible – literally a home-from-home – and the fancifully carved, seventeenth-century stern which dominates one of the rooms comes complete with a set of dainty mullion windows. There are oodles of nautical paintings too, some devoted to the achievements of Dutch trading ships, others showing heavy seas and shipwrecks and yet more celebrating the successes of the Dutch Navy. Willem van de Velde II (1633–1707) was the most successful of the Dutch marine painters of the period and there's a good sample of his work here – canvases that emphasize the strength and power of the Dutch warship, often depicted in battle. The final floor is devoted to the nineteenth and twentieth centuries and, in comparison, fails to excite. Outside, moored at the museum jetty, is a full-scale replica of an East Indiaman, the *Amsterdam*. It's crewed by actors, and another set of nautical thespians will be needed when the 78-metre *Stad Amsterdam* clipper is completed in the next couple of years.

Heading west from the Maritime Museum, it takes about fifteen minutes to reach Centraal Station, passing on the way the Nemo centre (see opposite). The Canal Bus (see p.61) does the same journey rather more pleasantly.

Strolling west along the waterfront Prins Hendrikkade, the foreground is dominated by a massive elevated hood that rears up above the entrance to the IJ tunnel. A good part of this hood is occupied by the large and lavish **NEMO** centre (Tues–Sun 10am–5pm, plus school holidays and July & Aug Mon 10am–5pm; €10; ⓦ www.e-nemo.nl) – just follow the signs for the ground-floor entrance. Recently rebranded, this is a young kids' attraction par excellence, with all sorts of interactive science and technological exhibits spread over six floors.

## The Museum Quarter and the Vondelpark

Amsterdam's three main museums lie on the edge of **Museumplein**, just south of the buzzing Leidseplein (see p.89). Museumplein's wide lawns, extending south from the Singelgracht to Van Baerlestraat, are used for a variety of outdoor activities, from visiting circuses to political demonstrations. The largest of the museums is the **Rijksmuseum**, which occupies a huge late nineteenth-century edifice built in an inventive historic style by Petrus Josephus Hubertus Cuypers, also the creator of Centraal Station, in the early 1880s. The museum possesses one of the most comprehensive collections of seventeenth-century Dutch paintings in the world, with twenty or so of Rembrandt's works, plus a healthy sample of canvases by Steen, Hals, Vermeer and their leading contemporaries. There are also representative displays of every other pre-twentieth-century period of Dutch and Flemish painting. Close by, the **Van Gogh Museum** boasts the finest assortment of Van Gogh paintings in the world, whilst the **Stedelijk Museum** focuses on modern and contemporary art. Together the three museums comprise one of Amsterdam's biggest pulls.

From Museumplein, it's a brief walk northwest along Van Baerlestraat to the sprawling greenery of the **Vondelpark**, Amsterdam's loveliest park.

### The Rijksmuseum

The **Rijksmuseum** (currently daily 10am–5pm, €9, but see box for details of ongoing renovation work; ⓦ www.rijksmuseum.nl) owns a small but eclectic collection of early Flemish – or more properly Netherlandish – paintings dating from the fifteenth and sixteenth centuries. The earliest paintings are the highly stylized works of the pre-Renaissance painters, traditionally known as the "**Flemish Primitives**", whose preoccupations were exclusively religious. Depicting biblical figures or saints, these are devotional snapshots, dotted with symbols that provided a readily-understood lexicon for the medieval onlooker. Thus, in the *Madonna Surrounded by Female Saints*, painted by an unknown artist referred to as thereafter as the "Master of the Virgin Among Virgins", each of the

---

### Rijksmuseum renovations

A major **renovation** of the Rijksmuseum will begin in December 2003 and is scheduled to last for no less than five years. During this period, most of the museum will be closed, though the kernel of the permanent collection - including the more important Rembrandts - will remain on view in the **Philips Wing**. Other works will be displayed in Amsterdam's Nieuwe Kerk (see p.75) and a few others in a new gallery at Schiphol airport, while yet more will be dispersed to other museums across the country. The projected **opening hours** of the Philips Wing during the refurbishment are longer than at present (Mon & Thurs 9am–5pm, Tues, Wed, Fri, Sat & Sun 9am–9pm), but admission prices have yet to be fixed.

saints wears a necklace that contains her particular symbol – St Barbara the tower of her imprisonment and so on. However, the most striking paintings in this group are by **Geertgen tot Sint Jans**. His *Holy Kindred*, painted around 1485, is a skilfully structured portrait of the family of Anna, Mary's mother, in which the Romanesque nave represents the Old Testament, the Gothic choir the New. Mary and Joseph in the foreground parallel the figures of Adam and Eve behind by the altar and Joseph holds a lily, emblem of purity, over Mary's head. Moving onto the sixteenth century, the Rijksmuseum possesses a voluptuous *Mary Magdalen* by **Jan van Scorel** and a memorable *Carrying of the Cross* by **Quinten Matsys**, long Antwerp's leading painter and a key transitional figure: Matsys was one of the first Netherlandish artists to be influenced by the Italian Renaissance.

The Rijksmuseum's forte is its collection of paintings from the **Dutch Golden Age**. The collection includes several wonderful canvases by **Frans Hals**, most notably his expansive *Marriage Portrait of Isaac Massa and Beatrix Laen*. Relaxing beneath a tree, a portly Isaac glows with contentment as his new wife sits beside him in a suitably demure manner. There's also **Dirck van Baburen**'s sensational *Prometheus in Chains* – a work from the Utrecht School, which used the paintings of Caravaggio as its model – and the miniatures of **Hendrick Avercamp**, noted for their folksy and finely detailed skating scenes. There are more thoroughly Dutch works in, for instance, the soft, tonal river scenes of the Haarlem artist **Salomon van Ruysdael** and the cool church interiors of **Pieter Saenredam**, not to mention **Ferdinand Bol**'s *Portrait of Elizabeth Bas*. Bol was a pupil of Rembrandt as was the more talented **Carel Fabritius**, who was killed in 1654 at the age of 32, when Delft's powder magazine exploded. Fabritius's *Portrait of Abraham Potter* is a restrained, skilful work of soft, delicate hues in stark contrast to the same artist's grisly *The Beheading of St John the Baptist*.

From the second half of the seventeenth century come the carousing peasants of **Jan Steen** – notably his *Feast of St Nicholas*, with its squabbling children making the festival a celebration of disorderly greed. There's also the drunken waywardness of Steen's *Merry Family* and *The Drunken Couple*, both of which verge on the anarchic. Steen was also capable of more subtle works, a famous example being his *Morning Toilet*, which is full of associations, referring either to sexual pleasures just had or about to be taken. **Vermeer** is well represented by *Love Letter*, which reveals a tension between servant and mistress – the lute on the woman's lap was a well-known sexual symbol – and *The Kitchen Maid*, an exquisitely observed domestic scene, literally right down to the nail (and its shadow) on the background wall. Similarly, in the precise *Young Woman Reading a Letter*, the map behind her hints at the far-flung places her loved one is writing from.

**Rembrandt**'s *The Night Watch* of 1642 is the Rijkmuseum's pride and joy. It is also the most famous and probably the most valuable of all the artist's pictures, restored after having been slashed in 1975. The painting is of a Militia Company and as such celebrates one of the companies formed in the sixteenth century to defend the United Provinces against Spain. As the Habsburg threat receded, so the militias became social clubs for the well-heeled, who were eager to commission their own group portraits as signs of their prestige. *The Night Watch* depicts Amsterdam's Kloveniersdoelen company, but the title is actually inaccurate – it got its tag in the eighteenth century when the background darkness was misinterpreted. Though not as subtle as much of the artist's later work, the painting is an adept piece, full of movement and carefully arranged. Paintings of this kind were collections of individual portraits as much as group pictures, and for the artist their difficulty lay in including each single face while simultaneously producing a coherent group scene. Rembrandt opted to show the company preparing to march off, a snapshot of military activity in which banners are unfurled, muskets primed and drums rolled. There are a couple of allegorical figures as well, most prominently a young, spotlit woman who has a bird hanging from her belt, a reference to the Kloveniersdoelen's traditional emblem of a claw.

Amongst the other Rembrandts is a late *Self-Portrait*, with the artist caught in mid-shrug as the Apostle Paul, a self-aware and defeated old man, and the finely detailed *Portrait of Maria Trip*. There's also his touching depiction of his cowled son, *Titus*, and *The Jewish Bride*, one of his very last pictures, finished in 1667. No one knows who the people are, nor whether they are actually married (the title came later), but the painting is one of Rembrandt's most telling, the paint dashed on freely and the hands touching lovingly, as Kenneth Clark wrote, in a "marvellous amalgam of richness, tenderness and trust".

## The Van Gogh Museum

**Vincent van Gogh** (1853–90) is arguably the most popular, most reproduced and most talked about of all modern artists, so it's not surprising that the **Van Gogh Museum** (daily 10am–6pm; €7; ⓦ www.vangoghmuseum.nl), comprising a fabulous collection of the artist's work, is one of Amsterdam's top tourist attractions. It's housed in two buildings: an angular 1970s structure designed by Gerritt Rietveld, a leading light of the De Stijl movement, and a flashy new extension added to the rear of the earlier structure in 1999 to a design by the Japanese architect Kisho Kurokawa. It's a well-conceived and beautifully presented introduction to the man and his art, with the kernel of the collection inherited from Vincent's art-dealer brother Theo. There is enough gallery space to allow for the regular rotation of works, so the description below should be treated with some caution. The museum is located a brief walk west of the Rijksmuseum on the north edge of Museumplein.

The museum starts on the ground floor with a group of works by some of Van Gogh's well-known friends and contemporaries, many of whom influenced his work – Gauguin, Millet, Adolph Monticelli and others. It then moves on to the works of the man himself, presented for the most part chronologically on the first floor. The first paintings go back to the artist's **early years** in Nuenen, in the south of the country, where he was born. These are dark, sombre works in the main, ranging from an assortment of drab grey and brown still-lifes to the gnarled faces and haunting, flickering light of *The Potato Eaters* – one of Van Gogh's best-known paintings, and the culmination of hundreds of studies of the local peasantry.

Across the hall, the sobriety of these early works is easily transposed onto the **Parisian** urban landscape, particularly in the *View of Paris*, where the city's domes and rooftops hover below Montmartre under a glowering, blustery sky. But before long, under the sway of fellow painters and influenced by the sheer colour of the city, his approach began to change. This is most noticeable in the views of Montmartre windmills and allotments, a couple of self-portraits, and the pictures from Asnières just outside Paris, where the artist used to travel regularly to paint. Look out also for *A Pair of Shoes*, a painting that used to hang in the house Van Gogh shared with Gauguin in Arles, the dazzling movement of *Wheatfield with a Lark* and the almost neurotic precision of his *Flowerpot with Chives*.

In February 1888, Van Gogh moved to **Arles**, inviting Gauguin to join him a little later. With the change of scenery came a heightened interest in colour, and the predominance of yellow as a recurring motif: it's represented best in such paintings as *Van Gogh's Bedroom* and the *Harvest at La Crau*, and most vividly in *The Yellow House*. A canvas from the artist's *Sunflowers* series is justly one of his most lauded works, intensely, almost obsessively, rendered in the deepest oranges, golds and ochres he could find. Gauguin told of Van Gogh painting these flowers in a near trance; there were usually sunflowers in jars all over their house.

Van Gogh committed himself to the asylum in **St Rémy** in 1889 after snipping off part of his ear and offering it to a local prostitute. Here, his approach to nature became more abstract: trees bent into cruel, sinister shapes and skies coloured purple and yellow, as in the *Garden of St Paul's Hospital*. The artist is at his most expressionistic here, the paint applied thickly, often with a palette knife, especially in the final, tortured paintings done at **Auvers**, where Van Gogh lodged for the last three months of his life. It was at Auvers that he painted the frantic *Ears of Wheat* and *Wheatfield with a Reaper*, in which the fields swirl and writhe under weird, light-green, moving skies. It was a few weeks after completing these last paintings that Van Gogh shot and fatally wounded himself.

The two floors above provide a back-up to the main collection: the second floor has a study area with computer access to an excessively detailed account of Van Gogh's life and times, and the third features a changing selection from the museum's vast stock of Van Gogh **drawings** and less familiar paintings, plus notebooks and letters. This floor also affords space to relevant temporary exhibitions illustrating Van Gogh's artistic influences, or his own influence on other artists. There's much more **temporary exhibition** space in the new extension, which is partly underground. It was financed by a Japanese insurance company – the same conglomerate that paid US$35 million for one of Van Gogh's *Sunflowers* canvases in 1987. The museum also has a shop and café, both located on the ground floor beside the main entrance.

### The Stedelijk Museum

Amsterdam's number one venue for modern art, the **Stedelijk Museum** (daily 11am–5pm; €5; Ⓦwww.stedelijk.nl), next door to the Van Gogh Museum, is still at the cutting edge after a hundred years or more. Its permanent collection is wide-ranging and its temporary exhibitions – based both on its own acquisitions and on loaned pieces, and regularly extending to photography and installations – are usually of international standard. It's housed in a grand neo-Renaissance building dating from 1895, but the interior is modern and a new wing was added in the 1950s. Note that the museum is closed until 2005 for renovation work (see box).

The museum's ground floor is usually given over to temporary exhibitions, often by living European artists. Contemporary Dutch art is a particular favourite, so keep an eye out for the work of such painters as Jan Dibbets, Rob Scholte and Marlene Dumas. Also on the ground floor are a couple of large-scale permanent attractions – **Karel Appel**'s *Bar* in the foyer, installed in the

### Stedelijk Museum renovations

The Stedelijk Museum is closed for refurbishment until late 2005. Until it re-opens, its permanent collection has been dispersed to other city museums, and some may be on display in the Nieuwe Kerk (see p.75).

1950s, and the same artist's wild daubings in the restaurant. Upstairs, the first floor is given over to a changing selection drawn from the museum's **permanent collection**. Broadly speaking, this starts off with drawings by Picasso, Matisse and their contemporaries, and moves on to paintings by major Impressionists (Manet, Monet, Bonnard) and Post-Impressionists (Ensor, Cézanne). Further on, Mondrian holds sway among the De Stijl group, from his early, muddy-coloured abstractions to the cool, boldly coloured rectangular blocks for which he's most famous. Kasimir Malevich is similarly well represented, his dense attempts at Cubism leading to the dynamism and bold, primary tones of his "Suprematist" paintings – slices, blocks and bolts of colour that shift around as if about to resolve themselves into some complex computer graphic. Elsewhere, depending on what's on show, you may come across some of the Stedelijk's wide collection of Marc Chagall paintings, and a number of pictures by American Abstract Expressionists Mark Rothko, Ellsworth Kelly and Barnett Newman, in addition to the odd work by Lichtenstein or Warhol. Jean Dubuffet, too, with his swipes at the art establishment, may well have a profile, and you might catch Matisse's large cutout, *The Parakeet and the Mermaid*.

## The Concertgebouw

Across Van Baerlestraat and just to the south of the Stedelijk Museum is the **Concertgebouw** (Concert Hall), home of the famed – and much recorded – Royal Concertgebouw Orchestra. When the German composer Brahms visited Amsterdam in the 1870s he was scathing about the locals' lack of culture and, in particular, their lack of a venue even halfway suitable for his music. In the face of such ridicule, a consortium of Amsterdam businessmen got together to fund the construction of a brand-new concert hall and the result was the Concertgebouw, completed in 1888. An attractive structure with a pleasingly grand Neoclassical facade, the Concertgebouw has become renowned among musicians and concert-goers for its marvellous acoustics, though it did have to undergo major repairs when it was discovered that the wooden piles on which it rested were rotting away. Although the Concertgebouw attracts the world's best orchestras and musicians, ticket prices can be surprisingly inexpensive – the venue operates an arts-for-all policy – and from September to May there are often free walk-in concerts at lunchtime.

## The Vondelpark

Amsterdam's city centre is short of green spaces, which makes the leafy expanses of the **Vondelpark**, just beyond Museumplein, doubly welcome. This is easily the largest and most popular of the city's parks, its network of footpaths used by a healthy slice of the city's population. The park dates back to 1864, when a group of leading Amsterdammers clubbed together to transform the soggy marshland that lay beyond the Leidsepoort into a landscaped park. The group, who were impressed by the contemporary English fashion for natural (as distinct from formal) landscaping, gave the task of developing the new style of park to the Zocher family, big-time gardeners who set about their task with gusto, completing their work in 1865. Named after the seventeenth-century poet Joost van den Vondel, the park proved an immediate success and was expanded to its present size (45 hectares) in 1877. It now possesses over 100 species of tree, a wide variety of local and imported plants, and – amongst many incidental features – a **bandstand** and excellent **rose garden**. Neither did the Zochers forget their Dutch roots: the park is latticed with ponds and narrow waterways, home to many sorts of wildfowl. There are other animals too: cows, sheep, hundreds of squirrels plus, bizarrely enough, a large colony of bright-green parakeets. The Vondelpark has several different children's **play areas** and during the summer regularly hosts free **concerts** and theatrical performances, mostly in its own specially designed open-air theatre.

# Eating

Amsterdam may not be Europe's culinary hotspot – Dutch cuisine is firmly rooted in the meat, potato and cabbage school of cooking – but in recent years the city has accumulated a string of excellent nouvelle **restaurants** and the Netherlands' colonial past accounts for many more. In the particular, Amsterdam is acclaimed for the best Indonesian food outside Indonesia, at characteristically hard-to-beat prices; *rijsttafel*, a selection of six or eight different dishes and hot sauces, is invariably an excellent choice. Other cuisines are also well-represented from French, Iberian and Italian through to Thai, Middle Eastern and Indian. Amsterdam also excels in the quantity and variety of its *eet-cafés* and **bars** (see p.110), which serve increasingly adventurous and inexpensive food in a wide range of attractive settings.

The city's **tearooms** (see p.109) – calling themselves this to steer clear of druggy "**coffeeshop**" connotations – correspond to the normal idea of a café: they are generally open all day, might serve alcohol but definitely aren't bars, don't allow dope-smoking, and serve up good coffee, sandwiches, light snacks and cakes.

## Restaurants

Unless otherwise stated, all the restaurants listed below operate similar **opening hours**, serving food daily from 5pm or 6pm until 10pm or 11pm. Note, however, that times may vary with the season and how busy things are.

### African

**Asmara** Jonas Daniel Meijerplein 8 ☎020/627 1002. Next to the Jewish Historical Museum (see p.96), a Coca-Cola sign indicates this small and very popular Ethiopian restaurant. Inexpensive.

**Pygmalion** Nieuwe Spiegelstraat 5a ☎020/420 7022. Good spot for both lunch and dinner, popular among local workers. South African dishes include crocodile steaks, and there's a good selection of sandwiches too. Near the Rijksmuseum. Moderate.

### The Americas

**Café Pacifico** Warmoesstraat 31 ☎020/624 2911. Quality array of Mexican (and Mexican–Californian) food in a cramped and crowded little joint only minutes from Centraal Station. Moderate.

**Iguazu** Prinsengracht 703, at Leidsestraat ☎020/420 3910. For carnivores only: a superb Argentinian–Brazilian restaurant, with some of the finest fillet steak in town. Daily noon–midnight. Moderate.

**Poco Loco** Nieuwmarkt 24 ☎020/624 2937. Cajun split-level restaurant with a friendly, cheerful atmosphere, and a menu including burritos, steaks and jambalaya. Inexpensive.

### Chinese, Thai and Filipino

**Dynasty** Reguliersdwarsstraat 30 ☎020/626 8400. Top-notch choice of Indo-Chinese food, with Vietnamese and Thai options too. Smart and subdued atmosphere. Near Rembrandtplein. Closed Tues. Expensive.

**Lana Thai** Warmoesstraat 10 ☎020/624 2179. Among the best Thai restaurants in town, with seating overlooking the Damrak. Quality food, chic surroundings – and high prices. Closed Tues. Expensive.

**Top Thai** Herenstraat 22 ☎020/623 4463. A popular restaurant that boasts some of the best Thai food in Amsterdam, with spicy, authentic dishes at good prices and in a friendly atmosphere. For complete burn-out try one of their chilli salads. Located at the north end of the Grachtengordel. Inexpensive.

## Restaurant prices

The following price categories indicate the average cost per person for a main course without drinks.

**Budget** Under €9
**Inexpensive** €9–13.50

**Moderate** €13.50–18
**Expensive** Over €18

### Dutch

**Claes Claesz** Egelantiersstraat 24 ☎020/625 5306. Exceptionally friendly Jordaan restaurant that attracts a good mixed crowd and serves excellent Dutch food. Live music from Thursday to Saturday, and Sunday's "theatre dinner" sees various Dutch theatrical/musical acts appearing between the courses. Closed Mon. Moderate.

**De Eettuin** 2e Tuindwarsstraat 10 ☎020/623 7706. Hefty portions of Dutch food, with salad from a serve-yourself bar. Non-meat eaters can content themselves with the large, if dull, vegetarian plate, or the delicious fish casserole. In the Jordaan. Inexpensive.

**Koevoet** Lindenstraat 17 ☎020/624 0846. The "Cow's-Foot" – or, alternatively, the "Crowbar" – is a traditional Jordaan *eetcafé* with a creative French menu and very tasty food. Closed Sun & Mon. Moderate.

**Piet de Leeuw** Noorderstraat 11 ☎020/623 7181. Amsterdam's best steakhouse, dating from the 1940s. Excellent steaks, and a mouth-watering Dame Blanche dessert. Mon–Fri noon–11pm, Sat & Sun 5–11pm. South of Rembrandtplein, off Vijzelgracht. Inexpensive.

**De Silveren Spiegel** Kattengat 4, off Spuistraat ☎020/624 6589. There's been a restaurant in this location – off the northern end of Spuistraat – since 1614, and the "Silver Mirror" is one of the best in the city, with a delicately balanced menu of Dutch cuisine. The proprietor lives on the coast and brings in the fish himself. Spectacular food, with a cellar of 350 wines to boot. Set menus and a la carte. Closed Sun. Expensive.

**'t Zwaantje** Berenstraat 12 ☎020/623 2373. Old-fashioned Dutch restaurant with a nice atmosphere and well-cooked, reasonably priced food. In the Grachtengordel, a five-minute walk southwest of the Dam. Moderate.

### Fish

**Albatros** Westerstraat 264 ☎020/627 9932. Family-run restaurant in the Jordaan serving some mouth-wateringly imaginative fish dishes. A place to splash out and linger over a meal. Closed Wed. Expensive.

**Éénvistwéévis** Schippersgracht 6 ☎020/623 2894. An uncomplicated central fish restaurant serving an interesting selection of seafood with delicious sauces; mussels too. Closed Mon.

**Lucius** Spuistraat 247 ☎020/624 1831. Bistro-style seafood specialist with prompt and efficient service. Stick to the excellent and reasonably priced daily specials – rather than dishes from the menu – both for taste and speed. Very popular. Closed Sun. Moderate.

**Le Pêcheur** Reguliersdwarsstraat 32 ☎020/624 3121. Beautiful restaurant with a well-balanced menu, both à la carte and set. Lovely garden terrace in the summer. Near Rembrandtplein. Open for lunch, but closed Sun. Moderate.

### French

**Bonjour** Keizersgracht 770 ☎020/626 6040. Classy French cuisine in a romantic setting; particularly good charcoal-grilled dishes. Set menus and à la carte. Closed Mon & Tues. In the Grachtengordel, east of Utrechtsestraat. Moderate.

**Christophe** Leliegracht 46 ☎020/625 0807. Classic Michelin-starred restaurant on a quiet and beautiful canal in the Grachtengordel, drawing inspiration from the olive-oil-and-basil flavours of southern France and the chef's early years in North Africa. His aubergine terrine with cumin has been dubbed the best vegetarian dish in the world. Reservations far outstrip capacity. Expect to pay €35 for two courses. Closed Sun. Expensive.

**Le Zinc… et les Dames** Prinsengracht 999 ☎020/622 9044. Wonderfully atmospheric little place serving good quality, simple French fare; there's a particularly good wine list as well. In the Grachtengordel, just west of Reguliersgracht. Closed Mon & Sun. Expensive.

### Indian

**Shiva** Reguliersdwarsstraat 72 ☎020/624 8713. The city's outstanding Indian restaurant in terms of quality and price, with a wide selection of dishes, all expertly prepared. Vegetarians well catered for too. Highly recommended. Near Rembrandtplein. Inexpensive.

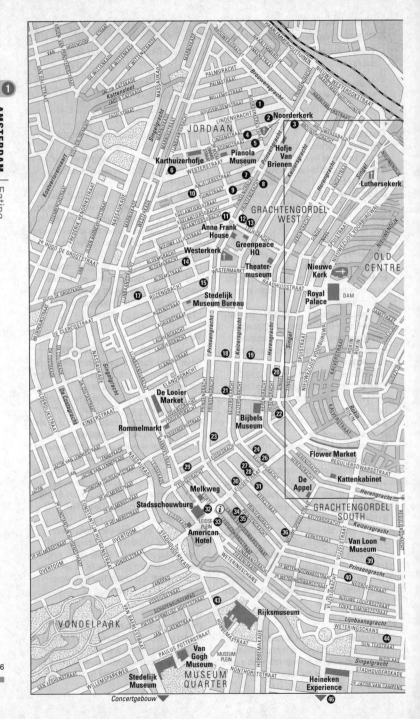

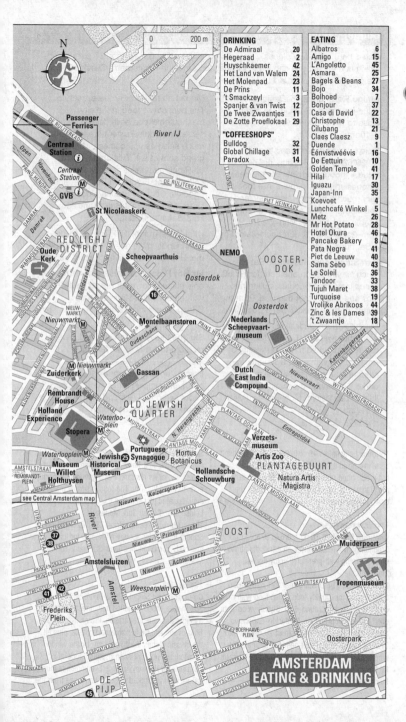

**DRINKING**

| | |
|---|---|
| De Admiraal | 20 |
| Hegeraad | 2 |
| Huyschkaemer | 42 |
| Het Land van Walem | 24 |
| Het Molenpad | 23 |
| De Prins | 11 |
| 't Smackzeyl | 3 |
| Spanjer & van Twist | 12 |
| De Twee Zwaantjes | 11 |
| De Zotte Proeflokaal | 29 |

**"COFFEESHOPS"**

| | |
|---|---|
| Bulldog | 32 |
| Global Chillage | 31 |
| Paradox | 14 |

**EATING**

| | |
|---|---|
| Albatros | 6 |
| Amigo | 15 |
| L'Angoletto | 45 |
| Asmara | 25 |
| Bagels & Beans | 27 |
| Bojo | 34 |
| Bolhoed | 7 |
| Bonjour | 37 |
| Casa di David | 22 |
| Christophe | 13 |
| Cilubang | 21 |
| Claes Claesz | 9 |
| Duende | 1 |
| Eénvistwéévis | 16 |
| De Eettuin | 10 |
| Golden Temple | 41 |
| Hilal | 17 |
| Iguazu | 30 |
| Japan-Inn | 35 |
| Koevoet | 4 |
| Lunchcafé Winkel | 5 |
| Metz | 26 |
| Mr Hot Potato | 28 |
| Hotel Okura | 46 |
| Pancake Bakery | 8 |
| Pata Negra | 41 |
| Piet de Leeuw | 40 |
| Sama Sebo | 43 |
| Le Soleil | 36 |
| Tandoor | 33 |
| Tujuh Maret | 38 |
| Turquoise | 19 |
| Vrolijke Abrikoos | 44 |
| Zinc & les Dames | 39 |
| 't Zwaantje | 18 |

**AMSTERDAM EATING & DRINKING**

## Budget eating

Listed here are a few places where it's possible to fill up for under €7 per person, which is the least you can expect to pay for a meal in Amsterdam. Check out, too, the pancake places on p.110.

**Amigo** Rozengracht 5. Basic, but good value-for-money Surinamese restaurant close to the Westerkerk. Tues–Sun 2–10pm.

**Bojo** Lange Leidsedwarsstraat 51 ☎020/622 7434. Possibly the best-value – though certainly not the best – Indonesian place in town. The food is very much a hit-and-miss affair, and you'll have to wait a long time both for a table and service. Mon–Wed 4pm–2am, Thurs & Sun noon–2am, Fri & Sat noon–4am.

**Dim Sum Court** Rokin 152. Eat as much as you can in one hour for €7.50. Dumplings, fried noodles, boiled noodles and a few other things all from the buffet, nothing special but a good filler.

**Mensa Atrium** Oudezijds Achterburgwal 237. Central self-service cafeteria attached to the University of Amsterdam, with extra discounts for students but open to all. Full meals for under €5, though the quality leaves a little to be desired. Mon–Fri noon–2pm & 5–7pm.

**Maoz Falafel** Reguliersbreestraat 45. The best street-food in the city: mashed chickpea balls deep-fried and served in Middle Eastern bread, with as much salad as you can eat, for the grand sum of €4. This branch is just off Rembrandtplein; others are at Leidsestraat, Ferdinand Bolstraat and opposite Centraal Station/Victoria Hotel. Mon–Thurs & Sun 11am–2am, Fri & Sat 11am–3am.

**Hilal** Rozengracht 154. Turkish fill-up with friendly owners and good shwarma. Popular with late-night revellers.

**Mr Hot Potato** Leidsestraat 44. The only place in town for baked potatoes, with nice Marilyn Monroe decor. Cheap, at around €2.50. Daily 10am–8pm.

**Sie Joe** Gravenstraat 24. Small café-restaurant that is great value for money. The Indonesian menu is far from extensive, but comprises well-prepared, simple dishes such as *gado gado*, *sateh* and *rendang*. Mon–Sat 11am–7pm, Thurs until 8pm.

**Tandoor** Leidseplein 19 ☎020/623 4415. Doesn't quite live up to its excellent reputation perhaps, but pretty good nonetheless. The tandoori dishes are highly recommended, and won't break the bank. Inexpensive.

## Indonesian

**Cilubang** Runstraat 10 ☎020/626 9755. Small Grachtengordel restaurant, with a friendly atmosphere, serving well-presented spicy dishes. Moderate.

**Kantjil en de Tijger** Spuistraat 291 ☎020/620 0994. Fresh, top-quality Indonesian food with main courses averaging around €25. Stylish wood-panelled bistro-like premises. Moderate–Expensive.

**Sahid Jaya** Reguliersdwarsstraat 26 ☎020/626 3727. Excellent restaurant near Rembrandtplein where you can eat outside surrounded by a beautiful flower garden. Helpful and friendly staff. Moderate.

**Sama Sebo** P.C. Hooftstraat 27 ☎020/662 8146. Amsterdam's best-known Indonesian restaurant, especially for its *rijsttafel* – and good value if you stick to the à la carte. The food is simply magnificent. Located just south of the Singelgracht from Leidseplein. Closed Sun. Moderate.

**Tujuh Maret** Utrechtsestraat 73 ☎020/427 9865. Superb Indonesian food, well-known for its rich and tasty combinations. Tues–Sat noon–10pm. Moderate.

## Italian

**Casa di David** Singel 426 ☎020/624 5093. Solid-value, wood-panelled Italian restaurant with a long-established reputation. Pizzas from wood-fired ovens and fresh hand-made pasta, plus all the classic dishes. Best seats are by the window. Located just north of Koningsplein. Moderate.

**L'Angoletto** Hemonystraat 2. Everyone's favourite Italian, always packed out – as you'll see from the condensation on the two big windows. The long wooden tables and benches create a very sociable atmosphere. No bookings, so just turn up and hope for the best. About ten minutes' walk south of Rembrandtplein. Closed Sat. Inexpensive.

### Japanese
**Hotel Okura** Ferdinand Bolstraat 333 ☎ 020/678 7111. The two restaurants in this five-star hotel located just south of the Heineken brewery – the sushi restaurant *Yamazato*, and the grill-plate restaurant *Teppan-Yaki Sazanka* – serve the finest Japanese cuisine in the city. Reckon on at least €50 per person. Both are open in the evening and for lunch noon–2.30pm. Expensive.
**Japan-Inn** Leidsekruisstraat 4 ☎ 020/675 9892. Warm and welcoming restaurant in the middle of the Leidseplein buzz. Kitchen open until midnight. Inexpensive.

### Spanish
**Centra** Lange Niezel 29 ☎ 020/622 3050. City-centre cantina, near Oude Kerk, with a wonderful selection of Spanish food, masterfully cooked and genially served. One of Amsterdam's best restaurants. Daily 1–11pm. Inexpensive.
**Duende** Lindengracht 62 ☎ 020/420 6692. Wonderful little tapas bar up in the Jordaan, with good quality and authentic tapas. Includes a small venue at the back for live dance and music. Mon–Thurs 4pm–1am, Fri 4pm–2am, Sat 2pm–2am, Sun 2pm–1am. Budget.

**Pata Negra** Utrechtsestraat 124 ☎ 020/422 6250. Big smoked hams hanging from the ceiling and an innkeeper who wants to know what you're drinking and how fast. Lovely tapas. Open from 2pm.

### Turkish
**Turquoise** Wolvenstraat 22 ☎ 020/624 2026. Good Turkish restaurant in the Grachtengordel with a beautiful long bar, giving it a café-like atmosphere. Inexpensive.

### Vegetarian
**Bolhoed** Prinsengracht 60 ☎ 020/626 1803. Something of an Amsterdam institution, this informal restaurant has a good range of vegan and vegetarian options from a daily changing menu; organic beer washes everything down. In the Grachtengordel, just south of Prinsenstraat. Daily noon–10pm. Moderate.
**Golden Temple** Utrechtsestraat 126 ☎ 020/626 8560. Laid-back place with a little more soul than the average Amsterdam veggie joint. Well-prepared lacto-vegetarian food without sugar and milk and pleasant, attentive service. No alcohol and non-smoking throughout. South of Rembrandtplein. Inexpensive.
**De Vrolijke Abrikoos** Weteringschans 76 ☎ 020/624 4672. All ingredients, produce and processes are organic or environmentally friendly in this restaurant that serves fish and meat as well as vegetarian dishes. Near Leidseplein. Closed Tues. Moderate.

## Tearooms

**Arnots** Singel 441. Basement lunchroom serving arguably the best coffees in town. Wholemeal sandwiches and freshly juiced drinks too, to absorb the caffeine. Just around the corner from Heiligeweg. Closed Sun.
**Bagels & Beans** Keizersgracht 504. Creative and delicious snacks that attract a youthful crowd: their version of strawberries and cream is a big favourite in the summer. The "Beans" refers to the coffee, which is very good too. In the Grachtengordel, near Leidsestraat.
**Café Esprit** Spui 10a. Swish modern café, with tasty sandwiches, rolls and superb salads.
**Gary's Muffins** Reguliersdwarsstraat 53. The first, and most authentic, New York bagels in town, with American-style cups of coffee (and half-price refills) as well as freshly baked muffins. Near

Rembrandtplein. Open until 3am.
**Lunchcafé Winkel** Noordermarkt 43. A popular café opposite the Noorderkerk, on the edge of the Jordaan. Something of a locals' meeting point on Saturday mornings, with the farmers' market in full flow. Serves up what many regard as the best apple pie in town.
**Metz** Keizersgracht 455. Enjoyable café on the top floor of the Metz department store, giving panoramic views over the city. The view is perhaps better than the food – stick to the simpler stuff. Near Leidseplein.
**Puccini** Staalstraat 21. Lovely cake- and chocolate-shop-cum-café, with wonderful handmade cakes, pastries and good coffee. In the Old Centre, close to Muntplein.

## Pancakes

**Pancakes** are a Dutch speciality – for fillers and light meals, you'd be hard pushed to find better. Although there are plenty of places dotted around town, those listed below are recommended. Expect to pay between about €4 and €7.

**Le Soleil** Nieuwe Spiegelstraat 56. Pretty little restaurant offering tasty pancakes – try the one with ginger and raisins. Open until 6pm.

**Pancake Bakery** Prinsengracht 191. In the basement of a good-looking canal house, this specialist place offers a large selection of filled pancakes from €5. Popular with tourists; located just south of Prinsenstraat. Daily noon–9.30pm.

**Pannekoekhuis Upstairs** Grimburgwal 2. Minuscule place in a tumbledown house, in the old centre opposite the university buildings, with sweet and savoury pancakes at low prices. Student discount. Wed–Fri noon–7pm, Sat & Sun noon–6pm.

# Drinking

Amsterdam is well known for its drinking, and with good reason: the selection of **bars** and **café-bars** is one of the real pleasures of the city. There are, in essence, two main kinds of Amsterdam bar. The traditional, old-style bar is the **brown café** (*bruin café* or *bruine kroeg*); these are cosy places, so called because of the dingy colour of their walls, stained by years of tobacco smoke. As a backlash, slick, self-consciously modern **designer bars** have sprung up, many of them known as "**grand cafés**", which tend to be as un-brown as possible and geared towards a young crowd. We've included details of the more established ones, although these places come and go – something like seventy percent are said to close down within a year of opening. Most **café-bars** (often called *eet-cafés*) and some bars sell food – anything from snacks to an extensive menu. Another type of drinking spot, though increasingly rare, is the **tasting-house** (*proeflokaal*), originally the sampling rooms of small private *jenever* distillers, now tiny, stand-up places that often only sell spirits and close around 8pm. For listings of gay bars, see p.119.

## Bars

**Bars**, either brown or designer, tend to open at either 10am or 5pm; those that open in the morning do not close at lunchtime, and both stay open until around 1am during the week, 2am at weekends (sometimes until 3am). **Prices** are fairly standard everywhere, and the only time you'll pay through the nose is when there's music, or if you're foolish (or desperate) enough to step into the obvious tourist traps around Leidseplein and along Damrak. Reckon on paying roughly €1.50 for a standard-measure small beer, called a *pils* (or, if you get it in a straight glass, a *fluitje*). A tiny beer chaser, called a *kleintje pils*, costs the same.

### Old Centre

**De Buurvrouw** St Pieterspoortsteeg 29. Dark, noisy bar near the Allard Pierson Museum with a wildly eclectic crowd.

**Cul de Sac** Oudezijds Achterburgwal 99. Down a long alley in what used to be a seventeenth-century spice warehouse, this is a handy retreat from the Red Light District. Small, quiet and friendly.

**De Drie Fleschjes** Gravenstraat 16. Tasting house behind the Nieuwe Kerk for spirits and liqueurs, which would originally have been made on the premises. No beer, and no seats either; its clients tend to be well heeled or well soused (often both). Closes 8pm.

**Droesem** Nes 41. On a thin, theatre-packed alley behind the Dam, this is a highly recommended wine-bar, with your selection arriving in a carafe filled from a barrel, along with a high-quality choice of cheeses and other titbits to help it on its way.

**De Engelbewaarder** Kloveniersburgwal 59. Once the meeting place of Amsterdam's bookish types, this is still known as a literary café. Relaxed and informal, it has live jazz on Sunday afternoons.

**Hoppe** Spui 18. One of Amsterdam's longest-established and best-known bars, and one of its most likeable, frequented by the city's office crowd on their wayward way home. Summer is especially good, when throngs of drinkers spill out on to the street.

**De Jaren** Nieuwe Doelenstraat 20. One of the grandest of the grand cafés: overlooking the Amstel next to the university, with three floors and two terraces, this place oozes artsy style. All kinds of English reading material, too – this is one of the best places to examine the Sunday papers. Also serves reasonably priced food and has a great salad bar. A short walk from Muntplein. Daily from 10am.

## Grachtengordel West

**De Admiraal** Herengracht 319, at Wolvenstraat. Large and uniquely comfortable *proeflokaal*, with a vast range of liqueurs and spirits to explore.

**'t Arendsnest** Herengracht 90. Dutch beers only and no less than eight from the tap, selected with true dedication by the owner, who delights in filling you in on the relative properties of each. Open from 4pm.

**Belhamel** Brouwersgracht 60. Kitschy bar/restaurant with an Art Nouveau-style interior and excellent, though costly, French food. The main attraction in summer is one of the most picturesque views in Amsterdam.

**Hegeraad** Noordermarkt 34. Lovingly maintained old-fashioned brown café with a fiercely loyal clientele. The back room, furnished with red plush and paintings, is the perfect place to relax with a hot chocolate.

**Het Molenpad** Prinsengracht 653. Just north of Leidsegracht, this is one of the most appealing brown cafés in the city: long, dark and dusty. Also serves remarkably good food. Fills up with a young, professional crowd after 6pm. Recommended.

**De Prins** Prinsengracht 124. Boisterous professionals bar, with a wide range of drinks and a well-priced menu. A great place to drink in a nice part of town. Food served from 10am to 10pm.

**'t Smackzeyl** Brouwersgracht 101. Uninhibited drinking hole on the fringes of the Jordaan – on the corner of Prinsengracht. One of the few brown cafés to have Guinness on tap; also an inexpensive menu of light dishes.

**Spanjer & van Twist** Leliegracht 60. A gentle place which comes into its own on summer afternoons, with chairs lining the most peaceful stretch of water in the city centre.

**De Twee Zwaantjes** Prinsengracht 114. Just north of Leliegracht, this tiny Jordaan bar has live accordion music and raucous singing – love it or hate it. Oompah-pah all the way.

## Grachtengordel South

**De Duivel** Reguliersdwarsstraat 87. Tucked away on a street of bars and coffeeshops near Rembrandtplein, this is the only hip-hop café in Amsterdam, with continuous beats and a clientele to match. Opposite the hip-hop coffeeshop *Free I*.

**De Heeren van Aemstel** Thorbeckeplein 5 ☎020/620 2173 ⓦwww.deheerenvanaemstel.nl. Warm, atmospheric café with swinging soul and funk gigs almost every day.

**Het Land van Walem** Keizersgracht 449. One of Amsterdam's nouveau-chic cafés, just north of Leidsestraat: cool, light, and vehemently un-brown. The clientele is stylish, and the food is a kind of hybrid French–Dutch; there's also a wide selection of newspapers and magazines, including some in English. Breakfast in the garden during the summer is a highlight. Usually packed.

**Huyschkaemer** Utrechtsestraat 137. Attractive small local bar-restaurant on a street renowned for its eateries, just south of Rembrandtplein. A favourite watering-hole of arty students and gay folk. At weekends the restaurant space is turned into a dance floor.

**Vive la Vie** Amstelstraat 7. Near Rembrandtplein, this small, campy bar is patronized mostly, but not exclusively, by women and transvestites.

**De Zotte Proeflokaal** Raamstraat 29. Belgian hangout just north of Leidseplein, with food, liqueurs and hundreds of different types of beer.

# Coffeeshops

In Amsterdam a "**coffeeshop**" is advertising just one thing: **cannabis**. You might also be able to get coffee and a slice of cake, but the main activity in a coffeeshop is smoking. There are almost as many different kinds of coffeeshops as there are bars: some are neon–lit, with loud music and day–glo decor, but there are plenty of others that are quiet, comfortable places to have a quiet smoke and take it easy. See p.37 for more advice on what to expect, including a rundown on the legal situation and how to go about making your purchase. The establishments listed here are better than the average; most of them open around 10am or 11am and close around midnight.

**The Bulldog** Leidseplein 15 & Korte Leidsedwarsstraat 49, ⊛ www.bulldog.nl. The biggest and most famous of the coffeeshop chains, and a long way from its pokey Red Light District dive origins. The main Leidseplein branch (the Palace), housed in a former police station, has a large cocktail bar, coffeeshop, juice bar and souvenir shop, all with separate entrances. It's big and brash, not at all the place for a quiet smoke, though the dope they sell (packaged up in neat little brand-labelled bags) is reliably good.

**Dampkring** Handboogstraat 29 off Spui. Colourful, central coffeeshop with loud music and laid-back atmosphere, known for its good-quality hash.

**Global Chillage** Kerkstraat 51, ⊛ www .globalchillage.nl. Celebrated slice of Amsterdam dope culture, always comfortably filled with tie-dyed stoneheads propped up against the walls, so chilled they're horizontal. Just south of Leidsestraat.

**Grey Area** Oude Leliestraat 2, ⊛ www.greyarea.nl. North of Raadhuisstraat, this high-class coffeeshop has the menu (and prices) to match.

**Homegrown Fantasy** Nieuwezijds Voorburgwal 87a, ⊛ www.homegrownfantasy.org. Attached to the Dutch Passion seed company, this sells the widest selection of marijuana in Amsterdam, most of it Dutch.

**Kadinsky** Zoutsteeg 9 & Rosmarijnsteeg 9, just north of Spui. Accurate deals weighed out to a background of jazz dance. Chocolate chip cookies to die for. Both in the Old Centre.

**The Otherside** Reguliersdwarsstraat 6. Gay, but not exclusively so (in Dutch, "the other side" is a euphemism for gay) – a very popular spot.

**Paradox** 1e Bloemdwarsstraat 2, ⊛ www .paradoxamsterdam.demon.nl. If you're fed up with the usual coffeeshop food offerings of burgers, cheeseburgers or double cheeseburgers, *Paradox* satisfies the munchies with outstanding natural food, including spectacular fresh fruit concoctions. In the Jordaan. Closes 8pm.

**Rusland** Rusland 16. One of the first Amsterdam coffeeshops, a cramped but vibrant place that's a favourite with both dope fans and tea addicts (it has 43 different kinds). A cut above the rest. Just north of Muntplein.

**Siberië** Brouwersgracht 11. Set up by the former staff of *Rusland* and notable for the way it's avoided the over-commercialization of the larger chains. Very relaxed, very friendly, and worth a visit whether you want to smoke or not.

# Entertainment and nightlife

The quality of music, theatre and film on offer in Amsterdam is high and benefits from substantial government subsidies. **Classical music** is a particular forte – the city hosts two excellent orchestras – and although the **rock-pop** scene is not a patch on, say, New York or London, Amsterdam's unusually youthful population ensures that you're almost bound to stumble across fringe events and an inventive variety of affordable entertainment. Good venues to start are the major **multimedia centres**, which offer a taste of everything (see box).

For information about what's on, a good place to start is the **Amsterdam Uitburo**, or **AUB**, the cultural office of the city council, which is housed in a corner of the Stadsschouwburg theatre on Leidseplein (daily 10am–6pm, Thurs until 9pm; ☎0900 0191). They offer advice on anything remotely cultural, sell tickets and have listings magazines, including their own monthly *Uitkrant*, which is comprehensive and free, but in Dutch, and the VVV's bland English-language *What's On In Amsterdam* (€1.50). Take a look, too, at the AUB's *Uitlijst* noticeboards, which include a weekly update

## Multimedia centres

**Arena** 's-Gravensandestraat 51
☎020/694 7444, ⍈www.hotelarena.nl.
Part of the major reorganization of what
used to be the *Sleep-In* hostel, the Arena
is a multimedia centre featuring live music
and cultural events, with a bar, coffeeshop
and restaurant. Awkwardly located out
to the east of the centre (trams #6 and
#10), the Arena's intimate hall tends to
feature underground bands from around
the world. Start time around 9.30pm.

**Melkweg** ("Milky Way")
Lijnbaansgracht 234a ☎020/624 1777,
⍈www.melkweg .nl. Probably
Amsterdam's most famous entertainment venue, and these days one of the
city's prime arts centres, with a young,
hip clientele. A former dairy (hence the
name) just round the corner from
Leidseplein, it has two separate halls
for live music, putting on a broad range
of bands covering everything from

reggae to rock, all of which lean
towards the "alternative". Late on
Friday and Saturday nights, excellent
offbeat disco sessions go on well into
the small hours, often featuring the
best DJs in town. As well as the gigs,
there's also a fine monthly film programme, a theatre, gallery, and bar and
restaurant (Marnixstraat entrance) open
Wed–Sun 2–9pm (dinner from 5.30pm).
Concerts start between 9pm and 11pm.

**Paradiso** Weteringschans 6–8
☎020/626 4521, ⍈www.paradiso.nl. A
converted church near the Leidseplein
with bags of atmosphere, featuring
bands ranging from the up-and-coming
to the Rolling Stones. It has been known
to host classical concerts, as well as
debates and multimedia events (often
in conjunction with the nearby Balie
centre). Bands usually get started
around 9pm.

music gigs. The Dutch newspaper on pop music events, or grab a copy of the
cigarette-sponsored *Camel Uitlijst* from any café for the latest live *Het Parool* has
a Wednesday entertainment supplement, *Uit en Thuis*. In addition, cinemas
stock the fold-out "Week Agenda", which gives details of all films showing in
the city that week (Thurs to Wed).

**Tickets** for most performances can be bought at the Uitburo (for a modest
fee) and VVV offices, or reserved by phone through the AUB Uitlijn (☎0900
0191) for a one-percent booking fee. You can also buy tickets for any live music
event in the country at the GWK bureau de change offices at the Leidseplein
and within the main post office at Singel 250, again for around a one-percent
fee. Avoid the fee by asking direct at the venue.

## Rock music

Amsterdam is a regular tour stop for many major artists, and something of a
testing ground for current rock bands. **Dutch rock** was formerly dire, but local
groups can nowadays lay claim to both quality and originality: look out for the
celebrated Urban Dance Squad, the Osdorp Posse and other members of the
dance/hip-hop scene, or try to catch rock bands like Bettie Serveert. Mathilde
Santing is a popular draw whenever she plays. Bear in mind, too, that
Amsterdam is often on the tour circuit of up-and-coming British bands – keep
a sharp eye on the listings.

With the construction of the 50,000-seat ArenA out in the southeastern suburbs, Amsterdam has finally gained the stadium **rock venue** it has craved for
years. However, it's taking some time to catch on, and, aside from the Tina
Turner/Michael Jackson brand of superstar, most major touring acts still
choose to play at Rotterdam's Ahoy sports hall. The three dedicated music venues in Amsterdam city centre – the **Paradiso**, the **Melkweg** and the **Arena**

(not to be confused with the ArenA) – are all much smaller, and supply a constantly changing seven-days-a-week programme of music to suit all tastes and budgets; see the box on p.113 for details of all three. Alongside the main venues, the city's clubs, bars and multimedia centres sporadically host performances by live bands.

As far as **prices** go, for big names you'll pay anything between €25 and €50 a ticket; ordinary gigs cost €6-15, although some places charge a membership (*lidmaatschap*) fee on top. If no price is listed, entrance is usually free.

**Arena** 's-Gravensandestraat 51 ☎020/694 7444, ⓦwww.hotelarena.nl. See box on p.113.

**De Buurvrouw** Pieterspoortsteeg 29 ☎020/625 9654. Eclectic alternative bar featuring loud local bands. Located east of the Dam.

**De Heeren van Aemstel** Thorbeckeplein 5 ☎020/620 2173 ⓦwww.deheerenvanaemstel.nl. Warm, atmospheric café with swinging soul and funk gigs almost every day.

**Maloe Melo** Lijnbaansgracht 163 ☎020/420 4592. A dark, low-ceilinged bar, with a small back room featuring local bluesy acts.

**Meander Café** Voetboogstraat 5 ☎020/625 8430.

Daily live music of the soul, funk and blues variety. South of Spui.

**Melkweg** Lijnbaansgracht 234a ☎020/624 1777, ⓦwww.melkweg.nl. See box on p.113.

**Paradiso** Weteringschans 6–8 ☎020/626 4521, ⓦwww.paradiso.nl. See box on p.113.

**Winston Kingdom** Warmoesstraat 123 ☎020/623 1380, ⓦwww.winston.nl. Adventurous small venue, next to an hotel, featuring everything from live Ghanean percussion and symphonic rock to R&B, punk/noise and club nights. Poetry night once a month on Monday.

## Folk and world music

The Dutch **folk music** tradition in Amsterdam is virtually extinct, although interest has been revived of late by the duo Acda and de Munnik, and there are still one or two touring folk singers who perform traditional Jordaan *smartlappen* (torchsongs) at the Carré theatre (see opposite). Aside from this, however, your best bet is to try and catch the small but thriving scene continuing in a few sympathetic cafés like the *Hof van Holland*. More accessible is **world music**, for which there are a couple of good venues, principally the Melkweg and Akhnaton.

**Akhnaton** Nieuwezijds Kolk 25, off Nieuwendijk ☎020/624 3396, ⓦwww.akhnaton.nl. A "Centre for World Culture", specializing in African and Latin American music and dance parties. On a good night, the place heaves.

**Hof van Holland** Rembrandtplein 7 ☎020/623 4650. Traditional brown café with Dutch music and live performances throughout the week.

**Melkweg** Lijnbaansgracht 234a ☎020/624 1777, ⓦwww.melkweg.nl. See box on p.113.

**De Twee Zwaantjes** Prinsengracht 114 ☎020/625 2729. Tiny Jordaan bar whose live accordion music and raucous singing you'll either love or hate. Fun, in an oompah sort of way.

## Jazz

For **jazz** fans, Amsterdam can be a treat. Since the 1940s and 1950s, when American musicians began moving to Europe to escape discrimination, the city has had a soft spot for jazz. There's an excellent range of venues for such a small city, varying from tiny bars staging everything from Dixieland to avant-garde, to the Bimhuis – the city's major jazz venue – which plays host to both international names and home-grown talent. Saxophonists Hans Dulfer, Willem Breuker and Theo Loevendie, and percussionist Martin van Duynhoven, are among the Dutch musicians you might come across – and they're well worth catching if you get the chance.

Café Alto Korte Leidsedwarsstraat 115 ⓣ020/626 3249, ⓦwww.jazz-cafe-alto.nl. It's worth hunting out this legendary little jazz bar just off Leidseplein for the quality modern jazz every night from 10pm until 3am (and often much later). It's big on atmosphere, though slightly cramped, but entry is free, and you don't have to buy a (pricey) beer to hang out and watch the band.

Bimhuis Oude Schans 73–77 ⓣ020/623 1361, ⓦwww.bimhuis.nl. The city's premier jazz venue for almost thirty years, with an excellent auditorium and modern bar. Concerts Thurs–Sat, free sessions Mon–Wed. There's also free live music in the bar on Sun at 4pm. Concert tickets are for sale on the day only.

Bourbon Street Leidsekruisstraat 6, near Leidseplein ⓣ020/623 3440. Friendly bar with a relaxed atmosphere and quality blues and jazz nightly until 3am.

De Engelbewaarder Kloveniersburgwal 59 ⓣ020/625 3772. Excellent live jazz sessions on Sunday afternoon and evening.

Le Maxim Leidsekruisstraat 35, near Leidseplein ⓣ020/624 1920. Intimate piano bar that's been going since the 1960s, with live music nightly.

## Classical music and opera

There's no shortage of **classical music** concerts in Amsterdam, with two major orchestras based in the city, plus regular visits by other Dutch orchestras. Amsterdam's Royal Concertgebouw Orchestra (ⓦwww.concertgebouworkest .nl) remains one of the most dynamic in the world, and occupies one of the finest concert halls to boot. The other resident orchestra is the Dutch Philharmonic (ⓦwww.orkest.nl), based at the Beurs van Berlage concert hall, which has a wide symphonic repertoire and also performs with the Dutch Opera (ⓦwww.dno.nl) at the Muziektheater. As far as smaller classical ensembles go, Dutch musicians pioneered the use of period instruments in the 1970s, and Ton Koopman's Amsterdam Baroque Orchestra (ⓦwww.tonkoopman.nl) and Frans Brüggen's Orchestra of the 18th Century (ⓦwww.orchestra18c.com) are two internationally renowned exponents. Koopman's Amsterdam Baroque Choir and the Amsterdam Bach Soloists are also pre-eminent. As well as the main concert halls, a number of Amsterdam's churches (and former churches) host regular performances of classical and chamber music; both types of venue are listed below.

The most prestigious venue for **opera** is the Muziektheater (otherwise known as the Stopera) on Waterlooplein, which is home to the Dutch Opera company as well as the National Ballet. Visiting companies sometimes perform here, but more often at the Stadsschouwburg and the Carré theatre.

The best multi-venue event is June's annual **Holland Festival** (ⓦwww .hollandfestival.nl), which attracts the best domestic mainstream and fringe performers in all areas of the arts, as well as an exciting international line-up. One of the more interesting music-oriented events is the **piano recital** held towards the end of August on a floating stage outside the *Pulitzer Hotel* on the Prinsengracht. The whole area is floodlit and filled with small boats, and every available spot on the banks and bridges taken up – altogether a thoroughly atmospheric evening.

Beurs van Berlage Damrak 213 ⓣ020/627 0466, ⓦwww.beursvanberlage.net. The splendid interior of the former stock exchange (see p.74) has been put to use as a venue for theatre and music. The resident Dutch Philharmonic and Dutch Chamber Orchestra perform in the huge but comfortable Yakult Zaal and the AGA Zaal, the latter a very strange, glassed-in room-within-a-room.

Carré Theatre Amstel 115–125, near Rembrandtplein ⓣ020/622 5225, ⓦwww.theater-carre.nl. A splendid century-old structure (originally built for a circus) which represents the ultimate venue for Dutch folk artists, and hosts all kinds of top international acts: anything from Russian folk dance to *La Cage aux Folles*, with reputable touring orchestras and opera companies squeezed in between.

Concertgebouw Concertgebouwplein 2–6

☎020/671 8345, ⊛www.concertgebouw.nl. After a facelift and the replacement of its crumbling foundations in the early 1990s, the Concertgebouw is now looking – and sounding – better than ever. The acoustics of the Grote Zaal (Large Hall) are unparalleled, and a concert here is a wonderful experience. The smaller Kleine Zaal regularly hosts chamber concerts, often by the resident Borodin Quartet. Though both halls boast a star-studded international programme, prices are on the whole very reasonable, rarely over €20. Free Wednesday lunchtime concerts are held from Sept to May (doors open 12.15pm, arrive early), and in July and August there's a heavily subsidized series of summer concerts. Look out also for occasional swing/jazz nights.

**Engelse Kerk** Begijnhof 48 ☎020/624 9665. The church with the most extensive music programme: three to four performances a week, lunchtime, afternoon and evening, with the emphasis on period instruments.

**Muziektheater** Waterlooplein ☎020/625 5455,

⊛www.muziektheater.nl. Part of the ugly modern complex that includes the city hall. The Muziektheater's resident company, Dutch Opera, offers the fullest, and most reasonably priced, programme of opera in Amsterdam: tickets go very quickly.

**Oude Kerk** Oudekerksplein 23 ☎020/625 8284, ⊛www.oudekerk.nl. Hosts organ and carillon recitals, as well as occasional choral events. In summer, in conjunction with the Amstelkring Museum (see p.78), the church organizes a series of "walking" concert evenings, consisting of three separate concerts at different venues, with time for coffee and a stroll between each.

**Stadsschouwburg** Leidseplein 26 ☎020/624 2311, ⊛www.stadsschouwburgamsterdam.nl. These days somewhat overshadowed by the Muziektheater, but still staging significant opera and dance (it's the home theatre of The Hague's innovative company, the Dutch Dance Theatre), as well as visiting English-language theatre companies.

## Theatre and cabaret

Surprisingly for a city that functions so much in English, there is next to no English-language **theatre** – though English-speaking touring companies do regularly visit. The Stalhouderij is the only company working in English, performing in a broom-cupboard of a theatre in the Jordaan. English-language **comedy** and **cabaret**, on the other hand, has become a big thing in Amsterdam, spearheaded by the resident and extremely successful Boom Chicago comedy company. During the summer in particular, a number of small venues host mini-seasons of English-language stand-up comedy and cabaret featuring touring British performers.

**De Balie** Kleine Gartmanplantsoen 10 ☎020/623 2904, ⊛www.balie.nl. A multimedia centre for culture and the arts, located off the Leidseplein, which often plays host to drama, debates, international symposia and the like, sometimes in conjunction with the Paradiso (see p.113) next door.

**Boom Chicago** Korte Leidsedwarsstraat 12 ☎020/423 0101, ⊛www.boomchicago.nl. Something of a phenomenon in Amsterdam in recent years, this rapid-fire improv comedy troupe performs nightly to crowds of both tourists and locals, and has received rave reviews. With inexpensive food and the cheapest beer in town (in pitchers, no less!), the comedy need not be funny – but it is. Near Leidseplein.

**Marionette Theatre** Nieuwe Jonkerstraat 8 ☎020/620 8027, ⊛www.marionet.demon.nl.

Continues an old European tradition with its performances of operas by Mozart and Offenbach. Although they're touring the Netherlands and the rest of Europe for most of the year, the wooden marionettes return to their Amsterdam theatre near Centraal Station around May, October and Christmas. Call for details of performances, and to find out about their opera dinners.

**Melkweg** Lijnbaansgracht 234a, near Leidseplein ☎020/624 1777, ⊛www.melkweg.nl. See box on p.113. At the centre of the city's cultural scene, this is often the first-choice venue for foreign touring companies.

**Stadsschouwburg** Leidseplein 26 ☎020/624 2311, ⊛www.stadsschouwburgamsterdam.nl. Often hosts productions on tour from London or New York.

# Film

Most of Amsterdam's commercial **cinemas** are huge multiplexes showing a selection of general releases. There's also a scattering of film houses (*filmhuizen*) showing revival and arthouse films plus occasional retrospectives. Pick up a copy of the "Week Agenda" from any cinema for details of all films showing in the city. Weekly programmes change on Thursdays. Almost all foreign movies playing in Amsterdam are shown in their original language and subtitled in Dutch; movies are rarely dubbed into Dutch, but if they are, *Nederlands Gesproken* will be printed in the listings. In all cases, prices are very reasonable. Amsterdam's only regular cinematic event is the fascinating International Documentary Film Festival in December (ⓦ www.idfa.nl).

**Desmet** Plantage Middenlaan 4a ☏ 020/627 3434. A *filmhuis* on the border between mainstream and arthouse, but still showing a lot of contemporary European films. Tram #7, #9, or #14.
**Kriterion** Roeterstraat 170 ☏ 020/623 1708, ⓦ www.kriterion.nl. Stylish duplex cinema close to Weesperplein metro. Shows arthouse and quality commercial films, with late-night cult favourites. Friendly bar attached. Tram #6, #7, #10.
**Melkweg** Lijnbaansgracht 234a ☏ 020/624 1777, ⓦ www.melkweg.nl. See box on p.113. As well as music, art and dance, the Melkweg manages to maintain a consistently good monthly film and video programme, ranging from mainstream fodder through to obscure imports. Near Leidseplein.

**The Movies** Haarlemmerdijk 161, near Brouwersgracht ☏ 020/624 5790, ⓦ www .themovies.nl. A beautiful Art Deco cinema, and a charming setting for independent films. Worth visiting for the bar and restaurant alone, fully restored to their original sumptuousness. Late shows at the weekend. Tram #3.
**Rialto** Ceintuurbaan 338 ☏ 020/675 3994, ⓦ www.rialtofilm.nl. The only fully authentic arthouse cinema in Amsterdam, showing an enormously varied programme of European and world movies, supplemented by themed series and classics. Located south of the centre in the De Pijp area. Tram #3, #24 or #25.

# Clubs

**Clubbing** in Amsterdam is not the style-conscious business it is in many other capitals: most Amsterdam clubs – even the hip ones – aren't very expensive or difficult to get into. As for the music itself, Amsterdam is not at the cutting-edge: house is definitely the thing backed up by hip-hop, modern and retro funk, jazz and underground trance and trip-hop. Consequently, unless you go looking for something special, a random dip into a club will probably turn up mellow, undemanding beats.

That said, the late 1990s saw a craze for pumped-up, 200bpm+ **"gabber"** (pronounced the Dutch way, with a throaty "kh" at the beginning), laid on at vast arenas for thousands of shaven-headed speed-freaks. If you can find a gabber event (check for flyers at Midtown Records, Nieuwendijk 104), expect to pay a hefty €30 or more for entry, although it'll go on until dawn. Incidentally, there are now practically no illegal raves or parties in and around Amsterdam, and the last squat venues have finally made way for apartment buildings.

Most clubs have very reasonable **entry prices**, hovering between €10 and €20 at weekends and then dropping to between €5 and €12 during the week. A singular feature of Amsterdam clubbing however is that you tip the bouncer: if you want to get back into the same place next week, €2 or €5 in the palm of his hand will do very nicely thank you. Drinks prices are slightly more expensive than in cafés but not excessively hiked up, and, as in the rest of the city, toilets cost €0.25 or €0.50. Dress codes are minimal or non-existent.

Although all the places listed below **open** at 10pm or 11pm, there's not much point turning up anywhere before midnight; unless stated otherwise, everywhere stays open until 4am, or 5am on Friday and Saturday nights. For news and flyers about clubs, upcoming parties and raves, drop in to places like Clubwear House, Herengracht 265, and the Hair Police and Conscious Dreams, next door to each other at Kerkstraat 115 and 117. Alternatively, pick up the *Camel Uitlijst* in any café, which gives a pretty definitive listing of live music venues and clubs. For gay club listings, see opposite.

**Escape** Rembrandtplein 11 ☏ 020/622 3542, ⓦ www.escape.nl. What once used to be a tacky disco is now home to Amsterdam's hottest Saturday night, "Chemistry", every so often featuring Holland's top DJ, Dimitri. A vast hangar, with room for 2000 people although you may still have to queue. Closed Sun.

**iT** Amstelstraat 24 ☏ 020/625 0111, ⓦ www.it.nl. Large disco with a superb sound system. Has popular and glamorous gay nights on the weekend and during the week and mixed gay/straight nights on Friday. Recently refurbished in a cool New York club style, but still attracting a dressed up, uninhibited crowd.

**Mazzo** Rozengracht 114 ☏ 020/626 7500, ⓦ www.mazzo.nl. One of the city's hippest and most laid-back clubs, with a choice of music to appeal to all tastes. Perhaps the easiest-going bouncers in town. Open nightly.

**Melkweg** Lijnbaansgracht 234a, near Leidseplein ☏ 020/624 1777, ⓦ www.melkweg.nl. See box on p.113. After the bands have finished, this multimedia centre plays host to some of the most enjoyable theme nights around, everything from African dance parties to experimental jazz-trance.

**Ministry** Reguliersdwarsstraat 12 ☏ 020/623 3981, ⓦ www.ministry.nl. A flourishing club near Rembrandtplein that tries to catch a wide brand of party people and featuring quality DJs playing speed garage, house and R&B. Monday night jam session with the local jazz talent. Open late.

**Paradiso** Weteringschans 6–8 ☏ 020/623 7348, ⓦ www.paradiso.nl. See box on p.113. One of the principal venues in the city, which on Fridays hosts an unmissable club night, from midnight onwards. Also hosts one-off events – check listings. Near Leidseplein.

**Panama** Oostelijke Handelskade 4 ☏ 020/311 8686, ⓦ www.panama.nl. Host to a wide variety of funky gigs and themed club nights, also with a theatre and restaurant. Well out from the centre in the Oosterdok.

# Gay and lesbian Amsterdam

No other city in Europe accepts **gay and lesbian** people quite as readily as Amsterdam. Here, more than anywhere, it's possible to be openly gay and accepted by the straight community. Furthermore, Amsterdam has become a magnet for the international gay scene and boasts a dense sprinkling of advice centres, bars and clubs. The COC (pronounced "say-oh-say"), the national gay and lesbian pressure group (see also p.47) is one of the longest-lived, and largest, groups of its kind in the world.

The city has four recognized gay areas: Reguliersdwarsstraat with its trendy bars and clubs tends to attract a young, lively crowd, while quieter Kerkstraat is populated as much by locals as visitors. The streets just north of Rembrandtplein and along Amstel are a camp focus, as well as being home to a number of rent-boy bars, while Warmoesstraat, in the heart of the Red Light District, is cruisy and mainly leather- and denim-oriented. Many bars and clubs have darkrooms, which are legally obliged to provide safe-sex information and condoms.

The **clubs** listed below cater either predominantly or exclusively to a gay clientele. Some venues have both gay only and mixed gay/straight nights; there are, however, very few **lesbian**-only nights or clubs and bars.

For more information, get hold of a copy of the widely available Columbia Fun Map of Amsterdam. You could also invest in a copy of the Best Guide to Amsterdam, a comprehensive gay guidebook (in English) available from most gay bookshops worldwide. Among the many local gay newspapers and magazines, *Gay & Night* (⒲www.gay-night.nl), which comes out monthly and costs €3 in newsagents, features interviews and news. The fortnightly *Gay Krant* (⒲www.gaykrant.nl) has all the details you could conceivably need, including up-to-the-minute listings, though it is in Dutch only. You can pick up free brochures and maps in most of the gay bars and businesses. There's also the **Gay and Lesbian Switchboard** (daily 2pm–10pm; ☎020/623 6565, ⒲www.switchboard.nl), an English-speaking service, which provides help and advice. **MVS Radio** (⒲www.mvs.nl), Amsterdam's gay and lesbian radio station, broadcasts daily from 6pm on 106.8FM (or 88.1 via cable) – try and catch the English-language talk show Aliens (Fri 7–8pm, Sun 6–7pm).

## Gay advice centres and bookshops

**American Book Centre** Kalverstraat 185 ☎020/625 5537, ⒲www.abc.nl. Large general bookstore with a fine gay and lesbian section.
**COC** Rozenstraat 14 ☎020/626 3087, ⒲www.cocamsterdam.nl. Amsterdam branch of the national gay and lesbian organization, offering advice, contacts and social activities, plus a meeting point (Sat 1–5pm) and a large notice board. The general COC café (Wed & Thur 8pm–midnight, Fri 8pm–3am) is also the venue for more specific "themed" nights. One of the most popular women-only nights in Amsterdam, *Just Girls*, is held regularly on Saturday in both the café (10pm–3am) and the nightclub (10pm–3am), for under 24s only.
**Intermale** Spuistraat 251 ☎020/625 0009, ⒲www.intermale.nl. Well-stocked gay bookshop, with a wide selection of English, French, German and Dutch literature, as well as cards, newspapers and magazines. They have a worldwide mail order service.
**Schorerstichting** P.C. Hooftstraat 5 ☎020/662 4206, ⒲www.schorer.nl. Gay and lesbian counselling centre offering professional and politically conscious advice on identity, sexuality and lifestyle. Its clinic, held at the GG&GD, provides STD examinations and treatment.
**Vrolijk** Paleisstraat 135 ☎020/623 5142, ⒲www.vrolijk.nu. "The largest gay and lesbian bookstore on the continent", with a vast stock of new and secondhand books and magazines, as well as music and videos.

## Gay nightlife

### Bars

**Amstel Taveerne** Amstel 54. Well-established traditional gay bar near Rembrandtplein with regular singalongs. Always packed, and at its most vivacious in summer when the crowds spill out onto the street.
**April** Reguliersdwarsstraat 37. Pleasant place off Rembrandtplein that's on the itinerary of almost every gay visitor to Amsterdam. Lively and cosmopolitan, with a good selection of foreign newspapers, cakes and coffee, as well as booze.
**Camp Café** Kerkstraat 45. Pleasant mix of friendly locals and foreign visitors. Worth a visit for the ceiling alone, which is covered with a collection of beer mugs from around the world.
**Downtown** Reguliersdwarsstraat 31, off Rembrandtplein. A favourite with visitors. Relaxed and friendly, with inexpensive meals.
**Le Shako** 's-Gravelandseveer 2. Friendly bar in a quiet street on the Amstel, that sometimes gives special parties for hairy or bearded men and their lovers.

**The Web** St Jacobsstraat 6. Strict rubber, leather and denim bar with a dance floor, darkrooms and a pool table. Bear hug on Saturday. From 2pm.

### Clubs

**COC** Rozenstraat 14. Amsterdam branch of the national gay lobby organization that runs a very popular women-only disco and café every Sat from 8pm called "Just Girls", popular with younger lesbians. Pumping on Friday nights too (mixed men/women).
**Cockring** Warmoesstraat 96. Amsterdam's most popular – and very cruisey – gay men's disco, open nightly, with a light show and bars on two levels. Get there early at the weekend to avoid queuing. Free.
**Exit** Reguliersdwarsstraat 42. Along with *iT* (see overleaf), the city's most popular gay club, located off Rembrandtplein. Current sounds play nightly to an upbeat, cruisey crowd. Predominantly male, though women are admitted. Free.

iT Amstelstraat 24. Saturday night here really is IT, as the city's most glamorous transvestites come out to play and the place gets packed out (men only). Thursday night is free if you're gay, and Friday is a popular gay/straight night. Near Rembrandtplein.

**Vive la Vie** Amstelstraat 7. Café mainly for women, which shifts its tables at the weekend to make room for a dance floor.

**You II** Amstel 178. Amsterdam's first and long-awaited official lesbian dance club, located near Rembrandtplein, which opened its doors in the summer of 1999. Men are welcome, as long as they're accompanied by a woman.

# Shopping

Amsterdam has some excellent, unusual **speciality shops** and a handful of great **street-markets**; where the city scores is in its convenience – the centre concentrates most of what's interesting within its tight borders. What's more, the majority of shops are still individual businesses rather than chains, which makes a refreshing change from many big cities.

Broadly, the Nieuwendijk/Kalverstraat strip is where you'll find mostly dull, high-street fashion and mainstream department stores. Here, just off Dam square, is Magna Plaza, a massive shopping mall spread over five floors, complete with espresso bars and teenagers joy-riding on the escalators. Elsewhere, Koningsplein and Leidsestraat used to be home to the most exclusive shops, but many of them have fled south, though there is still a surprisingly good selection of affordable designer shoe- and clothes-stores here. The Jordaan, by comparison, is where many local artists have set up shop and you can find much original stuff of genuine interest here, from arts and crafts to adventurous clothes shops and affordable antiques. Less affordable antiques – the cream of Amsterdam's renowned trade – can be found in the Spiegelkwartier, centred on Nieuwe Spiegelstraat, while to the south, P.C. Hooftstraat and Van Baerlestraat play host to designer clothiers, upmarket ceramics stores and confectioners.

As for **opening hours**, the majority of shops take Monday morning off, not opening up until noon or 1pm and closing again at 6pm. On Tuesday, Wednesday and Friday, hours are the standard 9am to 6pm, while Thursday is late-opening night (*koopavond*), with most places staying open until 9pm. Saturday hours are normally 8.30 or 9am to 5 or 5.30pm, and all except the larger shops on the main streets are closed on Sunday.

Most small and medium-sized shops – and even some of the larger ones – won't accept **payment** by credit card: don't take it for granted in anywhere but the biggest or most expensive places. Shops that do will accept the usual range of major cards (American Express, Visa, Mastercard, and the rest), but never travellers' cheques.

## Books and magazines

Virtually all Amsterdam **bookshops** stock at least a small selection of English-language books, though prices are always inflated (sometimes dramatically). In the city centre it's possible to pick up most English **newspapers** the day they come out, and English-language **magazines** are available, too, from both newsstands and bookshops. The secondhand and antiquarian booksellers listed below are only the most accessible; for a comprehensive list, pick up the *Antiquarian & Secondhand Bookshops of Amsterdam* leaflet from any of them.

Gabled houses in Amsterdam △

American Book Center Kalverstraat 185. Vast stock, all in English, with lots of imported US magazines and books. Especially good gay section. Students get a ten-percent discount.

Art Book Van Baerlestraat 126. The city's best source of high-gloss art books, situated near the Van Gogh Museum. Check out also the shops of the main museums, particularly the Stedelijk.

Athenaeum Spui 14. Excellent all-round bookshop with an adventurous stock. Also the best source of international newspapers and magazines.

Jacob van Wijngaarden Overtoom 97. The city's best travel bookshop, with knowledgeable staff and a huge selection of books and maps. West across the Singelgracht from Leidseplein.

Pegasus Singel 367. The best politics collection in the city; near Spui.

Scheltema Holkema Vermeulen Koningsplein 20. Amsterdam's biggest and best bookshop. Six floors of absolutely everything. Open late and on Sundays; just south of Spui.

Waterstones Kalverstraat 152. Dutch branch of the UK high-street chain, with four floors of books and magazines. A predictable selection perhaps, but prices are sometimes cheaper here than elsewhere.

## Comics

Lambiek Kerkstraat 78. Amsterdam's largest and oldest comic bookshop and gallery, with an international stock and an enormous "comiclopedia" on the web.

## Secondhand and antiquarian

Book Traffic Leliegracht 50. An excellent and well-organized selection, run by an American.

Brinkman Singel 319. Stalwart of the Amsterdam book trade, Brinkman has occupied the same premises for forty years. Near Spui.

De Kloof Kloveniersburgwal 44. Enormous higgledy-piggledy used bookshop on four floors. Great for a rummage. Open Thursday to Saturday.

Vrouwen In Druk Westermarkt 5. Secondhand books, all by women authors.

# Clothes

When it comes to **clothes**, good-value, if uninspiring, mainstream styles are to be found amongst the shops and stores of Kalverstraat and Nieuwendijk. Classier stuff is on sale along Rokin and Leidsestraat, and the top-range designer places are clustered to the south on P.C. Hooftstraat and Van Baerlestraat. More interestingly, a reasonable range of one-off youth-oriented and **secondhand clothing** shops are dotted around the Jordaan, on Oude and Nieuwe Hoogstraat, and along the narrow streets that connect the major canals west of the Old Centre. In addition, the Waterlooplein flea market (see opposite) is a marvellous hunting ground for secondhand bargains. What follows is a brief rundown of some of the more alluring outlets.

Antonia Gasthuismolensteeg 12. A gathering of adventurous Dutch designers under one roof. Good on shoes and bags too. Just south of Raadhuisstraat.

Clubwear House Herengracht 265. The place for everything to do with clubbing in Amsterdam, from flyers to fabulous clothes. DJs play in-store on Saturdays.

Exota Nieuwe Leliestraat 32 & Hartenstraat 10. Good, fairly priced selection of simple new and used clothing, in the Jordaan and Grachtengordel respectively.

Jojo Huidenstraat 23 & Runstraat 9. Decent secondhand clothes from all eras. Particularly good for trench coats and 1950s jackets. Both outlets in the Grachtengordel.

Kelere Kelder Prinsengracht 285, at Raadhuisstraat. Goldmine for used alternative clothing. Fri–Sun 1–6pm.

Local Service Keizersgracht 400, near Spui. Men's and women's fashions. Ultra-trendy and expensive.

Reflections P.C. Hooftstraat 66. The absolute *crème de la crème*, with price tags to match. Near the Rijksmuseum.

Zipper Huidenstraat 7 & Nieuwe Hoogstraat 10. Used clothes selected for style and quality – strong on jeans and flares. Prices are high, but it's very popular, and everything is in good condition.

## Markets

Visiting an Amsterdam **market** is a must. There's a fine central flea market on Waterlooplein, a number of vibrant street markets selling fresh veg as well as clothes plus smaller, specialist markets devoted to everything from stamps to flowers.

**Albert Cuypmarkt** Albert Cuypstraat, between Ferdinand Bolstraat and Van Woustraat. The city's principal general goods and food market, with some great bargains to be had – check out Hilten's stall partway down on the right for the best deals on vegetables. Mon–Sat 9am–5pm. South of the city centre; trams #4, 16, 20, 24 or 25 from Centraal Station.

**Amstelveld** Prinsengracht. Flowers and plants in a pleasant canalside location near Utrechtsestraat, but much less of a scrum than the Bloemenmarkt. Friendly advice on what to buy too. Mon 10am–3pm.

**Bloemenmarkt** Singel. Stretching between Koningsplein and Muntplein, this very popular market specializes in flowers and plants, ostensibly for tourists, but is frequented by locals too. Bulbs for export (with health certificate). Mon–Sat 9am–5pm, but some stalls open on Sunday as well.

**Boekenmarkt** Spui. Wonderful rambling collection of secondhand books, with many an interesting find lurking in the unsorted boxes. Fri 10am–3pm.

**Boerenmarkt** Noordermarkt. Next to the Noorderkerk, this organic farmers' market offers all kinds of organically grown produce, plus amazing fresh breads, exotic fungi, fresh herbs and home-made mustards. Sat 9am–4pm.

**Kunstmarkt** Spui & Thorbeckeplein. Low-key but high-quality art market in two locations, with much lower prices than you'll find in the galleries; prints and occasional books as well. Neither operates during the winter. Both Sun 10am–3pm.

**Noordermarkt** Noordermarkt. Next to the Noorderkerk, this is a junk-lover's goldmine, with a general market on Mondays full of all kinds of bargains, tucked away beneath piles of useless rubbish. Get there early. There's also a farmers' produce market (Sat 9am–4pm; see Boerenmarkt above) and a bird market (Sat 8am–1pm), though the latter is not for the squeamish. General market operates Mon 9am–1pm, Sat 8am–3pm.

**Waterlooplein** Behind the Stadhuis. A real Amsterdam institution, and the city's best flea market by a long chalk. Sprawling and chaotic, it's the final resting-place for many a pair of yellow corduroys, not to mention antique junk of every description and secondhand records. Mon–Sat 9am–5pm.

## Department stores

**De Bijenkorf** Dam 1. Dominating the northern corner of Dam square, this is the city's biggest and most diverse department store, a huge bustling place that has an indisputably wide range and little snobbishness. Departments to head for include household goods, cosmetics and kidswear; there's also a good range of newspapers and magazines.
**HEMA** Nieuwendijk 174. A kind of Dutch Woolworth's, but of a better quality: good for stocking up on toiletries and other essentials, and occasional designer delights – it's owned by De Bijenkorf, and you can sometimes find the same items at knockdown prices. Surprises include wine and cheese in the back of the shop.

**Metz & Co** Keizersgracht 455. Swanky store, with the accent on Liberty prints, stylish ceramics and designer furniture of the kind that's exhibited in modern art museums: just the place to pick up a Rietveld chair. If your funds won't stretch quite that far, settle for a cup of coffee in the top-floor restaurant, which gives great views over the city.
**Vroom & Dreesmann** Kalverstraat 203, entrance also from Rokin. The main Amsterdam branch of a middle-of-the-road nationwide chain, just near Muntplein. It's pretty unadventurous, but check out the listening stands in the CD section on the top floor – the best place for a free Mozart recital with a canal view.

# Food and drink

**Albert Heijn** Koningsplein 4, just west of Muntplein, ⓦ www.ah.nl. Amsterdam's main branch of a nationwide supermarket chain, but still small and crowded. There are other central branches at Nieuwmarkt 18 and Waterlooplein 131, but prices are marginally lower in those further out of the centre – Vijzelstraat 117 and Westerstraat 79 for instance. Variable opening hours; currently the Koningsplein branch operates Mon–Sat 10am–10pm, Sun noon–6pm.

**De Bierkoning** Paleisstraat 125, at Dam square. The "Beer King" is aptly named: 850 different beers, with matching glasses to drink them from.

**Bon Bon Jeanette** Centraal Station. Organic, handmade, additive- and preservative-free, low-sugar chocolates – surprisingly delicious.

**Gimsel** Huidenstraat 19. Very central, with a good selection of fruit and vegetables and excellent bread. A short walk west of Spui.

**'t Goede Soet** Keizersgracht at Herenstraat. Designer chocolates, including handmade bonbons and the best *Hagelslag* chocolate sprinkles ever tasted.

**De Kaaskamer** Runstraat 7. Friendly cheese shop, with tapas and olives too.

**Kwekkeboom** Reguliersbreestraat 36 & Ferdinand Bolstraat 119. One of the city's most famous pastry shops, showered with awards. Not cheap, but you're paying for the chocolatier's equivalent of Gucci. Serving coffee too.

**De Natuurwinkel** Weteringschans 133. ⓦ www.denatuurwinkel.nl. Main branch of a chain selling only organic food – and thus a little more expensive than the mainstream. Tasty fruit and vegetables, also grains, pulses and Bon Bon Jeanette chocolates. Superb bread. Mon–Sat 7am–8pm, Thurs till 9pm, Sun 11am–6pm.

**Paul Année** Runstraat 25. The best wholegrain and sourdough breads in town, bar none – all made from organic grains. Try their homemade muesli.

# Miscellaneous speciality shops

**Appenzeller** Grimburgwal at Nes. State-of-the-art design jewellery, watches and spectacles.

**Broekmans & Van Poppel** Van Baerlestraat 92. Classical music specialist, with historical recordings, smaller labels, opera and sheet music.

**Concerto** Utrechtsestraat 54. New and used records and CDs in all categories; equally good on baroque as on grunge. The best all-round selection in the city, with the option to listen before you buy.

**Condomerie Het Gulden Vlies** Warmoesstraat 141. Condoms of every shape, size and flavour imaginable, in the heart of the Red Light District. All in the best possible taste.

**DOM** Spuistraat 281. Large design giftshop with tables and couches too. Something for every price.

**D. Eberhardt** Damstraat 16. Chinese and southeast Asian crafts, ceramics, clothes and jewellery.

**Donald E. Jongejans** Noorderkerkstraat 18. Hundreds of old spectacle frames, all of them without a previous owner. Supplied the specs for Bertolucci's *The Last Emperor*.

**Droog Design** Rusland 3. Founded in 1993, and has since made a serious contribution to the international debate about – and reinvention of – design. Some of their products have ended up in museum collections, and now there is this gallery-cum-shop-cum-meeting place.

**Elisabeth Hendriks** Nieuwe Spiegelstraat 61. A whole shop devoted to snuff bottles.

**Gerda's** Runstraat 16. Amsterdam is full of flower shops, but this one is the most imaginative and sensual.

**Kawsara Fall** Kerkstraat 143. The brothers Kane from Senegal have set up a shop with an enormous range of imported African drums, textiles and art.

**'t Klompenhuisje** Nieuwe Hoogstraat 9a. Amsterdam's best and brightest range of clogs.

**1001 Kralen** Rozengracht 54. "Kralen" means beads, and 1001 would seem a conservative estimate in this place in the Jordaan, which sells nothing but.

**P.G.C. Hajenius** Rokin 92. Long-established tobacconist selling its own and other brands of cigars, tobacco, smoking accessories, and every make of cigarette you can think of.

**Santa Jet** Prinsenstraat 7. Hand-made Latin American items, from collectibles to humorous knick-knacks, as well as religious icons.

**Studio Spui** Spui 4. A dedicated photo shop with bags, cameras, a one-hour photo service and passport pictures.

**'t Winkeltje** Prinsengracht 228. Jumble of cheap glassware and crockery, candlesticks, antique tin toys, kitsch souvenirs, old apothecaries' jars and flasks. Perfect for browsing.

**Witte Tandenwinkel** Runstraat 5. The "White Teeth Shop" sells wacky toothbrushes and just about every dental hygiene accoutrement you could ever need.

# Listings

**Banks and exchange** Amsterdam's banks usually offer the best deals; hours are Mon–Fri 9am–5pm. Postbanks (located in every branch of the post office) also open on Saturday morning. Outside these times, you'll need to go to one of the many bureaux de change scattered around town. GWK, whose main branches are at Centraal Station (7am–11pm) and Schiphol Airport (7am–10pm), offers competitive rates, as does Thomas Cook at Dam 23 (daily 9.15am–6.15pm), Damrak 1–5 (daily 9am–8pm) and Leidseplein 31a (daily 8.45am–6.15pm). Beware of other agencies though, as some offer great rates but then slap on an extortionate commission, or, conversely, charge no commission but give bad rates. The VVV tourist office also changes money as does American Express at Damrak 66 (Mon–Fri 9am–5pm, Sat 9am–noon).

**Bike rental** You can rent bikes at the following outlets: Bike City, Bloemgracht 70 ☎020/626 3721; Damstraat Rent-a-Bike, Damstraat 20 ☎020/625 5029; Holland Rent-a-Bike, Damrak 247 ☎020/622 3207; Koenders Take-a-Bike, Stationsplein 12 ☎020/624 8391; MacBike, Mr Visserplein 2 ☎020/620 0985; Macbike Too, Marnixstraat 220 ☎020/626 6964.

**Car parks** The following are all 24hr city-centre car parks: De Bijenkorf, Beursplein, off Damrak; Byzantium, Tesselschadestraat 1, near Leidseplein; De Kolk, Nieuwezijds Kolk 20; Muziektheater, Waterlooplein (under City Hall); Parking Plus Amsterdam Centraal, Prins Hendrikkade 20a, east of Centraal Station.

**Car rental** Avis, Nassaukade 380 ☎020/683 6061; Budget, Overtoom 121 ☎020/612 6066; Europcar, Overtoom 51 ☎020/683 2123; Hertz, Overtoom 333 ☎020/612 2441.

**Children** The pick of the city's attractions that are especially popular with children are the Artis Zoo, Plantage Kerklaan 38–40 (tram #6, #9 or #14; see p.97), taking in aquariums, a planetarium and a Children's Farm; and NEMO (Oosterdok; see p.99), an Interactive "centre for human creativity". *The Pancake Bakery*, Prinsengracht 191 (☎020/625 1333), is a popular café that caters well for families, where kids are kept entertained at the table with pens and paper and free novelty toys.

**Consulates** UK, Koningslaan 44 ☎020/676 4343; USA, Museumplein 19 ☎020/575 5309. For full listings, see p.19.

**Emergencies** Police, Fire, Ambulance ☎112.
**Internet access** See box on p.59.
**Laundry** The Clean Brothers, Kerkstraat 56 (daily 7am–9pm) is the city's best self-service launderette (*wassalon*), with a sizeable load currently €4 to wash, €1 per 30min in the drier and soap for €0.50; they also do service washes, dry-cleaning, ironing, etc. There is also a branch at Jacob van Lennepkade 179. Other launderettes are to be found at: Elandsgracht 59 (Jordaan), Warmoesstraat 30 and Oude Doelenstraat 12 (Red Light District).
**Left luggage** Centraal Station has coin-operated lockers and a staffed left luggage office. See p.57.
**Lost property** For items lost on the trams, buses or metro, contact GVB Head Office, Prins Hendrikkade 108–114 (Mon–Fri 9am–4pm; ☎020/460 5858). For property lost on a train, go to the Gevonden Voorwerpen office at the nearest station; Amsterdam's is at Centraal Station, near the left luggage lockers (☎020/557 8544; 24hr). After three days all unclaimed property goes to the Central Lost Property Office at 2e Daalsedijk 4, Utrecht (☎030/235 3923), and costs €7 per item to pick up. If you lose something in the street or a park, try the police lost property at Stephensonstraat 18 (Mon–Fri noon–3.30pm; ☎020/559 3005). Schiphol Airport's lost and found number is ☎020/601 2325 (Mon–Fri 7.30am–5.30pm, Sat & Sun 9am–5pm).
**Moped rental** Moped Rental Service, Willemsstraat 133 ☎020/422 0266.
**Police** Headquarters at Elandsgracht 117 ☎020/559 9111.
**Post office** Main branch at Singel 250 (Mon–Fri 9am–6pm, Thurs until 8pm, Sat 10am–1.30pm), on the corner with Raadhuisstraat.
**Public transport** Information on ☎0900 9292.
**Women's contacts** Amsterdam has an impressive feminist infrastructure: there are support groups, health centres and businesses run by and for women. A good starting point to find out what's going on is Het Vrouwenhuis, Nieuwe Herengracht 95 (Mon–Fri 11am–4pm; ☎020/625 2066), an organizing centre for women's activities and cultural events. Xantippe Unlimited, Prinsengracht 290, is a women's bookshop with a wide selection of feminist titles in English.

# Travel details

## Trains

**Amsterdam CS (Centraal Station) to:** Alkmaar (every 15–20min; 30min); Amersfoort (every 30min; 35min); Apeldoorn (every 30min; 1hr); Arnhem (every 30min; 1hr 10min); Den Helder (every 30min; 1hr 10min); Dordrecht (every 30min; 1hr 30min); Eindhoven (every 30min; 1hr 30min); Enkhuizen (every 30min; 1hr); Groningen (every 30min; 2hr 20min); Haarlem (every 10min; 15min); The Hague/Den Haag (every 15–20min; 50min); Hoorn (every 30min; 40min); Leeuwarden (hourly; 2hr 25min); Leiden (every 15–20min; 35min); Maastricht (hourly; 2hr 30min); Nijmegen (every 30min; 1hr 30min); Rotterdam (every 30min; 1hr 10min); Schiphol Airport (every 15min; 20min); Utrecht (every 30min; 30min); Vlissingen (hourly; 2hr 45min); Zwolle (hourly; 1hr 20min).

## Buses

**Amsterdam CS (Centraal Station) to:** Edam (#110; every 30min; 40min); Marken (#111; every 30min; 30min); Monnickendam (#111; every 30min; 20min); Volendam (#110; every 30min; 30min). **Amsterdam Amstel Station to:** Muiden (#136; every 30min; 40min); Naarden (#136; every 30min; 55min).

# Noord-Holland

CHAPTER 2    # Highlights

✳ **Frans Hals Museum, Haarlem** Outstanding art gallery, set in this appealingly slow-paced town just west of Amsterdam. See p.134

✳ **Edam** Perhaps the prettiest village in the Netherlands, with a web of tiny canals overlooked by decoratively gabled houses. See p.140

✳ **Enkhuizen** A charming former Zuider Zee port at the end of the train line, with a good deal of character and a relaxed, easygoing air. See p.145

✳ **Die Drie Haringhe, Enkhuizen** Wonderful seafood restaurant, serving freshly caught pike and perch. See p.149

✳ **Zaanse Schans** Recreated eighteenth-century Dutch village, with seven working windmills. See p.151

✳ **Bergen-aan-Zee** Amiable coastal resort boasting a long, sandy beach and access to acres of pristine dunes and woodland. See p.155

✳ **Texel** Most accessible of the string of islands off the northern Dutch coast, offering brisk walks and bike-rides to blow the cobwebs away. See p.156

✳ **Naarden** Attractive fortified village, an easy day-trip just east of Amsterdam. See p.159

# Noord-Holland

S tretching north from Amsterdam to the island of Texel, the Dutch province of **NOORD-HOLLAND** is, with every justification, one of the country's most visited regions. Though not nearly as densely populated as its sister province Zuid-Holland to the south (see Chapter 3), it's still a populous area and boasts a string of prime attractions, detailed at Ⓦ www.noord-holland-tourist.nl. The landscape is typically Dutch, the countryside for the most part a familiar polder scene of flat fields, cut by trenches and canals, stretching far into the distance, the wide horizons broken only by the odd farmhouse or windmill. To the west, the province is protected from the sea by a long belt of sand dunes, which are themselves shielded by long and broad sandy beaches, while the province's east coast borders the Markermeer and IJsselmeer, formerly the Zuider Zee (see box on p.138). Here, along this deeply indented coast, lie a trio of old seaports, which sport the vestiges of a glorious past in their picturesquely preserved town centres.

The majority of Noord-Holland is easily visited by means of day-trips from Amsterdam, but such cursory explorations do the province few favours. The urban highlight is undoubtedly **Haarlem**, an easy day-trip west from Amsterdam but in itself definitely worth treating as an overnight stop. Haarlem also gives ready access to some wild stretches of dune and beach – at their prettiest amidst the **Nationaalpark de Kennemerduinen** – and one of the country's largest coastal resorts in **Zandvoort**.

For investigating the bulk of the province, however, there are two obvious routes: along the east coast or, inland, from Zaandam through to the island of Texel, with possible detours to several west-coast resorts along the way. The east-coast route starts with the villages nearest Amsterdam – **Marken** and **Volendam** – kitsch places full of tourists in search of clogs and windmills during summer, but with considerable charm if you can visit off-season. Neighbouring **Edam** is, however, even better – indeed, it's one of the region's most appealing country towns and one which has somehow managed to elude the tourist hordes. Further north, **Hoorn** and **Enkhuizen** were once major Zuider Zee ports, whose historic wealth, based on ship-building and the Baltic trade, is reflected in a liberal scattering of handsome old buildings. Modern development has hacked Hoorn around, but Enkhuizen remains a fascinating town and the possessor of one of the country's best open-air museums, the Zuiderzeemuseum. The inland route starts a short train ride from Amsterdam in the Zaanstad conurbation, whose chief attraction is the antique windmills and canals of the recreated Dutch village of **Zaanse Schans**. Further up the line, **Alkmaar** is usually visited as a day-trip for its much vaunted Friday cheese market, but is worth a longer visit if

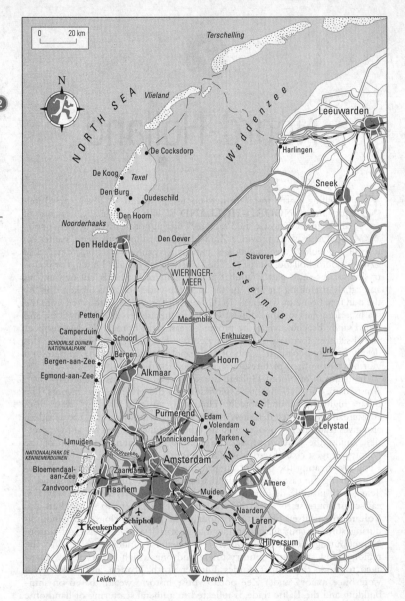

you're keen to experience small-town life. Alkmaar also makes a good base for visiting the west coast, especially the trim little resort of **Bergen-aan-Zee**. Beyond, in the far north of the province, the island of **Texel** is the most accessible and busiest of the Waddenzee islands. It's very crowded during summer, but don't be put off by the numbers: with a bit of walking you can readily find places well off the beaten track – and far away from the hustle and bustle of Amsterdam.

Most of Noord-Holland is located, logically enough, north of Amsterdam, but the borders of the province also dip round south of the city, taking in an assortment of leafy suburbs. Those to the southeast of Amsterdam are collectively known as **Het Gooi**, where the highlight is the old fortified town of **Naarden**.

Getting around Noord-Holland by **public transport** is easy enough, with **trains** linking all the major settlements and **buses** filling in the gaps. If you want to continue north out of the province, the two **dykes** that enclose the Markermeer and the IJsselmeer carry handy road links. The former connects Enkhuizen with Lelystad on the reclaimed Flevoland polders (see p.274), and the latter, the Afsluitdijk, makes the thirty-kilometre trip from Den Oever to the province of Friesland (see Chapter 4).

# Haarlem and around

Though only fifteen minutes from Amsterdam by train, **HAARLEM** has a very different pace and feel from its big-city neighbour. Founded on the banks of the River Spaarne in the tenth century, the town first prospered when the counts of Holland decided to levy shipping tolls here, but later it developed as a cloth-making centre. In 1572, the townsfolk sided with the Protestant rebels against the Habsburgs, a decision they must have regretted when a large Spanish army led by Frederick of Toledo besieged them in December of the same year. The siege was a desperate affair that lasted for eight months, but finally the town surrendered after receiving various assurances of good treatment – assurances which Frederick promptly broke, massacring over two thousand of the Protestant garrison and all their Calvinist ministers. Recaptured in 1577 by the Protestant army of William the Silent, Haarlem went on to enjoy its greatest prosperity in the seventeenth century, becoming a centre for the arts and home to a flourishing school of **painters**. Nowadays, it's an easily absorbed town of around 150,000 people, with a good-looking centre studded with fine old buildings and home to the outstanding **Frans Hals Museum**, located in the almshouse where the artist spent his last, and for some his most brilliant, years.

Well worth an afternoon in itself – maybe even an overnight stay if you're tired of the crowds and grime of Amsterdam – Haarlem is also a short train ride from two coastal resorts: the clumsy modern town of **Zandvoort-aan-Zee**, redeemed by its long sandy beach, and **Bloemendaal-aan-Zee**, where the beach is the main event. Both are within easy striking distance of the undeveloped dunes and seashore of the nearby **Nationaalpark de Kennemerduinen**.

## Arrival, information and accommodation

With fast and frequent services from Amsterdam, Haarlem's splendid **train station**, a fine example of the Amsterdam School of architecture, is located on the north side of the city centre, about ten minutes' walk from the main square, the Grote Markt. **Bike rental** is available at the train station for €6 per day. The **bus station** is in front of the train station on Stationsplein and the **VVV** is adjacent (April–Sept Mon–Fri 9am–5.30pm, Sat 9.30am–3.30pm; Oct–March Mon–Fri 9.30am–5.30pm, Sat 10am–2pm; ☏0900/616 1600, ⊕www.vvvzk.nl). The VVV issues free city maps and brochures and has a small supply of **private rooms**, but note that they are mostly on the outskirts of town. There are **campsites** dotted along the coast in and around Zandvoort; see p.136.

## Hotels

**Amadeus** Grote Markt 10 ☏ 023/532 4530, ⓦ www.amadeus-hotel.com. Friendly two-star family hotel with plain but perfectly comfortable en-suite rooms. The front bedrooms have enjoyable views over the main square, their only drawback being the pigeons thrashing around on the window sill. ❸

**Carillon** Grote Markt 27 ☏ 023/531 0591, ⓕ 531 4909. Inexpensive place opposite the Grote Kerk with frugal modern rooms, but friendly atmosphere. ❷

**Golden Tulip Lion d'Or** Kruisweg 34 ☏ 023/532 1750, ⓕ 532 9543. Smart chain hotel housed in a sturdy nineteenth-century building close to the train station. Very comfortable rooms, which offsets the dreariness of the setting. ❻

**Joops** Oude Groenmarkt 20 ☏ 023/532 2208, ⓕ 532 9549. Large if somewhat spartan rooms immediately behind the Grote Kerk. ❷

## Hostel

**Stayokay Haarlem** Jan Gijzenpad 3 ☏ 023/537 3793, ⓦ www.stayokay.com/haarlem. HI hostel near the sports stadium about 3km north of the town centre. Dorm beds €17. Take bus #2 from the station – a ten-minute journey.

# The Town

At the heart of Haarlem is the **Grote Markt**, a wide and attractive open space flanked by an appealing ensemble of Gothic and Renaissance architecture, including an intriguing if exceptionally garbled **Stadhuis**, whose turrets and towers, balconies and galleries were put together in piecemeal fashion between the fourteenth and the seventeenth centuries. At the other end of the Grote Markt stands a **statue** of a certain Laurens Coster (1370–1440), who, Haarlemmers insist, is the true inventor of printing. Legend tells of him cutting a letter "A" from the bark of a tree, dropping it into the sand by accident, and, hey presto, he realized how to create the printed word. The statue shows him earnestly holding up the wooden letter, but most historians agree that it was actually the German Johannes Gutenberg who invented printing, in the early 1440s.

The statue stands in the shadow of the **Grote Kerk** or **Sint Bavokerk** (Mon–Sat 10am–4pm; Sept–March closes 3.30pm; €2), a mighty Gothic structure supported by heavy buttresses. The church is surmounted by a good-looking lantern tower directly above the transept crossing, which is actually made of wood, but clad in lead – the original stone version had to be dismantled when, in 1514, it proved too heavy for its supports and threatened to crash down. Finally finished in 1538, after 150 years, the church dwarfs the surrounding clutter of higgledy-piggledy streets, and serves as a landmark from almost anywhere in town. If you've been to the Rijksmuseum in Amsterdam (see p.99), the Grote Kerk may seem familiar, at least from the outside, since it turns up in several paintings of Haarlem by the seventeenth-century artist Gerrit Berckheyde – only the black-coated burghers are missing.

The church **interior** is breathtakingly cavernous, its beauty enhanced by the stark, white power of the vaulting. The present entrance (round the back on Oude Groenmarkt) leads into the east end of the church, where the southern ambulatory contains the tombstone of the painter Pieter Saenredam and the choir that of Frans Hals. Nearby, next to the south transept, is the **Brewers' Chapel**, where the central pillar bears two black marks – one showing the height of a local giant, the 2.64m-tall Daniel Cajanus, who died in 1749, the other the 84cm-high dwarf Simon Paap from Zandvoort. Further west still, on the north side of the nave, is the **Dog Whippers' Chapel**, built for the men employed to keep dogs out of the church, and now separated from the nave by an iron grille. At the west end of the church, the mighty Christian Müller **organ** was four years in the making, completed in Amsterdam in 1738. It is

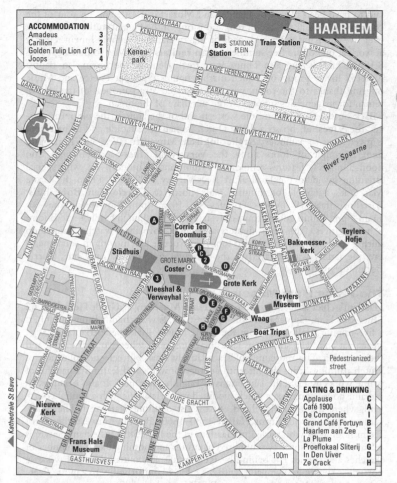

**ACCOMMODATION**

| | |
|---|---|
| Amadeus | 3 |
| Carillon | 2 |
| Golden Tulip Lion d'Or | 1 |
| Joops | 4 |

**EATING & DRINKING**

| | |
|---|---|
| Applause | C |
| Café 1900 | A |
| De Componist | I |
| Grand Café Fortuyn | B |
| Haarlem aan Zee | E |
| La Plume | F |
| Proeflokaal Sliterij | G |
| In Den Uiver | D |
| Ze Crack | H |

0     100m

## Excursions from Haarlem

Woltheus Cruises, by the river at Spaarne 11 (☎023/535 7723, ⓦwww
.woltheus-haarlem.nl), operate several **boat trips** from Haarlem, the most interesting of which is a once- or twice-weekly excursion to Zaanse Schans (July–Sept;
€14; takes 7hr; see p.151). Haarlem is also just a quick bus ride from the Keukenhof
Gardens (see p.172), which lie about 13km south of town.

Just north of Haarlem is the village of **Spaarndam**, which has little to recommend
it other than a well-known statue of **Hans Brinker**, the young lad who supposedly
saved the district from disaster by sticking his finger into a hole in the dyke.
Disappointingly, although the tale has the ring of truth, it's all fictitious – invented by
the American writer Mary Mapes Dodge in her 1873 children's book, *The Silver
Skates*. The monument to the heroic little chap was unveiled in 1950, more, it seems,
as a tribute to the opportunistic Dutch tourist industry than anything else.

said to have been played by Handel and Mozart (the latter on his tour of the country in 1766, at the age of ten) and is one of the biggest in the world, with over five thousand pipes and loads of snazzy Baroque embellishment. Hear it at work at one of the free summer **organ recitals** (mid-May to mid-Sept Tues 8.15pm; July & Aug also Thurs 3pm; free). Beneath the organ, Jan Baptist Xavery's lovely group of draped marble figures represent Poetry and Music offering thanks to the town, which is depicted as a patroness of the arts, in return for its generous support in the purchase of the organ.

Back outside, just beyond the western end of the church, the old meat market, the **Vleeshal**, boasts a flashy Dutch Renaissance facade and its basement is given over to a modest **Archeologisch Museum** (Wed–Sun 1pm–5pm; free). A couple of doors along, the **Verweyhal** (Tues–Sat 11am-5pm, Sun noon-5pm; €4) features temporary exhibitions of modern art, with special attention given to the local artist Kees Verwey (1900–95). From the Grote Markt, it's a couple of minutes' walk north to **Corrie Ten Boomhuis**, Barteljorisstraat 19 (May–Oct Tues–Sat 10am–4pm; Nov–April Tues–Sat 11am–3pm; 45min guided tours only; free), where a Dutch family – the Booms – hid fugitives, Resistance fighters and Jews above their watchmaking shop during World War II. The guided tour is instructive and moving in equal measure: the family was betrayed to the Gestapo in 1944 and only one, Corrie Boom, survived.

### The Frans Hals Museum

Haarlem's chief attraction, the **Frans Hals Museum** at Groot Heiligland 62 (Tues–Sat 11am–5pm, Sun noon–5pm; €5.40; Ⓦ www.franshalsmuseum.nl), is a five-minute stroll south from the Grote Markt – take pedestrianized Lange Veerstraat and keep straight as far as Gasthuispoort, where you turn right and then first left. The museum holds a relatively small but eclectic collection of Dutch paintings from the fifteenth century onwards and features a handful of prime works by Hals; the labelling is in English and Dutch. It also occupies an old almshouse complex, a much modified red-brick *hofje* with a central courtyard, where the aged Hals lived out his last destitute years on public funds. Little is known about **Frans Hals** (c.1580–1666). Born in Antwerp, the son of Flemish refugees who settled in Haarlem in the late 1580s, his extant oeuvre is relatively small – some two hundred paintings and nothing like the number of sketches and studies left behind by Rembrandt. His outstanding gift was as a portraitist, showing a sympathy with his subjects and an ability to capture fleeting expression that some say even Rembrandt lacked. Seemingly quick and careless flashes of colour characterize his work, blended into a coherent whole to create a set of marvellously animated seventeenth-century figures.

The museum begins with the work of other artists: first comes a small group of late fifteenth- and sixteenth-century paintings, the most prominent of which are a triptych from the **School of Hans Memling** and a polished *Adam and Eve* by **Jan van Scorel**. Afterwards, Room 10 features a couple of paintings by the **Haarlem mannerists**, including a work by **Karel van Mander** (1548–1606), leading light of the Haarlem School and mentor of many of the city's most celebrated painters. There's also a curious painting by Haarlem-born **Jan Mostaert** (1475–1555), his *West Indian Scene* depicting a band of naked, poorly armed natives trying to defend themselves against the cannon and sword of their Spanish invaders; the comparison with the Dutch Protestants is obvious. Moving on to Room 11, **Cornelis Cornelisz van Haarlem** (1562–1638) best followed van Mander's guidelines: his *Wedding of Peleus and Thetis* is an appealing rendition of what was then a popular subject, though

Cornelisz gives as much attention to the arrangement of his elegant nudes as to the subject. This marriage precipitated civil war amongst the gods and was used by the Dutch as a warning against discord, a call for unity during the long war with Spain. Similarly, and also in Room 11, the same artist's *Massacre of the Innocents* connects the biblical story with the Spanish siege of Haarlem in 1572.

**Frans Hals** was a pupil of van Mander too, though he seems to have learned little more than the barest rudiments from him. The Hals paintings begin in earnest in Room 21 amongst a set of "Civic Guard" portraits – group portraits of the militia companies initially formed to defend the country from the Spanish, but which later became social clubs for the gentry. Getting a commission to paint one of these portraits was a well-paid privilege – Hals got his first in 1616 – but their composition was a tricky affair and often the end result was dull and flat. With great flair and originality, Hals made the group portrait a unified whole instead of a static collection of individual portraits, his figures carefully arranged, but so cleverly as not to appear contrived. For a time, Hals himself was a member of the Company of St George, and in the *Officers of the Militia Company of St George* he appears in the top left-hand corner – one of his few self-portraits. Hals' later paintings are darker, more contemplative works, closer to Rembrandt in their lighting and increasingly sombre in their outlook. In Room 27, amongst several portraits of different groups of regents, is Hals' *Regents of St Elizabeth Gasthuis*, a serious but benign work of 1641 with a palpable sense of optimism, whereas his twin *Regents* and *Regentesses of the Oudemannenhuis*, currently displayed in Room 21 but often shunted around, is deep with despair. The latter were commissioned when Hals was in his eighties, a poor man despite a successful painting career, hounded for money by the town's tradesmen and by the mothers of his illegitimate children. As a result he was dependent on the charity of people like those depicted here: their cold, self-satisfied faces staring out of the gloom, the women reproachful, the men only marginally more affable. The character just right of centre in the *Regents* painting has been labelled (and indeed looks) drunk, although it is inconceivable that Hals would have depicted him in this condition; it's more likely that he was suffering from some kind of facial paralysis, and his jauntily cocked hat was simply a popular fashion of the time. There are those who claim Hals had lost his touch by the time he painted these pictures, yet their sinister, almost ghostly power as they face each other across the room, suggests quite the opposite. Van Gogh's remark that "Frans Hals had no fewer than 27 blacks" suddenly makes perfect sense.

Look out also for the geometric church interiors of **Pieter Saenredam** in Room 22 and a berserk *Dutch Proverbs* by **Pieter Brueghel the Younger** in Room 24.

### Along the River Spaarne

Beyond the Frans Hals Museum, at the end of Groot Heiligland, turn left along the canal and it's a short walk east to the **River Spaarne**, whose gentle curves mark the eastern periphery of the town centre. Turn left again, along riverside Turfmarkt and its continuation Spaarne, to reach the surly stonework of the **Waag** and then the country's oldest museum, the **Teylers Museum**, located in a grand old building at Spaarne 16 (Tues–Sat 10am–5pm, Sun noon–5pm; €4.50; ⓦ www.teylersmuseum.nl). Founded in 1774 by a wealthy local philanthropist, one Pieter Teyler van der Hulst, the museum should appeal to scientific and artistic tastes alike. It contains everything from fossils, bones and crystals to weird, H.G. Wells-type technology (including an enormous eighteenth-century electrostatic generator) and sketches and line drawings by

Michelangelo, Raphael, Rembrandt and Claude, among others. The drawings are covered to protect them from the light, but don't be afraid to pull back the curtains to take a peek. Look in, too, on the rooms beyond, filled with work by eighteenth- and nineteenth-century Dutch painters, principally Breitner, Israëls, Weissenbruch and, not least, Wijbrand Hendriks, who was once the keeper of the art collection here. Teyler also bestowed his charity on the riverside **Teylers Hofje**, a little way around the bend of the Spaarne at Koudenhorn 64. With none of the cosy familiarity of the town's other *hofjes*, this is a grandiose affair, a Neoclassical edifice dating from 1787 and featuring solid columns and cupolas. Nearby, the elegant fifteenth-century tower of the **Bakenesserkerk** (no public access), on Vrouwestraat, is a flamboyant, vaguely oriental protrusion on the Haarlem skyline.

### West of the centre

Two other sights that may help structure your wanderings are on the west side of the centre. Van Campen's **Nieuwe Kerk**, just west of the Frans Hals Museum on Kerkstraat, was added – rather unsuccessfully – onto Lieven de Key's bulbed tower in 1649, though the interior possesses a crisp soberness that acts as an antidote to the soaring heights of the Grote Kerk. Just beyond, and much less self-effacing, the Roman Catholic **Kathedrale St Bavo** (April–Sept Tues–Fri 10am–4pm, Sat-Mon 1-4pm; free) is one of the largest ecclesiastical structures in the Netherlands. Designed by Joseph Cuypers, son of P.J. Cuypers (see p.99), and built on the west bank of the Leidsevaart canal between 1895 and 1906, it is broad and spacious inside, with cupolas and turrets crowding around an apse reminiscent of Byzantine churches, the whole surmounted by a distinctive copper dome.

## Eating and drinking

Haarlem's best **restaurants** are conveniently clustered around the Grote Markt and on Oude Groenmarkt, round the back of the Grote Kerk. Excellent options include the *Applause*, a chic little bistro serving up Italian food at Grote Markt 23a (☎023/531 1425), with main courses hovering around €20, as well as the equally smart *De Componist*, whose Art Nouveau premises – and tasty Dutch menu - are at Korte Veerstraat 1 (☎023/532 8853). There's also the eccentric *Haarlem aan Zee*, Oude Groenmarkt 10 (☎023/531 4884), where the interior is done out like a Dutch beach and they serve a splendid range of seafood, with main dishes averaging around €20–25. Finally, the popular and very affordable *Restaurant La Plume*, Lange Veerstraat 1 (☎023/531 3202), offers a range of appetizing dishes from pastas through to traditional Dutch.

For a **drink**, *In Den Uiver*, just off the Grote Markt at Riviervismarkt 13, is a lively and extremely appealing bar offering occasional live music, while the *Grand Café Fortuyn*, Grote Markt 21, is a quieter, cosier café-bar with charming 1930s decor, including a tiled entrance and dinky little glass cabinets preserved from its days as a shop. Alternatively, the amenable and typically Dutch *Proeflokaal Sliterij* is an intimate bar at Lange Veerstraat 7, whilst *Café 1900*, Barteljorisstraat 10, has long been a popular café-bar, serving drinks and light meals in an attractive turn-of-the-century interior. Last of all, *Ze Crack*, at the junction of Lange Veerstraat and Kleine Houtstraat, is a dim, youthful and smoky bar with good sounds.

## Zandvoort and Bloemendaal-aan-Zee

Haarlem is just 5km from the coast at **ZANDVOORT**, a major seaside resort whose agglomeration of modern apartment blocks strings along the seashore behind a wide and sandy beach. As resorts go it's pretty standard – packed in summer, dead and gusty in winter – but the **beach** is excellent and the place also musters a casino and a car-racing circuit. What's more, Zandvoort is one of the few places on the Dutch coast with its own train station (see below): the journey from Amsterdam only takes thirty minutes, which makes it an easy day-trip – ideal for a spot of sunbathing.

Some 3km north along the coast from Zandvoort are the beachside shacks, dunes and ice cream stalls of **BLOEMENDAAL-AAN-ZEE**, a pocket-sized resort which possesses several campsites – and should not be confused with workaday Bloemendaal just inland. The resort is also located on the southern edge of the **Nationaalpark de Kennemerduinen**, whose pine woods, lagoons and dunes stretch north as far as the eminently missable industrial town of **IJMUIDEN**, at the mouth of the Nordzeekanaal. Maps of the park are widely available – from petrol stations and local VVVs, for example – and are useful if you intend to negotiate its network of footpaths and cycle trails, with everything on offer from an easy kilometre-long ramble to a full-scale 140km expedition. Bike rental is available in Haarlem and Zandvoort. The park's **visitor centre** is in its southeast corner, just off the N200 between Haarlem and Bloemendaal-aan-Zee, and reached from the former on bus #81.

## Practicalities

Half-hourly services from Haarlem pull in at **Zandvoort train station**, just a five-minute walk (if that) from the beach. There are buses from Haarlem too – the **bus station** is in the centre on Louis Davidsstraat. There's no strong reason to overnight here, but the **VVV** (April–Oct Mon–Fri 9am–5.15pm, Sat 9am–4pm; mid-July to mid-Aug Fri until 7pm; Nov–March Mon–Fri 9am–12.30pm & 1.30–5pm, Sat 10am–2pm; ☎023/571 7947), a short, signposted walk west of the train station at Schoolplein 1, has a full list of local accommodation. This includes several three- and four-star tower-block **hotels** dotted along the seashore, amongst which the large and slick *NH Zandvoort Hotel*, on the north side of the resort at Burgemeester van Alphenstraat 63 (☎023/576 0760, ⓕ571 9094; ❺) is perhaps the smartest. More modest but perfectly satisfactory options include the *Zuiderbad*, which, with its garish awnings, is on the shore at Boulevard Paulus Loot 5 (☎023/571 2613, ⓦwww.hotelzuiderbad.nl; ❸). The VVV also books **private rooms** (❶–❷), but these fill up fast in summer, so ask early or phone ahead.

Bloemendaal-aan-Zee has two good **campsites**, both among the dunes within comfortable reach of the beach: the sprawling *De Lakens*, Zeeweg 60 (☎0900/384 6226, ⓦwww.kennemerduincampings.nl; April–Oct), and *Bloemendaal*, Zeeweg 72 (☎023/573 2178, ⓕ573 2174; April–Sept). Bus #81 runs from Haarlem train station to Bloemendaal-aan-Zee along the N200; both campsites are just to the north of, and within easy walking distance of, this road.

# The east coast

The turbulent waters of the Zuider Zee were once busy with Dutch trading ships plying to and from the Baltic. This trade was the linchpin of Holland's prosperity in the Golden Age, revolving around the import of huge quantities of grain, the supply of which was municipally controlled to safeguard against famine. The business was immensely profitable and its proceeds built a string of prosperous seaports – including **Volendam**, **Hoorn** and **Enkhuizen** – and nourished market towns like **Edam**, while the Zuider Zee itself supported numerous fishing villages such as **Marken**. In the eighteenth century the Baltic

## The closing of the Zuider Zee

The towns and villages that string along the east coast of Noord-Holland flourished during Amsterdam's Golden Age, their economies buoyed up by shipbuilding, the Baltic sea trade and the demand for herring. They had access to the open sea via the waters of the **Zuider Zee** (Southern Sea) and, to the north, the connecting **Waddenzee** (Mud Sea). Both seas were comparatively new, created when the North Sea broke through from the coast in the thirteenth century: the original coastline is marked by Texel and the Frisian Islands. However, the Zuider Zee was shallow and tidal, part salt and part freshwater, and accumulations of silt began to strangle its ports – notably Hoorn and Enkhuizen – from the end of the seventeenth century, and shortly afterwards the Baltic trade slipped into decline. Indeed, by the 1750s the Zuider Zee ports were effectively marooned and the only maritime activity was fishing – just enough to keep a cluster of tiny hamlets ticking over, from Volendam and Marken on the sea's western coast, to Stavoren (see p.238) and Urk (see p.275) on the eastern side.

The Zuider Zee may have provided a livelihood for local fishermen, but most of the country was more concerned by the danger of flooding it posed, as time and again storms and high tides combined to breach the east coast's defences. The first plan to seal off and reclaim the Zuider Zee was proposed in 1667, but the rotating-turret wind-mills that then provided the most efficient way of drying the land were insufficient for the task and matters were delayed until suitable technology arrived – in the form of the steam-driven pump. In 1891, **Cornelis Lely** (1854–1929), after whom Lelystad (see p.276) was named, proposed a retaining dyke; his plans were finally put into effect after devastating floods hit the area in 1916. Work began on this dyke, the **Afsluitdijk**, in 1920 despite some uncertainty among the engineers, who worried about a possible rise in sea level around the islands of the Waddenzee. In reality, their concerns proved groundless and, on May 28, 1932, the last gap in the dyke was closed and the Zuider Zee simply ceased to exist, replaced by the freshwater **IJsselmeer**.

The original plan was to reclaim all the land protected by the Afsluitdijk, and three large-scale land-reclamation schemes were completed over the next forty years: **Noordoostpolder** in 1942 (48,000 hectares), **Oostelijk Flevoland** in 1957 (54,000 hectares) and **Zuidelijk Flevoland** in 1968 (44,000 hectares). In addition, a second, complementary dyke linking Enkhuizen with Lelystad was finished in 1976, thereby creating lake **Markermeer** – a necessary prelude to the draining of another vast stretch of the IJsselmeer. The engineers licked their contractual lips, but they were out of sync with the majority of the population, who were now opposed to any fur-ther draining of the lake. Partly as a result, the grand plan was abandoned and, after much governmental huffing and puffing, the Markermeer was left alone and thus most of the old Zuider Zee remained water.

There were many economic benefits to be had in the closing of the Zuider Zee. The threat of flooding was removed, the country gained great chunks of new and fertile farmland and the roads that were built along the top of the two main retaining dykes brought Noord-Holland within twenty minutes' drive of Friesland. The price was the demise of the old Zuider Zee **fishing fleet**. Without access to the open sea, it was inevitable that most of the fleet would go down the pan, though some skip-pers wisely transferred to the north coast before the Afsluitdijk was completed. Others learnt to fish the freshwater species that soon colonized the Markermeer and IJsselmeer, but in 1970 falling stocks prompted the government to ban trawling. This was a bitter blow for many fishermen and there were several violent demonstrations before they bowed to the inevitable. Today, villages such as Marken and Urk are shadows of their former selves, forced to rely on tourist kitsch to survive.

trade declined and the harbours silted up, leaving the ports economically stranded, and, with the rapid increase in the Dutch population during the nineteenth century, plans were made to reclaim the Zuider Zee and turn it into farmland. In the event, the Zuider Zee was only partly reclaimed (see box), creating a pair of freshwater lakes – the **Markermeer** and **IJsselmeer**.

These placid, steel-grey lakes are popular with day-tripping Amsterdammers, who come here in their droves to sail boats and visit a string of pretty little towns and villages. These begin on the coast just a few kilometres north of Amsterdam with the picturesque old fishing village of **Marken** and the former seaport of **Volendam**. In the summer, it's possible to travel between these two by boat, but the trip can also be made – if a little less conveniently – by bus via **Monnickendam**, another historic place (but of less interest) that has now become a sailing centre. Buses also link Volendam with **Edam**, a far prettier proposition and much less touristy. You don't necessarily need to make a choice though, since all three places can comfortably be visited in a day. A little way north of Edam, the Markermeer shore curves east to form a jutting claw of land at the base of which is **Hoorn**, an old Zuider Zee port whose compact centre, with its slender harbour and narrow streets, boasts a diverting assortment of Golden Age buildings. Though worth an hour or two of anyone's time, Hoorn is best viewed as a stop on the way to **Enkhuizen**, arguably the region's prettiest town, an engaging ensemble of narrow cobbled streets and slender waterways. Enkhuizen was once a flourishing port and its heritage is celebrated in the excellent, open-air Zuiderzeemuseum. It's also within easy striking distance of another old seaport, **Medemblik**, as well as to the Afsluitdijk over to Friesland (see Chapter 4).

## Marken, Monnickendam and Volendam

Once an island in the Zuider Zee, **Marken** was, until its road connection to the mainland in 1957, pretty much a closed community, supported by a small fishing industry. Despite its proximity to Amsterdam, its biggest problem was the genetic defects caused by close and constant intermarrying, but now it's how to contain the tourists, whose numbers increase yearly. That said, there's no denying the picturesque charms of the island's one and only village – also called **MARKEN** – where the immaculately maintained houses, mostly painted in deep green with white trimmings, cluster on top of artificial mounds raised to protect them from the sea. There are two main parts to the village, **Havenbuurt**, behind the harbour, and **Kerkbuurt** around the **church** (mid-May to Oct Mon–Sat 10am–5pm; free), an ugly 1904 replacement for its long-standing predecessor. Of the two, Kerkbuurt is the less touristy, its narrow lanes lined by ancient dwellings and a row of old eel-smoking houses, now the **Marker Museum**, Kerkbuurt 44 (April–Sept Mon–Sat 10am–5pm, Sun noon–4pm; Oct Mon–Sat 11am–4pm; €2), devoted to the history of the former island and its fishing industry. Across in the Havenbuurt, one or two of the houses are open to visitors, proclaiming themselves to be "typical" of Marken, and the waterfront is lined by snack bars and souvenir shops, often staffed by locals in traditional costume. It's all a tad prosaic, but now and again you get a hint of how hard life used to be – most of the houses on the waterfront are raised on stilts, allowing the sea to roll under the floors in bad weather, enough to terrify most people half to death.

If you are travelling from Marken to Volendam by bus (see overleaf), you have to change at **MONNICKENDAM** – so while you're here you may as well spend a few minutes nosing around. Once an important Zuider Zee port, Monnickendam has reinvented itself as a sailing centre and its large harbour heaves with hundreds of yachts. Reminders of its Golden Age heyday do, however, crop up here and there – nothing dramatic, but the long and spindly main street is adorned by an attractive **Waag** as well as the **Speeltoren**, the conspicuous brick tower of the old town hall, which comes complete with a sixteenth-century carillon. The local speciality is **smoked eel**, something of an acquired taste perhaps, but still worth a try – either from a shop or down at a harbour stall.

Larger but not nearly as quaint as Marken, the old fishing village of **VOLENDAM** has had, by comparison with its neighbour, some rip-roaring cosmopolitan times. In the early years of the twentieth century it became something of an artists' retreat, with both Picasso and Renoir spending time here. The artists, however, are long gone and nowadays Volendam is crammed with day-tripping tourists bobbing in and out of the souvenir stalls that run the length of the main street. Quiet places, never mind pretty ones, are hard to find, but narrow **Meerzijde**, one street back from the harbour, does have its moments in its mazy alleys and mini-canals. One curiosity to look out for is a **plaque** at the corner of Berend Demmerstraat and Josefstraat marking how high the floodwaters of 1916 rose here.

### Practicalities

**Marken** is accessible direct from Amsterdam on **bus** #111, departing from outside Centraal Station (every 15–30min; 30min). The bus drops passengers beside the car park on the edge of Marken village, from where it's a five-minute walk to the centre. Marken does not have a VVV and neither is there anywhere to stay. In season, a passenger **ferry** links Marken with Volendam (April–Oct daily every 30–45min 11am–5pm; 30min; €7; ☏0299/363 331), but at other times it's a fiddly **bus** trip: take bus #111 back towards Amsterdam, but get off at the Swaensborch stop on the edge of Monnickendam village. At Swaensborch, change to bus #110, which runs from Amsterdam to Volendam and Edam; or it's a five- to ten-minute walk to Monnickendam harbour.

In **Volendam** bus #110 from Monnickendam drops passengers on Zeestraat, just along the street from the **VVV**, at no. 37 (April–Sept daily 10am–5pm; Oct–March Mon–Sat 10am–3pm; ☏0299/363 747, ⓦwww.vvv-volendam.nl). From the VVV, it's a couple of minutes' walk to the waterfront. With Amsterdam just a short bus ride away and Edam even nearer (see below), there's absolutely no reason to **stay** overnight here, but if you do, the long-established *Best Western Spaander* on the waterfront at Haven 15 (☏0299/363 595, Ⓕ369 615; ❸) is the most attractive option. In the summertime, there is a regular **passenger ferry** to Marken (see above).

If you're planning to use more than a bus or two, you'd do well to buy a timetable at the nearest bus station before you set out.

## Edam

Just 3km from Volendam – and further along the route of bus #110 from Amsterdam – you might expect **EDAM** to be jammed with tourists considering the international fame of the rubbery red balls of cheese that carry its name. In fact, Edam usually lacks the crowds and is a delightful, good-looking and prosperous little town of neat brick houses, swing bridges and slender canals. Founded by farmers in the twelfth century it experienced a temporary boom in the seventeenth as a shipbuilding centre with river access to the Zuider Zee. Thereafter, it was back to the farm – and the excellent pasture land surrounding the town is still grazed by large herds of cows.

## Edam's cheese market

Nowadays, tourist office bumf notwithstanding, most Dutch Edam cheese is produced a long way from Edam village, even as far afield as Germany; "Edam" is the name of a type of cheese and not its place of origin. This does, of course, rather undermine the authenticity of Edam's open-air **cheese market**, held every Wednesday morning in July and August on the Kaasmarkt square (10.30am–12.30pm), but it's still a popular attraction and the only time the town heaves with tourists. Edam's cheese market is a good deal more humble than Alkmaar's (see p.153), but it follows the same format, with the cheeses laid out in rows before the buyers sample them. Once a cheese has been purchased, the cheese porters, dressed in the traditional white costumes and straw boaters, spring into action, carrying them off on their gondola-like trays.

At the heart of Edam is the **Damplein**, a pint-sized main square where an elongated humpbacked bridge has long vaulted in the Voorhaven canal, which once used to flood the town with depressing regularity. Also on the square is Edam's eighteenth-century **Stadhuis**, a severe Louis XIV-style structure whose plain symmetries culminate in a squat little tower, and the **Edams Museum** (Tues–Sat 10am–4.30pm, Sun 1.30–4.30pm; €2), housed in an attractive building whose crow-stepped gables date from 1530. Inside, a modest assortment of local bygones is redeemed by the curious floating cellar, supposedly built by a retired sea captain who could not bear the thought of sleeping on dry land. From Damplein, it's a short walk along Grote Kerkstraat to the rambling **Grote Kerk** (April–Oct daily 2–4.30pm; free), on the edge of the fields to the north of the village. This is the largest three-ridged church in Europe, with a huge organ built in 1663 and a vaulted ceiling constructed in wood in an attempt to limit the subsidence caused by the building's massive weight. A handsome, largely Gothic structure, it contains several magnificent **stained-glass windows** dating from 1606 to 1620, mostly heraldic but including historical scenes too. Unfortunately, the church's strong lines are disturbed by the almost comically stubby spire, which was shortened to its present height after a lightning strike started a fire in 1602.

Strolling back from the church, take Matthijs Tinxgracht – one street west of Grote Kerkstraat – along the canal and you'll soon reach the Kaasmarkt, site of both the cheese market (see box) and the **Kaaswaag**, whose decorative panels celebrate – you guessed it – cheese-making and bear the town's coat-of-arms, a bull on a red field with three stars. From here, it's a couple of hundred metres to the sixteenth-century **Speeltoren**, the elegant tower visible from all over town, and roughly the same distance again – south along Lingerzijde – to the impossibly picturesque **Kwakelbrug** bridge. This leads over to one of Edam's most charming streets, **Schepenmakersdijk**, a cobbled, canalside lane flanked by immaculate gardens and the quaintest of houses.

To explore Edam's every architectural nook and cranny, pop into the VVV, in the Stadhuis (see below), and buy their inexpensive booklet *A Stroll through Edam*.

### Practicalities

Leaving Amsterdam every half hour from outside Centraal Station, **bus #110** takes 35 minutes to reach Volendam and ten minutes more to get to Edam. Edam's **bus station** is on the southwest edge of town, on Singelweg, a five-minute walk from Damplein. There are no signs, but aim for the easily spotted

Speeltoren tower: cross the distinctive swing-bridge, turn right and follow Lingerzijde as it jinks left and right. From the Speeltoren, it's a few metres east to the Damplein, where the **VVV** (April–Oct Mon–Sat 10am–5pm, plus Sun in July & Aug 1–4.30pm; Nov–March Mon–Sat 10am–3pm; ℡0299/315 125, Ⓦwww.vvv-edam.nl) issues town maps and has the details of **boat trips** both along the local canals and out into the Markermeer. **Bike rental** is available at Ronald Schot, in the town centre at Grote Kerkstraat 7 (℡0299/372 155); a one-day rental costs about €7.

The VVV also has a selection of **private rooms**, which they will book on your behalf for free. Otherwise, there are three **hotels**, the pick being the charming *De Fortuna*, just round the corner from the Damplein at Spuistraat 3 (℡0299/371 671, Ⓦwww.fortuna-edam.nl; ❹). This three-star hotel, with its immaculate garden flowing down to a canal, has just thirty comfortable rooms distributed amongst six cosy little houses. An appealing second choice is the *Damhotel*, which occupies a modernized old inn opposite the VVV (℡0299/371 766, ℻374 031; ❸). The third hotel is the rather more modest, one-star *Harmonie*, in a plain but pleasant canalside house a couple of hundred metres east of the VVV at Voorhaven 92 (℡0299/371 664, ℻315 352; ❶). The nearest **campsite**, *Strandbad*, is east of town near the lakeshore at Zeevangszeedijk 7 (℡0299/371 994; April–Sept) – a twenty-minute walk east along the canal from Damplein.

For **eating**, *De Fortuna* has the best restaurant in town, but eating at the *Damhotel* is barely a hardship – and it's a good deal less expensive; both serve Dutch cuisine.

# Hoorn

The old Zuider Zee port of **HOORN**, some 15km north of Edam, "rises from the sea like an enchanted city of the east, with its spires and its harbour tower beautifully unreal" – or at least it did when the English travel writer E.V. Lucas passed through here in 1905. The trouble is that Hoorn has spent much of the last fifty years accruing humdrum suburbs and the town has now lost most of its looks. Nevertheless, there's no gainsaying its splendid past nor the fine ensemble of old merchants' houses whose tall and slender gables flank the convoluted streets down near the harbour. During the seventeenth century this was one of the richest of the Dutch ports, referred to by the poet Vondel as the "trumpet" of the Zuider Zee, handling the important Baltic trade and that of the Dutch colonies. The Dutch East India Company (see p.98) had one of its centres of operation here; *The Tasman* left its harbour to "discover" Tasmania and New Zealand; and in 1616 William Schouten sailed out of Hoorn to navigate a passage around South America, calling its tip "Cape Hoorn" after his native town. The harbour silted up in the early eighteenth century, however, stemming trade and gradually turning Hoorn into one of the so-called "dead cities" of the Zuider Zee – a process completed with the creation of the IJsselmeer (see box on p.138).

## The Town

At the centre of Hoorn is **Rode Steen**, literally "red stone", an unassuming square that used to hold the town scaffold and now focuses on a swashbuckling **statue** of Jan Pieterszoon Coen (1587–1629), founder of the Dutch East Indies Empire and one of the town's big shots in its seventeenth-century heyday. Coen was a headstrong and determined leader of the Dutch imperial effort and under him the country's Far East colonies were consolidated, and rivals,

## The Stoomtram

Hoorn is the starting point for the **Stoomtram**, an antiquated steam train that chugs off from Hoorn to Medemblik, a few kilometres to the north (see p.149). It's a popular family excursion and there are between one and four departures per day, except on Mondays, from April to June and in September and October. In July and August, the departures are daily and there are also a handful of Christmas departures. Advance booking is recommended on ☏0229/214 862, ⓦwww.museumstoomtram.nl. The journey time is one hour and a return ticket costs €13.75 (children of 4–12 years, €10.45). One-way is €8.35 (€6.35).

You can make a day of it by completing a round-trip, catching the ferry from Medemblik to Enkhuizen (April–Oct 2–3 daily; 1hr 30min; €8 one-way, €12 return), and then a normal train back to Hoorn (or on to Amsterdam). Savings can be made by buying a combined train and ferry ticket. Outside the summer season, catch bus #39 (hourly; 30min) to get from Hoorn to Medemblik.

like the English, kept at bay. His settling of places like the Moluccas and Batavia was something of a personal crusade, and his austere, almost puritanical way of life was in sharp contrast to the wild and unprincipled behaviour of many of his fellow colonialists. On one side of Rode Steen stands the early-seventeenth-century **Waag**, designed by Hendrik de Keyser and now a café-bar more enjoyable for its setting, amidst the ponderous wooden appliances that helped the weighing, than its food.

On the other side of Rode Steen, dominating the square, the **Westfries Museum** (Mon–Fri 11am–5pm, Sat & Sun 2–5pm; €6; ⓦwww.wfm.nl) is Hoorn's most prominent sight, housed in the elaborately gabled former West Friesland government building of 1632. The gable is decorated with the coats of arms of the house of Orange-Nassau and the region's towns. Now a district within the province of Noord-Holland, West Friesland incorporates the chunk of land between Alkmaar, Hoorn and Enkhuizen, but its origins were much grander. Speaking a distinctive German dialect, the **Frisians** once controlled a narrow sliver of seaboard stretching west from Bremerhaven in Germany to Belgium. Charlemagne conquered them in the 780s and incorporated their territory into his empire, chopping it down in size and dividing the remainder into seven regions, two of which – West Friesland and Friesland – are now in the Netherlands. Inside the museum, a string of period rooms convincingly re-creates the flavour of the seventeenth- and eighteenth-century seaport and along the way are numerous paintings, most memorably the militia portraits of **Jan Rotius** (1624–66) in the old Council Chamber (Room 7). Walk past the figure in the far right of the central painting and you'll see his foot change position from left to right – a nifty little trick that was much admired by Rotius's contemporaries. On the second floor, in Room 16, there's the charming *Landscape with a Peasant Cart* by **Jan van Goyen** (1596–1656) and a wooden fireplace carved with tiny scenes showing a whaling expedition – Hoorn was once a whaling port of some importance. Other items of interest include an unascribed view of Hoorn painted in 1622, a room containing portraits of various East India Company dignitaries, including one of a severe-looking Coen, and, on the top floor, mock-ups of seventeenth-century trades and shops – even a prison cell.

## Down to the harbour

Strolling east from Rode Steen, **Grote Oost** is shadowed by fine old mansions, many of which sport neat rococo balustrades. The most appealing amongst them is the **Bossuhuizen**, on the right at the corner with Slapershaven, its facade decorated with a long and slender frieze depicting a sea battle of 1573 – which Admiral Bossu actually lost. Continuing down Slapershaven, past some of the most comfortable houseboats imaginable – some have garages, others are even thatched – you soon reach the inner harbour, the **Binnenhaven**, with its clutter of sailing boats and antique barges. Overlooking the harbour, on Oude Doelenkade, is a long row of old warehouses, with their prim shutters and crow-stepped gables, whilst, just over the swing bridge and also beside the Binnenhaven, **Veermanskade** is fringed by elegant merchants' houses mostly dating from the seventeenth century. In particular, look out for the birthplace of **Willem Ysbrantzoon Bontekoe** (1587–1657), at Veermanskade 15 – the facade stone shows a particularly ugly spotted cow, as in *bonte* ("spotted") and *koe* ("cow"). A sea captain with the East India Company, Bontekoe published his journal in 1646, a hair-raising account of his adventures that proved immensely popular. Portraying himself as astute and brave in equal measure, Bontekoe's most eventful voyage included the snapping of the mainmast, an epidemic of scurvy and an explosion that forced the crew to abandon ship, all en route from Hoorn to Jakarta. At the end of Veermanskade rises the solid brickwork of the **Hoofdtoren**, a defensive watchtower from 1532, and at its base you'll find a friendly bronze sculpture of 1968 entitled *Three Ships' Boys*, by Jan van Druten.

Doubling back along Veermanskade, turn left at the swing bridge along Nieuwendam and it's a couple of minutes' walk round the canal to Appelhaven and the **Museum van de Twintigste Eeuw** (Museum of the Twentieth Century; Tues–Fri 10am–5pm, Sat & Sun noon–5pm; €3.50; ⓦwww .museumhoorn.nl), housed in two former cheese warehouses at Bierkade 4. Its permanent displays of daily life, though not exactly gripping, are supplemented by changing exhibits with titles such as "Travel Posters – A Nostalgic Journey" and "100 Years of Blokker" (Blokker is the Dutch equivalent of Woolworth's). A scale model of Hoorn in 1650 and an audio-visual display describing the role of the town in the Dutch Golden Age are perhaps a little more diverting, but not by much. From the museum, it's a couple of minutes' walk back to Rode Steen along narrow Grote Havensteeg.

### Practicalities

The easiest way to reach Hoorn from Amsterdam is by train (every 30min; 40min); from Edam, take bus #114 from the bus station (every 30min, hourly on Sun; 30min). Both leave you at Hoorn **train station**, on the northern edge of town about ten minutes' walk from the centre. To get to Rode Steen from here, veer right across the square in front of the station, turn left along Kleine Noord and keep going straight. Kleine Noord – along with its continuation, Grote Noord – is the main shopping street. The **VVV** is near the train at Veemarkt 4 (May–Aug Mon 1–6pm, Tues–Fri 9.30am–6pm, Sat 9.30am–5pm & Sun 1–5pm; Sept–April Mon 1–5pm, Tues–Sat 9.30am–5pm; ☎072/511 4284, ⓦwww.vvvhoorn.nl) - again, cut right across the square in front of the station and Veemarkt is on the left; it runs parallel to, and one block east of, Kleine Noord.

With Enkhuizen and Edam so near, there's no strong reason to stay in Hoorn, but the VVV does have a small supply of **private rooms** (at around €40 per double per night) and there are three recommendable **hotels** in the centre. First up is the three-star *De Keizerskroon*, in a well-kept, two-storey brick building near the station at Breed 31 (☎0229/212 717, ⓕ211 022; ❷). Alternatively, there's the *Petit Nord*, a smart four-star hotel in a boring location on the main shopping street at Kleine Noord 53 (℡0229/212 750, ℱ215 745; ❸), and the well-maintained, three-star *De Magneet*, beside a busy road down near the harbour at Kleine Oost 5 (℡0229/215 021, ℱ237 044; ❷).

For **food**, *Sweet Dreams*, metres from the Waag at Kerkstraat 1, is a very competent café offering delicious omelettes and Tex-Mex dishes – and it's open till late. There's also the excellent *De Eethoorn*, an appealingly cosy *eetcafé* serving standard Dutch food from its neat little premises beside the Grote Kerk at Kerkplein 7; main courses here start at €15. The *Isola Bella*, Grote Oost 65 (closed Mon), serves up very reasonably priced Italian food with pizzas from €6, and the more formal *Alpino*, Breed 32 (℡0229/218 567), offers tasty French specialities with main courses from €20.

## Enkhuizen

The beguiling little town of **ENKHUIZEN**, just 18km east along the coast from Hoorn and 25 minutes by train, was once one of the country's most important seaports. From the fourteenth to the early eighteenth century, when its harbour silted up, it prospered from the Baltic sea trade and North Sea herring fishing industry – and indeed its maritime credentials were second to none. It was home to Holland's largest fishing fleet and its citizens were renowned for their seamanship, with the Dutch East India Company always

During the summer you can travel from Enkhuizen by passenger **ferry** east across the IJsselmeer to either **Stavoren** (May–Sept 3 daily; late April & early Oct 2 daily; 1hr 20min; €7.50 one-way, €10 return; Ⓦ www.veerboot.info; see p.238) or **Urk** (late June to Aug Mon–Sat 3 daily; 1hr 45min; €8 one-way, €11 return; see p.275). Alternatively you can travel north to the village of **Medemblik** (April–Oct 2–3 daily; 1hr 30min; €8 one-way, €12 return; see p.149). All ferries leave from behind the train station, and you can buy tickets from the VVV, who also have timetables.

keen to recruit here. Enkhuizen was also the first town in Noord-Holland to rise against Spain, in 1572, but, unlike many of its Protestant allies, it was never besieged – its northerly location kept it safely out of reach of the Habsburg army. Subsequently, Enkhuizen slipped into a long-lasting economic reverie, becoming a remote and solitary backwater until, in recent years, tourism has revived its fortunes. About twenty minutes' walk from end to end, the town centre, with its ancient streets and slender canals, has preserved its medieval shape, a rough circle with a ring of bastions and moat on one side, and the old sea dyke on the other. Enkhuizen also possesses no less than three pretty harbours and a major attraction in the extensive **Zuiderzeemuseum**, which details the history and cultural significance of the sea to the region. It divides into two parts: the indoor **Binnenmuseum** and the rather more interesting **Buitenmuseum**, a well conceived recreation of life in the old Zuider Zee ports between 1880 and 1932. The town is also a good place to visit for its summer **ferry** connections to Stavoren (see p.238) and Urk (see p.275) across the IJsselmeer.

### Arrival, information and accommodation

**Trains** to Enkhuizen, which is at the end of the line, stop right opposite the head of the main harbour – the Buitenhaven, at the southeast corner of the town centre. **Buses** stop on one side of the train station, while on the other, about 100m to the east, is the **VVV**, at Tussen Twee Havens 1 (April–Oct daily 9am–5pm; Nov–March Mon 1–5pm, Tues–Fri 10am–12.30pm & 1–5pm, Sat 10am–12.30pm & 1.30–3pm; ☎0228/313 164, Ⓦ www.vvv-enkhuizen.nl). The VVV has a small supply of **private rooms**, with doubles costing around €40, issues free maps and has a list of all the town's accommodation.

Amongst the town's handful of **hotels**, the pick, by a long chalk, is the delightful, three-star *Recuer Dos*, Westerstraat 217 (☎0228/562 469, Ⓦ www.recuerdos.nl; ❸), in an immaculate Victorian residence on the west side of the centre, and with cosy rooms, an outside terrace and garden. Runners up are *Het Wapen van Enkhuizen*, Breedstraat 59 (☎0228/313 434, Ⓕ 320 020; ❷), an unassuming three-star hotel located right in the centre of town by the Stadhuis, and the three-star *Driebanen*, a modest, modern but spick-and-span little place at Driebanen 59 (☎0228/316 381, Ⓕ 321 454; ❷). In addition, there are two summer-only **campsites** handily located on the edge of the centre. The nearest is the *Enkhuizer Zand* on the far side of the Zuiderzeemuseum at Kooizandweg 4 (☎0228/317 289; April–Sept). The other is *De Vest*, Noorderweg 31 (☎0228/321 221; April–Sept), which fits snugly onto one of the old bastions. To get there, follow Vijzelstraat north off Westerstraat, continue down Noorderweg, and turn left by the old town ramparts; from the train station to the campground is about 1.5km.

## The Town

A good place to start an exploration of Enkhuizen's compact centre is **Westerstraat**, the town's spine, a busy pedestrianized street that is home to most of its shops and stores. At one end stands the **Westerkerk**, an early fifteenth-century Gothic church whose free-standing wooden tower is painted in violently incongruous colours – orangey-beige and green. The interior of the church, with its three naves of equal height, is distinguished by its rood-screen, a mid-sixteenth century extravagance whose six subtly carved panels show biblical figures – Moses, Joshua and the Evangelists. From the Westerkerk, it's a couple of minutes' walk south to the **Oude Haven** (old harbour) and its jangle of sailing boats and low-slung barges. The harbour stretches east in a gentle curve that leads round to the conspicuous **Drommedaris**, a heavy-duty brick watchtower built in 1540 to guard the enclosure. Immediately to the east is the oldest part of town, a narrow lattice of ancient alleys amongst which, in a wonderful tiny old house at Zuiderspui 1, is the pocket-sized **Flessenscheepjesmuseum** (April–Sept Mon–Fri 10am–5.30pm, Sat & Sun noon–5.30pm; Oct–March Mon 1–4pm, Tues–Fri 11am–4pm, Sat & Sun noon–5pm; €3), an establishment devoted to that ubiquitous maritime curiosity, the ship-in-bottle. Well presented and labelled, the exhibits are fascinating, with vessels ranging from East Indiamen to steamboats, and containers from a tiny scent bottle to a thirty-litre wine flagon.

Take comely Zuider Havendijk north from here along the canal and turn left at the end for the **Zuiderkerk**, a hulking Gothic pile with a massive tower. Close by, just to the east, is the solid, classically styled mid-seventeenth-century **Stadhuis**, an elegant and imposing Neoclassical edifice that still houses the city council.

### The Zuiderzeemuseum

From the Stadhuis, it's a short walk east to the indoor section of the **Zuiderzeemuseum**, the **Binnenmuseum**, at Wierdijk 18 (daily 10am–5pm; €5; joint ticket with Buitenmuseum €9; ⓦ www.zuiderzeemuseum.nl). This has separate sections on many aspects of Zuider Zee life, including trade and transport, boats and shipbuilding, fishing and whaling, land reclamation and the East India Company. One of the more curious exhibits is an ice-cutting boat from Urk, once charged with the responsibility of keeping the shipping lanes open between the island and the mainland. There are also several sections devoted to applied art, most notably some extravagant regional costumes, complete with fancy Dutch caps, and several beautiful examples of the painted furniture traditionally carved in Hindeloopen (see p.237).

Most people, however, give the indoor museum a miss and instead make straight for the **Buitenmuseum** (early April to late Oct daily 10am–5pm; joint ticket with Binnenmuseum €9), whose nearest entrance is about 200m to the north along Wierdijk. Note also that in high season – usually July and August – there's a free ferry service (every 15min) to the open-air museum from the train station, as there is from the museum car park to the south of the centre; just follow the signs as you drive into town. The Buitenmuseum itself stretches north along the seaward side of the old dyke that once protected Enkhuizen from the turbulent waters of the Zuider Zee. It contains over 130 dwellings, stores, workshops and even streets that have been transported here from every part of the region; together they provide the flavour – albeit rather antiseptically – of life hereabouts from 1880 to 1932. Highlights include the modest, precisely furnished interiors of a series of old fishermen's houses, a post office from Den Oever, a grocery store from Harderwijk and a bakery from Hoorn that sells pastries and chocolate. There are also regular demonstrations of traditional crafts, and goats and sheep roam the surrounding meadows.

△ Bicycling along the Dune Trail

## Eating and drinking

For a small town, Enkhuizen has a good supply of **restaurants**. Handy, town-centre options include the cosy *De Smederij*, Breedstraat 158 (☏0228/314 604), which offers a wide-ranging menu – from mussels to meat – with main courses averaging around €20, and the equally tasty Dutch food of the *Het Wapen Hotel*, Breedstraat 59 (☏0228/313 434). More upmarket but not much more expensive is the French cuisine of the first-rate *Restaurant d'Alsace*, Westerstraat 116 (☏0228/315 225; closed Sun & Mon), but the outstanding place in town is *Die Drie Haringhe*, Dijk 28 (☏0228/318 610; closed Tues), which serves imaginative seafood dishes that often feature local ingredients. Housed in a seventeenth-century building, the atmosphere is restrained but the food is magnificent, with main courses kicking off at around €20. This is the best place to try the local delicacy IJsselmeer pike (*snoek*). A good spot for a **drink** is the *'t Ankertje* pub at Dijk 4, an atmospheric, old-fashioned kind of place with nautical knick-knacks hanging on the walls.

## Medemblik and north

Just a few kilometres north along the coast from Enkhuizen, **MEDEMBLIK** is one of the most ancient towns in the Netherlands, a seat of pagan kings until the seventh century, though there's not a great deal to entice you here nowadays, unless you're madly into yachts. The only significant reminder of Medemblik's ancient origins is the **Kasteel Radboud**, perched by the harbour at Oudevaartsgat 8 (May to mid-Sept Mon–Sat 11am–5pm, Sun 2–5pm; rest of year Sun only 2–5pm; €2.50). It is named after the eighth-century baron who first fortified this spot, though the structure that survives is not his at all, but a much-restored thirteenth-century fortress built by Count Floris V, who was murdered in Muiden (see p.159) and buried in Alkmaar (see p.151). The restoration was planned by Petrus J.H. Cuypers, the architect responsible for Amsterdam's Centraal Station and Rijksmuseum. Inside the castle, exhibits outline the fort's history and there's a ragbag of archeological finds from local sites. The old train station, where the Stoomtram (see p.143) pulls in, houses Medemblik VVV (April–Oct Mon–Sat 10am–5pm; July & Aug also Sun same times; Nov–March Mon–Sat 10am–noon & 2–4pm; ☏0227/542 852, ⓦwww.vvvmedemblik.nl). Not far away, at Oosterdijk 4, the **Nederlands Stoommachinemuseum** (Dutch Steam Engine Museum; mid-Feb to Sept Tues–Sun 10am–5pm; €4; ⓦwww.stoommachinemuseum.nl) holds an assembly of thirty ancient steam engines in a former pumping station. Otherwise most people come to Medemblik to sail: the harbour is busy throughout summer with the masts of visiting and resident yachters and there is a ferry linking the place with Enkhuizen (see p.146).

North of Medemblik, the **Wieringermeer Polder** was reclaimed in the 1920s, filling in the gap between the former Zuider Zee island of Wieringen and the mainland. Towards the end of World War II, just three weeks before their surrender, the Germans flooded the polder, boasting they could return the Netherlands to the sea if they so wished. After the war, it was drained again, leaving a barren, treeless terrain that had to be totally replanted. Almost sixty years later, it's indistinguishable from its surroundings, a familiar landscape of flat, geometric fields, highlighted by neat and trim farmhouses. The polder leads north to the **Afsluitdijk** highway over to Friesland (see Chapter 4). The sluices on this side of the Afsluitdijk are known as the **Stevinsluizen**, after **Hendrick Stevin**, the seventeenth-century engineer who first had the idea of reclaiming the Zuider Zee. At the time, his grand plan was impracticable – the technology was unavailable – but his vision lived on, to be realized by **Cornelis Lely** (see box on p.138), though he too died before the structure was completed. There's a **statue** of Lely by the modern Dutch sculptor Mari Andriessen at the west end of the dyke. Further out along the dyke, at the point where the barrier was finally closed, there's an observation point on which an inscription reads "A nation that lives is building for its future" – a linking of progress with construction that read well in the 1930s, but seems rather dubious today.

# From Zaandam to Texel

The inland route north through the province begins with the build-up of settlements collectively known as Zaanstad, which trails northwest of Amsterdam on the far side of the River IJ. Two places are well worth visiting here – **Zaandam**, the urban core of Zaanstad, and the museum-village of **Zaanse Schans**, complete with its old wooden cottages and windmills. Stay on the train and it's another thirty minutes or so to **Alkmaar**, a pleasant old town with a clutch of handsome Golden Age buildings and a traditional open-air cheese market that is much admired by tourists. Nearby is the good-looking village of **Bergen**, home to the enjoyable Museum Kranenburgh of fine art, which itself lies close to the woods and dunes of the **Schoorlse Duinen Nationaalpark**. The latter rolls down to the coast near the seaside resort of **Bergen-aan-Zee**. It's another short haul to **Den Helder**, a humdrum port at the province's northern tip that is useful for the ferry over to the island of **Texel**.

As for public transport, a fast and frequent train service runs north from Amsterdam linking Zaandam, Koog-Zaandijk (for Zaanse Schans), Alkmaar and Den Helder. From each train station, buses run to the smaller communities that are not on the rail line, usually every hour or half-hour.

## Zaandam and Zaanse Schans

As observed from the train heading north from Amsterdam, the largely modern town of **ZAANDAM** is not especially enticing, but it does deserve a brief stop. The town was a popular tourist hangout in the nineteenth century, when it was known as "La Chine d'Hollande" for the faintly oriental appearance of its windmills, canals and row upon row of brightly painted houses. Monet spent some time here in the 1870s, and, despite being under constant police surveillance as a suspected spy, went on to immortalize the place in a series of paintings. To see something of Monet's Zaandam, follow the main street, Gedempte Gracht, east from the train station for five minutes, turn right down Damstraat, right again, and left down Krimp and you'll be rewarded with a pretty harbour, spiked with masts and fringed by wooden houses. On Krimp itself, at no. 23, is the town's main claim to fame, the **Czaar Petershuisje** (April–Oct Tues–Sun 1–5pm; Nov–March Sat & Sun only 1–5pm; €2), where the Russian tsar Peter the Great stayed when he came to study shipbuilding here. In those heady days, Zaandam was an important shipbuilding centre, and the Tsar made four visits, the first in 1697 when he arrived incognito and stayed in the simple home of one Gerrit Kist, who had formerly been employed by the Tsar. A tottering wooden structure enclosed within a brick shelter, the house is little more than two tiny rooms, decorated with a handful of portraits of a benign-looking emperor and the graffiti of tourists going back to the mid-nineteenth century. Among the few things to see is the cup-board bed in which Peter is supposed to have slept, together with the calling cards and pennants of various visiting Russian delegations; around the outside of the house is an exhibition on the shipbuilding industry in Zaandam. Napoleon is said to have remarked on visiting the house, "Nothing is too small for great men."

## Zaanse Schans

Most visitors to Zaanstad are on their way to the recreated Dutch village of **Zaanse Schans**. The village is made up of around thirty cottages, windmills and workshops assembled from all over the region, in an energetic and endear-ing attempt to reproduce a Dutch village as it would have looked in the eigh-teenth and early nineteenth centuries. Spread over a network of narrow canals beside the River Zaan, it's a pretty spot and deservedly popular, with the par-ticular highlight being the seven working **windmills**, giant industrial affairs used – amongst other things – to cut wood, grind mustard seeds and produce oil. This is the closest place to Amsterdam to see working windmills and there's a scattering of other attractions too, notably a Bakkerij (bakery), Kaasboerderij (cheese-making workshop) and a Klompenmakerij (clog-making workshop). Opening times vary, but almost every structure is open from April to October daily, except sometimes on Mondays, and from November to March at week-ends only. Precise times are available from the visitor centre, the **Bezoekerscentrum**, on the east side of the village beside the car park (daily 8.30am–5pm; ☎075/616 8218, ⓦwww.zaanseschans.nl). It's possible to walk round Zaanse Schans at any time, and in the evening or early morning you may well have the place pretty much to yourself. Finally, there are also enjoyable hour-long **boat trips** on the River Zaan from the jetty near the De Huisman mustard windmill (April–Oct daily 11am–4pm; €6).

It's about 800m to Zaanse Schans from the nearest **train station**, Koog-Zaandijk, two stops up the line from Zaandam.

# Alkmaar

Forty minutes from Amsterdam by train – and thirty from Koog-Zaandijk – the little town of **ALKMAAR** was founded in the tenth century in the middle of a marsh. It takes its name from the auk, a diving bird which once hung around here in numbers, as in *alkeen meer*, or "auk lake". Just like Haarlem, the town was besieged by Frederick of Toledo, but heavy rain flooded its surroundings and forced the Spaniards to withdraw in 1573, an early Dutch success in their long war of independence. Alkmaar's agreeable, partially canalized centre is still surrounded by its medieval moat, part of which has been incorporated into the Noordhollandskanaal, itself part of a longer network of waterways running north from Amsterdam to the Waddenzee near Den Helder – and beyond the Afsluitdijk.

## The Town

Even if you've only come for the cheese market (see box), it's well worth seeing something of the rest of the town before you leave. On the main square, the **Waag** was originally a chapel dedicated to the Holy Ghost – hence the imposing tower – but was converted and given its delightful east gable shortly after Alkmaar's famous victory against the Spanish. The gable is an ostentatious Dutch Renaissance affair bedecked with allegorical figures and decorated with the town's militant coat-of-arms. Nowadays, the Waag holds the VVV (see below) and the **Hollands Kaasmuseum** (Dutch Cheese Museum; April–Oct

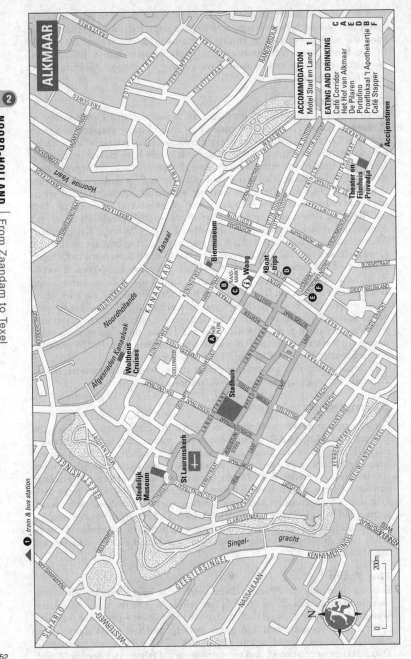

ALKMAAR

ACCOMMODATION
Motel Stad en Land          1

EATING AND DRINKING
Café Corridor              C
Het Hof van Alkmaar        A
De Pilaren                 E
Portofino                  D
Proeflokaal 't Apothekertje B
Café Stapper               F

200m

Mon–Thurs & Sat 10am–4pm, Fri 9am–4pm; €2.50; Ⓦwww.kaasmuseum.nl), with displays on the history of cheese, cheese-making equipment and suchlike. Just off the north side of the square, the **Biermuseum de Boom**, housed in the old De Boom brewery at Houttil 1 (April–Oct Tues–Fri 10am–4pm, Sat & Sun 1.30–4pm; Nov–March Tues–Sun 1–4pm; €2.50; Ⓦwww.biermuseum.nl), has displays tracing the brewing process from the malting to the bottling stage, aided by authentic props from this and other breweries. There's lots of technical equipment, enlivened by mannequins and empty bottles from once innumerable Dutch brewers – though few, curiously, from De Boom itself. It's an engaging museum, lovingly put together by enthusiasts, and there's a shop upstairs where you can buy a huge range of beers and associated merchandise, as well as a downstairs bar serving some eighty varieties of Dutch beer.

Heading south from the Waag along Mient, it's a few metres to the jetty from where boat trips (see overleaf) leave for a quick zip round the town's central canals. At the south end of Mient, the open-air **Vismarkt** (Fish Market) marks the start of the **Verdronkenoord** canal, whose attractive medley of facades and gables leads down to the spindly **Accijnstoren** (Excise Tower), part harbourmaster's office, part fortification built during the long struggle with Spain in 1622. Turn left at the tower along Bierkade and you'll soon reach **Luttik Oudorp**, another attractive corner of the old centre, a slender canal jammed with antique barges that leads back to the Waag.

One block south of the Waag, pedestrianized **Langestraat** is Alkmaar's main and mundane shopping street, whose only notable building is the **Stadhuis**, a florid affair, half of which (the Langestraat side and tower) dates from the early sixteenth century. At the west end of Langestraat lurks **St Laurenskerk** (June to mid-Sept Tues–Sat noon–5pm; free), a Gothic church of the late fifteenth century whose pride and joy is its huge organ, commissioned at the suggestion of the diplomat and political bigwig Constantijn Huygens in 1645. The case was designed by Jacob van Campen, the architect who was later to design Amsterdam's town hall (see p.75), and decorated with paintings illustrating the triumph of David by Caesar van Everdingen (1617–78). The artist's seamless brushstrokes and willingness to kowtow to the tastes of the burgeoning middle class were to make him a wealthy man. In the apse is the tomb of Count Floris V, penultimate in the line of medieval counts of Noord-Holland, who did much to establish the independence of the towns hereabouts and was murdered for his trouble by jealous nobles in 1296.

Across from the church, in the newly enlarged cultural centre, the **Stedelijk Museum** (Municipal Museum; Tues–Fri 10am–5pm, Sat & Sun 1–5pm; €3.40), displays pictures and plans of the siege of 1573, along with an assortment of seventeenth-century paintings. Amongst the latter is a striking *Holy Family* by Gerard van Honthorst (1590–1656), a Mannerist who specialized in glossy portraits of high officials. There's also work by Pieter Saenredam and Maerten van Heemskerck (1498–1574), a transitional figure who was tutored in the Dutch Mannerist style before a visit to Italy in 1532 changed the direction of his work. Greatly impressed by the Italians, Heemskerck returned home to paint in the style of Michelangelo, populating his large canvases with muscular men-of-action and buxom women.

### Practicalities

From Alkmaar's **train** and **bus station**, it's about ten minutes' walk to the centre of town: keep straight outside the station along Spoorstraat, take the first right down Snaarmanslaan and then left at busy Geesterweg, which leads over the old city moat to St Laurenskerk. From the church, it's another five minutes' walk east along Langestraat to the **VVV**, housed in the Waag on Waagplein (Mon–Fri 10am–5.30pm, Sat 9.30am–5pm; April–Oct Thurs until 9pm; ☏072/511 4284, ⓦ www.vvvalkmaar.nl). Alkmaar only takes an hour or two to explore, but if you decide to stay the VVV has plenty of **private rooms** for €32 per double per night, including breakfast, though most places are on the outskirts of town and en-suite rooms are rare. Failing that, there's one recommendable central **hotel**, the *Motel Stad en Land*, a plain and simple, trim and modern two-star establishment opposite the bus station, beside a busy road at Stationsweg 92 (☏072/512 3911, ⓕ 511 8440; ❸).

**Boat trips** around the town's central canals leave from the jetty on Mient (April–Oct daily, hourly 11am–5pm, plus additional departures during the cheese market; 25min; €4). There are also longer trips to Zaanse Schans (mid-May to late Oct 2–3 weekly; 6hr; €10 one-way, €15 return) and even to Amsterdam (mid-June to mid-Sept weekly; 9hr; €13 one-way, €21 return); ask at the VVV for further details or contact the operators, Woltheus Cruises, at the Kanaalkade jetty, on the north side of the centre (☏072/511 4840; ⓦ www.woltheuscruises.nl).

For **food**, Alkmaar is well served by *Het Hof van Alkmaar*, which occupies delightful old premises just off Nieuwesloot at Hof van Sonoy 1 (☏072/512 1222). During the day, this restaurant offers inexpensive sandwiches, snacks and pancakes, then at night it serves up tasty Dutch cuisine – it's the best choice in town. As a substitute, you might try *Portofino*, an old-fashioned Italian place close to the Waag at Mient 5; pizzas here begin at €6. As regards **drinking**, Alkmaar has two main groups of bars, one on Waagplein, the other around the Vismarkt, at the end of the Verdronkenoord canal. Among the former, the pick is *Proeflokaal 't Apothekertje*, an old-style bar, open until 2am, with an antique-cluttered interior and a laid-back atmosphere. Metres away, *Café Corridor* is younger and plays loud music late into the night. On Verdronkenoord, *De Pilaren* is another noisy place, though catering to a rather cooler crowd, some of whom take refuge in the *Café Stapper* next door if the music gets too much.

## Bergen and around

Bus #160 leaves Alkmaar train station every fifteen minutes or so – hourly on Sunday – for the ten-minute ride to **BERGEN**, a cheerful village whose main square, the **Plein**, is an amiable affair flanked by good-looking, vaguely rustic buildings. Bus #160 stops on the Plein and from here it's a couple of minutes' walk south along Breelaan to the **Gemeentemuseum Sterkenhuis** at Oude Prinsweg 21 (mid-May to Oct Tues–Sat 1–5pm, July & Aug also Sun 1–5pm; €1.50). Occupying a seventeenth-century mansion, the museum holds regular exhibitions of work by contemporary Dutch artists and has a section on a largely forgotten episode in the Napoleonic Wars, when a combined army of 30,000 English and Russian soldiers were defeated by a Franco-Dutch force here in 1799. From the Sterkenhuis, it's a short walk west to the **Museum Kranenburgh**, a fine arts museum housed in a handsome Neoclassical villa at Hoflaan 26 (Tues–Sun 1–5pm; €4.50). Bergen has been something of a retreat for artists since the late nineteenth century and the museum features the work of the Expressionist Bergen School, which was founded here in 1915. Greatly influenced by the Post-Impressionists, especially Cézanne, none of the group is original enough to stand out, but taken as a whole it's a delightful collection and one that is supported by an imaginative programme of temporary exhibitions. These often focus on the two contemporaneous Dutch schools that were to have much more artistic impact – De Ploeg and De Stijl (see p.374). In addition, and warming to this artistic past, the local council organizes all sorts of cultural events in Bergen, including open-air sculpture displays and concerts, whilst the village also boasts a scattering of chichi art-for-sale galleries.

From Bergen's Plein, local bus #410 (Mon–Sat 6 daily) makes the thirty-minute trip northwest to the hamlet of **SCHOORL**, travelling along the eastern border of the **Schoorlse Duinen Nationaalpark**, whose wooded dunes stretch 5km west to the sea – one of the widest undeveloped portions of the whole Dutch coastline. The park is criss-crossed by cycling and walking trails and for all but the briefest of visits, you should pick up a map from Bergen VVV, at Plein 1, before you set out (Mon–Fri 10am–5.30pm, Sat 10am–1pm; ☎072/581 3100). If you take a shine to Bergen, check out two good **hotels**, the smart, four-star *Best Western Hotel Marijke*, just five minutes' walk south of Plein at Dorpsstraat 23 (☎072/581 2381, ℻589 7771; ❸), and the rather more intimate, three-star *Villa Parkzicht*, right in the centre at Breelaan 24 (☎072/589 4600, ℻589 9132; ❷). Another option is to push on north from Schoorl, taking bus #151, which links Alkmaar with Den Helder (see p.156) via the coast, weaving through a string of small-scale resorts, the most agreeable of which are **Camperduin** and **Petten**.

## The coast: Bergen-aan-Zee and Egmond-aan-Zee

Heading west from Bergen, bus #262 (daily every 30min) takes ten minutes to travel the 5km to the coast at **BERGEN-AAN-ZEE**, a pleasant, pocket-sized resort where the main event is the long sandy beach with its thick border of grassy dunes. To either side is pristine coastline: the Schoorlse Duinen Nationaalpark (see above) stretches out to the north, while the woods and dunes of the **Noordhollands Duinreservaat**, with its abundance of footpaths and cycle trails, extends south. If you fancy a night here, the *Hotel Nassau-Bergen*, at Van der Wijckplein 4 (☎072/589 7541, ⓦwww.hotel-nassau.nl; ❹), has every convenience – from an outdoor swimming pool to tennis courts – and is situated just 50m from the beach. The **VVV** is just along the street at no. 8 (☎072/581 2400).

Another coastal option, just 11km from Bergen-aan-Zee, is the slightly larger resort of **EGMOND-AAN-ZEE**, in the middle of the dunes of the Noordhollands Duinreservaat and in the shadow of a whopping lighthouse. To get there, take bus #165 from Alkmaar train station (daily every 30min; 30min). Egmond has a **VVV** too, at Voorstraat 82a (☎072/506 1362).

# Den Helder

Forty minutes north from Alkmaar by train, **DEN HELDER** is a town of around 60,000, though it was little more than a fishing village until 1811, when Napoleon, capitalizing on its strategic position at the very tip of Noord-Holland, fortified it as a naval base. It's still the principal home of the Dutch navy, and national fleet days, or *Vlootdagen*, are held here on one weekend during the summer – usually in July – when, should you so desire, you can check out the bulk of the Dutch navy. For further details, contact the **VVV**, at Bernhardplein 18 (⊕0223/625 544, ⊚www.vvvkopvannoordholland.nl). Otherwise, the place holds little of interest: its centre is an uninspiring muddle of modern architecture prefacing a careworn older quarter down beside the harbour. Indeed, the only real reason to come here is to take one of the ferries over to the island of Texel and, if this is your plan, you can miss the town altogether by taking a bus direct from the train station to the ferry dock.

Otherwise, it's a two-kilometre walk through town from the station to the ferry and on the way, just 200m or so before the dock, you might drop by Den Helder's **Marinemuseum**, at Hoofdgracht 3 (Tues–Fri 10am–5pm, Sat & Sun noon–5pm; May–Oct also Mon 10am–5pm; €4.50). The museum makes a gallant attempt to conjure interest in what is, for most people, hardly a riveting subject, but to be fair the sections tracking through the history of the Dutch navy are well presented and entertaining. In particular, look out for the stuff on the naval heroes of yesteryear, especially Admiral Michiel de Ruyter (1607–76), who trounced in succession the Spaniards, the Swedes, the English and the French. His most daring exploit was a raid up the River Thames to Medway in 1667 and the seizure of the Royal Navy's flagship, *The Royal Charles*, a raid that drove Charles II almost to distraction. There's lots of technical information too – on shipbuilding techniques and the like – and several decommissioned vessels, including a 1960s submarine, the *Tonijn*, and the veteran World War II minesweeper, the *Abraham Crijnssen*.

# The island of Texel

The largest of the islands of the Waddenzee – and the easiest to get to – **Texel** (pronounced "tessel") is a lush, green thumb of land, speckled with small villages and patches of woodland, its fertile farmland fringed to the west by extensive dunes and long, sandy beaches. Now 24km long and 9km wide, the island was actually much smaller until the nineteenth century when its northeast corner was reclaimed from the ocean. A charming and infinitely relaxing place, it's no wonder that swathes of Netherlanders spend their summers here.

Ferries from the mainland (see p.158) drop you in the middle of nowhere at the southern tip of the island, but connecting buses take you onto **DEN BURG**, the main settlement – no more than a large village, but home to the island's VVV (details below). As for sights, there's precious little in Den Burg beyond a small local history museum, the **Oudheidkamer**, at Kogerstraat 1 (April–Oct Mon–Fri 10am–12.30pm & 1.30–3.30pm; €1.60), but it does make a decent base for exploring the rest of the island. The VVV has booklets detailing good **cycling routes**, as well as the best places to view the island's many **bird colonies**, protected in sanctuaries right across Texel – the island is one of the most important breeding grounds in Europe.

As regards other villages, **OUDESCHILD**, on the coast about 3km southeast of Den Burg, is worth a look for its **Maritiem en Juttersmuseum**,

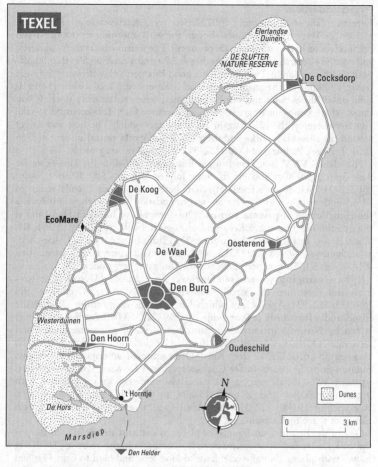

(Beachcombers Museum; Tues–Sat 10am–5pm, July & Aug also Mon 10am–5pm; €4.10), at Barentszstraat 21, which comprises a fascinating collection of marine junk recovered from offshore wrecks – everything from aeroplane engines to messages-in-bottles. Otherwise, in the opposite direction, **DE KOOG**, halfway up the west coast, is the island's main resort. It's a busy, popular spot equipped with a good, sandy beach, lots of restaurants and hotels, and a small army of campsites. De Koog also gives easy access to the circuitous streams, dunes and marshes of the delightful **De Slufter nature reserve** to the north and the **EcoMare** natural history museum and refuge for lost birds and seals about 2km to the south at Ruijslaan 92 (daily 9am–5pm; €7), is a small natural history museum. Moving on, the northern tip of Texel is occupied by the solitary hamlet of **DE COCKSDORP**, whose wedge of lonely little houses trail along a slender inlet. In the southern part of the island, **DEN HOORN** is another tiny place, surrounded by bulbfields and a handy base for exploring the thick mass of dunes that constitutes Texel's southern tip.

**Ferries** (daily 6.30am–9pm; ☎0222/369 691, ⓦwww.teso.nl) leave Den Helder for Texel roughly hourly, though the early-morning ferries don't run on Sundays or in the off-season (Sept–April). The journey takes thirty minutes, and costs €4 return; a bike adds another €2.70, and a car €38.50 (€26.50 off-peak and Nov–March). The island has a good **bus** network with fairly frequent services linking all the main villages; an inexpensive island-wide day pass is valid on all these buses and can be purchased when at the ferry dock. If you know where you want to go, you can also arrange for a **Telekomtaxi** to take you anywhere on the island; again ask at the ferry dock. The best way to get around the island is by **bike** and there are lots of **cycle rental** outlets: in Den Burg, F. Zegel, Parkstraat 14 (☎0222/312 150) will do very nicely.

The island's **VVV** is in Den Burg at Emmalaan 66 (Mon–Fri 9am–6pm, Sat 9am–5pm; April–Oct also Fri till 9pm; July & Aug also Sun 10am–1.30pm; ☎0222/314741, ⓦwww.texel.net). Staff here issue or sell a wide range of island information and operate an accommodation service; they also have a substantial cache of **private rooms**. One inexpensive **hotel** in Den Burg is the unassuming, two-star *'t Koogerend*, at Kogerstraat 94 (☎0222/313 301; ❷). There is also an **HI hostel** just outside Den Burg on the road to Oudeschild, at Schansweg 7 (☎0222/315 441, ⓦwww.stayokay.com; dorm bed €14.40–20.50). To get there, take bus #29 from the ferry dock.

If you're **camping**, you're spoilt for choice. In and around Den Burg are several sites: best are the small, well-run *De Koorn-Aar*, Grensweg 388 (☎0222/312 931; April–Oct), which has easy bus connections all over the island, and *'t Woutershok* at Rozendijk 38 (☎0222/313 080; April–Oct), which is run by Nivon, a nationwide organization devoted to culture, nature and recreation. Other sites dotted across the island include, in De Koog, *Kogerstrand*, Badweg 33 (☎0222/317 208; April–Oct), scattered among the dunes two minutes from the beach. In De Cocksdorp, there's *De Krim*, Roggeslootweg 6 (☎0222/390 111; all year), a comparatively upmarket vacation centre, with luxury bungalows and a pool. Finally, in Den Hoorn, *Loodsmansduin*, Rommelpot 19 (☎0222/319 203; April–Oct), is a large, isolated site with plenty of space for caravans.

One of the best of a small range of places to **eat and drink** in Den Burg is the café *De Worsteltent* at Smitsweg 6. By comparison, the resort of De Koog heaves with places, though you'd have to look long and hard to beat *Vogelhuis Oranjerie*, Dorpsstraat 204 (☎0222/317 279), an attractive restaurant where the emphasis is on local ingredients and prices for main courses hover around €16. If you make it as far as De Cocksdorp, you can refresh yourself with a drink, a pancake or a full meal at the *Paviljoen Vliezicht Restaurant* (☎0222/316 340; mid-March to Oct) on the beach.

# Het Gooi

The sprawling suburbs that spread southeast from Amsterdam towards Amersfoort (see p.211), known collectively as **Het Gooi**, are interrupted by open heaths, canals and woods, reminders of the time when this was a sparsely inhabited area largely devoted to sheep-farming. This changed after the Amsterdam–Amersfoort railway was constructed in 1874, when hundreds of prosperous Amsterdammers built their country homes here. Today, Het Gooi's low-key rural attractions remain popular with Dutch holidaymakers, but by and large the area is hardly essential viewing. That said, **Naarden**, encrusted by its star-shaped fortifications, is an agreeable little town, whilst both **Muiden** and **Hilversum**, the other two major places of interest, have some architectural high points – the first its old castle, the second the strikingly modern designs of Willem Dudok.

Getting around Het Gooi by public transport is straightforward. Only Hilversum is on the rail network, but bus #136 weaves a circuitous route through the area, beginning in Amsterdam and ending in Hilversum.

## Muiden

Heading southeast from Amsterdam, the first town you reach is **MUIDEN** (pronounced "mao-dn"), squashed around the River Vecht, which is packed with pleasure boats and dinghies primed to sail out into the Markermeer. It's the most famous sailing harbour in the Het Gooi area, not least because the royal yacht, *De Groene Draek*, is often moored here. Most of the sightseeing is done by weekend admirals eyeing up each other's boats, but an extra spark of interest is provided by the **Muiderslot** at Herengracht 1 (April–Oct Mon–Fri 10am–5pm, Sat & Sun 1–5pm; Nov–March Sat & Sun 1–4pm; guided tour €5.50; ⓦwww.muiderslot.nl). In the thirteenth century this was the home of Count Floris V, a sort of aristocratic Robin Hood who favoured the common people at the nobles' expense. They replied by kidnapping the count, imprisoning him in his own castle and stabbing him to death. Ransacked in the fourteenth century, Muiderslot's interior has now been returned to its seventeenth-century appearance in honour of a slightly more recent occupant, the poet Pieter Hooft. He was chatelain here from 1609 to 1647, a sinecure that allowed him to entertain a group of artistic and literary friends who became known as the Muiden Circle, and included Grotius, Vondel, Huygens and other Amsterdam intellectuals. The obligatory guided tour centres on this clique, in a restoration that is both believable and likeable – two things period rooms often aren't.

A fast and frequent **bus** service links Muiden with Amsterdam: bus #136 (every 30min; 30min) from Amstelstation continues on after Muiden to Naarden and Hilversum. Be warned that once you break free of Amsterdam, signs telling you where you are are few and far between and you can easily sail past Muiden without noticing – ask the driver to give you a shout. In Muiden, the bus drops you on the edge of town, a short, signposted walk from the Muiderslot and the **VVV** at Kazernestraat 10 (April to late Oct Mon–Fri 10am–5pm, Sat 10am–2pm; ☏0294/261 389). Once you've done the sights, there's no real reason to hang around unless, that is, you fancy pottering around in a **boat** – the Muiden Jachtverhuur Station (MYCS), at Naarderstraat 10 (☏0294/261 413) rents out sailboats. As far as eating and drinking goes, there are a couple of obvious places but you'd do better to carry on to Naarden, where there's a better choice.

## Naarden

Look at a postcard of **NAARDEN**, about 8km east of Muiden, and it seems as if the town was created by a giant pastry-cutter: the double rings of ramparts and moats, rare in Europe, were engineered between 1675 and 1685 to defend the eastern approaches to Amsterdam. They were still used in the 1920s, and one of the fortified spurs is now the wonderfully explorable **Nederlands Vestingmuseum** (Dutch Fortress Museum; March–Oct Tues–Fri 10.30am–5pm, Sat & Sun noon–5pm; June–Aug also Mon 10.30am–5pm;

Nov–Feb Sun noon–5pm only; €5; Ⓦ www.vestingmuseum.nl), at Westwalstraat 6, whose claustrophobic underground passages demonstrate how the garrison defended the town for nigh-on 300 years.

The rest of Naarden's tiny centre is peaceful and attractive. The small, low houses mostly date from after 1572 when the Spanish sacked the town and massacred the inhabitants, an act designed to warn others of the consequences of insurrection. Fortunately they spared the late Gothic **Grote Kerk** (June to mid-Sept Wed–Sun noon–5pm; free) and its superb vault paintings. Based on drawings by Dürer, these twenty wooden panels were painted between 1510 and 1518 and show an Old Testament story on the south side, paralleled by one from the New Testament on the north. To study the paintings without cricking your neck, borrow a mirror at the entrance. The church is also noted for its wonderful acoustics: every year there are several acclaimed performances of Bach's *St Matthew Passion* in the Grote Kerk in the days leading up to Easter – details from the VVV (see below). A haul up the 235 steps of the Grote Kerk's massive square **tower** gives the best view of the fortress. The elaborately step-gabled building opposite the church is the **Stadhuis** (April–Sept Mon–Sat 1.30–4.30pm; free), built in 1601 and still in use today.

Naarden also possesses the mildly absorbing **Comenius Museum** at Kloosterstraat 33 (Wed–Sun noon–5pm; €2.50; Ⓦ www.comeniusmuseum.nl). Jan Amos Komenski (1592–1670), his name latinized as Comenius, was a philosopher, cartographer and educational reformer who was born in Moravia, then part of the Holy Roman Empire and today part of the Czech Republic. A Protestant, he was expelled from the empire for his religious beliefs in 1621 and spent the next 36 years wandering round Europe preaching and teaching before finally settling in Amsterdam. The museum outlines Comenius' life and times and takes a stab at explaining his work, notably his government-commissioned plan to improve the Swedish educational system and his 1658 *Orbis Pictus* ("The World in Pictures"), the first-ever picture-book for children. Further sections relate his work to that of other philosophers of the day, principally the Frenchman René Descartes, who also lived in Amsterdam (from 1629 to 1649). After his death, Comenius was, for some unexplained reason, buried here in Naarden – hence the museum and the adjoining **mausoleum**, the last remnant of a medieval convent built on the site in 1438. In the 1930s the Dutch authorities refused the Czechoslovak government's request for the repatriation of the philosopher's remains, and instead sold them the building (and the land it stood on) for the symbolic price of one guilder: the mausoleum remains a tiny slice of Czech territory to this day. The museum-mausoleum is popular with Czech and Slovak tourists and Bratislava's Comenius University is named after the philosopher.

## Practicalities

Naarden is on the same **bus** #136 route as Muiden, with the journey from Amsterdam taking fifty minutes. The bus drops you off within sight of the Grote Kerk's tower – and within easy walking distance of all the sights. Everything is clearly signposted, including the **VVV**, about ten minutes' walk away at Adriaan Dortsmanplein 1b (May–Oct Mon–Fri 10am–5pm, Sat 10am–3pm, Sun noon–3pm; Nov–April Tues–Sun 1am–4pm; ℡035/694 2836). There is one central **hotel**, *Poorters*, in a trim little older house at Marktstraat 66 (℡035/694 4868, Ⓦ www.poorters.nl; ❷); advance reservations are advised – the hotel only has a handful of rooms.

For **food**, there's a concentration of places along the main shopping street, Marktstraat: from the bus stop, take Cattenhagestraat and you'll soon reach it.

**Café** options here include the *Salon de Thé Sans Doute* at no. 33, great for sandwiches and coffee, and the *Café De Doelen*, next to the Grote Kerk on the south side at no. 7, perfect for an inexpensive meal. The best **restaurant** in town is *Het Arsenaal*, in the old arsenal on the east side of the centre at Kooltjesbuurt 1 (☎035/694 9148), where the excellent Franco-Dutch main courses start at around €20.

## Hilversum and around

The main town of Het Gooi is **HILVERSUM**, a sprawling, leafy commuter suburb located just 7km south of Naarden and built for well-heeled Amsterdammers in the nineteenth century. In recent years, many of the old villas have been flashily modernized and some have been converted into studios for the Dutch media, reflecting the town's new role as the centre of the country's broadcasting industry.

Hilversum's main sight is the **Raadhuis** (town hall), about 700m west of the train station at Dudopark 1. Dating from 1931, the building is the work of Willem Marinus Dudok (1884–1974), an architect who was influenced by the innovative American Frank Lloyd Wright. The structure's design is based on a deceptively simple progression of straw-coloured blocks rising to a clock tower, with long, slender bricks giving it a strong horizontal emphasis. The interior is well worth seeing too: essentially a series of lines and boxes, its marble walls are margined with black, like a monochrome Mondrian painting, all coolly and immaculately proportioned. Dudok also designed the interior decorations, and though some have been altered, his style confidently prevails, right down to the ashtrays and lights. Long-time resident of Hilversum, Dudok worked for the city council for over thirty years, first as the director of public works and then as the city architect. If the Raadhuis whets your appetite, the VVV (see below) sells a guide to several of the other buildings he designed – a pleasant enough way to spend a couple of hours.

**Trains** leave Amsterdam's Centraal Station twice an hour for Hilversum, and take about thirty minutes to get there. **Bus** #136 also runs to Hilversum, departing from Amstelstation; departures are every half-hour, but the bus follows a meandering route and the journey takes all of two hours. Hilversum's train and bus stations are next door to each other and a short walk from the **VVV**, at Noordse Bosje 1 (mid-May to mid-Sept Mon–Fri 9.30am–5pm, Sat 10am–4pm; rest of year Mon–Fri 9am–5pm, Sat 9.30am–5pm; ☎035/624 1751). They have a small supply of private rooms, but with Amsterdam so close, and connections to more interesting towns so easy, there's little reason to stay. For **eating and drinking**, the pick of several inexpensive options near the train station is the *Grand Café Gooiland*, Emmastraat 2, which offers a good range of Dutch and French dishes. Alternatively, the excellent *Nusantara*, at Vaartweg 15a (☎035/623 2367), is a well established Indonesian restaurant. You can rent bikes, as usual, from the train station.

### Around Hilversum: exploring Het Gooi

Hilversum makes a good starting point for seeing the best of **Het Gooi** (which you can easily do in a day), and the VVV sells an excellent walking and cycling map of the area, the *Wandel- en fietskaart Gooi en Vechtstreek*. The text isn't in English, but the map is pretty easy to understand and on the ground the routes are well signposted. In particular, consider embarking on the "**Gooiroute**" – a scenic 30km-long cycle route that leads across the heathery heath to Laren, then via Blaricum to Huizen on the shore of the Gooimeer, and back via the woods to Hilversum. To get to the route from Hilversum train station, cross the rail line and continue along this road until just after you've crossed a round-about, where you'll find the first "Gooiroute" signpost at a small road to the right. If you don't fancy the idea of cycling, bus #136 (every 30min between Amsterdam and Hilversum) is almost like a guided tour, taking the most circuitous route possible through every town and village along the way.

The most attractive village hereabouts is **LAREN**, halfway between Hilversum and Huizen, if only because of its excellent **Singer Museum** of modern art at Oude Drift 1 (Tues–Sun 11am–5pm; admission varies with exhibition; Ⓦwww.singerlaren.nl); bus #136 stops outside. Once a drowsy sheep-farming community, Laren became fashionable with artists in the 1870s, notably those of the Impressionist Hague School, and the surrounding landscape, as well as the village's farmers and weavers, and even the interiors of their farmhouses, all appear in their paintings. In later years, Expressionist and Modernist painters also came to the Laren area, and their works were gathered together by the Singers, an American couple who moved here from Pittsburgh in 1901. The museum, which is based on their collection, opened in 1956 and offers an enterprising programme of temporary exhibitions. As for the rest of the village, its shady streets and diminutive houses centre around the **Brink**, the main square, which has several pleasant bars, an outdoor pancake restaurant and **St Jans Basiliek** (Mon–Thurs 9am–noon; free), a good-looking church built in 1925.

# Travel details

## Trains

**Alkmaar** to: Haarlem (every 30min; 25min); Hoorn (every 30min; 25min).
**Amsterdam CS** to: Alkmaar (every 30min; 30min); Den Helder (every 30min; 1hr); Enkhuizen (every 30min; 55min); Haarlem (every 15min; 15min); Hilversum (twice hourly; 30min); Hoorn (every 30min; 35min); Zaandam (every 15min; 10min).
**Haarlem** to: Alkmaar (every 30min; 25min); Hoorn (every 30min; 25min); Zandvoort (every 30min; 10min).
**Hilversum** to: Amersfoort (every 30min; 15min); Utrecht (every 20min; 20min).

30min; 40min); Naarden (every 30min; 55min); Volendam (every 30min; 30min); Zaandam (every 30min; 40min); Zaanse Schans (every 30min; 1hr).
**Edam** to: Hoorn (every 30min; 25min).
**Enkhuizen** to: Lelystad (every 2hr; 45min).
**Haarlem** to: Bloemendaal (every 30min; 15min); Zandvoort (every 15min; 20min).
**Hoorn** to: Medemblik (every 30min; 30–40min).
**Marken** to: Monnickendam (every 30min; 15min).
**Monnickendam** to: Volendam (hourly; 20min).
**Muiden** to: Hilversum (every 30min; 1hr 15min); Naarden (every 30min; 15min).

## Buses

**Alkmaar** to: Bergen (every 15min; 15min); Harlingen (hourly; 1hr 45min); Leeuwarden (hourly; 2hr 15min).
**Amsterdam** to: Edam (every 30min; 40min); Marken (every 30min; 30min); Muiden (every

## Ferries

**Den Helder** to: Texel (hourly; 30min).
**Enkhuizen** to: Medemblik (April–Oct 2–3 daily; 1hr 30min); Stavoren (May–Sept 3 daily; late April & early Oct 2 daily; 1hr 20min); Urk (late June to Aug Mon–Sat 3 daily; 1hr 45min).
**Marken** to: Volendam (April–Oct daily every 30-45min 11am–5pm; 30min).

# Zuid-Holland and Utrecht

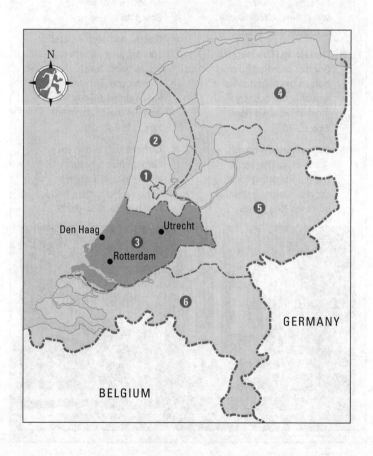

CHAPTER 3　Highlights

* **Leiden** Patterned by canals, this old university town has the museums to whet any historical or artistic palate. See p.167

* **Keukenhof gardens** Tight lines of colour reminiscent of Mondrian define the spring flowering season in the luxuriant Dutch bulbfields. See p.172

* **Den Haag (The Hague)** Sophisticated city that boasts the Mauritshuis, arguably the country's most impressive gallery. See p.173

* **Scheveningen beach** Acres of golden sand, the grand setting for a sand-sculpture festival in summer. See p.185

* **Delft** Lovely little town with one of the prettiest market squares in the country. See p.186

* **Rotterdam** Gritty and boisterous port city that has resurrected itself in flash modern style after extensive war damage. See p.191

* **Gouda** Archetypal Dutch country town, home of the famous round cheese and a splendid set of stained-glass windows in the St Janskerk. See p.199

* **Utrecht** Young and exuberant university town ideally placed halfway between Rotterdam and Amsterdam. See p.207

# Zuid-Holland
# and Utrecht

Zuid-Holland (pronounced "zowd"), or South Holland, is the most
densely populated province of the Netherlands, with a string of towns
and cities that make up most of the so-called **Randstad** (literally "Rim-
Town"). Careful urban planning has succeeded in stopping this from
becoming an amorphous conurbation, however, and each town has preserved
a pronounced identity. A short hop from Amsterdam is **Leiden**, a university
town par excellence, with an antique centre latticed by canals and dotted with
fine old buildings. Moving on, **Den Haag** (The Hague), once a humdrum
government town, has jazzed itself up and is now a very likeable city with a
string of good museums and an appealing, if low-key, bar and restaurant scene.
There's also **Delft**, a smaller place with just 100,000 inhabitants and the possessor of an extremely pretty centre, replete with handsome seventeenth-century buildings. Next it's on to the rough and tumble of big-city **Rotterdam**,
the world's biggest port, where an adventurous city council has stacked up a
string of first-rate attractions, from fine art through to harbour tours. From
here, it's a short journey inland to both **Gouda**, a good-looking country town
historically famed for its cheese market, and the tranquil charms of rural
**Oudewater**. Back on the coast, **Dordrecht** marks the southern edge of the
Randstad and is of interest as an ancient port and for its location, within easy
striking distance of the windmills of the **Kinderdijk** and the creeks and
marshes of the **Biesbosch**. Finally, the province of **Utrecht** holds two places
of some interest: **Utrecht** itself, a sprawling industrial city with a dramatic history and a bustling, youthful centre, and **Amersfoort**, half the size of its neighbour and home town of Piet Mondrian.

  Historically, Zuid-Holland is part of what was once simply Holland, the richest and most influential province in the country. Throughout the Golden Age,
Holland dominated the political, social and cultural life of the Republic, over-
shadowing its neighbours whose economies were dwarfed by Holland's
success. There are constant reminders of this pre-eminence in the province's
buildings: elaborate town halls proclaim civic importance and even the usually
sombre Calvinist **churches** allow themselves decorative excesses – the later
windows of Gouda's Janskerk being a case in point. Many of the great Dutch
**painters** either came from or worked here, too – Rembrandt, Vermeer, Jan
Steen – a tradition that continued into the nineteenth century with the paintings

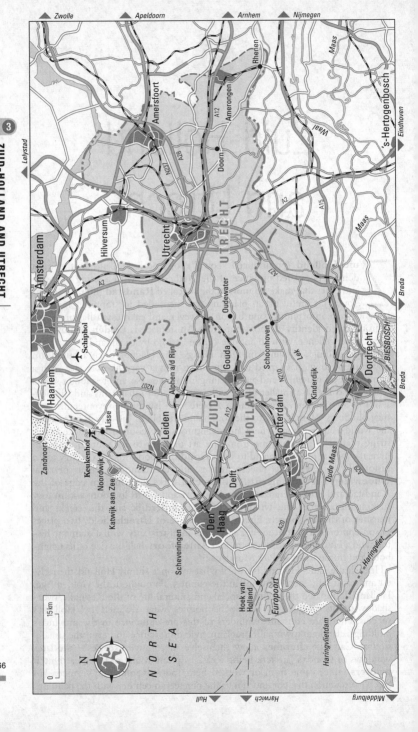

of the Hague School. All the towns offer good **museums** and galleries, most notably The Hague's Mauritshuis and Rotterdam's Boijmans-Van Beuningen. In addition, the coastal cities – especially Leiden and Den Haag – are only a short bus or tram ride from the wide sandy **beaches** of the North Sea coast, while the pancake-flat Randstad landscape is at least brightened by rainbow flashes of **bulbfields** in spring with the **Keukenhof gardens**, near Leiden, having the finest display.

A fast and efficient rail network makes travelling around Zuid-Holland extremely easy, and where the trains fizzle out, buses take over.

# Leiden and around

Ideal for a day-trip from Amsterdam, just 30km away and with fast and frequent train connections, **LEIDEN** has two main claims to fame: it possesses one of the most celebrated universities in Europe, and Rembrandt was born here in 1606. A lively and energetic place, Leiden's antique, sometimes careworn centre, with its maze of narrow lanes, is webbed by canals and encircled by a waterway that marks the line of the medieval walls. The centre is also liberally sprinkled with bars and restaurants and boasts a string of museums – too many to see in just a day.

Leiden may well have been founded by the **Romans** as a forward base on an important trade route running behind the dunes; it was certainly fortified in the ninth century when the local lords added a castle, among the marshes on an artificial mound. After Flemish weavers migrated here in the fourteenth century the town prospered as a cloth-making centre, but the town didn't make much of a mark until the foundation of its **university**, a gift from William the Silent as a reward for enduring a year-long siege by the Spanish. The town had emerged victorious on October 3, 1574, when William cut through the dykes around the town and sailed in with his fleet for a dramatic rescue. The event is still commemorated with an annual fair, fireworks, and the consumption of two traditional dishes: herring and white bread, which the fleet brought with them, and *hutspot*, a vegetable and potato stew, a cauldron of which was found simmering in the abandoned Spanish camp outside the walls.

## Arrival, information and accommodation

Leiden's ultra-modern **train station** is next to the **bus station** on the north-west edge of town, a five-minute walk from the Beestenmarkt at the west end of the centre. Halfway between is the **VVV**, at Stationsweg 2 (Mon–Fri 11am–7pm & Sat 11am–3pm; ☏0900/222 2333, Ⓦwww.leiden.nl), which has useful maps and brochures detailing walking tours of the town as well as a wide range of regional information.

Of the town's **hotels**, easily the most appealing is the excellent *Nieuw Minerva*, a cosy, very Dutch hotel which occupies a sequence of old canal-side houses in the centre at Boommarkt 23 (☏071/512 6358, Ⓦwww .nieuwminerva.nl; ❷). All their rooms are comfortable, in an undemanding sort of way, but the "honeymoon room" (❺) is up a notch, boasting a four-poster bed and fancy drapes. A reasonable second choice is the three-star, fifteen-room *De Doelen*, by another of the town's canals at Rapenburg 2 (☏071/512 0527, Ⓦwww.dedoelen.com; ❸). Finally, there's the bargain-basement *Hotel Rose*, at Beestenmarkt 16 (☏071/514 6630, ℻071/514 6630; ❶).

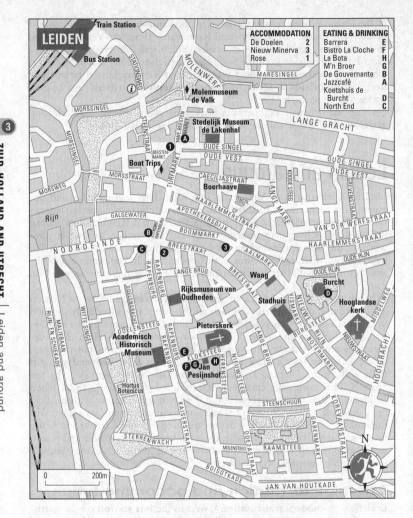

## The Town

The obvious place to start an exploration of the centre is the
**Beestenmarkt**, a large and really rather ugly open space that's long been a
major meeting point. The square is also the starting point for **canal trips**
around the centre – a pleasant enough way to spend forty minutes
(April–Sept 3–5 daily; €5). From here, it's a hop and a jump to **Rapenburg**,
a gentle, curving canal lined by some of Leiden's grandest mansions. In one
of the largest, at no. 28, is the town's most important museum, the
**Rijksmuseum van Oudheden** (National Museum of Antiquities; Tues–Fri
10am–5pm, Sat & Sun noon–5pm; €6; ⓦwww.rmo.nl), a leading archeological museum, holding extensive Egyptian and classical collections. You can
see one of its major exhibits, the Taffeh Temple, for free – it's located in the

covered atrium at the entrance. The temple was a gift from the Egyptian government, in gratitude for Dutch help with the 1960s UNESCO excavations, which uncovered a number of Nubian monuments. Dating back to the first century AD, the temple was adapted in the fourth century to the worship of Isis, eventually being sanctified as a Christian church four hundred years later. The Egyptians placed firm conditions on their legacy: no one should have to pay to see it, and the temperature and humidity were to be carefully regulated.

Inside the museum proper, there are oodles of classical Greek and Roman sculptures, including stolid busts, statues and friezes from Imperial Rome, plus the remains of a temple dedicated to Nehellania – a goddess of sailors – which was uncovered in Zeeland. The most enjoyable section, though, is the Egyptian one, beginning with wall reliefs, statues and sarcophagi from tombs and temples, and continuing with a set of mummies and sarcophagi as complete as you're likely to see outside Egypt. Particular highlights here include the exceptionally well-preserved *Three Figures of Maya* and the stunning stele from Hoey. There's also a Netherlands archeological section, which tracks through the history of the country from prehistoric to medieval times, but perhaps inevitably this suffers by comparison with what has gone before.

Further along Rapenburg, at no. 73, a three-sided courtyard complex includes – on the left – the building that became the university's first home, after previously being part of a medieval monastery. One room here contains the **Academisch Historisch Museum** (Sept–June Mon & Tues 9am–5pm, Wed 1–5pm; free), detailing the university's history. Through the courtyard, and much more interesting, is the **Hortus Botanicus** (April–Sept daily 10am–6pm; Oct–March Mon–Fri & Sun 10am–4pm; €4) lushly planted and subtly landscaped botanical gardens that stretch along the Witte Singel canal. Planted in 1587, this is one of the oldest botanical gardens in Europe, a mixture of carefully tended beds of shrubs and hothouses full of tropical foliage.

### Pieterskerk, the Stadhuis and the Waag

Cross Rapenburg from the Academisch Historisch Museum, and you're in the network of narrow streets that constitutes the medieval town, converging on a central square and the Gothic **Pieterskerk** (daily 1.30–4pm; free), Leiden's principal church. Deconsecrated now, it has an empty warehouse-like feel, but among the fixtures that remain are a simple and beautiful Renaissance rood screen and a host of memorials to the sundry notables buried here – including one to John Robinson (1575–1625), leader of the Pilgrim Fathers. Robinson lived in a house on the site of what is now the **Jean Pesijnshofje** at Kloksteeg 21, right beside the church. A curate in England at the turn of the seventeenth century, he was suspended from preaching in 1604, later fleeing with his congregation to pursue his Puritanism in the more amenable atmosphere of Calvinist Holland. Settling in Leiden, Robinson acted as pastor to growing numbers, but even here he found himself at odds with the religious establishment. In 1620, one hundred of his followers – the "Pilgrim Fathers" – sailed via Plymouth for the untrammelled wilderness of America, though Robinson died before he could join them; he's buried in the church.

From the church, it's a short stroll east to **Breestraat**, marking the edge of Leiden's commercial centre but undistinguished except for the **Stadhuis**, an imposing edifice whose Renaissance facade is a copy of the late sixteenth-century original destroyed by fire in 1929. Behind the Stadhuis, the canals that cut Leiden's centre into pocket-sized islands converge at the busiest point in town, the site of a vigorous general **market** on Wednesdays and Saturdays. Here, a tangle of narrow bridges is flanked by a number of buildings, from overblown Art Nouveau department stores to modest terrace houses. On the south side is the **Waag**, built to a design by Pieter Post (1608–69) and fronted with a naturalistic frieze showing a merchant watching straining labourers. Post was a successful architect, but his artist brother Frans was even better known for his major contribution to the *Historia Naturalis Brasiliae*, an influential ethnographic study of eastern Brazil, a Dutch colony from 1630 to 1654.

### The Hooglandsekerk and the Burcht

The general market sprawls right over the bridges and extends southeast along one of the town's prettiest canals, the **Nieuwe Rijn**. Ambling along its north bank, take the first left, Burgsteeg, and turn right at the end for the **Hooglandsekerk** on Nieuwstraat (mid-May to mid-Sept Mon 1–5pm, Tues–Fri 11am–3.30pm, Sat 11am–4pm; free). A light and lofty Gothic structure built in stages over a couple of hundred years, the church holds a monument to Pieter van der Werff, the heroic burgomaster of Leiden at the time of the 1573–74 siege. When the situation became so desperate that the people were all for giving up, the burgomaster, no doubt remembering the massacre at Haarlem, offered up his own body to be eaten. The invitation was declined, but it inspired new determination in the town's flagging citizens.

Doubling back to the end of Burgsteeg, follow the alley and you'll soon pass the steps up to the **Burcht** (daily 10am–10pm; free), the heavily restored stone shell of a medieval fortress perched high above the town on an artificial mound. This is where Leiden began, as an isolated ninth-century stronghold amongst the marshes; it's worth climbing up to the fort for a wide view of Leiden's roofs and towers. At the far end of the alley is the **Oude Rijn** canal, on the other side of which lies the blandly pedestrian **Haarlemmerstraat**, the town's main shopping street.

### Museum Boerhaave and the Stedelijk Museum de Lakenhal

A few metres to the north of Haarlemmerstraat, the **Museum Boerhaave** – the National Museum of the History of Science and Medicine – at Lange St Agnietenstraat 10 (Tues–Sat 10am–5pm, Sun noon–5pm; €3.50; Ⓦwww.museumboerhaave.nl) is named after a seventeenth-century Leiden surgeon, one Herman Boerhaave. It gives a brief but fairly absorbing overview of scientific and medical developments over the last five centuries, with particular reference to Dutch achievements, including some gruesome surgical implements, pickled brains and suchlike.

Five minutes' walk north from here, Leiden's **Stedelijk Museum de Lakenhal** (Tues–Fri 10am–5pm, Sat & Sun noon–5pm; €4; Ⓦwww.lakenhal .nl), housed in the old Cloth Hall at Oude Singel 32, has an engaging collection of fine and applied arts. On the ground floor, amongst a healthy sample of local sixteenth- and seventeenth-century paintings, are examples of the work of Jacob van Swanenburgh (first teacher of the young Rembrandt), Jan Lievens (with whom Rembrandt shared a studio), and Gerrit Dou (1613–75), whose exquisite *Astrologer* is in Room 8. Rembrandt's first pupil, Dou began by imitating his master, but soon developed his own style, pioneering the Leiden tradition of small, minutely detailed pictures of enamel-like smoothness. There's also Lucas van Leyden's (1494–1533) alarming and spectacularly unsuccessful *Last Judgement* triptych in Room 6, several paintings devoted to the siege of 1574 and the heroics of burgomaster Werff, plus mixed rooms of furniture, silver, tiles, glass and ceramics. Rembrandt himself, despite being born in Leiden, is poorly represented; he left his home town at the tender age of fourteen, and, although he returned in 1625, it was only for six years, after which he settled permanently in Amsterdam. Only a handful of his Leiden paintings survive, but there's one here, *Agamemnon before Palamedes*, a stilted and rather unsuccessful rendition of the classical tale, painted in 1626.

The other floors of the museum are of cursory interest only: the first floor holds several old guild rooms moved here from other parts of Leiden, the second floor is used for temporary exhibitions and the top floor has a series of modest displays on the town's history.

## The Windmill

At the west end of Oude Singel turn right and it's a couple of hundred metres to the **Molenmuseum de Valk** (Valk Windmill Museum; Tues–Sat 10am–5pm, Sun 1–5pm; €2.50; ⓦ home.wanadoo.nl/molenmuseum), a restored grain mill and the last survivor of the twenty-odd windmills built on the town's outer fortifications in the eighteenth century. On the ground floor are the millers' living quarters, furnished in simple period style, while upstairs are several different displays, the most interesting of which is a slide show and exhibition recounting the history of Dutch windmills.

### The Dutch bulbfields

The pancake-flat fields stretching north from Leiden towards Haarlem (see p.131) are the heart of the Dutch **bulbfields**, whose bulbs and blooms support a billion-euro industry and some ten thousand growers, as well as attracting tourists in their droves. Bulbs have flourished here since the late sixteenth century, when one Carolus Clusius, a Dutch botanist and one-time gardener to the Habsburg emperor, brought the first tulip bulb over from Vienna, where it had – in its turn – been brought from Asia Minor by an Austrian aristocrat. The tulip flourished in the Netherlands' sandy soil and was so highly prized that it became the subject of irrational speculation. At the height of the boom – in the mid-1630s – bulbs were commanding extraordinary prices: the artist Jan van Goyen paid 1,900 guilders and two paintings for ten rare bulbs, while a bag of one hundred bulbs was swapped for a coach and horses. When the government finally intervened in 1636, the industry returned to reality with a bang, leaving hundreds of investors ruined – much to the satisfaction of the country's Calvinist ministers who had railed against the excesses.

Other types of bulbs have also been introduced, and nowadays the spring flowering season begins in mid-March with **crocuses**, followed by **daffodils** and yellow **narcissi** in late March, **hyacinths** and **tulips** from mid-April through to May, and **gladioli** in August. The view from any train heading north from Leiden gives a brief taste of what's on offer – glorious fields divided into geometric blocks of pure colour – but you really need more time. Signed car and cycle routes guide visitors through the bulb fields and local VVVs sell pamphlets describing the routes in detail. You could also drop by the bulb growers' showpiece, the **Keukenhof** gardens (see p.172). Bear in mind also that there are any number of local flower festivals and parades in mid- to late April; every VVV has the details of these.

## Eating and drinking

Many of Leiden's choicest **cafés** and **restaurants** are concentrated around Pieterskerk. It's here you'll find *M'n Broer*, Kloksteeg 7, an agreeable, low-key café-bar offering a tasty range of light meals, and the rather more polished *Bistro La Cloche*, a French restaurant just along the street at no. 3 (℡071/512 3053; closed Sun). Nearby, *La Bota*, at Herensteeg 9, has some of the best-value local food in town as well as an excellent range of beers, while *Koetshuis de Burcht*, just below the Burcht at Burgsteeg 13 (℡071/512 1688), is a fashionable French/Dutch bistro working to an imaginative menu. Another good choice is the smart, bistro-style *Restaurant de Gouvernante*, Kort Rapenburg 17 (℡071/514 8818; closed Mon), which serves such delicacies as steak with truffles. Main courses here average €20–25 and reservations are advised.

There's no shortage of places to **drink**. The *North End English Pub* at Noordeinde 55, on the corner with Rapenburg, is a lively and popular spot as is *Barrera*, a fashionable café-bar and student favourite with a good beer menu on Rapenburg, opposite the entrance to the Hortus Botanicus. Otherwise, *Jazzcafé The Duke*, on the corner of Oude Singel and Nieuwe Beestenmarkt, has a busy bar and live jazz most nights.

## The Keukenhof gardens

The small town of **LISSE**, halfway between Leiden and Haarlem, is home to the largest flower gardens in the world, the **Keukenhof gardens** (late March to late May daily 8am–7.30pm; €11.50; Ⓦwww.keukenhof.com). The Keukenhof (literally, the "kitchen garden") was set up in 1949, designed by a group of prominent bulb growers to convert people to the joys of growing flowers from bulbs in their own gardens. Its site is the former estate of a fifteenth-century countess, who used to grow herbs and vegetables for her dining table here – hence the name. Some seven million flowers are on show for their full flowering period, complemented, in case of especially harsh winters, by 5000 square metres of glasshouses holding indoor displays. You could easily spend a whole day here, swooning among the sheer abundance of it all, but to get the best of it you need to come early, before the tour buses pack the place. There are several **restaurants** in the 28 hectares of grounds, and well-marked **paths** take you all the way through the gardens, which specialize in daffodils, narcissi, hyacinths and tulips.

To get to the Keukenhof by **public transport** from Leiden, catch either the special bus or regular bus #54 (every 30min; 30min) from the main bus station. To get there from Haarlem, the easiest way is to take the train to Leiden (every 20min; 20min) and then the bus.

## Katwijk-aan-Zee and Noordwijk-aan-Zee

Leiden has easy access to some fine **beaches**, and although the nearest seaside resorts aren't in themselves much to write home about, in good weather a trip out to the coast is enticing. The best local option is **KATWIJK-AAN-ZEE**, a thirty-minute ride west from Leiden station on bus #31 (every 15min, half-hourly on Sunday). There's something very civil about this unassuming resort, its low-slung houses strung along behind a wide sandy beach. Here and there, a row of cottages recalls the time when Katwijk was a busy fishing village, but there are no real sights as such with the possible exception of a chunky **lighthouse**, dating from 1610. The bus #31 terminus is next to the lighthouse, and close to an undeveloped expanse of dune that extends south along the shore toward Den Haag–

an ideal stretch for secluded sunbathing. If you decide to spend the night here, the **VVV** (April–Aug Mon–Sat 9am–6pm; July & Aug also Sun 11am–3pm; rest of year Mon–Fri 9am–5pm, Sat 9am–1pm; ☎071/407 5444), a few metres from the lighthouse at Vuurbaakplein 11, will do their best to help you out. They have a supply of **private rooms** (❶–❷) as well as a list of hotels and pensions, but even they may struggle to find a vacancy in July and August.

On the northern edge of the resort, beside the main bus route, are the **Katwijk Sluices**. Completed in 1807, this chain of gates regulates the flow of the Oude Rijn as it approaches the sea. Around high tide, the gates are closed and when they are re-opened, the pressure of the accumulated water brushes aside the sand deposited at the mouth of the river. This simple system has effectively fixed the course of the Oude Rijn, which for centuries had been continually diverted by the sand deposits, flooding the surrounding area.

**NOORDWIJK-AAN-ZEE**, some 4km up the coast and reachable by half-hourly bus #40 and #42 from Leiden station in thirty minutes, is larger and of less appeal than Katwijk. Indeed, it's not much more than a sequence of hotel developments built across the undulating sand dunes behind the coast. The one time it's worth coming to see the town is the last weekend in April, when a flower parade from Haarlem arrives and makes an illuminated tour.

# Den Haag and Scheveningen

**DEN HAAG** (**The Hague**) is different from any other Dutch city. Since the sixteenth century it's been the focus of national institutions (although Amsterdam is the present capital), in a country built on civic independence and munificence. Frequently disregarded until the development of central government in the nineteenth century, the city's older buildings are a comparatively subdued and modest collection, with little of Amsterdam's flamboyance. Indeed, the majority of the canal houses are demurely classical and exude that sense of sedate prosperity which prompted Matthew Arnold's harsh estimation of 1859: "I never saw a city where the well-to-do classes seemed to have given the whole place so much of their own air of wealth, finished cleanliness, and comfort; but I never saw one, either, in which my heart would so have sunk at the thought of living."

Nevertheless, much has changed since Arnold's days. His "well-to-do classes" – now mostly diplomats and top-flight executives – are still in evidence, inflating city-centre prices, but parts of the centre are now festooned with slick government skyrises and, more promisingly, Den Haag now holds a slew of lively and reasonably priced bars and restaurants. A creative city council has done much to jazz the city up too, organizing a lively programme of concerts and events, and Den Haag boasts several fascinating and outstanding museums, principally the wonderful Dutch paintings of the **Mauritshuis**, and more modern works of art at the **Gemeentemuseum**.

## Arrival, information and city transport

The city has two **train stations**: Den Haag HS (Hollands Spoor) and Den Haag CS (Centraal Station). Of the two, Den Haag CS is the more convenient, sited five minutes' walk east of the town centre. Most of the city's trams and buses stop here too. Den Haag HS is 1km to the south. There are frequent rail services between

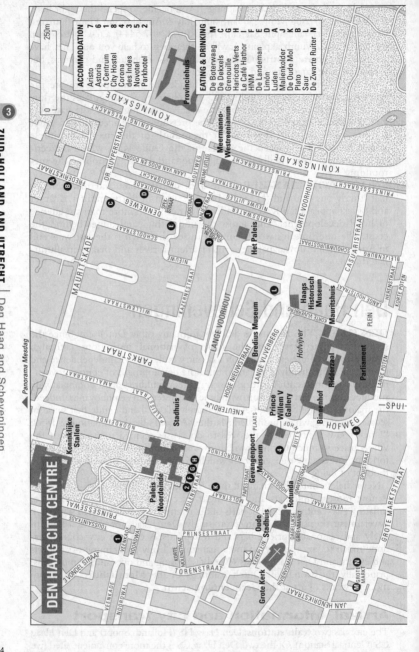

# DEN HAAG CITY CENTRE

3

▲ Panorama Mesdag

**ACCOMMODATION**

| | |
|---|---|
| Aristo | 7 |
| Astoria | 6 |
| 't Centrum | 1 |
| City Hostel | 8 |
| Corona | 4 |
| des Indes | 3 |
| Novotel | 5 |
| Parkhotel | 2 |

**EATING & DRINKING**

| | |
|---|---|
| De Boterwaag | M |
| De Dekxels | C |
| Grenouille | G |
| Haricots Verts | H |
| Le Café Hathor | F |
| HNM | E |
| De Landeman | D |
| Limón | A |
| Luden | J |
| Malienkolder | K |
| De Oude Mol | B |
| Plato | L |
| Saur | I |
| De Zwarte Ruiter | N |

250m

0

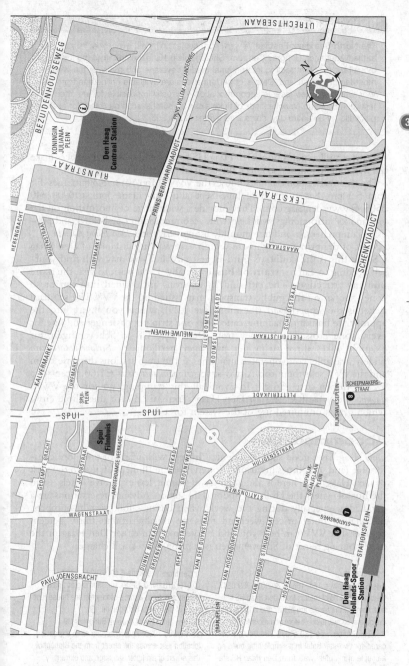

③

## North Sea Jazz Festival

The **North Sea Jazz Festival** (ⓦ www.northseajazz.nl), held every year in mid-July at the Nederlands Congres Centrum, Churchillplein 10, is the country's most prestigious jazz event, attracting international media coverage and many of the world's most famous musicians. Details of performances are available online and from the VVV, which will also reserve accommodation – virtually impossible to find after the festival has begun. Various kinds of tickets can be purchased; a *dagkaart*, for example, valid for an entire day, costs a very reasonable €55.

the two as well as trams from Den Haag HS to the centre – several services make the five-minute journey, so check the destination sign before hopping on.

The Centraal Station complex houses the **VVV** (Mon 10am–5.30pm, Tues–Fri 9am–5.30pm, Sat 10am–5pm; June–Sept also Sun 11am–3pm; ☎0900/340 3505, ⓦ www.denhaag.com). They provide a wide range of information on the city and its surroundings, will help with accommodation (see below), and publish a comprehensive and free monthly listings magazine, *Den Haag Agenda*.

Most of the principal sights are within easy walking distance of Den Haag CS, but this is the country's third-largest city and you may well find yourself needing to catch a **tram or bus**, especially if you want to visit the more outlying attractions. The city and its environs are divided into ten or so zones, shown on the public transport map issued by the VVV. The standard ticket is the *strippenkaart* (for more, see p.29), which you insert into the appropriate franking machine, cancelling one strip per passenger and one for every zone crossed: a journey from Den Haag CS to Scheveningen, for example, takes three strips per passenger per journey. *Strippenkaarts* are widely available: coin-operated machines at the train stations dispense them and the VVV sells them too. A two-strip *strippenkaart* costs €1.60, three-strip €2.40, fifteen-strip €6.20. To avoid all this stamping, go for the VVV's *dagkaart* (day-card; €5.50 for Den Haag centre, €7.50 for the whole city), which grants unlimited use of the system for a day.

## Accommodation

Den Haag has a good supply of central **hotels**, with many of the more comfortable (and sometimes luxurious) dotted near the Binnenhof, just to the west of Den Haag CS. There is also a cluster of plainer, less expensive hotels – and the **hostel** – near the Hollands Spoor (HS) station. Advance reservations are a good idea especially during the week when business folk visit in numbers, pushing up hotel prices: weekend rates are usually around thirty percent cheaper. The VVV can help you find a hotel room in either Den Haag or the neighbouring resort of Scheveningen (see p.185) for a small charge.

### Hotels

**Aristo** Stationsweg 164–166 ☎ & ☏070/389 0847. Clean and tidy hotel metres from Den Haag HS station; some of the rooms are bigger and brighter than the others, so ask to see before you register. ③
**Astoria** Stationsweg 139 ☎070/384 0401. Well cared-for two-star hotel in a simple little building a couple of minutes' walk from Den Haag HS station. One of the city's better budget options, but the rooms are small and there's no breakfast. ③

**'t Centrum** Veenkade 6 ☎070/346 3657 ☏070/310 6460. Small, unassuming but cosy two-star hotel in a three-storey terrace house just west of the Paleis Noordeinde. ③
**Golden Tulip Hotel Corona** Buitenhof 39 ☎070/363 7930, ⓦwww.corona.nl. In a great location just across the street from the Binnenhof, this smart chain hotel has large and extremely comfortable double rooms at €170; weekend discounts are often available. ⑥

Des Indes Lange Voorhout 54 ⊕070/361 2345, ⊛www.desindes.com. Luxurious five-star hotel that has long been – and still is – a favourite with visiting bigwigs. It was built in the 1850s as a private residence for a Dutch aristocrat, but became a hotel thirty years later. The interior is rich and ornate and comes complete with gilded scrollwork, columns and thick carpets. Double rooms cost €325, but some reach stratospheric rates much more than that. ❾

Novotel Den Haag Centrum Hofweg 5 ⊕070/364 8846, ⊛www.accorhotels.com. Efficient, four-star chain hotel with very comfortable rooms right in the centre of things, across the street from the Binnenhof. ❺

Parkhotel Molenstraat 53 ⊕070/362 4371, ⊛www.parkhoteldenhaag.nl. Smart and immacu-lately maintained chain hotel in a handy central location. From the outside, the hotel doesn't look anything special, but the interior is graced by all sorts of Art Deco flourishes. The hotel has over one hundred well-appointed rooms decorated in brisk modern style. Some rooms overlook the Paleis Noordeinde gardens next door. ❻

### Hostel

Stayokay Den Haag Scheepmakersstraat 27 ⊕070/315 7888, ⊛www.stayokay.com. This large and extremely comfortable HI hostel is located just 400m east of – and across the canal from – Den Haag HS station. A good range of facilities includes luggage storage, a café, Internet terminals, and a small library. Dorm beds are €22–25; smart doubles also available.

# The city centre

The prettiest spot in the centre of Den Haag – and the logical place to start a visit – is the north side of the **Hofvijver** (Court Pond), a placid lakelet that mirrors the attractive symmetries of the front facade of the extensive **Binnenhof** (Inner Court). Den Haag's oldest quarter and long home to the country's bicameral parliament, the Binnenhof occupies the site of a medieval castle (built by Count William II), the origins of a settlement known as the "Count's Domain" – *'s Gravenhage*, literally "Count's Hedge" – which is still Den Haag's official name, often printed on maps alongside "Den Haag" and "The Hague" as an alternative moniker for the city. William's descendants became the region's most powerful family, simultaneously acting as Stadholders (effectively provincial governors) of most of the seven United Provinces, which rebelled against the Habsburgs in the sixteenth century. In due course, one of the family, Prince Maurice of Orange-Nassau (1567–1625), established his main residence in Den Haag, which had become, to all intents and purposes, the country's political capital. As the embodiment of central rather than municipal power, the Binnenhof was at times feted, at others virtually ignored, until the nineteenth century when Den Haag officially shared political capital status with Brussels during the uneasy times of the United Kingdom of the Netherlands (1815–30). Thereafter it became the seat of government and home to a functioning legislature.

The lack of prestige in the modest brick buildings of the Binnenhof long irked Dutch parliamentarians; in 1992, they moved in to a flashy new extension next door. Much of the original Binnenhof – a broadly rectangular complex built around two connecting courtyards – is used for government offices and there's not that much to see. The exception is the **Ridderzaal** (Knights' Hall), a slender-turreted structure that looks distinctly church-like, but was built as a banqueting hall for Count William's son, Floris V, in the thirteenth century. Now used for state occasions, it's been a courtroom, market and stable, and so often renovated that little of the original remains. An uninspiring guided tour of the Ridderzaal and the chambers of parliament (often closed Mon & Tues) starts regularly from the information office at Binnenhof 8a (Mon–Sat 10am–4pm, last tour 3.45pm; €3).

## The Mauritshuis

To the immediate east of the Binnenhof, the **Mauritshuis**, Korte Vijverberg 8 (Tues–Sat 10am–5pm, Sun 11am–5pm; €7; ⊛www.mauritshuis.nl), is located in an elegant seventeenth-century mansion. Generally considered to be one of the finest galleries in Europe, it's famous for its eclectic collection of Flemish and Dutch paintings from the fifteenth to the eighteenth century, based on the hoard accumulated by Prince William V of Orange (1748–1806). All the major Dutch artists are represented and it's well laid out, with multilingual cards in each room providing background notes on all the major canvases.

The rooms are not numbered, so be sure to pick up a plan of the museum at the ground-floor information desk – one floor up from the basement entrance; the museum shop also sells an excellent guidebook for €12.50. Alternatively you can join one of the irregular and expensive conducted tours; prices depend on length, and you should ask at the information desk for times. During major exhibitions, expect the paintings to be moved around or removed altogether and the whole museum to be completely reorganized.

## The ground floor

The museum entrance is on the east side of the building in the basement. Head up the stairs to the **ground floor** and then walk back toward the old front doors and enter the room on the left – Room 2 on the museum plan. Here, the collection kicks off with **Hans Memling**'s *Portrait of a Man*, a typically observant work, right down to the scar on the nose, and **Rogier van der Weyden**'s *The Lamentation of Christ*, a harrowing picture of death and sorrow. Weyden has Christ's head hanging down toward the earth, surrounded by the faces of the mourners, each with a particular expression of anguish and pain. **Quentin Matsys** (1465–1530) was the first major artist to work in Antwerp, where he was made a Master of the Guild in 1519. An influential figure, the focus of his work was the attempt to imbue his religious pictures with spiritual sensitivity, and his *Descent from the Cross*, also displayed in Room 2, is a fine example – Christ's suffering face under the weight of the Cross contrasted with the grinning, taunting onlookers behind.

Proceeding in a counterclockwise direction, through a series of rooms on either side of the Italianate dining room, exhibits include two giant allegorical canvases by Jan Sanders van Hemessen and **Lucas Cranach the Younger**'s piercing *Man with a Red Beard*. There are also the busy, stick-like figures of the *Winter Scene* by **Hendrik Avercamp** (1585–1634), a deaf-mute artist from Kampen, and two fine canvases by **Hans Holbein the Younger** (1497–1543): a striking *Portrait of Robert Cheeseman*, where all the materials – the fur collar, the falcon's feathers and the cape – seem to take on the appropriate texture; and a *Portrait of Jane Seymour*, one of several pictures commissioned by Henry VIII, who sent Holbein abroad to paint matrimonial candidates. Holbein's vibrant technique was later to land him in hot water: an over-flattering portrait of Anne of Cleves swayed Henry into an unhappy marriage with his "Flanders mare" that was to last only six months.

Of a number of paintings by **Adriaen Brouwer** (1605–38), *Quarrel at a Card Table* and *Inn with Drunken Peasants*, both currently in Room 7, are two of the better known, with thick, rough brushstrokes recording contemporary Flemish lowlife. Brouwer could approach this subject with some authority, as he spent most of his brief life in either a tavern or prison. **Peter Paul Rubens** (1577–1640), the acclaimed painter and diplomat, was a contemporary of Brouwer, though the two could hardly be more dissimilar: Rubens' *Portrait of Isabella Brant*, his first wife, is a typically grand, rather statuesque work, not perhaps as intriguing as Room 8's *Adam and Eve in Paradise*, a collaboration between Rubens, who painted the figures, and **Jan Brueghel the Elder** (1568–1625), who filled in the dreamlike animals and landscape behind.

In the same room are two examples of the work of Rubens' chief assistant, **Anthony van Dyck** (1599–1641), a portrait specialist who found fame at the court of the English king Charles I. His *Pieter Stevens of Antwerp* and *Anna Wake* are good examples of his tendency to flatter and ennoble – this doubtless helped his career prospects no end. Nearby, and again showing the influence of Rubens, is the robust *Adoration of the Shepherds* by **Jacob Jordaens**.

## The upper floor

On the **upper-floor** landing are two immaculate nautical scenes by **Willem van de Velde** (1633–1707), that painter-propagandist for the Dutch navy.

On this floor, begin at the front of the house in the room on the right, Room 9, which is distinguished by the best known of the museum's works by **Rembrandt**, the *Anatomy Lesson of Dr Tulp*, the artist's first commission in Amsterdam, dating from 1632. The peering pose of the students who lean over the corpse solved the problem of emphasis falling on the body rather than the subjects of the portrait, who were members of the surgeons' guild. Hopefully Tulp's skills as an anatomist were better than his medical advice, which included the recommendation that his patients drink fifty cups of tea a day.

Moving on in a counterclockwise direction, Room 12 displays **Paulus Potter**'s lifelike *Young Bull*, a massive canvas complete with dung and a pair of fearsome testicles, whilst Room 14 chimes in with the broad brush-strokes of **Frans Hals**' *Laughing Boy* – a far cry from the restrained style he was forced to adopt in his more familiar paintings of the burghers of Haarlem. Here also is **Gerard Ter Borch**'s *Lice Hunt*, a vignette of seventeenth-century domestic life in striking contrast to Vermeer's detachment. Room 15 holds several of the museum's most treasured paintings, beginning with **Jan Vermeer**'s *View of Delft*, a superb townscape of 1658, with the fine lines of the city drawn beneath a cloudy sky, a patchwork of varying light and shade. Curiously enough, the dispassionate, photographic quality the painting has in reproduction is oddly lacking in the actual canvas.

**Carel Fabritius** (1622–54), pupil of Rembrandt and (possibly) teacher of Vermeer, was killed in a gunpowder explosion at Delft when he was only 22. Few canvases of his survive but an exquisite exception is Room 15's *The Goldfinch*, a curious, almost impressionistic work, with the bird reduced to a blur of colour. One of his Delft contemporaries was **Gerard Houckgeest**, who specialized in church interiors, like *The Tomb of William of Orange*, a minutely observed study of architectural lines lightened by expanses of white marble; it's displayed in Room 15 too.

Finally, dotted throughout the museum are no fewer than thirteen paintings by **Jan Steen** (1625–79), including a wonderfully riotous picture carrying the legend "The way you hear it, is the way you sing it" – a parable on the young learning bad habits from the old – and a typically salacious *Girl Eating Oysters*.

## Lange Voorhout and around

A few metres north of the Mauritshuis, the **Haags Historisch Museum**, Korte Vijverberg 7 (Tues–Fri 11am–5pm, Sat & Sun noon–5pm; €3.60; Ⓦ www.haagshistorischmuseum.nl), occupies a handsome Neoclassical mansion that was originally home to the city's leading militia company, the so-called Archers of St Sebastian. The museum traces the convoluted history of the city with a wide range of displays – everything from a hotchpotch of archeological finds to an intricate doll's house of 1910 – and is strong on medieval church silver and antique furniture. Best of all, however, are the assorted paintings of the city, notably those by Jan Steen and his father-in-law, Jan van Goyen (1596–1656), a pioneer of realistic landscape painting who is well represented by his enormous and finely detailed *View of The Hague*.

Across the street from the Historical Museum are the trees and cobblestones of **Lange Voorhout**, a wide L-shaped street-cum-square that is overlooked by a string of stately mansions, whose Neoclassical pretensions span the seventeenth and eighteenth centuries and now accommodate many major embassies. Most conspicuous is the *Hotel des Indes*, an opulent hotel where the ballerina Anna Pavlova died in 1931 and where today you stand a fair chance of being flattened by a chauffeur-driven limousine. Opposite, at no. 74, the **Escher in het Paleis Museum** (Tues–Sun 11am–5pm; €7.50) occupies another of these grand mansions and was a favourite royal residence from 1901 to 1934. Nowadays, it's devoted to the vibrantly kaleidoscopic work of the Dutch graphic artist, M.C. Escher (1898–1972).

The narrow streets and canals just to the east of Lange Voorhout comprise one of the prettiest corners of the city centre, a jumble of intimate old buildings that extends to the busy Prinsessegracht boulevard. There are several good bars and restaurants here and one specific sight, the **Museum Meermanno**, Prinsessegracht 30 (Tues–Fri 11am–5pm, Sat & Sun noon–5pm; €4; Ⓦ www.meermanno.nl), which possesses a small collection of remarkably well-preserved medieval illuminated manuscripts and bibles.

## Museum Bredius

Doubling back to the north side of Hofvijver, allow half an hour or so to visit the delightful **Museum Bredius**, Lange Vijverberg 14 (Tues–Sun noon–5pm; €4.50; Ⓦ www.museumbredius.nl), which displays the eclectic collection of paintings bequeathed to the city by a one-time director of the Mauritshuis, Abraham Bredius, in 1946. Packed together in this fine old house, with its stucco work and splendid staircase, are some exquisite works, notably several mini-canvases by **Rembrandt** including a *Christ's Head*, and an *Erection of the Cross* whose glutinous paintwork forms one of the artist's darkest, most melancholic works. Amongst the genre paintings is a characteristic *Boar Hunt* by **Roelandt Savery** (1576–1639), all green foliage and fighting beasts, and the careful draughtsmanship of **Aert van de Neer**'s (1603–77) *Festivities on the Ice*. There are also two noteworthy paintings by **Jan Steen**, the salacious *Couple in a Bedchamber* and the curious *Satyr and the Peasant*, a representation of a well-known Aesop fable in which the satyr, sat at the table with his hosts, is bemused by human behaviour. The creature's confusion is symbolically represented by two contrasting figures, one of whom blows on his soup to cool it down, while the other blows into his hands to keep them warm.

## Museum Gevangenpoort

A short walk from the Bredius Museum, on the west side of the Hofvijver, the **Museum Gevangenpoort**, Buitenhof 33 (Prisoner's Gate Museum; Tues–Fri 11am–4pm, Sat & Sun noon–4pm; hourly tours, last at 4pm; €3.60), was originally part of the city fortifications. Used as a prison until the nineteenth century, it now contains a display of instruments of torture and punishment centred around its Chamber of Horrors. As well as the guillotine blades, racks and gallows, the old cells are in a good state of preservation – including the *ridderkamer* for the more privileged captives. Here Cornelis de Witt, Burgomaster of Dordrecht, was imprisoned before he and his brother Johan, another staunch Republican and leader of the States of Holland, were dragged out and murdered by an Orangist mob in 1672. The brothers were shot, beheaded and cut into pieces that were then auctioned to the crowd; Johan's tongue is apparently preserved for a macabre posterity in the storerooms of the Gemeentemuseum.

The Gevangenpoort is popular; join the line about fifteen minutes before the tour begins to guarantee a place.

### Galerij Prince Willem V

Down the street at Buitenhof 35, the **Galerij Prins Willem V** (Tues–Sun 11am–4pm; €1.50) was created in 1773 as the private picture gallery of the eponymous prince and Stadholder of the United Provinces. On display is a diverting collection of seventeenth-century paintings including examples of the work of the prolific Jan Steen as well as Jacob Jordaens and Paulus Potter. There's also the folksy *Girl with a Lamp* by Gerard Dou, a pupil and companion of the young Rembrandt, and one of Willem van de Velde's (1633–1707) most successful maritime paintings, the *Warship at Sunset*. However, the gallery is perhaps more interesting as an example of an eighteenth-century "cabinet" picture gallery. The fashion then was to sandwich paintings together in a cramped patchwork from floor to ceiling, and though it's faithful to the period, this does make viewing difficult for eyes more used to spacious modern museums.

### The Oude Stadhuis and Grote Kerk

The lattice of narrow, mostly humdrum streets and squares stretching west of the Buitenhof zero in on the flamboyant Dutch Renaissance facade of the sixteenth-century **Oude Stadhuis** (Old City Hall), a good-looking affair complete with mullioned windows, shutters and decorative carvings. To the rear are the plodding symmetries of a later extension, and next door rises St Jacobskerk, or the **Grote Kerk** (July & Aug Mon–Fri 11am–4pm; free; otherwise closed except during exhibitions). Dating from the middle of the fifteenth century and easily the best of Den Haag's old churches, the building's cavernous interior, with its three naves of equal height, has an exhilarating sense of breadth and handsome timber vaulting. Like most Dutch churches, it's short on decoration, but there are one or two highlights, notably the **stained-glass windows** in the choir ambulatory. Two are particularly exquisite and may well be the work of Dirk Crabeth, one of the craftsmen responsible for the windows in Gouda's St Janskerk (see p.199). Of the two, one depicts the Annunciation, the other shows the Virgin descending from heaven to show the infant Jesus to a kneeling Emperor Charles V, who footed the bill. Nearby, in the choir, stands a memorial to Admiral Jacob van Opdam, who was blown up with his ship during the little-remembered naval battle of Lowestoft in 1665. Also look out for the Renaissance pulpit: similar to the one in Delft's Oude Kerk (see p.188), it has carved panels framing the apostles in false perspective.

From the Grote Kerk, it's a short walk north to the sixteenth- and seventeenth-century **Paleis Noordeinde** (no public access), the grandest of several royal buildings that lure tourists onto the expensive "Royal Tours" of Den Haag and its surroundings. Outside the palace's main entrance, on Noordeinde, is a jaunty equestrian statue of William the Silent.

## North of the city centre

Ten minutes' walk north of the Paleis Noordeinde, and accessible by tram #7 from Centraal Station, the **Panorama Mesdag**, Zeestraat 65 (Mon–Sat 10am–5pm, Sun noon–5pm; €4; ⓦ www.panorama-mesdag.com), was designed in the late nineteenth century by Hendrik Mesdag, banker-turned-painter and local citizen-become-Hague School luminary. For the most part, Mesdag painted unremarkable seascapes tinged with an unlikeable bourgeois sentimentality, but there's no denying the achievement of his panorama, a

▲ Ockenburgh Campsite & Hostel

**DEN HAAG (NORTH) AND SCHEVENINGEN**

depiction of Scheveningen as it appeared in 1881. Completed in four months with help from his wife and the young George Hendrik Breitner, the painting is so naturalistic that it takes a few moments for the skills of lighting and per-spective to become apparent.

Ten minutes' walk north, at Laan van Meerdervoort 7f, is the house Mesdag bought as a home and gallery. At the time it had a view over one of his favourite subjects, the dunes, the inspiration for much of his work; today it contains the **Museum Mesdag** (Tues–Sun noon–5pm; €4; ⓦwww.museummesdag.nl), accessible direct from Centraal Station on tram #17. His collection includes a number of Hague School paintings which, like his own work, take the seascapes of the nearby coast as their subject. There are also paintings by Corot, Rousseau, Delacroix and Millet, though none of them represents the artists' best achieve-ments. Perhaps the most interesting exhibits are the florid and distinctive paintings of Antonio Mancini, whose oddly disquieting subjects are reminiscent of Klimt.

### The Peace Palace

Round the corner from the Mesdag Museum, framing the Carnegieplein, the **Vredespaleis**, or Peace Palace (hourly guided tours usually Mon–Fri 10am,

11am, 2pm & 3pm; June–Sept also 4pm; €3.50; check with the VVV for times of tours in English; ⓦwww.vredespaleis.nl) is home to the International Court of Justice, and, for all the wrong reasons, a monument to the futility of war. Toward the end of the nineteenth century, Tsar Nicholas II called an international conference for the peaceful reconciliation of national problems. The result was the First Hague Peace Conference of 1899, whose purpose was to "help find a lasting peace and, above all, a way of limiting the progressive development of existing arms". This in turn led to the formation of a Permanent Court of Arbitration housed obscurely in Den Haag until the American industrialist Andrew Carnegie gave $1.5 million for a large new building – the Peace Palace. These honourable aims came to nothing with the onset of World War I: just as the donations of tapestries, urns, marble and stained glass were arriving from all over the world, so Europe's military commanders were preparing their offensives. Backed by a massive law library, fifteen judges still sit today, conducting trade matters in English and diplomatic affairs in French. Widely respected and generally considered neutral, their judgements are nevertheless not binding.

## The Gemeentemuseum and around

About 1.5km northwest of the Peace Palace, the **Gemeentemuseum**, Stadhouderslaan 41 (Tues–Sun 11am–5pm; €7; bus #4 or 14 from Centraal Station; ⓦwww.gemeentemuseum.nl), is easily the most diverse of Den Haag's many museums. Designed by Hendrik Petrus Berlage (1856–1934) and completed in 1935, the building itself is often regarded as his masterpiece, an austere but particularly appealing structure with brick facings superimposed upon a concrete shell. Unfortunately, the interior can be confusing and the labelling inconsistent, but there are some superb collections – such as the musical instruments (especially the harpsichords and early pianos) and the Islamic ceramics. The manageable delft collection is among the world's finest and the large Fashion Gallery hosts an ambitious range of temporary exhibitions on fashion and associated subjects. The modern art section outlines the development of Dutch painting since the 1860s, through the Romantic, Hague and Expressionist schools to the De Stijl movement. **Piet Mondrian** (1872–1944), the most famous member of the De Stijl group, dominates this part of the gallery and pride of place goes to *Victory Boogie Woogie*, his last and – some say – finest work. The museum has the world's largest collection of Mondrian paintings, though much of it consists of unfamiliar early works painted before he evolved the abstraction of form into geometry and pure colour for which he's best known.

On the same campus as the Gemeentemuseum, at Stadhouderslaan 43, is **GEM**, **Museum voor Actuele Kunst** (Tues–Sun 2–10pm; €5; ⓦwww.gem-online.nl), a new gallery of contemporary art featuring an enterprising programme of temporary exhibitions. In the same building – and costing no extra – is the **Fotomuseum** (Photography Museum; same hours), which puts on up to six exhibitions a year and in between times displays photographs from the Gemeentemuseum's permanent collection.

Also on the Gemeentemuseum campus is the **Museon** (Tues–Sun 11am–5pm; €6; ⓦwww.museon.nl), a sequence of non-specialist exhibitions dealing with human activities and the history of the earth – everything from rock formations to the use of tools. Self-consciously internationalist, it's aimed at school parties, as is the adjoining **Omniversum** or "Space Theatre" (Mon noon–5pm, Tues–Wed 10am–5pm, Thurs–Sun 10am–9pm; €8, children under 12 years €6; programme on ☎0900/666 4837, ⓦwww.omniversum.nl). A planetarium in all but name, it possesses all the technical gadgetry you'd expect.

## The Madurodam miniature town

Halfway between Den Haag and Scheveningen, the **Madurodam miniature town** (daily: April–June 9am–8pm; July & Aug until 10pm; Sept–March 9am–6pm; €11; Ⓦwww.madurodam.nl), reachable on tram #1 or #9 from Centraal Station, is heavily plugged by the tourist authorities, though its origins are more interesting than the rather trite and expensive present, a stylised version of a Dutch town constructed on a 1:25 scale. The money was put up by one J.M.L. Maduro, who wished to establish a memorial to his son, George, who had distinguished himself during the Nazi invasion of 1940 and died in Dachau concentration camp five years later. There's a memorial to him just by the entrance, and profits from the Miniature Town are still used for general Dutch social and cultural activities. The replica town itself is extremely popular – so be prepared to queue.

# Eating and drinking

Den Haag has an excellent range of **restaurants**, and although some are aimed squarely at the expense account, many more are very affordable, with main courses hovering between €15 and €20. There is a cluster of first-rate places just north and east of Lange Voorhout along and around Denneweg and Frederikstraat, and another on Molenstraat, near the Paleis Noordeinde: frankly, you need look no further. These two areas are good for **cafés** and **café-bars** too, though the liveliest **bars** are concentrated on and around the Grote Markt, south of the Grote Kerk.

## Restaurants

**De Dekxels** Denneweg 130 ☎070/365 9788. Coolly decorated, modern-chic café-cum-restaurant serving from a wide-ranging menu, featuring international and Dutch dishes. Main courses average €10–12.

**HNM** Molenstraat 21 ☎070/365 6553. Imaginatively decorated café serving a tasty range of Dutch, Indonesian, French and Italian snacks and meals. The daily specials are especially good value, beginning at just €7.

**Le Haricot Vert** Molenstraat 9 ☎070/365 2278. Nicely cosy French restaurant decorated in traditional bistro style. All the classics, and then some. Main courses in the region of €20–25.

**Limón** Denneweg 39a ☎070/356 1465. Atmospheric, pastel-painted Spanish tapas restaurant catering to a fashionable, youngish crowd. Great food; a popular spot.

**Luden** Frederikstraat 36 ☎070/360 1733. Classy little restaurant offering a Dutch/French menu which shows flair and imagination. Main courses from €17.

**Malienkolder** Maliestraat 9 ☎070/364 5542. Inexpensive bistro-style restaurant with French and Dutch dishes. A few metres from the end of Denneweg.

**Plato** Frederikstraat 32 ☎070/363 6744. Smart and cosy restaurant offering tasty and reasonably priced French/Dutch cuisine. Main courses at around €17.

**Saur** Lange Voorhout 47 ☎070/346 2565. This smart and formal, old-fashioned restaurant, with its Art Deco flourishes and French menu, serves some of the best steaks in town. The attached brasserie is a new, ultra-modern and informal addition – and the steaks are just as good. Not as expensive as you might expect. Closed Sun.

## Café-bars and bars

**De Boterwaag** Grote Markt 8a. Immensely appealing café-bar housed in an old and cavernous brick-vaulted weigh house. Very popular with a youthful crowd and offers a wide range of beers as well as inexpensive bar food, though this hardly inspires the palate.

**De Landeman** Denneweg 48. Mellow brown(ish) bar near the southern end of Denneweg with dark panelling and a clutter of bygones.

**Le Café Hathor** Maliestraat 22. Just 100m or so from the end of Denneweg, this agreeable, laid-back café-bar occupies charming old premises and has a lovely canalside terrace to boot. Convivial atmosphere; recommended.

**De Oude Mol** Oude Molenstraat. Good old traditional bar and neighbourhood joint down a narrow
sidestreet. Oodles of atmosphere and an enjoyable
range of beers.

**De Zwarte Ruiter** Grote Markt 27. This fashionable bar boasts a good selection of beers and ales,
and positively heaves on the weekend.

## Listings

**Bikes** Can be rented from either of Den Haag's
train stations at standard rates.
**Car rental** Avis, Theresiastraat 216 ☎070/385
0698; Europcar, Binckhorstin 297 ☎070/381
1811; Hertz, Binckhorstin 318 ☎070/381 8989.
**Embassies and consulates** Australia,
Carnegielaan 4 ☎070/310 8200, ⓦwww
.australian-embassy.nl; Canada, Sophialaan 7
☎070/311 1600, ⓦwww.canada.nl; Ireland, Dr
Kuijperstraat 9 ☎070/363 0993, ⓦwww
.irishembassy.nl; New Zealand, Carnegielaan 10
☎070/346 9324, ⓦwww.nzembassy.com; UK,
Lange Voorhout 10 ☎070/427 0427,
ⓦwww.britain.nl; US, Lange Voorhout 102
☎070/310 9209, ⓦwww.usemb.nl.

**Emergencies** Fire, Police, Ambulance ☎112.
**Markets** Food market on Markthof, Gedempte
Gracht/Spui (Mon 11am–6pm, Tues–Sat
9am–5pm, Thurs until 9pm). Antiques, books and
curios markets are on Lange Voorhout (May–Sept
Thurs 11am–7pm & Sun 11am–5pm) and on Plein
(Oct–May Thurs 11am–7pm).
**Pharmacy** Central pharmacy at Korte Poten 7a.
For information on night services, call ☎070/345
1000.
**Post office** Main post office on Kerkplein (Mon–Fri
9am–6pm, Thurs until 8pm, Sat 9am–4pm).
**Taxi** HTMC ☎070/390 7722; HCT City Taxi
☎070/383 0830.

# Scheveningen

Situated on the coast about 4km north of the centre of Den Haag, the old fishing port of **SCHEVENINGEN** is now the Netherlands' biggest coastal resort,
a sometimes tacky, often breezy place that attracts more than nine million visitors a year. It also has one curious claim to fame: during World War II, resistance groups tested suspected Nazi infiltrators by getting them to say
"Scheveningen" – an impossible feat for Germans, and not much
easier for English-speakers either (try a throaty *s-khay-ve-ning-uh*). Den Haag
and Scheveningen were once separated by a thick strip of forested dune, but
nowadays it's hard to know where one ends and the other begins. There is,
however, no mistaking Scheveningen's principal attraction, its **beach**
(ⓦwww.scheveningenbeach.nl), a long expanse of golden sand that is hard to
resist on a warm day, especially as it only takes about ten minutes to get there
on **tram #1** from either of Den Haag's train stations.

Scheveningen's main tram stop is a couple of hundred metres from its most
impressive building, the **Kurhaus** (see map p.182), a grand hotel of 1885, built
when this was one of the most fashionable resorts in Europe. Pop inside for a
peek at its central hall, a richly decorated affair with pendulous chandeliers and
rich frescoes bearing mermaids and semi-clad maidens cavorting high above
the diners and coffee-drinkers. Most of Scheveningen's other attractions are
within easy walking distance of the Kurhaus: the **casino** is next door; it's east
along the seashore to the cement **pier** and its amusement arcades; and west to
**Sea Life**, Strandweg 13 (daily 10am–6pm, July & Aug until 8pm; €9.50, children €6; ⓦwww.sealife.nl), a glorified aquarium complete with a seabed walk-
way and coral reef.

About 250m further west is the much more original **Museum Beelden-aan-
Zee**, at Harteveltstraat 1 (Tues–Sun 11am–5pm; €5; ⓦwww.beeldenaanzee.nl).
This features an intriguing assortment of modern sculptures arranged around a
pavilion built by King William I for his ailing wife, Wilhelmina, in 1826. There

are examples of the work of many leading sculptors, including Karel Appel and Wim Quist, Man Ray and Fritz Koenig, and although there is supposed to be a unifying theme – the human experience – it's the variety of forms and materials that impresses.

### Scheveningen harbour

Set apart at the west end of the resort, about 2km from the Kurhaus, is Scheveningen's sprawling **haven** (harbour), the focus of an industrial complex that incorporates a busy container depot and fish docks. The local trawler fleet is a shadow of its former self, but there are still several excellent seafood restaurants hereabouts – try the excellent *Ducdalf*, at Dr Lelykade 5 (℡070/355 7692), or the more straightforward and less expensive *Havenrestaurant* at Treilerdwarsweg 2 (℡070/354 5783). If you fancy trying to catch a meal yourself, plump for one of the North Sea **fishing trips** that head out during the summer from Dr Lelykade, the southern dock of the inner harbour – both the Scheveningen VVV (see below) and Den Haag VVV (see p.176) have details of these and other ocean-going excursions.

### Practicalities

Scheveningen is best visited as a day-trip from Den Haag, but if you do decide to stay, the **VVV**, by the seafront just east of the Kurhaus at Gevers Deynootweg 1134 (Mon 10am–5.30pm, Tues–Fri 9am–5.30pm & Sat 10am–5pm; April–Sept also Sun 1–5pm; ℡0900/340 3505, ⓦwww.denhaag com), issues a free brochure listing all the resort's hotels and pensions. Out of season, there are oodles of vacant rooms, but in the summer it's best to use the VVV's accommodation booking service.

Scheveningen also has an ambitious programme of special events, including an international **sand sculpture** competition in early May and a massive international **kite festival** that takes over the beach and much of the town in early June.

# Delft

The compact centre of **DELFT**, roughly midway between Den Haag and Rotterdam, has considerable charm: gabled red-roofed houses stand beside tree-lined canals, and the pastel colours of the brickwork and bridges give the place a faded, placid tranquillity. With justification, it's one of the most visited spots in the Netherlands, but although the tourist crowds can be oppressive in the height of the summer, there's no gainsaying the town centre's good looks or the appeal of its ancient buildings, several of which date from its medieval heyday. Taken altogether, Delft makes an ideal day-trip or, with its several good hotels, an enjoyable overnight stay.

Delft is also famous for its connection with **Jan Vermeer** (1632–75). The artist was born in the town and died here too – leaving a wife, eleven children and a huge debt to the local baker. He had given the man two pictures as security, and his wife subsequently bankrupted herself trying to retrieve them. Vermeer's most celebrated painting is his 1661 *View of Delft*, now displayed in the Mauritshuis in Den Haag (see p.177), but if you're after a townscape that even vaguely resembles the picture, you'll be disappointed – it doesn't exist and in a sense it never did. Vermeer made no claim to be a realist and his *View* accorded with the landscape traditions of his day in presenting an idealised Delft framed by a broad expanse of water and dappled by a cloudy sky.

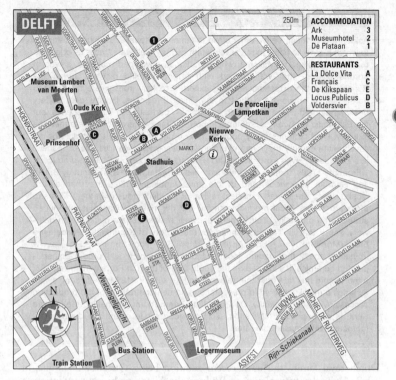

## The Town

The obvious place to start an exploration of Delft is the **Markt**, a central point of reference with the Stadhuis at one end and the Nieuwe Kerk at the other, with cafés and restaurants lined up in between and a **statue** of Delft's own Hugo Grotius in the middle. A well-known scholar and statesman, Grotius (1583–1645) was sentenced to life imprisonment by Maurice of Orange-Nassau during the political turmoil of the 1610s, but was subsequently rescued by his wife who smuggled him out of goal in a chest. Unfortunately, it didn't save Grotius from a sticky end – he died of exposure after being shipwrecked near Danzig.

The **Nieuwe Kerk** (April–Oct Mon–Sat 9am–6pm; Nov–March Mon–Fri 11am–4pm, Sat 11am–5pm; €2.50) is new only in comparison with the Oude Kerk (see overleaf), as there's been a church on this site since 1381. Most of the original structure was destroyed in the great fire that swept through Delft in 1536, and the remainder in an explosion a century later – a disaster, incidentally, which claimed the life of the artist Carel Fabritius, Rembrandt's greatest pupil and (debatably) the teacher of Vermeer. The most striking part of the restoration is the most recent: the 100-metre **spire** (same hours; €2), replaced in 1872 and from whose summit there's a great view of the town. Unless you're a Dutch monarchist, the church's interior is rather uninspiring: it contains the burial vaults of the

## Delftware

Aside from Vermeer, Delft's other claim to fame is **delftware**, the clunky ceramics to which it gave its name in the seventeenth century. Delftware traces its origins to the Balearic island of Mallorca, where craftsmen developed **majolica**, a type of porous pottery that was glazed with bright metallic oxides. During the Renaissance, these techniques were exported to Italy from where they spread north, first to Antwerp and then to the United Provinces. Initially, delft pottery designs featured Dutch and Italian landscapes, portraits and biblical scenes, but the East India Company's profitable import of Chinese ceramics transformed the industry. Delft factories freely copied Chinese designs and by the middle of the seventeenth century they were churning out blue-and-white tiles, plates, panels, jars and vases – even exporting to China, where they undercut Chinese producers.

From the 1760s, though, the delft factories were themselves undercut by British and German workshops, and by the time Napoleon arrived they had all but closed down. There was a modest revival of the delft industry in the 1870s and there are several local producers today, but it's mostly cheap mass-produced stuff of little originality. Delft's many souvenir shops are jam-packed with delftware, but if that isn't enough, head for the factory of **Koninklijke Porceleyne Fles** (Mon–Sat 9am–5pm; April–Oct also Sun 9am–5pm; €2.50; ⓦwww .royaldelft.com), the leading local manufacturer, which still produces hand-painted ceramics. It's located on the south side of town at Rotterdamseweg 196, a ten-minute bus ride from the train station (bus #63 or #129 to Jaffalaan); a visit includes a multilingual video presentation and demonstrations of the production process. More conveniently, **De Porcelijne Lampetkan**, just behind the Nieuwe Kerk, is an appealing little shop selling a good range of antique delftware at (comparatively) reasonable rates.

---

Dutch royal family, the most recent addition being Queen Wilhelmina, in 1962. Only the mausoleum of William the Silent grabs your attention, a hodgepodge of styles concocted by Hendrik de Keyser.

Keyser also designed the **Stadhuis** opposite, though its delightful facade, equipped with pert dormer windows, shutters, fluted pilasters and shell decoration, is dwarfed by the sulky stonework of the old medieval keep that he incorporated into the newer building.

### The Oude Kerk

Behind the Stadhuis, alongside the Wijnhaven canal, one of Delft's prettiest streets leads north along Hippolytusbuurt to the Gothic **Oude Kerk** (April–Oct Mon–Sat 9am–6pm; Nov–March Mon–Fri 11am–4pm, Sat 11am–5pm; €2.50), arguably the town's finest building. Simple and well-proportioned, despite its unhealthily leaning tower, the present edifice is the result of a succession of churches constructed here between the thirteenth and the seventeenth centuries. Inside, the unadorned vaulting proves interiors don't have to be elaborate to avoid being sombre. The pride of the church is its **pulpit** of 1548, intricately carved with figures emphasized in false perspective, but also notable is the modern **stained glass**, depicting and symbolizing the history of the Netherlands – particularly the 1945 liberation – in the north transept. If you're curious about the tombs, which include that of Admiral Maarten van Tromp, famed for hoisting a broom at his masthead to "sweep the seas clear of the English", take a look at the free *Striking Points* pamphlet available at the entrance. Incidentally, the English had the last laugh on Tromp, who was killed during a sea battle off Texel in 1653.

## The Prinsenhof

Opposite the Oude Kerk, down a passageway in the former Convent of St Agatha, is **Het Prinsenhof** (Tues–Sat 10am–5pm, Sun 1–5pm; €5), which served as the main residence of William the Silent of Orange-Nassau from 1572 to 1584. A rambling, somewhat confusing building with two floors, the Prinsenhof holds the municipal art collection, an appealing jumble of works whose highlights begin in the old refectory (Room 7) with the curious *Wretched State of the Netherlands*. This inflammatory canvas by an unknown seventeenth-century Protestant depicts the Habsburg commander, the Duke of Alva, in cahoots with the devil and the pope, enslaving the Low Countries with each province represented by one of the seventeen chained women before him. Meanwhile, in the background, Margaret of Parma, the region's Habsburg governor, can be seen fishing in a pool of blood.

Just beyond Room 7, the bottom of the old stone staircase marks the spot where **William the Silent** was assassinated on July 10, 1584. A former army commander of both Charles V and Philip II, William turned against the Habsburgs during Alva's persecution of the Protestants in 1567. He went on to lead the Protestant revolt against Philip, mustering a series of armies and organizing the *Watergeuzen*, a guerrilla unit that played a key role in driving back the imperial army. In return, Philip put a bounty of 25,000 gold crowns on William's head, but in the event the man who shot him was not a professional assassin but a fanatical Catholic, Balthazar Gerard, who did the deed for his religion. Two bullets passed right through William and the bullet holes are now protected by a glass sheet, put there to stop curious fingers wearing them down.

There's more fine and applied art upstairs, most notably a room full of anatomy paintings – *The Anatomy Lesson* of 1681 by Cornelis de Man is especially striking – and another of militia paintings. During the long war with Spain, every Dutch city had its own militia, but as the Habsburg threat diminished the militias devolved into social clubs, each of them keen to immortalize their particular company in a group portrait. The most famous of these is Rembrandt's *Night Watch* in Amsterdam's Rijkmuseum (see p.100), but there are several good examples here, particularly Michiel van Miereveld's *Banquet of the Delft Militia*.

## Museum Lambert van Meerten and Legermuseum

A few metres north of the Prinsenhof, the canalside **Museum Lambert van Meerten**, at Oude Delft 199 (Tues–Sat 10am–5pm, Sun 1–5pm; €3.50), exhibits the town's best collection of delftware. There are jars and vases, plates and panels, but the museum's speciality is its tiles – a fabulous hoard collected by the nineteenth-century industrialist after whom the museum is named. In particular, look out for the vibrant tile picture of the Battle of La Hogue – in which an Anglo-Dutch fleet worsted the French in 1692 – displayed on the staircase.

Heading south along Oude Delft, it's about 1km to the **Legermuseum**, housed in a pair of old arsenals and a warehouse at Korte Geer 1 (Mon–Fri 10am–5pm, Sat & Sun noon–5pm; €4.40). Here you'll find a display of weaponry, uniforms and military accoutrements labelled only in Dutch – which may sound dull, but isn't, even if you're not an enthusiast. The military history of the Netherlands is outlined from Roman times onwards, including detailed sections on the Spanish wars and the ill-advised colonialist enterprises of the 1950s, which are shown in surprisingly candid detail.

# Practicalities

From either of Den Haag's train stations, it only takes a few minutes to reach Delft **train station**, from where it's a ten-minute walk north to the Markt; the

△ The *kubuswoningen*, Rotterdam (see p.194)

**bus station** is adjacent. You can also make the trip on tram #1 from either of Den Haag's train stations; in Delft the tram rattles along Phoenixstraat/ Westvest between the train station and the centre. Delft **VVV** is currently closed, but when it re-emerges from reorganization it will almost certainly be on the Markt; in the meantime, Den Haag VVV (see p.176) can handle any queries.

Delft has several good **hotels**, beginning with the *Ark*, an attractive four-star place occupying three tastefully restored seventeenth-century canal houses at Koornmarkt 65 (☎015/215 7999, ⓦwww.deark.nl; ❺). Another appealing option is the *Best Western Delft Museumhotel*, which also has a canalside location, in sprucely converted premises close to the Prinsenhof at Oude Delft 189 (☎015/214 0930, ⓦwww.museumhotel.nl; ❺). A somewhat less expensive option is *De Plataan*, a comfortable three-star hotel in homely modern(ish) premises on a quiet square at Doelenplein 10 (☎015/212 6046, ⓦwww .hoteldeplataan.nl; ❹).

Many of the **cafés** and **restaurants** are geared up for day-trippers and serve pretty routine stuff, but there are also several excellent places, most notably *De Klikspaan*, Koornmarkt 85 (☎015/214 1562; closed Mon & Tues), a smart, polished restaurant with main courses around €20. Similar prices apply at the equally chic French *Restaurant Le Vieux Jean*, near the Oude Kerk at Heilige Geestkerkhof 3 (☎015/213 0433; closed Sun & Mon). Alternatively, *La Dolce Vita*, near the Stadhuis at Voldersgracht 8, has tasty pizzas from €6, and just along the street at no. 4 is the pleasant *Voldersvier*, which is good for snacks and cakes. For a **drink**, try *Locus Publicus*, Brabantse Turfmarkt 67, a popular hangout which serves a staggering array of beers and bar food too.

# Rotterdam

**ROTTERDAM** lies at the heart of a maze of rivers and artificial waterways that together form the outlet of the rivers Rijn (Rhine) and Maas (Meuse). After devastating damage during World War II, Rotterdam has grown into a vibrant, forceful city dotted with first-division cultural attractions. Redevelopment also hasn't obliterated the city's earthy character: its tough grittiness is part of its appeal, as are its boisterous bars and clubs.

An important **port** as early as the fourteenth century, Rotterdam was one of the major cities of the United Provinces and shared its periods of fortune and decline until the nineteenth century when it was caught unawares. The city was ill-prepared for the industrial expansion of the Ruhr, the development of larger ships and the silting up of the Maas, but prosperity did finally return in a big way with the digging of an entirely new ship canal (the "Nieuwe Waterweg") between 1866 and 1872. Rotterdam has been a major seaport ever since, though it has had difficult times, especially during World War II, when the Nazis bombed the city centre in 1940 and, in retreat, destroyed much of the harbour four years later, with Allied bombing doing much damage in between.

The postwar period saw the rapid reconstruction of the **docks**. When huge container ships and oil tankers made the existing port facilities obsolete, Rotterdammers promptly built an entirely new deep-sea port, the "**Europoort**", jutting out into the North Sea some 25km to the west of the old town. Completed in 1968, it can accommodate the largest of ships:

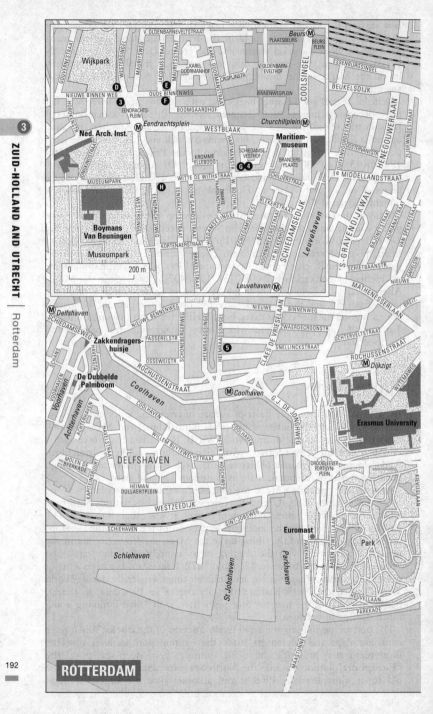

ROTTERDAM

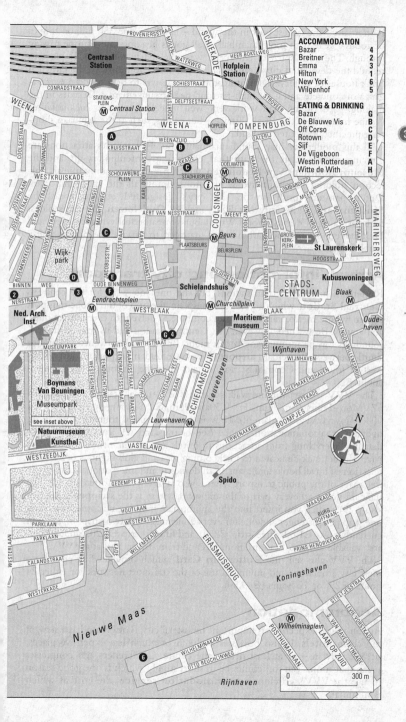

**ACCOMMODATION**

| | |
|---|---|
| Bazar | 4 |
| Breitner | 2 |
| Emma | 3 |
| Hilton | 1 |
| New York | 6 |
| Wilgenhof | 5 |

**EATING & DRINKING**

| | |
|---|---|
| Bazar | G |
| De Blauwe Vis | B |
| Off Corso | C |
| Rotown | D |
| Sijf | E |
| De Vijgeboon | F |
| Westin Rotterdam | A |
| Witte de With | H |

Rotterdam – the largest port in the world – handles some 350 million tonnes of goods a year, with more than half of all goods heading into Europe passing through. The same spirit of enterprise was reflected in the council's plans to rebuild the devastated **city centre**. There was to be no return to the crowded brick houses of yesteryear, but instead the centre was to be a modern extravaganza of concrete and glass, high-rise and pedestrianized areas. Decades in the making, parts of the plan work very well indeed – like the *kubuswoningen* ("cube houses") of the Blaak district – but others, such as the Lijnbaan shopping precinct, look tired and sad.

All this modernity may sound unalluring, but Rotterdam's attractions are enticing, most notably the **Kunsthal**, exhibiting contemporary art, and the **Museum Boijmans Van Beuningen**, which has an outstanding fine art collection holding representative works from almost all the most important Dutch painters; both are in the city's designated culture zone, the **Museumpark**. Other city highlights include **Oudehaven**, the city's oldest harbour, ravaged during World War II but sympathetically redeveloped, and **Delfshaven**, an antique harbour that managed to survive the bombs pretty much intact.

## Arrival, information and city transport

Rotterdam has several train stations, but the one you want for the centre is **Centraal Station**, which adjoins Stationsplein, the hub of the public transport system, whose metro, trams and buses combine to delve into every urban nook and cranny. Be warned, however, that Centraal Station and its immediate surroundings can be intimidating late at night. Bus #33 takes twenty minutes to shuttle between Rotterdam **airport** (Ⓦ www.rotterdam-airport.nl), just northwest of town, and Centraal Station. A taxi from the airport to the centre is about €20.

The **VVV** is a ten-minute walk southeast of Centraal Station at Coolsingel 67 (Mon–Thurs 9am–6pm, Fri 9.30am–9pm, Sat 9.30am–5pm; ☎010/414 0000, Ⓦ www.vvvrotterdam.nl). They issue all the usual tourist information, operate an accommodation service (see below) and sell a useful city guide detailing everything from attractions to hotels and restaurants (€2). They also have a leaflet rack dedicated to forthcoming gigs and club nights, stock a wide selection of travel books and maps, both domestic and international, and supply free maps of the public transport system (also at Ⓦ www.ret.rotterdam .nl). The standard ticket on every part of the transport system is the **strippenkaart** (see also p.29), which you insert into the appropriate franking machine, cancelling one strip per passenger and one for every zone crossed. A two-strip *strippenkaart* currently costs €1.60, three-strip €2.40, and fifteen-strip €6.20. *Strippenkaarts* are available at metro stations, from bus and tram drivers and at the VVV.

The VVV also sells the **Rotterdam Card**, which provides free entry into most city attractions and unlimited use of the transport network for either 24 hours (€25) or 72 hours (€49.50).

## Accommodation

As you might expect of an important industrial city, Rotterdam has a slew of big chain **hotels**. It also possesses a clutch of much less expensive places, occasionally in – or at least near – the centre. Conferences and congresses mean that rooms can sometimes be in short supply, which is one good reason to use the VVV's efficient **accommodation service**, the cost of which is minimal.

## Hotels

**Bazar** Witte de Withstraat 16 ☎010/206 5151, Ⓕ010/206 5159. Lively, very agreeable two-star hotel in a central location, near the Museumpark. Great, modernistic decor; adjoins an excellent café-restaurant. **❸**

**Breitner** Breitnerstraat 23 ☎010/436 0262, ⓦwww.hotelbreitner.nl. Unassuming three-star hotel on a quiet residential street, a short walk from Museumpark. Pleasant if somewhat spartan rooms. **❸**

**Emma** Nieuwe Binneweg 6 ☎010/436 5533, ⓦwww.hotelemma.nl. No great shakes, but this trim, modern three-star hotel has a central location and comfortable rooms. **❹**

**Hilton** Weena 10 ☎010/710 8000, ⓦwww .rotterdam.hilton.com. Luxurious five-star hotel with large and extremely well-appointed rooms. Occupies a classic early 1970s tower block with a wide sweeping foyer decorated by oceans of marble and a broken mirror motif on the walls. First-rate. **❼**

**New York** Koninginnenhoofd 1 ☎010/439 0500, ⓦwww.hotelnewyork.nl. Prestige four-star hotel occupying the grand nineteenth-century former head office of a shipping line. Situated across from the city centre on the south bank of the Nieuwe Maas. All the rooms are very well-appointed and most have smashing river views. Water taxi to and from the centre or reachable on the metro – the hotel is a five-minute walk from Wilhelminaplein station. **❹**

**Wilgenhof** Heemraadssingel 92–94 ☎010/425 4892, Ⓕ010/477 2611. Convivial three-star hotel occupying a pleasant canalside location to the west of the Museumpark. Tram #1 or #7 from Centraal Station. **❸**

# The City

From **Stationsplein**, outside Centraal Station, Kruisplein and then Westersingel/Mauritsweg cut south, dividing this part of the city into two: to the west is a largely working-class residential area, while to the east, hemmed in by Weena, Coolsingel and Westblaak, lies a jangle of modern high-rises and shopping streets. The layout is a tad baffling, but the focus of this second area – if indeed there is one – is the **Lijnbaan**, Europe's first pedestrianized shopping precinct, completed in 1953. The Lijnbaan is interesting as a prototype, but the dimensions are disconcerting: the street is too wide and the buildings are too low to create any sense of intimacy. Developers learnt lessons here.

To the east of Coolsingel, just north of Hoogstraat, another shopping strip, is the fifteenth-century **St Laurenskerk** or Grote Kerk (Tues–Sat 10am–4pm; free), a mighty brick pile rebuilt after bomb damage in 1940. The church has splendid bronze doors, the work of Giacomo Manzu in the 1960s, and you can climb the tower on the third Saturday of the month (April–Sept only, noon–2pm; free).

A short walk from the back of St Laurenskerk, along the wide and windy Binnenrotte, is **Blaak**, a pocket-sized area that was levelled in World War II, but has since been rebuilt in the full flush of modern design. The architectural highlight is a remarkable series of cube-shaped houses, the *kubuswoningen*, completed in 1984 to a design by the architect Piet Blom. One of them, the **Kijk-Kubus** (Show Cube; March–Dec daily 11am–5pm; Jan & Feb Fri–Sun same hours; €1.75; ⓦwww.kubuswoning.nl), at Overblaak 70, near Blaak train and metro station, is open to visitors, offering a somewhat disorientating tour of what amounts to an upside-down house.

Behind the cube houses is the **Oudehaven**, the city's first harbour, built in 1325, and now flanked by cafés and crowded with antique barges and boats.

## The Maritime Museum and the Museum Het Schielandshuis

Heading west from the Kijk-Kubus, it's about 600m along Blaak boulevard to Churchillplein and the **Maritiem Museum** (Tues–Sat 10am–5pm, Sun 11am–5pm; €3.50; ⓦwww.maritiemmuseum.nl), situated beside the waters of

## Cruises around the port

The shape and feel of the **Leuvehaven**, Rotterdam's first artificial harbour, has been transformed by the Boompjes freeway, which scoots along the top of the old enclosing sea dyke. Beside the Boompjes, at the south end of the Leuvehaven, is the departure point for **cruises** operated by Spido (℡010/275 9988, ⓦwww.spido.nl). They have several different tours of the surrounding waterways and port facilities, heading off past the wharves, landings, docks and silos of this, the largest port in the world. The standard **harbour tour** costs €8 (April–Oct 5–11 daily; Nov–March Thurs–Sun 3–4 daily; 1hr 15min). From April to September, there are also longer, less frequent trips to Dordrecht, the windmills of Kinderdijk and the Europoort, from between €15 and €30 per person.

The Spido excursion to the series of colossal dams that make up the **Delta Project**, along the seaboard southwest of Rotterdam, provides only the briefest of glances, and it's better to visit by bus, which takes two hours. To get there, take the metro to Spijkenisse (30min) and catch bus #104 for Vlissingen (Mon–Sat hourly, Sun every 2hr), which travels along the road that crosses the top of the three dams that restrain the Haringvliet, Grevelingen and Oosterschelde estuaries. For more on the Delta Project and Delta Expo, see p.314-315.

the Leuvehaven. The museum has an interesting display on the history of Rotterdam as a seaport and shipbuilding centre plus an entertaining section on the life of seamen in the seventeenth and eighteenth centuries. The outside area has been spruced up for the museum's prime exhibit: an immaculately restored mid-nineteenth-century ironclad, the *Buffel*, complete with communal sinks shaped to match the angle of the bows, a couple of ships' figureheads and a string of luxurious officers' cabins.

There's more on the history of Rotterdam at the **Museum Het Schielandshuis** (Tues–Fri 10am–5pm, Sat & Sun 11am–5pm; €2.70; ⓦwww.hmr.rotterdam.nl), housed in a seventeenth-century mansion at Korte Hoogstraat 31 – a brief stroll north of the Maritiem Museum on the far side of Blaak boulevard. The main historical display features original footage of the bombing of the city in World War II and the museum is also home to the *Atlas van Stolk* collection of drawings and prints, which includes fascinating sketches of pre-colonial Indonesia.

### Museumpark

Tram #8 serves the southern edge of **Museumpark**, a newly designated cultural zone where a string of museums fringe a wide, open area. In the south, bordering Westzeedijk, are the **Natuurmuseum** (Tues–Sat 10am–5pm, Sun 11am–5pm; €3; ⓦwww.nmr.nl), where all sorts of stuffed animals are displayed, and the excellent **Kunsthal** (Tues–Sat 10am–5pm, Sun 11am–5pm; €6.50; ⓦwww.kunsthal.nl), which showcases first-rate exhibitions of contemporary art, photography and design.

### Museum Boijmans Van Beuningen

A few minutes' walk from the Kunsthal, on the northern edge of Museumpark near Eendrachtsplein metro stop, is Rotterdam's top attraction, the **Museum Boijmans Van Beuningen** (Tues–Sat 10am–5pm, Sun 11am–5pm; €6; ⓦwww.boijmans.nl). Newly revamped, the museum spreads over two floors with the ground floor used for temporary exhibitions, the first floor for the vast permanent collection (with the older paintings being in one wing, the newer works – from the late nineteenth century onwards – in the other). The information desk provides an updated and simplified diagrammatic outline of the museum, necessary because the exhibits are frequently rotated.

Among the museum's earlier paintings is an excellent **Flemish and Netherlandish** section, where one highlight is the sumptuous *Christ in the House of Martha and Mary* by Pieter Aertsen. There are also four exquisite works by Hieronymus Bosch. Usually considered a macabre fantasist, Bosch was actually working to the limits of oral and religious tradition, where biblical themes were depicted as iconographical representations, laden with explicit symbols. In his *St Christopher*, the dragon, the hanged bear and the broken pitcher lurk in the background, representations of danger and uncertainty, whereas the Prodigal Son's attitude to the brothel behind him in *The Wanderer* is deliberately ambivalent. Bosch's technique never absorbed the influences of Renaissance Italy, and his figures in the *Marriage Feast at Cana* are static and unbelievable, uncomfortably arranged around a distorted table. Other works in this section include paintings by Jan van Scorel, who was more willing to absorb Italianate styles as in his *Scholar in a Red Cap*; the Bruges artist Hans Memling, whose capacity for detail can be seen in his *Two Houses in a Landscape*; Pieter Brueghel the Elder's mysterious, hazy *Tower of Babel*; and Geertgen tot Sint Jans' beautiful, delicate *Glorification of the Virgin*.

Moving on, a fascinating selection of **Dutch genre** paintings reflects the tastes of the emergent seventeenth-century middle class. The idea was to depict real-life situations overlaid with a symbolic moral content as typified by Jan Steen's *Extracting the Stone* and his *Physician's Visit*. There's also Gerrit Dou's *The Quack*, ostensibly just a passing scene, but littered with small cameos of deception – a boy catching a bird, the trapped hare – that refer back to the quack's sham cures. In this section also are a number of Rembrandts, including two contrasting canvases: an analytic *Portrait of Alotta Adriaensdr*, her ageing illuminated but softened by her white ruff, and a gloomy, powerfully indistinct *Blind Tobias and his Wife* painted twenty years later. His intimate *Titus at his Desk* is also in marked contrast to the more formal portrait commissions common to his day. Most of the work of Rembrandt's pupil Carel Fabritius was destroyed when he was killed in a Delft gunpowder explosion in 1654; an exception is his *Self-Portrait*, reversing his master's usual technique by lighting the background and placing the subject in shadow.

The museum's collection of **modern paintings** is perhaps best known for its Surrealists. *De rigueur* for students' bedrooms in the 1970s, it's difficult to appreciate Salvador Dali's *Spain* as anything more than the painting of the poster, but other works by the likes of René Magritte, Max Ernst and Giorgio de Chirico still have the power to surprise. Surrealism was never adopted by Dutch artists, though the Magic Realism of Carel Willink has its similarities in the precise, hallucinatory technique he uses to distance the viewer in *Self Portrait with a Pen*. Charley Toorop's *Three Generations* is also realism with an aim to disconcert: the huge bust of her father, Jan, looms in the background and dominates the painting. In this section, look out also for paintings from many of Europe's most famous artists, including Monet, Van Gogh, Picasso, Gauguin, Cézanne and Munch, as well as a representative sample of the Barbizon and Hague schools, notably J.H. Weissenbruch's *Strandgezicht*, a beautiful gradation of radiant tones.

## Delfshaven

If little in Rotterdam city centre can exactly be called picturesque, **DELFSHAVEN**, a couple of kilometres southwest of Centraal Station, goes part of the way to make up for it – to get there, catch tram #4 or #6 (direction

Schiedam, tram stop Spanjaardstraat), or take the metro to Delfshaven. Once the harbour that served Delft, it was from here that the **Pilgrim Fathers** set sail in 1620, changing to the more reliable *Mayflower* in Plymouth before continuing onward to the New World. However, despite this substantial claim to fame, Delfshaven was long a neglected corner until finally, in the 1970s, the city recognized its tourist potential and set about conserving and restoring. Most of the buildings lining the two narrow canals that comprise Delfshaven are eighteenth- and nineteenth-century warehouses, with the more fetching facades on the more westerly Voorhaven. It's here, at no. 12, you'll find the **Museum de Dubbelde Palmboom** (Tues–Fri 10am–5pm, Sat & Sun 11am–5pm; €2.70), once a jenever distillery and now an historical museum, with a wide-ranging, if unexceptional collection of objects representing work and leisure in the Maas delta. A few metres to the north, at Voorstraat 13, is the **Zakkendragershuisje** (Tues–Sat 10am–5pm, Sun 1–5pm; free), originally the guild room of the Grain Sack Carriers, who decided the allocation of duties by dice. Today, it's a privately owned, fully operational tin foundry, selling a variety of items made in the old moulds.

## Eating and drinking

Oude and Nieuwe Binneweg are lined with **cafés** and **café-bars** – try *De Vijgeboon* at Oude Binnenweg 146a, *Sijf* at Oude Binnenweg 115, on the corner with Jacobstraat, or *Rotown* at Nieuwe Binneweg 19: all have affordable dinner menus featuring tasty Dutch staples; *Rotown* offers regular **live music** too. Another good street to head for is Witte de Withstraat, where *The Bazar*, at no. 16, does excellent kebabs and vegetarian meals. There's also a very pleasant café at the Boijmans Museum. For something more luxurious, the *Hotel Westin Rotterdam*, close to Centraal Station at Weena 686 (☎010/430 2000), has an outstanding first-floor restaurant with enjoyable views back over to the station; main courses here average around €20–25. There are lots of **cannabis coffeeshops** around the centre; one to start with is *Witte de With* at Witte de Withstraat 92.

Rotterdam has a great **club scene**. Two current hotspots are *Off Corso*, near Centraal Station at Kruiskade 22 (🌐www.off-corso.nl), with top DJs and even art exhibitions, and *De Blauwe Vis* (🌐www.blauwevis.nl), underground in a disused underpass at the north end of the Lijnbaan. Tickets for gigs and concerts are on sale at the main post office, Coolsingel 42 (☎0900/300 1250, 🌐www .ticketservice.nl).

## Listings

**Car rental** Hertz, Schiekade 986 ☎010/404 6088; Europcar, Walenburghof 17 ☎010/465 6400; Sixt, at the Hilton, Weena ☎010/462 7221.
**Emergencies** Police, Ambulance & Fire ☎112.
**Flight enquiries** Rotterdam Airport ☎010/446 3444, 🌐www.rotterdam-airport.nl.
**Football** The local team is the famous Feyenoord (☎010/292 6888, 🌐www.feyenoord.nl) – bus #49 or Stadion train run from Centraal Station to the stadium. Most games are on Sundays; the VVV has details.
**Left luggage** Coin-operated lockers at the train station.
**Markets** General market, including antiques, on Mariniersweg (Tues & Sat 9am–5pm). Stamps, coins and books on Grotekerkplein (Tues & Sat 9.30am–4pm).
**Medical assistance** For a doctor, call ☎010/420 1100. The emergency municipal dentist is on ☎010/455 2155.
**Pharmacies** 24hr service details on ☎010/411 0370.
**Police** Headquarters is at Doelwater 5 ☎010/274 9911.
**Post office** Coolsingel 42 (Mon–Thurs 9am–6pm, Fri 9am–7pm, Sat 9am–1pm).
**Taxi** Rotterdamse Taxi Centrale ☎010/462 6060; airport taxis ☎010/262 0406.

# Gouda and around

A pretty little place some 25km northeast of Rotterdam, **GOUDA** is almost everything you'd expect of a Dutch country town: a ring of quiet canals encircling ancient buildings and old docks. More surprisingly, its **Markt**, a ten-minute walk from the train station, is the largest in the Netherlands, an attractive reminder of the town's prominence as a centre of the medieval cloth trade, and later of its success in the manufacture of cheeses and clay pipes.

Gouda's main claim to fame is its **cheese market**, held in the Markt every Thursday morning from June to August. Traditionally, some one thousand local farmers brought their home-produced cheeses here to be weighed, tested and graded for moisture, smell and taste. These details were marked on the cheeses, and formed the basis for negotiation between buyer and seller, the exact price confirmed using an elaborate code of hand-claps. Today, however, the cheese market is a shadow of its former self, a few locals in traditional dress standing outside the Waag, surrounded by modern, open-air stands. It's mercilessly milked by tour operators, who herd their crowds into this scene every week – but don't let this put you off a visit, since Gouda's charms lie elsewhere.

There's a jazz festival in town in early September and, if you happen to be in the area in mid-December, it's worth checking with the Gouda VVV to find out exactly when the town will be holding its splendid candlelit pre-Christmas festival. All electric lights are extinguished on the main square, which is lit up instead by thousands of candles.

## The Town

Slap-bang in the middle of the Markt, the **Stadhuis** is an elegant Gothic building dating from 1450, its facade fringed by statues of counts and countesses of Burgundy above a tinkling carillon that plays every half-hour. Nearby, on the north side of the square, the **Waag** is a tidy seventeenth-century building, decorated with a detailed relief of cheese-weighing and now holding a **Kaaswaag** (Cheese Museum; April–Oct Tues, Wed & Fri–Sun 1–5pm, Thurs 10am–5pm; €2).

To the south, just off the Markt, **St Janskerk** (March–Oct Mon–Sat 9am–5pm; Nov–Feb Mon–Sat 10am–4pm; €2) was founded in the thirteenth century and rebuilt three times after fires, most recently in the sixteenth century. The church is famous for its magnificent and stunningly beautiful **stained-glass windows**, which also witness the move from Catholicism to Calvinism. The biblical themes executed by Dirk and Wouter Crabeth between 1555 and 1571, when Holland was still Catholic, have an amazing clarity of detail and richness of colour. Their last work, *Judith Slaying Holofernes* (window no. 6), is perhaps the finest, the story unfolding in intricate perspective. By comparison, the post-Reformation windows, which date from 1572 to 1603, adopt an allegorical and heraldic style typical of a more secular art. *The Relief of Leiden* (window no. 25) shows William the Silent retaking the town from the Spanish, though Delft and its burgomasters take prominence – no doubt because they paid the bill for its construction. All the windows are numbered and a detailed guide is available at the entrance; binoculars will help you make out the detail.

By the side of the church, the flamboyant **Lazarus Gate** of 1609 was once part of the town's leper hospital, until it was moved to form the back entrance to the **Catharina Gasthuis**, a hospice till 1910. A likeable conglomeration of sixteenth-century rooms and halls, including an old isolation cell for the insane, the interior of the Gasthuis has been turned into a **fine art museum** (Mon–Sat 10am–5pm, Sun noon–5pm; €2.50). The collection incorporates an enjoyable sample of early religious art in The Chapel (room 13), notably a large triptych, *Life of Mary*, by Dirk Barendsz and a characteristically austere *Annunciation* by the Bruges artist Pieter Pourbus. Other highlights include a

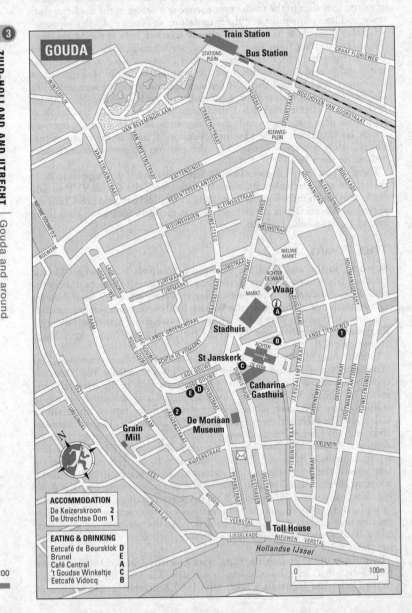

spacious hall, *Het Ruim* (room 10), that was once a sort of medieval hostel, but is now dominated by paintings of the Civic Guard, including two by the talented Ferdinand Bol. Here also is an intricate, silver-gilt chalice and eucharist dish presented to Gouda's Civic Guard in the early fifteenth century. Two later rooms have a modest selection of Hague and Barbizon School canvases, notably work by Anton Mauve and Charles Daubigny.

With time to spare, you might squeeze in a visit to another museum, **De Moriaan** (Mon–Fri 10am–5pm, Sat 10am–12.30pm & 1.30–5pm, Sun noon–5pm; €3.60; free with Gasthuis ticket). Located in a cosy old merchant's house at Westhaven 29, it holds a mixed bag of exhibits from clay pipes to ceramics and tiles. Westhaven itself is a winsome jumble of old buildings that head off toward the old **Tolhuis** (toll house) and a dilapidated mill beside the Hollandse IJssel river, on the southern edge of the town centre. There's a restored, fully operational grain mill, **Molen de Roode Leeuw** (Thurs 9am–2pm, Sat 9am–4pm; €1.20), five minutes' walk west of the Markt, at Vest 65.

## Practicalities

Gouda's **train** and **bus stations** are to the immediate north of the town centre, ten minutes' walk from the **VVV**, at Markt 27 (Mon–Fri 9am–5pm, Sat 10am–4pm; July & Aug also Sun noon–3pm; ☏0900/4683 2888, Ⓦwww.vvvgouda.nl). They have a limited supply of **private rooms** (❶–❷), and will make hotel reservations on your behalf for a small charge. There are two recommendable and reasonably priced **hotels** in the centre – the excellent-value *De Utrechtsche Dom*, in an airy and pleasantly renovated old building five minutes' walk from the station at Geuzenstraat 6 (☏0182/528 833, Ⓦwww.hotelgouda.nl; ❷), and *De Keizerskroon*, to the west of Westhaven at Keizerstraat 11–13 (☏0182/528 096; ❷).

Gouda has literally dozens of **cafés** and snack bars geared up for the day-trippers who descend on the town in droves during the summer. Among them, there are tasty pancakes at *'t Gouds Winkeltje*, Achter de Kerk 9a (closed Sun & Mon), and good quality Dutch food at the popular *Eetcafé De Beursklok*, in an attractively converted old shop at Hoge Gouwe 19. *Eetcafé Vidocq*, Koster Gijzensteeg 8, offers similar food – and both eetcafés are pleasant places for a **drink**, as is the more traditional *Café Central*, Markt 23. Arguably the best **restaurant** in town is *Bunel*, a smart French place at Hoge Gouwe 23 (☏0182/518 979), where main courses average about €20.

## Oudewater

In the countryside some 11km east of Gouda, and easily accessible by bike (rent one from the train station) or bus #180 (every 30min, hourly on Sun; takes 20min), **OUDEWATER** is a compact and delightful little town that holds a unique place in the history of Dutch witchcraft (see box on p.202). The town's sixteenth-century Waag has survived, converted into the **Heksenwaag** (Witches' Weigh House; April–Oct Tues–Sat 10am–5pm, Sun noon–5pm; €1.50; Ⓦwww.heksenwaag.nl), a family-run affair, where you can be weighed on the original rope and wood balance, as were women accused of witchcraft. The owners dress up in national costume and issue a certificate in olde-worlde English that states nothing, but does so very prettily. There's not much else to see in Oudewater, but it's a pleasant little place, whose traditional stepped gables spread out along the River Hollandse IJssel as it twists its way through town.

## Oudewater and the Dutch witch-hunts

It's estimated that over a million women across Europe were burned or otherwise murdered in the widespread **witch-hunts** of the sixteenth century – and not just from fear and superstition: anonymous accusation to the authorities was an easy way of removing a wife, at a time when there was no divorce. Underlying it all was a virulent misogyny and an accompanying desire to terrorize women into submission. There were three main methods for investigating accusations of witchcraft: in the first, **trial by fire**, the suspect had to walk barefoot over hot cinders or have a hot iron pressed into the back or hands. If the burns blistered, the accused was innocent, since witches were supposed to burn less easily than others; naturally, the (variable) temperature of the iron was crucial. **Trial by water** was still more hazardous: dropped into water, if you floated you were a witch, if you sank you were innocent – though very probably drowned. The third method, **trial by weight**, pre-supposed that a witch would have to be unduly light to fly on a broomstick, so many towns – including Oudewater – used the Waag (town weigh-house) to weigh the accused. If the weight didn't accord with a notional figure derived from a person's height, the woman was burned. The last Dutch woman to be burned as a witch was a certain Marrigje Ariens, a herbalist from Schoonhaven, whose medical efforts, not atypically, inspired mistrust and subsequent persecution. She died in 1597.

Oudewater gained its fame from the actions of Charles V (1516–52), who saw a woman accused of witchcraft in a nearby village. The weigh-master there, who'd been bribed, stated that the woman weighed only a few pounds, but Charles was dubious and ordered the woman to be weighed again in Oudewater, where the officials proved unbribable, pronouncing a normal weight and acquitting her. The probity of Oudewater's weigh-master impressed Charles, and he granted the town the privilege of issuing certificates, valid throughout the empire, stating: "The accused's weight is in accordance with the natural proportions of the body". Once in possession of the certificate, a woman could never be brought to trial for witchcraft again. Not surprisingly, thousands of women came from all over Europe for this life-saving piece of paper, and, much to Oudewater's credit, no one was ever condemned in the town.

The **VVV**, Markt-Oostzyde 8 (April–Sept Tues–Sat 10.30am–4.30pm, Sun 1–4.30pm; Oct–March Tues–Sat 10am–1pm; ℡0348/564 636), has details of several inexpensive **private rooms** (❶), and there is one central **hotel**, the *Abrona*, a well-maintained, two-star establishment at Broeckerstraat 20 (℡0348/567 466, ⓦwww.abrona.nl; ❷). For **food**, *Café 't Bactertje*, Markt-Oostzyde 14, does decent snacks and *Joia* is a quality brasserie serving Dutch cuisine at Havenstraat 1–2 (℡0348/567 150).

# Dordrecht and around

Some 15km southeast of Rotterdam, the ancient port of **DORDRECHT**, or "Dordt" as it's often called, is a likeable town beside one of the busiest waterway junctions in the world, where tankers and containers from the north pass the waterborne traffic of the Maas and Rijn. Eclipsed by the expansion of Rotterdam and left relatively intact by World War II, Dordrecht has also been spared the worst excesses of postwar development to emerge with a particularly beguiling centre adorned by a confusion of

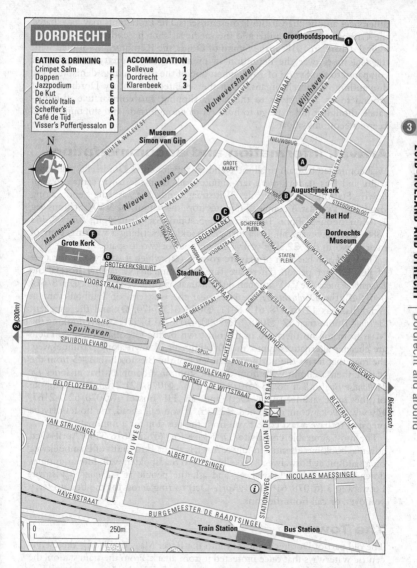

## DORDRECHT

**EATING & DRINKING**

| | |
|---|---|
| Crimpet Salm | H |
| Dappen | F |
| Jazzpodium | G |
| De Kut | E |
| Piccolo Italia | B |
| Scheffer's | C |
| Café de Tijd | A |
| Visser's Poffertjessalon | D |

**ACCOMMODATION**

| | |
|---|---|
| Bellevue | 1 |
| Dordrecht | 2 |
| Klarenbeek | 3 |

ancient buildings. Within easy reach also is some of the province's prettiest countryside, including the windmills of the **Kinderdijk** and the **Biesbosch** nature reserve.

Granted a town charter in 1220, Dordrecht was the most important and powerful town in Holland until well into the sixteenth century. One of the first cities to declare against the Habsburgs in 1572, it was the obvious site for the first meeting of the Free Assembly of the Seven Provinces, and for a series of doctrinal conferences that tried to solve a whole range of theological differences among the various Protestant sects. The Protestants may have hated the Catholics, but they inherited the medieval church's enthusiasm for theological debate; in 1618, at the Synod of Dordt, the Remonstrants argued with the Calvinists over the definition of predestination – pretty weighty stuff compared to the Synod of 1574, when one of the main rulings demanded the dismantling of church organs. From the seventeenth century, Dordrecht lost ground to its great rivals to the north, slipping into comparative insignificance, though it did manage to hold on to enough trade and shipbuilding to keep its economy afloat.

## Arrival, information and accommodation

Well connected by train to all the Randstad's major cities, Dordrecht's adjoining **train** and **bus** stations are a ten-minute walk from the town centre, straight down Stationsweg/Johan de Wittstraat and left at the end along Bagijnhof/Visstraat. A couple of minutes from the station, the **VVV**, Stationsweg 1 (Mon noon–5.30pm, Tues–Fri 9am–5.30pm, Sat 10am–4pm; ☎0900/463 6888; ⓦwww.vvvzhz.nl), has a first-rate booklet describing a **walking tour** of the city, worth the €2.50 if you've got an hour or two to spare.

The VVV also has a list of **private rooms** (❶), which it will reserve for a fee of just €1 per person. There are three recommendable central **hotels**: the *Klarenbeek*, near the VVV at Johan de Wittstraat 35 (☎078/614 4133, ☏078/614 0861; ❺); the *Dordrecht*, by the river near the west end of Spuiboulevard at Achterhakkers 12 (☎078/613 6011, ☏078/613 7470; ❹); and the excellent *Bellevue*, Boomstraat 37 (☎078/613 7900, ☏078/613 7921; ❹), overlooking the Maas from the northern tip of the old town by the Groothoofdspoort. There are cheaper alternatives approximately 4km east of town along Baanhoekweg, the road that forms the northern perimeter of the Biesbosch (bus #5 from the station, then a 20min walk from the last stop), in a complex that includes *De Hollandse Biesbosch* at no. 25 (☎078/621 2167, ☏078/621 2163; ❷), a campsite of the same name (April–Oct) and an HI **hostel** (☎078/621 2167, ⓦwww.stayokay.com; dorm bed €23.35). If you call ahead, the hostel may be prepared to have a taxi collect you from the bus stop for a minimal charge.

The most agreeable **campsite**, *De Kleine Rug* (☎078/616 3555; April–Oct; advance bookings essential in July & Aug), is about 1km south of Baanhoekweg on a sandspit at Loswalweg 1: take bus #3 to Stadspolder, walk fifteen minutes down to the end of Loswalweg and ask the people at *Camping 't Vissertje*, Loswalweg 3 (☎078/616 2751; April–Oct) to ring across for the boat to ferry you over, or call from the bank.

## The Town

The old part of Dordrecht juts out into the River Maas, divided by three concentric waterways that once protected it from attack. From the train station, the second canal is the heart of the town, flowing beside the **Voorstraat**, today's main shopping street. At the junction of Voorstraat and Visstraat, the Visbrug spans the canal with a heavy-handed monument to the de Witt brothers, Johan and Cornelius, prominent Dutch Republicans who paid for their principles when they were torn to pieces by an Orangist mob in Den Haag in 1672. To the right, Voorstraat bends its way northeast, a chaotic mixture of the old, the new and the restored, intersected by a series of tiny alleys that once served as the town's docks. Cutting off Voorstraat at Wijnbrug, the **Wijnhaven** was used by the city's merchants to control the import and export of wine when they held the state monopoly from the fourteenth to the seventeenth centuries.

At the end of Voorstraat, the **Groothoofdspoort** was once the main city gate, its grand facade, dating from 1618, pushed up against the *Hotel Bellevue*, with its fine views over the surrounding waterways.

The town's innermost canal is just along the waterfront from here, divided into two harbours and home to the cruisers, barges and sailing boats that ply up and down the Maas. Fringed by stately buildings and criss-crossed by rickety footbridges, it's an attractive setting for the **Museum Simon van Gijn**, Nieuwe Haven 29 (Tues–Sun 11–5pm; €5; ⓦwww.simonvangijn.nl), whose collection of local memorabilia and period rooms is of moderate interest. Best are the eighteenth-century Brussels tapestries and a fine Renaissance chimneypiece of 1550, transferred from the old guild house of the arquebusiers.

### The Grote Kerk and the Stadhuis
Near the southwest end of Nieuwe Haven, the **Grote Kerk** (April–Oct Tues–Sat 10.30am–4.30pm, Sun noon–4pm; Nov & Dec 1st & 3rd Sat of month 2–4pm; guided tour at 2.15pm; free) is visible from all over town, its fourteenth-century **tower** (April–Oct same hours; Nov–March Sat 1–4pm in fine weather only; €1) topped with incongruous seventeenth-century clocks. One of the largest churches in the country, it was built to emphasize Dordrecht's wealth and importance, but it's heavy and dull, despite its attractive environs, and there's only an elaborately carved choir inside to hold your interest. Climb the tower for a great view over the town and its surrounding waters.

From beside the church, Grotekerksbuurt leads to the stolid classicism of the **Stadhuis**, on the Voorstraat.

### Dordrechts Museum
A five- to ten-minute walk from the Stadhuis, to the southeast of the centre, the **Dordrechts Museum**, (Tues–Sun 11am–5pm; €5; ⓦwww .dordrechtsmuseum.nl) is at Museumstraat 4. Well presented and clearly labelled (in Dutch), the museum concentrates on the work of local artists, both in its permanent and temporary displays. Highlights of the permanent collection include a couple of finely drawn portraits by Jacob Cuyp (on the wall of the staircase as you leave), and a whole room (room 5) devoted to the work of his son, Albert. Born in Dordrecht, Albert Cuyp (1620–91) was influenced by those of his contemporaries who had visited Italy, modulating his work with the soft, yellowish tones of the Renaissance. Noted for his Italianate landscapes, seascapes and town scenes, his *Resting Riders in a Landscape* is representative of his work, in contrast to the muted tones of traditional Dutch landscape painting, as illustrated by Jan van Goyen's *View of Dordrecht*, the city's bustle restricted to the bottom section of the canvas, beneath a wide sky and flattened horizon.

A student of Rembrandt, Nicolaes Maes (1632–93) first specialized in informal domestic scenes, as in *The Eavesdropper* (room 6), turning his skills to portrait painting after his visit to Antwerp in 1670. A good example of his later work is his flattering picture of *Jacob de Witt the Elder* (room 7). More curiously, *De Dordtse Vierling* ("The Dordt Quadruplets") is an odd, unattributed seventeenth-century painting of a dead child and her three swaddled siblings, a simple, moving tribute to a lost daughter. High on the wall of the staircase nearby, the massive *Gezicht op Dordt* (View of Dordt) is a masterpiece of minutely observed naturalist detail by Adam Willaertz (1577–1644).

On the second floor, there's a selection of work by the later and lesser Ary Scheffer (1795–1858), who was born in Dordrecht, but lived in Paris from 1811. His much-reproduced *Mignon Pining for her Native Land* struck a chord in the sentimental hearts of the nineteenth-century bourgeoisie. Jozef Israels' *Midday Meal at the Inn* and G.H. Breitner's *Lauriergracht 1891* (room 14) are among a small collection of Amsterdam and Hague School paintings.

## Eating and drinking

Voorstraat is dotted with competent, reasonably priced **cafés** and **restaurants**, one of the better choices being *Piccolo Italia*, at no. 259 (☎078/614 4950), where tasty Italian dishes average around €12. Alternatively, *Visser's Poffertjessalon*, on the Groenmarkt, has a fine line in pancakes plus traditional Dutch snacks, and it's next door to *Scheffer's*, which does filling pub food. There's also *De Kut*, a fashionable, glass-sided tapas bar overlooking the canal on Scheffersplein. Moving upmarket, *Crimpet Salm*, near Visbrug at Visstraat 7 (☎078/614 5557), serves delicious seafood – and, appropriately enough, it occupies a handsome old building that once housed the fish merchants' guild.

For **drinking**, the atmospheric *Café de Tijd*, Voorstraat 170, has a good range of brews, as does *Dappen*, a lively place by the Grote Kerk on tiny Huoffuin. The *Jazzpodium*, Grotekerkplein 1 (☎078/614 0815), usually has **live music** on Wednesday, Friday and Saturday. Amongst Dordrecht's **cannabis coffee-shops**, *Asila* on Bagijnhof, near Vest, makes a friendly start.

## The Biesbosch

On November 18, 1421, Zuid-Holland's sea defences gave way and the St Elizabeth Day flood formed what is now the Hollands Diep sea-channel and the **Biesbosch** (Reed Forest), an expanse of river, creek, marsh and reed covering around fifteen square kilometres to the south and east of Dordrecht. It was a disaster of major proportions, with seventy towns and villages destroyed, and a death toll of around 100,000. The effect on the region's economy was catastrophic too, with the fracturing of links between Zuid-Holland and Flanders accelerating the shift in commercial power to the north. Those villages that did survive took generations to recover, subjected, as they were, to raids by the wretched refugees of the flood.

Inundated twice daily by the tide, the Biesbosch produced a particular **reed culture**, its inhabitants using the plant for every item of daily life, from houses to baskets and boats, and selling excess cuttings at the local markets. It was a harsh existence that lasted well into the nineteenth century, when machine-manufactured goods largely rendered the reeds redundant. Today, the Biesbosch is a national park whose delicate ecosystem is threatened by the very scheme that aims to protect the province from further flooding. The Delta Project dams (see p.314) have controlled the rivers' flow and restricted the tides' strength, forcing the reeds to give ground to other forms of vegetation incompatible with the area's bird and plant life. Large areas of reed have disappeared, and no one seems to know how to reconcile the nature reserve's needs with those of the seaboard cities, but vigorous attempts are being made.

### Practicalities

The park divides into two main sections, north and south of the Nieuwe Merwede channel, which marks the provincial boundary between Zuid-Holland and Noord-Brabant (see p.318). The undeveloped heart of the nature reserve is the **Brabantse Biesbosch**, the chunk of land to the south, whereas tourist facilities have been carefully confined to the north, on a strip just east of Dordrecht, along the park's perimeter. Here, rebuilt after being burnt to the ground, the **Bezoekerscentrum de Hollandse Biesbosch**, Baanhoekweg 53 (Visitors' Centre; Tues–Sun 9am–5pm; May & June also Mon 1–5pm; July & Aug daily 9am–5pm; ⓦwww.biesbosch.org; free), accessible by bus #5 from Dordrecht bus station, has displays on the flora and fauna of the region and a beaver observatory. **Boat trips** for the Brabantse Biesbosch leave from the jetty beside the Bezoekerscentrum (July & Aug daily; Sept & Oct Wed & Sun only). Prices vary according to the itinerary, starting at €13 for the day ("Dagtochten") or €5 for a two-hour excursion ("Rondvaarten").

Some of the longer excursions visit the **Biesboschmuseum**, on the southern shore of the Nieuwe Merwede at Hilweg 2 (Tues–Sat 10am–5pm, Sun noon–5pm; €2.75; ⓦwww.biesboschmuseum.nl), where there is further information on the ecology of the Biesbosch and the origins of its distinctive reed culture. Details of boat trips are available at the Dordrecht VVV and the visitors' centre.

The other way of visiting the nature reserve is by **bike**, for rent at standard rates from Dordrecht train station. The VVV sells detailed maps of the national park and brochures on suggested cycle routes. The ride from town to the Biesbosch takes about half an hour, via the shuttle passenger boat service that runs from the dock by Kop van 't Land, 5km southeast of the town centre, to a point about 1km northeast of the Biesboschmuseum.

## The Kinderdijk

Some 12km north of Dordrecht, the **Kinderdijk** (Child's Dyke; ⓦwww.kinderdijk.nl) sits at the end of a long drainage channel which feeds into the River Lek, whose turbulent waters it keeps from flooding the polders around Alblasserdam. Sixteenth-century legend suggests it takes its name from the time when a cradle, complete with cat and kicking baby, was found at the precise spot where the dyke had held during a particularly bad storm. A mixture of symbols – rebirth, innocence and survival – the story encapsulates the determination with which the Dutch fought the floods for hundreds of years.

Today, the Kinderdijk is famous for its picturesque, quintessentially Dutch **windmills**, all eighteen lining the main channel and its tributary beside the Molenkade for some three kilometres. Built around 1740 to drive water from the Alblasserwaard polders, the windmills are put into operation every Saturday afternoon in July and August plus the first Saturday of the month from May to December. In addition, one of the windmills is open to visitors from April to October, weather permitting (Mon–Sat 9.30am–5.30pm; €2.50) and they all swing into action on **National Windmill day**, April 30.

Without a car, the easiest way to explore the district from Dordrecht is by **bike**; alternatively, take bus #252 to Alblassendam, then bus #154 (direction Utrecht) to the mills. If you decide to **stay**, the tiny village of Kinderdijk is to the immediate west of the dyke, on the banks of the Lek. There's just one **hotel**, *Kinderdijk*, West Kinderdijk 361 (①078/691 2425, ②078/691 5071; ②). Advance booking is essential from June to August.

# Utrecht

"I groaned with the idea of living all winter in so shocking a place," wrote Boswell in 1763, and **UTRECHT** still promises little as you approach: surrounded by shopping centres and industrial developments, the town only

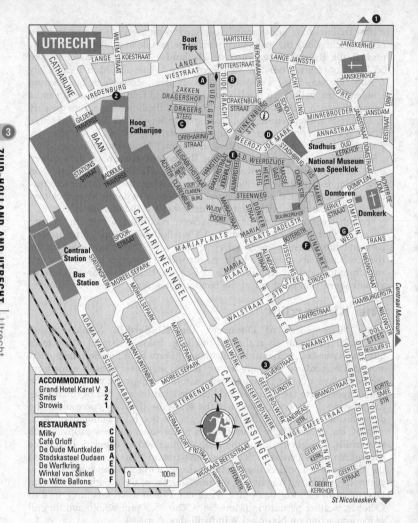

St Nicolaaskerk

begins to reveal itself to good advantage in the old area around the Domkerk, roughly enclosed by the Oude and Nieuwe Gracht – sunken canals dating from the fourteenth century. It is this area that has most appeal, partly on account of its scattering of historical sights, but also its lively atmosphere, thanks to its large student population. Indeed, although Utrecht seems a tad provincial when compared to Amsterdam, just half an hour away by train, there's enough youthful spirit to keep you here overnight – though the sights themselves can easily be explored in half a day.

Founded by the **Romans** in the first century AD, the city of Utrecht became home to a wealthy and powerful medieval bishopric, which controlled the surrounding region under the auspices of the German emperors. In 1527, the bishop sold off his secular rights and shortly afterwards the town council enthusiastically joined the revolt against Spain. Indeed, the **Union of Utrecht**, the agreement that formalized the opposition to the Habsburgs, was signed

"KLM launches the new loyalty programme."

"A lift-off for great new benefits."

Flying
Dutchman
KLM proudly introduces the all-new Flying Dutchman loyalty programme. Taking advantage has never been so easy! Every flight is now credited with a minimum of 500 Miles, and travellers receive double credit for flying in Business Class. Once you achieve Elite membership status, you also earn extra Award Miles every time you fly. And there are countless ways to raise your total even higher with the many airlines and service partners participating in the programme. Spending the Miles you earn (which never expires) is easier and more rewarding too. To find out more or to join the programme online, visit www.klm.com. And start counting down all the benefits you'll gain as a member.

The Reliable Airline

"Only the Dutch could manage
it 68 times a day."

More flights to Amsterdam than all
the other airlines put together.

No one serves Holland's capital like KLM.
We fly up to 68 times each weekday from 14
airports in the UK.

For more information or to book, visit
www.klm.com, call 08705 074 074 or contact
your travel agent.

The Reliable Airline

here in 1579. Some two hundred years later, the **Treaty of Utrecht** brought to an end some of Louis IV of France's grand imperial ambitions. In between, in 1636, **Utrecht University** was founded, making it the second oldest university in the country after Leiden.

## Arrival, information and accommodation

Utrecht's **train and bus stations** both lead into the mammoth Hoog Catharijne shopping centre, on the edge of the city centre; the main **VVV** office is a short walk away at Vinkenburgstraat 19 (Mon–Fri 9.30am–6.30pm, Sat 9.30am–5pm; ☎0900/128 8732, ⓦwww.utrechtstad .com). They have a range of information on the city and surroundings, and provide city maps as well as the comprehensive listings magazine *Uit Lopper*. Though the city is compact enough to explore on foot, touring the canals, either by boat or by cycling along towpaths, adds another dimension to a visit. **Bikes** can be rented from the train station at standard rates, while **canal trips** depart hourly from Oude Gracht at the corner of Lange Viestraat and Potterstraat near the Viebrug bridge, behind the main post office (daily 11am–6pm; €6.25).

As regards **accommodation**, the most ambient place is the *Strowis*, a budget hostel housed in a seventeenth-century building at Boothstraat 8 (☎030/238 0280, ⓦwww.strowis.nl; dorm beds €12; ❶), a fifteen-minute walk east from the station. The hostel has pleasant rooms and dorms with (limited) access for travellers with disabilities, plus guest cooking facilities and free email. They also have lots of info on what's happening, especially cultural events. The official **HI hostel** is 5km southeast of town in an old country manor house at Rhijnauwenselaan 14 in Bunnik (☎030/656 1277, ⓦwww.stayokay.com; dorm beds €20; ❷) – take bus #40 or #41 from Utrecht train station. Two recommendable **hotels** in Utrecht are the *Best Western Amrath*, a smart modern place right in the centre at Vredenburg 14 (☎030/233 1232, ⓦwww.amrath.nl; ❺), and the luxurious, five-star *Grand Hotel Karel V*, Geertebolwerk 1 (☎030/233 7555, ⓦwww.karelv.nl; ❽).

## The Town

The focal point of the centre is the **Domtoren**, at over 112m the highest church bell tower in the country. It's one of the most beautiful, too, its soaring, unbuttressed lines rising to a delicate, octagonal lantern, added in 1380. Guided tours (Mon–Sat 10am–4pm, Sun noon–4pm; tours hourly, or every 30min in July & Aug; €6) take you unnervingly near to the top, from where on a clear day you can see Rotterdam and Amsterdam. Below, only the eastern part of the great cathedral – the **Domkerk** – remains, the nave having collapsed (with what must have been an apocalyptic crash) during a storm in 1674. It's worth peeking inside (May–Sept Mon–Fri 10am–5pm, Sat 10am–3pm & Sun 2–4pm; Oct–April Sat 11am–3pm & Sun 2–4pm; free) to get a sense of the hangar-like space the building once had, and to wander through the **Kloostergang**, the fourteenth-century cloisters that link the cathedral to the chapter house. The **Kloostertuin**, or cloister gardens, are reckoned to be the best place in town to listen to the carillon concerts from the Domtoren.

Heading northwest from here, the grandiose nineteenth-century **Stadhuis** overlooks a bend in the Oude Gracht. Nearby is an unusual little museum, the **Nationaal Museum van Speelklok tot Pierement**, Buurkerkhof 10 (Tues–Sat 10am–5pm, Sun noon–5pm; €6), a collection of burping fairground organs and ingenious musical boxes worth an hour of anyone's time. The museum is housed in the **Buurkerk**, once the home of one sister Bertken, who was so ashamed of being the illegitimate daughter of a cathedral priest that she hid away in a small cell here for 57 years, until her death in 1514.

### Museum Catharijne Convent

The national collection of ecclesiastical art, the **Museum Catharijne Convent** (Tues–Fri 10am–5pm, Sat & Sun 11am–5pm; €6; Ⓦwww .catharijneconvent.nl), at Nieuwe Gracht 63, has a mass of paintings, manuscripts and church ornaments from the ninth century on, brilliantly exhibited in a complex built around the old convent. This excellent collection of paintings includes work by Geertgen tot Sint Jans, Rembrandt, Hals and, best of all, a luminously beautiful *Virgin and Child* by Van Cleve (room 15). The convent incorporates the late Gothic **St Catharijnekerk**, whose radiant white interior is enhanced by floral decoration.

### Centraal Museum

Keep walking down along Nieuwe Gracht and you reach the **Centraal Museum** at Agnietenstraat 1 (Tues–Sun 11am–5pm; €8; Ⓦwww .centraalmuseum.nl). Its claim to hold "25,000 curiosities" may be exaggerated, but it does have a good collection of paintings by Utrecht artists of the sixteenth and seventeenth centuries. Jan van Scorel (1495–1562) lived in Utrecht before and after he visited Rome, from where he brought the influence of the Renaissance back home. His paintings, especially the vividly individual portraits of the *Jerusalem Brotherhood*, combine Renaissance style with native Dutch observation. The central figure in white is van Scorel himself: he is thought to have made a trip to Jerusalem around 1520, which may account for his unusually accurate drawing of the city in *Christ's Entry into Jerusalem*. A group of painters influenced by another Italian, Caravaggio, became known as the **Utrecht School**. Such paintings as Honthorst's *The Procuress* adapt his chiaroscuro technique to genre subjects, and develop an erotic content that would itself influence later genre painters like Jan Steen and Gerrit Dou. Even more skilled and realistic is Terbrugghen's *The Calling of St Matthew*, a beautiful balance of gestures dramatizing Christ summoning the tax collector to become one of the twelve disciples.

Gerrit Rietveld, the De Stijl designer, was most famous for his brightly coloured geometrical chairs, displayed in the museum's **applied art** section. Part of the De Stijl philosophy (see Contexts, p.374) was the need for universality, though Rietveld's angular furniture is undoubtedly better to look at than to sit on.

### The Schröderhuis

There is more Rietveld furniture in the **Schröderhuis** (guided tours only; Wed–Sun 11am–4pm; €8; booking essential on ☏030/236 2310), out of town at Prins Hendriklaan 50, accessible on bus #4 from the train station. Rietveld designed and built the house in 1924 for one Truus Schröder and her family. It's hailed as one of the most influential pieces of modern architecture in Europe, demonstrating the organic union of lines and rectangles that was the hallmark of the De Stijl movement. The ground floor is the most conventional part of the building, since its design had to meet the rigours of the building licence; however, Rietveld was able to let his imagination run riot with the top floor living space, creating a flexible environment where only the outer walls are solid – indeed the entire top floor can be subdivided in any way, simply by sliding the modular walls.

## Eating and drinking

There are lots of good places to **eat** and **drink** along Oude Gracht, both on the street and below at canal level, where the brick cellars, which were once used as warehouses, have been converted into a string of cafés, bars and restaurants. Options include the inexpensive pancake bakery *De Oude Muntkelder* at no. 112 and the vegetarian *De Werfkring* at no. 123. Also check out the popular media hangout *Café Orloff*, by the junction of Oude Gracht and Wed, *Polman's Huis*, on the corner of Jansdam and Keistraat – if only for its fancy turn-of-the-century interior – and a more upmarket and exotic vegetarian place, *Milky*, at Zakkendragersteeg 22 (☎030/231 9616).

Amongst Oude Gracht's many **bars**, there's *Winkel van Sinkel*, at no. 158, a large and often crowded bar with regular weekend dance nights, plus a chill-out room downstairs in the cellars, and *Stadkasteel Oudaen*, at no. 99, which brews beer on the premises and serves reasonable Dutch food. Another good option is *De Witte Ballons*, a friendly, low-key spot at Lijnmarkt 10–12.

Most of Utrecht's thirty or so **cannabis coffeeshops** are on the outskirts of town, but one city-centre option is *Andersom*, at Vismarkt 23.

# East of Utrecht

The Utrechtse Heuvelrug (Utrecht Ridge) stretches across the eastern edge of the province of Utrecht, a wooded region that appeals to many locals for its gentle walking and cycling. **Amersfoort**, twenty minutes from Utrecht by train, is the main town hereabouts – an attractive and easygoing place with a handful of decent museums, and certainly worth a day, or at least half day's detour. The countryside south of Amersfoort is dotted with the remains of medieval castles, most of them subsequently converted into grand châteaux. The castles at **Doorn** and **Amerongen**, in particular, warrant a visit if you're heading east towards Arnhem (see p.288), while the little town of **Rhenen**, prettily set beside the Rhine, pulls in tourists aplenty to view the fifteenth-century church of St Cunera.

## Amersfoort

Near the provincial border between Utrecht and Gelderland, the town of **AMERSFOORT** was first fortified in the eleventh century and received its charter in 1259. Surprisingly, it managed to avoid the attentions of the rival armies during the Revolt of the Netherlands, and some of today's centre dates from the fifteenth century, lying at the heart of a series of twisting canals that once served to protect the town from attack. The main square, the **Hof**, where the market is held on Friday and Saturday, is edged by the giant hulk of the **St Joriskerk** (mid-June to mid-Sept Mon–Sat 2–4.30pm; free), an unusual, predominantly Gothic edifice finished in 1534. The nave and aisles are of equal height, and only the south porch stops the exterior from resembling an aircraft hangar. Like most churches of the period, it was an enlargement of an earlier building, but here the original Romanesque tower was left inside the later fifteenth-century construction.

A few minutes' walk northeast along Langestraat, the **Kamperbinnenpoort** is a turreted thirteenth-century gate, extensively renovated in the 1930s. To the north and south of the gate runs **Muurhuizen** – literally "wall houses", after the habit of attaching dwellings to what was once the city's medieval rampart.

At the northern end of Muurhuizen, the **Museum Flehite**, Westsingel 50 (Tues–Fri 11am–5pm, Sat & Sun 1–5pm; €4; ⓦwww.museumflehite.nl), is located in one of these wallhouses, a fancifully gabled building of neo-Renaissance design. This is the town's main museum, but it's packed with a dreary assortment of items of strictly local interest. The museum also has a bizarre annexe across the canal, the chapel and male ward of a medieval hospice, the **St Pieters-en-Bloklands Gasthuis** (Tues–Fri 10–5pm, Sat & Sun 2–5pm; same ticket). From here, it's just a couple of hundred metres north to the highly picturesque **Koppelpoort**, a fifteenth-century town gate, which defended Amersfoort's northern approach by dropping down a wooden panel and sealing off the canal.

## Onze Lieve Vrouwekerk and the Mondriaanhuis

Back on Westsingel, 500m south of the Museum Flehite, all that remains of Amersfoort's other main church, the **Onze Lieve Vrouwekerk** (July & Aug Tues–Fri 10am–5pm, Sat noon–5pm; €3), is the fifteenth-century tower – the rest was accidentally blown up in 1797. The original church was paid for by pilgrims visiting the Amersfoort Madonna, a small and much-revered medieval wooden figure. Legend has it that, in 1444, a young girl threw the statuette into the town canal when she was on her way to enter one of the city's convents. It wasn't that she minded becoming a nun, but rather that she was ashamed of the simplicity of her Madonna. In the manner of such things, a dream commanded her to retrieve the statue, which subsequently demonstrated miraculous powers. Part-morality play, part-miracle, the story fulfilled all the necessary criteria to turn the figure into a revered object, and the town into a major centre of medieval pilgrimage.

Piet Mondrian (1872–1944), the leading light of De Stijl and internationally famous for his geometric paintings, was born in Amersfoort. The house where he was born, along with the adjacent school where his father was the headteacher, are now the **Mondriaanhuis**, located by the canal a short walk southeast of the Onze Lieve Vrouwekerk, at Kortegracht 11 (Tues–Fri 10am–5pm, Sat & Sun 1–5pm; €3; ⓦwww.mondriaanhuis.nl). The house features a retrospective of the artist's life and work – an enjoyable collection.

## Practicalities

Amersfoort **train station** is 400m from the **VVV** at Stationsplein 9 (May–Sept Mon–Fri 9am–5.30pm, Sat 10am–4pm; Oct–April Mon–Fri 9am–5.30pm, Sat 9am–2pm; ℡0900/112 2364, ⓦwww.vvvamersfoort.nl) – turn left out of the station building. From the station, it's a good ten minutes' walk east to the town centre. In the unlikely event you decide to stay, the VVV has a good supply of **private rooms** (❶) and will call ahead to make a booking, though most are way out of the town centre. Amersfoort has several reasonably priced **hotels**, the most recommendable being the family-run *De Tabaksplant* at Coninckstraat 15 (℡033/472 9797, ℻033/470 0756; ❷). To get there, go out of the town centre through the Kamperbinnenpoort and take the first major turn on the left.

For **food**, there are a number of snack bars along the main shopping street, Langestraat, and outdoor cafés around Hof and Groenmarkt, including *Onder de Linde* at Groenmarkt 15. Two other good spots for light meals are *Café de Blauwe Engel*, on the Hof, and the bagel specialists *Willy's Bagel Store*, just west of the Hof at Krommestraat 10. In the evening, *De Kluif*, at Groenmarkt 3 (℡033/463 3729; closed Mon) is one of the most popular spots in town for tasty Dutch food.

There are some first-rate **bars** in town, among them the buzzing *'t Nonnetje* on Groenmarkt 3, the ancient *In den Grooten Slock* on the corner of Hof and Langestraat at Zevenhuisen, and the atmospheric *Mariposa*, off Langestraat at Valkestraat 10. The last has the best beer selection in town. Finally, *Trenchtown* at Krommestraat 41 is an agreeable and handy **cannabis coffeeshop**.

## Doorn

Just beyond the A12/E35 motorway some 12km south of Amersfoort, from where it's reachable by bus, **DOORN** holds one of the more awkward skeletons in the Netherlands' historical cupboard. The **Kasteel Huis Doorn** (mid-March to Oct Tues–Sat 10am–5pm, Sun 1–5pm; Nov to mid-March Sun 1–5pm; guided tours only; €4; last entry 1hr before closing; ⓦwww .huisdoorn.nl), a medieval castle converted into a classical manor house in 1792, was home to Kaiser Wilhelm II from 1920 to 1941, following his flight from Germany at the end of World War I. At a time when the British government was mounting a "Hang the Kaiser" campaign, the Dutch, who had been neutral during the war, allowed Wilhelm to live in their country; although he was supposedly under house arrest, you won't feel much sympathy when you see the manor's comfortable rooms and extensive grounds. The guided tour takes in the usual trappings of a stately home – elegantly decorated rooms, furnished here in the style of the 1920s – and, among Wilhelm's personal souvenirs, an extraordinary collection of snuffboxes from the era of Frederick the Great. There's a bust of the Kaiser in the gardens and House of Hohenzollern tea-cloths in the souvenir shop.

There is no real reason to hang around Doorn after visiting the castle, but the **VVV**, nearby at Dorpsstraat 4 (April–Sept Mon–Fri 9.30am–5pm, Sat 9am–2pm; Oct–March Mon–Fri 9.30am–12.30pm & 1.30–5pm; ☏0343/412 015), has a small supply of **private rooms** (❶–❷).

## Amerongen

Some 8km east of Doorn, the most interesting feature of **AMERONGEN** is its **castle** (April–Oct Tues–Fri 10am–5pm, Sat & Sun 1–5pm; €2.50), built in the thirteenth century, but largely remodelled in the 1680s by one Godard van Reede. Like many Dutch aristocrats, the Van Reedes did well when William of Orange became king of England in 1688 – in this case, one of the family became Earl of Athlone after he helped defeat the Irish at the Battle of the Boyne in 1690. The Amerongen castle stayed in the family's hands until 1879, when it was inherited by the German Count van Aldenburg – first host to Kaiser Wilhelm after he left Germany in November 1918 – and is now owned by the state. It's rather a stuffy place, awash with tedious family portraits, but the splendid painted ceilings in the state room and the hall do partly redeem matters. They include a cheerful white elephant, recalling Godard's membership of the Danish Order of the Elephant, a sort of ambassadorial club. The castle also displays a number of fine Flemish tapestries and a giant eighteenth-century backgammon set in the master bedroom – the latter contrasting nicely with the room's tiny furniture. The VVV office (☏0343/452 020) adjoins the entrance to the castle at Drostestraat 20.

## Rhenen

Strategically positioned on the north bank of the Rhine 11km east of Amerongen, the pint-sized town of **RHENEN** has ancient origins – as evidenced by the prehistoric pottery and burial urns displayed at the enjoyable

**Gemeentemuseum Het Rondeel**, Kerkstraat 1 (Tues–Fri noon–5pm, Sat 1–5pm; July & Aug also Sun 1–5pm; €1.50). The museum also holds Merovingian weapons and jewellery plus a collection of gargoyles and assorted statuary from the town's **Sint Cunerakerk** (July to mid-Sept Mon–Sat 2–3.30pm; free), a late Gothic church with an imposing 84-metre tower. According to legend, St Cunera was a fifth-century English princess, who was kidnapped when she was on a pilgrimage to Rome. Radboud, king of Rhenen, promptly rode out and rescued her and afterwards Cunera stayed around, becoming hugely popular on account of her work with the poor and the sick – though Radboud's wife was distinctly unimpressed. Green with envy, the queen had Cunera murdered, but that was just the beginning of her problems. Cunera's ghost appeared again and again, churning out the odd medical miracle and attracting so many pilgrims that Rhenen was able to build the Cunerakerk in honour of the saint.

# Travel details

## Trains

**Amersfoort** to: Amsterdam CS (every 15min; 35min); Utrecht (every 15min; 20min); Zwolle (every 30min; 35min).
**Den Haag** to: Amersfoort (every 20min; 1hr); Delft (every 15min; 12min); Dordrecht (every 30min; 40min); Gouda (every 20min; 20min); Rotterdam (every 15min; 25min); Utrecht (every 20min; 40min).
**Leiden** to: Amsterdam CS (every 30min; 35min); Den Haag CS (every 30min; 35min).
**Rotterdam** to: Dordrecht (every 10min; 20min); Gouda (every 20min; 20min); Utrecht (every 20min; 45min).

**Utrecht** to: Amersfoort (every 15min; 20min); Arnhem (every 15min; 30min); Leeuwarden (hourly; 2hr); Zwolle (every 30min; 1hr).

## Buses

**Amersfoort** to: Doorn (hourly; 30min).
**Gouda** to: Oudewater (hourly; 20min).
**Den Haag** to: Katwijk (every 30min; 25min).
**Leiden** to: Katwijk (every 10min; 25min); Noordwijk (every 30min; 40min).
**Utrecht** to: Doorn (hourly; 25min).

# The north and the Frisian Islands

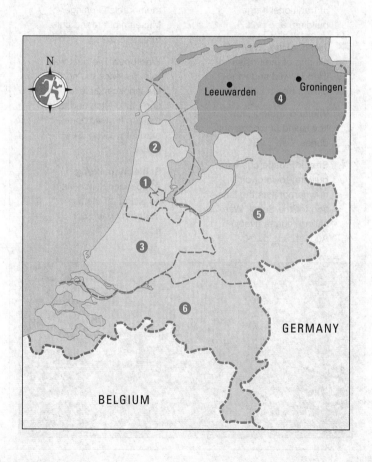

# CHAPTER 4

# Highlights

✳ **Fries Museum, Leeuwarden** A fine insight into the culture of Friesland, in the heart of this easygoing market town. See p.224

✳ **Harlingen** Far-flung harbour, with a long history of traditional barge-building. See p.227

✳ **Terschelling** The most alluring of the Frisian islands, wild and wind-blown. See p.229

✳ **Vlieland** Tranquil, low-key island of woods and dunes. See p.232

✳ **Sneek** Prosperous ship-building town of old, now famous as the location for the Sneek Week sailing regatta every August. See p.233

✳ **Ameland** Popular holiday island, with long, sandy beaches and big skies. See p.241

✳ **Groningen** Dynamic university town in the far north, with a cosmopolitan outlook and the memorable Groninger Museum of art and culture. See p.242

✳ **Wadlopen** The best way to experience the northern landscapes is to copy the Dutch and take a guide for *wadlopen* – mudflat walking. See p.251

✳ **Schiermonnikoog** Atmospheric, little-visited island off the far northern coast. See p.251

# 4

# The north and the Frisian Islands

U
p until the early twentieth century, the north of the Netherlands was a relatively remote area, a distinct region of small provincial towns far removed from the mainstream life of the Randstad. The year 1932 saw the opening of the **Afsluitdijk**, a 30km-long sea wall bridging the mouth of the Zuider Zee, once the corridor for the great trading ships of the Golden Age. Since the completion of the dyke, the cultural gap between the north and west of the Netherlands has narrowed, and now fashion and custom seem all but identical. The main exception is linguistic: Friesland has its own language, more akin to Low German than Dutch, and its citizens are keen to use it.

One of the three northern provinces, **Friesland**, is a deservedly popular tourist stopover. Attracting an increasing number of visitors, it offers the cluster of duneswept **Frisian Islands** and a chain of eleven immaculate, history-steeped "cities", such as **Hindeloopen** and **Sloten**, each with a distinct charm and trade. Church towers, cobbled streets, narrow canals, wooden barges and bright window-boxes are typical details that add colour to these smartly kept settlements. Like much of the Netherlands, the scenery is predominantly green, bisected by a network of canals and dotted with black and white cattle – Friesians, of course. Breaking the dead flat monotony of the landscape, sleek wind turbines, or American windmills as they're called, make the most of the strong westerlies, a modern counterpart to the last working windmills in the area.

East of Friesland, the province of **Groningen** has comparatively few attractions. But whilst its villages are less charismatic and more suburban, the university town of Groningen more than makes up for them with its vibrant ambience, hip fashions, an array of affordable bars and restaurants, a growing international performance art festival and the best nightlife in the region. Also home to the Groninger Museum, a striking and controversial vision of urban architecture and art, it makes a definite highlight to the region.

South of Groningen lies **Drenthe**, little more than a barren moor for much of its history. During the nineteenth century, the face of much of the province was changed by the founding of innumerable peat colonies, whose labourers drained the land and dug the peat to expose the subsoil below. As a result of

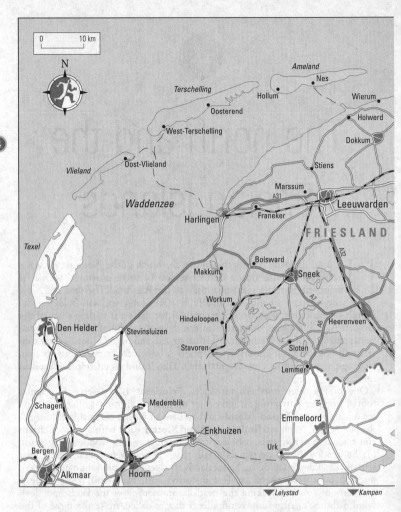

their work, parts of Drenthe are given over to prosperous farmland, with agriculture the dominant local industry. Sparsely populated and the least visited of the Dutch provinces, today Drenthe is popular with homegrown tourists, who are drawn by its quiet natural beauty, swathes of woods, wide cycling paths and abundant walking trails. The two main towns have only a couple of attractions that might bring you this far off the beaten track: the capital **Assen** has the Drents Museum, with a superb collection of prehistoric finds, while **Emmen** is the best place to see Drenthe's most original feature – its *hunebeds*, or megalithic tombs.

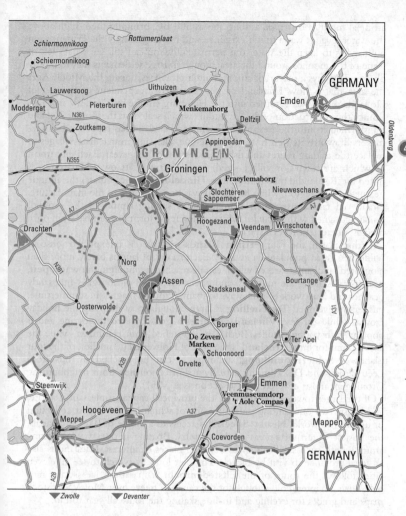

# Friesland

A region that prospered during the sixteenth-century heyday of the Zuider Zee trade, **Friesland** is focused around eleven historic cities and seven lakes, the latter symbolized by the seven red hearts on the region's flag, which proudly flutters in many a back garden.

Friesland once occupied the whole of the north. In the eighth century, Charlemagne recognized three parts: West Frisia, equivalent to today's West Friesland, across the IJsselmeer; Central Frisia, today's Friesland; and East Frisia, now Groningen province. At the time, much of the region was prey to inundation by the sea. Houses and sometimes entire settlements would be built on artificial mounds or *terpen*, as long ago as 500 BC, bringing them high above the water level. It was a tough existence, and not surprisingly the Frisians soon built dykes to keep the water out permanently. You can still see what's left of some of the mounds around the area, though in large settlements they're mostly obscured. Always a maverick among Dutch provinces, during the Middle Ages the area that is now Friesland proper remained independent of the rest of Holland, until it was absorbed into the Habsburg empire by Charles V in 1523.

Since the construction of the Afsluitdijk, which sealed off the Zuider Zee and transformed it into the freshwater IJsselmeer, Friesland has relied on holiday-makers drawn to its rich history, picturesque lakes and immaculate villages to replace the trading routes and fishing industries of yesteryear. Each city (most of which are town- or village-sized) has a charm of its own: **Harlingen** is noted for its splendid merchant houses, **Hindeloopen** encapsulates the antique neatness of the region, while **Makkum** was once a centre of tile manufacture. Grand old farmhouses, their thatched roofs sloping almost to the ground, remain crowned with *uleburden*, white gables in the form of a double swan once used as a deterrent to evil spirits.

Further north, the four **Frisian Islands** preserve an unexpected sense of wilderness in so populated a country. Each strand of land is barely more than elongated sandbank (parts of which can be reached by indulging in **wadlopen**, hearty walks along the mudflats) and offers kilometres of hourglass-fine sandy beaches and a network of cycleways to roam. A tourist magnet in summertime, busy and developed **Terschelling** is large enough to swallow up the holiday crowds while car-free **Vlieland** resembles a grass-covered dunescape and is popular with young families. Both can be reached from Harlingen, while the access point for busy **Ameland** is the port of Holwerd. The smallest of the four islands is **Schiermonnikoog**; although it can be reached by bus from Leeuwarden and Dokkum, it's actually a shorter journey from neighbouring Groningen, and is covered in that section (see p.251).

Of the larger towns, **Leeuwarden**, the provincial capital, is pleasant if sedate, and boasts two outstanding museums, one of which has the largest collection of tiles in the world. Nearby **Sneek** has access to a tangle of lakes and canals, the busiest watersports areas in the country. Boating is one way of getting around; with such small distances between places of interest, Friesland is also an ideal province to visit by bicycle. The best loop by which to see all eleven cities follows the route of the **Elfstedentocht**, a marathon ice-skating race held during winters cold enough for the canals to freeze over. Most VVVs stock maps and guides for cycling and in-line skating the route all year round.

# Leeuwarden

An old market town at the heart of an agricultural district, **LEEUWARDEN** was formed from the amalgamation of three *terpen* that originally stood on an expanse of water known as the Middelzee. Later it was the residence of the powerful Frisian Stadholders, who vied with those of Holland for control of the United Provinces. These days it's Friesland's capital, a university town with a provincial air, its centre a discordant blend of modern glass architecture and traditional design. While it lacks the concentrated historic charm of many other Dutch towns, it does have a number of grand buildings and two outstanding museums. Most appealing is a compact town centre, almost entirely surrounded and dissected by water, along which big barges nudge their way through.

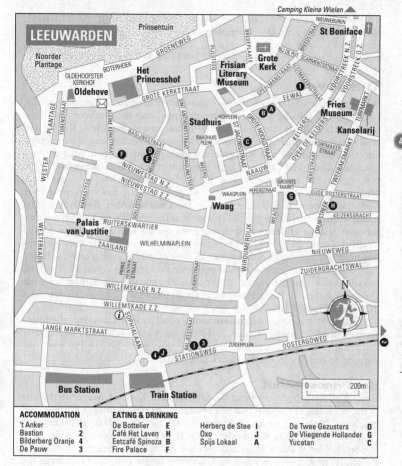

| ACCOMMODATION | | EATING & DRINKING | | | | | |
|---|---|---|---|---|---|---|---|
| 't Anker | 1 | De Bottelier | E | Herberg de Stee | I | De Twee Gezusters | D |
| Bastion | 2 | Café Het Leven | H | Oxo | J | De Vliegende Hollander | G |
| Bilderberg Oranje | 4 | Eetcafé Spinoza | B | Spijs Lokaal | A | Yucatan | C |
| De Pauw | 3 | Fire Palace | F | | | | |

## Arrival, information and accommodation

Leeuwarden's **train** and **bus stations** virtually adjoin each other, five minutes' walk south of the town centre; behind them is **car parking** at €2.50 a day. The **VVV** is on the ground floor of the Achema Tower, the grey skyscraper 200m north of the train station at Sophialaan 4 (Mon–Fri 9am–5.30pm, Sat 10am–2pm; June–Aug Sat until 4pm; ☎0900/202 4060). They publish a map detailing walking tours of the centre (€1.15, ask for accompanying English leaflet) and have a short list of private **rooms** that covers the whole of Friesland, as well as information on guided boat trips to the Frisian lakes.

There are only two reasonably priced **hotels** in town: the slightly musty *De Pauw*, Stationsweg 10 (☎058/212 3651, ℻216 0793; ❶), is convenient and comfortable enough; the *Hotel 't Anker*, Eewal 69–75 (☎058/212 5216, ℻212 8293; ❶), is a popular and more central alternative, though it does sometimes get full: book in advance if you can. The *Bastion* is a reliable fallback, though it's a good walk east of town at Legedijk 6 (☎058/289 0112, ℻289 0512; ❷).

The plushest option is *Bilderberg Oranje*, Stationsweg 4 (☎058/212 6241, ⓦwww.bilderberg.nl; ④). **Camping** *Kleine Wielen*, De Groene Ster 14 (☎0511/431 660; closed Oct–March) is about 6km out towards Dokkum, nicely sited by a lake; take bus #10, #13, #51 or #62 from the station.

## The Town

If you've just arrived from Friesland's immaculate coast and countryside towns, Leeuwarden is initially a bit of a disappointment, with the southern part of the town centre near the station an indeterminate, careless mixture of the old and new. Heading north, high-rise blocks and shopping centres line Wirdumerdijk into the centre of town at **Waagplein**, a long, narrowing open space cut by a canal and flanked by cafés and large department stores. The **Waag** itself, now converted into a restaurant and bank, dates from 1598. Walking west, **Nieuwestad** is Leeuwarden's main shopping street, from where Kleine Kerkstraat, a turn on the right, leads to the **Oldehoofster Kerkhof**, a large square-cum-car park near the old city walls, at the end of which stands the precariously leaning **Oldehove**. Something of a symbol for the city, this is part of a cathedral started in 1529 but never finished because of subsidence, a lugubrious mass of disproportion that defies all laws of gravity and geometry. To the right stands a statue of the Frisian politician and trade unionist P.J. Troelstra, who looks on impassively, no doubt admonishing the city fathers for their choice of architects. For a better view, climb the 40m-high tower (May–Sept Tues–Sat 2–5pm; €1.20).

A little further east is the **Prinsentium**, a small park that was once the pleasure garden of the ruling Nassaus. It is still a quiet place to wander by the river and admire, on the other side, the rather thoughtful bronze Friesian cow, donated to the city by the Friesian Cattle Syndicate.

### Het Princessehof

Grote Kerkstraat leads east from the Oldehoofster Kerkhof, following the line of the track that connected two of Leeuwarden's original *terpen*, Oldehove and Nijehove. Near the square, at Grote Kerkstraat 11, is **Het Princessehof** (Tues–Sun 11am–5pm; €5), a house from 1650 that was once the residence of the Stadholder William Friso and also the birthplace of graphic artist M.C. Escher. It's now a ceramics museum, with the largest collection of tiles in the world, though the layout is a little confusing and there are no English-language guidebooks available.

Of the many displays, two are outstanding. The first, through the ornamental arch at the reception desk and up the stairs to the third floor, is the collection of **Chinese**, **Japanese** and **Vietnamese ceramics**, which outlines the rise and fall of Far Eastern china production. In the sixteenth century Portuguese traders first began to bring back Chinese porcelain for sale in Europe. It proved tremendously popular, and by the seventeenth century the Dutch, among others, had begun to muscle in. Ships crammed with plates and dishes shuttled back and forth to the coast of China, where European merchants bargained with local warlords for *hongs*, or trade and territorial concessions (hence "Hong Kong"). The benefits of the trade were inevitably weighted in favour of Western interests, and the Chinese could only watch with dismay as the bottom fell out of the market when European factories began to reproduce their goods. The Dutch soon modified the original, highly stylized designs to more naturalistic patterns with a lighter, plainer effect, with the result that Chinese producers were forced to make desperate attempts to change their designs to fit Western tastes.

The earliest pieces on display in this section date from the sixteenth century, notably several large blue and white plates of naive delicacy, decorated with swirling borders and surrealistic dragons. Although Chinese producers began to work to European designs in the early eighteenth century, it was many years before the general deterioration in manufacture became apparent. Some of the most exquisite examples of Chinaware date from as late as the middle of the eighteenth century – not least those from the Dutch merchantman *Geldermalsen*, which sank in the waters of the South China Sea in 1752 and was salvaged in 1983. Some 150,000 items of cargo were retrieved, and there's a small sample here, including a magnificent dish of bright-blue entwined fish bordered by a design of flowers and stems – in stark contrast to the crude, sad-looking Chinese imitations of Western landscapes and coats of arms across the room.

On the second floor, to the left of the stairs, you'll find another room devoted to the development of **Chinese porcelain** from prehistory onward, with representative examples illustrating major trends. The finest work dates from the Ming Dynasty (1368–1644), with powerful open-mouthed dragons, billowing clouds, and sharply drawn plant tendrils. This room leads to the other section you shouldn't miss, a magnificent array of **Dutch tiles**, with good examples of all the classic designs – soldiers, flowers, ships, and so forth – framed by uncomplicated borders. Well documented and clearly laid out, the earliest tiles date from the late fifteenth century, the work of Italians based in Antwerp who used a colourful and expensive tin-glazing process. By the seventeenth century, tiles were no longer exclusive to the wealthy, and the demands of a mass market transformed the industry. Popular as a wall covering – the precursor of wallpaper – thousands of identical tiles were churned out by dozens of Dutch factories; there were seven in Friesland alone. The emphasis was on very simple designs, characteristically blue-on-white, the top end of the market distinguished by extra colours or the size of the design: the more tiles it took to make the "picture", the more expensive the tile.

The collection of **European ceramics and porcelain** slots awkwardly around the other exhibits; best are the Art Deco and Art Nouveau pieces on the second floor and the modern work in the basement. More interesting, if you're not too exhausted, is the small collection of **Middle Eastern tiles** in the basement, including thirteenth-century pieces from Persia and a few flamboyant sixteenth-century Iznik tiles.

## Along Grote Kerkstraat

East of the museum along Grote Kerkstraat, the **Frysk Letterkundich Museum** (Frisian Literary Museum; Mon–Fri 9am–12.30pm & 1.30–5pm; €0.90) is housed at no. 212 in the building where Mata Hari, something of a local heroine, spent her early years. Her old home has become a repository for a whole range of Frisian documents and a handful of pamphlets in English on the Frisian language. A permanent display details P.J. Troelstra, the Frisian socialist politician and poet, who set up the Dutch Social Democratic party in 1890 and headed the Dutch labour movement until 1924.

At the far end of Grote Kerkstraat, the **Grote** or **Jacobijner Kerk** (June–Sept Tues–Fri 2–4pm), though restored in recent years, remains an unremarkable Gothic construction. Another victim of subsidence, the whole place tilts slightly toward the newer south aisle, where you can see some fragmentary remnants of sixteenth-century frescoes. In front of the church a modernistic monument remembers Leeuwarden's wartime Jewish community, based on the classroom registers of 1942; it's an imaginative and harsh reminder of suffering and persecution. Three minutes' walk west of the church, the **Fries Natuurmuseum**, Schoenmakersperk 2 (Tues–Sat 10am–5pm & Sun 1–5pm; €2.70; Ⓦwww.friesnatuurmuseum.nl) has exhibitions on local flora and fauna.

## The Fries Museum

South of here, on Turfmarkt, the **Fries Museum** (Tues–Sun 11am–5pm; €5; Ⓦwww.friesmuseum.nl) is one of the Netherlands' best regional museums. Founded by a society that was established in the nineteenth century to develop interest in the language and history of Friesland, the museum traces the development of Frisian culture from prehistoric times up until the present day. It also incorporates the Frisian Resistance Museum, with its story of the local resistance to Nazi occupation, and an exhibition on the infamous Mata Hari.

The museum's extensive collection of **silver** is concentrated on the ground floor of the main building. Silversmithing was a flourishing Frisian industry throughout the seventeenth and eighteenth centuries, most of the work commissioned by the local gentry, who were influenced by the fashions of the Frisian Stadholder and his court. The earliest piece is an elegant drinking horn of 1397, and there are some particularly fine examples of chased silver in Baroque style, where each representation is framed by a fanciful border or transition. This distinctive "Kwabornament" design flourished in Friesland long after it had declined in the rest of the Netherlands. Some of the more curious exhibits date from the mid-seventeenth century when it was fashionable to frame exotic objects in silver: a certain Lenert Danckert turned a coconut into a cup, while Minne Sikkes fitted silver handles to a porcelain bowl to create a brandy cup. Most of the later exhibits are ornate, French-style tableware.

Upstairs, on the first floor, there's a selection of early **majolica**, many examples of different sorts of **porcelain** and a collection of seventeenth-century Frisian **painting**. Rather more interesting are the rooms devoted to the island of Ameland and the painted **furniture** of Hindeloopen: rich, gaudy and intense, patterned with tendrils and flowers on a red, green or white background. Most peculiar of all are examples of the bizarre headgear of eighteenth-century Hindeloopen women: large cartwheel-shaped hats known as *Deutsche muts* and the less specifically Frisian *oorijzers*, gold or silver helmets that were an elaborate development of the hat-clip or brooch. As well as an indication of social standing, a young girl's first *oorijzer* symbolized the transition to womanhood.

The top floor of the main building has a chronological exhibition tracing the early days of the **Nazi invasion**, through collaboration and resistance on to the Allied liberation. A variety of photographs, Nazi militaria, Allied propaganda and tragic personal stories illustrate the text, but the emphasis is very much on the local struggle rather than the general war effort.

Back by the ticket desk downstairs, a passage leads through to the museum's second building where you'll find the exhibition on **Mata Hari**. A native of Leeuwarden, Mata Hari's name has become synonymous with the image of the *femme fatale*. A renowned dancer, she was arrested in 1917 by the French on charges of espionage and subsequently shot, though what she actually did remains a matter of some debate. In retrospect it seems likely that she acted as a double agent, gathering information for the Allies while giving snippets to the Germans. Photographs, letters and other mementoes illustrate the rather pathetic story.

## The Kanselarij and around

Near the Fries Museum stands one of the most striking buildings in Leeuwarden – the **Kanselarij**, a superb gabled Renaissance structure of 1571, which hosts art exhibitions in the summer. The original plan placed the gable and the corresponding double stairway in the centre of the facade, but they are in fact slightly off-centre to the right because the money ran out before the work was finished. Just south of the Fries Museum, at Turfmarkt 48, the wonderful 1930s **Utrecht Building** today contains a restoration workshop. A little way north of Turfmarkt is the Catholic church of **St Boniface**, a belated apology to an English missionary killed at nearby Dokkum, along with 52 other Christians, by the pagan Frisians in 754. It's a neo-Gothic building of 1894 designed by P.J.H. Cuypers, its ornamented spire imposing itself on what is otherwise a rather flat skyline. The spire was almost totally destroyed in a storm of 1976 and many people wanted to take the opportunity to pull the place down altogether – even to replace it with a supermarket. Fortunately the steeple was replaced at great expense and with such enormous ingenuity that its future seems secure, making it one of the few Cuypers churches left in the Netherlands.

## Eating and drinking

One of the most popular places to **eat** in Leeuwarden is *Eetcafé Spinoza* at Eewal 50–52, a youthful, reasonably priced restaurant with a range of vegetarian dishes. Next door is the intimate and friendly *Spijs Lokaal*, with mains for €15. The slightly seedy Groente Markt nearby (and Uniabuurt which runs off it) offer a few restaurants including *De Vliegende Hollander*, with chunky wooden tables and *dagschotels* for around €7.50. There's Mexican food at the *Yucatan* on St Jacobsstraat and, further east, at the rather smart *Café Het Leven*, Druifstreek 57a. The *Oranje* hotel, Stationsweg 4, has two excellent restaurants; expect to pay around €30 for three courses at the bistro and the same for one course at the main restaurant. Next door, and much cheaper, *Oxo* has *dagschotels* for around €13.50, as well as a couple of **Internet** terminals.

For **drinking** in a quiet atmosphere, settle down amidst the delightful old furniture at the bar of the *Hotel De Pauw*, Stationsweg 10; boisterous types prefer the *Herberg De Stee*, next door. In the centre of town, the *Fire Palace*, Nieuwestad N.Z. 49, overlooking the canal, is a big bar that doubles as the town's main disco at weekends. There's a series of lively bars on Doelesteeg, most with loud music; quieter drinking spots across the bridge on Nieuwesteeg include *De Bottelier* and *De Twee Gezusters*. There are **cinemas** on Nieuwestad.

## Listings

**Bike rental** From the *Fietspoint* next to the train station (€5.20/day).
**Books** Van der Velde, Nieuwstad 90, has a good stock of English-language titles.
**Car rental** AutoRent, Valeriusstraat 2 ☎058/299 8882, ⊛www.autorent-europaservice.nl.
**Internet access** At the VVV and the Bibliotheek, Wirdumerdijk 34 ☎058/234 7777.
**Left luggage** Lockers at the station (daily 6am–10pm; €2/day).

**Market** General market on Fridays at Wilhelminaplein.
**Pharmacy** Details of nearest (emergency) pharmacy on ☎058/213 5295.
**Police** Holstmeerweg 1 ☎058/213 2423.
**Post office** Oldehoofster Kerkhof 4 (Mon–Fri 7.30am–6pm, Thurs until 8pm, Sat 7.30am–1.30pm).
**Taxi** Leeuwarder Taxicentrale ☎058/212 2222.

## Popta Slot

On the western outskirts of Leeuwarden, the tiny village of **MARSSUM** incorporates **Popta Slot** (guided tours only: July & Aug Mon–Sat hourly 11am–5pm; June Mon–Fri 11am, 2pm & 3pm; April, May, Sept & Oct

Mon–Fri 2.30pm; €3.50), a trim, onion-domed eighteenth-century manor house that sits prettily behind its ancient moat; inside, the period rooms are furnished in the style of the local gentry. Dr Popta was an affluent lawyer and farmer who spent some of his excess wealth on the neighbouring **Popta Gasthuis**, neat almshouses cloistered behind an elaborate portal of 1712. Buses #71 and #91 head to Marssum from Leeuwarden bus station.

# West of Leeuwarden

West of Leeuwarden, the train line heads straight for **Harlingen**, though if you're travelling by road the small town of **Franeker**, with its fascinating eighteenth-century planetarium, makes a worthwhile detour. Seventeenth-century Harlingen was very much a naval centre and it remains an important port today, primarily to ferry tourists from the mainland to the Frisian islands of **Terschelling** and **Vlieland**. With a resurgence in the last few decades in its tradition of ceramic manufacture, and a strong maritime heritage, Harlingen makes a pleasant stopover for the night en route to the islands.

## Franeker

About 17km west of Leeuwarden, **FRANEKER** was the cultural hub of the northern Netherlands until Napoleon closed the university in 1810. Nowadays it's a quiet country town with a spruce old centre, the highlight of which is its intriguing Planetarium. The **train station** is five minutes' walk southeast of the centre; follow Stationsweg round to the left and over the bridge, first left over the second bridge onto Zuiderkade and second right along Dijkstraat. Buses from Leeuwarden drop off passengers on Kleijenburg, at the northwest corner of the old town centre.

All the key sights are beside or near the main street, **Voorstraat**, a continuation of Dijkstraat, which runs east–west to end in a park, **Sternse Slotland** – the site of the medieval castle. Near the park at Voorstraat 51, the VVV is housed in the **Waag** of 1657, which also serves as the entrance to the nextdoor **Museum 't Coopmanshus** (Tues–Sat 10am–5pm; May–Sept also Sun 1–5pm; €2), whose ground floor has bits and pieces relating to the university and its obscure alumni. In the old senate room, there is a pile of slim boxes carved to resemble books that contain dried samples of local flora and fauna, the gift of Louis Bonaparte.

Heading east along Voorstraat, past the stolid **Martenahuis** of 1498, the Raadhuisplein branches off to the left; opposite, above the Friesland Bank, is the **Kaatsmuseum** (May–Sept Tues–Sat 1–5pm; €2), devoted to the Frisian sport of *Kaatsen* ("Dutch tennis"). The nearby **Stadhuis** (Mon–Fri 1.30–5pm; free), with its twin gables and octagonal tower, is rather more interesting. It's a magnificent mixture of Gothic and Renaissance styles built in 1591 and worth a peek upstairs for the leather-clad walls – all the rage until French notions of wallpaper took hold in the eighteenth century.

Opposite the Stadhuis, at Eise Eisingastraat 3, there's the fascinating eighteenth-century **Planetarium** (Tues–Sat 10am–5pm; mid-April to mid-Sept also Sun & Mon 1–5pm; €3) built by a local woolcomber, Eise Eisinga, and now the oldest working planetarium in the world. Born in 1744, Eisinga was something of a prodigy: he taught himself mathematics and astronomy, and published a weighty arithmetic book when aged only seventeen. In 1774, the unusual conjunction of Mercury, Venus, Mars and Jupiter under the sign of Aries prompted a local paper to predict the end of the world. There was panic in the countryside, and an appalled Eisinga embarked upon the construction of his planetarium, in order to dispel superstition by demystifying the workings of the cosmos. It took him seven years, almost as long as he had to enjoy it before his disdain for the autocratic Frisian Stadholder caused his imprisonment and exile. His return signalled a change of fortunes. In 1816 he was presented with the order of the Lion of the Netherlands, and, two years later, a royal visit persuaded King Willem I to buy the planetarium for the state, granting Eisinga a free tenancy and a generous annual stipend until his death in 1828.

The planetarium isn't of the familiar domed variety but was built as a false ceiling in the family's living room, a series of rotating dials and clocks indicating the movement of the planets and associated phenomena, from tides to star signs. The whole apparatus is regulated by a clock, driven by a series of weights hung in a tiny alcove beside a half-size cupboard-bed. Eisinga wasn't short, but he believed that sleeping sitting up improved blood circulation to the brain. Above the face of the main dials, the mechanisms – hundreds of hand-made nails driven into moving slats – are open for inspection. A detailed guidebook explains every aspect and every dial and there's an explanatory video in English, shown on request.

## Practicalities

Franeker's **VVV** is at Voorstraat 51 (Tues–Sat 10am–5pm; April–Sept also Sun 1–5pm; ☎0517/392 696 & ☎0900/540 0001, ⓦwww.friesekust.nl), five minutes' walk northwest of the train station. Of the town's **hotels**, your first choice should be the friendly *De Stadsherberg*, on the continuation of Stationsweg at Oude Kaatsveld 8 (☎0517/392 686, Ⓕ398 095; ❸); failing that, *Pension De Klokgevel*, opposite the modern church at Godsacker 20 (☎0517/392 246; ❷) or the more basic *De Bleek*, near the station at Stationsweg 1 (☎0517/392 124, Ⓕ392 124; ❶). The town **campsite**, *Bloemketerp* (☎0517/395 099, ⓦwww.bloemketerp.nl; April–Sept) is ten minutes' walk north of the station at Burg. J. Dijkstraweg 3: up Stationsweg, Oud Kaatsveld and Leeuwarderweg, then left. For **snacks**, try the croissanterie *La Terraz*, Zilverstraat 7, or coffee and cakes at *De Tuinkamer*, beside the Planetarium at Eise Eisingastraat 2 – the building dates back to 1745, and has fine wooden counters, a mosaic floor and original coffee cabinets from 1910, as well as a beautiful back garden. Of the **restaurants**, the upmarket, canalside *De Grillerije*, Groenmarkt 14, offers a set menu for €20.50, or you could try *De Doelen*, on the same square, which has main courses for around €15. *De Bogt Fen Gune*, Vijverstraat 1, is the oldest student **bar** in the country, worth dropping in for a drink.

# Harlingen

Just north of the Afsluitdijk, 30km west of Leeuwarden, **HARLINGEN** is a more compelling stop than Franeker. An ancient and historic port that serves as the ferry terminus for the islands of Terschelling and Vlieland, Harlingen is something of a centre for traditional Dutch **sailing barges**, a number of which are usually moored in the harbour. A naval base from the seventeenth century, the town straddles the Vliestroom channel, once the easiest way for shipping to pass from the North Sea through the shallows that surround the Frisian islands and on into the Zuider Zee. Before trade moved west, this was the country's lifeline, where cereals, fish and other foodstuffs were brought in from the Baltic to feed the expanding Dutch cities.

Harlingen has two **train stations**: one on the southern edge of town for trains from Leeuwarden, the other, Harlingen Haven, right next to the docks, handling trains connecting with boats to the islands. From Harlingen Haven the old town spreads east, sandwiched between the pretty Noorderhaven and more functional Zuiderhaven canals, a mass of sixteenth- to eighteenth-century houses that reflect the prosperity and importance of earlier times. However, Harlingen is too busy to be just another cosy tourist town: there's a fishing fleet, a small container depot, a shipbuilding yard and a resurgent ceramics industry. The heart of town is the **Voorstraat**, a long, tree-lined avenue that's home to an elegant eighteenth-century **Stadhuis**, the VVV and the **Hannemahuis Museum** at no. 56 (July to mid-Sept Tues–Sat 10am–5pm & Sun 1.30–5pm; April–June & mid-Sept to Oct Mon–Fri 1.30–5pm; €1.55). Sited in an eighteenth-century merchant's house, the museum concentrates on the history of the town and includes some interesting displays on shipping and some lovely locally produced tiles.

Harlingen's tile-making industry flourished until it was undermined by the rise of cheap wallpaper. The last of the old factories closed in 1933, but the demand for traditional crafts later led to something of a recovery, and the opening of new workshops during the 1970s. If you like the look of Dutch tiles, this is a good place to buy. The **Harlinger Aardewerk en Tegelfabriek**, Voorstraat 84, sells an outstanding range of contemporary and traditional styles – if you've got the money (Dutch handicrafts don't come cheap). On Thursdays Voorstraat fills with market stalls selling cheap clothing and general bric-a-brac, with food stalls at the fringes. The **Galerie de Vis**, Noordehaven 40 (Wed–Fri 1–5pm, Sat 11am–5pm) has occasional displays of local art and some international exhibitions.

## Practicalities

No great bargains on the accommodation front in Harlingen. The **VVV**, Voorstraat 34 (July & Aug Mon–Fri 9.30am–12.30pm & 1.30–5.30pm, Sat 9.30am–5pm; April–June & Sept Mon 1–5pm, Tues–Fri 10am–noon & 1–5pm, Sat 10am–4pm; Oct Tues–Fri 10am–noon & 1–5pm, Sat 9.30am–4pm; Nov–March Tues–Fri 1–4pm, Sat 10am–2pm; ☏0900/540 0001, ⓦwww.friesekust.nl) has a list of **rooms** and **pensions**, many of which you'll spot by walking down Noordehaven. Of the **hotels**, the *Heerenlogement* is on the eastern continuation of Voorstraat at Frankereind 23 (☏0517/415 846, ℻412 762; ❷–❸), while the slightly more expensive *Anna Casparii* (☏0517/412 065, ℻414 540; ❸) is more central, on the canal at Noordehaven 6. Third choice is the *Zeezicht*, by the harbour at Zuiderhaven 1 (☏0517/412 536, ℻419 001; ❸), which, despite its higher rates, isn't in such a nice location.

The nearest **campsite**, *De Zeehoeve* (☏0517/413 465, ℻416 971; April–Sept), is a twenty-minute walk along the sea dyke to the south of town at Westerzeedijk 45 – follow the signs from Voorstraat. If you've got your own transport, you're better off heading about 4km south to Kimswerd, to the delightful mini-camping *Popta Zathe* (☏0517/641 205; also a cheap B&B; €32), something of a metropolis close to the sea wall. There's a small plot of grass, a beautiful garden and bike rental; the sunsets are great and it's a lovely ride along the top of the dyke into town.

As you'd expect, Harlingen's speciality is fresh **fish**, and there are fish stands, fish restaurants and snack bars dotted around the centre of town. Best is *De Tjotter* on the edge of the Noorderhaven at St Jacobstraat 1, a combined snack bar and restaurant with a wide range of North Sea delicacies. Alternatives are

*De Gastronoom* next to the VVV, *Café 't Noorderke* at Noorderhaven 17–19, which has good-value daily specials, and the hotel restaurants. **Nightlife** is quiet but there are several decent **bars**, including *'t Skutsje* on the corner of Frankereind and Heiligeweg.

# The islands of Terschelling and Vlieland

A highlight of any visit to Friesland is a trip to **Terschelling** or **Vlieland**, two of the five inhabited islands strung out along the Netherlands' north coast that include neighbouring Texel in Noord-Holland (see p.156). With kilometres of empty beach and grass-covered dunes, these low-lying sandbanks are popular with Dutch tourists in the holiday season, and havens too for scores of plants and animals that thrive in their unique ecological habitat. Known for their unpredictable weather, the islands are frequently swept by storms throughout the year, though the summer months can boast high temperatures and clear blue skies.

Less than a two-hour ferry ride from Harlingen, both islands preserve a sense of isolated wilderness. Of the two, Terschelling is by far the more developed, and busier for it. Visitors' cars are not allowed on smaller and quieter Vlieland, but in any case the best way of exploring all the Frisian islands is by **bike**. There are rental companies near the ferry terminals on both islands, charging roughly €4.50 per day for a basic bike – although given the sometimes steep, stony hills, it's worth shelling out a bit more for a machine with decent gears.

## Terschelling

Of all the Frisian islands, **TERSCHELLING** is both the largest – some 30km long and 3.5km wide – and the easiest to reach. Despite its reputation as a teenage hangout in summer months, it does offer wilderness, peace and tranquillity: you just have to head away from main centres to find them. Quite simply, the further east you go the more attractive the island becomes; eighty percent of the island is a nature reserve area, dominated by beach, dunes, forest and polder. Although summer temperatures can soar, out of season Terschelling's wild weather seems to mirror its wild landscape, storms lending it a brooding air.

The ferry docks next to the colourful fishing harbour at **WEST-TERSCHELLING**, a tourist resort in its own right that's packed throughout the summer with tourists sampling the restaurants and bars that line the main

---

### Ferries to Terschelling and Vlieland

From Harlingen, **ferries** cross to Terschelling and Vlieland at least three times daily in summer and twice daily in winter (takes 1hr 45min). A return fare is €17.86 for either island (not including nominal taxes), plus €8.93 per bike (and per dog). Boats dock at West-Terschelling and Oost-Vlieland, the islands' main settlements. There's also a fast **hydrofoil** service from Harlingen (May–Sept 3 daily to Terschelling, twice daily to Vlieland; rest of year twice daily to Terschelling only). It costs an extra €7.26 return, but saves you an hour each way in travelling time, so worth it if you're planning a day trip.

From May to the end of September there's also a ferry running between Terschelling and Vlieland (€5.36 one-way, €5.50 for a bike).

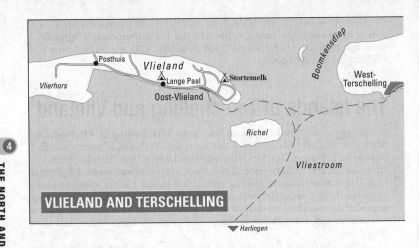

Posthuis · Vlierhors · Vlieland · Lange Paal · Oost-Vlieland · Stortemelk · Richel · Vliestroom · Boomkensdiep · West-Terschelling

**VLIELAND AND TERSCHELLING**

Harlingen

streets, Torenstraat in particular. West-Terschelling today is a rather unappealing sprawl of chalets, bungalows and holiday complexes that spread out from what remains of the old village, belying its past importance as a port and safe anchorage on the edge of the Vliestroom channel, the main shipping lane from the Zuider Zee. This strategically positioned town boomed throughout the seventeenth century as a centre for supply and repair of ships and with its own fishing and whaling fleets; it paid the price for its prominence when the British razed it in 1666. The islanders were renowned sailors, much sought after by ships' captains who also needed them to guide vessels through the treacherous shallows and shifting sandbanks that lay off the Vliestroom. Shipwrecks were common all along the island's northern and western shores (the VVV sells a sketch of the island marked with all the known disasters); the most famous victim was the *Lutine*, which sank while carrying gold and silver to British troops stationed here during the Napoleonic wars. The wreck lies still at the bottom of the sea, and only the ship's bell was recovered – now in Lloyd's of London, it's still rung whenever a big ship goes down.

The best place to investigate Terschelling's past is the excellent **Museum 't Behouden Huys**, near the ferry terminus at Commandeurstraat 30 (April–Oct Mon–Fri 10am–5pm; mid-June to Sept also Sat & Sun 1–5pm; €3). Prime exhibits here include maps of the old coastline illustrating Terschelling's crucial position, various items from the whaling fleet, lots of sepia photos of bearded islanders and a shipwreck diving room. There's also a rather half-hearted tribute to the local explorer Willem Barents, who hit disaster when pack ice trapped his ship in the Arctic in 1595. Undaunted, he and his crew managed to survive the whole winter on the ice, sailing back in the spring. Barents mounted other, more successful expeditions into the Arctic regions, discovering Spitzbergen and naming the Barents Sea, all in the fruitless search for the northwest passage to China. He died in the Arctic in 1597. If you're extra-keen on things aquatic, aim for the tiny **Museum "Aike van Stien"**, a fishing museum at the back of a shop on Raadhuisstraat (Mon–Sat 10am–12.30pm & 2–5pm; €2), as well as, just east of town, the **Centrum voor Natuur en Landschap**, Burg Reedekerstraat 11 (Nature and Landscape; April–Oct Mon–Fri 9am–5pm, Sat & Sun 2–5pm; at other times, check hours at VVV; €4), which contains a decent aquarium.

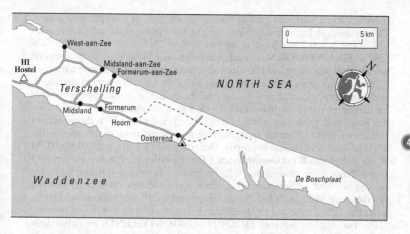

## West-Terschelling practicalities

The **VVV** (Mon–Sat 9.30am–5.30pm; ☎0562/443 000, ⓦwww.vvv
-terschelling.org), near the ferry port, provides a full list of pensions and
**rooms** and operates a booking service. They also take bookings for the rest of
the island, offer a variety of walking tours, sell a good **map** of the island
(€2.70) that includes towns, beaches and cycleways, and can give information
on cycling routes and seal-watching excursions.

You can **rent bikes** from Haant Jes, located 50m to the right of the ferry terminal, beyond the VVV – either single-speed (€4.50/day, €22/week) or
geared bikes (€6.50/day, €27/week); they have various drop-off points around
the island, and a handy cycling map. There are other bike-rental shops down
by the harbour and at the ferry terminal. The island's **bus** service leaves from
right next to the ferry terminus (every 1hr 10min), taking 35 minutes to travel
along the south coast to Oosterend.

**Accommodation** in West-Terschelling is hard to come by in July and
August when all the cheaper places tend to be booked up months in advance.
At other times you have a wide choice – try the *Hotel Buren*, Burg Mentzstraat
20 (☎0562/442 226, ⓕ444 020; ❷) or the similarly priced *Pension Altijd Wad*,
Trompstraat 6 (☎0562/442 050; ❷), both not far from the ferry terminus.
There's a newly renovated HI **hostel** overlooking the harbour at Burgmeester
van Heusdenweg 39 (☎0562/442 338, ⓦwww.stayokay.com; April–Sept; ❶),
with dorm beds (€21) and ensuite doubles: it's a 1.5km walk eastwards along
the coast, or you can take any bus to the Dellewal stop. There are also a number of shoreside **campsites** east of town that are popular with the hordes of
partying teenagers who descend on the island in summer.

For a quick bite to **eat**, the fish-and-chips takeaway at Boomstraat 12 offers
the usual fishy suspects fresh from the North Sea, including fried *lekkerbek* for
€2.75. At *Strandpaviljoen De Walvis*, at Groene Strand on the western edge of
West Terschelling, you can buy snacks and drinks while taking in the sea view.

## Around the island

From West-Terschelling, plenty of visitors cycle off for the day to the beach 5km
away at **WEST-AAN-ZEE** where there's a café, *Zilver Meeuw*, and as much
empty beach as you're prepared to look for. There are two cycle routes to get

there, the more northerly passing through a cemetery in a wood, with a small Commonwealth forces graveyard; as ever, the inscriptions make sad reading, with few of the downed bombardiers aged more than 25. Further round is the *Palm Café* at **KAAP HOORN**, a beach reachable only by bicycle along a narrow forested trail, the variety of bikes locked around trees proof of its popularity.

Terschelling's other villages stretch out along the southern part of the island, sheltered from winter storms by the sand dunes and occasional patches of forest that lie to the immediate north. Cycle routes are almost always traffic-free. For peace and quiet, aim to stay in one of the pensions between the villages of Formerum and Oosterend, far enough east to escape most of the crowds; the VVV in West-Terschelling has details. Definitely worth a visit in **FORMERUM** is the delightful **Wrakkenmuseum "De Boerderij"**, Formerum Zuid 13 (April–Nov daily 10am–5pm; €2): its ground floor is an atmospheric bar decked out with all things nautical, while upstairs there's a collection of items salvaged from the island's beaches and shipwrecks, including cannons and coins, relics from the *Lutine*, and the Netherlands' largest collection of diving helmets.

The two final settlements, **HOORN** and **OOSTEREND**, are particularly pleasant, within easy reach of empty tracts of beach and the nature reserve **De Boschplaat**, where thousands of waterfowl congregate in the marshy shallows of the southeastern shore. Seeking peaceful nesting, they include gulls, oyster-catchers, green plovers and spoonbills. To help protect the birds, De Boschplaat is closed during the breeding season (mid-March to mid-Aug), although the VVV runs guided tours for bird enthusiasts. Around the island, wild American cranberries are harvested for wine, liqueur and juice, from September until the first frost. As well as a handful of **campsites**, Oosterend also has one of the best **places to eat** on the island, the café *De Boschplaat*. Signed 2km north is the *Heartbreak Hotel*, Strandpaviljoen Tordelenweg 2 (March–Nov daily 10am–2am; ☎0562/448 634), an American-style **diner**, wall-to-wall with 1950s memorabilia, in a superb location overlooking kilometres of white sand and sea; meal prices range are around €10–15, and there are live Fifties bands every night during July and August. Alternatively, it's a great spot to relax in the dunes with a bottle of wine and watch the sun slipping into the sea.

## Vlieland

Compared to its lively neighbour, **VLIELAND** is laid-back and low key. All but car free, it has just one settlement, **OOST-VLIELAND** – little more than a tree-lined street with a string of pavement cafés, bike-rental agencies and a few hotels and B&Bs. Historically isolated by a complex pattern of sandbanks, the island was of minor importance during the Zuider Zee trade; its only other village was swept away by the sea in the eighteenth century and never rebuilt. These days, there's not much to do but enjoy the country walks and relax along the 12km of sandy beach – a sedate lifestyle that is popular with Dutch families, who load up their bikes with panniers, tents, children and animals, and head for one of the island's two campsites.

Oost-Vlieland offers all the necessities, including a choice of eateries, bars and supermarkets. There's also a maritime centre geared towards children, the **Centrum "De Noordwester"**, Dorpsstraat 150 (July & Aug Mon–Sat 10am–5pm; hours vary out of season; €2.50), displaying an assortment of shells, an explanation of dune formation, a couple of aquariums with crabs and rays, and an unexpected elf forest (information is in Dutch only). The village's **Tromps Huys** museum, Dorpsstraat 99 (Mon–Sat 10am–noon & 2–5pm; €2), has a collection of antiques and Vlieland bygones.

Accommodation is limited, and virtually impossible to find throughout the summer unless you're camping. The **VVV**, Havenweg 10 (Mon 8.30am–5pm, Tues–Fri 9am–5pm, Sat 9.15–11.45am & 3.30–4.45pm, Sun 10.30–11.45am; also open for brief periods daily to coincide with ferry arrivals; ☎0562/451 111, ⓦwww.vlieland.net) does its best with the few private rooms, and will help groups rent apartments and "dune houses"; it also has information on birdwatching expeditions. Cheapest of the **hotels** and pensions is the *Duin en Dal*, Dorpsstraat 163 (☎0562/451 684; ❶); along the road is the more comfortable *Badhotel Bruin*, Dorpsstraat 88 (☎0562/451 301, ⓔbadhotelbruin@wxs.nl; ❸) and the smart *De Wadden*, Dorpsstraat 61 (☎0562/452 626, ⓦwww.hoteld ewadden.nl; ❹). The **campsite** *De Stortemelk*, Kampweg 1 (☎0562/451 225, ⒻƑ451 259), is on the dunes behind the beach, about half an hour's walk or a ten-minute bike ride northeast of the village. More peaceful is the Staatsbosbeheer site a few kilometres west at *Lange Paal* (☎0562/451 639); it's set in the forest clearing of a nature reserve, with carved log furniture and vine-like ropes for children to swing on. Facilities are simple but clean and there's a relaxed, friendly atmosphere. Bring some insect repellent though: the mosquitoes here are ruthless.

To explore the island's woods and dunes, follow one of the many **bike** routes that run the length of the island, criss-crossing a succession of wide sandy beaches on the northern shore. The VVV can provide you with details in English of two routes, and there are also plenty of marked **walking** trails. You can rent bikes, tandems and trailers – for kids as well as canines – all over town, including at Fietsenverhuur Frisia, Dorpsstraat 17 & 113. A limited **bus** service travels along the southern shore from near the ferry terminus. Private operators organize day-trips to the northern tip of the neighbouring island of Texel (see p.156) by means of a tractor-like lorry, which crosses the great expanse of sand (the "Vliehors") on Vlieland's western extremity to connect with a boat.

# South to Stavoren

Trains from Leeuwarden to **Stavoren** pass through a series of small Frisian towns with a speed that gainsays the earlier isolation of these places. Until well into the nineteenth century, the lakes, canals and peat diggings south and east of Sneek made land communications difficult, and the only significant settlements were built close to the sea or on major waterways. Dependent on waterborne commerce, these communities declined with the collapse of the Zuider Zee trade, but, because of their insularity, some maintained particular artistic and cultural traditions – from the painted furniture and distinctive dialect of **Hindeloopen** to the style and design of many of **Makkum**'s tiles. Passing through by train, the tiny old towns resemble what in fact they once were: islands in the shallow marshes. Nowadays all are popular holiday destinations; **Sneek**, the centre of a booming pleasure-boat industry, is by far the busiest.

## Sneek

Twenty minutes by train from Leeuwarden, **SNEEK** (pronounced *snayk*) was an important shipbuilding centre as early as the fifteenth century, a prosperous maritime town protected by an extensive system of walls and moats. Postwar development has robbed the place of some of its charm but there are still some buildings of interest. At the beginning of August, crowds flock in for **Sneek Week**, an annual regatta, when the flat green expanses around town are thick with the white of slowly moving sails.

Sneek's train and bus stations are five minutes' walk from the old centre. Stationsstraat leads to the main square, **Martiniplein**, whose ponderous sixteenth-century **Martinikerk** (mid-June to mid-Sept Mon–Sat 2.30–5pm; mid-July to mid-Aug also Tues–Fri 7.30–9pm; free) is edged by an old wooden belfry. Around the corner at the end of Grote Kerkstraat, the **Stadhuis**, Marktstraat 15 (mid-July to mid-Aug Mon–Fri 2–4pm), is all extravagance, from the Rococo facade to the fanciful outside staircase; inside there's an indifferent display of ancient weapons in the former guardroom. Heading east along Marktstraat, veer right after the VVV and follow the signs to the nearby **Scheepvaart Museum en Oudheidkamer**, Kleinzand 14 (Mon–Sat 10am–5pm, Sun noon–5pm; €2; www.friesscheepvaartmuseum.nl), a well-displayed collection of maritime models, paintings and related miscellany. There's also a room devoted to the Visser family, who made a fortune during the eighteenth century by transporting eels to London. A little further along, at Kleinzand 32, the Weduwe Joustra shop has an original nineteenth-century interior, worth a glance for its old barrels and till, even if you decide not to indulge in a bottle of *Beerenburg*, a herb-flavoured gin that is a local speciality (from €2.90). Turn right at the end of Koemarkt and you reach the grandiose **Waterpoort**, all that remains of the seventeenth-century town walls.

To see more of the lakes outside town, **boat trips** (July & Aug) leave from the Oosterkade, over the bridge by the east end of Kleinzand. Itineraries and prices vary and there's no fixed schedule of sailings: you can request anything from a quick tour of the town's canals to venturing out into the open sea. Contact the VVV or the boat owners at the dock for up-to-date details.

## Practicalities

Sneek can get exceptionally busy, and accommodation is impossible to find during Sneek Week in early August. At other times, the central **VVV**, near the Stadhuis at Marktstraat 18 (Mon–Fri 9am–6pm, Sat 9am–5pm; Sept–May Mon–Fri closes 5.30pm; ☎0515/414 096, ✉vvvsneek@tref.nl), can arrange private **rooms** for a small fee. **Hotels** aren't cheap. The *Douldersplaats*, by the station at Stationsstraat 64 (☎0515/413 175, ℻425 455; ❸), is comfortable, while *De Wijnberg*, Marktstraat 23 (☎0515/412 421, ℻413 369; ❷) is good value and central. The HI **hostel** *Wigledam*, Oude Oppenhuizerweg 20 (☎0515/412 132, www.stayokay.com; April–Oct; €19) is some 2km south-east of the centre; head east to the end of Kleinzand, turn right down Oppenhuizerweg, and it's the first major road on the left (bus #98 or #99 from the station). The nearest **campsite** is *De Domp*, Domp 4 (☎0515/412 559; April–Oct), 2km northeast of the centre on Sytsingawiersterleane, a right turn off the main road to Leeuwarden; no buses run near. *Camping De Potten*, Paviljoenweg (☎0515/415 205; April–Oct), lies some 5km east beside the pretty Sneekemeer, the nearest of the Frisian lakes; in July and August, it's served by a bus from town (check at the station for details). *De Potten* rents a good range of watersports equipment at reasonable prices; the VVV can give you a list of other outlets.

Sneek has a large number of **restaurants**, few of which have much character: Leeuwenburg, behind the VVV, is the best place to look for reasonably priced *dagschotels* (try *Van der Wal*), while *'t Stoofje*, Oude Koemarkt 11, has a variety of tasty pancakes. *Hinderlooper Kamer*, Oosterdijk 10, is a smart, cheerful bistro with reasonably priced Dutch food; *Klein Java*, Wijde Noorderhorne 18, offers Indonesian meals. The best **bars** are on Leeuwenburg too, including *Amicitia*, with a cinema next door providing distraction from the quiet nightlife.

# Bolsward

Some 10km west of Sneek, and served by regular buses #98 and #99 from Sneek train station, **BOLSWARD** (pronounced *bozwut* in the local dialect) is less touristy and has a wider ethnic diversity than the surrounding villages and towns. Founded in the seventh century, this was a bustling and important textile centre in the Middle Ages, though its subsequent decline has left a population of around ten thousand and only a handful of worthwhile sights. Your first stop should be the **Stadhuis**, Jongemastraat 2 – a magnificent red-brick, stone-trimmed Renaissance edifice of 1613. The facade is topped by a lion holding a coat of arms over the head of a terrified Turk, and below a mass of twisting, curling carved stone frames a series of finely cut cameos, all balanced by an extravagant external staircase. Inside there's a small **museum** (April–Oct Thurs & Fri 9am–noon & 2–4pm; July & Aug Mon–Fri 10am–5pm; €1) of local historical bits and pieces. Ten minutes' walk away, the fifteenth-century **Martinikerk** at Groot Kerkhof (Mon–Fri 10am–noon & 2–4pm; July & Aug also Sat 2–4pm; €1.50) was originally built on an earthen mound for protection from flooding. Some of the wood carving inside is quite superb: the choir with its rare misericords from 1470 and, particularly, the seventeenth-century pulpit, carved by two local men from a single oak tree. Its panels depict the four seasons: the Frisian baptism dress above the young eagle symbolizes spring, while the carved ice skates (winter) on the other side are thought to be unique. The Reformation was a little less iconoclastic here than elsewhere, and the only visible damage is the odd smashed nose on some of the figures. The stone font dates from around 1000, while the stained-glass windows at the back depict occupation by the Nazis and subsequent liberation by the Canadians.

Bolsward is also home to the **Friese Bierbrouwerij**, Snekerstraat 43 (Frisian Brewery; Mon, Tues, Thurs & Fri 3–6pm, guided tour at 4pm; Sat 10am–6pm, guided tours hourly; €3.50). The smallest brewery in the country, it produces eight different kinds of *Us Heit* beer, and you can learn all about the production process before sampling the product.

The **VVV**, Marktplein 1 (Mon 1.30–5pm, Tues–Fri 9.30am–12.30pm & 1.30–5pm, July & Aug also Sat 10am–2pm; ☎0900/123 4888), has a handful of private **rooms**. There are two convenient **hotels**, the *Stads Herberg Heeremastate*, Heeremastraat 8 (☎0515/573 063, ℱ573 974; ❸), and *De Wijnberg*, Marktplein 5 (☎0515/572 220, ℱ572 665; ❷).

# Makkum

Immaculate houses, church towers, cobbled streets, flower pots and wooden boats sum up the agreeable town of **MAKKUM**. It's saved from postcard prettiness by a working harbour, although, as the centre of traditional Dutch **ceramics** manufacture, the town can be overwhelmed by summer tourists. The local product rivals the more famous delftware in quality, varying from the bright and colourful to more delicate pieces. Ceramic enthusiasts can visit the Tichelaar family workshops, Turfmarkt 65 (Mon–Fri 9am–4.30pm; ☎0515/231 341), take a guided tour (Mon–Fri 11am, 1.30pm & 3pm; €3.50), or just browse through their shop.

Makkum is served by the irregular **minibus** #102 from Workum train station, and by the much easier bus #98 from Bolsward (which you must book in advance ☎0900/1961). Makkum **VVV**, Pruikmakershoek 2 (July & Aug Mon–Fri 9.30am–12.30pm & 1.30–5pm, Sat 9.30am–5pm; April–June, Sept & Oct Mon–Fri 10am–12.30pm & 1.30–5pm, Sat 10am–4pm; ☎0900/540

0001, ⓦwww.friesekust.nl) is sited in the old Waag and can arrange **private rooms** for a €2.50 fee. The **campsite** *De Weeren* (☏0515/321 374), 2km out of town on the road to Wons (bus #98 or #99 towards Bolsward) is basic but clean and quiet. Otherwise, try the pleasantly located **hotel** *De Waag*, Markt 13 (☏0515/231 447, ☏232 737; ❶), with a low-priced **restaurant**. *It Posthus*, in the old post office building at Plein 15, has main courses averaging around €15; for cheaper snacks try *Lunchroom De Halte*, Markt 8.

## Workum

Ten minutes southwest of Sneek by train, **WORKUM**, a long, straggly town with an attractive main street, has the appearance of a comfortable city suburb, protected by several kilometres of sea defences. In fact, until the early eighteenth century it was a seaport, though nowadays indications of a more adventurous past are confined to the central square, 2km from the train station, with its seventeenth-century **Waag** at Merk 4, which contains a standard nautical-historical collection (April–Oct Tues–Fri 10am–5pm, Sat–Mon 1–5pm; €2). Immediately behind, the **St Gertrudskerk** (Mon–Sat 11am–5pm; hours vary out of season; €1), the largest medieval church in Friesland, contains a small collection of mostly eighteenth-century odds and ends. If you're into religious art, explore the **Museum Kerkelijke Kunst** in the neo-Gothic St Werenfridus Kerk, Noard 175 (June to mid-Sept Mon–Sat 1.30–5pm; €1). Just down the road at Noard 6, the likeable **Jopie Huisman Museum** (April–Oct Mon–Sat 10am–5pm, Sun 1–5pm; March & Nov daily 1–5pm; €3) is devoted to paintings by Huisman, a contemporary local artist, most of which have an appealingly unpretentious focus on Frisian life.

### The Elfstedentocht

The **Elfstedentocht** ("Eleven Towns Race") is Friesland's biggest spectacle, a gruelling **ice-skating** marathon around Friesland that dates back to 1890, when one Pim Muller, a local sports journalist, skated his way around the eleven official towns of the province, simply to see whether it was possible. It was, and twenty years later the first official Elfstedentocht was born, contested by 22 skaters. Weather – and ice – permitting, it has taken place just fifteen times in the last hundred years, most recently in 1997, and attracts skaters from all over the world.

The race is organized by the Eleven Towns Association, of which you must be a member to take part; the high level of interest in the race means that membership is very difficult to obtain. The route, which measures about 200km in total, takes in all the main centres of Friesland, starting in Leeuwarden in the town's Friesland Hall, from where the racers sprint – skates in hand – 1500m to the point where they get onto the ice. The first stop after this is Sneek, after which the race takes in Hindeloopen and the other old Zuider Zee towns before finishing in Dokkum in the north of the province. The event is broadcast live on national TV, the route lined with spectators. Of the 17,000 or so people who take part, usually no more than three hundred are professional skaters. Casualties are inevitably numerous; the worst year was 1963, when 10,000 skaters took part and only seventy finished, the rest beaten by the fierce winds, extreme cold and snowdrifts along the way. Generally, however, something like three-quarters of the starters make it to the finishing line.

If you're not around for the race itself, the route makes a popular bike ride and is signposted by the ANWB as one of their national cycling routes; four or five days will allow enough time to sightsee as well as cycle.

The **VVV** (July & Aug Mon–Fri 9.30am–12.30pm & 1.30–5.30pm, Sat 9.30am–5pm; rest of year Mon 1.30–5pm, Tues–Fri 9.30am–12.30pm & 1.30–5pm, Sat 9.30am–4pm; Nov–March closed Mon; ☏0900/540 0001, ⓌWwww.friesekust.nl) across from the Merk at Noard 5, has a limited number of **private rooms**. Alternatively, head for the *Gulden Leeuw*, Merk 2 (☏0515/542 341, Ⓕ543 127; €54) where facilities include a decent **restaurant**, or the *Herberg van Oom Lammert en Tante Klaasje*, next door at Merk 3 (☏ & Ⓕ0515/541 370; €64). The **campsite** *It Soal* (☏0515/541 443, Ⓕ543 640; April–Oct) is located on the IJsselmeer, 3km south of the centre.

From Workum, it's just 6km to Hindeloopen, a pleasant bike-ride across fields, past a windmill and along a dyke. It's a popular route with families, well signposted and steers clear of busy roads.

## Hindeloopen

Next stop down the rail line, the village of **HINDELOOPEN** juts into the IJsselmeer, twenty minutes' walk west of its train station. A highlight of the tour bus trail during the summer months, it's an appealing little town that blossoms with elderly visitors on sunny weekends. A tidy jigsaw of old streets, canals and wooden bridges make an attractive stroll, but unless you visit out of high season it's too quaint and touristy to linger for long.

Until the seventeenth century, Hindeloopen prospered as a Zuider Zee port, concentrating on trade with the Baltic and Amsterdam. The combination of rural isolation and trade created a specific culture within this tightly knit community, with a distinctive dialect (Hylper – Frisian with Scandinavian influences) and sumptuous local **dress**. Adopting materials imported into Amsterdam by the East India Company, the women of Hindeloopen dressed in a florid combination of colours where dress was a means of personal identification: caps, casques and trinkets indicated marital status and age, and the quality of the print indicated social standing. Other Dutch villages adopted similar practices, but nowhere were the details of social position so precisely drawn. However, the development of dress turned out to be a corollary of prosperity, for the decline of Hindeloopen quite simply finished it off. Similarly, the local **painted furniture** showed an ornate mixture of Scandinavian and Oriental styles superimposed on traditional Dutch carpentry. Each item was covered from head to toe with painted tendrils and flowers on a red, green or white background, though again the town's decline resulted in the lapsing of the craft. Tourism has revived local furniture-making, and countless shops now line the main street selling modern versions, though even the smallest items aren't cheap, and the florid style is something of an acquired taste.

Hindeloopen's characterfully wonky **church** – a seventeenth-century structure with a medieval tower – has some graves of British airmen who perished in the Zuider Zee, while the small **Schaats Museum**, Kleine Wiede 1 (Mon–Sat 10am–6pm & Sun 1–5pm; Ⓦwww.schaatsmuseum.nl; €1.50), displays some skating mementoes relating to the great Frisian ice-skating race "De Friese Elfstedentocht" (see box opposite), as well as plenty of painted Hindeloopen-ware in its shop. You can see original examples of this in the small village museum, the **Hidde Nijland Stichting Museum**, beside the church (March–Oct Mon–Sat 10am–5pm, Sun 1.30–5pm; €2.50), although there's a wider display at the Fries Museum in Leeuwarden. At Buren 25 is Galerie Telgenhof (Thurs–Sun 2–5pm; July & Aug Tues–Sun same hours), displaying a collection of locally made jewellery and contemporary Frisian paintings.

Hindeloopen's popularity makes finding **accommodation** a problem during the summer, and the town's lodgings – *De Stadsboerderij*, Nieuwe Weide 9 (℡0514/521 278, 🅕523 016; ❷), and *Pension De Twee Hondjes*, Paardepad 2 (℡0514/522 873; ❶) – tend to fill up early. If you're really caught short, try the prefab *Skips Appartmenten & Dormettes*, in the yachting marina at Oosterstrand 22 (℡0514/524 500, 🅕524 551, 🅦www.skipsmaritiem.nl; ❶). The **VVV**, Nieuwstad 26 (July & Aug Mon–Sat 9.30am–12.30pm & 1.30–5pm; April–June, Sept & Oct Mon, Wed & Sat 11am–4pm, June also Fri; ℡0514/522 550 & ℡0900/540 0001, 🅦www.friesekust.nl) can organize the odd private **room**. The only alternative is the **campsite** *Hindeloopen* (℡0514/521 452, 🅕523 221; April to mid-Oct), 1km or so south near the coast at Westerdijk 9. For **eating**, the smart *De Gasterie*, just off the harbour at Kalverstraat 13, is a lovely place to dine in the evening; *De Brabander*, Nieuwe Wiede 7, has main dishes for under €20 and a wide array of excellent pancakes for under €5. Failing that, the stands on the harbour serve fresh fishy snacks during the day for around €5, with grassy verges to picnic on and plenty of passing boat trade for people-watching.

## Sloten

With its thicket of boat masts poking out above the rooftops, it's easy to spot **SLOTEN** from afar. It's something of a museum piece, though the village's 700 inhabitants are proud to call Sloten one of Friesland's eleven "cities", and a medieval one at that. The town comprises little more than a few pavement cafés fronting a central canal, strips of manicured lawn, a windmill, old locks and colourful flower boxes, although it's encircled by water and is a popular spot with Dutch and German tourists. The adjoining milk-powder factory may seem a blip in this picture-perfect setting, but if anything it lends the place a welcome sense of realism.

Reaching Sloten can be a little awkward; the easiest way is to take bus #42 from Sneek train station to the bus change-over point on the motorway at Spannenburg (takes 35min), where connecting service #41 continues west to Sloten, and #44 runs on to Sloten and Bolsward. Alternatively, it's a 19km bike ride from Sneek, with all manner of cycling permutations to be had in the region.

There's a small **museum** (Tues–Fri 10am–5pm; €3) in the town hall on Heerenval, but otherwise it's just a case of wandering the cobbled alleyways and admiring the gabled facades. The **VVV**, Koestraat 44 (July & Aug Mon–Sat 9.30am–12.30pm & 1.30–5pm; May & June Mon, Tues & Fri 10am–3pm; April, Sept & Oct Wed & Fri 10am–3pm; ℡0514/531 583 & ℡0900/540 0001, 🅦www.friesekust.nl), can suggest a few **places to stay**, including the *Pension 't Brechje*, Voorstreek 110 (℡0514/531 298; ❶). A couple of **restaurants** by the bridge on the canal do good light lunches and more expensive evening meals, and have nice outdoor seating.

The closest **campsite** is *Lemsterpoort*, Jachthaven 3 (℡0514/531 668), but if you have your own transport, it's worth striking out 2km to neighbouring Wijckel: turn left opposite the church, bear right at the first fork, follow the road round, and just past the cow postbox lies the friendly mini-camping *De Tjasker*, Iwert 17 (℡0514/605 869), with its own thatched barn and spotless lawn.

## Stavoren

Named after the Frisian god Stavo, **STAVOREN** is the oldest town in Friesland and was once a prosperous port; it's now the point from where **ferries** make the crossing to Enkhuizen (see p.146 for frequencies and prices, and connecting trains to Amsterdam). Strung out along the coast, Stavoren is an eclectic mix of old and new: the harbour is flanked by modern "Legoland" housing while the shipyards are linked by cobbled backstreets. Popular with yachty types, it's a great place to admire the painstakingly restored seventeenth- to nineteenth-century vessels that once plied the Zuider Zee, now moored up and awaiting hire. On a sunny day, watching the old wooden ships go by and listening to the clink of halyards is an enjoyable pastime as any. At the southern end of town, squat turbines encased in glass, once the largest in the world, can be seen pumping water out of Friesland and into the IJsselmeer.

The glass-shelled **VVV** is on the harbour, two minutes' walk from the station (July & Aug Mon–Sat 9.30am–noon & 1–4.30pm & 5.30–6.45pm, Sun 9.30–10.30am & 1.30–2.30pm & 5.30–6.45pm; April–June, Sept & Oct Mon–Sat 9.45am–noon & 1.30–4.30pm & 5.45–6.30pm; ☎0900/540 0001, Ⓦwww.friesekust.nl) and has details of pensions and private rooms (around €20). Next door, Zeilvloot Lemmer-Stavoren (☎0514/681 818, Ⓦwww .zeilvloot.nl) can provide details on renting **sailboats**, though ideally you'll need to be in a group: keeping up tradition doesn't come cheap.

The best place to **stay** is the hotel *De Vrouwe van Stavoren*, Havenweg 1 (☎0514/681 202, ℱ681 205, Ⓦwww.hotel-vrouwevanstavoren.nl; April–Oct; ➊), attractively sited by the harbour and surprisingly good value. Nearby Smidstraat has a pizzeria, café, ice cream shop and supermarket; Vishandel Doede Bleeker at no. 21 (daily 11am–7pm) offers a platter of tasty fish and chips for €3.50.

Situated at the end of the train line, Stavoren is a good base for **cycling** (you can rent bikes from Annie's Winkeltsje, Smidstraat 14). Options include following the coastal cycleway north 10km to Hindeloopen, or south 5km to Laaksum, past dark green and marine blue lagoons with banks of reeds rustling in the wind. For a longer ride, continue through Laaksum and pick up the signposts to Oudemirdum, with its swathes of forest criss-crossed by cycleways and wooden bridges spanning pea-soupy canals. This 40km loop makes a pleasant day-trip, but bear in mind the winds can be forceful along the coast, and generally blow from the southwest.

# North to Ameland

Edged by the Lauwersmeer to the east and protected by interlocking sea-dykes to the north, the strip of Friesland **north of Leeuwarden** is dotted with tiny agricultural villages that were once separated from each other by swamp and marsh. The area was sparsely inhabited, and the first settlers were forced to confine themselves to whatever higher ground was available, the terpen which kept the treacherous waters at bay. It's home to one of Friesland's oldest towns, **Dokkum**; of interest too are the coastal hamlets of **Moddergat** and **Wierum**. Further west, the unprepossessing port of **Holswerd** provides access to the island of **Ameland**, reached directly from Leeuwarden by a bus service that connects with the ferry. Note too that while the island of Schiermonnikoog can also be reached from Dokkum and Leeuwarden, the quickest and most direct route is from Groningen (for full information on Schiermonnikoog, see p.251).

## Dokkum, Moddergat and Wierum

From Leeuwarden, the scenic national **bike** route LF3b heads northeast, following the contours of a meandering canal; flat, narrow and predominantly

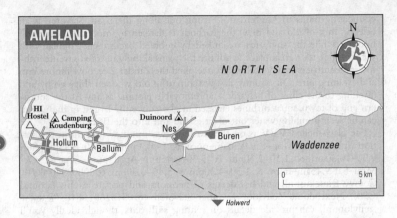

carless, its only challenges are the minute (but near-vertical) wooden hump-back bridges, hiccups in the surrounding calm. Before you reach Holwerd, follow signs branching off to **DOKKUM**, half-an-hour from Leeuwarden by bus #50 & #51. This is the only significant settlement in the area, and one of Friesland's oldest towns: the English missionary St Boniface and 52 of his companions were murdered here in 754 while trying to convert the pagan Frisians to Christianity. In part walled and moated, Dokkum has kept its shape as a fortified town, best appreciated by the side of the Het Grootdiep canal, which cuts the town into two distinct sections. This was the commercial centre of the old town and is marked by a series of ancient gables, including that of the **Admiraliteitshuis** which serves as the town's **museum** (April–Sept Tues–Fri 10am–5pm, Sat 1–5pm; €2). There's not much else: a couple of windmills, quiet walks along the old ramparts and all sorts of things named after St Boniface.

The **VVV**, Op de Fetze 13 (Mon 1–5pm, Tues–Fri 9am–6pm, Fri also 7–9pm, Sat 9am–5pm; ℡0519/220 690, ⓦwww.lauwersland.net) has a map of the city that covers the outlying towns of Holwerd and Wierum too, as well as a supply of private rooms. The best-value **hotel** is the *Van der Meer*, Woudweg 1 (℡0519/292 380, ℉221 006; ❶). The closest campsite, *Harddraverspark*, is just five minutes', walk east of the centre at Harddraversdijk 1a. At **lunchtime** *De Waegh*, Grote Breedstraat 1, serves medieval-style food – big servings of mostly meat, bread and potatoes – and large cups of coffee; *'t Keerpunt*, a lunch and snack bar a few doors further along at no. 13, offers a selection of pancakes and soups, while in the evening your best bet is *'t Raedhus* on Nauwstraat, or *Pizzeria Romana* (closed Mon), just off the main canal at Koornmarkt 8.

Of all the tiny hamlets in north Friesland, two of the most interesting lie on the Waddenzee. **MODDERGAT**, the more easterly of the two, spreads out along the road behind the seawall 10km north of Dokkum, merging with the village of Paesens. At its western edge, a memorial commemorates the 1893 tragedy when seventeen ships sank during a storm, with the loss of 83 lives. Opposite, the **'t Fiskerhuske Museum**, Fiskerpad 4–8 (March–Nov Mon–Sat 10am–5pm; €1.75) comprises three restored fishermen's cottages with displays on the history and culture of the village and details of the disaster: as such small museums go, it's pretty good. Huddled behind the sea-dyke 5km to the west, **WIERUM** has one main claim to fame: its twelfth-century church with a saddle-roof tower and (as in Moddergat) a golden ship on the weather vane. The dyke offers views across to the islands and holds a monument of twisted anchors to the fishermen who died in the 1893 storm and the dozen or so claimed in the century since. The **Wadloopcentrum Fryslân** here (☎0519/562 516, ⓦwww.wadlopen.net) organizes guided walks across the mud flats: times vary with conditions and tides.

Moddergat and Wierum are on the same bus #52 route from Dokkum (you must book on ☎0900/1969 at least an hour in advance of the sched-uled time to ensure that the bus will arrive at the stop). If you've rented a bicycle from Leeuwarden and ridden to Dokkum, follow the signposted cycleway; it's around 8km to Moddergat and a few kilometres more to Wierum. There are a couple of **places to stay**, the farmhouse pension *Recreatiebedrijf Meinsma*, at Meinsmaweg 5 in Moddergat (☎0519/589 396; ❶), which also offers mini-camping and self-contained bungalows, or the pension *'t Sloepke*, Pastoriestraat 1 in Wierum (☎0519/589 727; ❶), also with mini-camping.

## The island of Ameland

Easy to reach from the tiny port of Holwerd, a few kilometres from Wierum, the island of **AMELAND** is one of the major tourist resorts of the north Dutch coast, with a population that swells from 3000 to a staggering 35,000 during summer weekends. Not that the sun is always shining: at times, clouds bustle for position and the colour of the sky can mirror that of the water. It's during the storms that the island is at its moodiest, the flatness of the land accentuating the action in the sky above.

Boats dock near the main village, **NES**, a tiny place that nestles among the fields behind the dyke. Once a centre of the Dutch whaling industry, Nes has its share of cafés, hotels and tourist shops, though quite a bit of the old village survives. High-rise development has been forbidden, and there's a focus instead on the seventeenth- and eighteenth-century captains' houses, known as *Commandeurshuizen*, which line several of the streets. Perhaps surprisingly, the crowds rarely seem to overwhelm the village, but rather to breathe life into it – which is just as well as there's not a lot to do other than wander the streets and linger in cafés. Even if you do hit peak season, it's fairly easy to escape the crowds on all but the busiest of days, and you can **rent bikes** at a number of shops in the village. If it's raining, you might consider the **Natuurcentrum**, Strandweg 38 (Mon–Fri 10am–5pm & 7–9pm, Sat & Sun 10am–5pm; €3.25), an aquarium and natural history museum – look out for the life-size whale – with no information in English.

Nes has a wide range of **accommodation**, but prices do rise dramatically in summer, when many places are full. You should call ahead if you're visiting in July or August. For a small charge, the **VVV**, Rixvan Doniastraat 2 (Mon–Fri 9am–12.30pm & 1.30–6pm, Sat & Sun 10am–5pm; ☎0519/546 546, ⓦwww.ameland.nl) will fix you up with a pension or private room anywhere on the island. Failing that, you could try the rather basic **pension** *Domingo*, De Worteltuin 3 (☎0519/542 371; ❶), the central **hotel** *De Jong*, Reeweg 29 (☎0519/542 016; ❷) or the luxurious *Golden Tulip Resort Noordsee*, Strandweg 42 (☎0519/546 654, ⓦwww.westcordhotels.nl; ❺). The best-appointed **campsite** is the sprawling *Duinoord* (☎0519/542 070; April–Oct); go 1km north out of Nes, then follow Strandweg all the way to the sea, bearing left to enter the camping complex.

A summer **bus** service, connecting with ferry arrivals, runs to the principal villages. There's a variety of **boat** excursions from Nes, including trips to the islands of Terschelling (see p.229) and Schiermonnikoog (see p.251), and to the sandbanks to watch seals. Details can be had from the VVV or tour operators in Nes.

### Around the island

Ameland is just 2km wide but 25km long, and its entire northern shore is made up of a fine expanse of sand and dune laced by foot and cycle paths. The east end of the island is the most deserted, and you can cycle by the side of the marshy shallows that once made up the whole southern shore before the seadyke was built.

Of the smaller villages that dot the island, the prettiest place to stay is **HOLLUM**, a sedate settlement of old houses and farm buildings west of Nes. Its **VVV**, Fabrieksweg 6 (April–Oct Mon–Fri 9am–noon & 2–5.30pm, Sat 10am–noon; Nov–March Mon–Fri 10am–noon & 3–5.30pm & Sat 10am–noon; ☎0519/546 546) can offer the same services as the Nes VVV and is generally less crowded. If you're an aquatic addict there are a couple of small museums here: the **Sorgdragermuseum**, Herenweg 1 (Mon–Fri 10am–5pm, Sat & Sun 1.30–5.30pm; €2.05), an old *commandeurshuis*, and the **Reddingsmuseum Abraham Fock**, Oranjeweg 18 (Mon–Fri 10am–5pm, Sat & Sun 1.30–5pm; €2.05), devoted to the local lifeboat teams and the horses that used to drag the boats to the sea. The lighthouse is now, sadly, closed to the public after being ravaged by a fire.

Hollum's best-value place to stay is the homely *Pension Ambla*, Westerlaan 33a (☎0519/554 537; ❷). Alternatives include the **campsite** *Koudenburg Oosterhiemweg* (☎0519/554 367), by the heath to the north at Oosterhemweg 2. Further west, situated dramatically at the tip of the island past the lighthouse and between pine forest and dunes, is the *Waddencentrum Ameland* – a good HI **hostel** (☎0519/555 353, ⓦ www.stayokay.com; dorm bed €21.50), with bike-rental (from €4.50/day). To get there take bus #130 to the last stop.

# Groningen

The most exciting city in the north Netherlands, **GRONINGEN** comes as something of a surprise in the midst of the province's quiet, rural surroundings.

| ACCOMMODATION | | EATING & DRINKING | | | | Schimmelpennink Huys | **M** |
|---|---|---|---|---|---|---|---|
| Auberge Corps de Garde | **2** | Brussels Lof | **J** | Four Roses | **N** | Soestdijk | **I** |
| City Hotel Groningen | **4** | Café Hooghoudt | **H** | Kleine Moghul | **A** | De Spieghel | **K** |
| Garni Friesland | **5** | Café Kachel | **C** | Maoz Falafel | **O** | Ugly Duck | **E** |
| Garni Groningen | **3** | Café d'Opera | **D** | Metamorphose | **B** | Warung Jawa | **P** |
| Simplon Jongerenhotel | **1** | De Drie Gezusters | **F** | Het Pakhuis | **G** | De Witz | **L** |

Hip, streetwise fashions, a cosmopolitan feel and thriving student life imbue the city with vigour. Competitively priced restaurants dish up exotic curries and fresh falafel alongside the standard Dutch staples, and the arts scene is vibrant, particularly during the academic year. Virtually destroyed during the Allied liberation in 1945, Groningen is now a jumble of arts and architectures: from traditional canal-side townhouses to colourful art-deco tilework parading along the upper facades of the shopping streets. This eclecticism culminates in the innovative Groninger Museum, resplendent in acid-greens and golds on its own little island; its controversial design encases a superb collection of contemporary art, set off by numerous and varied exhibitions.

Groningen was once an important centre of trade, nominally a fiefdom of the bishops of Utrecht from 1040 until 1536, but in reality an autonomous merchant state ruled by a tightly defined oligarchy, whose power was exercised through the city council, or *Raad*. In 1536 Charles V forced the town to submit to his authority, but Groningen was nevertheless still hesitant in its support of the Dutch rebellion against his successors. The dilemma for the city fathers was that, although they stood to gain economically from independence, the majority of the town's citizens were Catholic, deeply suspicious of their Protestant neighbours. In the end, the economic argument won the day, and the town became the capital of its own province in 1594.

# Arrival, information and accommodation

Groningen's **bus** and **train** stations are side by side on the south side of town. The VVV is ten minutes' walk away in the centre at Grote Markt 25 (Mon–Fri 9am–6pm, Thurs until 8pm, Sat 10am–5pm; July & Aug also Sun 11am–3pm; ☎0900/202 3050, ⊛www.vvvgroningen.nl). It offers a range of services, from tourist information on the town and province to tickets for visiting bands, theatre groups and orchestras. They also have a short list of **private rooms** in both Groningen and the surrounding area, though hardly any are near the centre.

Groningen has plenty of good, reasonably priced **accommodation**, though it's a good idea to call ahead to reserve a room. The *Garni Friesland*, Kleine Pelsterstraat 4 (☎ & ℗050/312 1307; ❶) is a decent budget choice. Ten minutes' walk east of Gedempte Zuiderdiep, a street of cheap eating places that gets scruffier the further east you go, the *Garni Groningen*, Damsterdiep 94 (☎050/313 5435; ❶) is friendly if a little spartan, and a good alternative if the more central hotels are full. Two more upmarket options are the *Auberge Corps de Garde*, Oude Boteringestraat 72–74 (☎050/314 5437, ⊛www .corpsdegarde.nl; ❹) and *City Hotel Groningen*, Gedempte Kattendiep 25 (☎050/588 6565, ⊛www.edenhotelgroup.com; ❹). The lowest prices in town are at the *Simplon Jongerenhotel*, Boterdiep 73 (☎050/313 5221, ℗360 3139; ❶), which boasts clean doubles as well as well-kept dorms (€11.60); from the Grote Markt follow Oude Ebbingestraat north over the canal, turn first right and then first left. If you're **camping**, catch bus #2 from the main square via Piezerweg for the ten-minute journey to *Stadspark*, Campinglaan 6 (☎050/525 1624, ⊛www.campingstadspark.nl; mid-March to mid-Oct).

# The Town

Groningen's **train station** was built in 1896 at enormous cost; it was one of the grandest of its day, decorated with the strong colours and symbolic designs of Art Nouveau tiles from the Rozenburg factory in The Hague. The grandeur of much of the building has disappeared under a welter of concrete, glass and plastic suspended ceilings, but the old first- and second-class waiting rooms have survived pretty much intact, and have been refurbished as restaurants. The epitome of high Gothic style, the oak-panelled walls are edged by extravagantly tiled chimneypieces, while a central pillar in each room supports a papier-mâché fluted ceiling. The third-class waiting room is now a travel agency, but a yellow, blue and white tiled diagram of the Dutch rail system still covers one wall, and even the adjoining burger joint gets the stained-glass treatment.

## Pedal power in Groningen

One of the best things about Groningen is the lack of motor traffic: much of the centre is **car-free**, the result of municipal decisions dating back to the mid-1970s, when the city suffered some of the worst road congestion in Europe. In typically bold but sensible Dutch fashion, local authorities dismantled a huge motorway intersection in the city centre, closed most of its roads to cars and invested heavily in a network of cycle paths and bus lanes. Today the park-and-ride scheme goes from strength to strength and two-thirds of residents travel regularly by **bike**, the highest percentage in the country. Groningen is now one of the most popular and appealing cities in the Netherlands in which to live, and the council is planning even more restrictions on cars.

# The Groninger Museum

The town's main draw is the excellent **Groninger Museum** (Tues–Sun 10am–5pm; July & Aug also Mon 1–5pm; €6; ⓦ www.groninger-museum.nl), set on its own island on the southern edge of the centre, directly across from the train station. It consists of six pavilions, each designed in a highly individual style. The museum entrance is under the shimmering golden tower of the central pavilion: think Gaudí on holiday in Miami, and you'll have some inkling of the interior decor. Beyond the stylish café and museum shop, a striking mosaic stairwell flummoxes most visitors by sweeping downwards, depositing you among bulbous lemon-yellow pillars on a baby-blue floor. From here moat-level corridors head off to pavilions either side: east to Mendini, Mendini 1 and Coop Himmelb(l)au, west to Starck and De Ploeg.

Highlights of the museum include Rubens' energetic *Adoration of the Magi* among a small selection of seventeenth-century works, Isaac Israels' inviting *Hoedenwinkel* from a modest sample of Hague School paintings, and a number of later works by the Expressionists of the Groningen *De Ploeg* association, principally Jan Wiegers, whose *Portrait of Ludwig Kirchner* is typically earnest. An adventurous acquisition policy has also led the museum to dabble in some of the more unusual trends in modern art, like Carel Visser's 1983 collage *Voor Dali* and the bizarre *Can the Bumpsteers while I Park the Chariot* by Henk Tas. The paintings are regularly revolved, so don't pin your hopes on catching any particular item. The entire archeology and history collection is presently in storage, with no firm future plans for permanent display.

To the west, the **Philippe Starck pavilion** is a giant disc clad in vertical aluminium plating. A simple vase motif on the exterior hints at the collection of **East Asian ceramics** within, beautifully displayed in circular glass cases, softened by gauzy drapes. A notable exhibit is a 200-piece sample of porcelain rescued from the *Geldermalsen*, which sank in the South China Sea in 1572. Of the examples on display, several have been "re-sunk" in an aquarium on the museum's floor, still encrusted with accumulated detritus, but others have been cleaned and polished to reveal designs of delicate precision: fine drawings of flowers and stems, and bamboo huts where every stick is distinct.

Starck's disc pavilion sits atop the **De Ploeg pavilion**, created by Michele De Lucchi in the form of a trapezium constructed from red bricks, a traditional local building material. The De Ploeg art movement began in Groningen in 1918, and is characterized by intense colour contrasts, exaggerated shapes and depiction of landscapes. As founding member Jan Altink put it:

△ Sneek Week Regatta (see p.233)

## Festival Noorderzon

Every year in mid-August Groningen hosts the increasingly popular **Festival Noorderzon** (✆www.noorderzon.nl), a ten-day blend of theatre, music, film and performance art. About a third of the events are free, many of them staged in the Noorderplantsoen park, a fifteen-minute walk north along Nieuwe Kijk in 't Jatstraat. Come night-time, food-stalls and drinking-holes surround the lake in the park, while folk stroll along the lantern-lit paths, or chill on the lake's stone steps to the sound of Afrobeat, Latin, funk, rock, jazz or ambient music. Other entertainment includes circuses, mime, puppetry, videos and installations. Hotels get busy, so if you're planning to visit around this time you'd do well to book in advance.

"There wasn't much going on in the way of art in Groningen, so I thought of cultivation and thus also of ploughing. Hence the name *De Ploeg*." The group often depicted the landscape north of Groningen in their works; the museum information desk can provide cycle routes which take in scenes depicted in the art collection.

To the east of the mosaic stairway, three pavilions house the museum's collection of **contemporary art**. On the lower and ground levels, the **Mendini pavilion** is dedicated to temporary exhibitions. The **Mendini 1 pavilion**, on the first floor, displays a selection of the museum's collection of contemporary visual art, with particular emphasis on art, architecture, design, graffiti and photography. The galleries are individually colour-schemed: cool blues and purples, or toastier cherry and peach.

A large concrete stairway links Mendini 1 to the final, and most controversial, pavilion. Designed by Wolfgang Prix and Helmut Swiczinsky, who together call themselves **Coop Himmelb(l)au**, this is a Deconstructivist experiment: double-plated steel and reinforced glass jut out at awkward angles, and skinny aerial walkways criss-cross the exhibition space. It all feels – probably deliberately – half-built. Look out for the glass walkholes, where the concrete floor stops and suddenly between your feet the canal gapes, two storeys below. This pavilion is given over to temporary exhibitions which exist in a harsh industrial soundscape, created by the movement of visitors through metal doors and on the unworked concrete and resonating steel gantries.

## Grote Markt and around

The effective centre of town is **Grote Markt**, a wide open space that was badly damaged by wartime bombing and has been rather unimaginatively reconstructed. At its northeast corner is the tiered tower of the **Martinikerk** (June–Aug Tues–Sat noon–5pm; at other times, check hours with VVV; €1). Though the oldest parts of the church go back to 1180, most of it dates from the mid-fifteenth century, the nave being a Gothicized rebuilding undertaken to match the added choir. The vault paintings in the nave are beautifully restored, and in the old choir there are two series of frescoes on the walled-up niches of the clerestory. On the right, a series of eight depicts the story of Christmas, beginning with an Annunciation and ending with a portrayal of the young Christ in the temple. On the left, six frescoes complete the cycle with the story of Easter. Also in the choir is a maquette of the city centre as it looked before wartime destruction: fifteen years in the making, it's painstakingly accurate.

Adjoining the church is the essentially seventeenth–century **Martinitoren** (daily: April–Nov 11am–5pm; rest of year noon–4pm; €2.20) which offers a view that is breathtaking in every sense of the word. Behind the church is the lawn of the Kerkhof, an ancient piece of common land that's partly enclosed by the Provinciehuis, a rather grand neo-Renaissance building of 1915, seat of the provincial government. On the opposite side of the Grote Markt, the classical **Stadhuis** dates from 1810, tucked in front of the mid-seventeenth-century **Goudkantoor** (Gold Office); look out for the shell motif above the windows, a characteristic Groningen decoration.

### Around the A-kerk

From the southwest corner of the Grote Markt, the far side of Vismarkt is framed by the **Korenbeurs** (Corn Exchange) of 1865. The statues on the facade represent, from left to right, Neptune, Mercurius (god of commerce) and Ceres (goddess of agriculture). Just behind, the **A-kerk** is a fifteenth-century church with a Baroque steeple, attractively restored in tones of yellow, orange and red. The church's full name is Onze Lieve Vrouwekerk der A ("Our Dear Lady's Church of the A"), the A being a small river which forms the moat encircling the town centre.

Just west of the church along A-Kerkhof N.Z., the **Noordelijk Scheepvaart Museum**, Brugstraat 24–26 (Tues–Sat 10am–5pm, Sun 1–5pm; €2.75), is one of the best-equipped and most comprehensive maritime museums in the country, tracing the history of north Holland's shipping from the sixth to the twentieth centuries. Housed in a warren of steep stairs and timber-beamed rooms, each of the museum's twenty displays deals with a different aspect of shipping, including trade with the Indies, the development of peat canals and a series of reconstructed nautical workshops. The museum's particular appeal is its imaginative combination of models and original artefacts, which are themselves a mixture of the personal (seamen's chests, quadrants) and the public (figureheads, tile designs of ships). In the same building is the much smaller **Niemeyer Tabaksmuseum** (same hours and ticket), devoted to tobacco smoking. Exhibits include a multitude of pipes and a great collection of snuff paraphernalia in all sorts of materials, from crystal and ivory to porcelain and silver. The Niemeyer family built their fortune on the tobacco trade, and here you can see the origins of those familiar blue tobacco packets.

A little south, the **Natuurmuseum**, Praediniussingel 59 (Tues–Fri 10am–5pm, Sat & Sun 1–5pm; Ⓦwww.natuurmuseum.org; €2.80), has a permanent exhibition (in Dutch) on the Ice Age, complete with woolly mammoths, and a display on wildlife, geology and land reclamation in the local area.

### Smaller museums

Of the smaller museums, there's contemporary art at the **Centrum Beeldende Kunst** (Visual Arts Centre) in the Oosterpoort, Trompsingel 27 (Tues–Fri 10am–5pm, Sat & Sun 1–5pm; free), while the **Grafisch Museum**, Rabenhauptstraat 65 (Tues–Sun 1–5pm; €3), southeast of the train station, has everything from a nineteenth-century steam-driven printing press to word-processors.

Northwest of Grote Markt, down a passage off Zwanestraat, the **Universiteitsmuseum** (Wed–Fri noon–4pm, Sun 1–4pm; €1.50) gives a taste of the university's history, with exhibits ranging from scientific equipment to photos of derby-hatted students clowning around at the turn of last century. Further north still, at Nieuwe Kijk in 't Jatstraat 104, the **Volkenkundig Museum Gerardus van der Leeuw** (Ethnological museum; Tues–Fri 10am–4pm, Sat & Sun 1–5pm; free) has collections from Asia, Africa, the Pacific and South America.

# Eating, drinking and nightlife

Groningen's nicest places to **eat and drink** are concentrated in three loosely defined areas, each only a couple of minutes' walk from the next. Best of the three is centred on **Poelestraat**, just east of Grote Markt, where an array of open-air cafés pulls in a mainly young crowd. *Café d'Opera* at no. 17 has good Dutch food; around the corner, *Het Pakhuis*, Peperstraat 8, offers cheapish meals and a lively bar in a marigold-coloured traditional warehouse; just to the south, the elegant *Schimmelpennink Huys*, Oosterstraat 53, has excellent and moderately priced daily specials, while for Tex-Mex food visit *Four Roses* at the junction of Oosterstraat and Gedempte Zuiderdiep. East across the canal from Poelestraat, the tiny boisterous *Café Kachel*, Schuittendiep 62, is the best of the town's traditional Dutch **bars**; there are several other decent places to drink nearby.

On the south side of the Grote Markt, the best of a flank of **outdoor cafés** are the cosy *De Witz* at no. 47, the civilized *De Drie Gezusters* at no. 39, with a great old interior, and *Café Hooghoudt* in the old Lloyds Insurance building at no. 42; this last also contains a night café serving food until 4am at weekends.

Northwest of the Grote Markt, around Zwanestraat, the *Ugly Duck* at no. 28 has fish and Dutch food, including a good-value tourist menu; just to the west, *Soestdijk*, Grote Kromme Elleboog 6, is pricier and posher; while *Brussels Lof*, A-Kerkstraat 24, is a **vegetarian** restaurant with good fondues. While you're in this area, hunt down the superb **applecake** on offer at A-Kerkhof 43, and the old-fashioned *Postema* at A-Kerkhof 9, which has been selling coffee since 1917.

A little further north, in the genteel university surroundings, is the coffeehouse *Metamorphose*, Oude Boteringestraat 53 – a chilled hangout popular with locals. Two streets to the west, **Oude Kijk in 't Jatstraat** is a student stomping-ground, lined with cheap cafés, secondhand clothes stores and bookshops. A ten-minute walk further north over the bridge is the *Kleine Moghul*, Niewe Boteringestraat 62, an excellent-value and busy Indian takeaway and restaurant that's well worth the trek for its kitsch decor.

West of the Pathé cinema on Gedempte Zuiderdiep, there's an assortment of inexpensive cafés and takeaways doing Turkish and Surinamese food, such as *Warung Jawa* at no. 110. Best value of all is *Maoz Falafel* at no. 23: their Middle Eastern-style falafel-stuffed pitta sandwiches can fill you up for €3.50.

For **live music** try *De Vestibule*, Oosterstraat 24; *Vera*, Oosterstraat 44; or *Troubadour*, Peperstraat 19. The jazz café *De Spieghel*, Peperstraat 11, has live performances most nights (including some reasonably big names), and there's a nightly piano bar, *Café Koster*, at Hoogstraat 7. Most of the bigger visiting bands play in the Stadsschouwburg, Turfsingel 86 (℡050/312 5645), or De Oosterpoort, Trompsingel 27 (℡050/313 1044), just east of the train station. The *Palace*, Gelkingestraat 1, is a good **club** that occasionally hosts live bands. The VVV's free *Uitgaanskrant* has listings of all events.

# Listings

**Bike rental** At the train station (€5.20/day, €21/week; ℡050/312 4174).

**Boat trips** Along the old town moat (€6.50 for 1hr 15min). Bookings and schedules at the VVV.

**Books** A good range of English-language titles is at Scholtens-Wristers on Guldenstraat.

**Cinema** Images, Poelestraat 30 (℡050/312 0433, ⓦwww.images.nu) is an arthouse cinema with a pleasant open-air café. Mainstream films are shown at the Pathé Megabioscoop, Gedempte Zuiderdiep 78 (℡050/5844050).

**Emergencies** ℡112.

Laundry Self or service wash at Handy Wash, Schuitendiep 56 ☏ 050/318 7587.

Left luggage At the train station (€4 for 24hr; no access 2–5am).

Markets Vegetables, fruit, flowers, fish and fabrics at A-Kerkhof (Tues, Fri & Sat 9am–5pm). Organic food market at Vismarkt (Wed 9am–5pm). Non-

food general market at the Grote Markt (Thurs 1–9pm).

Pharmacy Apotheek Hanzeplein, Hanzeplein 122 (open 24hr; ☏ 050/311 5020).

Police Herebinnsingel 2 ☏ 0900/8844.

Post office By the A-kerk on Munnekeholm (Mon 10am–6pm, Tues–Fri 9am–6pm, Sat 10am–1.30pm).

Taxi TaxiCentrale ☏ 050/366 6663.

# Around Groningen

A patchwork of industrial complexes and nondescript villages, Groningen province has few major attractions; unless you fancy a night in the country near the old monastery at Ter Apel, there's nowhere that really warrants a stay. The easiest trip is to the **botanical gardens** at **HAREN** (daily 9.30am–5pm, Nov–March 9am–5pm; €3.50) a few kilometres south by train or bus #51 or #54. From the train station it's a signed, 25-minute walk. There's a small Chinese garden, an English garden and some extensive rose gardens, although the real highlight is the tropical greenhouse complex, with a range of cacti and some wonderful old cycads, as well as the more familiar palms, bananas and ferns.

## Uithuizen

For day-tripping from Groningen city, the most agreeable journey is to the village of **UITHUIZEN**, 25km north, where the moated manor house of **Menkemaborg** (June–Sept daily 10am–5pm; March–May Tues–Sun 10am–noon & 1–5pm; Oct–Jan Tues–Sun 10am–noon & 1–4pm; €4.50; ⓦwww.menkemaborg.nl) is a signed ten-minute walk from the station. Dating from the fifteenth century and surrounded by formal gardens in the English style, the house has a sturdy, compact elegance and is one of the very few mansions, or borgs, of the old landowning families to have survived. The interior consists of a sequence of period rooms furnished in the style of the seventeenth century, displaying some of the Groninger Museum's applied art and history collection. The specialist-interest **Museum 1939–1945**, Dingeweg 1 (May–Oct daily 9am–6pm; €5), has an excellent collection of World War II military artefacts: uniforms, weapons, secret radios and more.

The trip to Uithuizen can be combined with *wadlopen* (see box opposite) – a guided walk across the coastal mud flats to the uninhabited sand-spit island of **Rottumeroog**. Excursion buses head out to the coast from Menkemaborg three or four times monthly (June–Sept); the trip costs from €20 per person, and booking is essential – contact Stichting Uithuizer Wad (ⓦwww .wadlopen-suw.nl). Without a guide, it's too dangerous to venture onto the mud flats, but it is easy enough to **walk** along the enclosing dyke that runs behind the shoreline for the whole length of the province. There's precious little to see, but when the weather's clear, the browns, blues and greens of the surrounding land and sea are unusually beautiful. From Uithuizen, it's a good hour's stroll north to the nearest point on the dyke, and you'll need a large-scale map (available from Groningen VVV) for directions.

Wadlopen, or mudflat walking, is a popular and strenuous Dutch pastime, and the stretch of coast on the northern edge of the provinces of Friesland and Groningen is one of the best places to do it: twice daily, the receding tide uncovers vast expanses of mud flat beneath the Waddenzee. It is, however, a sport to be taken seriously, and far too dangerous to do without an experienced guide: the depth of the mud is variable and the tides inconsistent. In any case, channels of deep water are left even when the tide has receded, and the currents can be perilous. The timing of treks depends on weather and tidal conditions, but most start between 6am and 10am. It's important to be properly equipped; recommended gear includes shorts or a bathing suit, a sweater, wind jacket, knee-high socks, high-top trainers and a complete change of clothes stashed in a watertight pack. In recent years, *wadlopen* has become extremely popular, and as excursions are infrequent, between May and August it's advisable to book a place at least a month in advance.

Prices are €15–25 a head, and include the cost of a return ferry crossing; the VVVs in Leeuwarden (see p.221), Dokkum (see p.240) and Groningen (see p.244) can provide details, or you could contact one of the *wadlopen* organizations direct: Dijkstras Wadlopencentrum, Hoofdstraat 118, Pieterburen (☏ 0595/528 345, ⓦ www.wadloop-dijkstra.nl), has the most multilingual guides; there's also Stichting Wadloopcentrum Pieterburen, Hoofdstraat 68, Pieterburen (☏ 0595/528 300, ⓦ www.wadlopen.com). The Wadloopcentrum Fryslân (☏ 0519/562 516, ⓦ www.wadlopen.net) is based in Wierum (see p.241).

# The Lauwersmeer

Some 35km northwest of Groningen, the **Lauwersmeer** is a broken and irregular lake that spreads across the provincial boundary into neighbouring Friesland. Once an arm of the sea, it was turned into a freshwater lake by the construction of the Lauwersoog dam, a controversial 1960s' project that was vigorously opposed by local fishermen, who ended up having to move all their tackle to ports on the coast. Spared intensive industrial and agricultural development because of the efforts of conservationists, it's a quiet and peaceful region with a wonderful variety of sea birds, and increasingly popular with anglers, windsurfers, sailors and cyclists.

The local villages are uniformly dull, however; the most convenient base is **ZOUTKAMP**, near the southeast corner of the lake on the River Reitdiep, accessible by bus #65 from Groningen. The VVV, Dorpsplein 1 (April–Sept Mon–Fri 9am–5pm, Sat 10am–noon & 1–4pm, Sun 1–4pm; Oct–March Mon–Fri 9am–noon & 1–4.30pm; ☏ 0595/401 957) houses a small museum (€2), with changing displays on the maritime history and traditions of the area, including an old-fashioned fishing boat. There is a limited supply of private rooms, which can be reserved here or at Groningen VVV.

At the mouth of the lake, some 10km north of Zoutkamp, the desultory port of **LAUWERSOOG** is where **ferries** leave for the fifty-minute trip to the island of Schiermonnikoog.

# The island of Schiermonnikoog

Until the Reformation, the island of **SCHIERMONNIKOOG** belonged to the monastery of Klaarkamp on the mainland; its name means literally "island of the grey monks". Nothing remains of the monks, however, and these days

SCHIERMONNIKOOG

NORTH SEA

Seedune

Schiermonnikoog

Waddenzee

0          5 km

N

▼ *Lauwersoog*

Schiermonnikoog's only settlement is a prim and busy village bordering on long stretches of muddy beach and sand dune to the north and farmland and mudflats to the south. At low tide, these motionless pools of water reflect the colours in the sky, particularly atmospheric at dawn and dusk. Schiermonnikoog is the smallest of the Frisian islands at 16km long and 4km wide, and, once you're clear of the weekend homes that fringe the village, it's a wild, uncultivated place, criss-crossed by cycle paths – a popular spot for day-trippers.

Ferries from Lauwersoog (see box below) dock at the island jetty, some 3km from the village; a connecting bus drops you off outside the VVV in the centre. It's even possible to walk to the island across the mud flats from Kloosterburen, a distance of about 8km, but you must do this accompanied by a guide; see the box on p.251 for details.

Finding **accommodation** is difficult to find in season, when prices rise sharply; it's essential to ring ahead. The **VVV** (Mon–Fri 9am–1pm & 2–6pm, Sat 9.30am–1pm & 2–4.30pm; Oct–April Mon–Fri closes 30min earlier; ☎0519/531 900, ⓦwww.vvvschiermonnikoog.nl) will help by booking private rooms and pensions. The cheapest **hotel** is *De Tjattel* (☎0519/531 133, ⓦwww.detjattel.nl; ❷), in the heart of the village at Langestreek 94; the *Strandhotel Noderstraun* (☎0519/531 111, ⒻF531 857; ❹), about twenty minutes' walk from the VVV and overlooking the beach at Badweg 32, is a more luxurious alternative; the large *Van der Werff*, Reeweg 2 (☎0519/531 203, ⒻF531 748; ❸) is a third possibility. Schiermonnikoog's **campsite**, *Seedune* (☎0519/531 398, ⓦwww.seedune.nl), is to the north, in the woods just east of

**Ferries to Schiermonnikoog**

For **Schiermonnikoog**, bus #63 runs 5 times daily from Groningen (1hr) and bus #51 from Dokkum (30min) and Leeuwarden (1hr 30min), to the port of Lauwersoog, from where ferries make the crossing (basic schedule: Mon–Sat 6.30am, 9.30am, 1.30pm & 5.30pm, Sun 9.30am, 3.30pm & 5.30pm; extra sailings in summer: June Sat 11.30am; July & Aug daily 11.30am, Sun 7.30pm; no sailing Nov–Feb Sat 1.30pm; 45min; €11.60 return). The returning boat leaves from the island one hour *later* in each case. Taking your bike over will cost extra. Only residents' cars are allowed on Schiermonnikoog.

Badweg at Seeduneweg 1. On the east side of the village at Knuppeldam 2, fifteen minutes' walk from the VVV, is the *Herberg Rijsbergen*, a non-HI **hostel** (T0519/531 257, Wwww.herbergrijsbergen.nl; dorm bed €25; doubles available; ➊).

The *Strandhotel* has windsurfing equipment for rent; bikes are available from several small shops in the village, and the VVV sells good maps. Places to eat and drink are scattered along Langestreek and Badweg to the north of the VVV.

## East of Groningen

Some 20km east of Groningen on the northern edge of the small town of **SLOCHTEREN**, accessible by bus #78 from Groningen station, the typically northern **Fraeylemaborg** (March–Dec Tues–Fri 10am–5pm, Sat & Sun 1–5pm; €4.50) is a well-preserved, seventeenth-century moated mansion, set within extensive parkland.

More interesting, some 60km southeast of Groningen close to the German frontier, **BOURTANGE** is a superbly restored fortified village. Founded by William of Orange in 1580 to help protect the eastern approaches to Groningen, Bourtange fell into disrepair during the nineteenth century, only to be entirely refurbished as a tourist attraction in 1964. The design of the village is similar to that of Naarden, outside Amsterdam (see p.159), and is best appreciated as you walk round the old bastions of the star-shaped fortress. Bus #71 from Groningen drops you by the car park, from where you enter the village through the VVV building and information centre (April–Oct Mon–Fri 9am–5.30pm, Sat & Sun noon–5.30pm; Nov–March Mon–Fri 9am–noon; T0599/354 600). Entry to the village is free, but there is a charge of €4 if you want to see the slide-show which gives a history of Bourtange and to visit the various exhibitions depicting traditional life in the village. There's a **campsite**, *'t Plathuis*, Vlagtwedderstraat 88 (T0599/354 383; mid-March to Oct) and one **hotel**, *De Staakenborgh*, up the road at no. 33 (T0599/354 216, Wwww.staakenborgh.nl; ➊).

### Ter Apel

South from Bourtange in the small town of **TER APEL** near the German border, the **Museum Klooster** (Mon–Sat 10am–5pm, Sun 1–5pm; Nov–April closed Mon; €4.50), is the definite highlight in this part of the country, served by bus #270 from Bourtange. This was the monastery of the Crutched Friars, built in 1465, and probably unique among rural monasteries in surviving the Reformation intact, after the enlightened local authorities allowed the monks to remain here during their lifetimes. The chapel, superbly restored, preserves a number of unusual features, including the tripartite sedilia, where the priest and his assistants sat during Mass, and a splendid roodscreen that divides the chancel from the nave. Elsewhere, the east wing is a curious hybrid of Gothic and Rococo styles, the cloister has a small herb garden and the other rooms are normally given over to temporary exhibitions of religious art. The monastery is surrounded by extensive beech woods and magnificent old horse-chestnut trees; follow one of the marked walks or simply ramble at your leisure. Opposite, the **hotel** and **restaurant** *Boschhuis* (T0599/581 208, Wwww.hotelboschhuis.nl; ➊) is ideal for a good meal, or for spending a quiet night in the country.

# Drenthe

Until the early nineteenth century, the sparsely populated province of **Drenthe** was little more than a flat expanse of empty peat bog, marsh and moor. Today it's the country's least populated province, popular with visitors for its woods and countryside. Its only conspicuous geographical feature is a ridge of low hills that runs northeast for some 50km from Emmen toward Groningen. This ridge, the **Hondsrug**, was high enough to attract prehistoric settlers whose *hunebeds* (megalithic tombs) have become Drenthe's main tourist attraction. **Assen**, the provincial capital, is a dull place with a good museum, and **Emmen**, the other major town, can only be recommended as a convenient base for visiting some of the *hunebeds* and three neighbouring open-air folk culture museums.

Governed by the bishops of Utrecht from the eleventh century, Drenthe was incorporated into the Habsburg empire in 1538. The region sided with the Protestants in the rebellion against Spain, but it had little economic or military muscle and its claim to provincial status was ignored until the days of the Batavian Republic. In the nineteenth century, work began in earnest to convert the province's peat bogs and moors into farmland. *Veenkulunies* (peat colonies) were established over much of the south and east of Drenthe, where the initial purpose of the labourers was to dig drainage canals (*wiels*) and cut the peat for sale as fuel to the cities. Once cleared of the peat, the land could be used to grow crops, and today the region's farms are some of the most profitable in the country.

## Assen

**ASSEN**, about 16km south of Groningen, is a possible first stop, though not somewhere you're likely to want to stay. Its train and bus station are about five minutes' walk from the centre of town, moving straight ahead across the main road down Stationsstraat. On the eastern side of the central square, Brink is home to both parts of the **Drents Museum** (Tues–Sun 11am–5pm; €5; Ⓦ www.drentsmuseum.nl), which, spread over a pleasant group of old houses, is the only thing that makes a stop in town worthwhile. Of the buildings, the Ontvangershuis at Brink 1 has on its second floor an extraordinary assortment of prehistoric bodies, clothes and other artefacts that have been preserved for thousands of years in the surrounding peat bogs. The bodies are the material remains of those early settlers who built the *hunebeds*, and the museum has a modest display covering their customs and culture. There's also the much vaunted Pesse Canoe, the oldest water vessel ever found, dating from about 6800 BC and looking its age.

Assen's VVV was closed indefinitely at the time of writing. The cheapest **place to stay** is the *Christerus* (☎0592/313 517; ❶), on the way in from the station at Stationsstraat 17. The *De Nieuwe Brink Hotel*, Brink 13, has a reasonable **restaurant**.

If you have your own transport, you might want to detour to the **Herinneringscentrum Kamp Westerbork** (Mon–Fri 10am–5pm, Sat & Sun 1–5pm; July & Aug Sat & Sun also 11am–1pm; €3.85) a little south of town, on the road between the villages Amen and Hooghalen. It was here, before and during World War II, that the Nazis assembled Dutch Jews before transporting them to the death camps in the east. Although little remains of the camp itself, the documents and artefacts on display are deeply affecting.

# Emmen and around

To all intents and purposes **EMMEN** is a new town, a twentieth-century amalgamation of strip villages that were originally peat colonies. The centre is a modernistic affair, mixing the remnants of the old with lumpy boulders, trees and shrubs and a job lot of concrete and glass.

Emmen is known for two things: its *hunebeds* and its zoo. The **zoo** (daily 10am–6pm; Oct–May closes 4.30pm; €14.50), right in the middle of town at Hoofdstraat 18, boasts an imitation African savanna, where the animals roam "free", a massive sea-lion pool – the biggest in Europe – and a giant hippo house. The best of Emmen's *hunebeds* is the clearly signed **Emmerdennen Hunebed**, in the woods 1km or so east of the station along Boslaan. This is a so-called passage-grave, with a relatively sophisticated entrance surrounded by a ring of standing stones. The other interesting *hunebed* within easy walking distance is the **Schimmer-Es**, a large enclosure containing two burial chambers and a standing stone about 2km north of the centre; to get there follow Hoofdstraat north from the VVV, take a left down Noorderstraat, right along Noordeinde, left along Broekpad, and first right at Langgrafweg. The VVV sells detailed maps of a circular car route along the minor roads to the north of town that covers all the principal remains.

Emmen's **train** and **bus** stations adjoin each other, five minutes' walk north of the town centre: head straight down Stationsstraat into Boslaan and turn left down Hoofdstraat, the main drag. The **VVV**, Hoofdstraat 22 (Mon 1–5.30pm, Tues–Fri 9.30am–5.30pm, Sat 10am–4pm; ☎0591/613 000, ⓦwww.vvvemmen.nl), can arrange **accommodation** at pensions, private rooms and hotels. Cheapest pension is *De Wanne*, Stortweg 1 (☎0591/611 250, ⓦwww.hoteldewanne.nl; ❶–❷), 1.5km southwest of the zoo. For a little more you could stay in the cheapest hotel, the *Boerland*, Hoofdstraat 57 (☎0591/613 746, ⓦwww.stads-hotelboerland.nl; ❷), which is immediately behind the train station. For food, try the upper-floor café of the *Boerland*.

## Around Emmen

**BORGER**, some 20km northwest of Emmen, has the largest *hunebed* in the country on the northeast edge of the village, at 25m long; its origins are explained at the adjoining information centre (Mon–Fri 10am–5pm, Sat & Sun 11am–5pm; €2.80). You'll need, too, to use some imagination: these bulges in the ground, sprouting tufts of grass and small trees, aren't up to much. Back in town, the *hunebed* theme is everywhere, from streetnames and pancakes to special menus. Should you decide to stay, the **VVV** (July & Aug Mon–Sat 9.30am–5pm, Sun 10am–3pm; April–June Mon–Sat 9.30am–4.30pm; Sept–March Mon–Sat 10am–4pm; ☎0599/234 855) has a list of private rooms, or you could try the **hotel** *Nathalia*, Hoofdstraat 87 (☎0599/234 791; ❷). For **camping**, *Minicamping de Zwerf Ke*, at Bij de Boer SVR, is friendly and not that far out of town: from the centre, head west under the N34 road, and at the junction to Rolde, cross straight over onto Stregenweg, and the campsite is 1.5km down the road on the right. As well as producing potatoes, sweet beet and maize, the farmers of Borger also make a mean football pitch – the immaculate, billiard-green fields around you are where the turf used for pitches around the country (including league champions Ajax of Amsterdam) originates. Bus #59 runs to Borger on its way between Emmen and Groningen; from Assen, take bus #24.

About 11km east of Emmen, toward the German border, the **Veenmuseumdorp 't Aole Compas** (daily: July & Aug 10am–6pm; Easter–Oct 10am–5pm; €9; ⓦwww.veenpark.nl), served by bus #45 hourly from Emmen station (30min) is a massive open-air museum-village that traces the history and development of the peat colonies of the moors of southern Groningen and eastern Drenthe. The colonies were established in the nineteenth century, when labour was imported to cut the thick layers of peat that lay all over the moors. Isolated in small communities, and under the thumb of the traders who sold their product and provided their foodstuffs, the colonists were harshly exploited and lived in abject poverty until well into the 1930s. Built around some old interlocking canals, the museum consists of a series of reconstructed villages that span the history of the colonies. It's inevitably a bit folksy, but very popular, with its own narrow-gauge railway, a canal barge, and working period bakeries, bars and shops. A thorough exploration takes a full day.

Some 13km northwest of Emmen, on the northern edge of the village of **SCHOONOORD** and served by bus #21 from Emmen, **Ellert en Brammert** (April–Oct daily 9am–6pm; €3.50) is another open-air museum concerned with life in Drenthe. Exhibits here concentrate on the late nineteenth century and cover a wide range of traditional community activities – from sheep farming to education and carpentry. About 7km west, tiny **ORVELTE** (July & Aug daily 9am–5.30pm; April–Oct Mon–Fri 10am–5pm, Sat & Sun 11am–5pm) is another village-museum, fully operational and actually inhabited, though certain buildings may be closed at any time. Owned by a trust which exercises strict control over construction and repair, Orvelte's buildings date from the seventeenth to the nineteenth centuries and include examples of a toll house, a dairy, a farmhouse and a number of craft workshops. Most are open to the public, but you really need a car to get here: bus #27 from Emmen to Zweeloo (20min) and then bus #22 to Orvelte (10min) may get you here, but you should call ⓣ0900/1475 for up-to-date information before attempting the journey to improve your chances of making successful connections.

# Travel details

## Trains

**Emmen** to: Zwolle (every 30min; 50–60min).
**Groningen** to: Amsterdam (every 30min; 2hr 20min); Assen (every 20min; 20min); Leeuwarden (every 30min; 50min); Uithuizen (hourly; 35min); Zwolle (every 20min; 1hr 10min).
**Leeuwarden** to: Amsterdam (every 30min; 2hr 20min); Franeker (every 30min; 15min); Groningen (every 30min; 50min); Harlingen (every 30min; 25min); Hindeloopen (hourly; 40min); Sneek (every 30min; 20min); Stavoren (hourly; 50min); Zwolle (every 30min; 50min–1hr 5min).

## Buses

**Bolsward** to: Makkum (Mon–Sat hourly, Sun every 2hr; 20min).
**Bourtange** to: Ter Apel (hourly; 30min).
**Dokkum** to: Wierum & Moddergat (Mon–Sat 7 daily, Sun 2 daily; 25min & 35min).
**Groningen** to: Bourtange (Mon–Fri hourly; 1hr); Emmen (hourly; 1hr 10min); Zoutkamp (hourly; 1hr).
**Leeuwarden** to: Alkmaar (hourly; 2hr 20min); Dokkum (Mon–Fri 3 per hour, Sat & Sun hourly; 30–50min); Franeker (hourly; 25min); Marssum (Mon–Sat every 30min, Sun hourly; 10min).

**Sneek** to: Bolsward (Mon–Sat every 20min, Sun hourly; 15min).

**Workum** to: Makkum (Mon–Sat every 2–3hr; 30min).

## Buses to connecting ferries

**Groningen** to: Lauwersoog (bus #63: 5 daily; 1hr) for boats to Schiermonnikoog.

**Leeuwarden** to: Holwerd (bus #66: 5–7 daily; 50min) for boats to Ameland; and to Lauwersoog (bus #51: 4–7 daily; 1hr 30min) for boats to Schiermonnikoog.

## Ferries and hydrofoils

**Harlingen** to: Terschelling (2–3 ferries daily; 1hr 45min; 3–4 hydrofoils daily; 50min direct, 1hr 20min via Vlieland); Vlieland (2–3 ferries daily; 1hr 45min; 2–3 hydrofoils daily; 45min direct, 1hr 30min via Terschelling).

**Holwerd** to: Ameland (4–8 ferries daily; 45min).

**Lauwersoog** to: Schiermonnikoog (2–6 ferries daily; 50min).

**Stavoren** to: Enkhuizen (May–Sept 3 ferries daily; 1hr 20min).

**Terschelling** to: Vlieland (2–3 ferries daily; 1hr 5min; 1–2 hydrofoils daily; 30min).

**Vlieland** to: Terschelling (2–3 ferries daily; 1hr 5min; 1–2 hydrofoils daily; 30min).

THE NORTH AND THE FRISIAN ISLANDS | Travel details

# The eastern Netherlands

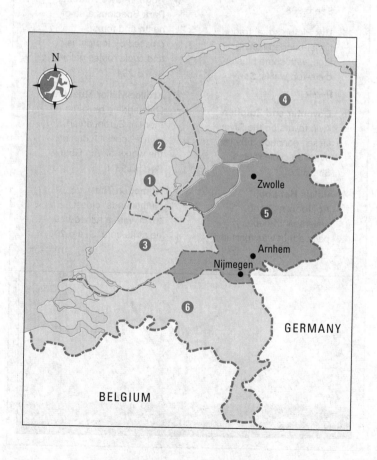

# CHAPTER 5

# Highlights

✳ **Giethoorn** Gentle village set amidst lakes and wetlands – ideal for messing about on the water. See p.265

✳ **Zwolle** Ancient fortified town, capital of the province of Overijssel. See p.268

✳ **Urk** Picturesque, traditional-minded fishing village, with some blustery dyke-top walks. See p.275

✳ **Deventer and Zutphen** Twin towns on the River IJssel, connected by lazy riverside cycle routes. See p.281

✳ **Paleis Het Loo, Apeldoorn** Grand, seventeenth-century palace that was formerly home to the Dutch royal family. See p.286

✳ **Arnhem** Garden city with a tragic wartime history, a good base for exploring this attractive region. See p.288

✳ **Hoge Veluwe National Park** Spacious area of heath and forest, crossed by footpaths and cycle routes galore. See p.294

✳ **Kröller-Müller Museum** Outstanding museum of modern European art, with a special focus on the works of Van Gogh. See p.295

✳ **Nijmegen** The Netherlands' oldest town, with a ruined castle at its core. See p.296

# 5

# The eastern Netherlands

n the eastern provinces of the Netherlands, the flat polder landscapes of the north and west of the country begin to disappear, the countryside growing steadily more undulating as you head toward Germany. Coming from the north, **Overijssel** is the first province you reach, "beyond the [River] IJssel", which forms the border with Gelderland to the south. Its more appealing western reaches are a typically Dutch area, in part cut by lakes and waterways around the picturesque water-village of **Giethoorn**, at the heart of a series of towns – **Kampen**, **Deventer**, **Zutphen** and the provincial capital of **Zwolle** – which enjoyed a period of immense prosperity during the heyday of the Zuider Zee trade, from the fourteenth to the sixteenth centuries. Lying at the junction of trade routes from Germany, Scandinavia and South Holland, all were keen to outdo their rivals in architectural grandeur. The bubble burst in the seventeenth century, when trade moved west and prices were undercut by the great merchant cities of South Holland; today, all are well worth a visit for their ancient centres, splendid churches and extravagant defensive portals. Southeast of here, **Twente** – an industrial region of old textile towns – is one of the least visited parts of the country and with good reason: only **Enschede**, the main town, provides a reason to visit, with an excellent local museum and a lively music scene.

The boundary separating Overijssel from the pancake-flat reclaimed lands of **Flevoland** runs along the old shoreline of the Zuider Zee. Divided into two halves (the drab Noord-Oost Polder in the east and the Flevoland Polder to the west), it doesn't have much to attract the visitor, although the fishing village of **Urk** – an island until the land reclamation scheme got under way – is an unusual historical relic. The provincial capital is **Lelystad**, a pretty dire modern town redeemed by some fine museums and an impressive reconstruction of an early-seventeenth-century trading ship.

**Gelderland**, spreading east from Utrecht to the German frontier, takes its name from the German town of Geldern, its capital until the late fourteenth century. As a province it's a bit of a mixture, varying from the uninspiring agricultural land of the **Betuwe** (Good Land), south of Utrecht, to the more distinctive – and appealing – **Veluwe** (Bad Land), an expanse of heath, woodland and dune that sprawls down from the old Zuider Zee coastline to **Arnhem**. Infertile and sparsely populated in medieval times, today the Veluwe constitutes

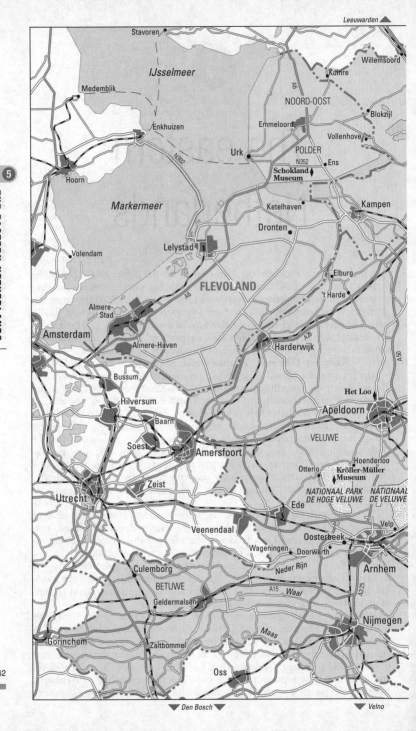

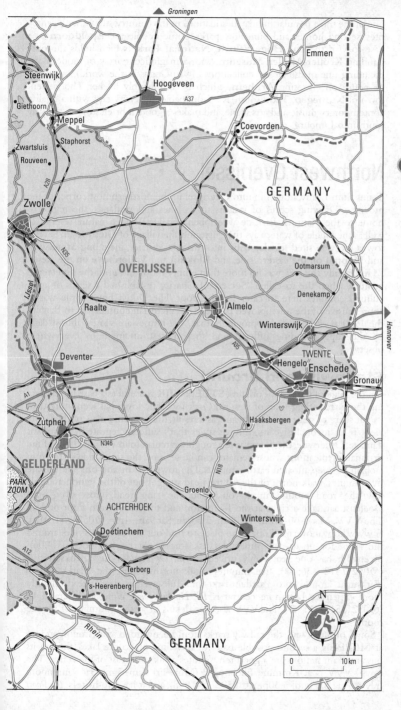

▲ Groningen

Steenwijk

Hoogeveen

A37

Giethoorn

Meppel

Emmen

Coevorden

Zwartsluis
Staphorst

Rouveen

A28

Zwolle

GERMANY

IJssel

N35

OVERIJSSEL

Ootmarsum

Raalte

Almelo

Denekamp

Winterswijk

A35

TWENTE

Deventer

Hengelo
Enschede

A1

Gronau

Zutphen

N346

Háaksbergen

GELDERLAND

PARK
ZOOM

N18

Groenlo

ACHTERHOEK

Winterswijk

Doetinchem

A12

Terborg

s-Heerenberg

Rhein

GERMANY

N

► Hannover

0        10 km

one of the most popular holiday destinations in the country, strewn with camp-sites, second homes and bungalow parks. Some people use **Apeldoorn** as a base to visit the fine **Hoge Veluwe National Park** (which holds the out-standing **Kröller-Müller Museum**, with a magnificent array of modern art, including one of the largest collections of Van Goghs in the world), but you'd be better off choosing **Arnhem**, which is considerably livelier. The ancient town of **Nijmegen**, 21km south, is a fashionable university city, with a quality contemporary music and arts scene, and makes a good, if brief, stop on the way south into Limburg.

# Northwest Overijssel

Trains from Leeuwarden slip into Overijssel in the northernmost corner of the province. Drawing scores of visitors to its lakes and wetlands, the region is home to the National Park de Weeribben and De Wieden nature reserve, as well as the tangle of waterways that surround the village of **Giethoorn**. Several towns are well sited for day trips into this lake district, including **Steenwijk** and **Meppel** on the eastern side, and **Blokzijl** and **Vollenhove** on the west.

Historically, the area was no more than empty moorland until the nineteenth century, when the so-called "Society of Charity" established a series of agri-cultural colonies here to cater for the poor. The Dutch bourgeoisie was as apprehensive of the unemployed pauper as its Victorian counterpart in Britain: the 1900 *Baedeker* noted approvingly that "the houses are visited almost daily by the superintending officials and the strictest discipline is everywhere observed".

## Steenwijk and around

On the edge of the old moorlands, **STEENWIJK** is useful as a base for explor-ing the surrounding lakes of western Overijssel. The town has seen more than its fair share of siege and assault, and, as a result, the towering mass of the Grote Kerk is an inconclusive mixture of styles that's suffered repeatedly from war damage. Otherwise, the centre is still roughly circular, following the lines of the original fortifications whose remains can be seen on the south side of town in a chain of steep, moated earth ramparts. The town's **train** and **bus** stations are five minutes' walk north of the centre; head straight out of the station and fol-low the road around until you reach the ring road, cross over onto Doelenstraat, take a right at the T-junction and the Markt is in front of you. The **VVV**, Markt 60 (Mon–Fri 9am–5.30pm, Sat 9am–4pm; ☎0521/512 010, ⓦ www.kopvanoverijssel.nl), is the place to find out about bus services around the lakes; for up-to-date timetables, ask for the Arriva bus book (€4.06). Steenwijk has one reasonably priced **hotel**, *De Gouden Engel*, Tukseweg 1 (☎0521/512 436; ❶), five minutes' walk northwest of the Markt: follow Kerkstraat around into Paardenmarkt and Tukseweg is dead ahead. Slightly more expensive but more central is *De Hiddingerberg*, Woldmeentherand 15 (☎0521/512 311; ❷). The VVV also has details of a small number of private rooms.

South of Steenwijk, the railway tracks from Leeuwarden and Groningen join at **MEPPEL**, a second possible base for travelling on to the lakes, though its bus and train stations are a good ten minutes' walk southeast of the centre. The town's VVV is at Kromme Elleboog 2 (Mon–Fri 9am–5pm, Sat 9am–noon; July & Aug Sat until 5.30pm; ☎0522/252 888), and it has two **hotels**, *De Poort* *van Drente*, Parallelweg 25 (℡0522/251 080; ❷) and *De Reisiger*, Dirk Jacobstraat 6 (℡0522/256 649, ℱ255 514; ❸). Something of a quiet backwater, the town livens up on market day each Thursday. Those with a sweet tooth might enjoy the local calorie-packed speciality, *Meppelentorengebak*, a chocolate cake featuring the Meppel tower painted in white chocolate. A cycle loop around the De Wieden nature reserve will help work it off; bikes can be rented for €5.20 a day from the Rijwiel shop next to the train station. It's an easy ten-kilometre signposted ride to the lakes of Beulakerwidje and Belterwidje, set amongst an expanse of wetlands known for their abundant birdlife, including black terns and great warblers. Equally appealing is the ride around Bovenwijde Lake to Giethoorn, some 12km away, along signposted cycleways.

Beyond Meppel lie the elongated villages of **STAPHORST** and **ROUVEEN**, tiny squares of brightly shuttered and neatly thatched farmhouses – by local custom painted in vicious shades of green and sky blue – that line some 10km of road in the shadow of the motorway. Despite significant industrial development in the last decade, both these communities still have strong and strict Calvinist traditions: most people still observe the Sabbath and many continue to wear traditional costume as a matter of course – and do not wish to be photographed.

## Giethoorn and the lakes

Meppel and Steenwijk in the east and the old seaports of Vollenhove and Blokzijl in the west rim an expanse of lake, pond, canal and river that's been formed by centuries of haphazard peat digging. Although it's a favourite holiday spot for watersports enthusiasts, public transport is limited and in any case you really miss the quiet charm of the region if you aren't travelling by **boat**. These are available for rent at the best-known and most picturesque lakeland village, **GIETHOORN**, which flanks a series of interlocking canals that lie some 200m east of the minor N334 road from Steenwijk to Zwolle – not to be confused with the modern village of the same name on the main road itself. See the box below for details of buses around the lake from Steenwijk, Meppel and Zwolle train stations; "Travel Details" on p.300 has full information. Bus #70 from Steenwijk station travels right through modern Giethoorn before reaching the VVV beyond; make sure the driver lets you off at the old village.

Giethoorn's origins are rather odd. The marshy, infertile land here was given to an obscure sect of flagellants in the thirteenth century by the lord of Vollenhove. Isolated and poor, the colonists were dependent on local peat deposits for their livelihood, though their first digs only unearthed the horns of hundreds of goats who had been the victims of prehistoric flooding, leading to the settlement being named Geytenhoren ("goats' horns"). Nowadays

---

### Buses around the lakes

**From Steenwijk train station** Bus #70 to Giethoorn (15min), Zwartsluis (30min) and Zwolle (1hr); change at Zwartsluis for connecting bus #71 to Vollenhove (20min). Also bus #75 from Steenwijk to Blokzijl (15min).

**From Meppel train station** Bus #79 to Zwartsluis (20min); change at Zwartsluis for Vollenhove, as above.

**From Zwolle train station** Bus #70 or #71 to Zwartsluis (30min) – the #71 continues to Vollenhove (50min), the #70 continues to Giethoorn (45min) and Steenwijk (1hr).

Giethoorn's postcard-prettiness of thatched houses and narrow canals criss-crossed by arching footbridges draws plenty of visitors, Dutch and German weekenders swarming into the village throughout summer to jam the busy footpaths and clog the waterways in search of some sort of northern Venice. Despite its popularity, Giethoorn still offers a peaceful escape, with its network of narrow, reed-fringed waterways perfect for waterborne exploration, shared with gangs of noisy ducks hoping for picnic leftovers.

**Water taxis** leave from pretty much everywhere and cost about €5 per hour for a trip round the village. Most of the campsites and hotels **rent boats**, in a variety of shapes and sizes, from canoes to motorboats and dinghies (and the VVV can provide details of more than a dozen other operators). Prices vary, but reckon on €10–15 per hour for a whisper boat (a quiet, environmentally friendly, electric-powered motorboat) down to €5–6 per hour for a canoe. The other alternative is to come on a **boat trip** from Kampen (see p.270): itineraries vary, but once or twice weekly from mid-July to mid-August, boats sail from Kampen to Vollenhove, Blokzijl and Giethoorn. Kampen VVV has further details.

### Giethoorn practicalities

Giethoorn's **VVV** (mid-May to mid-Sept Mon–Sat 9am–6pm, Sun 10am–5pm; mid-Sept to Oct & March to mid-May Mon–Sat 9am–5pm; Nov–March Mon–Fri 9.30am–5pm; ☏0521/361 248, ⓦwww.kopvanoverijssel .nl), based in a houseboat on Beulakerweg roughly 2km further along the N334, can book private **rooms** and **pensions** for you; clarify the exact location of the place beforehand, or you could end up walking for miles. Accommodation is very tight between June and August. Two of the more convenient hotels lie beside Giethoorn's central canal: *'t Centrum*, Ds. Hylkemaweg 39 (☏0521/361 225, ⓕ362 429; ❷; April–Oct) and *De Pergola* nearby at no. 7 (☏0521/361 321, ⓦwww.hotel-depergola.nl; ❷). Alternatives include *De Waterlelie*, Petersteeg 2 (☏0521/361 317, ⓦwww.dewaterlelie.nl; ❸), and *De Jonge*, Beulakerweg 30 (☏0521/361 360, ⓦwww.hoteldejongegiethoorn.com; ❷). On the eastern edge of old Giethoorn, Lake Bovenwijde has no fewer than six **campsites** on its western shore; the two nearest ones, at the end of the main canal, are *Botel Giethoorn*, Binnenpad 49 (☏0521/361 332, ⓦwww.botel.giethoorn.nl) and *De Kragge*, Binnenpad 113 (☏0521/361 319); both are open April to October.

For **eating**, most of the hotels have reasonable restaurants. Alternatively, you could try the *Achterhuis*, on the main canal at no. 43, or *Café Fanfare*, further east at Binnenpad 68, which has cheap daily dishes on its wide-ranging menu. **Nightlife** tends to be pretty quiet, although there are jazz and blues festivals over succeeding weekends in August.

### Zwartsluis

South of Giethoorn, bus #70 travels the length of the dyke across Lake Belterwijde before cutting down into **ZWARTSLUIS**, once the site of an important fortress at the junction of waterways from Zwolle and Meppel. There's nothing much to the place today, but a couple of minutes' walk east of the bus station, at the bottom of Dawarsstraat, off Handelskade, is a small Jewish **cemetery** with a touching memorial to those locals who died in the concentration camps.

### Vollenhove

At the bus station on the edge of Zwartsluis, you can change for the journey west to **VOLLENHOVE**, one of the most agreeable little towns in the area.

Once a maritime fortification guarding the approach to Zwolle, Vollenhove spreads out east from the Vollenhover Kanaal that marks the path of the old Zuider Zee coastline. Buses stop on Clarenberglaan, a five-minute walk away from the main square (straight up Doelenstraat), where the Onze Lieve Vrouwekerk is a confusion of towers, spires and gables. The elegant, arcaded Stadhuis is attached to the church, and, across Kerkplein, the weathered stone gateposts outside the bank were originally part of the entrance to the Latin School. Around the corner from the church is the town's charming ancient harbour, a cramped, circular affair encased in steep grass banks.

Vollenhove **VVV** (July & Aug Mon–Fri 10am–noon & 1.30–5pm, Sat 10am–noon & 2–4pm; April–June & Sept Mon–Sat 10am–noon & 1.30–4pm; Oct–March Wed 10am–noon & 2–4pm; ☎0527/241 700, ⓦwww .kopvanoverijssel.nl) is beside the harbour. It can't offer much help with accommodation, but does **rent bikes** (€5/day). There's just one **hotel**, the *Herberg*, Kerkplein 1 (☎0527/243 466, ⓦwww.de-herberg.nl; ❷). Of the two local **campsites**, the nearest is *'t Akkertien op de Voorst*, Noordwal 3 (☎0527/241 452, ⓦwww.akkertien.nl), five minutes' walk southwest of the VVV along the canal. The **restaurant** *De Vollenhof*, Kerkplein 12, serves good fish dishes and has a three-course menu. More appealing – and more expensive – is the *Seidel* restaurant in the old Stadhuis at Kerkplein 3; if you can't afford a meal, pop in for a coffee: the decor is delightfully antique.

## Blokzijl

Some 6km north of Vollenhove, **BLOKZIJL** is more beguiling still, an orange-pantiled cobweb of narrow alleys and slim canals surrounding a trim little harbour. Formerly a seaport, it now finds itself between the nature reserve of De Wieden to the south, and the National Park De Weerribben to the north, which together offer 15,000 hectares of unspoilt moorland and over 400km of waterways to explore. It's easily reached in summer by **boat** from Vollenhove and Zwartsluis, while **bus** #75 from Steenwijk (see box on p.265) drops you on the north edge of town, five minutes' walk from the harbour.

Blokzijl has scores of restored seventeenth-century houses reflecting its mercantile past; one of the grandest has been converted into the **hotel** *Kaatje bij de Sluis*, Zuiderstraat 1 (☎0527/291 833, ⓦwww.kaatje.nl; ❼), overlooking the main canal. The town is stuffed with **restaurants**: the *Kaatje bij de Sluis* hotel has the finest food for miles around, but it is expensive and its restaurant is closed all day on Monday and Tuesday and at lunchtime on Saturday. Cheaper choices for local food include the *Prins Mauritshuis* on the harbourside at Brouwerstraat 2, and basic accommodation is available through the **VVV**, Kerkstraat 9a (July & Aug Mon–Sat 9am–12.30pm & 1.30–5.30pm; April–June & Sept–Oct Mon–Sat 10am–12.30pm & 1.30–4pm; ☎0527/ 291 414, ⓦwww.kopvanoverijssel.nl), but it's wise to book in advance in season. To the northeast *Tussen de Diepen*, Duiningermeerweg 1a (☎0527/291 565, ⓦwww.tussendediepen.nl; April–Oct) offers **camping** on the water's edge, with canoes and motorboats for rent.

Blokzijl also makes a good base for exploring the surrounding countryside, in particular the **National Park De Weerribben**, a chunk of protected canal and marshland starting about 3km to the northeast of the town. The VVV can suggest cycle routes through the park, linking up with any of a number of motorboat trips. The Bezoekerscentrum, at Hoogweg 27 (Tues–Fri 10am–5pm, Sat & Sun noon–5pm), on the north edge of the park, has information on the local flora and fauna.

# Zwolle

The first major rail junction as you come from the north, **ZWOLLE** is the compact capital of Overijssel. An ancient town, it achieved passing international fame when Thomas à Kempis settled here in 1399; throughout the fifteenth century Zwolle prospered as one of the principal towns of the Hanseatic League, its burghers commissioning an extensive programme of public works designed to protect its citizens and impress their rivals. Within the city walls, German textiles were traded for Baltic fish and grain, or more exotic products from Amsterdam, like coffee, tea and tobacco. The boom lasted for some two hundred years, but by the middle of the seventeenth century the success of Amsterdam and the general movement of trade to the west had undermined its economy – a decline reflected in Zwolle's present-day status as a small market town of no particular significance.

Refortified in successive centuries, Zwolle's centre is still in the shape of a star fortress, nine roughly triangular earthen bulwarks encircling both the old town and its harbour, whose waters separate a northern sector off from the rest. The approach from the train station is particularly pleasant, as fountains play in the moat and the city walls are clearly visible behind the trees. For the ultimate citadel feeling, turn right at Burg Van Roijensingel, cross the bridge and enter via the magnificent Sassenpoort defensive portal.

## The Town

In the centre of Zwolle's Grote Markt stands the restored **Grote Kerk**, dedicated to St Michael, patron saint of the town. If the exterior seems spartan it's because the church has been dogged by ill luck. Its bell tower used to be one of the highest in the country, and was struck by lightning three times (in 1548, 1606 and 1669). After the third time it was never rebuilt and eventually the bells were sold. Inside you'll find the familiar austerity of Dutch Protestantism, with the choir bare and dusty and the seats arranged on a central pulpit plan. The pulpit itself is an intricate piece of Renaissance carving by the German Adam Straes, where the grace of Christ is emphasized by the brutal ugliness of the faces of the sinners.

Attached to the church is the **Hoofdwacht** of 1614, an ornately gabled building which once served as a guardhouse. In front was the place of public execution, the remaining inscription *Vigilate et Orate* ("Watch and Pray") a stern piece of advice to the crowds who gathered to witness these bloody spectacles. The building later housed the town's main police station.

A little way west, down an alley off the Grote Markt, the primly restored **Onze Lieve Vrouwekerk** (May–Sept Mon–Sat 10.30am–4.30pm; Oct Mon–Sat 1.30–4.30pm; Nov–April Mon–Sat 1.30–3.30pm; free; tower €0.91) is a discordant mixture of styles dating from the fifteenth century. Once again, the church has been plagued with difficulties: the original building contractor ran off with his advance payment and the tower was rebuilt after a fire in 1815 with an odd-looking turret on top, giving rise to its nickname *Peperbus* ("pepperpot"); it's climbable for the views.

From beside the Grote Kerk, Sassenstraat twists and turns its way southeast toward the old city walls. No. 33, the **Karel V Huis**, is all that's left of the mansion built for the emperor Charles V in case he decided to pay the town a visit. He never did, but then all the major cities of his empire were obliged to construct similarly grand buildings for his possible convenience. Strangely, the bas-relief medallion of Charles on the gable is dated 1571 – thirteen years after his death. At the end of the Sassenstraat, the massive **Sassenpoort** (Wed–Fri

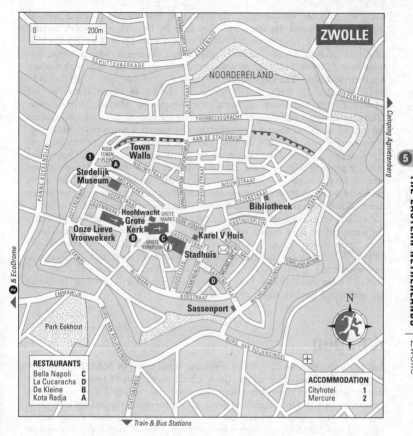

2–5pm, Sat–Sun noon–5pm; €1) is a fine example of a fifteenth-century defensive portal, complete with machicolation; it gives some idea of just how grand the medieval town must have been.

North of the Grote Markt, Roggenstraat and subsequently Vispoortenplas lead to a bridge over what was once the city harbour. On its south side much of the old **town wall** has been restored, including sections with a covered defensive parapet and a couple of fortified towers – principally the Wijndragerstoren ("wine-porters' tower"), which dates from the fourteenth century.

Fifteen minutes' walk east of the station, the **EcoDrome**, Willemsvaart 19 (April–Oct daily 10am–5pm; Nov–March Wed, Sat & Sun 10am–5pm; €7.25) is of interest, particularly for children. The park comprises a nature museum, prehistoric animal display including a 150-million-year-old Allosaurus, an aqua tunnel, butterfly garden, plus rides for kids along with exhibitions on all things ecological. Allow about two hours or so for a visit.

## Practicalities

Well connected by train to many of the Netherlands' major cities and by bus to most of Overijssel's tourist attractions, Zwolle's **train** and **bus** stations are some ten minutes' walk south of the centre on Stationsweg. If you're intending to travel around the lakes and Flevoland by bus, it's well worth buying timetables from the bus station's kiosk (Mon–Fri 8am–6pm). Zwolle's **VVV** is at Grote Kerkplein 14 (Mon 10am–5.30pm, Tues–Fri 9am–5.30pm, Sat 9am–4pm; ☏0900/112 2375, ⓦwww.vvvzwolle.nl) and can help with finding **accommodation**. The dependable *Cityhotel*, Rode Torenplein 10 (☏038/421 8182, ⓕ422 0829; ❸), is just northwest of the Grote Markt at the end of Melkmarkt. A little out of town, the functional *Mercure Hotel Zwolle*, Hertsenbergweg 1 (☏038/421 6031, ⓦwww.mercure.nl; ❹) sometimes offers cut-priced deals on rooms at weekends. The town's **campsite**, *Agnietenberg*, Haersterveerweg 22 (☏038/453 1530, ⓦwww.campingagnietenberg.nl; April–Sept), is by the River Vecht on the northeastern outskirts of town and difficult to reach without a car. Take the Meppel bus #40 from Zwolle station and ask for the campsite – you'll be let off on the east side of the bridge across the Vecht on the A28; immediately east of the bus stop, Ordelseweg goes under the A28 and leads north to the campsite, a distance of about 2km.

Zwolle is surprisingly short of interesting **places to eat**. Grote Kerkplein has the inexpensive *Bella Napoli*, offering pizzas from €7, and *De Kleine* (closed Sun), with cheap snacks available all day. The *Kota Radja*, Melkmarkt 50 (☏038/421 3534), has reasonable Chinese/Indonesian food, and *La Cucaracha*, Sassenstraat 54 (☏038/421 8172), has a standard Mexican selection. Of Zwolle's **bars**, *Het Wijnhuis* is the best bet on Grote Kerkplein, while *De Docter* at Voorstraat 3 has live music at the weekend.

# Kampen

Just ten minutes from Zwolle by train, the small town of **KAMPEN** strings along the flat flood-plain of the IJssel, a bold succession of towers and spires that, together with the other towns along the river, enjoyed a period of real prosperity in the fourteenth and fifteenth centuries. Equipped with its own fleet, Kampen enjoyed trade with the Hanse as well as their competitors, Holland and Flanders, although when war broke out between the Hanse and Holland in the mid-fifteenth century, Kampen aligned itself with the Hanseatic League. Success was short-lived, and by the late sixteenth century trade moved west and Amsterdam mopped up what was left by undercutting prices. Indeed, the IJssel towns slipped into obscurity just as Amsterdam rose to the full height of its glory. Storehouses from the Hanseatic period can still be seen on Voorstraat, while old-fashioned wall advertisements in the town centre contrast with the modern shops underneath.

## The Town

Sidelined by history, Kampen nowadays is little more than four roughly parallel streets edging the river, dotted with the remnants of the town's heyday. Orientation is very easy: the town centre is compacted between Onze Lieve Vrouwekerk and St Nicolaaskerk to the north and south, with the IJssel river and Burgel moat to the west and east. A bridge from beside the station spans the IJssel, leading directly into the centre. Clearly visible to the right of the bridge is a leaning tower with a bizarre top that resembles a hollowed-out onion, part of the Stadhuis. Just across the street is a second tower, the seventeenth-century **Nieuwe Toren**, which becomes Kampen's main attraction for one morning each year, usually in mid-July (contact the VVV for the exact date and time), when the "Kampen cow" is pulled up to its top. The story goes that when grass began growing at the top of the tower, local farmers asked if they could graze their cattle up there. To commemorate this daft request, an animal has been hoisted up the tower every year ever since, though thankfully it's now been replaced by a stuffed model.

The **Stadhuis** (Mon, Tues & Thurs 9am–12.30pm & 1.30–4pm, Fri 9am–12.30pm; free) is divided into two parts: the Oude Raadhuis was built in 1543, the Nieuwe Raadhuis added during the eighteenth century. Of the two, it's the old building which has most of interest, namely the Schepenzaal ("Magistrates' Hall"), a claustrophobic medieval affair with dark-stained walls capped by a superbly preserved barrel-vault roof. The magnificent stone chimneypiece – a grandiloquent, self-assured work – was carved by Colijn de Nole in tribute to Charles V in 1545, though the chimney's typically Renaissance representations of Justice, Prudence and Strength speak more of municipal pride than imperial glory. To the right, the magistrate's bench is the work of a more obscure local carpenter, a Master Frederik, who didn't get on with de Nole at all: angry at not getting the more important job of the chimneypiece, his legacy can be seen on the left-hand pillar, where a minute, malevolent satyr laughs maniacally at the chimney. Near the Stadhuis, the **Gotische Huis**, Oudestraat 158, is an attractive fifteenth-century merchant's house, which is also home to a collection of local bits and pieces in the **Stedelijk Museum** (Tues–Sat 11am–12.30pm & 1.30–5pm; June–Sept also Sun 1–5pm; €2.50).

Sited in a nineteenth-century cigar factory nearby, the **Kamper Tabaksmuseum**, Botemarkt 3 (April–Sept Thurs & Fri 11am–12.30pm & 1.30–5pm; €1.20), has a singular claim to fame: "The Giant", allegedly the largest cigar in the world at 278cm long, 32.4cm wide and a hefty 27.3kg. In addition, the museum displays the old-fashioned machines and paraphernalia from the heydays of Kampen's tobacco industry, as well as demonstrations of cigar making. Tobacco aficionados could also visit De Olifant, Voorstraat 104, a recently reopened tobacco factory with a wholesale shop at the rear (accessed from Oudestraat).

In the other direction, Oudestraat leads directly south to the St Nicolaaskerk, or **Bovenkerk** (May to mid-Sept Tues 1–4.30pm, Wed–Fri 10am–4.30pm; rest of year Tues–Fri 1–4pm; free), a lovely Gothic church with a light, spacious sandstone interior. Generally regarded as one of the most important Dutch medieval churches, its choir – with thirteen radiating chapels – was the work of Rotger of Cologne, a member of the Parler family of masons who worked on Cologne Cathedral. In the south transept an urn contains the heart of Admiral de Winter, a native of Kampen who fought to rid his country of what he considered to be the yoke of the House of Orange. A staunch Republican, he took part in the successful French invasion of 1795 that created the Batavian Republic; the rest of him lies in the Pantheon in Paris. Beside the Bovenkerk is the earliest of Kampen's three surviving gates, the fourteenth-century **Koornmarktpoort**. The others – the **Cellebroederspoort** and the **Broederpoort** – are of a later, more ornamental design and lie on the west side of town along Ebbingestraat, reached from the Bovenkerk via Schoolstraat.

## Practicalities

It takes ten minutes by train from Zwolle to reach Kampen **station**, five minutes' walk from the town centre. Finding somewhere to stay can be difficult as the town has only one **hotel** – the riverside *Van Dijk*, IJsselkade 30 (☎038/331 4925, ℱ331 6508; ❷) – and it's often full in high season. The nearest **campsite** is the *Seveningen* (April–Sept; ☎038/331 4891) some 3km northeast of town at Frieseweg 7: heading out of Kampen, cross the bridge and turn left, then follow the main road around until it crosses the Ganzendiep canal and the campsite is just beyond – watch out for signs. The *Roggebotsluis* site (☎038/331 7351; April–Sept) is 4km out of town towards Dronten, next to the yacht harbour at Reeveweg 1. The Kampen **VVV**, on the main street at Oudestraat 151 (Mon–Fri 9am–5.30pm, Sat 9am–4pm; ☎038/331 3500, Ⓦwww.vvvkampen .nl), has a very short list of private rooms.

If you do manage to get fixed up, Kampen makes a good base for **day-trips** into Flevoland and the Noord-Oost Polder. Throughout July and August **boat trips** from Kampen explore the surrounding waterways; prices vary according to the itinerary, and you can get up-to-date schedules, and book, at the VVV. Alternatively, you can, as always, **rent bikes** from the train station or from Potkamp, Oudestraat 152 (☎038/331 3495; €5/day). For **food**, there's pancakes and snacks at *'t Trappetje*, Oudestraat 25, Chinese/Indonesian meals at *Kota Radja*, Oudestraat 119, or the fish and Dutch specialities of *D'Olde Vismark*, IJsselkade 45. **Concerts** are held in the Bovenkerk on Saturday afternoons in July and August at 3pm (€5).

# Elburg

Half an hour southwest of Zwolle by bus, just across the provincial boundary in Gelderland, the tiny coastal town of **ELBURG** once looked out across the Zuider Zee, whose perimeter is now marked by the path of the Veluwemeer as it snakes its way between the mainland and the polders of Flevoland. These days the town is one of the most popular day-trip destinations in this part of the Netherlands, awash with visitors throughout the season, here to enjoy the seaside flavour and to tour the homeopathic gardens on the outskirts. Famous too is the local delicacy of smoked eel, a tradition from the days when eels were native to these waters, before the IJssel was dammed.

Elburg was a successful port with its own fishing fleet from as early as the thirteenth century. However, in 1392 the governor, a certain Arent thoe Boecop, moved the whole town inland as a precaution against flooding. Familiar with the latest developments in town planning, Boecop and his overlord, the count of Zutphen, laid out the new town as a grid, encircled by a protective wall and moat. Not all of Elburg's citizens were overly impressed – indeed the street by the museum is still called Ledigestede, literally "Empty Way" – but the basic design, with the notable addition of sixteenth-century ramparts and gun emplacements, survived the decline that set in when the harbour silted up, and can still be observed today. Elburg's two main streets are Beekstraat, which forms the north–south axis and Jufferenstraat/Vischpoortstraat, which runs east–west; they intersect at right angles to form the main square, the Vischmarkt. All of Elburg's streets radiate from one or the other.

Buses drop you just outside the old town, a couple of minutes' walk from the **Gemeentemuseum**, Jufferenstraat 6–8 (Tues–Fri 10am–noon & 2–5pm; April–Sept also Mon 2–5pm; joint ticket including Vischpoort & Kazematten €2), housed in an old convent, with period rooms and objects of local interest. Heading north across Jufferenstraat, the **St Nicolaaskerk** (June–Aug Mon–Fri 2–4.30pm, Tues also 10am–noon; tower €0.75) dominates the landscape, even without its spire, which was destroyed by lightning in 1693. West of the church, down Van Kinsbergenstraat, is the old **Stadhuis**, which once served as Boecop's home. At the end of Van Kinsbergenstraat, turn left into Beekstraat for the town's main square, the Vischmarkt, from where Vischpoortstraat leads straight to the best preserved of the medieval town gates, the **Vischpoort**, a much restored brick rampart tower dating from 1594. Inside there's a modest exhibition on the local fishing industry (April–Sept Mon 2–4.30pm, Tues–Fri 10am–noon & 1–4.30pm; joint ticket as above).

Outside the gate, the pattern of the sixteenth-century defensive works is clear to see – from interior town wall, to dry ditch, to earthen mound and moat. The interior of one of the subterranean artillery **Kazematten** (Casements) is open in summer (mid-June to Aug Mon 2–5pm, Tues–Fri 10am–5pm; joint ticket as above). Cramped and poorly ventilated, it's easy to see why the Dutch called such emplacements Moortkuijl, literally "Pits of Murder". From the Kazematten, a stroll right around the ramparts takes about an hour.

Ten minutes' walk northwest from the Vischpoort – turn right along Havenkade and take the second left – lie the **Alfred Vogel Tuinen** (Homeopathic Gardens; April–Oct Mon–Fri 10am–5pm; June–Aug also Sat 10am–5pm; €2.50), six hectares of land that hold a comprehensive collection of homeopathic plants. The Bezoekerscentrum (visitors' centre), at Industriestraat 15, has a variety of illustrative displays and a mock-up of an old chemist's, but it's all in Dutch and the surrounding gardens are of far more interest. They form part of a successful business and are Elburg's main tourist attraction; in the summer, subject to demand, there are free two-hour guided tours, starting from the visitors' centre. It's easy to tag onto any of the groups visiting the gardens, although you may want to call ahead (℡0525/687 373) to enquire about times for tours in English.

## Practicalities

From Zwolle, **bus** #100 heads to Elburg in 35 minutes. The nearest **train station** to Elburg is 8km southeast at 't Harde, on the Zwolle–Amersfoort line, but as bus connections are poor, a better option is to get the train to the larger town of Nunspeet and pick up bus #100 on its return routing towards Zwolle (20min).

Elburg's **VVV** is around the corner from the Gemeentemuseum at Ledigestede 31 (May–Aug Mon–Fri 9am–5pm & Sat 10am–4pm; Sept–April Mon noon–5pm, Tues–Fri 9am–5pm, Sat noon–4pm; ℡0525/681 520, Ⓦwww.vvvelburg.nl). It has a list of private rooms and will phone around to make a booking; try to get a room in the old centre and come early in the day in high season, when accommodation is tight. The one **hotel**, Elburg, Smedestraat 5 (℡0525/683 877, ℻683 549; ❸) is just off Beekstraat on the southwest side of the centre. The nearest **campsite** is Old Putten, Zuiderzeestraatweg 65 (℡0525/681 938; April–Oct), some 500m east of the VVV; head out of the old town along Zwolseweg and take the first turn on the right.

Of Elburg's many **restaurants** it's difficult to find any of real note. However, 't Olde Regthuys, Beekstraat 33, serves a reasonable range of fish dishes beneath fishing nets and models of ships suspended above; da Pietro, Vischpoorstraat 20, has good pizzas starting at €10; and de Tapperij at the Hotel Elburg has dagschotels for €12. Elburg's local speciality – for a change from rollmops – is paling, a smoked eel in a jelly casing available at any number of pavement stalls. It's sold by weight – a pond is 500g – working out at roughly €2 per eel. Should you have a thirst to slake, the Beekzicht, Beekstraat 39, has a broad selection of beers.

For **boat trips**, there are hour-long excursions from Elburg around the Veluwemeer throughout the summer (€4 per person). There are also day-trips to Urk (July & Aug 4 weekly) and occasional sailings to Ketelmeer and Harderwijk, among other destinations. It's also possible to rent a traditional wooden fishing boat for the day (from €110 for 1hr 30min, maximum 12 people). The VVV has the latest details and will make bookings on your behalf.

The strip of coast on both sides of the Veluwemeer around Elburg is popular with Dutch holidaymakers for its watersports, nature reserves and forests. The whole region is dotted with campsites and the best way to explore it all is by bike. You can **rent bikes** and tandems in Elburg at De Oosthoek, Vackenordestraat 3 (℡0525/683 957; €5 per day). The VVV has a comprehensive range of suggested cycle routes.

# Flevoland

The damming of the Zuider Zee and the creation of the IJsselmeer (see box on p.138) transformed the coastline north and west of Kampen and Elburg, creating two new polder areas, the **Oostelijk** and **Zuidelijk Flevoland** polders, which form an island of reclaimed land in front of the old shoreline and make up the greater part of Holland's twelfth and newest province – **FLEVOLAND**. To the north, the reclaimed land mass of the **Noord-Oost Polder** forms the rest of the new province, the small towns that mark the line of the old coast – Vollenhove, Blokzijl and Kuinre – cut off from open water and now marking the provincial boundary between Flevoland and Overijssel.

## The Noord-Oost Polder

The **Noord-Oost Polder** was the first major piece of land to be reclaimed as part of the Zuider Zee reclamation scheme (see p.138), which began in earnest with the Zuider Zee Reclamation Act of 1918. The key to the project was the completion of the Afsluitdijk between Den Oever in North Holland and Zurich in Friesland in 1932, which separated the Zuider Zee from the open sea, thereby changing it from brine into the freshwater IJsselmeer lake. The draining of the polder was completed in 1936: once dried out, it provided 119,000 acres of new agricultural pasture, which the government handed out under an incentive scheme to prospective settlers. The original aims of the project were predominantly agricultural and (unlike later polders) little consideration was given to the needs of the settlers, with the result that most of the Noord-Oost Polder is an unimaginably boring landscape (the only town of any size, **Emmeloord**, is like a vast housing development) and it's no surprise that, even with the incentives, there were difficulties in attracting settlers. Also, a number of design faults soon became apparent. Without enough trees, the land was subject to soil erosion, and the lack of an encircling waterway meant the surrounding mainland also dried out and began to sink – problems that have persisted until the present day.

The only appeal is its startlingly artificial feel. Even a map of the polder looks like a circuit diagram, with dead straight roads kinking off at 45-degree angles every few kilometres, and trees planted with almost mathematical precision. While on a rainy day the effect is all the more depressing, the sunsets on a clear evening can be breathtaking, a 360-degree panorama of sky broken only by banks of wind turbines spinning in the distance.

## Schokland Museum

The Noord-Oost Polder incorporates the former Zuider Zee islands of Urk and Schokland, which in Roman times were connected as one. Schokland, however, was abandoned in the nineteenth century because of the threat of flooding and only the church of 1834 has survived, converted into the **Schokland Museum** (April–Nov Tues–Sun 11am–5pm; July & Aug also Mon 11am–5pm; rest of year Sat & Sun 11am–5pm; €2.30; Ⓦ www.natuurlijkseholland .nl), with displays of all sorts of bits and pieces found during the draining of the polders. From beside the museum, a circular foot- and cycle-path follows the old shoreline of the island, a distance of about 10km.

It's an awkward journey without a car: the museum is 400m south of the minor road between Ens and Nagele/Urk, some 3km west of Ens. Buses from Zwolle or Kampen go to Ens bus station, from where you're better off walking the 3km as the connecting bus on its way to Urk is infrequent.

## Urk

The only place really worth a visit in the Noord-Oost Polder is **URK**, a trim harbour and fishing port, formerly an island, that was a reluctant addition to the mainland. Centuries of hardship and isolation bred a tight-knit island fishing community here, with its own distinctive dialect and version of the national costume – aspects that have inevitably become diluted by connection to the mainland. However, the island's earlier independence does to some extent live on, rooted in a fishing industry which marks it out from the surrounding agricultural communities. **Buses** run to Urk from Kampen and Zwolle; ask the driver to drop you off at the stop nearest the centre. In July and August, **ferries** (Mon–Sat) shuttle across the IJsselmeer between Enkhuizen and Urk two or three times a day, taking around ninety minutes – check with any VVV for times and prices. Ferries no longer run to Lelystad, as is suggested on some maps.

There's nothing spectacular about Urk but its setting is attractive, its waterfront a pleasant mixture of the functional and the ornamental; a series of narrow lanes of tiny terraced houses indicate the extent of the old village, with a

### Urk irked

The damming of the Zuider Zee (see box on p.138) posed special problems for the islanders of Urk and it's hardly surprising that they opposed the IJsselmeer scheme from the beginning. Some feared that when the Noord-Oost Polder was drained they would simply be overwhelmed by new settlers, but their biggest concern was that their fishing fleet would lose direct access to the North Sea. After futile negotiations at national level, the islanders decided to take matters into their own hands: the larger ships of the fleet were sent north to fish from ports above the line of the Afsluitdijk, particularly Delfzijl, and transport was organized to transfer the catch straight back for sale at the Urk fish auctions. In the meantime, other fishermen decided to continue to fish locally and adapt to the freshwater species of the IJsselmeer. These were not comfortable changes for the islanders and the whole situation deteriorated when the Dutch government passed new legislation banning trawling in the IJsselmeer in 1970. When the inspectors arrived in Urk to enforce the ban, years of resentment exploded in ugly scenes of dockside violence and the government moved fast to sweeten the pill by offering substantial subsidies to compensate those fishermen affected. This arrangement continues today and the focus of conflict has moved to the attempt to impose EU quotas on the catch of the deep-sea fleet.

busy little port of working shipyards where you can watch the boats being repaired. A surprising number of the islanders still wear traditional costume, further examples of which are on display in the **Museum Het Oude Raadhuis**, Wijk 2, no. 2 (April–Oct Mon–Sat 10am–5pm; €2.25).

Adjoining the museum, Urk's **VVV** (April–Oct Mon–Fri 10am–5pm, Sat 10am–1pm; Nov–March Mon–Fri 10am–4pm; ℡0527/684 040), will help arrange **accommodation**. There are several cheap pensions near the harbour: *De Kroon*, Wijk 7, no. 54 (℡0527/681 216; ❷), *De Kaap*, Wijk 1, no. 5 (℡0527/681 509; ❷) and the unnamed pension of *Mw. J. Bakker*, Wijk 3, no. 76 (℡0527/682 363; ❶). The nearest **campsite** is the enormous *Hozevreugd*, Wormtweg 9 (℡0527/681 785; April–Oct), in the woods some 4km north of Urk along the coastal road.

Urk is a great place to eat **fresh fish**: *De Kaap* (see above), does good lunch specials and all-you-can-eat deals in the evening and has fine views over the IJsselmeer from its window tables; there are also plenty of affordable snack bars along Raadhuisstraat, as well as the more expensive *De Zeebodem*, by the harbour at Wijk 1, no. 67. With its fish processing factories, Urk is also the **rollmop** capital of the Netherlands; fresh herrings washed down with onion chasers are only €1 apiece.

If you feel like a breath of fresh air, follow the 5km **walk** north along the dyke to one of the area's wind farms: fifty perfectly aligned wind turbines stretch over 6km in distance, well sited to catch the stiff breeze for which the polder is known. It's a strange experience to stand in the midst of them, listening to the hypnotic swoosh of their blades.

## The Flevoland polders

The Dutch learned from their mistakes on the Noord-Oost Polder when, in the 1950s and 1960s, they drained the two polders that make up the western portion of the province of Flevoland, ringing the new land with a water channel to stop the surrounding land drying out and sinking. The government also tried hard to make these polders attractive – they're fringed by trees and watersports facilities – but it remains an uphill struggle and people have moved here reluctantly, only persuaded by very cheap housing. **Lelystad**, along with the other new town of Almere, 25km to the west, is where most of them end up, and it's to Lelystad, if anywhere, that you're likely to come, as a handful of attractions on its outer edge repay a short visit.

### Lelystad

Home to some of Amsterdam's most poorly paid workers, the town of **LELYSTAD** is a largely characterless expanse of glass and concrete surrounded by leafy suburbs. It takes its name from the pioneer engineer who had the original idea for the Zuider Zee scheme, but is something of a disaster. Far removed from the organic centres of many Dutch towns, Lelystad is the epitome of 1960s and early 1970s urban design. Approaching by car or bike, the landscape starts to repeat itself – a main road below, a flyover above, a canal and a bridge – in every direction, making for the most extraordinary city map in the Netherlands. Within this maze, a series of cul-de-sacs radiate from the centre, each designed in a distinct architectural style with bizarre cuboids, wooden A-frames and even coloured streets. Lelystad is well served by trains from Amsterdam CS, and bus #143 from Kampen.

On the outskirts of town, **Batavia Werf**, Oostvaardersdijk 1–9 (daily 10am–5pm; joint ticket with Nationaal Scheepshistorisch Centrum €8;

## Energy from the wind

Strung along the shores of the IJsselmeer, and propping up many rural horizons, **wind turbines** dot the modern Dutch landscape from Friesland to Zeeland. In the countryside, solitary turbines provide electricity for farmers, while on the coast and out to sea, banks of turbines harness the incoming weather systems, providing electricity for thousands of households.

The heyday of the windmill was in seventeenth-century Holland, when gangs of them were used to grind grain, pump water, saw wood and manufacture paper. By the nineteenth century there were around 12,000 examples throughout the country, but their place in industry was usurped by the steam engine, and they were all but forgotten in the Industrial Revolution. The first wind turbines provided electricity in the 1930s for remote communities across the great plains of the US and in the Australian outback. Their full potential wasn't realized until research into cleaner forms of energy, carried out in Denmark and Germany during the 1970s, produced mechanisms that were more efficient and more powerful. Ideally suited to the flat, windswept polders of the Netherlands, the first Dutch turbines generated 40 kilowatts of electricity. Output is now a beefier 600 kilowatts – enough for a single wind farm of 50 turbines to provide power to 6500 households.

ⓦ www.bataviawerf.nl), is a working yard for traditional shipbuilding. Its principal attraction is the 56-metre *Batavia*, a reconstruction of a merchant ship – one of the largest of its time – built in 1628 for the Dutch East India Company to bring home exotic cargo from Holland's new colonies in Asia. Heavily armed and loaded with 341 crew and passengers, many of them soldiers employed by the company to ward off pirates, the original *Batavia* sank on its maiden voyage off the west coast of Australia. The reconstruction project began in 1985, but because of the traditional materials and methods used, it was not until 1995 that the new Batavia was officially launched by Queen Beatrix. In 1999 she left for a two-year holiday outside the National Maritime Museum in Sydney, returning here to her home port in 2001. From Lelystad station, bus #9 and #150 run to Batavia Werf (15min), in the absence of which you'll have to pay €3.50 for the train-taxi, cough up €10 for a conventional taxi, or hike the 5km on foot.

You're free to clamber all over the ship at will. The **hold**, down below, has mountains of space for the anticipated freight of wine, coffee, wood and spices, while the **orlop deck** above demonstrates the suffocatingly cramped living space of the soldiers, in stark contrast with the comfortably proportioned quarters of the captain and officers. Up on the **gundeck**, replicas of the *Batavia's* 32 cannon were cast in moulds created to the design of the seventeenth-century originals. Throughout, it's the attention to detail that really catches the eye, particularly in the late-Renaissance style carving, from the bright-red Dutch lion figurehead to the golden heroes on the stern – William of Orange alongside Julius Civilis, leader of the Batavians in their revolt against the Romans in 69 AD. Once you've finished on board, you can check out the latest work-in-progress, a reconstruction of the man-o'-war *The Seven Provinces*, the seventeenth-century flagship of Admiral Michiel Adriaensz De Ruyter. A lack of funding and shipwrights brought construction to a halt in 2001, and although work has recently recommenced, it looks unlikely to make the original completion date of 2005.

While you're in the area there are a few good museums worth catching. **The Nieuw Land Poldermuseum**, opposite Batavia Werf at Oostvaardersdijk

1–13 (Mon–Fri 10am–5pm, Sat & Sun 11.30am–5pm; €4.30), is the country's definitive museum on land reclamation. It gives the background on the Zuider Zee plan, and uses photos, old maps, models, historical film footage and interactive computer programmes to illustrate the ongoing struggle with the sea. There's a free leaflet in English. The excellent **Nationaal Scheepshistorisch Centrum**, Oostvaardersdijk 1–4 (National Centre for Maritime History; same hours and ticket as Batavia Werf) has a collection of material retrieved from the extraordinary number of ships that foundered in the treacherous shallows of the Zuider Zee. The museum's centrepiece is the hull of a thirty-metre early seventeenth-century merchant ship, while the contents of the *Lutina*, which went down with its two-man crew in a storm in 1888, are touching in their simplicity – a cargo of clay pipes from Gouda, silver coins and sundry personal effects. You can also watch the archeologists working on the conservation of the wrecks and artefacts. Five minutes' walk back up the main road is the worthwhile **Nederlands Sportsmuseum Olympion**, Museumweg 10 (Tues–Fri 10am–5pm, Sat & Sun noon–5pm; €4.50). Photographs and exhibits cover every sport the Dutch have ever been involved in, and interactive displays let you test your skill at fencing and other events.

You probably won't want to spend the night in Lelystad but, if you have to, consult with the **VVV**, opposite the station at Stationsplein 186 (Mon–Fri 9am–5pm, Sat 9am–3pm; Sept–March Sat closes 1pm; ☏0320/243 444, ⓦwww.vvvflevoland.nl).

# Twente

Southeast of Zwolle, the flat landscape is replaced by the lightly undulating, wooded countryside of **Twente**, an industrial region within the province of Overijssel whose principal towns – **Almelo**, **Hengelo** and **Enschede** – were once dependent on the textile industry. Hit hard by cheap East Asian imports, they have been forced to diversify their industrial base with mixed success: the largest town, Enschede, still has a serious unemployment problem.

## Enschede

If you visit anywhere in Twente it should really be the university town of **ENSCHEDE**. Laid waste by fire in 1862, it has a desultory modern centre that's been refashioned as a large shopping precinct, but it's a lively place, with regular festivals and exhibitions as well as a museum with an excellent collection of Dutch art and some interesting 1930s architecture. All in all it's a worthwhile detour if you're heading east.

Five minutes' walk south of the train station, **Langestraat** is Enschede's main street. At its northern end, **Markt** is the town's main square, home to the nineteenth-century **Grote Kerk** (July & Aug Sat 2–4pm) in the middle, with its Romanesque tower, and the **St Jacobuskerk** across the way, completed in 1933 on the site of a previous church that burned down in 1862. The severe rectangular shape of the St Jacobuskerk is punctured by angular copper-green roofs, huge circular windows and a series of Gothic arches; it's built in a beautiful domed and cloistered neo-Byzantine style, with some good modern sculpture and stained glass. The **Stadhuis**, a couple of minutes away down Langestraat, was finished in the same year and is also something of an architectural landmark, its brown brick tower topped by four eye-catching blue and gold clocks. No expense was spared in its construction and the interior is richly decorated with mosaics and, again, stained glass.

From beside the Stadhuis, it's a ten-minute walk southwest to the **Museum Jannink** (Tues–Fri 10am–5pm, Sat & Sun 1–5pm; €2), at the junction of Haaksbergerstaat and Industriestraat (head straight down Van Loenshof, turn right at Boulevard 1945 and take the first left), housed in a former mill and devoted to portraying everyday life in Twente from the nineteenth century onward. The most intriguing displays are a series of representative living rooms and a bewildering variety of looms reflecting the development of the textile industry from its origins as a cottage industry to large-scale factory production. The **Natuurmuseum**, De Ruyterlaan 2 (Tues–Fri 10am–5pm, Sat & Sun 1–5pm; €2), is also worth a quick look: there's a vivarium on the second floor, some well-presented fossils on the first floor and a mineralogy section in the basement. It's a five-minute walk from the station; turn right on exiting and then down the first major road on the left.

## Rijksmuseum Twente

Fifteen minutes' walk north of the centre at Lasondersingel 129 – over the railway tracks at the crossing beside the station, first right, second left and follow the road to the end – is the **Rijksmuseum Twente** (Tues–Sun 11am–5pm; €4), housed in an Art Deco mansion of 1929, the gift to the nation of a family of mill owners, the Van Heeks, who used the profits they made from their workers to build up one of the eastern Netherlands' finest art collections. The museum contains three main sections: fifteenth- to nineteenth-century art, modern art (primarily Dutch, with the emphasis on Expressionism), and applied art, based on exhibits from the region of Twente – prehistoric and medieval artefacts, tiles and porcelain, tapestries and a reconstructed farm.

It's the **paintings** that provide the most interest, especially the Dutch and Flemish sections. Among a fine sample of early religious art are seven brilliant blue and gold fragments from a French hand-illuminated missal; a primitive twelfth-century wood carving, *Christ on Palm Sunday*; a delightful cartoon strip of contemporary life entitled *De Zeven Werken van Barmhartigheid* ("The Seven Acts of Charity"); and an extraordinary pair of fifteenth-century altar doors by one Tilman van der Burch, where a deep carved relief of a pastoral scene resembles a modern pop-up book. Of later canvases, Hans Holbein's *Portrait of Richard Mabott* is typical of his work, the stark black of the subject's gown offset by the white cross on his chest and the face so finely observed it's possible to make out the line of his stubble. Pieter Brueghel the Younger's *Winter Landscape* is also fastidiously drawn, down to the last twig, and contrasts with the more loosely contoured bent figures and threatening clouds of his brother Jan's *Landscape*. Lucas Cranach's studies of a bloated *Frederick Grootmoedige* and the spectacularly ugly *Barbara van Saksen* must have done little for the self-confidence of their subjects. Jan Steen's *The Alchemist* is all scurrilous satire, from the skull on the chimneypiece to the lizard suspended from the ceiling and the ogre's whispered advice, and compares with the bulging breasts and flushed countenance of the woman in his *Flute Player*, where the promise of forthcoming sex is emphasized by the vague outline of tussling lovers on the wall in the background.

The modern section, too, has a few highlights: Monet's volatile *Falaises près de Pourville*; a characteristically unsettling canvas by Carel Willink, *The Actress Ank van der Moer*; and examples of the work of less well-known Dutch modernists like Theo Kuypers, Jan Roeland and Emo Verkerk.

## Practicalities

Enschede's most central **accommodation** is the *Amadeus*, Oldenzaalsestraat 103 (℡053/435 7486, ℻430 4383; ❸). Alternatively, the *Parkhotel*, Hengelosestraat 200 (℡053/435 3855, ℻433 0155; ❷) and the *Rodenbach*, Parkweg 39 (℡053/480 0200, ℻433 0155; ❷), are a short walk out of the city centre. The **VVV**, in the centre of town at Oude Markt 31 (Mon 10am–5.30pm, Tues–Fri 9am–5.30pm, Sat 9am–4pm; ℡053/432 3200, ⓦwww.vvvenschede.nl), has details of a limited number of private rooms.

For **food**, stick to the Markt and the streets around. *Crash*, Markt 6, and *Eetcafe Sam Sam* by the Grote Kerk both have good daily specials; popular bars nearby include *De Kater* and *De Geus*. There's also a friendly bar and a varied menu at the *Twentse Schouwberg*, the town's principal venue for plays, dance, films and occasional live music, located around the corner from the St Jacobuskerk on Langestraat. Watch out for the blue figurines scaling its exterior and hanging off the eaves.

# Around Enschede

Some 10km northwest of Enschede, **HENGELO** has about eighty thousand inhabitants and is Twente's second town, a grim place whose old centre was destroyed during World War II. **ALMELO**, a further 17km northwest, is the region's third-largest town, but also has few attractions: the only buildings of any real interest are the centrally sited Waag, whose stepped gables date, surprisingly enough, from 1914, and, in a park east of the Marktplein, the stately seventeenth-century mansion Huize Almelo (no public access).

North of Enschede things pick up a little with **OLDENZAAL**, the most agreeable of Twente's other settlements. Founded by the Franks, it was a medieval city of some importance and it was from here, too, that Overijssel's textile industry began its rapid nineteenth-century expansion, spurred on by the introduction of the power loom by Englishman Thomas Ainsworth. The town's principal sight, the **St Plechelmusbasiliek** (June–Aug Tues & Thurs 2–3pm, Wed 2–4pm; free), is right in the centre, an impressive, essentially Romanesque edifice dating from the thirteenth century. Named after St Plechelm, the Irish missionary who brought Christianity here, the interior (visits organized by the VVV) is an exercise in simplicity – strong, sturdy pillars supporting a succession of low semicircular arches. Above, the bell tower is the largest in Europe with a carillon of no less than 46 bells.

From Enschede, **bus** #60 goes direct to Oldenzaal; by **train**, you must change at Hengelo. Oldenzaal's **train station** is ten minutes' walk south of the centre – head down Stationsplein, turn right at the end onto Haerstraat and first left along Wilhelminastraat. The central **VVV**, St Plechelmusplein 5 (Mon–Fri 9am–5pm, Sat 10am–4pm; ℡0541/514 023, ⓦwww.vvvoldenzaal.nl), has information on private rooms. There are several **hotels**, including *De Kroon*, Steenstraat 17 (℡0541/512 402; ❸), and the central *Herberg de Gulden Kroes*, Marktstraat 1 (℡0541/512 102; ❸). Markt is lined with **bars** and **restaurants** that liven up dramatically on weekend evenings: the best is *De Engel*, Markt 14; *Las Carretas* at no. 21 has a three-course Mexican blow out for €23.

Oldenzaal is a good base for visiting the wooded countryside that gently undulates northeast to the German border. This is a holiday area, littered with campsites, summer cottages, and bungalow parks, and is a popular cycling destination: three-geared **bikes** can be rented for €8 a day from B.J. Siemerink, Steenstraat 18 (closed Sun & Mon). From the VVV, follow the signs for the Springendalroute, a 48-kilometre signposted loop that takes in heathland and forest.

The village of **OOTMARSUM** (bus #64) is noted for its half-timbered houses and quaint Markt. The VVV at Markt 1 (May–Oct Mon–Fri 9am–5pm, Sat 10am–1.30pm, Sun 1.30–4pm; July & Aug same hours, Sat 10am–12.30pm & 1–4pm; Nov–April Mon–Fri 10am–12.30pm & 1–4pm, Sat 10am–1.30pm, Sun 1.30–4pm; ☎0900/202 1981) can help with accommodation.

By comparison, **DENEKAMP** (bus #52) is rather drab, though the elegant classicism of the Kasteel Singraven, some 2km west of the centre, partly makes up for it. Details of guided tours around the castle (mid-April to Oct) are available from the Denekamp VVV, Kerkplein 2 (May–Aug Mon 1.30–5pm, Tues–Fri 9am–12.30pm & 1.30–5pm; July & August also Sat 10am–1pm; Sept–April Mon 1.30–4pm, Tues–Fri 10am–12.30pm & 1.30–4pm; ☎0541/351 205, ⓦwww.vvv-denekamp.demon.nl). While you're up at the castle, look out for the watermill on the banks of the river, built in 1448 and still functioning.

# Deventer and Zutphen

South of Zwolle, the River IJssel marks out the boundary between Overijssel and Gelderland. Twisting its way through flat, fertile farmland and fringed with weeping willows, the river makes a welcome change from the regimented canals synonymous with the Dutch polders. For two hundred years the towns of the lower IJssel, **Deventer** and **Zutphen**, shared with Zwolle and Kampen a period of tremendous prosperity at the junction of trade routes from Germany, the Baltic and Amsterdam. Although both towns suffered grievously during the wars with Spain, the underlying reasons for their subsequent decline were economic: they could do little to stop the movement of trade to the west and could not compete with the great cities of South Holland. By the eighteenth century, they had slipped into provincial insignificance.

## Deventer

Only 25 minutes by train from Zwolle, **DEVENTER** sits calmly on the banks of the IJssel, an intriguing and – in tourist terms – rather neglected place, whose origins can be traced to the missionary work of the eighth-century Saxon monk, Lebuinus. An influential centre of medieval learning, it was here in the late fourteenth century that Gerrit Groot founded the Brotherhood of Common Life, a semi-monastic collective that espoused tolerance and humanism within a philosophy known as *Moderne Devotie* ("modern devotion"). This progressive creed attracted some of the great minds of the time, and Thomas à Kempis and Erasmus both studied here. Appropriately, on the first Sunday of August, Deventer is the venue for the biggest book market held in Europe.

Five minutes from the train station, the centre of town is **Brink**, a vast, cobbled marketplace that runs roughly north to south. Traffic-free and lined with pavement cafés, it divides the old town in two. The **Waag** edges the southern end of the elongated square, a late-Gothic edifice (undergoing restoration until 2004) that retains an ancient dignity despite its somewhat rickety appearance. Inside, a small **museum** (Tues–Sat 10am–5pm, Sun 1–5pm; joint ticket including Speelgoed en Blikmuseum €2.30) has a thin collection of portrait paintings and a few antique bicycles. More intriguing is the large pan that's nailed to the outside of the Waag's western wall. Apparently, the mintmaster's assistant was found making a tidy profit by debasing the town's coins, so he was put in the pan and boiled alive. The bullet holes weren't an attempt to prolong the

> ### Cycling along the IJssel
>
> Crossing the Wilhelminabrug in Deventer, a signposted **cycleway** follows the banks of the IJssel 20km south to Zutphen. It's a gentle ride through farmland and along quiet, winding lanes. With plenty of places to stop for a picnic, there are some fine views of the river and weeping willows that thrive along its banks. Once in Zutphen, the return journey can either be made on the opposite shore, bringing the total distance to around 45km, or direct by train. You can rent bikes for the day from the Rijwiel shop in Deventer train station.

agony, but the work of idle French soldiers taking, quite literally, "pot shots". Behind the Waag, the **Speelgoed en Blikmuseum** (Toy and Tin Museum; Tues–Sat 10am–5pm, Sun 1–5pm; €2.30, including Waag musuem) specializes in mechanical dolls.

Walking west from here, Assenstraat's **window cuts** were completed in the early 1980s by a local artist, J. Limburg. Precise and entertaining, each illustrates a particular proverb or belief: at no. 119 the hedgehog's inscription translates as "Thrift yields big revenues" and at no. 81, on a house called *Gevaarlijke Stoffen* ("Dangerous Materials"), a totem pole is surrounded by slogans including *E pericolose sporcare* ("It's dangerous to pollute"). Continuing to the west along Assenstraat and veering left down Grote Poot ("Big Leg"), the **Lebuïnuskerk** (Mon–Sat 1pm–5pm; €1.25) is one of the most impressive Gothic buildings in the east of the country and is an expression of Deventer's fifteenth-century wealth and self-confidence. Carefully symmetrical, the massive nave is supported by seven flying buttresses, trimmed by an ornate stone parapet. The interior has been restored and today the expanse of white stone is startling, high arched windows and slender pillars reaching up toward a distant timber roof. Below, the church has two magnificent Baroque organs, the delicate remnants of some medieval murals and an eleventh-century crypt with a simple vaulted roof supported by Romanesque spiral columns. The rear of the Lebuïnuskerk is joined to the fourteenth-century **Mariakerk**. Services haven't been held here since 1591 and the town council considered demolishing it as early as 1600, but in the event it survived as the town's arsenal and now houses a smart restaurant.

Back at Brink, east of the Waag, Rijkmanstraat takes you into the **Bergkwartier**, an area of fairly ancient housing that was tastefully refurbished during the 1960s, one of the Netherlands' first urban renewal projects. Turning left onto Kerksteeg, there's a small piece of iron, the remnants of a ring, embedded in a hole on the right-hand wall: the 1570s were desperate times for the inhabitants of Deventer, fearful of marauding Spanish armies, and, in their efforts to reinforce the town's defences, iron rings were embedded in the walls of many of the streets so that chains could be hung across them. At the end of Kerksteeg, the **Bergkerk** is fronted by two tall towers dating from the thirteenth century, the differences in the colouring of the brick indicating the stages of construction. From the church, Roggestraat leads downhill to the east side of Brink; opposite is a tiny triangle edged by the **Penninckshuis**, whose florid Renaissance frontage is decorated with statuettes of six virtues. The inscription *Alst Godt behaget beter benyt als beclaget* is smug indeed: "If it pleases God it is better to be envied than to be pitied".

South of Brink, a stroll across the **Wihelminabrug**, an impressive iron girder bridge spanning the IJssel, affords fine views of the swirling river, surrounding farmland and the Lebuïnuskerk, rising head and shoulders above the rest of town.

## Practicalities

Deventer's **bus** and **train** stations are a five-minute walk north of the town centre – turn left out of the station and first right straight down Keizerstraat to reach the Brink. The **VVV** is at Keizerstraat 22 (Mon–Sat 9.30am–5pm, summer Thurs until 9pm; ☎0570/691 410, ⊛www.vvvdeventer.nl), with information on a walking tour of the city and details of **boat trips** up the IJssel leaving from the jetty near the Vispoort: a weekly programme throughout July and August includes excursions to Enkhuizen, Urk, Kampen, Zwolle and Zutphen.

For a town of this size, **accommodation** is thin: there are two central hotels, the grimly modern *Royal*, Brink 94 (☎0570/611 880; ❷) and the slightly more expensive but excellent *Gilde*, housed in an old convent at Nieuwstraat 41 (☎0570/641 846, ⑤641 819; ❸). The other alternative is the **campsite** *De Worp* (☎0570/613 601; April–Sept), west of the centre in the fields across the IJssel; a boat service shuttles across the river from the landing-stage at the bottom of Vispoort, and on the other side the campsite is a five-minute walk down the first turn on the right, Langelaan.

**Bars** and **restaurants** line both sides of Brink: *De Waagschaal*, no. 77, is a pleasant brown café, and *La Balance*, no. 72, has a varied French and Dutch menu. There are Dutch meals at *De Drie Nissen*, Grote Poot 19, and good if pricey Portuguese fare at *Chez Antoinette*, Roggestraat 8 (closed Mon). The local speciality, *Deventer koek*, is a sort of honey gingerbread, and the best place to try it is the antique cake shop, Bussink, at Brink 84. Take a stroll to Menstraat 7 to explore an extraordinary shop festooned with household artefacts of yesteryear, including scrubbing brushes made from Russian pig and Chinese skunk hair.

# Zutphen and around

A sleepy little town some 15km by road south of Deventer, over in Gelderland, **ZUTPHEN** was founded in the eleventh century as a fortified settlement at the confluence of the Berkel and IJssel rivers. It took just a hundred years to become an important port and today's tranquillity belies an illustrious and sometimes torrid past; the town was sacked on numerous occasions. The massacre of its citizens by Spanish forces in 1572 became part of Protestant folklore, strengthening their resolve against Catholic cruelty and absolutism. It was also here that Sir Philip Sidney, the English poet, soldier and courtier, met his death while fighting with the Earl of Leicester's forces against the Spanish in 1586. Sir Philip personified the "Renaissance man" and even managed to die with some measure of style: mortally wounded in the thigh after having loaned his leg-armour to a friend, Sir Philip offered his last cup of water to yet another wounded comrade, uttering "thy need is greater than mine".

The effective centre of Zutphen, five minutes' walk from the train station, is the **Wijnhuis**, a confused building of pillars and platforms that was begun in the seventeenth century. All the old town's main streets radiate from here and although there aren't many specific sights, the place does have charm, a jangle of architectural styles within much of the medieval street plan.

Around the corner from the Wijnhuis, Lange Hofstraat cuts down to the **Grote Kerk** of St Walburga (May–Sept Mon 2–4pm, Tues–Sat 11am–4pm; €3), an indifferent, though immense, Gothic church. Inside, the most impressive features are an extravagant brass baptismal font and a remarkable medieval **library**, sited in the sixteenth-century chapterhouse. Established in 1560, the library has a beautiful low-vaulted ceiling that twists around in a confusion of sharp-edged arches rising above the original wooden reading desks. It has all the feel of a medieval monastery, but it was in fact one of the first Dutch libraries to be built for the general public, a conscious effort by the Protestant authorities to dispel ignorance and superstition. The collection is wonderful, ranging from early illuminated manuscripts to later sixteenth-century works, a selection of which are still chained to the lecterns on which they were once read. There are also two manuscript volumes, one a beautiful sixteenth-century illuminated missal, the other an original manuscript attributed to Thomas à Kempis. Curiously, the tiles on one side of the floor are dotted with paw marks, which some contemporaries attributed to the work of the Devil.

Down the alleys east of the church entrance is the fifteenth-century **Drogenapstoren**, one of the old city gates. This is a fine example of a brick rampart tower, taking its name from the time when the town trumpeteer, Thomas Drogenap, lived here.

Heading back toward the Wijnhuis along the Zaadmarkt, you'll come to the **Museum Henriette Polak** at no. 88 (Tues–Fri 11am–5pm, Sat & Sun 1.30–5pm; €2.30) which has a modest collection of twentieth-century Dutch paintings, notably *Landschap* by Wim Oepts, a profusion of strong colours, roughly brushed, that manages a clear impression of a Dutch landscape. The **Stedelijk Museum** (same hours and ticket), on the other side of town toward the station at Rozengracht 3, is housed in the shell of a thirteenth-century Dominican monastery and has a fairly predictable selection of shards, armour and silver. In the old refectory on the second floor there's an altarpiece from around 1400, originally from the Grote Kerk. Finally, the **Grafisch Museum**, near the Grote Kerk at Kerkhof 16 (Wed–Fri 1–4.30pm, Sat 11am–3pm; €2.50) merits a quick stop for its collection of printing presses and other paraphernalia relating to the industry.

### Practicalities

Zutphen's **VVV**, Stationsplein 39 (Mon 10am–5.30pm, Tues–Fri 9am–5.30pm, Sat 10am–4pm; ☎0900/269 2888, ⓦwww.vvvzutphen.nl), has details of a couple of centrally situated rooms, though in July and August it's advisable to arrive early as they disappear fast. Of the **hotels**, the best value options are the pension-like *Berkhotel*, Marschpoortstraat 19 (☎0575/511 135, ⓔberkhotel@tebenet.nl; ❷) and the spotless *'t Volkhuis*, Houtmarkt 62 (☎0575/513 580, ⓦwww.volkshuis.nl; ❷). Alternatively, try the rather more comfortable, but less personal *Hotel Inntel*, De Stoven 37 (☎0575/525 555, ⓕ529 676, ⓦwww.hotelinntel.com; ❹).

There are two good and reasonably priced **restaurants** in Zutphen: *Pizzeria da Enzo*, near the Drogenapstoren at Pelikaanstraat 1a, and the *Berkhotel*'s vegetarian café *De Kloostertuin*, Marschpoortstraat 19 (closed Mon). For **bars**, try the lively *Camelot*, Groenmarkt 34, or the quieter *De Korenbeurs*, Zaadmarkt 84.

In July and August, **boat trips** run north up the IJssel (schedules from the VVV). Prices vary according to the route, but a day-trip will cost about €13.

### Bronkhorst

If you've got your own transport, the village of **BRONKHORST**, lying 10km south of Zutphen on the banks of the IJssel, makes for an appealing visit. With its cobbled streets and thatched cottages, this pretty village is a honeypot in summertime, popular with Dutch tourists enjoying its cafés, galleries and fine cheese shop De Olde Schuure. It's also home to the eccentric "Dickens Corner", Onderstraat 2, a museum packed with memorabilia including original programmes and the author's cane.

Gardens of Het Loo, Apeldoorn (see p.286) △

## The Achterhoek

Extending some 30km southeast from Zutphen to the German border, the **Achterhoek** ("Back Corner") is aptly named, a dozy rural backwater whose towns and villages have little to hold your attention. The easy hills have, however, made it a popular spot for cyclists, and the area is compact enough to tour from Zutphen. There are no really noteworthy monuments, with the possible exception of the old frontier settlement of **'s-Heerenberg**, whose modern centre edges the medieval town hall, church and castle that once belonged to the counts Van de Bergh. Of the three, it's the castle – the Huis Bergh – that dominates, its impressive red-brick walls, rising abruptly above the moat, bedecked with shutters. Its present appearance was acquired in 1912 when an Enschede industrialist, J.H. van Heek, bought the place and had it restored. Guided tours (July & Aug daily, otherwise call ☎0314/661 281 for times; €5) whisk you round an interior littered with sundry late medieval paintings, statues, prayer books and other paraphernalia installed by van Heek. The quickest way to reach 's-Heerenberg is to take a train to Doetinchem, where you can pick up bus #24a from the train station.

# Through the Veluwe

Extending west of the River IJssel, the **Veluwe** (literally "Bad Land") of the province of Gelderland is an expanse of heath, woodland and dune edged by **Apeldoorn** and Amersfoort to the east and west and the Veluwemeer and Arnhem to the north and south. For centuries these infertile lands lay almost deserted, but today they make up the country's busiest holiday centre, a profusion of campsites, bungalow parks and second homes that extends down to the Hoge Veluwe National Park (see p.294), a protected zone in the southeast corner that is much the prettiest part and the best place to experience the area – though, unless you're camping, it's more sensibly seen from Arnhem (see p.288).

## Apeldoorn

The administrative capital of the Veluwe, **APELDOORN** was no more than a village a century ago, but it's grown rapidly to become an extensive garden city, a rather characterless modern place that spreads languidly into the surrounding countryside. However, as one-time home of the Dutch royal family, Apeldoorn is a major tourist centre in its own right, popular with those Dutch senior citizens who like an atmosphere of comfortable, rather snobbish privilege. The only sign of life is the annual jazz festival, the **Jazztival**, usually held on the first Friday in June, with jazz musicians performing in the bars and clubs around town; get details from the VVV.

Apeldoorn is most famous for the **Paleis Het Loo** (Tues–Sun 10am–5pm; €9; ⓦ www.hetloo.nl) situated on the northern edge of town and reachable by half-hourly bus #1, #102 or #104 from the station. Looking something like an imposing military academy, it was designed in 1685 by Daniel Marot for William III and his queen, Mary, shortly before he acceded to the throne of England and Scotland. The palace was later the favourite residence of Queen Wilhelmina, who lived here until her death in 1962. No longer used by the Dutch royal family – they moved out in 1975 – it was opened as a national museum in the early 1980s to illustrate three hundred years of the history of the House of Orange-Nassau. Years of repair work have restored an apparently endless series of bedrooms, ballrooms, living rooms and reception halls to their former glory. A self-guided tour, with information in English, leads you along a warren of passageways from one room to the next, packed with displays of all things royal, from lavish costumes and silk hangings to documents and medals, via roomfuls of austere portraits and curly antlers. It's a fascinating and infinitely detailed snapshot of royal life, and you can view the rooms of William and Mary, including their colourful individual bedchambers, as well as the much later study of Queen Wilhelmina.

After immersing yourself in a bygone era, the formal **gardens** (both William and Mary were apparently keen gardeners), make for a relaxing place to wander. A maze of miniature hedgerows and a series of precise and neatly bordered flowerbeds are accessible by long walkways ornamented in the Dutch Baroque style, with tiered fountains, urns, statuettes and portals. The other part of the palace, the Royal Stables of 1906, has displays of some of the old cars and carriages of past monarchs, including a baby carriage that's rigged up against gas attack.

The town's second draw is the **Apenheul** monkey reserve (April–Oct daily 9.30am–5pm; June–Aug until 6pm; €12), just west of town on bus #2. The highlight is the gorillas – among the world's largest colonies of the creatures – living on wooded islands that isolate them from the visitors and from the dozen or so species of monkey that roam around the rest of the park. It's best to go early to catch the young gorillas fooling around and antagonizing the elders; as the day warms up they all get a bit more slothful. The park is well designed, with a reasonable amount of freedom for most of the animals (at times it's not obvious who is watching who) and you'll see other wildlife including otters, deer and capybara.

If you're staying, it's worth catching the spectacular *Lumido* light show held at the Natuurpark Berg En Bos (July & Aug nightly 10–11pm; gates open 7.30pm; €3.50), complete with music, illuminated fountains and gondolas on the water. A **film festival** takes place in the same park during August, and features international films but with only Dutch subtitles; details are available from the VVV and at ⓦwww.recreatif.nl. Finally, in July and August an old **steam train** is put back into service between Apeldoorn and Dieren (a 75-minute ride), facilitating a pleasant half-day journey Apeldoorn–Dieren–Zutphen–Apeldoorn by steam train, boat and regular train.

## Practicalities

The Apeldoorn **VVV**, Stationstraat 72 (Mon 9.30am–5.30pm, Tues–Fri 9am–5.30pm, Sat 9am–5pm; ⓣ0900/168 1636, ⓦwww.vvvapeldoorn.nl), stocks maps of the town and the surrounding area and lists of **rooms** – in season it's advisable to ask them to ring ahead to confirm vacancies. The most reasonably priced **hotel** near the centre is the *Abbekerk*, Canadalaan 26, a ten-minute walk north (ⓣ055/522 2433, ⓕ521 1323; ❶): head up Stationstraat and Canadalaan is the fourth left turn after the Marktplein. There's also an **HI hostel**, 4km west at Asselsestraat 330 (ⓣ055/355 3118, ⓦwww.stayokay.com; €23 for a dorm bed), which is open year-round and reachable with bus #4 or #7 to the Chamavenlaan stop. The nearest **campsite** is *De Parelhoeve*, Zwolseweg 540 (ⓣ055/312 1332, ⓦwww.deparelhoeve.nl) in the village of Wenum Wiesel some 5km north of Apeldoorn centre (bus #96 from the train station). The VVV also has a list of nearby mini-campings.

Don't expect a lot of night-time excitement. The main hive of evening activity is the **Caterplein**, where Hoofdstraat meets Nieuwstraat. *Tipico*, an excellent

Italian place with food for all budgets, is nearby at Kapelstraat 11, while *Eetcafé 't Pakhuys*, Beekpark 9, has reasonable Dutch food; there are also plenty of cheap kebab joints nearby. Further south on Hoofdstraat, Raadhuisplein has several good café-bars. The *Blues Café* on Nieuwstraat has occasional live music.

An easy way to see the countryside around town is by **bike**. Details of suggested routes are available from the VVV and bikes can be rented from the station (€5.50/day, or €6.50 for a 3-geared bike). The VVV can also provide details of walking trails in the forests around the Paleis Het Loo.

# Arnhem

Around 20km south of Apeldoorn, on the far side of the heathy Hoge Veluwe National Park, **ARNHEM** was once a wealthy resort, a watering hole to which the merchants of Amsterdam and Rotterdam would flock to idle away their fortunes. Last century it became better known as the place where thousands of British and Polish troops died in the failed Allied airborne operation of September 1944, codenamed Operation Market Garden (see box); the town is most famous for its bridge, a key objective in Field Marshal Montgomery's audacious attempt to shorten the war by dropping parachute battalions behind enemy lines in an attempt to secure a string of advance positions across the rivers of southeast Gelderland. Much of the city was destroyed as a result of the operation, and most of what you see today is a postwar reconstruction. Arnhem is now something of a place of pilgrimage for English visitors, who flock here every summer to pay their respects to the soldiers who died and visit the crucial sites of the battle. However, it's a lively town that makes a good centre for seeing the numerous attractions scattered around its forested outskirts – the war museums and memorials near **Oosterbeek**, the **Nederlands Openluchtmuseum**, and one of the highlights of the area, the **Hoge Veluwe National Park** itself, incorporating a superb collection of modern art at the **Kröller-Müller Museum**.

## The Town

Predictably, postwar rebuilding has left Arnhem a patchy place with the usual agglomerations of concrete and glass; however, five minutes' walk southeast from the train station is the **Korenmarkt**, a small square which escaped much of the destruction. The streets which lead off it are choc-a-block with restaurants and bars, while the **Filmhuis**, at Korenmarkt 42, has an excellent programme of international films and late-night showings, and a small gallery on the ground floor.

Arnhem deteriorates as you walk southeast from the Korenmarkt and into the area most badly damaged by the fighting. Here stands the "Bridge too Far", the **John Frostbrug**, named after the commander of the battalion that defended it for four days. It's a plain modern bridge, but it remains a symbol of people's remembrance of the battle, Dutch and British alike. Around its north end you can see the results of the rebuilding: wide boulevards intersect broad open spaces edged by haphazardly placed tower blocks and car parks. Overlooking this rather desolate spot, at the end of the characterless **Markt**, is the church of **St Eusabius** (summer Tues–Sat 10am–5pm, Sun noon–5pm; winter Tues–Sat 11am–4pm, Sun noon–4pm; free), with the dainty fifteenth-century **Stadhuis** tucked in behind. The church is a fifteenth- to sixteenth-century structure

## Operation Market Garden

By September 1944 most of France and much of Belgium had been liberated from Nazi occupation. Fearing that an orthodox campaign would take many months and cost many lives, Field Marshal Montgomery decided that a pencil thrust north through the Netherlands and subsequently east into the Ruhr, around the back of the Siegfried line, offered a good chance of ending the war early. To speed the advance of his land armies, Montgomery needed to cross several major rivers and canals in a corridor of territory stretching from Eindhoven, a few kilometres north of the front, to Arnhem. The plan, codenamed **Operation Market Garden**, was to parachute three airborne Divisions behind enemy lines, each responsible for taking and holding particular bridgeheads until the army could force their way north to join them. On Sunday, September 17, the 1st British Airborne Division parachuted into the fields around Oosterbeek, their objective to seize the bridges over the Rhine at Arnhem. Meanwhile, the 101st American Airborne Division was dropped in the area of Veghel to secure the Wilhelmina and Zuid-Willemsvaart canals, and the 82nd was dropped around Grave and Nijmegen, for the crossings over the Maas and the Waal.

The American paratroopers were successful, and by the night of September 20, sections of the main British army, 30 Corps, had reached the American bridgehead across the River Waal at Nijmegen. However, the landings around Arnhem ran into serious problems: Allied Command had estimated that opposition was unlikely to exceed three thousand troops, but as it turned out, the entire 2nd SS Panzer Corps was refitting near Arnhem just when the 1st Division landed. Taking the enemy by surprise, 2nd Parachute Battalion, under Lieutenant-Colonel John Frost, did manage to capture the north end of the road bridge across the Rhine, but it proved impossible to capture the southern end. Surrounded, out-gunned and out-manned, the 2nd Battalion held their position from September 17th to the morning of the 21st, a feat of extraordinary heroism. Meanwhile, other Polish and British battalions had concentrated around the bridgehead at Oosterbeek, which they held at tremendous cost under the command of General Urquhart. By the morning of the 25th it was apparent that reinforcements in sufficient numbers would not be able to get through in support, so under cover of darkness, a dramatic withdrawal saved 2163 soldiers out of an original force of 10,005.

surmounted by a valiantly attempted but rather obvious replacement tower and was extensively renovated for the fiftieth anniversary of Operation Market Garden in 1994; you can take a lift to the top (€2.50) for fine views around the surrounding area.

From outside the train station, it's a fifteen-minute walk west along Utrechtsestraat (or take bus #1 direction Oosterbeek) to the **Museum voor Moderne Kunst**, Utrechtseweg 87 (Tues–Fri 10am–5pm, Sat & Sun 11am–5pm; Ⓦwww.mmkarnhem.nl; €5), whose speciality is exhibitions of modern Dutch art. The nucleus of the permanent collection is the work of the Magic Realists, particularly Carel Willink and Pyke Koch, whose *Vrouwen in de Straat* is a typically disconcerting canvas, the women's eyes looking out of the picture in a medley of contrasting emotions. The paintings of Reinier Lucassen, for example *The Kiss* of 1976, establish the stylistic link between the Magic Realism of the 1930s and Dutch contemporary art, the familiar once again given a disturbing and alienating slant.

The more centrally located **Historische Museum** (Tues–Fri 10am–5pm & Sun 11am–5pm; €3.50) is located in an old orphanage at Bovenbeekstraat 21. The collection includes numerous archeological finds from the surrounding area; a display of Chinese, Japanese and Delft ceramics from the seventeenth

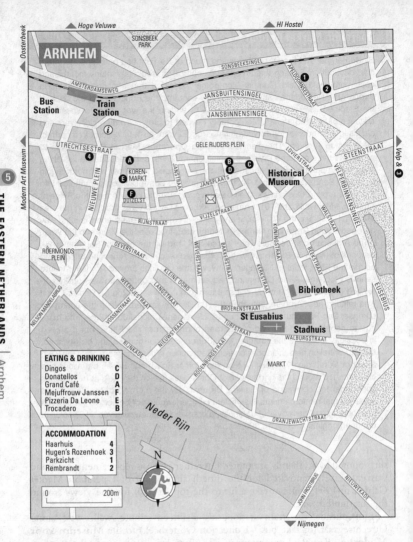

**ARNHEM**

Oosterbeek

▲ Hoge Veluwe     ▲ HI Hostel

SONSBEEK PARK

SONSBEEKSINGEL

APELDOORNSESTRAAT

❶
❷

Bus Station

Train Station

ⓘ

AMSTERDAMSEWEG

JANSBUITENSINGEL

JANSBINNENSINGEL

UTRECHTSESTRAAT

GELE RIJDERS PLEIN

LOVIERSTRAAT

STEENSTRAAT

Velp & 3 ▶

Modern Art Museum

❹

Ⓐ KOREN-MARKT

Ⓔ

Ⓕ DUIZELST

Ⓑ
Ⓓ Ⓒ

JANSTRAAT

JANSPLAATS

Historical Museum

VELPERBINNENSINGEL

WALSTRAAT

NIEUWE PLEIN

VIJZELSTRAAT

KONINGSTRAAT

KERKSTRAAT

BEEKSTRAAT

EUSEBIUS

RIJNSTRAAT

RÖERMONDS PLEIN

OEVERSTRAAT

WEVERSTRAAT

BAKKERSTRAAT

NELSON MANDELABRUG

VOSSENSTRAAT

WEERDJESSTRAAT

KLEINE OORD

LANGSTRAAT

NIEUWSTRAAT

BROERENSTRAAT

Bibliotheek

RIJNKADE

RODENBURGSTRAAT

St Eusabius

TURFSTRAAT

WALBURGSTRAAT

Stadhuis

MARKT

Neder Rijn

ORANJEWACHTSTRAAT

N

JOHN FROSTBRUG

NIEUWEKADE

▼ Nijmegen

**EATING & DRINKING**

| Dingos | C |
| Donatellos | D |
| Grand Café | A |
| Mejuffrouw Janssen | F |
| Pizzeria Da Leone | E |
| Trocadero | B |

**ACCOMMODATION**

| Haarhuis | 4 |
| Hugen's Rozenhoek | 3 |
| Parkzicht | 1 |
| Rembrandt | 2 |

0        200m

and eighteenth centuries; Dutch silver, notably several guild beakers, whose size and degree of decoration indicated the status of the owner; and a modest selection of paintings from the sixteenth to the nineteenth centuries, with the emphasis on views of the landscape, villages and towns of Gelderland.

## Practicalities

Arnhem is a major rail junction. The town's **train** and **bus stations** are only a few minutes' walk from the centre and the **VVV**, Willemsplein 8 (Mon 11am–5.30pm, Tues–Fri 9am–5.30pm & Sat 10am–4pm; ☎0900/202 4075, ⓦ www.vvvarnhem.nl), which has a good selection of Dutch maps, books on Operation Market Garden, brochures and up-to-date cultural information. **Walking** is the best way to get around the centre, although to see any of the outlying attractions and for some of the accommodation, you'll need at some point to use a **bus**. Arnhem has a rather odd system of trams which describe a figure-of-eight pattern over town. This means there'll often be two buses at the station with the same number and different destinations, so it's important to get the direction as well as the number right.

The VVV operates an **accommodation**-booking service – useful in July and August when Arnhem's handful of reasonably priced pensions and hotels can fill up early. The cheapest rooms in town are at *Parkzicht*, Apeldoornsestraat 16 (☎026/442 0698, ⓕ443 6202; ❶) and the friendly *Rembrandt* nearby, Paterstraat 1 (☎026/442 0153; ❷). Both are a ten-minute walk east from the station. If money's not too tight, there's the reassuringly comfortable *Haarhuis* opposite the train station at Stationsplein 1 (☎026/442 7441, ⓦwww.hotelhaarhuis.nl; ❺), while, if you're on a budget, aim for the **HI hostel** some 5km north at Diepenbrocklaan 27 (☎026/442 0114, ⓦwww.stayokay.com; €23 for a dorm bed; ❷; bus #3, direction Altaveer, to the Rijnstaete hospital stop). The nearest **campsite** is *Camping Warnsborn*, 6km northwest of the centre at Bakenbergseweg 257 (☎026/442 3469, ⓦwww.campingwarnsborn.nl; bus #2, direction Schaarsbergen), attractively situated on a large estate and hemmed in by beech and oak trees. You can **rent bikes** here for the lovely cycle ride through the trees to the Hoge Veluwe National Park, 5km further north. There are many other campsites around the edge of the park, including one by the Hoenderloo entrance in the park itself (April–Oct; ☎0555/378 2232) – an ideal spot for a quiet night's camping.

If you have problems finding something, there's a good alternative outside the city proper: in the leafy suburb of **Velp**, served by half-hourly trains, is *Hugen's Rozenhoek*, Rozendaalselaan 60 (☎026/364 7290, ⓕ361 7588; ❸). Untouched by the war, parts of Velp are still much as they were a century ago – comfortable country mansions and landscaped streets and gardens.

Arnhem has plenty of decent places for reasonably priced **food** and a range of good **bars**. The cheapest food can normally be found on the Jansplein near the post office; *Trocadero* at no. 49 and *Donatellos* at no. 50 offer Mexican and Italian food respectively from €6 per head. Carnivores should make for the popular *Eetcafe Mejuffrouw Janssen* at Duizelsteeg 7, just south of Korenmarkt, while *Pizzeria Da Leone* at Korenmarkt 1 has pasta dishes for around €7. Most people head for the pavement cafés of Korenmarkt for their drinking; *Le Grand Café* is probably the most popular but there are a dozen others to choose from. *Dingos*, Boyenbeekstraat 28, a couple of minutes' walk to the east, is another good bar and has cheap food on Tuesdays and Thursdays (6–10pm). There's often **live music** at one or other of the bars on Korenmarkt; get hold of a copy of the listings magazine *Uit Loper* for details of what's on.

# Around Arnhem

Most people who visit Arnhem do so for the attractions outside the city: you could certainly spend several days here visiting the wartime sites of Operation Market Garden around **Oosterbeek**, taking in the countryside of the **Hoge Veluwe** park (and its superb modern art collection, the **Kröller-Müller Museum**), not to mention the **Nederlands Openluchtmuseum**, a huge open-air museum of Dutch vernacular architecture – the country's largest – and a castle or two.

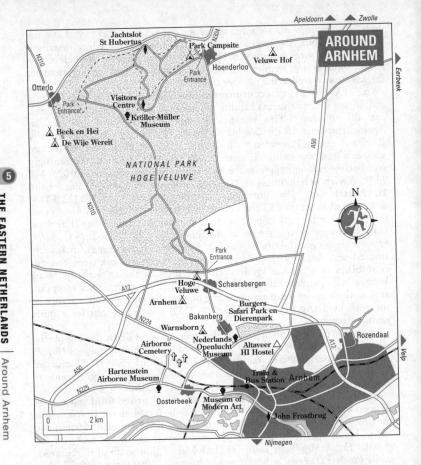

## Two castles: Doorwerth and Rosendaal

For the most part the banks of the River Rhine near Arnhem are rather dull, though there's an appealing stretch to the west, where you'll find the massive, moated thirteenth-century **Kasteel Doorwerth** (April–Oct Tues–Fri 10am–5pm, Sat & Sun 1–5pm; last entry 4pm; €4.50), carefully reconstructed after war damage. To get there, take bus #88 from the station and ask to be dropped at the stop nearest the Kasteel, from where it's a thirty-minute walk along the river. There's an excellent and pricey **restaurant** there too, which for most people is more of an attraction than the collection of stuffed carcasses and old weapons at the Nature Museum which occupies the castle.

On the opposite side of Arnhem, lying on the edge of the suburbs of Velp, is the **Kasteel Rosendaal** (mid-April to Oct Tues–Sat 10am–5pm, Sun 1–5pm; €5.50; bus #31 direction Velp Zuid) – an attractive mixture of medieval and eighteenth-century architecture, set in its own parkland. Not far away, on the west side of Velp, the **Museum Bronbeek**, Velperweg 147 (Tues–Sun 10am–5pm; €2.30; bus #1 direction Velp), occupies a building donated to ex-soldiers by William III in 1859. The collection has all sorts of curious relics left over from the Dutch occupation of Surinam and Indonesia.

# Oosterbeek's World War II memorials

The area around Arnhem is scattered with the graveyards of thousands of soldiers who died during Operation Market Garden (see box on p.289). Arnhem VVV sells specialist books on the campaign for devotees of battlegrounds and battle plans, and provides details of organized tours (minimum 20 people). Otherwise, the easiest way to get some idea of the conflict and its effect on this part of the Netherlands is to visit **OOSTERBEEK**, once a small village and now a prosperous suburb of Arnhem (train or bus #1).

Following the signs from beside Oosterbeek train station, it's a five-minute walk east to the **Airborne Cemetery**, a neat, symmetrical tribute to nearly two thousand paratroopers, mostly British and Polish, whose bodies were brought here from the surrounding fields. It's a quiet, secluded spot; the personal inscriptions on the gravestones are especially poignant. Ten minutes' walk (or bus #1) south of the station down Stationsweg, the village proper has spruced lawns and walls dotted with details of the battle – who held out where and for how long – as the Allied forces were pinned back within a tighter and tighter perimeter.

The **Airborne Museum**, Utrechtseweg 232 (April–Oct Mon–Sat 10am–5pm, Sun noon–5pm; Nov–March Mon–Sat 11am–5pm, Sun noon–5pm; €4; ⓦ www.airbornemuseum.com) is just to the west of the village centre along Utrechtseweg, reachable direct from Arnhem on bus #1, housed in the former Hotel Hartenstein, where the British forces were besieged by the Germans for a week before retreating across the river. With the use of an English commentary, photographs, dioramas and original military artefacts – from rifles and light artillery to uniforms and personal memorabilia – the museum gives an excellent outline of the battle and, to a lesser extent, aspects of World War II as it affected the country as a whole. The Army Film and Photographic Unit landed with the British forces, and it's their photographs that stick in the memory: grimly cheerful soldiers hauling in their parachutes, tense tired faces during the fighting, and shattered Dutch villages.

# The Nederlands Openluchtmuseum

Immediately north of Arnhem, the **Nederlands Openluchtmuseum**, Schelmseweg 89 (Dutch Open-Air Museum; April–Oct daily 10am–5pm; Nov–March Tues–Sun 10am–4.30pm; €6; ⓦ www.openluchtmuseum.nl), reachable by bus #3 direction Alteveer (every 20min), or direct by special bus #13 (July & Aug only; every 20min), is a huge collection of Dutch buildings open to public view. One of the first of its type, the museum was founded in 1912 in order to "present a picture of the daily life of ordinary people in this country as it was in the past and has developed in the course of time". Over the years, original and representative buildings have been taken from all over the country and assembled here in a large area of the Veluwe forest. Where possible, buildings have been placed in groups that resemble the traditional villages of the different regions of the Netherlands – from the farmsteads of Friesland to the farming communities of Zuid-Holland and the peat colonies of Drenthe. There are about 120 buildings in all, including examples of every type of Dutch windmill, most sorts of farmhouse, a variety of bridges and several working craftshops, demonstrating the traditional skills of papermaking, milling, baking, brewing and bleaching. Other parts of the museum incorporate one of the most extensive regional costume exhibitions in the country and a modest herb garden. The giant snail building houses *Hollandrama*, which shows visual footage of typical Dutch scenes through the ages.

All in all, it's an imaginative attempt to recreate the rural Dutch way of life over the past two centuries. The museum's guidebook costs €5 and explains everything with academic attention to detail; it's by no means essential, though, as most of the information is repeated on plaques outside each building.

## The Hoge Veluwe National Park

Spreading north from the Open-Air Museum is the **Hoge Veluwe National Park** (ⓦwww.hogeveluwe.nl), an area of sandy heath and thick woodland. Just ninety minutes by train from Amsterdam, the impressive **Kröller-Müller Museum** and Europe's largest sculpture garden lie at the heart of 5500 hectares of national park. Cycle paths wind through this beautiful nature reserve, home to wild game and inland sand dunes as well as over a thousand free white bicycles which can be used to explore it all. Today, the park is one of the region's most popular day-trip destinations, with its perfect blend of nature and art.

The park was formerly the private estate of Anton and Helene Kröller-Müller. Born near Essen in 1869, Helene Müller came from a wealthy family whose money was made in the blast-furnace business. She married Anton Kröller of Rotterdam, whose brother ran the Dutch side of their trading interests, and the couple's fortunes were secured when the death of her father and his brother's poor health placed Anton at the head of the company at the age of 27. Apart from extending their business empire and supporting the Boers in South Africa, they had a passionate desire to leave a grand bequest to the nation, a mixture of nature and culture which would, she felt, "be an important lesson when showing the inherent refinement of a merchant's family living at the beginning of the century". She collected the art, he the land, and in the 1930s ownership of both was transferred to the nation on the condition that a museum was built in the park. The museum opened in 1938 and Helene acted as manager until her death in 1939.

### Park practicalities

The park has three entrances: one near the village of **Otterlo** on the northwest perimeter, another near **Hoenderloo** on the northeast edge, and a third to the south at Rijzenburg, near the village of **Schaarsbergen**, only 7km from Arnhem. It has long **opening hours** (daily: June & July 8am–10pm; May & Aug 8am–9pm; April 8am–8pm; Sept 9am–8pm; Oct 9am–7pm; Nov–March 9am–5.30pm). **Admission** is €5 (park only) or €10 (park and Kröller-Müller museum); cars cost an extra €5. During the deer rutting season in September and early October, certain areas of the park are off-limits.

As there are very few roads in the national park, the best way to explore is on one of the 1300 **white bicycles** which lie in wait at each of the park's three entrances and are free to use. These famous white bikes come in all shapes and sizes for the whole family, and several have children's seats at the front and rear. There are also trikes, tandems and wheelchair bikes available from next to the **Bezoekerscentrum** (Visitors' Centre; daily 10am–5pm), located in the middle of the park near the museum.

There are a number of ways to get to De Hoge Veluwe by **bus**. From Arnhem, bus #107 runs hourly to Otterlo; here, you can change to bus #110, which runs 4km east to the Kröller-Müller Museum, or you can walk to the park entrance (5min) and pick up a free white bike. On its full trip, bus #110 runs hourly on a handy route between Ede-Wageningen and Apeldoorn, stopping midway at the Otterlo entrance, the Bezoekerscentrum and the Hoenderloo entrance.

Alternatively, you can **rent a bike** at Arnhem train station and cycle yourself; note, though, that the round trip from Arnhem station to the Kröller-Müller museum and back is a total of about 28km.

## Around the park

At Eikenzoom 12 in Otterlo village, ten minutes' walk from the park entrance and across from the VVV, is the small **Tegel Museum** (Tile Museum; Tues–Fri 10am–5pm, Sat & Sun 1–5pm; €2.70), worth an hour of your time. Displays trace the development of the Dutch tile from the sixteenth to the twentieth century, and include themes such as biblical scenes, shipping and sea monsters. Slideshows and guided tours in English are available on request.

Cycle paths wind through the park's heathland, woodland, sand dunes and lakes, with some themed routes such as the 14km "Images in the Landscape" taking in the best of the open-air art (map available from the Bezoekerscentrum; €1). Or you can just make it up as you pedal along – you won't get lost thanks to the mushroom-like kilometre stones with directions and distances at every twist and turn.

While Helene collected art, her husband, Anton Kröller, imported animals such as moufflons (wild sheep from Corsica) and bought up land. The parkland is now carefully managed for its unusual ecosystems, such as wandering inland dunes, which form unexpected desert vistas, and the endangered species that survive in them. Hides are dotted throughout the park, from where you can observe bigger game such as red deer, roe deer and wild boar. To understand the environment you're cycling through, don't miss the **Museonder** (same hours; free), beneath the Bezoekerscentrum (see above). This engrossing subterranean museum brings to life the unusual ecosystems of the park through an array of interactive presentations – great for children, and adults will find themselves morbidly fascinated too. Look out for the giant beetle-mites, a rabbit morgue and a 23m-long beech tree banister.

Apart from the Kröller-Müller Museum (see below), point your handlebars towards the **Jachtslot St Hubertus** (open only for guided tours, book at the Bezoekerscentrum; April–Oct every 30min 11.30am–5pm; Feb, March, Nov & Dec daily 2pm & 3pm; free), some 3km north of the Visitors' Centre, a hunting lodge and country home built in 1920 for the Kröller-Müllers by the modernist Dutch architect H.P. Berlage. Dedicated to the patron saint of hunters, it's an impressive Art Deco monument, with lots of plays on the hunting theme. The floor plan – in the shape of branching antlers – is representative of the stag bearing a crucifix that appeared to St Hubert, the adopted patron of hunters, while he was hunting and each room of the sumptuous interior symbolizes an episode in the saint's life: all in all, a somewhat unusual commission for a committed socialist who wrote so caustically about the haute bourgeoisie.

## The Kröller-Müller Museum

Most people who visit the Hoge Veluwe Park come for the **Kröller-Müller Museum** (Tues–Sun 10am–5pm; free with park admission; Ⓦwww.kmm.nl), made up of the private art collection of the Kröller-Müllers. It's one of the country's finest museums, a wide cross-section of modern European art from Impressionism to Cubism and beyond, housed in a low-slung building that was built for the collection in 1938 by the Belgian architect Van de Velde.

The bulk of the collection is in one long wing, starting with the most recent Dutch painters and working backward. There's a good set of paintings, in particular some revealing self-portraits by Charley Toorop, one of the most skilled and sensitive of twentieth-century Dutch artists. Her father Jan also gets a good showing throughout the museum, from his pointillist studies to later, turn-of-the-century works more reminiscent of Aubrey Beardsley and the Art

Nouveau movement. Piet Mondrian is well represented too, his 1909 *Beach near Domburg* a good example of his more stylized approach to landscape painting, a development from his earlier sombre-coloured scenes in the Dutch tradition. In 1909 Mondrian moved to Paris, and his contact with Cubism transformed his work, as illustrated by his *Composition* of 1917: simple flat rectangles of colour with the elimination of the object complete, the epitome of the De Stijl approach. Much admired by Mondrian and one of the most influential of the Cubists, Fernand Léger's *Soldiers Playing Cards* is typical of his bold, clear lines and tendency toward the monumental. One surprise is an early Picasso, *Portrait of a Woman*, from 1901, a classic post-Impressionist canvas very dissimilar from his more famous works.

The building as a whole gravitates toward the works of **Vincent van Gogh**, with one of the most complete collections of his work in the world, housed in a large room around a central courtyard and placed in context by accompanying contemporary pictures. The museum owns no fewer than 278 Van Gogh pieces and doesn't have the space to show them all at any one time; consequently exhibits are rotated (with the exception of his most important paintings). Of earlier canvases, *The Potato Eaters* and *Head of a Peasant with a Pipe* are outstanding: rough, unsentimental paintings of labourers from around his parents' home in Brabant. From February 1886 to early 1888, Van Gogh lived in Paris, where he came into contact with the Impressionists, whose work – and arguments – convinced him of the importance of colour. His penetrating *Self-portrait* is a superb example of his work of this period, the eyes fixed on the observer, the head and background a swirl of grainy colour and streaky brush-strokes. One of his most famous paintings, *Sunflowers*, dates from this period also, an extraordinary work of alternately thick and thin paintwork in dazzlingly sharp detail and colour.

The move to Arles in 1888 spurred Van Gogh to a frenzy of activity, inspired by the colours and light of the Mediterranean. The joyful *Haystacks in Provence* and *Bridge at Arles,* with its rickety bridge and disturbed circles of water spreading from the washerwomen on the river bank, are from these months, one of the high points of his troubled life. The novelty of the south quickly wore off, however, and Van Gogh's desperate sense of loneliness intensified. At the end of the year he had his first attack of madness – and committed his famous act of self-mutilation. In and out of mental hospital until his suicide in July of the following year, his *Prisoners Exercising* of 1890 is a powerful, sombre painting full of sadness and despair: heads bent, the prisoners walk around in a pointless circle as the walls around them seem to close in.

Finally, outside the museum, behind the main building, there's a **Sculpture Garden** (Tues–Sun 10am–4.30pm; free), recently doubled in size and now the largest in Europe. Some frankly bizarre creations reside within its 21 hectares, as well as works by Auguste Rodin, Alberto Giacometti, Jacob Epstein and Barbara Hepworth. In contrast to the carefully conserved paintings of the museum, the sculpture-garden pieces are exposed to the weather and the touches of visitors – you can even clamber all over Jean Dubuffet's *Jardin d'e-mail*, one of his larger and more elaborate jokes.

# Nijmegen

The oldest town in the Netherlands, **NIJMEGEN**, some 20km south of Arnhem, was built on the site of the Roman frontier fortress of *Novio Magus*, from which it derives its name. Situated on the southern bank of the Waal, just to the west of

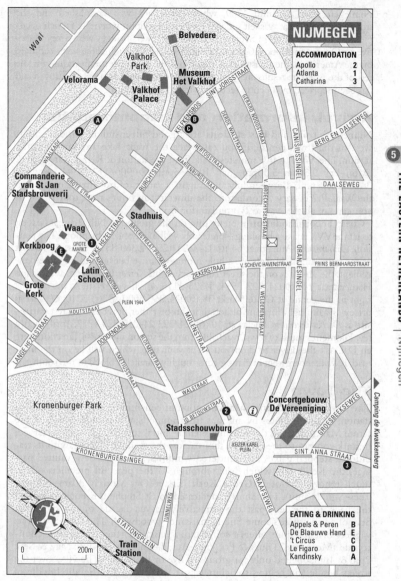

**NIJMEGEN**

**ACCOMMODATION**

| | |
|---|---|
| Apollo | 2 |
| Atlanta | 1 |
| Catharina | 3 |

Camping de Kwakkenberg

**EATING & DRINKING**

| | |
|---|---|
| Appels & Peren | B |
| De Blaauwe Hand | E |
| 't Circus | C |
| Le Figaro | D |
| Kandinsky | A |

its junction with the Rhine, the town's location has long been strategically important. The Romans used Nijmegen as a buffer against the unruly tribes to the east; Charlemagne, Holy Roman Emperor from 800 to 814, made the town one of the principal seats of his administration, building the **Valkhof Palace**, an enormous complex of chapels and secular buildings completed in the eighth century. Rebuilt in 1155 by another emperor, Frederick Barbarossa, the complex dominated

Nijmegen right up until 1769, when the palace was demolished and the stonework sold; what was left suffered further demolition when the French occupied the town in 1796. In September 1944, the town's bridges were a key objective of Operation Market Garden (see p.289) and although these were captured by the Americans, the disaster at Arnhem put the town on the front line for the rest of the war. The results are clear to see: the old town was largely destroyed and has been replaced by a centre reconstructed to a new plan.

## Arrival, information and accommodation

Nijmegen's **train** and **bus stations** are a good fifteen-minute trudge southwest of the town centre; if you can't face the walk, take any bus from the station. The **VVV** is five minutes' walk from the station at Keizer Karelplein 2 (Mon–Fri 9.30am–5.30pm, Sat 10am–5pm; ℡0900/112 2344, Ⓦwww .vvvnijmegen.nl). Between July and August, a variety of **boat trips** operate on the Waal. Prices vary according to the itinerary: an hour's river tour is €3, or you can sail all the way to Rotterdam for €35.

Cheap **accommodation** is pretty thin on the ground in Nijmegen; it's easiest to let the VVV make a booking – preferably well in advance – by phone. The pension *Catharina*, St Annastraat 64 (℡024/323 1251, Ⓕ360 8534; ❷) is not far east of the train station. **Hotels** are a little more expensive but tend to be more convenient: the *Apollo* is on the street running east off Keizer Karelplein, at Bisschop Hamerstraat 14 (℡024/322 3594, Ⓕ323 3176; ❸). If you're stuck, the *Atlanta*, right in the centre at Grote Markt 38 (℡024/360 3000, Ⓕ360 3210; ❸), isn't as pricey as you might imagine, although it can be rather noisy. The nearest **campsite** is *De Kwakkenberg*, Luciaweg 10 (℡024/323 2443, Ⓕ323 4772; April–Oct), a few kilometres south of town, reachable from the station by bus #8, direction Berg en Dal. Ask the driver to drop you off at your stop, which will be on the main road, Kwakkenbergweg; Luciaweg runs roughly parallel, a block to the south.

## The Town

The town centre is **Grote Markt**, a good fifteen-minute walk from the train station, or five minutes by any bus from immediately outside. Much of the Grote Markt survived the wartime shelling and is surprisingly well preserved, in stark contrast to the modern shops across the road. The **Waag**, with its traditional stepped gables and shuttered windows, stands beside a vaulted passage, the Kerkboog, which leads through to the peaceful precincts of the much-renovated Gothic **Grote Kerk** (Easter–Oct Mon 10.30am–1.30pm, Tues–Sun 1–4pm). The church, dedicated to St Stephen, is entered around the back to the left, past the attractively carved facade of the old Latin School; inside there's some fine Renaissance woodwork. The **tower**, with its vaguely oriental spire, offers a commanding vista over the surrounding countryside (Mon, Tues, Thurs & Fri: June–Aug 11am, 2pm & 4pm; May & Sept 2pm & 4pm; opened only for groups of five or more; €2). The view over the streets beside and behind the church isn't what it used to be: the huddle of medieval houses that sloped down to the Waal was almost totally destroyed during World War II and has been replaced by a hopeful but rather sterile residential imitation.

A few metres away, down toward the river, the **Commanderie van St Jan** is more authentic-looking, a reconstruction of a seventeenth-century building that now houses the **Stadsbrouwerij De Hemmel**, Franse Plaats 1 (Tues–Sun noon–8pm; free; guided tours €4.50), which features a brewery museum and tasting room.

Bike-bods must not miss the **Velorama Nationaal Fietsmuseum**, just a few minutes' walk north at Waalkade 107 (National Bicycle Museum; Mon–Sat 10am–5pm, Sun 11am–5pm €2.80; ⓦ www.velorama.nl), with the largest collection of bicycles and other human-powered vehicles in Western Europe. The recently renovated museum devotes three floors to over 200 contraptions dating from the early nineteenth-century to the present day. There are bicycles delicately carved from wood, a tandem for five people, penny-farthings, recumbents and quadricycles – anything and everything that has helped shape bicycle design in the last few centuries. Lovingly restored and beautifully displayed, it's the perfect museum to visit in a country where the bicycle rules.

## To the Valkhof

From the Grote Markt, Burchtstraat heads east roughly parallel to the river, past the dull reddish-brown brick of the **Stadhuis**, a square, rather severe edifice with an onion-domed tower, another reconstruction after extensive war damage.

A couple of minutes away, in a park beside the east end of Burchtstraat, lie the scanty remains of the **Valkhof Palace** – a ruined fragment of the Romanesque choir of the twelfth-century palace chapel and, just to the west, a sixteen-sided chapel built around 1045, in a similar style to the palatinate church at Charlemagne's capital, Aachen. These bits and pieces are connected by a footbridge to a **belvedere**, which was originally a seventeenth-century tower built into the city walls; today it's a restaurant and a lookout platform with excellent views over the river.

The modern-looking **Museum Het Valkhof**, Kelfkensbos 59 (Tues–Fri 10am–5pm, Sat & Sun noon–5pm; €4.50; ⓦ www.museumhetvalkhof.nl) houses a variety of exhibits with a local flavour, including innumerable paintings of Nijmegen and its environs – none particularly distinguished except for Jan van Goyen's *Valkhof Nijmegen*, which used to hang in the town hall. Painted in 1641, it's a large, sombre-toned picture – pastel variations on green and brown – where the Valkhof shimmers above the Waal, almost engulfed by sky and river. Also contained in the museum is the collection of the eminent archeologist G.M. Kam, who died in 1922. Alongside his Roman discoveries are other more recent artefacts; together they form a comprehensive picture of the first Roman settlements in the area and elsewhere in the Netherlands.

## Nearby museums

Southeast of Nijmegen on the road to Groesbeek, the **Bijbels Openluchtmuseum**, Profetenlaan 2 (Biblical Open-Air Museum; Easter–Oct daily 9am–5.30pm; ⓦ www.bijbelsopenluchtmuseum.nl; €8), is accessible by bus #5 (destination Groesbeek) from beside the train station. Ask the driver to indicate your stop on Nijmeegsebaan, from where it's a two-minute walk northeast along Meerwijkselaan to the museum. Here you'll find a series of reconstructions of the ancient Holy Land, including a Galilean fishing village, a complete Palestinian hamlet, a town street lined with Egyptian, Greek, Roman and Jewish houses and, strangely enough, "Bedouin tents of goats' hair as inhabited by the patriarchs". An experience not to be missed on any account.

There's another unusual museum 2km east of here, along Meerwijkselaan – the **Afrika Museum** at Postweg 6, Berg en Dal (April–Oct Mon–Fri 10am–5pm, Sat & Sun 11am–5pm; Nov–March Tues–Fri 10am–5pm, Sat & Sun 1–5pm; ⓦ www.afrikamuseum.nl; €6), where there's a purpose-built West African village, a small animal park and a museum full of totems, carved figurines and musical instruments. You can get here on bus #8 (destination Berg en Dal), though from the bus stop it's still a twenty-minute walk to the museum.

## Eating, drinking and nightlife

As you'd expect in a student town, Nijmegen has a wide range of places to eat and drink at sensible prices. For **food**, Kelfkensbos is a good place to start: *'t Circus* at no. 21 has excellent Dutch fare, while the Dutch-French food at *Appels & Peren* at no. 30 is a notch up in price. There are several decent places around the Waag, including the popular *de Waagh*. For drinking, head down Grote Straat to the waterfront; *Kandinsky Café* at Waalkade 65 is usually a lively spot, or you could try *Le Figaro* at Waalkade 47. If you don't want to be outdoors, try *Café in de Blaauwe Hand* – a cosy little bar behind the Grote Kerk and, supposedly, the oldest bar in town.

Every inch a fashionable town, Nijmegen attracts some top-name rock **bands**, especially during the academic year. Most perform at the Concertgebouw De Vereeniging, Keizer Karelplein 2/D or the Stadsschouwburg, Keizer Karelplein 32/H; for latest what's-on details, check with the VVV. For **films**, the Lux, Marienburg 38–39, has a good international programme of independent films and some late-night shows.

# Travel details

## Trains

**Apeldoorn** to: Amersfoort (every 30min; 25min); Deventer (every 30min; 10min); Zutphen (every 30min; 15min).

**Arnhem** to: Amsterdam CS (every 20min; 1hr 10min); Nijmegen (every 15min; 15min); Roosendaal (every 30min; 1hr 45min–2hr 10min); Velp (every 30min; 10min).

**Enschede** to: Amsterdam CS (every 30min; 2hr); Zutphen (every 30min; 55min).

**Lelystad** to: Amsterdam CS (every 20min; 40min).

**Zutphen** to: Arnhem (every 30min; 25min); Deventer (every 30min; 15min).

**Zwolle** to: Amersfoort (every 30min; 35–50min); Amsterdam CS (every 30min; 1hr 10min–1hr 35min); Arnhem (every 30min; 1hr); Deventer (every 30min; 20min); Emmen (every 30min; 55min); Groningen (3 hourly; 1hr–1hr 15min); Kampen (every 30min; 10min); Leeuwarden (every 30min; 55min–1hr 5min); Meppel (every 30min; 15min); Nijmegen (every 30min; 1hr 15min); Schiphol airport (4 hourly; 1hr 20min–1hr 45min); Steenwijk (every 30min; 15min); Zutphen (every 30min; 35min).

## Buses

**Doetinchem** to: 's-Heerenberg (Mon–Fri every 30min, Sat & Sun hourly; 20min).
**Enschede** to: Oldenzaal (Mon–Sat every 30min, Sun hourly; 20min).

**Kampen** to: Lelystad (Mon–Sat every 30min, Sun hourly; 55min); Urk (Mon–Sat every 30min, 3 on Sun after 4pm; 1hr).

**Lelystad** to: Enkhuizen (every 30min; 35min); Kampen (Mon–Sat every 30min, Sun hourly; 55min).

**Meppel** to: Zwartsluis (Mon–Fri 13 daily, Sat 6 daily, Sun 5 daily; 20min).

**Oldenzaal** to: Denekamp (hourly; 30min); Ootmarsum (hourly; 15min).

**Steenwijk** to: Blokzijl (Mon–Fri hourly, Sat 4 daily, Sun 3 daily; 15min); Giethoorn (Mon–Fri hourly, Sat 8 daily, Sun 4 daily; 15min); Zwartsluis (Mon–Fri hourly, Sat 8 daily, Sun 4 daily; 30min); Zwolle (Mon–Fri hourly, Sat 8 daily, Sun 4 daily; 1hr).

**Zwartsluis** to: Vollenhove (Mon–Fri every 30min, Sat & Sun hourly; 20min).

**Zwolle** to: Elburg (Mon–Sat every 30min, Sun hourly; 35min); Ens (Mon–Fri every 30min, Sun hourly; 1hr); Giethoorn (Mon–Fri hourly, Sat 8 daily, Sun 4 daily; 45min); Kampen (hourly; 20min); Steenwijk (Mon–Fri hourly, Sat 8 daily, Sun 4 daily; 1hr); Urk (Mon–Sat every 30min, 3 on Sun after 4pm; 1hr 10min); Vollenhove (Mon–Sat every 30min, Sun every 2hr; 50min); Zwartsluis (Mon–Sat every 30min, Sun every 2hr; 30min).

## Ferries

**Urk** to: Enkhuizen (July & Aug 3 daily; 1hr 30min).

6

# The south and Maastricht

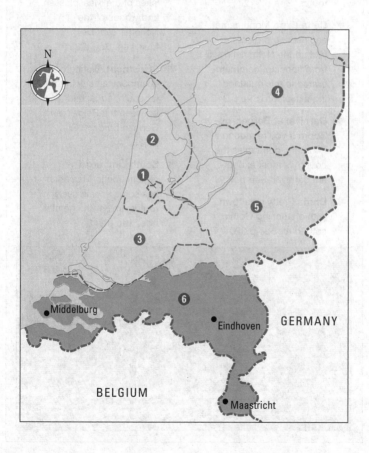

# CHAPTER 6

# Highlights

* **Middelburg** Pleasant maritime town, capital of the watery province of Zeeland. See p.306

* **The Walcheren coast** Zeeland's windswept coast has some dramatic footpaths and cycle routes. See p.312

* **Delta Expo** Monumental engineering project protecting the Netherlands from flooding, commemorated in this outstanding exhibition. See p.315

* **Carnival at Bergen-op-Zoom** If you're around in February, don't miss the country's most exuberant carnival. See p.319

* **Breda** Pretty little town with a stunning Gothic cathedral. See p.320

* **'s Hertogenbosch** Lively market town with a picturesque old quarter of alleys and little bridges. See p.324

* **Roermond** Popular holiday spot, a good base for exploration of nearby lakes of the Maasplassen and woods of the National Park De Meinweg. See p.331

* **Maastricht** Alluringly cosmopolitan city in the far south, squashed between the Belgian and German borders. See p.335

* **South Limburg** The region around Maastricht has some scenic cycle routes amidst the gentle hills. See p.343

# The south and Maastricht

Three widely disparate provinces make up the southern Netherlands. **Zeeland** is a scattering of villages and towns whose wealth, survival and sometimes destruction have long depended on the vagaries of the sea. Secured only in 1986, when the dykes and sea walls of the Delta Project were finally completed, many settlements seem held in suspended animation from a richer past, like the regional market centre of **Middelburg** and the small wool settlement of **Veere**.

As you head across the arc of towns of **Noord–Brabant** the landscape slowly fills out, rolling into a rougher countryside of farmland and forests, unlike the precise rectangles of neighbouring provinces. Though the change is subtle, there's a difference in the people here, too – less formal and for the most part Catholic, a fact manifest in the magnificent churches of **Breda** and **'s-Hertogenbosch**. But it's in solidly Catholic Limburg that a difference in character is really felt.

Continental rather than Dutch, **Limburg** has only been part of the Netherlands since the 1830s, but way before then the presence of Charlemagne's court at neighbouring Aachen greatly influenced the identity of the region. As Frankish emperor, Charlemagne had a profound effect on early medieval Europe, revitalizing Roman traditions and looking to the south for inspiration in art and architecture. Some of these great buildings remain, like **Maastricht**'s St Servaas. Indeed, the city is far and away the highlight of the province, with its unique blend of Catholic history and modern day cosmopolitan panache. As Belgium and Germany press closer, the landscape steepens sharply and you're within sight of the Netherlands' first and only hills.

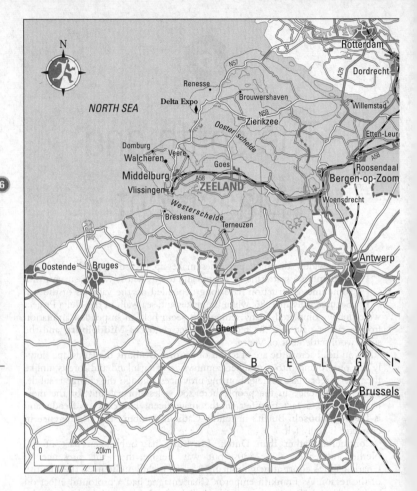

# Zeeland

*Luctor et Emergo*, reads **Zeeland**'s slogan: "I struggle and I emerge", a reference to the eternal battle waged with the sea. As its name suggests, the southwestern corner of the Netherlands is bound as much by water as by land. Comprising three main peninsulas submerged by the delta of the Rijn (Rhine), the Schelde and the Maas, each consists of a cluster of islands and semi-islands linked by kilometres of dykes. This concrete web not only gives protection from flooding but also forms the main lines of communication between each slither of land. The northernmost landmass, **Goeree-Overflakkee**, a little south of Rotterdam, is connected by two dams to

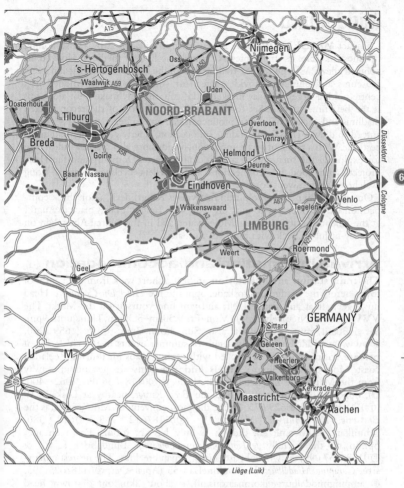

▲ Düsseldorf ▶ Cologne

▼ Liège (Luik)

**Schouwen-Duiveland**, while further south are Noord and Zuid **Beveland**, the western tip of which, site of Middelburg and traversed by a narrow canal, is **Walcheren**. Furthest south of all is **Zeeuws Vlaanderen**, lying across the blustery waters of the Westerschelde on the Belgian mainland.

Before the Delta Project (see p.314) secured the area, silting up and fear of the sea's encroachment had prevented any large towns developing; Zeeland remains a condensed area of low dunes and nature reserves, popular with holidaymakers escaping the cramped conurbations nearby. The province also has more sun than anywhere else in the Netherlands: the winds blow the clouds away, with spectacular sunsets guaranteed, beams of sunlight puncturing fast-moving clouds. Getting around is easy, with bus services making up for the lack of north–south train connections, though undoubtedly the best way to see these islands is to **cycle**, using **Middelburg** as a base and venturing out to the surrounding smaller towns.

# Middelburg

Compact **MIDDELBURG**, the largest town in Zeeland, is by any reckoning the most likeable. Its streets preserve some snapshots of medieval Holland, its cobbled alleyways echo the sea-trading days of the sixteenth century, and a few museums and churches provide targets for your wanderings. Middelburg's centre holds a large Thursday market and if you can only make it for a day, this is the best time to visit. Set to the imposing backdrop of the reconstructed Stadhuis and packed with local produce, it's an atmospheric event that's guaranteed to draw a crowd – including, on occasion, elderly couples in traditional costume. With a range of accommodation, Middelburg also makes an ideal base for exploring the surrounding area, including Veere, Domburg and the Delta project, with good bus connections and excellent cycling potential along Walcheren's windswept coast.

One of the town's most colourful **festivals** is Ringrijderij, a horseback competition where riders try to pick off rings with lances. It takes place in August at the Koepoort city gate near Molenwater, and in the central Abdijplein on one day in July. Check with the VVV for dates.

## Arrival, information and accommodation

The **train station** and **bus station** are just a short walk from the centre of town, across the bridge on Loskade, opposite the *Hotel Du Commerce*. Head up Segeersstraat and Lange Delft and you find yourself on the Markt. The **VVV** office at Nieuweburg 40 (Mon–Fri 9.30am–5.30pm, Thurs until 9pm, Sat 9.30am–5pm, April–Oct also Sun noon–3pm; ☎0118/659 900, ⓦwww.vvvmiddelburg.nl) has details of summer events in the city, a list of **private rooms** and is well stocked with cycling maps for touring Zeeland's coast. Most of Middelburg's **hotels and pensions** are just minutes away from the Markt: the *Du Commerce*, Loskade 1 (☎0118/636 051, ⓕ626 400; ❹), opposite the train station, and the *Beau Rivage*, nearby at Loskade 19 (☎0118/638 060, ⓕ629 673; ❸), are the most convenient. More central is the *Brasserie De Huifkar*, Markt 19 (☎0118/612 998, ⓕ612 386, ⓔhuifkar@mahoco.nl; ❸), though it only has six rooms. For a cheaper option, try the friendly *de Koningin van Lombardije*, Blindehoek 12 (☎ & ⓕ0118/637 099; ❷), which boasts a gargantuan breakfast. The nearest **campsite**, *Camping Middelburg*, Koninginnelaan 55 (April–Oct; ☎0118/625 395, ⓔcampingmiddelburg@komnaarons.nl), is about 2km out of town: head down Zandstraat and Langeviele Weg, or take bus #57 (every 30min) from the station.

The VVV has a guided **walking tour** (April–Oct daily 1.30pm; €3.65) which leaves from their office and lasts one and a half hours, taking in the city's main landmarks. **Horse-drawn carriage rides** also operate from outside the office (June–Sept Mon–Sat 11am–5pm, Sun 1–5pm; 20min; €3). The VVV can also sell you the *Middelburg City Guide* (€2.99), a booklet which offers walking information, a basic map and discounts on museums and boat tours.

Open-top **boats** offer trips on the canals, leaving from the Lange Viele bridge on Achter de Houttuinen (mid–May to mid–Sept Mon–Sat 10am–5pm, Sun noon–4pm; April & Oct Mon–Sat 11am–4pm; €4.50). The return boat trip to Veere (May–Sept daily 10.15am & 2pm; €10.50) leaves from near the train station.

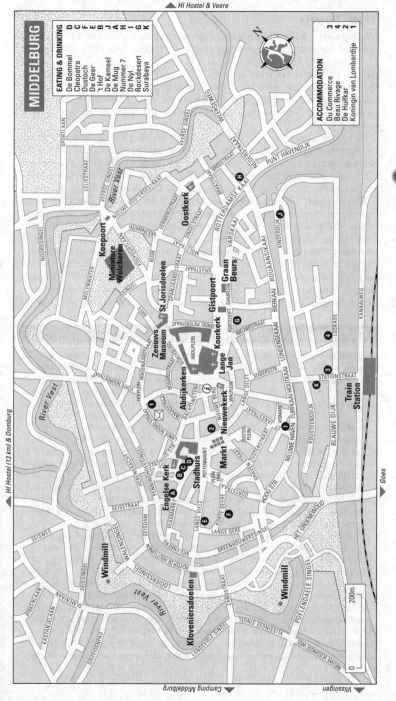

**MIDDELBURG**

**EATING & DRINKING**

| | |
|---|---|
| De Bommel | D |
| Cleopatra | C |
| Dustoch | F |
| De Geer | E |
| 't Hof | B |
| De Kameel | J |
| De Mug | A |
| Nummer 7 | I |
| De Nyl | G |
| Rockdesert | H |
| Surabaya | K |

**ACCOMMODATION**

| | |
|---|---|
| Du Commerce | 3 |
| Beau Rivage | 4 |
| De Huifkar | 2 |
| Koningin van Lombardije | 1 |

# The Town

Middelburg is an appealing town to explore, small enough to cover on foot and scattered with architectural clues to its rich, sea trading past. The town owed its early growth to its position on a bend in the River Arne, making it easy to defend. The slight elevation gave the settlement protection from the sea and its streets slope down to the harbour, protecting the centre from flooding. Look out for the surviving stone blocks at the end of Brakstraat, into which wooden planks were slotted then bolstered with sand banks, acting as a temporary dyke.

Though its abbey was founded in 1120, Middelburg's isolation restricted its development until the late Middle Ages, when, being at the western end of the Scheldt estuary, it began to get rich off the back of Antwerp, Bruges and Ghent. Conducting its own trade in wool and cloth, it became both the market and administrative centre of the region. The town's street names – Houtkaai ("Timber Dock"), Korendijk ("Grain Dyke"), Bierkaai ("Beer Dock") – reveal how diverse its trade became, while house names like "London" and "Samarkand" tell of the routes Middelburg's traders plied. Kuiperspoort ("Barrelmaker's Port") is an alleyway off Rouaansekaai along which warehouses have been impressively restored, many of which are now occupied by artists and musicians.

Once a town of wood and thatch, Middelburg's newly acquired wealth bought bricks and tiles to clothe its timber-framed buildings. In "de Laurier Boom", Rouaansekaai 2, chunky wooden rafters can be seen on the first floor, as can exposed oak beams at Spanjaardstraat 3a and 49. Indeed, with oak an

## Cycling around the Walcheren

Countless cycling options are available to make the most of the Walcheren's stunning coastline, with plenty of refreshments en route. With limited transport for bikes, most routes are best completed as loops. As a rule of thumb, red cycleway signs indicate utility paths, often parallel to a main road, while the green signs favour more scenic alternatives. The VVV sells a yellow booklet covering 22 rides around Zeeland (€6.50); if you intend to explore further, try the ANWB Fietsmap Zeeland, a pack with twenty suggested routes and four handy 1:60,000 maps for €11.50.

Possible day-trips include cycling west to Domburg, picking up signs to the Domburg HI hostel and continuing through the woods to Breezand. A cycleway follows the polder to Veere, from where you can ride alongside the Walcheren canal, cutting back to Middelburg. Alternatively, pick up the same canal out of town to Vlissingen, joining the cycleway that runs between dune and woodland to Zoutelande and Westkapelle: there's a fabulous stretch of dyke to cycle along, in the direction of Domburg, with spectacular sunsets out to sea and a photogenic lighthouse. A red-signposted cycle path leads directly back to Middelburg.

If Zeeland's well-founded reputation for blustery winds is putting you off, pay a visit to one of Middelburg's more unusual factories. **M5**, at Nieuwe Kleverskerkseweg 23 (☎0118/628 759, ⊛www.m5-ligfietsen.com), is a company at the cutting edge of bicycle technology: they specialize in **recumbents**, or *ligfietsen* in Dutch. With their low-slung riding position, recumbents are not only fun and comfortable to ride but will also slice through Zeeland's fiercest headwinds – though it might take a few minutes to learn to ride one. You can rent from M5 for around €20 a day (plus €136 deposit), with significant discounts for a week or more. Otherwise, you can **rent bikes** from the train station. Alternatively, head for Delta Cycles at Zusterplein 8 (down the alleyway next to the ING bank on Marktplein; ☎0118/639 245). Part of a project that places people with mental disabilities in employment, they rent single-speed bikes at €4.55 per day.

increasingly scarce and valued material for shipbuilding – supplies were sought out from as far as the Baltic - inhabitants even recycled hulls and rigging, salvaged from old or damaged ships, to build their homes.

Most interesting buildings date from this period, though the **Stadhuis**, generally agreed to be Zeeland's finest, is a wonderfully eclectic mix of architectural styles. The towering Gothic facade is especially magnificent, dating from the mid-fifteenth century and designed by the Keldermans family from Mechelen. Inside is the **Vleeshal**, a former meat hall that now houses changing exhibitions of contemporary art which can be visited on conducted tours. Hour-long **tours** of the Stadhuis (April–Oct Mon–Sat 11am–5pm, Sun noon–5pm; check notice board outside for exact times; €2.75) take in the mayor's office, council chambers and various reception rooms.

The Stadhuis' impressive pinnacled tower was added in 1520, but it's as well to remember that this, along with the Stadhuis itself and much of Middelburg's city centre, is only a reconstruction of the original. On May 17, 1940 the city was all but flattened by German bombing in the same series of raids that destroyed Rotterdam. In 1944, in an attempt to isolate German artillery in Vlissingen, Walcheren's sea defences were breached, which resulted in severe flood damage to Middelburg's already treacherous streets. Restoration was a long and difficult process, but so successful that you can only occasionally tell that the city's buildings have been patched up. Bricks were made locally from sea clays: when fired in the kiln, salts form a natural glaze of reds, greens or yellows; these hues can be seen on the corner of Nieuwstraat and Korte Delft, glinting in the sun.

### The Abdijkerken and around

Middelburg's most distinctive tower, that of the **Abdijkerken** ("Abbey Churches") on Onderdentoren, collapsed under German bombing, destroying the churches below. Today the abbey complex – really three churches in one (May–Sept Mon–Fri 10am–5pm; free) – is quite bare inside, considering it's been around since the twelfth century. There's a reason for this: Middelburg was an early convert to Protestantism following the uprising against the Spanish, and in 1574 William the Silent's troops threw out the Premonstratensian monks and converted the abbey to secular use. Occupied by various unlikely syndicates, including a gun manufacturer and a mint, the abbey's three churches were then adapted back to Protestant worship.

The **Nieuwe Kerk** has an organ case of 1692, and the **Wandel Kerk** the outrageously triumphalistic tomb of admirals Jan and Cornelis Evertsen, brothers killed fighting in a naval battle against the English in 1666. The **Koor Kerk**, on the eastern side of the tower, retains the oldest decoration, including a Nicolai organ of 1478. Best of all is to climb the 207 steps of the tower (April–Oct Mon–Sat 11am–5pm, Sun noon–5pm; €2.25), known locally as *Lange Jan* (Long John). In clear weather, the view from its 91-metre summit across over Walcheren and as far as the Zeelandbrug and the eastern Scheldt, gives a good sense of how vulnerable the province is to the sea. The history of the abbey is presented in the **Historama**, in the cloister at Abdijplein 9 (April–Oct Mon–Sat 11am–5pm, Sun noon–5pm, €1.80). The **carillon** of *Lange Jan* plays every quarter-hour, with additional concerts year-round (Thurs noon–1pm; May to mid–Sept also Sat 11am–noon).

At the rear of the abbey, housed in what were once the monks' dormitories, the **Zeeuws Museum** (closed for renovation at time of writing; check with VVV; ⓦ www.zeeuwsmuseum.nl) holds a mixed bag of collections and finds from the Zeeland area. The museum has a tiny but choice collection of twentieth-century paintings by Mesdag, Jan and Charley Toorop and other (local) artists. Elsewhere in the museum are some lively tapestries, commissioned by the local authorities between 1591 and 1604 to celebrate the naval battles against the Spanish, and a comprehensive display of local costumes.

The **Roosevelt Study Centre**, Abdij 9 (Mon–Fri 10am–12.30pm & 1.30–4.30pm), a centre for the study of twentieth-century American history (one of the largest in Europe), has a permanent exhibition on presidents Theodore and Franklin Delano Roosevelt and the latter's remarkable wife Eleanor.

East of the abbey, **Damplein** was restored to its original breadth by the demolition of a couple of rows of houses. It forms a quieter focus for bars than the Markt and is the site of the **Graanbeurs**, a grain exchange rebuilt in the nineteenth century and today containing some intriguing and humorous stone plaques by international artists – a project known as "Podio del Mondo per l'Arte".

Directly north of Damplein on Molenwater, **Miniature Walcheren** (daily: April–Oct 10am–6pm; July–Aug 9am–7pm; €7) has scaled-down models of Walcheren island's best buildings that might entertain kids for an hour or so. Further east, the distinctive profile of the domed, octagonal **Oostkerk** (May–Oct Thurs 10am–4pm; free) stands high above the surrounding suburbs, near the main road to Veere: built in 1647 to designs by Pieter Post and others, it was one of the first churches in the Netherlands to be built expressly for Protestant use. What's more, its construction was financed by taxes raised on beer, a profitable commodity to tax: in seventeenth-century Middelburg, water was so dirty that the whole population, children included, drank light beer instead.

## Kloveniersdoelen

While the streets around the Abdijkerken and Stadhuis are the most atmospheric, it's worth walking to the western edge of town to reach the landmark of the **Kloveniersdoelen** at the end of Langeviele. Built in 1607 in exuberant Flemish Renaissance style, this was the home of the city's civic guard, the Arquebusiers, until the end of the eighteenth century, later becoming the local headquarters of the East India Company, and later still a military hospital. Restored in 1969 (as you might have guessed if you spotted the weather vane), it's now a recital hall and is renowned for presenting new and experimental music (there's a festival every year in July; call ☎0118/623 650 for details). A short walk north or south of the Kloveniersdoelen, by the edge of Middelburg's old star-shaped defensive canal, are a couple of eighteenth-century **windmills**: De Hoop mill to the south was once a barley peeling mill; De Seismolen to the north a cereal mill, though it's not possible to enter either today.

## Eating and drinking

Vlasmarkt, running northwest of Markt, has Middelburg's widest selection of **restaurants**, including *De Mug*, Vlasmarkt 56, with good Dutch–French cooking at moderate prices, an excellent array of beers, and occasional live jazz. A little pricier but still good value, *Nummer 7*, east of Damplein at Rotterdamsekai 7, and *De Kameel*, by the canal at Kinderdijk 82, both have fabulous local food. If your budget is tight, there are a couple of decent shwarma joints: *De Nyl*, at St Janstraat 45 and *Cleopatra* at Vlasmarkt 2. Most other restaurants are situated on or around Markt and many are tourist-orientated and pricey for what you get.

Elsewhere in town, *Surabaya*, Stationstraat 20, is an Indonesian restaurant with reasonably priced *rijsttafels*, and a €16 evening buffet. The colourful and cheap café *Dustoch* at Korte Geere 16 is part of a project placing people with mental disabilities in jobs (as with Delta Cycles, see Listings), and includes a children's menu. For something a little different, try the house at Rotterdamsekai 13; every other Saturday the owner opens up an organic café (3–6pm), where you can eat well for €6. On Thursdays the market stands supply limitless cheap and tasty snacks, especially fresh fish and seafood. Look out for *bolus*, a circular sweet bread brought to Middleburg by Portuguese Jews, best served hot with butter and a cup of coffee.

**Bars** and **cafés** are also concentrated on or near the Markt; *De Bommel* is the pick of the bars here, although there's not much to choose between them at the weekends. At the bottom of Vlasmarkt, *'t Hof* is excellent and gets occasional live bands. Damplein is another good stretch for drinking: *Rockdesert* at no. 20 is young and noisy while *De Geer*, Lange Viele 55, has the cheapest beer in town.

## Listings

Bookshop De Drukkerij, Markt 51, has a wide selection of books, Internet access and a popular café centred around a communal table.
Markets General market on the Markt is on Thursday (8.30am–4pm); there's also a flower and produce market on Saturday (same hours). Vismarkt has a flea market on the first Sat of the month (except Jan) 9am–4pm, and an antique and curio market in summer (June–Aug Thurs 9am–4pm).
Police Achter de Houttuinen 10 ☏0118/688 000.
Post office Lange Noordstraat 48 (Mon 10am–6pm, Tues–Fri 9am–6pm, Thurs until 6pm, Sat 9am–12.30pm).
Taxi Taxicentrale ☏0118/612 600 or 613 200.

# Vlissingen

**VLISSINGEN** (Flushing), 5km south of Middelburg, was previously an important ferry terminus, but its role as a hub for transport to Belgium has been reduced by the impending completion of the tunnel between Ellewoutsdijk and Terneuzen a little upstream to the east. There's not an awful lot to see in the town, although a new maritime museum warrants a couple of hours of exploration, and the shipping trade that plies the choppy Westerschelde estuary has an appeal of its own.

The VVV is at Oude Markt 3 (Mon 1–6pm, Tues–Fri 10am–6pm, Sat 10am–5pm; ☏0118/422 190, ⓦwww.vvvvlissingen.nl). It has a list of pensions, including the nearby *Pension Marijke*, Coosje Buskenstraat 88 (☏ & Ⓕ0118/415 062; ❶) and *Belgische Loodsen Societeit*, on the seafront at Boulevard de Ruyter 4 (☏0118/413 608, Ⓕ410 427; ❷), near the end of Nieuwendijk, and has information on local cycling routes. The town centre itself is less attractive, with the unremarkable **St Jacobskerk** on Kleine Markt (July & Aug Mon–Sat 10am–noon; free) and the improbably named **Cornelia Quackhofje**, an eighteenth-century almshouse for sailors just north of the Lange Zelke shopping precinct.

For more atmosphere, head for the **harbour**. Popular with Dutch and German tourists in the summer and school holidays, it's awash with pavement cafés and fresh fish and chip stalls. The brand new **Zeeuws Maritiem "Muzeeum"** at Nieuwendijk 15 (Mon–Fri 10am–5pm, Sat & Sun 1–5pm; €6) is the place to gen up on Zeeland's rich maritime tradition. The museum is divided into four themes – the sea, trade, glory and adventure. Multimedia presentations (in Dutch) explain the sea's crucial role in shaping Zeeland's

At the time of writing, the 6.6km **tunnel** beneath the Westerschelde, linking Ellewoutsdijk and Terneuzen, was nearing completion. Once completed (in 2003), the tunnel will be open 24 hours a day; the toll for cars is expected to be around €5. The **ferry** across the Westerschelde between Vlissingen and Breskens (takes 20min) will continue to carry foot passengers and bicycles. Bus #56, #57 and #58 from Vlissingen town centre, via the train station, run to the port. Ferry departures from Vlissingen are daily (every hour 7am–9pm), and there are buses on the other side from Breskens to the Belgian town of Bruges. In the opposite direction, the ferry departs Breskens daily (every hour 7.30am–9.30pm). Tickets are €2 per person, with a 70c surcharge for bicycles. For more details, call ☏0118/465 905.

livelihood, while excellent audio-visuals reconstruct scenes of naval battles to dramatic effect. Displays include wares shipped along the trading routes of the Dutch East Indies – nutmeg, ginger, salt, tea, silver, porcelain and even bricks. A thriving port in the Golden Age, Vlissingen was the hometown of Admiral Michiel de Ruyters, famous throughout the Netherlands – his face even appears on Pilsner bottles – though the town was renowned too for spawning its fair share of marauding pirates. Not that some ships needed pillaging: so overloaded was the Asia-bound 't Vliegent Hart in 1735, it didn't even make it further than the Westerschelde; most of its cargo was retrieved in 1982 and is now on display in the museum.

Families will enjoy **Het Arsenaal**, on Arsenaalplein (June–Sept daily 10am–8pm; Feb–May & Oct–Dec Tues–Sun 10am–7pm; last admission 2hr before closing; €8.50; ⓦwww.arsenaal.com), a theme park where you can go on a simulated sea voyage, climb an observation tower and walk on a mocked-up seabed among tanks of sharks.

The blustery **walk** along the Nieuwendijk offers views of the enormous vessels that sail the Westerschelde. Keeping to a narrow, often tortuous path, these enormous container ships must negotiate the shallow waters and shifting sandbanks that regularly reveal centuries-old wrecks. Further round the harbour, the promenade has a pleasant seaside feel, with a beach at the end. Alternatively, you could rent a bike from the train station next to the ferry terminal – it has a wide selection, including recumbents – and continue past the promenade on the green-signposted cycle path to Dishoek and Zouteland; along the way there are plenty of opportunities to lock your bike and hike up and over the dunes, emerging onto a beach that runs for miles.

# The West Zeeland coast

The coastline west of Middelburg offers some of the Netherlands' finest beaches and makes for excellent walking and cycling country, although on midsummer weekends parts of it virtually disappear beneath the crowds of Dutch and German holidaymakers. Bus #53 from Middelburg station (hourly) runs through **OOSTKAPELLE**, notable for its striking church tower, before passing the thirteenth-century **Kasteel Westhove**, now home to the fine Domburg **HI hostel** (☏0118/581 254, ⓦwww.stayokay.com; dorms €26; April–Oct) – complete with moat and set amid a nature reserve. You can rent bikes from here (€4/day). Next door, the *Zeeuws Biologisch Museum* (April–Oct

Mon & Sat noon–5pm, Tues–Fri & Sun 10am–5pm; July & Aug daily 10am–6pm; Nov–March Tues–Sun noon–5pm; €3.50) has an aquarium and displays on local flora and fauna. Oostkapelle's **VVV** is at Duinweg 2a (April–Oct Mon–Sat 10am–4.30pm; July & Aug until 6pm; Nov–March Mon–Fri 10am–3pm; ☎0118/582 910, ⓦwww.vvvwnb.nl).

A couple of kilometres further on, **DOMBURG**, 14km northwest of Middelburg, is the area's principal resort, a favourite haunt for artists since early last century when Jan Toorop gathered together a group of like-minded painters (including, for a while, Piet Mondrian), inspired by the peaceful scenery and the fine quality of the light. Toorop built a pavilion to exhibit the paintings and the building has been recreated as the **Museum Domburg**, Ooststraat 10a (April–Nov Tues–Sun 1–5pm; €2.25), where exhibitions continue to display works by members of the group. Parts of the Domburg church, including the tower, date from the thirteenth century, although it's off-limits to visitors at present. On the whole, though, you'd come here to walk on the dunes and through the woods or to cycle the coast path. An easy ride 7km west of Domburg is **Westkapelle**, a quieter beach resort with a picturesque lighthouse and a critical spot where the dyke was breached during the 1953 flood.

Domburg's **VVV** is at Schuitvlotstraat 32 (April–Oct Mon–Sat 9.30am–5pm; July & Aug Mon–Fri 9.30am–6pm, Sat 9.30am–6pm, Sun 2–4pm; Nov–March Mon–Fri 9.30am–4.30pm, Sat 930am–1pm; ☎0118/581 342, ⓦwww.vvvwnb.nl); ask the bus driver to drop you nearby. They'll help with accommodation and provide you with a map of the village. Staff can recommend dozens of **pensions** – *Duinliust* is a safe bet at Badhuisweg 28 (☎0118/582 970, ⓔlosnoordzee@zeelandnet.nl; ❶). There are several **campsites**, the nearest being *Hof Domburg* at Schelpveg 7 (☎0118/588 200, ⓕ583 668), a few minutes' walk west of town. Domburg has plenty of simple **cafés**; for something a little different try the great pizzas at *Pizzeria Milano* on Ooststraat. *Tramzicht* on Stationstraat is the best bar. The other resorts also have plenty of pensions and campsites, although you may need to book rooms through one of the VVVs at busy times.

# Veere and around

Some 8km northeast of Middelburg, **VEERE** is a picturesque little town by the banks of the Veerse that makes an ideal day-trip. Today it's a centre for all things maritime, its small harbour jammed with yachts and its cafés packed with weekend admirals, but a handful of buildings and a large church point to a time when Veere was rich and quite independent of other, similar towns in Zeeland. To reach Veere from Middelburg, catch bus #53 (timetable changes regularly, check with VVV), or rent a bike from Middelburg train station and take either the cycle path beside the main road or the circuitous but more picturesque routes from the north of the town.

Veere made its wealth through a fortuitous Scottish connection: in 1444 Wolfert VI van Borssele, the lord of Veere, married Mary, daughter of James I of Scotland. As part of the dowry, van Borssele was granted a monopoly on trade with Scottish wool merchants; in return, Scottish merchants living in Veere were granted special privileges. A number of their houses still stand, best of which are those on the dock facing the harbour: *Het Lammetje* (The Lamb) and *De Struys* (The Ostrich), dating from the mid-sixteenth century, were combined offices, homes and warehouses for the merchants; they now house the **Museum Schotse Huizen** (April–Oct Mon–Fri noon–5pm, Sun 1–5pm; €2.50), a rather lifeless collection of local costumes, old books, atlases and furniture, along with an exhibit devoted to fishing. Elsewhere there are plenty of Gothic buildings, whose rich decoration leaves you in no doubt that the Scottish wool trade earned a bundle for the sixteenth and seventeenth-century burghers of Veere: many of the buildings (which are usually step-gabled with distinctive green and white shutters) are embellished with whimsical details that play on the owners' names or their particular line of business. The **Stadhuis** at Markt 5 (open by arrangement; ☎0118/583 615) is similarly opulent, dating from the 1470s, with an out-of-scale Renaissance tower added a century later. Its facade is decorated with statues of the lords of Veere and their wives (Wolfert VI is third from the left), and, inside, a small museum occupies what was formerly the courtroom, pride of place going to a goblet that once belonged to Maximilian of Burgundy.

Of all Veere's buildings the **Grote Kerk** (April–Oct Mon–Sat 10am–5pm, Sun 1–5pm; €2) seems to have suffered most: finished in 1560, it was badly damaged by fire a century later and restoration removed much of its decoration. In 1808 invading British troops used the church as a hospital and three years later Napoleon's army converted it into barracks and stables, destroying the stained glass, bricking up the windows and adding five floors in the nave. Despite all this damage, the church's blunt 42-metre **tower** (same hours and ticket; last admission 4.30pm) adds a glowering presence to the landscape, especially when seen across the misty polder fields. According to the original design, the tower was to have been three times higher, but even as it stands there's a great view from the top, back to the pinnacled skyline of Middelburg and out across the breezy Veerse Meer.

Veere fell from importance with the decline of the wool trade. The opening of the Walcheren Canal in the nineteenth century, linking the town to Middelburg and Vlissingen, gave it a stay of execution, but the construction of the Veersegatdam and Zandkreekdam in the 1950s finally sealed the port to seagoing vessels, and simultaneously created a freshwater lake ideal for watersports.

The **VVV**, Oudestraat 28 (mid-July to mid-Sept daily noon–4pm; mid-April to mid-July & mid-Sept to Nov Mon–Sat noon–4pm; rest of year Mon & Wed–Fri 1.30–4pm; ☎0118/501 365), can advise on the rental of all types of watercraft and has details of **private rooms**. The cheaper of Veere's two **hotels** is *'t Waepen van Veere* at Markt 23–27 (☎0118/501 231; ❷), while the *De Campveerse Toren*, Kade 2, is beautifully situated overlooking the water (☎0118/501 291, ☎501 695; ❸). There are a few cafés around the Markt including the *Suster Anna Pannekoekhuis* (summer daily; winter Sat & Sun only), which serves pancakes, sandwiches and cakes.

## The Delta Project

On February 1, 1953, a combination of an exceptionally high spring tide and powerful northwesterly winds drove the North Sea over the dykes to **flood** much of Zeeland. The results were catastrophic: 1855 people drowned, 47,000 homes and 500km of dykes were destroyed and some of the country's most fertile agricultural land was ruined by salt water. Towns as far as Bergen-op-Zoom and Dordrecht were flooded and Zeeland's road and rail network was wrecked. The government's response was immediate and on a massive scale. After patching up the breached dykes, work was begun on the **Delta Project**, one of the largest engineering schemes the world has ever seen and one of phenomenal complexity and expense.

The plan was to ensure the safety of Zeeland by radically shortening and strengthening its coastline. The major estuaries and inlets would be dammed, thus preventing unusually high tides surging inland to breach the thousands of kilometres of small dykes. Where it was impractical to build a dam – such as across the Westerschelde or Nieuwe Waterweg, which would have closed the seaports of Antwerp and Rotterdam respectively – secondary dykes were to be reinforced. New roads across the top of the dams would improve communications to Zeeland and Zuid-Holland and the freshwater lakes that formed behind the dams would enable precise control of the water table of the Zeeland islands.

It took thirty years for the Delta Project to be completed. The smaller, secondary dams – the **Veersegat**, **Haringvliet** and **Brouwershaven** – were built first to provide protection from high tides as quickly as possible, a process that also enabled engineers to learn as they went along. In 1968, work began on the largest dam, intended to close the Oosterschelde estuary that forms the outlet of the Maas, Waal and Rijn rivers. It soon ran into intense opposition from environmental groups, who pointed out that the mudflats were an important breeding ground for birds, while the estuary itself was a nursery for plaice, sole and other North Sea fish. Local fishermen too, saw their livelihoods in danger: if the Oosterschelde were closed the oyster, mussel and lobster beds would be destroyed, representing a huge loss to the region's economy.

The environmental and fishing lobbies argued that strengthening the estuary dykes would provide adequate protection; the water board and agricultural groups raised the emotive spectre of the 1953 flood. In the end a compromise was reached, and in 1976 work began on the **Stormvloedkering** ("Storm Surge Barrier"), a gate that would stay open under normal tidal conditions, allowing water to flow in and out of the estuary, but close ahead of potentially destructive high tides.

### Delta Expo

It's on the Stormvloedkering, completed in 1986, that the fascinating **Delta Expo** (April–Oct daily 10am–5.30pm; €11.50; Nov–March Wed–Sun 10am–5pm; €8.50), signposted as Waterland Neeltje Jans, is housed. Only once you're inside the Expo itself, though, do you get an idea of the scale of the project. It's best to start with the half-hour video presentation before taking in the exhibition itself, which is divided into three areas: the historical background of the Netherlands' water management problems; the technological developments that enabled the country to protect itself; the environmental consequences of applying the technologies and the solutions that followed. The Surge Barrier (and the Delta Project as a whole) has been a triumphant success: computer simulations predict most high tides, but if an unpredicted rise does occur, the sluice gates close automatically in a matter of minutes.

**Transport** to the Delta Expo is easy: from Middelburg take hourly bus #104 (twice hourly in summer) from Hof van Tange on the west side of town (10min walk from the VVV near the Kloveniersdoelen building), or you can easily cycle it (takes 1hr 30min), following national cycleway LF16 (nord), alongside open beaches and dunes, past wind turbines and onto the storm barrier itself; there are ample opportunities to peer into the sluice gates and appreciate the full scale of the project. Allow for blustery winds on the way back. From Rotterdam, take the metro to Spijkenisse and then bus #104; tell the driver you want the Waterland stop.

# Schouwen-Duiveland

The Storm Surge Barrier spans the mouth of the Oosterschelde estuary over to **SCHOUWEN-DUIVELAND**. Most of the Dutch and German tourists who come here head directly to the western corner for the acres of beach, pine forest and dune between **Burgh-Haamstede** and **Renesse**, two villages situated 6km apart. In the summer, this western flank of the island is packed with families and predominantly young holidaymakers, making the most of its waterborne activities. **Zierikzee** further east is a more traditional affair, a miniature Middelburg that makes an appealing base for exploring the island, with some fine trips through the countryside and one of Europe's longest (and perhaps windiest) bridges nearby.

If you're coming for peace and quiet, you should steer clear of the school holidays in July and August for the best chance of finding suitable accommodation. Travel over the season's bookends in June and September and you'll find you have much of the long, pristine beaches to yourself, though the weather can be varied: facilities dwindle with the approach of autumn, and storms blot the sky.

## Renesse and around

En route to Renesse, the village of **BURGH-HAAMSTEDE** is well placed to explore the Beschermd Natuur-Monument around Westerschouwen, a large expanse of forest and dune run by the Staatsbosbeheer. With a network of bicycle tracks and walking trails, it's a lovely spot to get lost in for a couple of hours – which is probably what will happen, as the signposting is pretty confusing. You can rent a geared bike for €6.15 a day from Fiets en Hengelsport Bouwman, Noordstraat 17.

About 6km north, **RENESSE** is a modern sprawl of bungalows, set just a kilometre from the beach, that makes a more appealing base. Popular with the surfing and windsurfing crowd, its sixteen-kilometre beach is divided in summer into sectors, catering for families, surfers, kite-flyers and naturists. A free open-top electric bus (9am–7pm) plies the length of the beach, linking hotels, campsites and the "Transferium" – the modern bus station on the edge of town that offers changing rooms, showers and bike rental, in an attempt to encourage holidaymakers to abandon their cars at the free car park alongside. Parking at the beach (€0.80/hr) is limited to two hours. **Surfboards** cost €35 a day and **skimboards** (miniature boards that glide into the surf) are €5 an hour from Windsurfing Renesse, De Zoom 15 (⊛www.windsurfingrenesse.nl); they'll also provide lessons. Windsurfs can be rented too, but the best spot for windsurfing is at the Brouwersdam, 8km away (see below). Jonker Funsports, Zeeanemoonweg 8 (⊛www.jonkerfunsports.nl) rents blades and protective gear (€12/day). These shops are often only open on the weekends in winter. To tap into the town's historical roots, consult the VVV about tours to **Slot Moermond** (mid-June to mid-Aug; ℡0111/460 360), a castle built for the local lords just north of Renesse.

The area is teeming with hotels, campsites, mini-campings and holiday homes, many of which run B&Bs. If you're planning on visiting over the summer, you should contact the **VVV**, Zeeanemoonweg 4a (Mon–Sat 9am–5pm; hours vary out of season; ℡0111/460 360, ⊛www.vvvschouwenduiveland.nl) well in advance for a list of available accommodation; travel with a tent and you're more likely to find a plot of grass to squeeze onto. Central accommodation includes *Am-Re Cottage*, Laône 23 (℡0111/461 205, ✉amre@zeelandnet

.nl; **❶**) and the larger *Hotel de Logerij*, Laône 15 (☏0111/462 570, 🅦www
.delogerij.nl; **❸**). The English website 🅦www.renesse.nl includes lists of
accommodation and services. The VVV sells an excellent map detailing beach
allotment, as well as walking and cycling trails on the island (€2) and has a free
booklet *Toegankelijk Schouwen-Duiveland* on areas suitable for the disabled or
those in wheelchairs.

It's a 45-minute journey on bus #104 from Middelburg to Renesse, five
minutes less if you get off at Burgh-Haamstede. The same bus continues onto
Spijkenisse, from where you can catch the metro into Rotterdam.

### Surfcentrum

The **Surfcentrum**, at Ossenhoek 1, Kabbellaarsbank (☏0111/671 480,
🅦www.brouwersdam.nl) is an invigorating detour from Renesse, with views
across the Grevelingenmeer inlet. Reached by bus #104 (ask the driver for the
Port Zélande stop), it's situated halfway along the Brouwersdam, linking
Schouwen-Duiveland to Goeree-Overflakkee. The centre offers excellent
windsurfing on one side, and one of Europe's cleanest beaches on the other –
renting a board and wetsuit costs €50 a day, or €75 for a weekend. Tuition,
small sailboats and four-bed dorms (€50 per room) are also available.

### Brouwershaven

Back on dry land, **BROUWERSHAVEN** is an attractive village, reached by
bus #134 hourly from Renesse. Until the building of the Nieuwe Waterweg
linking Rotterdam to the coast, Brouwershaven was a busy seaport – boats
could sail right into the centre of town. Today it's a pretty town with yachts
tethered on the main square. There's not much to see, other than the gabled
houses flanking the harbour and a few narrow streets around the Markt,
though the Stadhuis is an attractive Flemish Renaissance building of 1599.

## Zierikzee and around

Schouwen-Duiveland's most interesting town lies to the south.
**ZIERIKZEE**'s position at the intersection of shipping routes between
England, Flanders and Holland led to it becoming an important port in the late
Middle Ages as it traded with the towns of the Hanseatic League. It was also
famed for its salt and madder – a root that, when dried and ground, produces
a brilliant red dye. Nowadays, it's a picturesque town of narrow cobbled streets
and traditional gabled facades, an ideal base for exploring the area.

Encircled by a defensive canal and preferably entered by one of two sixteenth-
century watergates, Zierikzee's centre is small and easily explored, easier still if
you arm yourself with a map from the **VVV** at Nieuwe Haven 7 (May–Sept
Mon–Fri 10am–4pm, Sat 10am–2pm; hours vary out of season; ☏0111/412
450, 🅦www.vvvschouwenduiveland.nl). A few minutes' walk from the office,
the Gothic **'s Gravensteen** building at Mol 25 (April–Oct Mon–Sat
10am–5pm, Sun noon–5pm; €2) was once the jail and is today home to a
maritime museum, although the building is more interesting than the exhibits:
the removal of plaster walls from the old prison cells in 1969 uncovered graffiti and drawings by the prisoners, and the basements contain torture chambers
and iron cage cells built to contain two prisoners. Zierikzee's **Stadhuis** is easy
enough to find – just head for the tall spire on Meelstraat 6. Inside, the
**Gemeentemuseum** (May–Oct Mon–Sat 10am–5pm, Sun noon–5pm; €2)
has collections of silver, costumes and a regional history exhibition. Also worth
seeing is the **Monstertoren** (April to mid–Sept Mon–Sat 11am–4pm, Sun

noon–4pm; €1.50), a tower designed by the Keldermans family on which work was stopped when it reached 97 of its planned 167 metres.

The VVV has details of **private rooms**, including a lovely self-contained apartment at Minderbroederstraat 36–38 (☎0111/416 759; ●). Alternatives include the *Pension Klaas Vaak*, Nieuwe Bogerdstraat (☎0111/414 204; ●) and the *Hotel Van Oppen China Garden*, Verrenieuwstraat 11 (☎0111/412 288, ℱ417 202; ●). Book early during the summer; like the rest of the island Zierikzee is a magnet for Dutch, German and Belgian tourists. Bus #132 shuttles between Goes and Zierikzee in half an hour; it's an hour and a quarter to Rotterdam on twice-hourly bus #133.

### Around Zierikzee

If you have your own transport – or rent a bike from Bike Totaal, Weststraat 5–7 – you have plenty of scope for discovering the surrounding countryside and coastline. **Dreischor**, 8km northeast, makes a pleasant half-day ride. There, the fourteenth-century St Adriaanskirche lies surrounded by a moat and plush green lawns, encircled by a ring of attractive houses. Complete with waddling geese and a restored *travalje* (livery stable), it's an idyllic setting – although busy on weekends. A wander round the Ring will reveal several appealing B&Bs, such as at Ring 5 (☎0111/401 801; ●).

If you still have the energy, 6km out of Zierikzee in the opposite direction, the simple but atmospheric **Ouwekerk Museum** (mid-April to Nov Mon–Sat 1–5pm; hours variable, check with VVV; €3) commemorates the great floods of 1953 (see p.314), the catalyst for the massive Delta Project. Atmospherically set in a desolate *caisson*, one of the original concrete bunkers manoeuvred into plugging a break in the dyke, it houses construction machinery used in the 1950s, scale models showing the extent of the damage, old photographs and original newsreel footage beamed onto the wall.

Finally, to put colour in your cheeks you could follow the bike lane over the wind tunnel-like **Zeelandbrug**, a graceful bridge that spans the Oosterschelde south of Zierikzee. Refreshments are available in Colijnsplaat on the other side, where you can rest up, having cycled one of the longest bridges in Europe, at 5022m. Prevailing winds will be against you on the way out; expect the journey back to be half the time and twice as speedy.

# Noord-Brabant

**Noord-Brabant**, the Netherlands' largest province, stretches from the North Sea to the German border. While it's unlikely to form the focus of an itinerary, the instantly likeable provincial capital of **Den Bosch** is well worth a lingering visit. Along with **Breda**, its cobbled and car-free centre enjoys a lively market, pulling crowds that spill into the adjoining streets.

Originally part of the independent Duchy of Brabant, Noord-Brabant was taken over by the Spanish, and eventually split in two when its northern towns joined the revolt against Spain. This northern part was ceded to the United Provinces in 1648; the southern half formed what today are the Belgian provinces of Brabant and Antwerp. As a result, a Catholic influence is still strong here: the region takes its religious festivals seriously and if you're here in February and March, the boozy **carnivals** (especially in **Bergen-op-Zoom** and Den Bosch) are must-sees – indeed, it's difficult to miss them. Geographically, woodland and heath form most of the natural scenery, the gently undulating arable land a welcome change from the watery polders of the west.

# Bergen-op-Zoom

**BERGEN-OP-ZOOM**, only 30km north of Antwerp, is an untidy town, a jumble of buildings old and new that are the consequence of being shunted between various European powers from the sixteenth century onwards. In 1576 Bergen-op-Zoom sided with the United Provinces against the Spanish and as a result was under near-continuous siege until 1622. This war-ravaged theme continued: the French bombarded the city in 1747 and took it again in 1795, though it managed to withstand a British attack in 1814. Unless you're coming for the town's famous February carnival (see overleaf), there's little reason for more than a passing visit.

Walk straight out of the train station and you'll soon find yourself on the **Grote Markt**, most cheerful during summer when it's decked out with openair cafés and the like. The **Stadhuis**, on the north side of the square (by appointment only, contact VVV), is Bergen's most attractive building, spruced up in recent years and comprising three separate houses: to the left of the gateway an alderman's house of 1397, to the right a merchant's house of 1480 and on the far right a building known as "De Olifant" whose facade dates from 1611. All of this is a lot more appealing than the blunt ugliness of the **Grote Kerk**, a uniquely unlucky building that's been destroyed by siege, fire and neglect innumerable times over the last four hundred years.

To the left of the Stadhuis, Fortuinstraat leads to the **Markiezenhof Museum**, Steenbergsestraat 8 (April–Sept Tues–Sun 11am–5pm; Oct–March Tues–Sun 2–5pm; €2.27), a first-rate presentation of a collection that has a little of everything: domestic utensils and samplers from the sixteenth century onward, sumptuous period rooms, architectural drawings, pottery and galleries of modern art. All this is housed in a palace built by Anthonis Keldermans between 1485 and 1522 to a late-Gothic style that gives it the feel of an Oxford college. Of the rest of old Bergen-op-Zoom, little remains: at the end of Lievevrouwestraat, near the entrance to the Markiezenhof, the **Gevangenpoort** is practically all that remains of the old city defences, a solid-looking fourteenth-century gatehouse that was later converted to a prison.

## Practicalities

The **VVV**, at Stationsstraat 4 (Mon noon–5.30pm, Tues–Fri 9am–5.30pm, Sat 10am–5pm; ℡0900/202 0336, ⊛www.vvvboz.nl) has details of **private rooms**, along with a map of the centre. The cheapest **hotel** is *De Lantaarn*, Bredasestraat 8 (℡0164/236 488, ℻246 879; ❶) while the **HI hostel** (℡0164/233 261, ⊛www.stayokay.com; dorms €23; April–Oct) is 4km out of town at Boslustweg 1; take bus #21 or #22 from the station and it's a five-hundred-metre walk from the Lievensberg stop. There's a variety of **restaurants** grouped around the Grote Markt and, while the town's drinking scene is not exactly buzzing, *Kunst-en Proeflokaal de Hemel* is a lively spot at Moeregrebstraat 35, just off Steenbergsestraat.

In February each year Bergen-op-Zoom hosts one of the southern Netherlands' most vibrant **carnivals**, with virtually every inhabitant – as well as revellers from all over Europe – joining in the Tuesday procession. It's a great time to be in the town if you can manage it, although you shouldn't expect to find any accommodation – the town gets packed; just do as the locals do and party all night. Contact the VVV for the exact dates.

# Breda

**BREDA**, one of the prettier towns of Noord-Brabant, is a pleasant, easygoing place to while away a day. The centre is compact, largely pedestrianized and eminently strollable. A magnificent Gothic cathedral looms above the three-storey buildings that front its stone-paved square, crammed with stallholders and shoppers on market days. There's a range of well-priced accommodation, inexpensive restaurants and lively bars, though ultimately it's less appealing than Den Bosch as a base for exploring central Noord-Brabant.

While there's little evidence of it today, Breda developed as a strategic fortress town and was badly damaged following its capture by the Spanish in 1581. The local counts were scions of the House of Nassau, which in the early sixteenth century married into the House of Orange. The first prince of the Orange-Nassau line was **William the Silent**, who spent much of his life in the town and would probably have been buried here, had Breda not been in the hands of the Spanish at the time of his assassination in Delft. In 1566 William was among the group of Netherlandish nobles who issued the **Compromise of Breda** – an early declaration against Spanish domination of the Low Countries. The town later fell to the Spanish, was retaken by Maurice, William's son, captured once more by the Spanish, but finally ceded to the United Provinces in 1648.

King Charles II of England lived in the town for a while (it was here that he issued his **Declaration of Breda** in 1660, the terms by which he was prepared to accept the throne), as did – though less reliable historically – Oliver Cromwell and Daniel Defoe. Breda was last fought over in 1793, when it was captured by the French, who hung on to it until 1813.

## Arrival, information and accommodation

The **VVV** office, Willemstraat 17–19 (Mon 1–6pm, Tues–Fri 9am–6pm, Sat 9am–5pm; ☎0900/522 2444, ⓦwww.vvvbreda.nl) is straight outside the **train station**, about five minutes' walk from the Grote Markt and the town centre. It sells the handy *Strolling through Breda* (currently a €1 photocopied booklet).

**Hotels** and **pensions** include the *Pension Singel,* Delpratsingel 14 (☎076/521 6271; ❶). The others are all too far to reach on foot – take a yellow #130 bus from the station and ask to be dropped off at Duivelsbruglaan, where you'll find the *Aardster* at no. 92 (☎076/565 1666; ❷) and the cheaper *Donkers* at no. 72 (☎076/565 4332; ❶). The conveniently located but expensive *De Klok* is at Grote Markt 26–28 (☎076/521 4082, ⓕ514 3463; ❸–❹), though it fills quickly in summer; the *Van Ham,* Van Coothplein 23 (☎076/521 5229; ❷) is an alternative. The nearest **campsite**, *Liesbos* (☎076/514 3514, ⓔliesbos@worldonline.nl; April–Sept), is 8km out of town on the route of bus #111. The nearest **HI hostel** is 15km away at Chaam, Putvenweg 1 (☎0161/491 323, ⓦwww.stayokay.com; dorms €22; April–Oct) – take bus #132 and it's a 3km walk further.

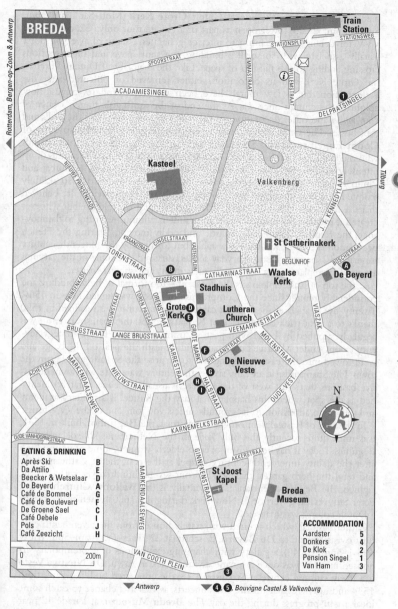

EATING & DRINKING

| Après Ski | B |
| Da Attilio | E |
| Beecker & Wetselaar | D |
| De Beyerd | A |
| Café de Bommel | G |
| Café de Boulevard | F |
| De Groene Sael | C |
| Café Oebele | I |
| Pols | J |
| Café Zeezicht | H |

ACCOMMODATION

| Aardster | 5 |
| Donkers | 4 |
| De Klok | 2 |
| Pension Singel | 1 |
| Van Ham | 3 |

▼ Antwerp    ▼ **4**. **5**. Bouvigne Castel & Valkenburg

## The Town

From the train station and VVV, head down Willemstraat and cross the park for the town centre. The **Grote Markt** is the focus of life, site of a general **market** every Tuesday and Friday morning and a secondhand market every Wednesday morning, when stalls loaded with books, bric-a-brac, clothes and small furniture pieces push up against the pocket-Gothic **Grote Kerk** (Mon–Sat 10am–5pm, Sun 1–5pm; €1.75; tower open as part of a guided tour only; €2; contact the VVV for details), whose intimate interior generates a sense of awe you don't usually associate with so small a building, the short nave and high, spacious crossing adding to the illusion of space. Like the majority of Dutch churches, the Grote Kerk had its decorations either removed or obscured after the Reformation, but a few murals have been uncovered and reveal just how colourful the church once was. At the end of the south aisle there's a huge *St Christopher* and other decorations in the south transept embellish the walls and roof bosses. The Grote Kerk's most remarkable feature is the **Mausoleum of Count Engelbrecht II**, a Stadholder and Captain-General of the Netherlands who died in 1504 of tuberculosis – vividly apparent in the drawn features of his intensely realistic face. Four kneeling figures (Caesar, Regulus, Hannibal and Philip of Macedonia) support a canopy that carries his armour, so skilfully sculpted that their shoulders seem to sag slightly under the weight. It's believed that the mausoleum was the work of Tomaso Vincidor of Bologna, but whoever created it imbued the mausoleum with grandeur without resorting to flamboyance; the result is both eerily realistic and oddly moving. During the French occupation the choir was used as a stable, but fortunately the sixteenth-century misericords, showing rustic everyday scenes, survived. A couple of the carvings are modern replacements – as you'll guess from their subject matter.

At the top of Kasteelplein sits the **Kasteel** – too formal to be forbidding and considerably rebuilt since the Compromise of Breda was signed here in 1566. Twenty-five years later the Spanish captured Breda, but it was regained in 1590 thanks to a neat trick by Maurice of Nassau's troops: the Spanish garrison was regularly supplied by barge with peat, so, using the Trojan Horse strategy, seventy troops under Maurice's command hid beneath the peat on the barge and were towed into the castle, jumping out to surprise the Spanish and regain the town. The Spanjaardsgat, an early sixteenth-century watergate with twin defensive bastions that's just west of the Kasteel, is usually (but inaccurately) identified as the spot where this happened. Today the Kasteel is a military academy and there's no admission to its grounds, unless you join one of the VVV tours.

To the east of Kasteelplein on Catherinastraat, the **Begijnhof**, built in 1531, was until quite recently the only *hofje* in the Netherlands still occupied by Beguines. Today it has been given over to elderly women, some of whom look after the dainty nineteenth-century chapel at the rear, the St Catherinakerk, and tend the herb garden that was laid out several hundred years ago. To the right of the Begijnhof entrance, incidentally, is the **Walloon Church**, where Peter Stuyvesant, governor of New York during the 1600s when that city was a Dutch colony, was married.

Catherinastraat, which is lined with stately houses from the seventeenth century, twists around to **De Beyerd**, Boschstraat 22 (Tues–Fri 10am–5pm, Sat & Sun 1–5pm; €3.40), a gallery with changing exhibitions of contemporary art housed in what was once a lunatic asylum. Back in town, **De Nieuwe Veste** is a lively cultural centre at St Janstraat 18; the converted building dates from 1534 and offers regular theatre and concerts, as well as a chance to catch some local art-in-progress during the day. The **Breda Museum**, at Parade 12 near Oude Vest (Tues–Sun 10am–5pm; €3.50) holds a forgettable collection of exhibits concerning the town's history.

Finally, 5km out of town, the village of **ULVENHOUT** is the start of some stunning cycling, along narrow cycleways that twist and turn through dense forest. Bikes can be rented at Breda train station; follow LF13b in the direction of Alphen, a national cycleway that eventually leads to the Rhine.

## Eating and drinking

Breda has a decent range of places to **eat**. Centrally placed, *Da Attilio* is a good pizzeria at Grote Markt 35, while *Café de Boulevard*, further down the square at Grote Markt 10, has a wide variety of dishes. Less pricey is the popular *Beecker & Wetselaar* by the Grote Kerk. Cheaper still is *Pols*, Halstraat 15, a small and excellent *eetcafé* adjoining an old, rickety theatre, with three courses for a bargain €9. Beside the upmarket *Café Zeezicht* at Halstraat 2a is *Café Oebele*, with funky music and 70s decor. Kebab joints and Turkish pizzas are plentiful at Havermarkt, a square packed with hole-in-the-wall eateries for late-night snacks.

For down-to-earth **drinking**, try *De Groene Sael*, Havermarkt 8, an unpretentious bar serving draught Palm beer and with a small dance floor at the back; *Nickelodeon*, Halstraat 2, is a more upmarket affair, with a swish interior. Connoisseurs of Low Countries' beer generally make for *De Beyerd*, Boschstraat 26, while, back in the centre, *Café de Bommel* at Halstraat 3 is a large and lively café-bar with a mix of customers. *Après Ski*, Reigerstraat 20, is a somewhat tacky disco and bar.

# Tilburg and De Efteling

**TILBURG**, 20km east of Breda, is a faceless industrial town, its streets a maze of nineteenth-century houses and anonymous modern shopping precincts. The main reason you might find yourself passing through is to change transport on your way to the action-packed **De Efteling** theme park (see overleaf). However, four decent museums within easy walking distance of the train station provide a worthwhile detour. No need to explore further – if that's as far as you get, you haven't missed much.

Tilburg developed as a textile town, though today most of its mills have closed in the face of cheap competition from India and southeast Asia. The **Nederlands Textielmuseum** is housed in an old mill at Goirkestraat 96 (out of the station, walk west along Spoorlaan, turn right along Gasthuisring and Goirkestraat is the fourth turn on the right; Tues–Fri 10am–5pm, Sat & Sun noon–5pm; €4.50), and displays aspects of the industry relating to design and textile arts. It also houses a collection of textile designs by Dutch artists and demonstrations of weaving and spinning, as well as a range of looms and weaving machines from around the world. The **Scryption**, Spoorlaan 434a (Tues–Fri 10am–5pm, Sat & Sun 1–5pm; €2.70) is a fancy name for a collection of writing implements – everything from lumps of chalk to word processors. Particularly interesting are the old, intricate typewriters, some of which you can operate yourself. Next door, the **Noordbrabants Natuurmuseum** (Tues–Fri 10am–5pm, Sat & Sun 1–5pm; €3.20) is basically a load of dead animals and (live) creepy crawlies. The **De Pont** modern art museum (Tues–Sun 11am–5pm; €3.50), a ten-minute walk behind the station at Wilheminapark 1, has both a permanent international collection and annual exhibitions. A converted woolspinning mill, its main gallery space is complemented by more intimate side rooms, previously used for storage of wool. There's a library, reading room and a free guided tour (Sun 3pm, except July & Aug); book at least a week ahead to have it in English.

The **VVV** office is at Spoorlaan 364 (Mon 1–6pm, Tues–Fri 9am–6pm, Sat 10am–4pm; ☎0900/202 0815, ⊛www.vvvtilburg.nl), a few minutes' walk from the station – cross the main road and head left. You'll need their detailed town map to have any chance of finding the **Poppenmuseum** at Telefoonstraat 13–15 (Wed–Sat, 1–4pm; €3.20), a small private collection of dolls. There's little reason to **stay** in Tilburg, but, for the record, the least expensive room in town is at the *Het Wapen van Tilburg* hotel, next to the VVV at Spoorlaan 362 (☎013/542 2692; ❷). There are several good **cafés** around Korte Heuvel/Piusplein.

## De Efteling

Hidden in the woods fifteen minutes' drive north of Tilburg, the **De Efteling** theme park (April–Oct daily 10am–6pm; July to mid-Aug until 9pm; €21) is one of the country's principal attractions. It's an excellent day out, and not just for children. The setting is superbly landscaped, especially in spring when the tulips are out. And whilst it's not Disney, it's certainly vast enough to swallow up the crowds.

Of the rides, *Python* is the most hair-raising, a rollercoaster twister with great views of the park before plunging down the track; *De Bob*, a recreation bobsleigh run, is almost as exhilarating although over far too quickly, especially if you've queued for ages. *Piranha* takes you through some gentle whitewater rapids (expect to get wet). Of the quieter moments, *Villa Volta* is a slightly unsettling room that revolves around you, after a rather lengthy introduction in Dutch. For kids, the *Fairy-Tale Wood*, where the park began – a hop from Gingerbread House to Troll King to Cinderella Castle – is popular. *Carnaval Festival* and *Droomvlucht* are the best of the rides, and there are afternoon shows in the Efteling Theatre. In addition, there are a number of fairground attractions, canoes and paddle-boats, and a great view over the whole shebang and the surrounding woods from the *Pagoda*. A sedate way to check whether you've missed anything is to take the steam train around the park. Prepare yourself for long queues on summer weekends; if you're not up to doing it all, skip the disappointing *Haunted Castle* and the *Fata Morgana*.

**Bus** #136 and #137 run to De Efteling every half-hour from Tilburg (15min), and from Den Bosch (40min); in summer, the direct services #182 from Tilburg and #181 from Den Bosch are slightly faster. The park is well signposted just off the A261 between Tilburg and Waalwijk; parking costs €5. Though there's little need to **stay**, if you're eager for another day's fun, the *Efteling Hotel* is right by the park (☎0416/287 111, ⊛www.efteling.nl; ❺). There are plenty of **maps** posted around the complex, and snack-bars and refreshment stops at every turn.

# 's Hertogenbosch (Den Bosch)

Capital of Noord-Brabant, **'S HERTOGENBOSCH** is a lively town, particularly on Wednesdays and Saturdays, when its medieval Markt fills with traders from all over the province. Better known as **Den Bosch** (pronounced "bos"), it merits exploration over a day or two. The town's full name – "the Count's Woods" – dates from the time when Henry I, Duke of Brabant, established a hunting lodge here in the twelfth century. Beneath the graceful townhouses of the old city flows the Binnendieze, its gloomy depths spanned by small wooden bridges. Staggered crossroads, winding streets and the twelfth-century town walls are vestiges of conflict with Holland, Gelderland and the far north and south of today's Netherlands. The town's history is written into its street and

house names: "Corn Bridge", "The Gun Barrel", "Painters' Street" and more, while its most famous son is the fifteenth-century artist **Hieronymous Bosch**, whose statue now stands, palette in hand, in the middle of the Markt.

## Arrival, information and accommodation

Den Bosch's centre is fifteen minutes' walk east of the **train station**. Stop by the **VVV** office, housed in *De Moriaan*, the oldest brick-building in town, at Markt 77 (Mon 1–6pm, Tues–Fri 9am–6pm, Thurs until 9pm, Sat 9am–5pm; ℡0900/112 2334, ⓦwww.vvvs-hertogenbosch.nl) to pick up the useful *Tourist Information Guide* (€1.35) and *Walking tour 's-Hertogenbosch* (€1.60), which unearths all kinds of historical and architectural nuggets.

There are two hotels to the west of town by the train station: most convenient is the *Terminus* at Boschveldweg 15 (℡073/613 0666, ⓦwww.hotel-terminus.nl; ❷) above a folk pub of the same name. The *Jo van de Bosch*, Boschdijkstraat 39a (℡073/613 8205, ⓦwww.jovandenbosch.nl; ❸) is further out and more expensive. In the centre of town is the basic but friendly *All Inn* (℡073/613 4057; ❶), off the Markt at Gasselstraat 1, while the *Eurohotel* is round the corner at Hinthamerstraat 63 (℡073/613 7777, ⓦwww.bestwestern.nl; ❸).

For a different way to see a lot of the town, there's a variety of **boat trips**. Traditional open boats depart from Molenstraat 15a, next to *Café van Puffelen* (twice hourly; April–Oct Mon 2–5.20pm, Tues–Sun 10am–5.20pm; mid-July to mid-Sept also 6pm daily; reserve on ☎0900/202 0178; €5). Closed boats depart from St Janssingel near the Wilhelmina bridge, and tours taken in the River Aa, Dommel and the Oude Dieze (May–Sept daily 11am, 12.30pm, 2pm & 3.30pm; €4.50). *Rederij Wolthuis*, Leunweg 17 (☎073/631 2048, ⓦwww.rederijwolthuis.nl), has information and reservations for closed-boat tours.

## The Town

If you were to draw a picture of the archetypal Dutch marketplace, it would probably look like the one in Den Bosch. It's broad and cobbled, home to the province's largest market (Wed & Sat) and is lined with typical seventeenth-century houses. The sixteenth-century **Stadhuis** (Mon–Thurs 8am–5pm, Fri 8am–noon) has a carillon that's played every Wednesday between 10 and 11am and that chimes the half-hour to the accompaniment of a group of mechanical horsemen.

### St Janskathedraal

From just about anywhere in the centre of town it's impossible to miss **St Janskathedraal** (Mon–Sat 10am–4.30pm, Sun 1pm–4.30pm; restricted entrance during services). Generally regarded as the finest Gothic church in the country, it was built between 1330 and 1530 and has recently undergone a massive restoration. But if Breda's Grote Kerk is Gothic at its most intimate and exhilarating, then St Jan's is Gothic at its most gloomy, the garish stained glass – nineteenth-century or modern – only adding to the sense of dreariness that hangs over the nave. You enter beneath the oldest and least well-preserved part of the cathedral, the western **tower** (open May–Aug; €3.50): blunt and brick-clad, it's oddly prominent amid the wild decoration of the rest of the exterior, which includes some nasty-looking creatures scaling the roof – symbols of the forces of evil that attack the church.

Inside, there's much of interest. The **Lady Chapel** near the entrance contains a thirteenth-century figure of the Madonna known as *Zoete Lieve Vrouw* ("Sweet Dear Lady"), famed for its miraculous powers in the Middle Ages and still much venerated today. The brass **font** in the southwest corner was the work of Alard Duhamel, a master mason who worked on the cathedral in the late fifteenth century. It's thought that the stone pinnacle, a weird twisted piece of Gothicism at the eastern end of the nave, was the sample piece that earned him the title of master mason.

Almost filling the west wall of the cathedral is an extravagant **organ case**, assembled in 1602. It was described by a Victorian authority as "certainly the finest in Holland and probably the finest in Europe... it would be difficult to conceive a more stately or magnificent design." Equally elaborate, though on a much smaller scale, the south transept holds the **Altar of the Passion**, a retable (a piece placed behind and above the altar to act as a kind of screen) made in Antwerp in around 1500. In the centre is a carved Crucifixion scene, flanked by Christ bearing the Cross on one side and a Lamentation on the other. Though rather difficult to make out, a series of carved scenes of the life of Christ run across the retable, made all the more charming by their attention to period (medieval) costume detail.

Though a few painted sections of the cathedral remain to show how it would have been decorated before the Reformation, most of its paintings were destroyed in the iconoclastic fury of 1566. These included several by the late

Gothic painter **Hieronymus Bosch**, who lived in the town all his life: his fantastically vivid and tormented religious paintings won him the epithet "The master of the monstrous… the discoverer of the unconscious" from Carl Jung. However, only two works by Bosch remain in the cathedral (in the north transept) and even their authenticity is doubtful. What is more certain is that Bosch belonged to the town's Brotherhood of Our Lady, a society devoted to the veneration of the Virgin, and that as a working artist he would have been expected to help adorn the cathedral. None of his major works remain in Den Bosch today, but there's a collection of his prints in the town's Noordbrabants Museum (see below).

## The rest of the town

Opposite the cathedral at Hinthamerstraat 94, the **Zwanenbroedershuis** (Tues & Thurs 1.30–4.30pm; €3.50) has an intriguing collection of artefacts, liturgical songbooks and music scores that belonged to the Brotherhood of which Bosch was a member. Founded in 1318, there's nothing sinister about the Brotherhood: membership is open to all and its aim is to promote and popularize religious art and music.

South and east of the cathedral, the **Museum Slager**, Choorstraat 16 (Tues–Sun 2–5pm; €3; ⓦ www.museum-slager.nl), contains the works of three generations of the Slager family who lived in Den Bosch. The paintings of the family's doyen, P.M. Slager (1841–1912), such as *Veterans of Waterloo*, have the most authority, but some of the other works are competent, encompassing the major trends in European art as they came and went. Over the decades they have been active, the Slager family seems to have spent most of its time painting either Den Bosch or their own relatives.

A few minutes' walk southwest of the cathedral, the **Noordbrabants Museum**, Verwersstraat 41 (Tues–Fri 10am–5pm, Sat & Sun noon–5pm; ⓦ www.noordbrabantsmuseum.nl; €5.70), is housed in an eighteenth-century building that was once the seat of the provincial commissioner and has been enlarged with two new wings and complemented by a sculpture garden. The good-looking collection of local art and artefacts from prehistory to the present is uniformly excellent and interesting, and the downstairs galleries often hold superb temporary exhibitions of modern art. The permanent collection includes drawings and prints by Hieronymus Bosch, works by other medieval painters and assorted early torture equipment. There's also a rare *Schandhuik* or "Cloak of Infamy", a wooden cloak carved with adders and toads, symbols of unchastity; in the seventeenth century, women who had been unfaithful to their husbands were paraded in it through the city streets on a cart.

Just down the road from the museum, St Jorisstraat leads down to the site of the old city walls, which still marks the southern limit of Den Bosch. The **Bastion Oranje** once defended the southern section of the city walls, but, like the walls themselves, it has long gone. Still remaining is a large cannon, **De Boze Griet** ("The Devil's Woman"), cast in 1511 in Cologne and bearing the German inscription "Brute force I am called, Den Bosch I watch over". The only action she sees now is from the cows, chewing serenely in the water-meadows below.

For the rest, the backstreets of Den Bosch are a mass of intriguing buildings and facades. Particularly pleasant is the **Uilenburg** quarter, with pint-size houses squashed up against each other; look out for the restored farmhouse opposite Molenstraat 29, and the picturesque Uilenburgstraatje bridge. Finally, just north of the Zuid Willems Vaart canal, the **Museum Het Kruithuis** at Citadellaan 7 (closed for reconstruction until 2004) has an international collection of modern art and design; ceramics and jewellery are particular strengths, with works by Braque, Chagall, Miró and Picasso. Until the main site reopens, the museum shop and a small educational exhibition are housed on the south side of town at Hekellaan 2 (Wed–Sun 1–5pm; free).

## Eating and drinking

Den Bosch's **restaurants** can be pricey: many of those in the centre are geared to expense-accounts and are poor value for money. *Da Peppone* at Kerkstraat 77 and *Taormina*, Verwersstraat 58, are both inexpensive pizzerias. *Bagatelle*, Hinthamerstraat 29, has well-priced Dutch food, as does *Hof van Holland* at Kolperstraat 12. *De Opera*, Hinthamerstraat 115–117, offers a range of wonderful Dutch–French cooking in a relaxed setting: well worth a splurge. *Dry Hamerkens*, Hinthamerstraat 57 (closed Tues), is similarly expensive; you dine in the elegant ambience of a seventeenth-century house that looks as if it's lifted straight from a Vermeer canvas. A fairly short distance from the centre of town, *Van Puffelen* at Van Molenstraat 4 is an attractive *eetcafé* above a canal, with affordable *dagschotels*.

For **drinking**, it's easy enough to wander up and down Hinthamerstraat or the streets that radiate from the Markt and find somewhere convivial. *Keulse Kar*, Hinthamerstraat 101, is as good a starting point as any, a fairly conservative bar near the cathedral; the nearby *Basilique* on the corner of Torenstraat is also a decent spot. At Hinthamerstaat 97, *'t Bonte Palet* is a tiny, popular bar that's good for a swift drink as you're working your way along the street. Up a few notches on the trendiness scale, *Café Cordes*, Parade 4 (just southwest of the cathedral), is a stylish, aluminium-clad café-bar that brings in Den Bosch's bright young things. *De Blauwe Druif*, at the corner of Markt and Kolperstraat, is a big, boozy pub that takes off on market days. *Geen Flauw Idee* at Kolperstraat 13 is a friendly place to drink and smoke dope. *Duvelke*, Verwersstraat 55, is a deftly decorated bar near the Noordbrabants Museum.

# Eindhoven and around

You might wonder why a town the size of **EINDHOVEN** merits only a page in a guidebook; half an hour there, and a few statistics, will tell you why. In 1900 Eindhoven's population was approximately 4700. A century later it had passed 200,000. What happened in between was **Philips**, the multinational electrical firm: the town is home to Philips' research centre (the manufacturing plant had such trouble recruiting here, it relocated to the more popular Amsterdam), and the name of Eindhoven's benevolent dictator is everywhere – on bus stops, parks, even the stadium of the famous local football team, PSV Eindhoven. Once you've penetrated the ring roads, the centre is charmless; on the plus side, the cycle lanes are spacious and it's almost impossible to get lost, but ultimately, most visitors come here for business, not pleasure – and it shows.

If you do find yourself in Eindhoven, visit the recently expanded **Van Abbe Museum**, Vonderweg 1 (Tues–Sun 11am–5pm; €8.50), with its superb collection of modern paintings that includes works by Picasso, Klein, Chagall, Kandinsky and Bacon. Try to come between June and September, since at other times most of the collection disappears and the place has rotating exhibitions of modern art.

Eindhoven's **VVV** (Mon 10am–5.30pm, Tues–Thurs 9am–5.30pm, Fri 9am–6.30pm, Sat 10am–5pm; ☎0900/112 2363, ⊛www.vvveindhoven.nl) is outside the train station. It can provide a handy brochure on the city and a list

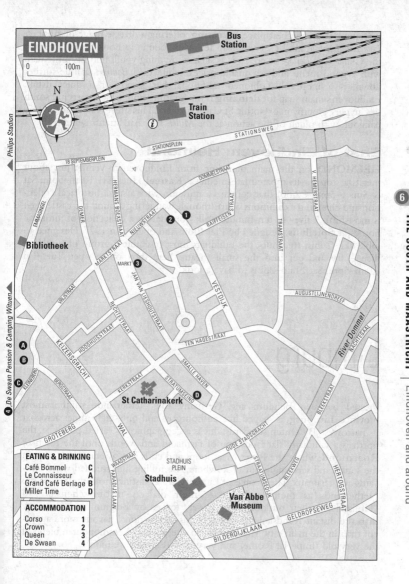

**EINDHOVEN**

0       100m

N

*Philips Stadion*

Bus
Station

Train
Station
*(i)*

STATIONSWEG

STATIONSPLEIN

18 SEPTEMBERPLEIN

DOMMELSTRAAT

RAIFFEISENSTRAAT

V. HEMESSTRAAT

TRAMSTRAAT

**Bibliotheek**

DEMER

HERMANS BOEKSTRAAT

NIEUWSTRAAT

MARKTSTRAAT

PARMASINGEL

VRIJSTRAAT

MARKT **③**

**②  ①**

JAN VAN LIESHOUTSTRAAT

VESTDIJK

AUGUSTIJNENDREEF

*De Swaan Pension & Camping Witven*

KEIZERSGRACHT

HOOGHUISSTRAAT

RECHTESTRAAT

TEN HAGESTRAAT

SMALLE HAVEN

River Dommel

NACHTEGAAL

**Ⓐ**
**Ⓑ**

**Ⓒ**

KLEINBERG

BERGSTRAAT

KERKSTRAAT

STRATUMSEIND

**Ⓓ**

BLEEKSTRAAT

**St Catharinakerk**

GROTEBERG

WAL

WAAGSTRAAT

OUDE STADSGRACHT

STRATUMSEDIJK

BLEEKWEG

HERTOGSTRAAT

**EATING & DRINKING**

Café Bommel    C
Le Connaisseur    A
Grand Café Berlage    B
Miller Time    D

**ACCOMMODATION**

Corso    1
Crown    2
Queen    3
De Swaan    4

PARADIJSLAAN

STADHUIS
PLEIN

**Stadhuis**

**Van Abbe
Museum**

GELDROPSEWEG

BILDERDIJKLAAN

of pensions – *De Swaan*, above Broodje Smits, Wilhelminaplein 5 (☎040/244 8992; **①**), is friendly and quite central. The hotels are even better placed: *Corso*, Vestdijk 17 (☎040/244 9131, ℱ245 7399; **②**) is the cheapest; the *Crown* opposite at no. 14–16 (☎040/844 4000, ⓦwww.crownhoteleindhoven.nl; **⑤**) caters to a mostly corporate clientele; and the *Queen* is above a pleasant café at Markt 7 (☎040/245 2480, ⓦwww.queeneindhoven.nl; **④**). Many hotels have weekend deals all year round, offering discounts of up to twenty percent. There's a **campsite**, *Witven* (☎040/253 2727, ℱ255 4099; April–Oct), 5km southwest of the city at Runstraat 40 in Veldhoven; bus #150 runs from the station.

Kleine Berg is the best place for **eating**, offering a diverse range of cuisines: *Le Connaisseur* at no. 12 serves cheap Tex-Mex food in its bookshelved interior; the *Grand Café Berlage* at no. 16 is as slick as anything you'll find in Amsterdam with a good menu and reasonable prices; while *Café Bommel*, a little further down, is a more old-fashioned traditional bar, good for a quiet drink. Eindhoven's main strip for **drinking** is the Stratumseind, which starts just south of Cuypers' gloomy neo-Gothic St Catherinakerk. This street is a prime teenage hangout, with much of the action at the *Miller Time* bar, Stratumseind 51.

### East of Eindhoven: Helmond

**HELMOND**, on the main train line from Eindhoven to Venray, just about merits a stop for its moated late-medieval **Kasteel** (Tues–Fri 10am–5pm, Sat & Sun 1–5pm; €2.50) that contains a museum with a small historical collection and changing exhibitions of art (though wandering around the castle itself is most fun). A five- to ten-minute walk from here is a collection of futuristic houses, **'t Spielhuis**, designed by Piet Blom and opened in 1977. Designed to look like Cubist tree-huts, the buildings most resemble a group of tumbling dice – try and get into the small theatre here (box office open Tues–Fri 11am–5pm, Sat 11am–2pm) to have a look.

# Limburg

Pressed between Belgium and Germany, the Netherlands' southernmost province, **Limburg**, is shaped like an hourglass and only eight miles across at its narrowest. By Dutch standards, this is a geographically varied province: the north is a familiarly flat landscape of farmland and woods until the town of **Roermond**, where the River Maas loops and curls its way across the map; in the south, and seemingly out of nowhere, rise rolling hills studded with vineyards and châteaux. The people of Limburg are as distinct from the rest of the Netherlands as their landscape – their dialects incomprehensible to "Hollanders", their outlook more closely forged by Belgium and Germany than the distant Randstad. Nowhere is this international flavour more apparent than in the main city, **Maastricht**, an energetic and cosmopolitan blend of the very old (Imperial Rome) and very new (European Union).

## Venlo and around

Just a few kilometres from the German border, **VENLO** has been repeatedly destroyed and recaptured throughout its history, particularly during the last war, when most of its ancient buildings were knocked down during the Allied invasion of Europe. As a result the town is short of sights, but makes a good base for the National War and Resistance Museum at Overloon.

The cramped streets of Venlo's centre wind medievally around the town's architectural highlight, the fancily turreted and onion-domed **Stadhuis**, a much-amended building dating from the sixteenth century. Nearby, along Grote Kerkstraat, is the louring pile of **St Martinus Kerk** (Mon–Sat 10am–noon & 2–4pm, Sun 2–4pm; free), rebuilt after bombing in 1944, but still holding a brilliant golden seventeenth-century reredos. Near the station is the **Limburgs Museum**, Keulsepoort 5 (Tues–Fri 10am–4.30pm, Sat & Sun 2pm–5pm; €5), the city's historical collection. Best exhibit is the nineteenth-century kitchenware, the largest such assortment in western Europe. Venlo's other museum, the **Van Bommel Van Dam**, Deken van Oppensingel 8 (Tues–Sun 11am–5pm; €2), has changing exhibitions of the work of contemporary, mostly local artists; from the train station, take the third right off the roundabout.

Venlo's **VVV**, Koninginneplein 2 (Mon–Fri 9.30am–6pm, Sat 9.30am–5pm; ☎077/354 3800, ⓦ www.vvvvenlo.nl), opposite the train station, has details of **boat trips** and can help find accommodation. Flanking the train station are *Hotel Wilhelmina*, Kaldenkerkerweg 1 (☎077/351 6251, ℻351 2252; ❸), and the cheaper *Stationshotel*, Keulsepoort 16 (☎077/351 8230, ⓦ www .stationshotel.nl; ❷). For **eating and drinking**, try the *D'n Dorstigen Haen* at Markt 26, for snacks and a few samples of their huge range of beers. Otherwise, there are cheap light lunches at several cafés around the Stadhuis.

From beside the train station, bus #83 makes the 10km trip north along the Maas to the village of Arcen, home to the **Kasteeltuinen** (April to late-Oct daily 10am–6pm, weekends in Nov 11am–5pm; €10), a trim seventeenth-century moated castle surrounded by a fine series of formal gardens set beside narrow canals and a string of tiny lakes.

## National War and Resistance Museum

The cosy residential town of Venray, a few minutes north of Venlo by train, is a stepping-stone to **OVERLOON**, site of the **Nationaal Oorloogs- en Verzetsmuseum** (National War and Resistance Museum). To reach the museum from Venray, you have to take the *treintaxi* (€3.50 each way), as there is no bus service. Alternatively, you could rent a bike from Venlo and follow route LF33, turning off at Venray to cycle the last 6km through fields of wheat to Overloon. Either way, you'll cross back into Noord-Brabant to reach this affluent little town that was rebuilt following destruction in the last war during a fierce battle in October 1944 in which 2400 men died. The final stages took place in the woods to the east, where hand-to-hand fighting was needed to secure the area and it's on this site that the **museum** (daily: June–Aug 9.30am–6pm; Sept–May 10am–5pm; €6.50) now stands, founded with the military hardware that was left behind after the battle. Its purpose is openly didactic: "Not merely a monument for remembrance, it is intended as an admonition and warning, a denouncement of war and violence." This the museum powerfully achieves, with the machinery of war (which includes tanks, rocket launchers, armoured cars, a Bailey bridge and a V1 flying bomb) a poignant prelude to the excellent collection of documents and posters. To tour the whole museum takes a couple of hours and is a moving experience.

# Roermond and around

**ROERMOND**, the focal point of central Limburg, is something of an oddity. Whilst not especially exciting, it does have a rich Catholic heritage, as numerous shrines to the Virgin suggest – a legacy of 250 years of Habsburg rule

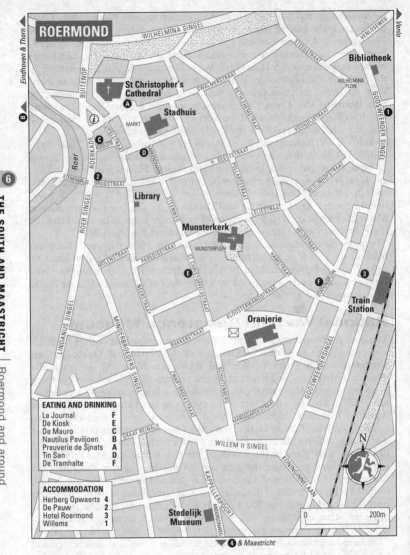

Wilhelmina Singel

Venlo

Eindhoven & Thorn

Venloseweg

Steegstraat

**Bibliotheek**

Buitenop

St Christopher's Cathedral

Swalmerstraat

Wilhelmina Plein

Goodsweerder Singel

Bethlehemstraat

Voogdijstraat

**A**

**Stadhuis**

Roerkade

**B**

**i**

MARKT

Koolstr

**C**

Dawerschmarkt

H. Geeststraat

Begijnhofstraat

**D**

Roer

Steenenbrug

**2**

Brugstraat

Roer Singel

**Library**

Steenweg

Pollartstraat

Leliestraat

**Munsterkerk**

Munsterplein

Lindanus Singel

Molenstraat

Paredisstraat

St Christoffelstraat

Hamstraat

Veldstraat

**E**

Neerstraat

**F**

Steenweg

**3**

**Train Station**

Minderbroeders Singel

Kloosterwandstraat

**Oranjerie**

✉

Bakkerstraat

Zwartbroekstraat

Schuitenberg

Goodsweenderssingel

**EATING AND DRINKING**

| Le Journal | F |
| De Kiosk | E |
| De Mauro | C |
| Nautilus Paviljoen | B |
| Preuverie de Sjnats | A |
| Tin San | D |
| De Tramhalte | F |

Graaf Reinald

Mariagardestraat

**Willem II Singel**

Koninginnelaan

**ACCOMMODATION**

| Herberg Opwaerts | 4 |
| De Pauw | 2 |
| Hotel Roermond | 3 |
| Willems | 1 |

Kappellerpoort

Andersonweg

**Stedelijk Museum**

**N**

0        200m

**4** & Maastricht

that ended only in 1839 with the unification of the Netherlands. Indeed it was here that the architect P.J.H. Cuypers, who crowded the country with Gothic-revival Catholic churches, lived and worked. Today, the town's greatest asset is its position: Roermond lies on the banks of the River Maas, at the point where it meanders into the small, artificial lakes of the **Maasplassen**. Come summertime, these lakes fill with small boats, windsurfs and water-skis as holidaymakers take to the water or fish under the town's skyline. For those less aquatically inclined, it's only 9km to **De Meinweg**, the Netherlands' largest national park, with forests and fens that extend to the German border. Roermond is also useful as a base for visiting nearby **Thorn,** and a handy stopover on the way to Maastricht and the south, or Aachen, Düsseldorf and Cologne in Germany.

Though it looks straightforward enough on the map, Roermond is a confusing place to walk around, its series of wide streets and broad squares all too similar to the unacquainted. Use the Munsterkerk and river as landmarks and you shouldn't get lost for too long.

## The Town

Walk into town from the train station and you'll come to the **Munsterkerk** (Fri 10am–noon & 2–5pm, Sat 10am–4pm; free) on Munsterplein, built in Romanesque style in the thirteenth century, but much altered and gothicized by Cuypers in the nineteenth century. Inside, the chief thing to see is the polychrome thirteenth-century tomb of Gerhard III and his wife Margaret of Brabant. From here it's a short walk to the large sloping square of the **Markt**, on the eastern side of which is the early eighteenth-century **Stadhuis**, a dull building that's easily overlooked. More noticeable (though not more interesting), **St Christopher's Cathedral** (April–Oct daily 2–5pm; free) was rebuilt following damage in World War II.

Making your way down the larger streets leading south from the Markt – Marktstraat, Neerstraat and Minderbroeders Singel – you'll come across some later and much more attractive architecture. Wherever you are in town, it's worth keeping an eye open for Roermond's alluring twentieth-century **facades**: the majority are Art Nouveau, often strongly coloured with heavily moulded vegetal patterns and designs, sometimes with stylized animal heads and grotesque characters. Some examples can be found at Neerstraat 38 and 10.

Roermond's principal architectural claim to fame is celebrated at the **Stedelijk Museum**, Andersonweg 2–8 (Tues–Fri 11am–5pm, Sat & Sun 2–5pm; €2). P.J.H. Cuypers (1827–1921) was the Netherlands' foremost ecclesiastical architect in the nineteenth century, his work paralleling that of the British Gothic revivalist, Augustus Pugin. Almost every large city in the country has a Catholic church by him – those in Eindhoven, Leeuwarden and Hilversum are notable – though his two most famous buildings are secular: the Rijksmuseum and Centraal Station in Amsterdam. Roermond's museum is the building in which Cuypers lived and worked for much of his life and preserves a small private chapel as well as a large extension in which masses of decorative panels, mouldings and fixtures were produced. Other exhibits show his plans and paintings, along with a collection of works by other local artists, chiefly Hendrik Luyten.

## Practicalities

The **VVV** office, Kraanpoort 1, behind Markt (Mon–Fri 9.30am–6pm, Sat 9.30am–5pm; ☏0475/335 847, ⊛www.vvvroermond.nl) is a fair walk from the train station, so booking your accommodation before you arrive – so that you can go straight to your hotel from the station without visiting the VVV – is worth considering. A good range of **hotels** includes *Willems*, above a café of the same name on Godsweerdersingel 58 (☏0475/333 021; ❷); and the more expensive *Hotel Roermond*, Stationsplein 9 & 13 (☏0475/332 325, ⊛www .hotelroermond.nl; ❸). Other possibilities include *De Pauw*, Roerkade 1–2 (☏0475/316 597, ℻316 400; ❷), and a single **pension**, *Herberg Opwaerts*, Hagelkruisweg 7, St Odilienberg (☏0475/536 540, ⊛www.herbergopwaerts .nl; ❶), 5km south of the town. Take bus #80 from the station.

The three main areas to **eat** and **drink** are those around the Markt, the Munsterkerk and the train station. On Stationsplein, *Le Journal* and *De Tramhalte*, both at no. 17, are inexpensive café-bars catering to an older crowd. The restaurant of the *Hotel Roermond*, although pricey for dinner, is worth checking out for its fixed-price €15 lunches. *Tin San* is the best of several Chinese places, just south of the Markt at Varkensmarkt 1. A fun place to eat Italian food is *De Mauro*, Koolstraat 8, while *De Kiosk*, a brasserie at Sint Christoffelstraat 4 has a pleasant verandah. In summertime, the *Nautilus Paviljoen* at Maasboulevard 2 is a popular café overlooking the yachts moored up in the marina. Roermond lacks first-rate **watering holes**. The cafés at Stationsplein are often the liveliest nightspots; otherwise try *Preuverie de Sjnats*, Markt 24, for a good range of beers. For a more artistic night out, check out the *Orangerie*, a multicultural centre at Kloosterwandplein 12–16.

**Fishing** and **boat trips** along the River Maas (April–Sept) are also possible; ask at the VVV for details (and licences for the former). If you want to rent a boat of your own, visit Watersportschool Frissen, Haacenboer 75 (☏0475/327 873), where a five-person boat costs €60 a day.

## National Park De Meinweg

Roermond makes a good base for exploring the nearby **National Park De Meinweg**, an excellent region for walking and cycling hard up against the German border. It comprises 1600 hectares of oak, birch and pine trees, dotted with small lakes, heather, adders and shy wild boars. If you get really lost, you'll either find yourself in Germany, or on the private estate of the Maharishi Mahesh Yogi, famous as the Beatles' guru in the 1960s. Entrance to De Meinweg is free, and the Bezoekerscentrum (visitors' centre), just before the park entrance, sells maps with routes and starting points for walkers and cyclists, and has a small nature museum.

To get to the park, you'd be best off using your own transport as bus connections aren't great – rent a bike from the Rijwielshop at Roermond station (€6.85/day for a 3-geared bike) and cycle the 9km, following signs to the village of Herkenbosch, or drive. From Herkenbosch, follow Keulsebaan, then turn left down Meinweg to reach the Bezoekerscentrum (April–Oct daily 10am–5pm) and entrance to the park (open daily, unlimited access). In Herkenbosch, Manege de Venhof, Venhof 2 (☏0475/531 495), can arrange group horse-riding in the park (€10/hr).

## Thorn

The village of **THORN** makes for an enjoyable half-day outing from Roermond. Regular buses link the two, but it's more fun to rent a bike from the train station and cycle alongside the River Maas, following LF Route 5b (Roermond to Thorn). Take a map though (available at the Roermond VVV), as the signposting can be patchy. To return, follow the 5a signs; a round trip is roughly 30km.

Once you get here, it's easy to see why Thorn is a favourite for travel agents' posters, and something of a tourist honeypot. Its houses and farms are all painted white, a tradition for which no one seems to have a credible explanation, but which has a photogenic effect. The farms intrude right into the village itself, giving Thorn a barnyard friendliness that's enhanced by its cobblestone streets, the closed-shuttered propriety of its houses and, at the centre, the **Abdijkerk** (March–Oct daily 10am–5pm; Nov–Feb Sat & Sun noon–5pm; €2). The abbey was founded at the end of the tenth century by a powerful count,

Ansfried, and his wife Hilsondis, as a sort of religious retirement home after Ansfried had finished his tenure as bishop of Utrecht. Under his control the abbey and the land around it was granted the status of an independent principality under the auspices of the Holy Roman Empire and it was in the environs of the abbey that the village developed.

The abbey was unusual in having a double cloister that housed both men and women (usually from local noble families), a situation that carried on right up until the French invasion of 1797, after which the principality of Thorn was dissolved, the monks and nuns dispersed and all the abbey buildings save the church destroyed. Most of what can be seen of the church today dates from the fifteenth century, with some tidying up by P.J.H. Cuypers in the nineteenth. The interior decoration, though, is congenially restrained Baroque of the seventeenth century, with some good memorials and side chapels. If you're into the macabre, aim for the crypt under the chancel, which has a couple of glass coffins containing conclusively dead members of the abbey from the eighteenth century: this and other highlights are described in the notes that you can pick up on entry (in English) for a self-guided walking tour.

Thorn has one small museum, the **Museum Land of Thorn**, in the historic heart of the village at Wijnguard 14 (March–Nov daily 10am–4.30pm; rest of year Tues–Sun 11am–4pm; €2), which details the history of Thorn, hosts temporary exhibitions of art and houses a three-dimensional painting of the village.

### Practicalities

The **VVV**, at the entrance to the museum at Wijnguard 14 (same hours; ☎0475/562 761) can help with regional information. Thorn makes a great place to stay if you want to get away from it all: the cheaper of two **hotels** is the *Crasborn*, Hoogstraat 6 (☎0475/561 281, ⊛www.stadsherberg-crasborn.nl; ❸), though the atmospheric *Hostellerie La Ville Blanche*, Hoogstraat 2 (☎0475/562 341, ℻562 828; ❹) offers surprisingly affordable luxury. There's also a private **campsite**, *Viverjerbroek*, Kessenicherweg 20 (☎0475/561 914, ℻565 565; April–Oct), reached by turning right halfway down Hofstraat.

# Maastricht

**MAASTRICHT** made world headlines in 1992, when the signing of the Maastricht Treaty created the European Union. With its cobbled streets and fashionable boutiques in the old town, contemporary architecture in the Céramique district, a fantastic art fair and excellent cuisine, Maastricht is one of the most vibrant cities in the Netherlands. Add in its continental feel, the multilingual population and close proximity to Belgium and Germany and it's no wonder why the Eurocrats signed the treaty here: Maastricht epitomizes the most positive aspects of European union.

Keen to promote itself as the oldest town in the Netherlands (a title mildly contested by Nijmegen), Maastricht was first settled by the **Romans**, who took one look at the River Maas and dubbed the town *Mosae Trajectum* or "Crossing of the Maas". An important stop-off on the trading route between Cologne and the North Sea, the town boasted a Temple of Jupiter; that and other relics are now on view in a hotel basement. A millennium later, **Charlemagne's** legacy is two churches – some of the best surviving examples of the Romanesque in the Low Countries. Politically, the landscape around Maastricht has always consisted of small states ruled by powers as remote as

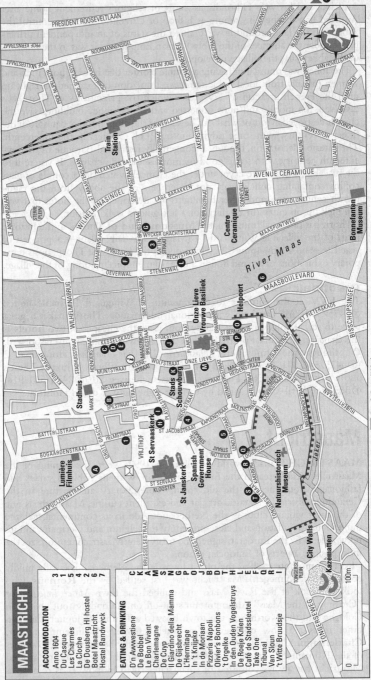

Austria and Spain in the eighteenth century. Once dependent on its natural resources, the closure of the last coalmines in the 1960s sent Maastricht into a sharp decline and unemployment was rife. A massive **regeneration** scheme turned the city around, and generous subsidies and aid programmes attracted foreign investors and businesses. Now Maastricht has become something of a call-centre capital, hosting the likes of Mercedes Benz and DHL. Redevelopment continues apace today within the "City Centre in Motion" scheme, whose most recent contribution is **'t Bassin**, a spruced up inland harbour north of the Markt, with restaurants, cafés, shops and galleries.

To the Dutch, Maastricht and the province of Limburg have an almost foreign flavour: being twice as far away from Amsterdam as from Brussels, and in the centre of a constellation of Liège, Cologne and Düsseldorf, the attitude here is breezily cosmopolitan. In fact, it's a popular day-trip destination not only for the Dutch but also Belgians and Germans, who hop over the borders to fill the all-year pavement cafés for which Maastricht is renowned. The town is also a temporary home to students and professionals from around the world, studying at over 40 international institutes, including the European Journalism Centre and the University of the United Nations, all of which boosts the vivacity of the place no end.

## Arrival, information and tours

The centre of Maastricht is on the west bank of the river and most of the town spreads out from here toward the Belgian border. You're likely to arrive, however, on the east bank, in the district known as **Wijk**, a sort of extension to the centre that's home to the **train** and **bus stations** and many of the city's hotels. The train station itself is about ten minutes' walk from the St Servaas bridge, which takes you across the river into the centre. All local buses connect with Markt from here, but really, if you have no heavy luggage, it's easy enough to walk. Maastricht **airport** is 12km north of the city at Beek, connected to Markt and the train station by a twenty-minute ride on bus #61 (bus #51 on Sun); a taxi costs about €25. Arriving by **car**, follow signs for Q-Parking; there's no free parking in the town centre. The VVV has a detailed "Parking in Maastricht" leaflet.

The main **VVV** (May–Oct Mon–Sat 9am–6pm, Sun 11am–3pm; Nov–April Mon–Fri 9am–6pm, Sat 9am–5pm; ☎043/325 2121, ⓦwww.vvvmaastricht.nl) is housed just across the river in the Dinghuis, a tall, late-fifteenth-century building at Kleine Straat 1, at one end of the main shopping street. As well as information on the city and on film, theatre and music events around town, they have decent maps and good walking guides. In July and August they organize **walking tours** (in English) which leave from the office daily at 12.30pm (€3) and last about an hour and a half. You can also buy VVV Gift Vouchers here (in denominations of €5 upwards), which gives discounts in over 100 shops and restaurants around town, and may be worth buying if you plan to do a lot of shopping.

You only really need to use **city buses** to get from the station to the town centre at Markt, or out to St Pietersburg; otherwise it's easy to walk everywhere. Between mid-May and September, Stiphout (ⓦwww.stiphout.nl) runs hourly cruises from the bottom of Graanmarkt down the Maas (Mon–Sat 10am–5pm, Sun 1–5pm; 50min; €5.50), and offers trips taking in the St Pietersberg caves (3hr; €8.75) or even as far as Liège (day-trip €17.50). Since not all cruises are available every day, phone ☎043/351 5319 to confirm, or ask at the VVV.

## Accommodation

For **accommodation**, there's nothing super-cheap. The VVV has a list of **private rooms** and will either book them for you at the usual fee or sell you the list. There are several good **pensions**, including *Anno 1604*, Kattenstraat 11 (☎043/325 0165; ❷) and *Hostel Randwyck*, Endepolsdomein 30 (☎043/361 6835, ⨍361 9007; ❷). **Hotels** include *La Cloche*, Bredestraat 41 (☎043/321 2407, ✉rachel@mail.cobweb.nl; ❷), the more comfortable *Les Charmes*, Lenculenstraat 18 (☎043/312 7400, ⨍325 8574; ❸), and *Botel Maastricht* (☎043/321 9023, ⨍325 7998; ❶), moored on the river at Maasboulevard, not far from the Helpoort, and with an excellent breakfast. Up a notch in price is the very central *Du Casque*, Helmstraat 14 (☎043/321 4343, ⨍325 5155; ❹).

The *De Dousberg* **campsite**, Dousbergweg 102 (☎043/343 2171, ⨍343 0556; April–Oct), almost in Belgium on the far western side of town, is large and well equipped; take bus #11 (Mon–Fri), #8 or #18 (Sat & Sun) from the train station. If you're travelling after 6.30pm, you'll need to take bus #28. The same buses also take you to the **HI hostel** at Dousbergweg 4 (☎043/346 6777, ⨆www.stayokay.com; dorms €22), which is sited within a sports complex – guests have free use of the swimming pools.

## The Town

The busiest of Maastricht's squares is the **Markt**, which transforms on Wednesday and Friday mornings from a car park into a busy general market. At the centre of the square, the **Stadhuis** (Mon–Fri 8.30am–12.30pm & 2–5.30pm; free) of 1664 was designed by Pieter Post, a square, grey limestone building that is a fairly typical slice of mid-seventeenth-century Dutch civic grandeur. Its double staircase was designed so that the rival rulers of Brabant and nearby Liège didn't have to argue about who should go first on the way in. Inside, the building has an imposing main hall, which gives way to a rear octagonal dome supported by heavy arches.

On your way to Vrijthof, the second of the town's main central squares, pop your head into the thirteenth-century **Dominicanerkerk**, just off Helmstraat, for a bit of a surprise. No reredos here, or elaborate altarpiece – but at €0.50 a day, this must be the Netherlands' cheapest, and most historic, supervised bike park. **Vrijthof** is just west of the Markt, a larger, rather grander open space flanked by a couple of churches on one side and a line of cafés on the other, with tables taking over the wide pavement in summer. During the Middle Ages, Vrijthof was the scene of the so-called "Fair of the Holy Relics", a seven-yearly showing of the bones of St Servaas, the first bishop of Maastricht, which brought plenty of pilgrims into the town but resulted in such civil disorder that it was eventually banned.

The church which holds the saint's relics now, the **St Servaaskerk** (April–Oct daily 10am–5pm; July & Aug until 6pm; Nov–March Mon–Sat 10am–5pm, Sun 12.30–5pm; €2), dominates the west side of Vrijthof. Dating from 950, it's the elaborate amalgamation of an earlier shrine dedicated to St Servaas and the site of his burial in 384. Only the crypt remains of the tenth-century church, containing the tomb of the saint himself, and the rest is mostly of medieval or later construction. You enter on the north side of the church, where a fifteenth-century Gothic cloister leads into the **treasury**, which holds a large collection of reliquaries, goblets and liturgical accessories, including a bust reliquary of St Servaas, decorated with reliefs telling the saint's story, which is carried through the town in Easter processions. There's also a coffin-reliquary of the saint, the so-called "Noodkist", dating from 1160 and bristling with saints, stones and ornate copperwork, as well as a jewelled crucifix from 890 and a twelfth-century Crucifixion in ivory. Beyond the Treasury is the entrance to the rich and imposing interior, the round-arched nave supporting freshly painted Gothic vaulting. Don't miss the mid-thirteenth-century Bergportaal on the south side of the church, the usual entrance during services.

The second most prominent building on the square, next door, is Maastricht's main Protestant church, the fourteenth-century **St Janskerk** (April–Oct daily except Sun 11am–4pm), the baptistery of the church of St Servaas when it was a cathedral and nowadays competing for attention with its high and faded, delicate red fifteenth-century Gothic tower. The church has some medieval murals, but a climb up the tower (€1.15) is the church's main appeal. On the south side of the square, the sixteenth-century **Spanish Government House** (guided tours only; Tues–Sun 1–5pm; €2.50) has an attractive Renaissance arcade and a number of period rooms furnished in Dutch, French and the more local Liège–Maastricht style. Among various exhibits are statues and figurines, porcelain and applied arts and a handful of seventeenth-century paintings.

Maastricht's other main church, the **Onze Lieve Vrouwe Basiliek**, is a short walk south of Vrijthof, down Bredestraat, in a small, shady square crammed with café tables in summer. It's unusual for its fortified west front, with barely more than one or two slits for windows. First built around the year 1000, it's a solid, dark and eerily devotional place after the bright Protestant churches of the north – or even the relative sterility of the St Servaaskerk. The Gothic vaulting of the nave springs from a Romanesque base, while the galleried choir is a masterpiece of proportion, raised under a high half-dome, with a series of capitals exquisitely decorated with Old Testament scenes. Off the north aisle, the **treasury** (Easter to mid-Sept Mon–Sat 11am–5pm, Sun 1–5pm; €1.60) holds the usual array of reliquaries and ecclesiastical garments, most notably the dalmatic of St Lambert – the evangelical bishop of Maastricht who was murdered at Liège in 705, allegedly by a local noble whom he had rebuked for adultery. Entrance to the church is through a side chapel on the Onze Lieve Vrouweplein, which houses the statue of Stella Mare, an object of pilgrimage for centuries and which attracts as many devotees as the church itself.

## Stokstraat Kwartier and the city walls

Around the corner from the Onze Lieve Vrouweplein is a district of narrow streets known as the **Stokstraat Kwartier** after its main gallery- and boutique-lined spine, Stokstraat. This quarter has an intimate feel, with its vermilion townhouses, scattered sculptures and Maasland-Renaissance style houses in warm Namur stone. On Plankstraat, the **Museumkelder Derlon** (Sun noon–4pm; free), in the basement of the hotel of the same name, contains one of the few remnants of Roman Maastricht – the remains of a temple to Jupiter, a well and several layers of pavement, discovered before the building of the present hotel in the mid-1980s.

On the other side of Onze Lieve Vrouweplein lies another of Maastricht's most appealing quarters, narrow streets winding out to the remains of the town battlements alongside the fast-flowing River Jeker, which weaves in and out of the various houses and ancient mills. The best surviving part of the walls is the **Helpoort** of 1229, close to a stretch overlooking the river at the end of St Bernadusstraat; and from here you can walk along the top of the walls almost as far as the **Natuurhistorisch Museum** at De Bosquetplein 6–7 (Mon–Fri 10am–5pm, Sat & Sun 2–5pm; €3), where there's a small collection on the geology, flora and fauna of the surrounding area, along with a small, lush garden display.

A little way southwest of here, the **Kazematten** (Casemates) in the Waldeck Park (tours July–Sept daily 12.30pm & 2pm; Oct–June Sun 2pm;

€3) are further evidence of Maastricht's once-impressive fortifications, a system of galleries created through mining between 1575 and 1825 that were used in times of siege for surprise attacks on the enemy. There used to be many more casemates around the town, but only these survive, making for a fairly draughty way to spend an hour. Tours take you through a small selection of the 10km or so of damp passages. Trivia buffs might be interested to know that the famous fourth "musketeer", d'Artagnan, was killed here, struck down while engaged in an attack on the town as part of forces allied to Louis XIV in 1673.

## The east bank

Ten minutes' walk south of the St Servaas bridge, the **Bonnefanten Museum**, Avenue Céramique 250 (Tues–Sun 11am–5pm, Ⓦ www.bonnefanten.nl; €7) is one of Maastricht's highlights. Named after the Bonnefanten monastery where it once was housed, the museum now inhabits an impressive modern building, designed by Aldo Rossi. On the banks of the Maas, its space rocket-style cupola is instantly recognizable, zooming skywards. Inside is a permanent collection of old masters and contemporary fine art, including works from the Minimal Art and Arte Povera movements. The rest of the museum is given over to various temporary exhibitions, superbly displayed: you could find anything from giant spider installations to Titians. Don't miss the cupola space, which is usually given over to a single piece of art.

Not far from the Bonnefanten Museum on Plein 1992, with its low horizons and euro symbols studded into the paving stones, is the **Centre Céramique**, Avenue Céramique 50 (Mon–Fri 10.30am–5.30pm, Tues & Thurs until 8.30pm, Sat 10.30am–3pm, Sun 1–5pm; Ⓦ www.centreceramique.nl). This huge modern building is home to the European Journalism Centre, the city archives and the library (which has free Internet access).

## Outside the centre: St Pietersberg

There are more dank passageways to explore fifteen minutes' walk from the casemates on the southern outskirts of Maastricht, where the flat-topped hill of **St Pietersberg** rises to a height of about 110m – a popular picnic spot on warm summer weekends. Again these aren't so much caves as galleries created by quarrying, hollowed out of the soft sandstone, or marl, which makes up the hill – an activity which has been going on here since Roman times. Nowadays, there are more than 20,000 passages; they still claim the lives of people (usually children) who enter without a guide and never find their way out. Of the two cave systems, the **Zonneberg** is probably the better, situated on the far side of the St Pietersberg hill at Casino Slavante (guided tours in English: July & Aug daily 2.45pm; €3). The caves here were intended to be used as air-raid shelters during World War II and were equipped accordingly, though they were only in fact utilized during the last few days before Maastricht's liberation. There is some evidence of wartime occupation, plus what everyone claims is Napoleon's signature on a graffiti-ridden wall. Also on the walls are recent charcoal drawings, usually illustrating a local story and acting as visual aids for the guides, not to mention the ten varieties of bat that inhabit the dark (and cold) corridors.

The other, more northerly system of caves, the **Grotten Noord** (€3) is easier to reach (15min walk from the centre of town), but it has less of interest, and no guided tours in English. The entrance is at Chalet Bergrust, on the near side of St Pietersberg close by **Fort St Pieter**, a low brick structure, pentagonal in shape and built in 1702, which nowadays houses a pricey restaurant –

troglophobes would do well to nurse a drink on the restaurant's terrace, which gives panoramic views over the town and surrounding countryside.

## Eating, drinking and nightlife

Maastricht has some of the best cooking in the Netherlands, Michelin-starred restaurants and three or four major breweries, so options abound for good **eating** and **drinking**. Regional delicacies include asparagus, cave mushrooms and Rommedou cheese.

There are a number of inexpensive **restaurants** around the Markt, including *Pizzeria Napoli* at no. 71 (which gives a twenty percent student discount), while in Wijk *De Roeje Knien*, Rechtsraat 76, serves good Dutch food. *Charlemagne* on Onze Lieve Vrouweplein also has reasonably priced steaks, chicken and ribs, while *Il Giardino della Mamma*, Onze Lieve Vrouweplein 15, has good pizzas and pasta from €10. *L'Hermitage*, St Bernardusstraat 13, around the corner and near the Helpoort, has Mexican food from €15; and *In 't Knijpke*, opposite, has a pleasant bar/restaurant and great onion soup. A few minutes from the centre is Tongersestraat, located in the university district, which has cheapish cafés, and two slightly more expensive Dutch/French restaurants: *'t Orgelke*, at no. 40, and *De Cuyp* at no. 30. More upmarket still is *Le Bon Vivant*, Capucijnenstraat 91 (☎043/321 0816), where a three-course meal in the seventeenth-century vault costs from €34.

Late-night snack attacks can be assuaged at *'t Witte Bruudsje*, Platielstraat 12 (between the VVV and Vrijthof), which stays open until 2am (Fri & Sat 3am), serving up baguettes, salads and hot staples such as chilli con carne and fish and chips. Chocolate lovers shouldn't miss *Olivier's Bonbons*, Kesselskade 55 (Mon 1–6pm, Tues–Fri 10am–6pm, Sat 10am–5pm) with its wicked chocolate concoctions, delicate displays and old-fashioned ambience.

For drinking, the **bars** on the east side of the Vrijthof have most pulling-power, particularly in summer when the pavement cafés are packed; *In den Ouden Vogelstruys*, on the corner of Platielstraat, is one of the nicest. Away from the Vrijthof crowds, *De Bobbel*, on Wolfstraat just off Onze Lieve Vrouweplein, is a bare-boards place, lively in the early evening, while *In de Moriaan*, Stokstraat 12, is a delight – possibly the smallest bar in the country and with a cosy terrace in the summer. The no-frills *Café de Stadssleutel*, Kesselskade 60, has the cheapest beer in town, and the student quarter around Tongesestraat has a couple of excellent bars in *Van Sloun* at no. 3 and *Tribunal* opposite. On the other side of the river, *De Gijsbrecht*, toward the station on Wycker Brugstraat, is a very busy bar while *Take One*, Rechtstraat 28, is a good bet for beer connoisseurs. There are DJs playing **music** throughout the year at *D'n Auwestiene*, Kesselkade 43 (Wed–Sun 10pm–5am).

The Lumière Filmhuis, Bogaardenstraat 40b (☎043/321 4080), regularly shows interesting **movies**, often English or American and always subtitled in Dutch.

## Listings

**Bike rental** Aon de Stasie, Stationsplein (Mon–Fri 6am–midnight, Sat & Sun 6am–1am; ☎043/321 1100; from €7/day plus €100 deposit).
**Books** There's a branch of De Slegte at Grote Straat 53, good for secondhand English-language paperbacks and much else besides. Try also Bergmans on Nieuwestraat, off Markt, which has a good selection of new English-language titles.

**Bureau de change** There's a GWK office at the train station, open daily.
**Car rental** Europcar, Sibemaweg 1 (☎043/361 2310, ℱ408 4337). The major companies also have desks at the airport.
**Post office** On Keizer Karelplein, just off the northwest corner of Vrijthof.
**Taxi** Crals, Ankerkade 275 ☎043/363 8484.

△ Path leading into the hills of Limburg

# Around South Limburg

**South Limburg** boasts the Netherlands' only true **hills** and as such is a popular holiday area for the Dutch, many of the villages crammed in summer with walkers from the north taking in the scenery. Several long-distance walking routes converge on Maastricht, including the popular and scenic Grand Randonné 5 "Traject der Ardennen", the Pieterpad (from St Pietersberg to Groningen's Pieterburen), and the Krijtlandpad, which winds its way to the German border. The countryside is green and rolling, studded with castles (many of which have been converted to hotels), seamed with river valleys and dotted with the crooked timber-framed houses that are unique to the area. Everywhere is within easy reach of Maastricht, although since public transport connections are patchy it makes more sense to take a **car**. This puts you in easy reach of Liège in Belgium (Luik in Dutch) and Aachen in Germany, and just an hour away from the cities of Brussels, Düsseldorf and Cologne – or the wild river valleys and peaks of Belgium's Ardennes.

**Valkenburg** is South Limburg's main resort, perhaps the easiest place to visit as it's on the main train line from Maastricht to Aachen, though it does get packed throughout the summer. Further east down the train line, **Heerlen** and

---

## A day's cycling in South Limburg

On a leisurely cycle route from Maastricht east to Vaals, right on the border on the edge of Aachen, scenic villages nestle among vineyards and orchards, linked by quiet lanes dotted with shrines. The pace of life is slow – the pony and trap is still a common sight – and cycling is a perfect way to appreciate this peaceful landscape and its un-Dutch hills. Allow a day for this seventy-kilometre round-trip ride, and carry a Limburg province map from the VVV.

From Maastricht train station, follow the river south to **Gronsveld**, picking up signs to the eleventh-century St Geertruid. The black and white half-timbered farmsteads in these villages are known as *vakwerkhuisjes*, built from clay, wood and dried dung. The road snakes over hills draped with vineyards before swooping into the villages **Mheer**, **Norbeek** and **Slenaken** – all highly picturesque and popular with walkers throughout the year. Each can conjure up accommodation, should you decide to spend longer in the area. At Slenaken, the road develops some hairpin tendencies as it climbs the valley side above, overlooked by grazing sheep. Continue through **Eperheide** and **Epen**, with sweeping views across to the rolling valleys of Belgium on the right. Between Epen and **Vaals**, there's a gradual eight-kilometre climb on narrow roads, winding between woods of red oaks, with glimpses of bright green farmland below. For a six-kilometre round-trip to the highest point in the Netherlands, follow the signs to the **Drielandenpunt** (see p.344) from Vaals – the monument celebrating 321m of altitude is just in front of the concrete observation tower. Otherwise, follow the main road out of Vaals (there's a dedicated cycle lane), turning left to **Vijlen** where ploughed fields and potatoes take up as much space as the main street as the houses. Surrounding you is a panoramic view over Belgium, Germany and the Netherlands, beautiful on a clear day, presided over by the wind turbines in the distance. From eleventh-century **Mechelen** and **Gulpen**, you're in striking distance of **Valkenburg** to the north, approached through the old town. Climb the steep but brief Cauberg hill to return to Maastricht, enjoying a speedy descent between orchards and farmland with the city locked in your sights. Once on the outskirts, follow the cycle route signs to bring you back to the station.

An alternative (and shorter) return route is to continue from Gulpen to Maastricht on a straight route via **Margraten** and **Cadier en Keer**.

**Kerkrade** are also easily reached, though neither is any great shakes. To the south of the train line, toward the Belgian border, the countryside is wilder and more impressive, with expansive views all around.

## East of Maastricht

Some 5km east of Maastricht, the first stop on the #54 bus route – which eventually goes to Vaals on the German border – **CADIER-EN-KEER** is a small suburb best known for its **Africa Centre** (Tues–Fri 1.30–5pm, Sat & Sun 2–5pm; €4), ten minutes' walk off to the left of the main road (follow the signs). Housed in the headquarters of the African Missionaries Society, this contains a small museum of mainly West African artefacts, masks, jewellery and statuary arranged by tribe and dating back as far as the thirteenth century – as well as giving details on the contemporary way of life of African peoples.

Bus #54 continues to **MARGRATEN**, where just before the town proper there's an **American War Cemetery** (daily sunrise–sunset), a peaceful and moving memorial to over eight thousand American servicemen who died in the Dutch and Belgian campaigns of late 1944 and 1945. Buses stop right outside. The centrepiece is a stone quadrangle recording the names of the soldiers, together with a small visitors' room and a pictorial representation and narrative describing the events in this area leading up to the German surrender, while beyond the quadrangle, the white marble crosses that mark the burial places of the soldiers cover a depressingly huge area.

There's not much else to Margraten, nor is there to **GULPEN**, a few kilometres beyond, a nondescript place with good bus connections all over South Limburg. The town is known for its Gulpener beer, the name of which you see all over the province and indeed the rest of the country, though that aside the only thing that distinguishes Gulpen is the 161m-high Gulpenberg, which rises roundly behind the town and is home to a campsite. At the end of the #54 route, the small town of **VAALS** is perched on a hillside whose peak is the highest point in the Netherlands, at a lofty 321m. Just a few metres further on are three flags in a graffiti-covered concrete block symbolising the "**Drielandenpunt**", where the borders of Belgium, Germany and the Netherlands meet. A nearby labyrinth (€2.75), observation tower (€2.50), car parks and fast-food outlet contrive to make this a truly underwhelming experience.

South of Gulpen, the countryside makes for a pretty route back to Maastricht, either driving yourself or via the #57 bus route from Gulpen's bus station, taking in the scenically sited villages of **Mechelen**, **Epen** and **Slenaken**.

## Valkenburg

Set in the gently wooded valley of the River Geul, **VALKENBURG**, ten minutes east of Maastricht by train, is southern Limburg's major tourist resort. A medieval castle, its ruins starkly silhouetted on crags above the town, surveys the fake castle train station, garish centre and bus-loads of tourists throughout the summer heading for its innumerable hotels, restaurants and casino. While you wouldn't want to stay here, it's certainly a change from the rest of the Netherlands, with a feel more akin to a Swiss or Austrian alpine resort. Valkenburg is also famed for its Christmas-season markets, held in Fluwelengrot and Gemeentegrot, with all manner of special foodstuffs, decorations and street entertainment.

**Theodoor Dorrenplein**, five minutes' walk from the train station, is the centre of town, fringed with cafés and home to the VVV. From here the main Grote Straat leads up through the pedestrianized old centre through the old **Grendelpoort** arch to **Grendelplein**, which provides a second focus, with streets leading off to Valkenburg's main attractions. A great many of these are directed at children – things like bobsleigh runs, a fairytale wood, a hopeful reconstruction of Rome's catacombs – and even those that aren't are still the kind of things kids enjoy.

It's worth a walk up to the **castle** (April–Oct daily 10am–5pm; €2.60; joint ticket with Fluwelengrot €5.90; entrance off Grendelplein). The edifice was blown up in 1672 on the orders of William III, after he had retrieved it from its French occupiers. Repair and restoration began in 1921 and continue still, uncovering a series of underground passages that served as an escape route in times of siege. These form part of the **Fluwelengrot** (guided tours only; Jan–March Mon–Fri 11am & 1pm, Sat & Sun 11am–3pm on the hour; April–Oct daily 11am–4pm on the hour; July & Aug daily 10.30am–5pm every half-hour and at 8pm; closed Nov & Dec for Christmas market; €4.40; joint ticket with castle €5.90), further up the road on the left, a series of caves formed – like those of St Pietersberg in Maastricht – by the quarrying of marl, which has been used for much of the building in this area over the years. On the whole they're a damp, cold way to spend an hour, the most interesting features the signatures and silhouettes of American soldiers who wintered here from 1944 to 1945 and a clandestine chapel that was used during the late eighteenth-century French occupation.

If you particularly like caves, or can't be bothered to walk around the Fluwelengrot, the **Gemeentegrot** (April–Oct Mon–Sat 9am–5pm, Sun 10am–5pm; Nov–March Mon–Fri 2pm, Sat & Sun 10am–4pm; €4), just off Grendelplein on Cauberg, is similar, but has a train which whips you around its charcoal drawings, memorials to local dignitaries, giant sculptures of dinosaurs and fish hewn out of the rock, and, most engagingly, a weirdly, brightly lit underground lake. The whole tour by train takes about thirty minutes.

Further up the same road as the Fluwelengrot, on the left, the **Steenkolemijn** (guided tours only: April–Oct daily 10am–5pm; Nov–March Mon–Fri 2pm, Sat & Sun 1pm, 2pm & 3pm; €5.75) is a reconstruction of a coal mine whose 75-minute tours include a short film on coal-mining, some fake mine-workings and a small fossil museum – again, good for the kids but not exactly riveting viewing.

If the idea of trudging around dank underground passages doesn't appeal to you, you can ascend to the top of the hill above the castle by way of a **cable car** (daily: April–Oct 10am–5pm; Nov–March 1–5pm; €3 return), five minutes' walk down Berkelstraat from the top of Grote Straat – or you can cut through the passage between the castle and the Fluwelengrot. This, a fairly primitive structure of the kind used for ski lifts, with two-person open cars, takes you up to the **Wilhemina Toren**, where you can enjoy the view from the terrace of the inevitable bar-restaurant.

For a trip further afield, you can take a sightseeing excursion from Valkenburg to Kerkrade by steam or diesel **train** (all year Sun 11am; ☎045/544 0018).

## Practicalities

The **VVV**, Theodoor Dorrenplein 5 (April–Oct Mon–Fri 9am–5.30pm, Sat 9am–5pm, Sun 10am–3pm; Nov–March Mon–Fri 9am–5.30pm, Sat 9am–1pm; ☎043/609 8600, ⓦwww.vvvzuidlimburg.nl) has maps and information on all Valkenburg's attractions, as well as lists of the dozens of **hotels** and **pensions**. Among the cheapest hotels are *De Grendel*, Grendelplein 17

(①043/601 4868; ②) and *Casa* (next to *Havana*, a noisy bar pumping out dance music to teenagers) at Grotestraat 25–27 (①043/601 2180; ②). Slightly upmarket are the *Hostellerie Valckenborgh*, Hovetstraat 3 (①043/601 2484, ⑩www .valckenborgh.nl; ③), the *Gaudi*, Grendelplein 14 (①043/601 5333, ⑩www .hotelgaudi.nl; ③) and *De Uitkijk*, Broekhem 68 (①043/601 3589, ⑤601 4744; ④). The nearest **campsite** is *Den Driesch*, a short walk up Dahlemerweg from Grendelplein on the left (①043/601 2025, ⑩www.campingdendriesch.nl; April–Nov), which attracts a young crowd. An alternative is *Camping Cauberg 29* (①043/601 2344; March–Nov). As virtually every second building in Valkenburg is a restaurant, there's little point in listing specific places to **eat**. Suffice to say you can dine cheaply and fairly reasonably at most of the places in the centre.

For a break from sightseeing, head to **Thermae 2000**, the Netherlands' first official spa, located up a steep hill on Cauberg (daily 9am–11pm; €15.50 for 2hr, €26.50 for whole day). It has a sauna complex, eucalyptus steam rooms, indoor and outdoor pools (with views over the Limburg countryside), plus relaxation and yoga rooms, and a range of face and body treatments. The adjoining hotel, *Thermaetel*, has free use of all these facilities – but at a staggering €203 a night, you'd better get that relaxation treatment booked in advance.

## Heerlen and Kerkrade

**HEERLEN**, ten minutes northeast of Valkenburg by train, is quite different, an ugly modern town that sprawls gracelessly over the rolling countryside. But it has one definite attraction in the excellent **Thermen Museum**, Coriovallumstraat 9 (daily 10am–5pm, ⑩www.thermenmuseum.nl; €3.50), which incorporates the excavations of a bath complex from the Roman city of Coriovallum here – a key settlement on the Cologne–Boulogne trade route. These have been enclosed in a gleaming, purpose-built hi-tech structure, with walkways leading across the ruins and tapes (in English) explaining what's what. An adjacent room displays finds and artefacts from the site, including glasswork from Cologne, shards of pottery, tombstones and coins, all neatly labelled. To get to the museum, follow Saroleastraat from the station as far as Raadhuisplein and turn right.

Fifteen minutes on from Heerlen by the German border lies **KERKRADE**, again an unappealing place, but worthy of a visit for its **Abdij van Rolduc** complex (opening hours vary, call ①045/546 6888), situated on the far side of town, about a twenty-minute walk from the station. Originally founded by one Ailbert, a young priest who came here in 1104, this is now almost entirely sixteenth-century, used as a seminary and conference centre, but it does preserve a fine twelfth-century church, a model of simplicity and elegance, with contemporary frescoes and a marvellous mosaic floor. The clover leaf-shaped crypt, dark and mysterious after the church and with pillar capitals carved by Italian craftsmen, contains the relics of Ailbert, brought here from Germany where he died. Kerkrade also has, beside the train station, the **Industrion** (Tues–Sun 10am–5pm; €5), an interesting museum which traces the nation's industrial development, with a focus on paper, graphics, ceramics and coal-mining.

# Travel details

## Trains

**Breda** to: Dordrecht (every 20min; 20min); 's Hertogenbosch (every 30min; 30min); Middelburg (every 30min; 1hr 15min); Maastricht (every 30min; 1hr 50min).

**Eindhoven** to: Roermond (every 30min; 30min); Venlo (every 30min; 35min).

**'s Hertogenbosch** to: Eindhoven (every 15min; 25min).

**Maastricht** to: Amsterdam (every 30min; 2hr 35min); Den Haag/The Hague (every 30min; 2hr 45min); Roermond (every 30min; 40min).

**Middelburg** to: Bergen-op-Zoom (every 30min; 40min); Goes (every 30min; 13min); Roosendaal (every 30min; 50min).

**Roermond** to: Venlo (every 30min; 24min).

**Roosendaal** to: Breda (every 30min; 19min); Dordrecht (every 20min; 25min).

**Tilburg** to: Eindhoven (every 20min; 35min); 's Hertogenbosch (every 30min; 15min).

**Vlissingen** to: Middelburg (every 30min; 8min).

## Buses

**Middelburg** to: Delta Expo (hourly; 30min); Renesse (hourly; 45min); Veere (Mon–Sat hourly, Sun every 2hr; 10min).

**Renesse** to: Brouwershaven (hourly; 30min).

**Zierikzee** to: Goes (every 30min; 30min).

## Ferries

**Vlissingen** to: Breskens (hourly; 30min).

# Contexts

# Contexts

# The historical framework

The country now known as the Netherlands didn't reach its present delimitations until 1830. Until then the borders of the entire region, formerly known as the Low Countries and including present-day Belgium and Luxembourg, were continually being redrawn following battles, treaties and alliances. Inevitably, then, what follows is, in its early parts at least, an outline of the history of the whole region, rather than a straightforward history of the Netherlands as such. Please note, incidentally, that the term "Holland" refers to the province – not the country – throughout.

## Beginnings

Little is known of the **prehistoric** settlers of the Netherlands. Their visible remains are largely confined to the far north of the country, where mounds known as *terpen* were built to keep the sea at bay in Friesland and Groningen. In Drenthe, megalithic tombs, *hunebeds*, stretch scattered across a low ridge of hills, the Hondsrug, north of Emmen.

Clearer details of the region begin to emerge at the time of Julius Caesar's conquest of Gaul in 57 to 50 BC. He found three tribal groupings living in the region: the mainly Celtic **Belgae** (hence the nineteenth-century term "Belgium") settled by the Rhine, Maas and Waal to the south; the Germanic **Frisians** living on the marshy coastal strip north of the Scheldt; and the **Batavi**, another Germanic people, inhabiting the swampy river banks of what is now the southern Netherlands. The Belgae were conquered and their lands incorporated into the imperial province of **Gallia Belgica**, but the territory of the Batavi and Frisians was not considered worthy of colonization. These tribes were granted the status of allies, a source of recruitment for the Roman legions and curiosity for imperial travellers. In 50 AD **Pliny** observed: "Here a wretched race is found, inhabiting either the more elevated spots or artificial mounds… When the waves cover the surrounding area they are like so many mariners on board a ship, and when again the tide recedes their condition is that of so many shipwrecked men."

The Roman occupation of Gallia Belgica continued for 500 years until the legions were pulled back to protect the heartlands of their crumbling empire. As the empire collapsed in chaos and confusion, the Germanic **Franks**, who had been settling within Gallia Belgica from the third century, filled the power vacuum, establishing a **Merovingian** kingdom around their capital Tournai (in modern Belgium) with their allies the Belgae. A great swathe of forest extending from the Scheldt to the Ardennes separated this Frankish kingdom from the more confused situation to the north and east, where other tribes of Franks settled along the Scheldt and Leie, Saxons occupied parts of Overijssel and Gelderland, and the Frisians clung to the shore.

Towards the end of the fifth century, the Merovingian king Clovis was converted to **Christianity** and the faith slowly filtered north, spread by energetic missionaries like St Willibrord, first bishop of Utrecht from about 710, and St Boniface, who was killed by the Frisians in 754 in a final act of pagan resistance before they too were converted. Meanwhile, after the death of the last distinguished Merovingian king, Dagobert, in 638, power passed increasingly to the so-called "mayors of the palace", a hereditary position whose most outstanding occupant was **Charles Martel** (c.690–741). Martel dominated a large, but all-too-obviously shambolic, kingdom whose military weakness he determined to remedy. Traditionally, the Merovingian (Frankish) army was comprised of a body of infantry led by a small group of cavalry. Martel replaced this with a largely mounted force of highly trained knights, who bore their own military expenses in return for land – the beginnings of the **feudal system**. These reforms came just in time to save Christendom: in 711 an extraordinary Arab advance, which had begun early in the seventh century, reached the Pyrenees and a massive Muslim army occupied southern France in preparation for further conquests. In the event, Martel defeated the invaders outside Tours in 732, one of Europe's most crucial engagements and one that saved France from Arab conquest for good. Ten years after Martel's death, his son, Pepin the Short, formally usurped the Merovingian throne with the blessing of the pope, becoming the first of the **Carolingian** dynasty, whose most famous member was **Charlemagne**, son of Pepin and king of the west Franks from 768. In a dazzling series of campaigns, Charlemagne extended his empire south into Italy, west to the Pyrenees, north to Denmark and east to the Oder. His secular authority was bolstered by his coronation as the first **Holy Roman Emperor** in 800, a title bestowed on him by the pope in order to legitimize his claim as the successor to the emperors of Imperial Rome.

The strength and stability of Charlemagne's court at Aachen spread to the Low Countries, bringing a building boom that created a string of superb Romanesque churches like Maastricht's St Servaas, and a trading bonanza, utilizing the region's principal rivers. However, unlike his Roman predecessors, Charlemagne was subject to the divisive inheritance laws of the Salian tribe of Franks, and after his death in 814, his kingdom was divided between his grandsons into three roughly parallel strips of territory, the precursors of France, the Low Countries and Germany.

## The growth of the towns

The tripartite division of Charlemagne's empire placed the Low Countries between the emergent French- and German-speaking nations, a dangerous location which was subsequently to decide much of its history. Amidst the cobweb of local alliances that made up **early feudal western Europe** in the ninth and tenth centuries, however, this was not apparent. During this period, French kings and German emperors exercised a general authority over the region, but power was effectively in the hands of local lords who, remote from central control, brought a degree of local stability. From the twelfth century, feudalism slipped into a gradual decline, the intricate pattern of localized allegiances undermined by the increasing strength of certain lords, whose power and wealth often exceeded that of their nominal sovereign. Preoccupied by territorial squabbles, this streamlined nobility was usually willing to assist the growth of towns by granting charters that permitted a certain amount of **autonomy** in exchange for tax revenues, and military and labour services. The first major cities were the cloth towns of Flanders – Bruges, Ieper (Ypres) and Ghent. Meanwhile, their smaller northern neighbours concentrated on trade, exploiting their strategic position at the junction of several of the major waterways and trade routes of the day, Amsterdam being a case in point.

## Burgundian rule and the Habsburgs

By the late fourteenth century the political situation in the Low Countries was fairly clear: five lords controlled most of the region, paying only nominal homage to their French or German overlords. In 1419 **Philip the Good** of

Burgundy succeeded to the countship of Flanders and by a series of adroit political moves gained control over Holland, Zeeland, Brabant and Limburg to the north, and Antwerp, Namur and Luxembourg to the south. He consolidated his power by establishing a strong central administration in Bruges and restricting the privileges granted in the towns' charters. During his reign Bruges became an emporium for the Hanseatic League, a mainly German association of towns who acted as a trading group and protected their interests by an exclusive system of trading tariffs. Philip died in 1467 to be succeeded by his son, **Charles the Bold**, who was killed in battle ten years later, plunging his carefully crafted domain into turmoil. The French seized the opportunity to take back Arras and Burgundy and before the people of Flanders would agree to fight the French they kidnapped Charles's daughter, Mary, and forced her to sign a charter that restored the civic privileges removed by her grandfather Philip.

After her release, Mary married the **Habsburg** Maximilian of Austria, who assumed sole authority when Mary was killed in a riding accident in 1482. **Maximilian** continued to implement the centralizing policies of Philip the Good, but in 1494, when he became Holy Roman Emperor, he transferred control of the Low Countries to his son, Philip the Handsome. The latter died in 1506 and his territories were passed on to Maximilian's grandson **Charles V**, who in turn became King of Spain and Holy Roman Emperor in 1516 and 1519 respectively. Charles was suspicious of the turbulent burghers of Flanders and, following in Maximilian's footsteps, favoured Antwerp at their expense; it soon became the greatest port in the empire, part of a general movement of trade and prosperity away from Flanders to the cities to the north.

Through sheer might, Charles systematically bent the merchant cities of the Low Countries to his will, but regardless of this display of force, a spiritual trend was emerging that would soon question not only the rights of the Emperor but also rock the power of the Catholic Church itself.

## Stirrings of the Reformation

An alliance of Church and State had dominated the medieval world: pope and bishops, kings and counts were supposedly the representatives of God on earth, and they combined to crush religious dissent wherever it appeared. Much of their authority depended on the ignorance of the population, who were entirely dependent on their priests for the interpretation of the scriptures, their view of the world carefully controlled.

There were many complex reasons for the **Reformation**, the stirring of religious revolt that stood sixteenth-century Europe on its head, but certainly the **development of typography** was key. For the first time, printers were able to produce relatively cheap bibles in quantity, and the religious texts were no longer the exclusive property of the Church. A welter of debate spread across much of western Europe, led initially by theologians who wished to cleanse the Catholic Church of its corruptions, superstitions and extravagant ceremony; only later did many of these same thinkers decide to support a breakaway church. Humanists like **Erasmus of Rotterdam** (1465–1536) saw man as the crowning of creation rather than the sinful creature of the Fall; and, most importantly, in 1517 **Martin Luther** produced his 95 theses against indulgences, rejecting among other things Christ's presence in the sacrament of the Eucharist, and denying the Church's monopoly on the interpretation of the Bible. His works and Bible translations were printed in the Netherlands and his ideas gained a following in a group known as the Sacramentarians. They, and other reforming groups branded as **Lutheran** by the Church, were persecuted and escaped the towns to form fugitive communes where the doctrines of another reformer, **John Calvin** (1509–64), became popular. Luther stated that the Church's political power was subservient to that of the state; Calvin emphasized the importance of individual conscience and the need for redemption through the grace of Christ rather than the confessional. The seeds of Protestantism fell on fertile ground among the merchants of the cities of the Low Countries, whose wealth and independence could not easily be accommodated within a rigid caste society. Similarly, their employees, the guildsmen and their apprentices, had a long history of opposing royal authority, and many were soon convinced of the need to reform an autocratic, venal church. In 1555, Charles V abdicated, transferring his German lands to his brother Ferdinand, and his Italian, Spanish and Low Countries territories to his son, the fanatically Catholic **Philip II**. In the short term, the scene was set for a massive confrontation, while the dynastic ramifications of the division of the Habsburg Empire were to complicate European affairs for centuries.

## The revolt of the Netherlands

On his father's abdication, Philip decided to teach his heretical subjects a lesson. He garrisoned the towns of the Low Countries with Spanish mercenaries, imported the Inquisition and passed a series of anti-Protestant edicts. The opposition to these measures was, however, so widespread that he was pushed into a tactical withdrawal, recalling his soldiers and transferring control to his sister **Margaret of Parma** in 1559. Based in Brussels, the equally resolute Margaret implemented the policies of her brother with gusto. In 1561 she reorganized the Church and created fourteen new bishoprics, a move that was construed as a wresting of power from civil authority, and an attempt to destroy the local aristocracy's powers of religious patronage. Protestantism and Protestant sympathies spread to the nobility, who now formed the "League of the Nobility" to counter Habsburg policy. The League petitioned Philip for moderation but were dismissed out of hand by one of Margaret's Walloon advisers, who called them *ces geux* ("those beggars"), an epithet that was to be enthusiastically adopted by the rebels. In 1565 a harvest failure caused a winter famine among the workers, and in many towns, particularly Antwerp, they ran riot in the churches, sacking them of their wealth and destroying their rich decoration in the **Iconoclastic Fury**.

The ferocity of this outbreak shocked the upper classes into renewed support for Spain, and Margaret regained the allegiance of most nobles – with the principal exception of the country's greatest landowner, Prince William of Orange-Nassau, known as **William the Silent** (though William the Taciturn is a better translation). Of Germanic descent, he was raised a Catholic but the excesses and rigidity of Philip had caused him to side with the Protestant movement. A firm believer in individual freedom and religious tolerance, William became a symbol of liberty; but after the Fury had revitalized the pro-Spanish party, he prudently slipped away to his estates in Germany.

Philip II saw himself as responsible to God for the salvation of his subjects and therefore obliged to protect them from heresy. In 1567, keen to take advantage of the opportunity provided by the increased support for Margaret, he appointed the **Duke of Alva**, with an army of 10,000 men, to enter the Low Countries and suppress his religious opponents absolutely. Alva's arrival prompted Margaret to withdraw in a huff, and the Low Countries came under military rule. Alva's first act was to set up what the Protestants soon called the

**Council of Blood**, a kangaroo court which tried and condemned 12,000 of those who had taken part in the rioting of the year before. Initially the repression worked: in 1568, when William attempted an invasion from Germany, the towns, garrisoned by the Spanish, offered no support. William waited and conceived other means of defeating Alva. In April 1572, a band of privateers entered Brielle on the Maas and captured it from the Spanish. This was one of several commando-style attacks by the so-called **Waterguezen** or sea-beggars, who were at first obliged to operate from England, although it was soon possible for them to secure bases in the Netherlands, whose citizens had grown to loathe Alva and his Spaniards.

After the success at Brielle, the revolt spread rapidly: by June the rebels controlled most of the province of Holland and William was able to take command of his troops in Delft. Alva and his son Frederick fought back, taking Gelder, Overijssel and the towns of Zutphen and Naarden, and in June 1573 Haarlem, massacring the Calvinist ministers and most of the defenders. But the Protestants retaliated: utilizing their superior naval power, the dykes were cut and the Spanish forces, unpaid and threatened with destruction, were forced to withdraw. Frustrated, Philip replaced Alva with **Luis de Resquesens**, who initially had some success in the south, where the Catholic majority was more willing to compromise with Spanish rule than their northern neighbours.

William's triumphant relief of Leiden in 1574 increased the confidence of the rebel forces, and when de Resquesens died in 1576, his unpaid garrison in Antwerp mutinied and attacked the town, slaughtering some eight thousand of its people in what was known as the **Spanish Fury**. Though Spain still held several towns, the massacre alienated the south and pushed its peoples into the arms of William, whose troops now controlled most of the Low Countries. Momentarily, it seemed possible for the whole region to unite behind William, and the various provinces signed the **Pacification of Ghent** in 1576, an agreement that guaranteed freedom of religious belief. However, differences between Protestant north and Catholic south proved irreconcilable, with many Walloons and Flemings suspicious both of William's ambitions and his Calvinist cronies. Consequently, when another army arrived from Spain, under the command of Alexander Farnese, Duke of Parma, the south was reoccupied without much difficulty, beginning a separation that would lead, after many changes, to the creation of three modern countries – Belgium, Luxembourg and the Netherlands.

In 1579 seven provinces (Holland, Zeeland, Utrecht, Groningen, Friesland, Overijssel and Gelderland) signed the **Union of Utrecht**, an alliance against Spain that was to be the first unification of the Netherlands as an identifiable country – the so-called **United Provinces**. The agreement stipulated freedom of belief within the provinces, an important step since the struggle against Spain wasn't simply a religious one: many Catholics disliked the Spanish occupation and William did not wish to alienate this possible source of support. This liberalism did not, however, extend to freedom of worship, although a blind eye was turned to the celebration of Mass if it was done privately and inconspicuously – giving rise to the "hidden churches" found throughout the country.

## The United Provinces 1579–1713

In order to follow the developments of the sixteenth and seventeenth centuries in what is now the Netherlands, it's necessary to have an idea of the organization of the **United Provinces**. Holland, today comprising Noord- and Zuid-Holland, was by far the dominant province economically and politically, and although the provinces maintained a decentralized independence, as far as the United Provinces as a whole were concerned, what Holland said, pretty much went. The assembly of these United Provinces was known as the **States General**, and met at Den Haag (The Hague); it had no domestic legislative authority, and could only carry out foreign policy by unanimous decision, a formula designed to make potential waverers feel more secure. The role of **Stadholder** was the most important in each province, roughly equivalent to that of governor, though the same person could occupy this position in any number of provinces – and mostly did, with the Orange-Nassaus characteristically picking up five or six provinces at any one time. The Council Pensionary was another major post. The man who held either title in Holland was a centre of political power. Pieter Geyl, in his seminal *Revolt of the Netherlands*, defined the end result as the establishment of a republic which was "oligarchic, erastian (and) decentralized".

In 1584, a Catholic assassinated William the Silent at his residence in Delft. It was a grievous blow to the provinces and, as William's son **Maurice** was only 17, power passed to **Johan van Oldenbarneveldt**, the country's leading statesman and Council Pensionary of Rotterdam and later, Holland. Things were going badly in the war against the Spanish: Nijmegen had fallen and Henry III of France refused help even though the States General had made him tentative offers of sovereignty. In desperation, Oldenbarneveldt turned to **Elizabeth I** of England, who suggested the Earl of Leicester as governor general. Leicester was accepted, but completely mishandled the military situation, alienating the Dutch into the bargain. Short of options, Oldenbarneveldt and Maurice stepped into the breach and, somewhat to their surprise, drove the Spanish back. International events then played into their hands: in 1588, the English defeated the Spanish Armada and, the following year, the powerful and ambitious king Henry III of France died. Most important of all, Philip II of Spain, the scourge of the Low Countries, died in 1598, a necessary preamble to the **Twelve Year Truce** (1609–21) signed between the Habsburgs and the United Provinces, which grudgingly accepted the independence of the new republic.

## The early seventeenth century

In the breathing space created by the truce, the **rivalry** between Maurice and Oldenbarneveldt intensified and an obscure argument within the Calvinist church on predestination proved the catalyst for Oldenbarneveldt's downfall. The quarrel, between two Leiden theologians, began in 1612: Armenius argued that God gave man the choice of accepting or rejecting faith; Gomarus, his opponent, that predestination was absolute – to the degree that God chooses who will be saved and who damned with man powerless in the decision. This row between the two groups (known respectively as Remonstrants and Counter-Remonstrants) soon became attached to the political divisions within the republic. When a synod was arranged at Dordrecht to resolve the doctrinal matter, the province of Holland, led by Oldenbarneveldt, refused to attend, insisting on Holland's right to decide its own religious orthodoxies. At heart, he and his fellow deputies supported the provincial independence favoured by Remonstrant sympathisers, whereas Maurice sided with the Counter-Remonstrants, who favoured a strong central authority. The Counter-Remonstrants won at Dordrecht and Maurice, with his troops behind him, quickly overcame his opponents and had Oldenbarneveldt arrested. In May 1619 Oldenbarneveldt was **executed** in Den Haag "for having conspired to dismember the states of the Netherlands and greatly troubled God's church".

With the end of the Twelve Year Truce in 1621, fighting with Spain broke out once again, this time part of the more general **Thirty Years' War** (1618–48), a largely religious-based conflict between Catholic and Protestant countries that involved most of western Europe. In the Low Countries, the Spanish were initially successful, but they were weakened by war with France and by the fresh attacks of Maurice's successor, his brother **Frederick Henry**. From 1625, the Spaniards suffered a series of defeats on land and sea that forced them out of what is today the southern part of the Netherlands, and in 1648 they were compelled to accept the humiliating terms of the **Peace of Westphalia**. This was a general treaty that ended the Thirty Years' War and under its terms the independence of the United Provinces was formally recognized. What's more, the Dutch were able to insist that the Scheldt estuary be closed to shipping, an action designed to destroy the trade and prosperity of Antwerp, which – along with the rest of modern-day Belgium – remained part of the Habsburg empire. By this act, the commercial expansion and pre-eminence of Amsterdam was assured, and the Golden Age began.

## The Golden Age

The brilliance of **Amsterdam**'s explosion onto the European scene is as difficult to underestimate as it is to detail. The size of the city's merchant fleet carrying Baltic grain into Europe had long been considerable and even during the long war with Spain it had continued to expand. Indeed, not only were the Spaniards unable to undermine it, but they were, on occasion, even obliged to use Dutch ships to supply their own troops – part of a burgeoning cargo trade that was another key ingredient of Amsterdam's economic success.

It was, however, the emasculation of Antwerp by the Treaty of Westphalia that launched a period of extraordinarily dynamic growth – the so-called **Golden Age** – and Amsterdam quickly became the emporium for the products of north and south Europe and the new colonies in the East and West Indies. Dutch banking and investment brought further prosperity, and by the mid-seventeenth century Amsterdam's wealth was spectacular. The Calvinist bourgeoisie indulged themselves in fine canal houses, and commissioned images of themselves in group portraits. Civic pride knew no bounds: great monuments to self-aggrandizement, such as Amsterdam's new town hall, were hastily erected, and, if some went hungry, few starved, as the poor were cared for in municipal almshouses. The arts flourished and religious tolerance extended even to the traditional scapegoats, the Jews, and in particular the Sephardic Jews, who had been hounded from Spain by the Inquisition but were guaranteed freedom from religious persecution under the terms of the Union of Utrecht of 1579. By the end of the eighteenth century, Jews accounted for ten percent of the city's inhabitants. Guilds and craft associations thrived, and in the first half of the seventeenth century the city's population quadrupled. Furthermore, although Amsterdam was the centre of this boom, economic ripples spread across much of the United Provinces. Dutch farmers were, for instance, able to sell all they could produce in the expanding city and a string of Zuider Zee ports cashed in on the flourishing Baltic trade.

Throughout the Golden Age, one organization that kept the country's coffers brimming was the **East India Company**. Formed in 1602, this Amsterdam-controlled enterprise sent ships to Asia, Indonesia, and as far as China to bring back spices, woods and other assorted valuables. The States General granted the company a trading monopoly in all lands east of the Cape of Good Hope and, for good measure, threw in unlimited military powers over the lands it controlled. As a consequence, the company became a colonial power in its own right, governing, at one time or another, Malaya, Ceylon and parts of modern-day Indonesia. In 1621, the **West India Company** was inaugurated to protect Dutch interests in the Americas and Africa. However, this second company never achieved the success of its sister, expending most of its energies in waging war on Spanish and Portuguese colonies from its base in Surinam. The company was dismantled in 1674, ten years after its small colony of New Amsterdam had been captured by the British and renamed **New York**. Elsewhere, the Netherlands held on to its colonies for as long as possible: Java and Sumatra remained under Dutch control until 1949.

Although the economics of the Golden Age were dazzling, the **political climate** was dismal. The United Provinces were dogged by interminable wrangling between those who hankered for a central, unified government under the pre-eminent **House of Orange-Nassau** and those who championed provincial autonomy. Frederick Henry died in 1647 and his successor, William II, lasted just three years before his death from smallpox. A week after William's death, his wife bore the son who would become William III of England, but in the meantime the leaders of the province of Holland seized their opportunity. They forced measures through the States General abolishing the position of Stadholder, thereby reducing the powers of the Orangists and increasing those of the provinces, chiefly Holland itself. Holland's foremost figure in these years was **Johan de Witt**, Council Pensionary to the States General. He guided the country through wars with England and Sweden, concluding a triple alliance between the two countries and the United Provinces in 1678. This didn't last, however, and when France and England marched on the Provinces two years later, the republic was in deep trouble – previous victories had been at sea, and the army, weak and disorganized, could not withstand an attack. In panic, the country turned to **William III of Orange** for leadership and Johan de Witt was brutally murdered by a mob of Orangist sympathizers in Den Haag. By 1678 William had defeated the French and made peace with the English – and was rewarded (along with his wife Mary) with the English crown ten years later.

## The United Provinces in the eighteenth century

Though King William had defeated the French, Louis XIV retained designs on the United Provinces and the pot was kept boiling in a long series of dynastic wars that ranged across northern Europe. In 1700, Charles II of Spain, the last of the Spanish Habsburgs, died childless, bequeathing the Spanish throne and control of the Spanish Netherlands to Philip of Anjou, Louis' grandson. Louis promptly forced Philip to cede the latter to France, which was, with every justification, construed as a threat to the balance of power by France's neighbours. The **War of the Spanish Succession** ensued, with the United Provinces, England and Austria forming the Triple Alliance to thwart the French king. The war itself was a haphazard, long-winded affair distinguished by the spectacular victories of the Duke of Marlborough at Blenheim, Ramillies and Malplaquet. It dragged on until the **Treaty of Utrecht** of 1713 in which France finally abandoned its claim to the Spanish Netherlands.

However, the fighting had drained the United Provinces' reserves and its slow economic and political decline began, accelerated by a reactive trend towards conservatism. This in turn reflected the development of an increasingly socially static society, with power and wealth concentrated within a small elite. Furthermore, with the threat of foreign conquest effectively removed, the Dutch ruling class divided into two main camps – the **Orangists** and the pro-French "**Patriots**" – whose interminable squabbling soon brought political life to a virtual standstill. The situation deteriorated even further in the latter half of the century and the last few years of the United Provinces present a sorry state of affairs.

## French occupation & the United Kingdom of the Netherlands

In 1795 the French, aided by the Patriots, invaded, setting up the **Batavian Republic** and dissolving the United Provinces – and much of the hegemony of the rich Dutch merchants. Effectively part of the Napoleonic empire, the Netherlands were obliged to wage unenthusiastic war with England, and in 1806 Napoleon appointed his brother **Louis** as their king in an attempt to create a commercial gulf between the country and England. Louis, however, wasn't willing to allow the Netherlands to become a simple satellite of France; he ignored Napoleon's directives and after just four years of rule was forced to abdicate. The country was then formally incorporated into the French Empire, and for three gloomy years suffered occupation and heavy taxation to finance French military adventures.

Following Napoleon's disastrous retreat from Moscow, the Orangist faction once more surfaced to exploit weakening French control. In 1813, Frederick William, son of the exiled William V, returned to the country and eight months later, under the terms of the **Congress of Vienna**, was crowned King William I of the **United Kingdom of the Netherlands**, incorporating both the old United Provinces and the Spanish (Austrian) Netherlands. A strong-willed man, he spent much of the latter part of his life trying to control his disparate kingdom, but he failed primarily because of the Protestant north's attempt to dominate the Catholic south. The southern provinces revolted against his rule and in 1830 the Kingdom of Belgium was proclaimed.

# From 1830 to World War II

A final invasion of Belgium in 1839 gave William most of Limburg, and all but ended centuries of territorial change within the Low Countries. The Netherlands benefited from this new stability, the trade surplus picked up and canal building linked both Rotterdam and Amsterdam to the North Sea. The outstanding political figure of the times, **Jan Rudolph Thorbecke**, formed three ruling cabinets (1849–53, 1862–66 and 1872, in the year of his death) and steered the Netherlands through a profound change. The political parties of the late eighteenth century had wished to resurrect the power and prestige of the seventeenth-century Netherlands; Thorbecke and his allies resigned themselves to the country's reduced status and eulogized the advantages of being a small power. For the first time, from about 1850, liberty was seen as a luxury made possible by the country's very lack of power, and the malaise which had long disturbed public life gave way to a positive appreciation of the very narrowness of its national existence. One of the results of Thorbecke's liberalism was a gradual extension of the franchise, culminating in the **Act of Universal Suffrage** of 1917.

The Netherlands remained neutral in **World War I** and the privations resulting from the Allied blockade of German war materials were offset by the advantages concomitant with continuing to trade with both sides. Similar attempts to remain neutral in **World War II** however, failed: the Nazis invaded on May 10, 1940, destroying Rotterdam four days later, a salutary lesson that made prolonged resistance inconceivable. The Dutch army was quickly overwhelmed, Queen Wilhelmina fled to London to set up a government in exile, and opposition to Nazi occupation was continued by the **Resistance**. Instrumental in destroying German supplies and munitions, they also helped many downed airmen escape back to England, but at a heavy price: 23,000 resistance fighters and sympathisers were killed in the war years. In Amsterdam, the old Jewish community, swollen by those who had fled Germany to escape the persecution of the 1930s, was obliterated, leaving the deserted Jodenhoek and the diary of Anne Frank as testament to the horrors.

Liberation began in autumn 1944 with **Operation Market Garden**. This was a British plan to finish the war quickly by creating an Allied corridor stretching from Eindhoven to Arnhem. This would have secured control of the country's three main rivers, isolate the occupying forces to the west, and facilitate an advance straight into Germany. It was a gamble, but if it had been successful, it would have speeded the end of the war. On September 17, 1944, the 1st Airborne Division parachuted into the countryside around Oosterbeek, a small village near the most northerly target of the operation, the bridge at Arnhem. Nazi opposition was much stronger than expected, and after heavy fighting the Allied forces could only take the northern end of the bridge. The advancing British army was unable to break through fast enough, and after four days the decimated battalion defending the bridge was forced to withdraw.

With the failure of Operation Market Garden, the Allies were obliged to resort to more orthodox military tactics. In their push towards Germany, they slowly cleared the east and south of the country in the winter and spring of 1944–45, leaving the coastal provinces pretty much untouched, though here lack of food and fuel created desperate conditions, with hundreds starving to death. Finally, on April 5, 1945, the remains of the German army in the Netherlands surrendered to the Canadians at Wageningen.

## From 1945 to the present day

The postwar years were spent patching up the damage of occupation and liberation. Rotterdam was rapidly rebuilt, and the dykes blown in the war – both by the Allies to slow the German advance and by the German army itself – were repaired. Two events were, however, to mar the late 1940s and early 1950s: the former Dutch **colonies** of Java and Sumatra, taken by the Japanese at the outbreak of the war, were now ruled by a nationalist Republican government that refused to recognize Dutch sovereignty. Following the failure of talks between the Dutch government and the islanders in 1947, the Dutch sent the troops in, a colonial enterprise that soon became a bloody débâcle. International opposition was intense and, after much condemnation and pressure, the Dutch reluctantly surrendered their most important Asian colonies, which were incorporated as **Indonesia** in 1950. Back at home, tragedy struck on February 1, 1953, when an unusually high tide was pushed over Zeeland's sea defences by a westerly wind, flooding 40,000 acres of land and drowning over 1800 people. The response was to secure the area's future with the **Delta Project**, closing off the western part of the Scheldt and Maas estuaries with massive sea dykes. A brilliant and graceful piece of engineering, the main storm surge barrier on the Oosterschelde was finally completed in 1986.

Elsewhere rebuilding continued; in Amsterdam all the land projected in 1947 for use by the year 2000 was in fact used up by the "garden cities" of the dormitory suburbs by 1970. Similarly, the reclaimed polders of Flevoland were soon built upon to absorb more of the excess urban population – Lelystad, the

## The Provos and the Kabouters

Amsterdam's reputation as a wacky, offbeat city rests largely on its experiences in the 1960s, when social and political discontent began to coalesce into opposition to the city council's redevelopment plans. In common with similar movements in Paris and the US, these Amsterdam protests developed a playful aspect, and, as a consequence, garnered substantial public support. One of the popular groupings that emerged, led by one Roel van Duyn and called the **Provos** (a name derived from "provocation"), took to holding small "happenings" around the 't Lieverdje statue on the Spui. In 1965, a clumsy attempt by the police to break up one of these happenings provoked a riot, but this disturbance was nothing compared with the scenes a few months later when, in March 1966, Princess (now Queen) Beatrix married an ex-Nazi, Claus von Amsberg. The Provos objected to the massive cost of the event as well as the Fascist connection and while the wedding procession was passing through the city, rioters clashed with police amidst smoke bombs and tear gas. Amsberg himself was jeered with the refrain "Give us back the bikes!" – a reference to the commandeering of hundreds of bikes by the retreating German army in 1945. The rioting continued throughout the summer, prompting Amsterdam's police chief to resign, followed by the mayor.

In 1966, the Provos won over two percent of the vote in municipal elections, and gained a seat on the city council. They brought with them their wide-ranging and imaginative **White Plans**, whose most famous proposal was to ban cars from the centre of Amsterdam and provide 20,000 white bicycles instead. The bicycles were to be distributed for people to use free of charge, who would leave them at their journey's end for someone else, but trials didn't really work and the plan was never implemented. By 1967, the Provos' plans for the rejuvenation of Amsterdam had become over-idealistic and unmanageable, and the group split. Van Duyn promptly founded a group called the **Kabouters**, after a helpful gnome in Dutch folklore. The Kabouters' manifesto described their form of socialism as "not of the clenched fist, but of the intertwined fingers, the erect penis, the escaping butterfly..." In the local elections of 1970, they met with some success, taking five council seats, but again implementation of the White Plans proved problematic. The Kabouters modified the White Bicycle Plan into a similar idea involving small, economical white cars, but trials in 1974 received poor public support and the plan was abandoned. In 1981, after ten years or so on the margins of Amsterdam politics, the Kabouters finally disintegrated.

main town, now has a population of around 80,000. But growth wasn't only physical: the social consciousness and radicalism of the 1960s reached the country early, and the flower-power, psychedelic revolution was quick to catch on. It was quick to fade, too, replaced by the cynicism of the 1970s, but one manifestation of the radical brouhaha that did produce tangible change was the **squatting movement**. The squatters and associated activists objected to the wholesale destruction of low-cost (often old) urban housing as envisaged by most municipal planning departments, arguing that the country's city centres should not become the preserve of big business, holed up in mighty glass and concrete towers. Their campaign precipitated major riots in Amsterdam and other cities from the late 1960s into the early 1980s, and although individual actions rarely defeated the developers, the squatters won the argument: by the mid-1980s urban planning had, by and large, become a much more thoughtful, consultative affair with due (or at least some) attention given to both the urban environment in general and the need to keep people living in the city centres in particular.

Politically, the country's finely balanced system of **proportional representation** forces almost continuous compromise and debate, but brings little rapid change. Consequently, politics and politicking has long seemed a bland if necessary business conducted between the three main parties, the Protestant-Catholic CDA coalition, the Liberal VVD and the Socialist PvdA. The thunder-bolt came in the May elections of 2002 when a brand new Rightist grouping – Leefbaar Nederlands ("Livable Netherlands") – led by **Pim Fortuyn**, swept to second place behind the CDA, securing seventeen percent of the national vote. Stylish and witty, openly gay and a former Marxist, Fortuyn managed to cover several popular bases at the same time, from the need for law and order through to tighter immigration controls. Most crucially, he also attacked the liberal establishment's espousal of multi-culturalism even when the representa-tives of these same minority groups were deeply reactionary, anti-gay and sexist. Politically, it worked a treat, but a year later Fortuyn was assassinated and his party rapidly unravelled, losing almost all its seats in the general election of January 2003. Since then, normal political service seems to have been resumed, with the CDA, the PvdA and the VVD once again the largest parties, though Fortuyn's popularity is likely to push certain sorts of social debate, particularly on immigration, to the right.

One of the reasons for Fortuyn's electoral success reflected the other shock to the Dutch system, which came with the publication of a damning report on the failure of the Dutch army to protect the Bosnian Muslims ensconced in the UN safe-haven of **Srebrenica** in 1995. Published in 2002, the report told a tale of extraordinary incompetence: the Dutch soldiers were inadequately armed, but still refused American assistance, and watched as Serb troops sepa-rated Muslim men and women in preparation for the mass executions, which the Dutch then did nothing to stop (though they were never involved). In a country that prides itself on its internationalism, the report was an especially hard blow and the whole of the PvdA-led government under **Wim Kok** promptly resigned.

# Dutch art

Designed to serve only as a quick reference, the following outline is the very briefest of introductions to a subject that has rightly filled volumes. Inevitably, it covers artists that lived and worked in both the Netherlands and Belgium, as these two countries have – along with Luxembourg – been bound together as the "Low Countries" for most of their history. For in-depth and academic studies, see the recommendations in "Books" on p.376. For a list of where to see some of the paintings mentioned here, turn to the box at the end of this section.

## Beginnings: the Flemish Primitives

Throughout the medieval period, **Flanders**, in modern-day Belgium, was one of the most artistically productive parts of Europe and it was here that the solid realist base of later Dutch painting developed. Today the works of these early Flemish painters, the **Flemish Primitives**, are highly prized and although examples are fairly sparse in the Netherlands, all the leading museums – especially Amsterdam's Rijksmuseum and Den Haag's Mauritshuis – have a sample.

**Jan van Eyck** (1385–1441) is generally regarded as the first of the Flemish Primitives, and has even been credited with the invention of oil painting – though it seems more likely that he simply perfected a new technique by thinning his paint with (the newly discovered) turpentine, thus making it more flexible. His most famous work still in the Low Countries is the altarpiece in Ghent cathedral (debatably painted with the help of his lesser-known brother, Hubert), which was revolutionary in its realism, for the first time using elements of native landscape in depicting Biblical themes. Van Eyck's style and technique were to influence several generations of Low Countries artists.

Firmly in the Eyckian tradition were the **Master of Flemalle** (1387–1444) and **Rogier van der Weyden** (1400–64), one-time official painter to the city of Brussels. The Flemalle master is a shadowy figure: some believe he was the teacher of Van der Weyden, others that the two artists were in fact the same person. There are differences between the two, however: the Flemalle master's paintings are close to Van Eyck's, whereas Van der Weyden shows a greater degree of emotional intensity in his religious works. Van der Weyden also produced serene portraits of the bigwigs of his day that were much admired across a large swath of western Europe. His style, never mind his success, influenced many painters with one of the most talented of these being **Dieric Bouts** (1415–75). Born in Haarlem but active in Leuven, Bouts is recognizable by his stiff, rather elongated figures and horrific subject matter, all set against carefully drawn landscapes. **Hugo van der Goes** (d.1482) was the next Ghent master after Van Eyck, most famous for the Portinari altarpiece in Florence's Uffizi gallery. After a short painting career, he died insane, and his late works have strong hints of his impending madness in their subversive use of space and implicit acceptance of the viewer's presence.

Few doubt that **Hans Memling** (1440–94) was a pupil of Van der Weyden: active in Bruges throughout his life, he is best remembered for the pastoral charm of his landscapes and the quality of his portraiture, much of which survives on the rescued side panels of triptychs. **Gerard David** (1460–1523) was a native of Oudewater, near Gouda, but he moved to Bruges in 1484, becoming the last of the great painters to work in that city, before it was outstripped by Antwerp, producing formal religious works of traditional bent. Strikingly different, but broadly contemporaneous, was **Hieronymus Bosch**

(1450–1516), who lived for most of his life in Holland, though his style is linked to that of his Flemish contemporaries. His frequently reprinted religious allegories are filled with macabre visions of tortured people and grotesque beasts, and appear at first faintly unhinged, though it's now thought that these are visual representations of contemporary sayings, idioms and parables. While their interpretation is far from resolved, Bosch's paintings draw strongly on subconscious fears and archetypes, giving them a lasting, haunting fascination.

## The sixteenth century

At the end of the fifteenth century, Flanders was in economic and political decline and the leading artists of the day were drawn instead to the booming port of Antwerp. The artists who worked here soon began to integrate the finely observed detail that characterized the Flemish tradition with the style of the Italian painters of the Renaissance. **Quentin Matsys** (1464–1530) introduced florid classical architectural details and intricate landscapes to his works, influenced perhaps by the work of Leonardo da Vinci. As well as religious works, he painted portraits and genre scenes, all of which have recognizably Italian facets – and paved the way for the Dutch genre painters of later years. **Jan Gossart** (1478–1532) made the pilgrimage to Italy too, and his dynamic works are packed with detail, especially finely drawn classical architectural backdrops. He was the first Low Countries artist to introduce the subjects of classical mythology into his works, part of a steady trend through the period towards secular subject matter, which can also be seen in the work of **Joachim Patenier** (d.1524), who painted small landscapes of fantastical scenery.

The middle of the sixteenth century was dominated by the work of **Pieter Bruegel the Elder** (c.1525–69), whose gruesome allegories and innovative interpretations of religious subjects are firmly placed in Low Countries settings. Pieter also painted finely observed peasant scenes, though he himself was well-connected in court circles in Antwerp and, later, Brussels. **Pieter Aertsen** (1508–75) also worked in the peasant genre, adding aspects of still life: his paintings often show a detailed kitchen scene in the foreground, with a religious episode going on behind. Bruegel's two sons, **Pieter Bruegel the Younger** (1564–1638) and **Jan Bruegel** (1568–1625), were lesser painters: the former produced fairly insipid copies of his father's work, while Jan developed a style of his own – delicately rendered flower paintings and genre pieces that earned him the nickname "Velvet". Towards the latter half of the sixteenth century highly stylized Italianate portraits became the dominant fashion, **Frans Pourbus the Younger** (1569–1622) the leading practitioner. Frans hobnobbed across Europe, working for the likes of the Habsburgs and the Medicis.

Meanwhile, there were artistic rumblings in Holland. Leading the charge was **Geertgen tot Sint Jans** (Little Gerard of the Brotherhood of St John; d.1490), who worked in Haarlem, initiating – in a strangely naive style – an artistic vision that would come to dominate the seventeenth century. There was a tender melancholy in his work very different from the stylized paintings produced in Flanders and, most importantly, a new sensitivity to light – and lighting. **Jan Mostaert** (1475–1555) took over after Geertgen's death, developing similar themes, but the first painter to effect real changes in northern painting was **Lucas van Leyden** (1489–1533). Born in Leiden, his bright colours and narrative technique were refreshingly novel, and he introduced a new dynamism into what had become a rigidly formal treatment of devotional subjects. There was rivalry, of course. Eager to publicize Haarlem as the artistic capital of the northern Netherlands, Carel van Mander (see opposite) claimed

Alkmaar native **Jan van Scorel** (1495–1562) as the better painter, complaining, too, of Van Leyden's dandyish ways. Certainly Van Scorel's influence should not be underestimated. Like many of his contemporaries, Van Scorel hot-footed it to Italy to view the works of the Renaissance, but in Rome his career went into overdrive when he found favour with Pope Hadrian VI, one-time bishop of Utrecht, who installed him as court painter in 1520. Van Scorel stayed in Rome for four years and when he returned to Utrecht, armed with all that papal prestige, he combined the ideas he had picked up in Italy with those underpinning Haarlem realism, thereby modifying what had previously been an independent artistic tradition once and for all. Amongst his several students, probably the most talented was **Maerten van Heemskerck** (1498–1574), who went off to Italy himself in 1532, staying there five years before doubling back to Haarlem.

## The Golden Age

The seventeenth century begins with **Carel van Mander**, Haarlem painter, art impresario and one of the few contemporary chroniclers of the art of the Low Countries. His *Schilderboek* of 1604 put Flemish and Dutch traditions into context for the first time, and in addition specified the rules of fine painting. Examples of his own work are rare – though Haarlem's Frans Hals Museum weighs in with a couple – but his followers were many. Among them was **Cornelius Cornelisz van Haarlem** (1562–1638), who produced elegant renditions of biblical and mythical themes; and **Hendrik Goltzius** (1558–1616), who was a skilled engraver and an integral member of Van Mander's Haarlem academy. These painters' enthusiasm for Italian art, combined with the influence of a late revival of Gothicism, resulted in works that combined Mannerist and Classical elements. An interest in realism was also felt, and, for them, the subject became less important than the way in which it was depicted: biblical stories became merely a vehicle whereby artists could apply their skills in painting the human body, landscapes, or copious displays of food. All of this served to break religion's stranglehold on art, and make legitimate a whole range of everyday subjects for the painter.

In Holland (and this was where the north and the south finally diverged) this break with tradition was compounded by the **Reformation**: the austere Calvinism that had replaced the Catholic faith in the United (ie northern) Provinces had no use for images or symbols of devotion in its churches. Instead, painters catered to the burgeoning middle class, and no longer visited Italy to learn their craft. Indeed, the real giants of the seventeenth century – Hals, Rembrandt, Vermeer – stayed in the Netherlands all their lives. Another innovation was that painting split into more distinct categories, such as genre, portrait, and landscape, and artists tended (with notable exceptions) to confine themselves to one field throughout their careers. So began the greatest age of Dutch art.

### Historical and religious painting

The artistic influence of Renaissance Italy may have been in decline, but Italian painters still had clout with the Dutch, most notably Caravaggio (1571–1610), who was much admired for his new realism. Taking Caravaggio's cue, many artists – Rembrandt for one – continued to portray classical subjects, but in a way that was totally at odds with the Mannerists' stylish flights of imagination. The Utrecht artist **Abraham Bloemaert** (1564–1651), though a solid Mannerist throughout his career, encouraged these new ideas, and his students –

Gerard van Honthorst (1590–1656), Hendrik Terbrugghen (1588–1629) and **Dirck van Baburen** (1590–1624) – formed the nucleus of the influential **Utrecht School**, which followed Caravaggio almost to the point of slavishness. Honthorst was perhaps the leading figure, learning his craft from Bloemaert and travelling to Rome, where he was nicknamed "Gerardo delle Notti" for his ingenious handling of light and shade. In his later paintings, however, this was to become more routine technique than inspired invention, and though a supremely competent artist, Honthorst is somewhat discredited among critics today. Terbrugghen's reputation seems to have aged rather better: he soon forgot Caravaggio and developed a more individual style, his later, lighter work having a great influence on the young Vermeer. After a jaunt to Rome, Baburen shared a studio with Terbrugghen and produced some fairly original work – work which also had some influence on Vermeer – but today he is the least studied member of the group and few of his paintings survive.

Above all others, **Rembrandt van Rijn** (1606–69) was the most original historical artist of the seventeenth century, also chipping in with religious paintings throughout his career. In the 1630s, the poet and statesman Constantijn Huygens procured for him his greatest commission – a series of five paintings of the Passion, beautifully composed and uncompromisingly realistic. Later, however, Rembrandt received fewer and fewer commissions, since his treatment of biblical and historical subjects was far less dramatic than that of his contemporaries and he ignored their smooth brushwork, preferring a rougher, darker and more disjointed style. It's significant that while the more conventional Jordaens, Honthorst and Van Everdingen were busy decorating the Huis ten Bosch near Den Haag for the Stadholder Frederick Henry, Rembrandt was having his monumental *Conspiracy of Julius Civilis* – painted for the new Amsterdam Town Hall – thrown out. The reasons for this ejection have been hotly debated, but it seems probable that Rembrandt's rendition was thought too pagan an interpretation of what was an important event in Dutch history: Julius had organised a revolt against the Romans, which had obvious resonance in a country just freed from the Habsburgs. Even worse, perhaps, Rembrandt had shown Julius to be blind in one eye, which was historically accurate but not at all what the city's burghers had in mind for a Dutch hero.

Finally, **Aert van Gelder** (1645–1727), Rembrandt's last pupil and probably the only one to concentrate on historical painting, followed the style of his master closely, producing shimmering biblical scenes well into the eighteenth century.

## Genre painting

Often misunderstood, the term **genre painting** was initially applied to everything from animal paintings and still lifes through to historical works and landscapes, but later – from around the middle of the seventeenth century – came to be applied only to scenes of everyday life. Its target market was the region's burgeoning middle class, who had a penchant for non-idealized portrayals of common scenes, both with and without symbols – or subtly disguised details – making one moral point or another. One of its early practitioners was Antwerp's **Frans Snijders** (1579–1657), who took up still-life painting where Aertsen (see p.364) left off, amplifying his subject – food and drink – to even larger, more sumptuous canvases. Snijders also doubled up as a member of the Rubens art machine (see p.371), painting animals and still-life sections for the master's works. In the north, in Utrecht, Hendrik Terbrugghen and Gerard Honthorst adapted the realism and strong chiaroscuro learned from Caravaggio to a number of tableaux of everyday life, though they were more concerned with religious works, whilst Haarlem's Frans Hals dabbled in genre too, but is better known as a portraitist. The opposite is true of one of Hal's pupils, **Adriaen Brouwer** (1605–38), whose riotous tavern scenes were well received in their day and collected by, among others, Rubens and Rembrandt. Brouwer spent only a couple of years in Haarlem under Hals before returning to his native Flanders, where he influenced the inventive **David Teniers the Younger** (1610–90), who worked in Antwerp, and later in Brussels. Teniers' early paintings are Brouwer-like peasant scenes, although his later work is more delicate and diverse, including *kortegaardje* – guardroom scenes that show soldiers carousing. **Adriaen van Ostade** (1610–85), on the other hand, stayed in Haarlem most of his life, skilfully painting groups of peasants and tavern brawls, though his later acceptance by the establishment led him to water down the realism he had learnt from Brouwer. He was teacher to his brother **Isaak van Ostade** (1621–49), who produced a large number of open-air peasant scenes, subtle combinations of genre and landscape work.

The English critic E.V. Lucas dubbed Teniers, Brouwer and Ostade "coarse and boorish" compared with **Jan Steen** (1625–79), who, along with Vermeer, is probably the most admired Dutch genre painter. You can see what he had in mind: Steen's paintings offer the same Rabelaisian peasantry in full fling, but they go their debauched ways in broad daylight, and nowhere do you see the filthy rogues in shadowy hovels favoured by Brouwer and van Ostade. Steen offers more humour, too, as well as more moralizing, identifying with the hedonistic mob and reproaching them at the same time. Indeed, many of his pictures are illustrations of well-known proverbs of the time: popular epithets on the evils of drink or the transience of human existence that were supposed to teach as well as entertain.

Leiden's **Gerrit Dou** (1613–75) was one of Rembrandt's first pupils. It's difficult to detect any trace of the master's influence in his work, however, as Dou initiated a style of his own: tiny, minutely realized and beautifully finished views of a kind of ordinary life that was decidedly more genteel than Brouwer's, or even Steen's. He was admired, above all, for his painstaking attention to detail: he would, it's said, sit in his studio for hours waiting for the dust to settle before starting work. Among his students, **Frans van Mieris** (1635–81) continued the highly finished portrayals of the Dutch bourgeoisie, as did **Gabriel Metsu** (1629–67) – perhaps Dou's most talented pupil – whose pictures often convey an overtly moral message. Another pupil of Rembrandt's, though a much later one, was **Nicholaes Maes** (1629–93), whose early works were almost entirely genre paintings, sensitively executed and again with an obvious didacticism. His later paintings show the influence of a more refined style of portrait, which he had picked up in France.

As a native of Zwolle, **Gerard ter Borch** (1619–81) found himself far from all these Leiden/Rembrandt connections; despite trips abroad to most of the artistic capitals of Europe, he remained very much a provincial painter. He depicted Holland's merchant class at play and became renowned for his curious doll-like figures and his enormous ability to capture the textures of different cloths. His domestic scenes were not unlike those of **Pieter de Hooch** (1629–after 1684), whose simple depictions of everyday life are deliberately unsentimental, and have little or no moral commentary. De Hooch's favourite trick was to paint darkened rooms with an open door leading through to a sunlit courtyard, a practice that, along with his trademark rusty red colour, makes his work easy to identify and, at its best, exquisite. That said, his later pictures reflect the encroaching decadence of the Dutch Republic: the rooms are more richly decorated, the arrangements more contrived and the subjects far less homely.

It was, however, **Jan Vermeer** (1632–75) who brought the most sophisticated methods to painting interiors, depicting the play of natural light on indoor surfaces with superlative skill – and the tranquil intimacy for which he is now famous the world over. Another recorder of the better-heeled Dutch households and, like De Hooch, without a moral tone, he is regarded (with Hals and Rembrandt) as one of the big three Dutch painters, though he was, it seems, a slow worker. Only about forty paintings can be attributed to him with any certainty. Living all his life in Delft, Vermeer is perhaps the epitome of the seventeenth-century Dutch painter – rejecting the pomp and ostentation of the High Renaissance to record quietly his contemporaries at home, painting for a public that demanded no more than that: bourgeois art at its most complete.

## Portraits – and Rembrandt

Predictably enough, the ruling bourgeoisie of Holland's flourishing mercantile society wanted to record and celebrate their success, and consequently portraiture was a reliable way for a young painter to make a living. **Michiel Jansz Miereveld** (1567–1641), court painter to Frederick Henry in Den Haag, was the first real portraitist of the Dutch Republic, but it wasn't long before his stiff and rather conservative figures were superseded by the more spontaneous renderings of **Frans Hals** (1585–1666). Hals is perhaps best-known for his "corporation pictures" – portraits of the members of the Dutch civil guard regiments that were formed in most of the larger towns during the war with Spain, but subsequently becoming social clubs. These large group pieces demanded superlative technique, since the painter had to create a collection of individual portraits while retaining a sense of the group, and accord prominence based on the relative importance of the sitters and the size of the payment each had made. Hals was particularly good at this, using innovative lighting effects, arranging his sitters subtly, and putting all the elements together in a fluid and dynamic composition. He also painted many individual portraits, making the ability to capture fleeting and telling expressions his trademark; his pictures of children are particularly sensitive. Later in life, however, his work became darker and more akin to Rembrandt's, spurred – it's conjectured – by his penury.

**Jan Cornelisz Verspronck** (1597–1662) and **Bartholomeus van der Helst** (1613–70) were the other great Haarlem portraitists after Frans Hals – Verspronck recognizable by the smooth, shiny glow he always gave to his sitters' faces, Van der Helst by a competent but unadventurous style. Of the two, Van der Helst was the more popular, influencing a number of later painters and leaving Haarlem as a young man to begin a solidly successful career as portrait painter to Amsterdam's burghers.

The reputation of **Rembrandt van Rijn** (1606–69) is still relatively recent – nineteenth-century connoisseurs preferred Gerard Dou – but he is now justly regarded as one of the greatest and most versatile painters of all time. Born in Leiden, the son of a miller, he was a boy apprentice to Jacob van Swanenburgh, a then quite important, though singularly un-inventive, local artist. Rembrandt shared a studio with Jan Lievens, a promising painter and something of a rival, though now all but forgotten, before venturing forth to Amsterdam to study under the fashionable Pieter Lastman. Soon he was painting commissions for the city elite and became an accepted member of their circle. The poet and statesman Constantijn Huygens acted as his agent, pulling strings to obtain all of Rembrandt's more lucrative jobs, and in 1634 the artist married Saskia van Ulenborch, daughter of the burgomaster of Leeuwarden and quite a catch for a relatively humble artist. His self-portraits from this period show the confident face of security – on top of things and quite sure of where he's going.

Sassenpoort gateway, Zwolle (see p.268) △

Rembrandt would not always be the darling of the Amsterdam burghers, but his fall from grace was still some way off when he painted *The Night Watch*, a group portrait often – but inaccurately – associated with the artist's decline in popularity. Indeed, although Rembrandt's fluent arrangement of his subjects was totally original, there's no evidence that the military company who commissioned the painting was anything but pleased with the result. More likely culprits are the artist's later pieces, whose obscure lighting and psychological insights took the conservative Amsterdam merchants by surprise. His patrons were certainly not sufficiently enthusiastic about his work to support his taste for art collecting and his expensive house on Jodenbreestraat, and in 1656 he was declared bankrupt. Rembrandt died thirteen years later a broken and embittered old man, as his last self-portraits indicate. Throughout his career he maintained a large studio, and his influence pervaded the next generation of Dutch painters. Some – Dou and Maes – more famous for their genre work, have already been mentioned. Others turned to portraiture.

**Govert Flinck** (1615–60) was perhaps Rembrandt's most faithful follower, and he was, ironically enough, given the job of decorating Amsterdam's new Town Hall after his teacher had been passed over. Unluckily for him, Flinck died before he could execute his designs and Rembrandt took over, but although the latter's *Conspiracy of Julius Civilis* was installed in 1662, it was discarded a year later. The early work of **Ferdinand Bol** (1616–80) was so heavily influenced by Rembrandt that for centuries art historians couldn't tell the two apart, though his later paintings are readily distinguishable, blandly elegant portraits, which proved very popular with the well-heeled. At the age of 53, Bol married a wealthy widow and promptly stopped painting; perhaps because he knew how emotionally tacky his work had become. Most of the pitifully slim extant work of **Carel Fabritius** (1622–54) was portraiture, but he too died young, before he could properly realize his promise as perhaps the most gifted of all Rembrandt's students. Generally regarded as the teacher of Vermeer, he forms a link between the two masters, combining Rembrandt's technique with his own practice of painting figures against a dark background, prefiguring the lighting and colouring of the Delft painter.

## Landscapes

Aside from Pieter Bruegel the Elder, whose depictions of his native surroundings make him the first true Low Countries landscape painter, **Gillis van Coninxloo** (1544–1607) stands out as the earliest Dutch landscapist. He imbued his native scenery with elements of fantasy, painting the richly wooded views he had seen on his travels around Europe as backdrops to biblical scenes. In the early seventeenth century, **Hercules Seghers** (1590–1638), apprenticed to Coninxloo, carried on his mentor's style of depicting forested and mountainous landscapes, some real, others not: his work is scarce but is believed to have had considerable influence on the landscape work of Rembrandt. **Esaias van der Velde**'s (1591–1632) quaint and unpretentious scenes show the first real affinity with the Dutch countryside, but while his influence was likewise considerable, he was soon overshadowed by his pupil **Jan van Goyen** (1596–1656). A remarkable painter, who belongs to the so-called "tonal phase" of Dutch landscape painting, Van Goyen's early pictures were highly coloured and close to those of his teacher, but it didn't take him long to develop a marked touch of his own, using tones of green, brown and grey to lend everything a characteristic translucent haze. His paintings are, above all, of nature, and if he included figures it was just for the sake of scale. A long neglected artist, Van Goyen only received recognition with the arrival of the Impressionists, when his fluid and rapid brushwork was at last fully appreciated.

Another "tonal" painter, Haarlem's **Salomon van Ruisdael** (1600–70) was also directly affected by Esaias van der Velde, and his simple and atmospheric, though not terribly adventurous, landscapes were for a long time consistently confused with those of Van Goyen. More esteemed is his nephew, **Jacob van Ruysdael** (1628–82), generally considered the greatest of all Dutch landscapists, whose fastidiously observed views of quiet flatlands dominated by stormy skies were to influence European landscapists right up to the nineteenth century. Constable, certainly, acknowledged a debt to him. Ruysdael's foremost pupil was **Meindert Hobbema** (1638–1709), who followed the master faithfully, sometimes even painting the same views (his *Avenue at Middelharnis* may be familiar).

**Nicholas Berchem** (1620–83) and **Jan Both** (1618–52) were the "Italianizers" of Dutch landscapes. They studied in Rome and were influenced by the Frenchman Claude Lorraine, taking back to Holland rich, golden views of the world, full of steep gorges and hills, picturesque ruins and wandering shepherds. **Allart van Everdingen** (1621–75) had a similar approach, but his subject matter stemmed from travels in Norway, which, after his return to the Netherlands, he reproduced in all its mountainous glory. **Aelbert Cuyp** (1620–91), on the other hand, stayed in Dordrecht all his life, painting what was probably the favourite city skyline of Dutch landscapists. He inherited the warm tones of the Italianizers, and his pictures are always suffused with a deep, golden glow.

Of a number of specialist seventeenth-century painters who can be included here, **Paulus Potter** (1625–54) is rated as the best painter of domestic animals. He produced a surprisingly large number of paintings in his short life, the most reputed being his lovingly executed pictures of cows and horses. The accurate rendering of architectural features also became a specialized field, in which **Pieter Saenredam** (1597–1665), with his finely realized paintings of Dutch church interiors, is the most widely known exponent. **Emanuel de Witte** (1616–92) continued in the same vein, though his churches lack the spartan crispness of Saenredam's. **Gerrit Berckheyde** (1638–98) worked in Haarlem soon after, but he limited his views to the outside of buildings, producing variations on the same scenes around town. Nautical scenes in praise of the Dutch navy were, on the other hand, the speciality of **Willem van der Velde II** (1633–1707), whose melodramatic canvases, complete with their churning seas and chasing skies, are displayed to greatest advantage in the Nederlands Scheepvaartsmuseum in Amsterdam.

A further thriving category of seventeenth-century painting was the still life, in which objects were gathered together to remind the viewer of the transience of human life and the meaninglessness of worldly pursuits. Thus, a skull would often be joined by a book, a pipe or a goblet, and some half-eaten food. Again, two Haarlem painters dominated this field: **Pieter Claesz** (1598–1660) and **Willem Heda** (1594–1680), who confined themselves almost entirely to these carefully arranged groups of objects.

## Rubens and his followers

Back down to the south, in Antwerp, **Pieter Paul Rubens** (1577–1640) was easily the most important exponent of the Baroque in northern Europe. Born in Siegen, Westphalia, he was raised in Antwerp, where he entered the painters' guild in 1598. He became court painter to the Duke of Mantua in 1600, and until 1608 travelled extensively in Italy, absorbing the art of the High Renaissance and classical architecture. By the time of his return to Antwerp in 1608 he had acquired an enormous artistic vocabulary: like his Dutch contemporaries, the paintings of Caravaggio were to influence his work strongly. His first major success was *The Raising of the Cross*, painted in 1610 and displayed today in Antwerp cathedral. A large, dynamic work, it caused a sensation at the time, establishing Rubens' reputation and leading to a string of commissions that enabled him to set up his own studio.

The division of labour in Rubens' studio, and the talent of the artists working there (who included Antony van Dyck and Jacob Jordaens) ensured an extraordinary output of excellent work. The degree to which Rubens personally worked on a canvas would vary, and would determine its price. From the early 1620s onwards he turned his hand to a plethora of themes and subjects – religious works, portraits, tapestry designs, landscapes, mythological scenes, ceiling paintings – each of which was handled with supreme vitality and virtuosity. From his Flemish antecedents he inherited an acute sense of light, and used it not to dramatize his subjects (a technique favoured by Caravaggio and other Italian artists), but in association with colour and form. The drama in his works comes from the vigorous animation of his characters. His large-scale allegorical works, especially, are packed with heaving, writhing figures that appear to tumble out from the canvas.

The energy of Rubens' paintings was reflected in his private life. In addition to his career as an artist, he also undertook diplomatic missions to Spain and England, and used these opportunities to study the works of other artists and – as in the case of Velázquez – to meet them personally. In the 1630s, gout began to hamper his activities, and from this time his painting became more domestic and meditative. Hélène Fourment, his second wife, was the subject of many portraits and served as a model for characters in his allegorical paintings, her figure epitomizing the buxom, well-rounded women found throughout his work.

Rubens' influence on the artists of the period was enormous. The huge output of his studio meant that his works were universally seen and also widely disseminated by the engravers he employed to copy his work. Chief among his followers was the portraitist **Anthony van Dyck** (1599–1641), who worked in Rubens' studio from 1618, often taking on the depiction of religious figures in his master's works that required particular sensitivity and pathos. Like Rubens, van Dyck was born in Antwerp and travelled widely in Italy, though his initial work was influenced less by the Italian artists than by Rubens himself. Eventually van Dyck developed his own distinct style and technique, establishing himself as court painter to Charles I in England, and creating portraits of a nervous elegance that would influence the genre there for the next hundred and fifty years. **Jacob Jordaens** (1593–1678) was also an Antwerp native who studied under Rubens. Although he was commissioned to complete several works left unfinished by Rubens at the time of his death, his robustly naturalistic works have an earthy – and sensuous – realism that is quite distinct in style and technique.

## The eighteenth and nineteenth centuries

Accompanying Holland's economic decline was a gradual deterioration in the quality and originality of Dutch painting. The delicacy of some of the classical seventeenth-century painters was replaced by finicky still lifes and minute studies of flowers, or finely finished portraiture and religious scenes, as in the work of **Adrian van der Werff** (1659–1722). Of the era's big names, **Gerard de Lairesse** (1640–1711) spent most of his time decorating a rash of brand new civic halls and mansions, but, like the buildings he worked on, his style and influences were French. **Jacob de Wit** (1695–1754) continued where Lairesse left off, painting burgher ceiling after ceiling in flashy style. He also benefited from a relaxation in the laws against Catholics, decorating several of their (newly-legal) churches. The period's only painter of any true renown was **Cornelis Troost** (1697–1750) who, although he didn't produce anything really original, painted competent portraits and some neat, faintly satirical pieces that have since earned him the title of "the Dutch Hogarth". Cosy interiors also continued to prove popular and the Haarlem painter **Wybrand Hendriks** (1744–1831) satisfied demand with numerous proficient examples.

**Johann Barthold Jongkind** (1819–91) was the first important artist to emerge in the nineteenth century, painting landscapes and seascapes that were to influence Monet and the early Impressionists. He spent most of his life in France and his work was exhibited in Paris with the Barbizon painters, though he owed less to them than to Van Goyen and the seventeenth-century "tonal" artists. Jongkind's work was a logical precursor to the art of the **Hague School**. Based in and around Den Haag between 1870 and 1900, this prolific group of painters tried to re-establish a characteristically Dutch national school of painting. They produced atmospheric studies of the dunes and polders around Den Haag, nature pictures that are characterized by grey, rain-filled skies, windswept seas, and silvery, flat beaches – pictures that, for some, verge on the sentimental. **J.H. Weissenbruch** (1824–1903) was a founding member, a specialist in low, flat beach scenes dotted with stranded boats. The banker-turned-artist **H.W. Mesdag** (1831–1915) did the same but with more skill than imagination, while **Jacob Maris** (1837–99), one of three artist brothers, was perhaps the most typical with his rural and sea scenes heavily covered by grey, chasing skies. His brother **Matthijs Maris** (1839–1917) was less pre-dictable, ultimately tiring of his colleagues' interest in straight observation and going to London to design windows, while the youngest brother **Willem Maris** (1844–1910), is best-known for his small, unpretentious studies of nature.

**Anton Mauve** (1838–88) is better-known, an exponent of soft, pastel land-scapes and an early teacher of Van Gogh. Profoundly influenced by the French Barbizon painters – Corot, Millet, *et al* – he went to Hilversum in 1885 to set up his own group, which became known as the "Dutch Barbizon". **Jozef Israëls** (1826–1911) has often been likened to Millet, though it's generally agreed that he had more in common with the Impressionists, and his best pic-tures are his melancholy portraits and interiors. Lastly, **Johan Bosboom**'s (1817–91) church interiors may be said to sum up the romanticised nostalgia of the Hague School: shadowy and populated by figures in seventeenth-century dress, they seem to yearn for Holland's Golden Age.

**Vincent van Gogh** (1853–90), on the other hand, was one of the least "Dutch" of Dutch artists, and he lived out most of his relatively short painting career in France. After countless studies of peasant life in his native Noord-Brabant – studies which culminated in the sombre *Potato Eaters* – he went to live in Paris with his art-dealer brother Theo. There, under the influence of the Impressionists, he lightened his palette, following the pointillist work of Seurat and "trying to render intense colour and not a grey harmony". Two years later he went south to Arles, the "land of blue tones and gay colours", and, struck by the brilliance of Mediterranean light, his characteristic style began to develop. A disastrous attempt to live with Gauguin, and the much-publicized episode when he cut off part of his ear and presented it to a local prostitute, led even-tually to his committal in an asylum at St-Rémy. Here he produced some of his most famous, and most expressionistic, canvases – strongly coloured and with the paint thickly, almost frantically, applied. Now one of the world's most popular, and popularized, painters, Van Gogh has his own museum in Amsterdam.

Like Van Gogh, **Jan Toorop** (1858–1928) went through multiple artistic changes, though he did not need to travel to do so; he radically adapted his technique from a fairly conventional pointillism through a tired Expressionism to Symbolism with an Art-Nouveau feel. Roughly contemporary, **George Hendrik Breitner** (1857–1923) was a better painter, and one who refined his style rather than changed it. His snapshot-like impressions of his beloved Amsterdam figure among his best work and offered a promising start to the new century.

## The twentieth century

Each of the major modern art movements has had its followers in the Netherlands and each has been diluted or altered according to local taste. Of many lesser names, **Jan Sluyters** (1881–1957) stands out as the Dutch pioneer of Cubism, but this is small beer when compared with the one specifically Dutch movement – **De Stijl** (The Style). **Piet Mondriaan** (1872–1944) was De Stijl's leading figure, developing the realism he had learned from the Hague School painters – via Cubism, which he criticized for being too cowardly to depart totally from representation – into a complete abstraction of form which he called Neo-Plasticism. He was something of a mystic, and this was to some extent responsible for the direction that De Stijl, and his paintings, took: canvases painted with grids of lines and blocks made up of the three primary colours and white, black and grey. Mondriaan believed this freed the work of art from the vagaries of personal perception, making it possible to obtain what he called "a true vision of reality".

De Stijl took other forms too: there was a magazine of the same name, and the movement introduced new concepts into every aspect of design, from painting to interior design and architecture. But in all these media, lines were kept simple, colours bold and clear. **Theo van Doesburg** (1883–1931) was a De Stijl co-founder and major theorist. His work is similar to Mondriaan's except for the noticeable absence of thick, black borders and the diagonals that he introduced into his work, calling his paintings "contra-compositions" – which, he said, were both more dynamic and more in touch with twentieth-century life. **Bart van der Leck** (1876–1958) was the third member of the circle, identifiable by white canvases covered by seemingly randomly placed interlocking coloured triangles. Mondriaan split with De Stijl in 1925, going on to attain new artistic extremes of clarity and soberness before moving to New York in the 1940s and producing atypically exuberant works such as *Victory Boogie Woogie* – named for the artist's love of jazz and now exhibited at Den Haag's Gemeentemuseum.

During and after De Stijl, a number of other movements flourished, though their impact was not so great and their influence largely confined to the Netherlands. The Expressionist **Bergen School** was probably the most localized, its best-known exponent **Charley Toorop** (1891–1955), daughter of Jan, developing a distinctively glaring but strangely sensitive realism. **De Ploeg** (The Plough), centred in Groningen, was headed by **Jan Wiegers** (1893–1959) and influenced by Kirchner and the German Expressionists; the group's artists set out to capture the uninviting landscapes around their native town, and produced violently coloured canvases that hark back to Van Gogh. Another group, known as the **Magic Realists**, surfaced in the 1930s, painting quasi-surrealistic scenes that, according to their leading light, **Carel Willink** (1900–83), revealed "a world stranger and more dreadful in its haughty impenetrability than the most terrifying nightmare".

Postwar Dutch art began with **CoBrA**: a loose grouping of like-minded painters from Denmark, Belgium and the Netherlands, whose name derives from the initial letters of their respective capital cities. Their first exhibition at Amsterdam's Stedelijk Museum in 1949 provoked a huge uproar, at the centre of which was **Karel Appel** (b.1921), whose brutal Abstract Expressionist pieces, plastered with paint inches thick, were, he maintained, necessary for the era – indeed, inevitable reflections of it. "I paint like a barbarian in a barbarous age," he claimed. In the graphic arts the most famous twentieth-century Dutch figure was **Maurits Cornelis Escher** (1898–1972), whose Surrealistic illusions and allusions were underpinned by his fascination with mathematics.

As for today, there's as vibrant an art scene as there ever was, with all the major cities possessing at least a couple of art galleries that feature regular exhibitions of contemporary art. Among contemporary Dutch artists, look out for the abstract work of **Edgar Fernhout** and **Ad Dekkers**, the reliefs of **Jan Schoonhoven**, the multimedia productions of **Jan Dibbets**, the glowering realism of **Marlene Dumas**, the imprecisely coloured geometric designs of **Rob van Koningsbruggen**, the smeary expressionism of **Toon Verhoef**, and the exuberant figures of **Rene Daniels** – to name just a few of the more important figures.

---

### Dutch galleries: a hit list

In **Amsterdam**, the Rijksmuseum (see p.99) gives a complete overview of Dutch art up to the end of the nineteenth century, in particular the work of Rembrandt, Hals, and the major artists of the Golden Age, while the Van Gogh Museum (see p.101) has the world's most comprehensive collection of van Goghs. In **Haarlem**, the Frans Hals Museum (see p.134) holds some of the best work of Hals and the Haarlem School, whilst **Leiden**'s Stedelijk Museum de Lakenhal (see p.170) weighs in with a healthy sample of lesser-known sixteenth- and seventeenth-century Dutch painters, featuring the likes of Jan Lievens, Gerrit Dou and Lucas van Leyden. In **Utrecht**, the Centraal (see p.210) has paintings by van Scorel and the Utrecht School, and the Catharijne Convent Museum (see p.210) boasts an excellent collection of works by Flemish artists and by Hals and Rembrandt.

**Den Haag**'s Gemeentemuseum (see p.183) owns the country's largest set of Mondrians, while the outstanding Mauritshuis (see p.177) exhibits the work of all the major painters of the Golden Age, especially Rembrandt and Vermeer. In **Rotterdam**, the Boijmans-Van Beuningen (see p.196) has a weighty stock of Flemish primitives and surrealists, as well as works by Rembrandt and other seventeenth-century artists, and in nearby **Dordrecht**, the Dordrechts Museum (see p.205) offers an assortment of seventeenth-century paintings that includes work by Aelbert Cuyp, and later canvases by the Hague School and Breitner. In the east of the country, the Rijksmuseum Kröller-Müller (see p.295), just outside **Arnhem**, is probably the country's finest modern art collection, and has a superb collection of van Goghs; a little further east, **Enschede**'s Rijksmuseum Twente (see p.279) has quality works from the Golden Age to the twentieth century. In the north, **Groningen**'s outstanding Groninger Museum (see p.295) – as striking for its innovative architecture as its art – holds several examples of the Hague School, a fine survey of the local *De Ploeg* expressionists and a broad range of contemporary works in all media.

# Books

M
ost of the following books should be readily available in bookshops or online, though you may have a little more difficulty tracking down those few titles we mention which are currently out of print, signified o/p. Titles marked with the ▣ symbol are especially recommended.

## Art and architecture

**Svetlana Alpers** *Rembrandt's Enterprise*. Intriguing 1988 study of Rembrandt, positing the theory – in line with findings of the Leiden-based Rembrandt Research Project – that many previously accepted Rembrandt paintings are not his at all, but merely the products of his studio. Bad news if you own one.

⭐ **Anthony Bailey** *A View of Delft*. Concise, startlingly well-researched book on Vermeer complete with an accurate and well-considered exploration of his milieu.

⭐ **R.H. Fuchs** *Dutch Painting*. As complete an introduction to the subject – from Flemish origins to the present day – as you could wish for, in just a couple of hundred pages.

**R.H. Fuchs et al** *Flemish and Dutch Painting (from Van Gogh, Ensor, Magritte and Mondrian to Contemporary)*. Excellent, lucid account giving an overview of the development of Flemish and Dutch painting.

**Walter S. Gibson** *Bosch* and *Bruegel*. Two wonderfully illustrated Thames & Hudson titles on these most famous allegorical painters. The former contains everything you wanted to know about Hieronymus Bosch, his paintings and his late fifteenth-century milieu, while the latter takes a detailed look at Pieter Bruegel the Elder's art, with nine well-argued chapters investigating its various components.

**H.L.C. Jaffe** *De Stijl: Visions of Utopia*. A good, informed introduction to the twentieth-century movement and its philosophical and social influences. Well illustrated too.

**Melissa McQuillan** *Van Gogh*. Extensive, in-depth look at Vincent's paintings, as well as his life and times. Superbly researched and illustrated; published by Thames & Hudson.

**Simon Schama** *Rembrandt's Eyes*. Published in 1999, this erudite work received good reviews, but it's very long – and often very long-winded.

**Irving Stone** *Lust for Life: the Life of Vincent van Gogh*. Everything you ever wanted to know about Van Gogh in a pop genius-is-pain biography.

**Dirk de Vos** *Rogier van der Weyden*. One of the most talented and influential of the Flemish Primitives, Weyden was the official city painter to Brussels in the middle of the fifteenth century. This 400-page volume details everything known about him and carries illustrations of all his works – but then no more than you would expect from such an expensive tome.

⭐ **Mariet Westerman** *The Art of the Dutch Republic 1585–1718*. This excellently written, well illustrated and enthralling book tackles its subject thematically, from the marketing of works to an exploration of Dutch ideologies. Highly recommended.

**Christopher White** *Rembrandt.*
This is the most widely available
– and wide-ranging – study of the
painter and his work. Well illustrated,
as you would expect of a Thames &
Hudson publication, plus a wonderfully incisive and extremely detailed
commentary. Also by White is *Peter
Paul Rubens: Man and Artist* (o/p),
a beautifully illustrated introduction to both Rubens' work and
social milieu.

## Literature

**Tracey Chevalier** *Girl with a Pearl
Earring.* Chevalier's book is a fanciful
piece of fiction, building a story
around the subject of one of
Vermeer's most enigmatic paintings.
It's an absorbing read, if a tad too
detailed and slow-moving for some
tastes, and it paints a convincing picture of seventeenth-century Delft
and Holland, exploring its social
structures and values. Has proved a
popular novel.

**Rudi van Dantzig** *For a Lost
Soldier.* Honest and convincing tale,
largely autobiographical, that gives
an insight into the confusion and
loneliness of the approximately
50,000 Dutch children evacuated to
foster families during the war. The
novel's leading character is Jeroen, an
11-year-old boy from Amsterdam
who is sent away to live with a family in Friesland. During the
Liberation celebrations, he meets an
American soldier, Walt, with whom
he has a brief sexual encounter; Walt
disappears a few days later. One of
the Netherlands' most famous chore-
ographers, Van Dantzig was the artistic director of the Dutch National
Ballet until 1991. This was his debut
novel.

**Anne Frank** *The Diary of a Young
Girl.* Lucid and moving, the most
revealing book you can read on the
plight of Amsterdam's Jews during
the war years.

**Nicolas Freeling** *Love in
Amsterdam; Dwarf Kingdom; A
City Solitary; Strike Out Where Not
Applicable; A Long Silence.* Freeling
writes detective novels, and his most
famous creation is the rebel cop Van
der Valk. These are light, carefully
crafted tales, with just the right
amount of twists to make them classic cops 'n' robbers reading – and
with good Amsterdam (and Dutch)
locations. London-born, Freeling
hasn't actually been resident in
Amsterdam for years, but he still
evokes Amsterdam (and
Amsterdammers) as well as any
writer ever has, subtly and unsenti-
mentally using the city and its people as a vivid backdrop to his fast-
moving action.

**Etty Hillesum** *An Interrupted Life:
the Diaries and Letters of Etty
Hillesum, 1941–43.* The Germans
transported Hillesum, a young Jewish
woman, from her home in
Amsterdam to Auschwitz, where she
died. As with Anne Frank's more
famous journal, penetratingly written – though on the whole much
less readable.

**Arthur Japin** *The Two Hearts of
Kwasi Boachi.* Inventive recreation of a true story in which the
eponymous Ashanti prince was dispatched to the court of King
William of the Netherlands in 1837.
Kwasi and his companion Kwame
were ostensibly sent to Den Haag to
further their education, but there
was a strong colonial sub-text.
Superb descriptions of Ashanti-land
in its pre-colonial pomp.

**Sylvie Matton** *Rembrandt's Whore.*
Taking its cue from Chevalier's *Girl
with a Pearl Earring* (see above), this

slim novel tries hard to conjure Rembrandt's life and times with some success. Matton certainly knows her Rembrandt onions – she worked for two years on a film of his life.

**Margo Minco** *The Fall; An Empty House; The Glass Bridge; Bitter Herbs: Vivid Memories of a Fugitive Jewish girl in Nazi-occupied Holland.* One of the best-known of Amsterdam's modern writers, the prolific Margo Minco has written widely and well about the city's Jewish community, particularly during the German occupation. She herself was a Holocaust survivor, spending several years in hiding – unlike the rest of her family, who were dispatched to concentration camps where they all died. One of Minco's favourite hideaways was Kloveniersburgwal 49, which served as a safe house for various Dutch artists and later as the inspiration for *An Empty House.* Published in 1991, *Bitter Herbs* is her testament.

**Harry Mulisch** *The Assault.* Set part in Haarlem, part in Amsterdam, this novel traces the story of a young boy who loses his family in a reprisal-raid by the Nazis. A powerful tale, made into an excellent and effective film. Also, *The Discovery of Heaven,* a gripping yarn of adventure and happenstance, and 2002's offering, *The Procedure,* featuring a modern-day Dutch scientist investigating strange goings-on in sixteenth-century Prague.

**Multatuli** *Max Havelaar, Or, The Coffee Auctions of the Dutch Trading Company.* Classic nineteenth-century Dutch satire of colonial life in the East Indies. Eloquent and intermittently amusing. If you have Dutch friends, they should be impressed (dumbstruck) if you have read it, not least since it's 352 pages long.

**Deborah Moggach** *Tulip Fever.* At first Deborah Moggach's novel seems no more than an attempt to build a story out of her favourite domestic

Dutch interiors, genre scenes and still life paintings. But ultimately the story is a basic one – of lust, greed, mistaken identity, and tragedy. The Golden Age backdrop is well realized, but almost incidental.

**Cees Nooteboom** *Rituals.* Cees Nooteboom is one of the country's best-known writers. He published his first novel in 1955, but only really came to public attention after the publication of his third novel, *Rituals,* in 1980. The central theme of all his work is the phenomenon of time: *Rituals* in particular is about the passing of time and the different ways of controlling the process. Inni Wintrop, the main character, is an outsider, a well-heeled, antique-dabbling "dilettante" as he describes himself. The book is almost entirely set in Amsterdam, and although it describes the inner life of Inni himself, it also paints a strong picture of the decaying city. Bleak but absorbing. Born in Den Haag in 1933, Nooteboom lives by turn in Germany, Spain and the Netherlands.

⭐ **Janwillem van de Wetering** *Hard Rain; Corpse on the Dyke; Outsider in Amsterdam; Amsterdam Cops – Collected Stories.* Off-beat detective tales set in Amsterdam and the provinces. Humane, quirky and humorous, Wetering's novels have inventive plots and feature unusual characters in interesting locations.

**David Veronese** *Jana.* A hip thriller set in the underworld of Amsterdam and London.

**Jan Wolkers** *Turkish Delight.* Wolkers is one of the Netherlands' best-known artists and writers, and this is one of his early novels, a close examination of the relationship between a bitter, working-class sculptor and his young, middle-class wife. A compelling work, at times misogynistic and even offensive, by a writer who seeks reaction above all. If you like it, try Wolkers' *Horrible Tango.*

# History and politics

**J.C.H. Blom (ed.)** *History of the Low Countries*. Books on Dutch history are fairly thin on the ground, so this heavyweight volume fills a few gaps, though it's hardly sun-lounge reading. A series of historians weigh in with their specialities, from Roman times onwards. Taken as a whole, its forte is in picking out those cultural, political and economic themes that give the region its distinctive character.

**Mike Dash** *Tulipomania*. An examination of the introduction of the tulip into the Low Countries at the height of the Golden Age, and the extraordinarily inflated and speculative market that ensued. There's a lot of padding and scene-setting, but it's an engaging enough read, and has nice detail on seventeenth-century Amsterdam, Leiden and Haarlem.

★ **Pieter Geyl** *The Revolt of The Netherlands 1555–1609* and *The Netherlands in the Seventeenth Century 1609–1648*. Geyl presents a concise account of the Netherlands during its formative years, chronicling the uprising against the Spanish and the formation of the United Provinces. Without doubt the definitive book on the period.

**Christopher Hibbert** *Cities and Civilisation*. Includes a diverting chapter on Amsterdam in the age of Rembrandt. Hibbert, one of the UK's best historians, is always a pleasure to read.

★ **Carol Ann Lee** *Roses from the Earth: the Biography of Anne Frank*. Amongst a spate of recent publications trawling through and over the life of the young Jewish diarist, this is probably the best, written in a straightforward and insightful manner without sentimentality. Working the same mine is the same author's *The Hidden Life of Otto Frank* – clear, lucid and equally as interesting.

**Geert Mak** *Amsterdam: A Brief Life of the City*. Published in 2001, this is a readable and evocative social history of Amsterdam written by a leading Dutch journalist. It's light and accessible enough to read from cover to cover, but its index of places makes it useful to dip into as a supplement to this guide, too.

★ **Geoffrey Parker** *The Dutch Revolt*. Compelling account of the struggle between the Netherlands and Spain. Quite the best thing you can read on the period. Also *The Army of Flanders and the Spanish Road 1567–1659*. The title may sound academic, but this book gives a fascinating insight into the Habsburg army which occupied the Low Countries for well over a hundred years – how it functioned, was fed and moved from Spain to the Low Countries along the so-called Spanish Road.

**John Leslie Price** *Culture and Society in the Dutch Republic in the 17th Century*. An accurate, intelligent account of the Golden Age.

**Simon Schama** *The Embarrassment of Riches: An Interpretation of Dutch Culture in the Golden Age*. Long before his reinvention on British TV, Schama had a reputation as a specialist in Dutch history and this chunky volume draws on a huge variety of archive sources. Also by Schama, *Patriots and Liberators: Revolution in the Netherlands 1780–1813* focuses on one of the less familiar periods of Dutch history and is particularly good on the Batavian Republic set up in the Netherlands under French auspices. Both are heavyweight tomes and leftists might well find Schama too reactionary by half.

**Andrew Wheatcroft** *The Habsburgs*. Excellent and well-researched trawl through the family's history, from eleventh-century beginnings to its eclipse at the end of World War I.

# Travel and general

**A. Burton et al** *Smokers Guide to Amsterdam.* Exactly what it says – a dope-smokers' guide to the city with no leaf unturned.

**Richard Huijing (ed. & trans.),** *The Dedalus Book of Dutch Fantasy.* A fun and artfully selected collection of stories that contains contributions from some of the greats of Dutch literature, including a number whose work does not, as yet, appear in translation anywhere else.

**Simon Kuper** *Ajax, the Dutch, the War: Football in Europe in the Second World War.* Great idea, but a tad cumbersome in its execution. Some intriguing details.

**Sir William Temple** *Observations upon the United Provinces of The Netherlands.* An entertaining and evocative account of the country written by a seventeenth-century English diplomat.

**Tim Webb** *Good Beer Guide to Belgium & Holland.* Detailed and enthusiastic guide to the best bars, beers and breweries, including a strong showing for Amsterdam. A good read, and extremely well informed to boot. Undoubtedly the best book on its subject on the market. Published in 2002.

**David Winner** *Brilliant Orange – The Neurotic Genius of Dutch Football.* Great title, great cover and great idea – zeroing in on the fine Dutch footballers of the 1960s and 1970s, including super-talented Johan Cruyff, and the way they – and their style of play – reflect Dutch culture and history. The problem is that sometimes the inferences and conclusions seem too obtuse, or at least unconvincing. Seven out of ten.

★ **Manfred Wolf (ed.)** *Amsterdam: A Traveler's Literary Companion.* Published by an independent American press, Whereabout Press, these anthologies aim to get to the heart of the modern cities they cover, and this well-chosen mixture of travel pieces, short fiction and reportage does exactly that, uncovering a low-life aspect to the city of Amsterdam that exists beyond the tourist brochures. A high-quality and evocative selection, and often the only chance you'll get to read some of this material in translation.

# Language

# Language

# Dutch

I n the Netherlands, the native language is Dutch. Most Dutch-speakers, however, particularly in the bigger towns and the tourist industry, speak English to varying degrees of excellence. The Dutch have a seemingly innate talent for languages, and your attempts at speaking theirs may be met with some bewilderment – though this can have as much to do with your pronunciation (Dutch is very difficult to get right) as their surprise that you're making an effort.

Dutch is a Germanic language – the word is a corruption of "Deutsche", a label inaccurately given by English sailors in the seventeenth century. Though the Dutch are at pains to stress the differences between the two languages, if you know any German you'll spot many similarities. As noted above, English is very widely spoken, but in smaller towns and in the countryside, where things aren't quite as cosmopolitan, the following words and phrases of Dutch should be the most you'll need to get by. We've also included a basic food and drink glossary, though menus are nearly always multilingual and where they aren't, ask and one will almost invariably appear.

As for **phrasebooks**, the *Rough Guide to Dutch* is pocket-sized, and has a good dictionary section (English–Dutch and Dutch–English) as well as a menu reader; it also provides a useful introduction to grammar and pronunciation.

# Pronunciation

Dutch is **pronounced** much the same as English. However, there are a few Dutch sounds that don't exist in English, which can be difficult to get right without practice.

## Consonants

Double-consonant combinations generally keep their separate sounds in Flemish: **kn**, for example, is never like the English "knight". Note also the following consonants and consonant combinations:

**v** is like an English f
**w** is like an English v
**j** is an English y
**ch** and **g** indicate a throaty sound, as at the end of the Scottish word loch. The Dutch word for canal – *gracht* – is especially tricky, since it has two of these sounds – it

comes out along the lines of *khrakht*. A common word for hello is *Dag!* – pronounced like *daakh*

**ng** as in bri**ng**
**nj** as in o**ni**on
**y** is not a consonant, but another way of writing **ij**

## Vowels and diphthongs

A good rule of thumb is that doubling the letter lengthens the vowel sound.

**a** is like the English apple

**aa** like cart

**e** like let

**ee** like late

**o** as in pop

**oo** in pope

**u** is like the French tu if preceded by a consonant; it's like wood if followed by a consonant

**uu** is the French tu

**au** and **ou** like how

**ei** and **ij** as in fine, though this varies strongly from region to region; sometimes it can sound more like lane

**oe** as in soon

**eu** is like the diphthong in the French leur

**ui** is the hardest Dutch diphthong of all, pronounced like how but much further forward in the mouth, with lips pursed (as if to say "oo").

# Words and phrases

## The basics

| | | | |
|---|---|---|---|
| yes | **ja** | Do you speak English? | **Spreekt u Engels?** |
| no | **nee** | I don't understand | **Ik begrijp het niet** |
| please | **alstublieft** | women/men | **vrouwen/mannen** |
| thank you | **dank u** or **bedankt** | children | **kinderen** |
| hello | **hallo** or **dag** | men's/women's toilets | **heren/dames** |
| good morning | **goedemorgen** | I want... | **Ik wil...** |
| good afternoon | **goedemiddag** | I don't want to... | **Ik wil niet...** (+verb) |
| good evening | **goedenavond** | I don't want any... | **Ik wil geen...** (+noun) |
| goodbye | **tot ziens** | | |
| see you later | **tot straks** | How much is...? | **Wat kost...?** |

## Travel and shopping

| | | | |
|---|---|---|---|
| post office | **postkantoor** | railway platform | **spoor** or **perron** |
| stamp(s) | **postzegel(s)** | ticket office | **loket** |
| money exchange | **geldwisselkantoor** | here/there | **hier/daar** |
| cash desk | **kassa** | good/bad | **goed/slecht** |
| How do I get to...? | **Hoe kom ik in...?** | big/small | **groot/klein** |
| Where is...? | **Waar is...?** | open/closed | **open/gesloten** |
| How far is it to...? | **Hoe ver is het naar...?** | push/pull | **duwen/trekken** |
| | | new/old | **nieuw/oud** |
| When? | **Wanneer?** | cheap/expensive | **goedkoop/duur** |
| far/near | **ver/dichtbij** | hot/cold | **heet** or **warm/koud** |
| left/right | **links/rechts** | with/without | **met/zonder** |
| straight ahead | **rechtuit gaan** | | |

# Useful cycling terms

| | | | |
|---|---|---|---|
| tyre | **band** | pedal | **trapper** |
| puncture | **lek** | pump | **pomp** |
| brake | **rem** | handlebars | **stuur** |
| chain | **ketting** | broken | **kapot** |
| wheel | **wiel** | | |

# Numbers

| | | | |
|---|---|---|---|
| 0 | **nul** | 19 | **negentien** |
| 1 | **een** | 20 | **twintig** |
| 2 | **twee** | 21 | **een en twintig** |
| 3 | **drie** | 22 | **twee en twintig** |
| 4 | **vier** | 30 | **dertig** |
| 5 | **vijf** | 40 | **veertig** |
| 6 | **zes** | 50 | **vijftig** |
| 7 | **zeven** | 60 | **zestig** |
| 8 | **acht** | 70 | **zeventig** |
| 9 | **negen** | 80 | **tachtig** |
| 10 | **tien** | 90 | **negentig** |
| 11 | **elf** | 100 | **honderd** |
| 12 | **twaalf** | 101 | **honderd een** |
| 13 | **dertien** | 200 | **twee honderd** |
| 14 | **veertien** | 201 | **twee honderd een** |
| 15 | **vijftien** | 500 | **vijf honderd** |
| 16 | **zestien** | 525 | **vijf honderd vijf en twintig** |
| 17 | **zeventien** | | |
| 18 | **achttien** | 1000 | **duizend** |

# Days and times

| | | | |
|---|---|---|---|
| Sunday | **Zondag** | week | **week** |
| Monday | **Maandag** | day | **dag** |
| Tuesday | **Dinsdag** | hour | **uur** |
| Wednesday | **Woensdag** | minute | **minuut** |
| Thursday | **Donderdag** | What time is it? | **Hoe laat is het?** |
| Friday | **Vrijdag** | It's... | **Het is...** |
| Saturday | **Zaterdag** | 3.00 | **drie uur** |
| yesterday | **gisteren** | 3.05 | **vijf over drie** |
| today | **vandaag** | 3.10 | **tien over drie** |
| tomorrow | **morgen** | 3.15 | **kwart over drie** |
| tomorrow morning | **morgenochtend** | 3.20 | **tien voor half vier** |
| year | **jaar** | 3.25 | **vijf voor half vier** |
| month | **maand** | 3.30 | **half vier** |

| | | | |
|---|---|---|---|
| 3.35 | vijf over half vier | 8am | acht uur 's ochtends |
| 3.40 | tien over half vier | 1pm | een uur 's middags |
| 3.45 | kwart voor vier | 8pm | acht uur 's avonds |
| 3.50 | tien voor vier | 1am | een uur 's nachts |
| 3.55 | vijf voor vier | | |

# A Dutch menu reader

## Basic terms

| | | | |
|---|---|---|---|
| boter | butter | peper | pepper |
| boterham/broodje | sandwich/roll | pindakaas | peanut butter |
| brood | bread | sla/salade | salad |
| dranken | drinks | smeerkaas | cheese spread |
| eieren | eggs | stokbrood | french bread |
| gerst | barley | suiker | sugar |
| groenten | vegetables | vis | fish |
| honing | honey | vlees | meat |
| hoofdgerechten | main courses | voorgerechten | starters/hors d'oeuvres |
| kaas | cheese | vruchten | fruit |
| koud | cold | warm | hot |
| nagerechten | desserts | zout | salt |

## Starters and snacks

| | | | |
|---|---|---|---|
| erwtensoep/snert | thick pea soup with bacon or sausage | patates/frites | chips/french fries |
| | | soep | soup |
| huzarensalade | potato salad with pickles | uitsmijter | ham or cheese with eggs on bread |
| koffietafel | light midday meal of cold meats, cheese, bread, and perhaps soup | | |

## Meat and poultry

| | | | |
|---|---|---|---|
| biefstuk (hollandse) | steak | gehakt | minced meat |
| biefstuk (duitse) | hamburger | ham | ham |
| eend | duck | kalfsvlees | veal |
| fricandeau | roast pork | kalkoen | turkey |
| fricandel | frankfurter-like sausage | karbonade | a chop |
| | | kip | chicken |

| kroket | spiced veal or beef in hash, coated in breadcrumbs | **lever** | liver |
| | | **rookvlees** | smoked beef |
| | | **spek** | bacon |
| **lamsvlees** | lamb | **worst** | sausages |

## Fish

| **forel** | trout | **oesters** | oysters |
| **garnalen** | prawns | **paling** | eel |
| **haring** | herring | **schelvis** | haddock |
| **haringsalade** | herring salad | **schol** | plaice |
| **kabeljauw** | cod | **tong** | sole |
| **makreel** | mackerel | **zalm** | salmon |
| **mosselen** | mussels | | |

## Cooking terms

| **belegd** | filled or topped, as in **belegde broodjes** (bread rolls topped with cheese, etc) | **gekookt** | boiled |
| | | **geraspt** | grated |
| | | **gerookt** | smoked |
| | | **gestoofd** | stewed |
| **doorbakken** | well-done | **half doorbakken** | medium-done |
| **gebakken** | fried or baked | **Hollandse saus** | hollandaise sauce |
| **gebraden** | roast | **rood** | rare |
| **gegrild** | grilled | | |

## Vegetables

| **aardappelen** | potatoes | **rijst** | rice |
| **bloemkool** | cauliflower | **sla** | salad, lettuce |
| **bonen** | beans | **stampot andijvie** | mashed potato and endive |
| **champignons** | mushrooms | | |
| **erwten** | peas | **stampot boerenkool** | mashed potato and cabbage |
| **hutspot** | mashed potatoes and carrots | | |
| | | **uien** | onions |
| **knoflook** | garlic | **wortelen** | carrots |
| **komkommer** | cucumber | **zuurkool** | sauerkraut |
| **prei** | leek | | |

# Indonesian dishes and terms

| | | | |
|---|---|---|---|
| ajam | chicken | nasi rames | a **rijsttafel** on a single plate |
| bami | noodles with meat/ chicken and vegetables | pedis | hot and spicy |
| | | pisang | banana |
| daging | beef | rijsttafel | collection of different spicy dishes served with plain rice |
| gado gado | vegetables in peanut sauce | | |
| goreng | fried | sambal | hot, chilli-based sauce |
| ikan | fish | | |
| katjang | peanut | satesaus | peanut sauce to accompany meat grilled on skewers |
| kroepoek | prawn crackers | | |
| loempia | spring rolls | | |
| nasi | rice | seroendeng | spicy shredded and fried coconut |
| nasi goreng | fried rice with meat/chicken and vegetables | | |
| | | tauge | beansprouts |

# Sweets and desserts

| | | | |
|---|---|---|---|
| appelgebak | apple tart or cake | pannekoeken | pancakes |
| drop | Dutch liquorice, available in **zoet** (sweet) or **zout** (salted) varieties – the latter an acquired taste | pepernoten | Dutch ginger nuts |
| | | poffertjes | small pancakes, fritters |
| | | (slag)room | (whipped) cream |
| | | speculaas | spice and honey-flavoured biscuit |
| gebak | pastry | stroopwafels | waffles |
| ijs | ice cream | taai-taai | Dutch honey cake |
| koekjes | biscuits | vla | custard |
| oliebollen | doughnuts | | |

# Fruits and nuts

| | | | |
|---|---|---|---|
| aardbei | strawberry | hazelnoot | hazelnut |
| amandel | almond | kers | cherry |
| appel | apple | kokosnoot | coconut |
| appelmoes | apple purée | peer | pear |
| citroen | lemon | perzik | peach |
| druiven | grape | pinda | peanut |
| framboos | raspberry | pruim | plum/prune |

# Drinks

| | | | |
|---|---|---|---|
| anijsmelk | aniseed-flavoured warm milk | melk | milk |
| | | met ijs | with ice |
| appelsap | apple juice | met slagroom | with whipped cream |
| bessenjenever | blackcurrant gin | pils | Dutch beer |
| chocomel | chocolate milk | proost! | cheers! |
| citroenjenever | lemon gin | sinaasappelsap | orange juice |
| droog | dry | thee | tea |
| frisdranken | soft drinks | tomatensap | tomato juice |
| jenever | Dutch gin | vruchtensap | fruit juice |
| karnemelk | buttermilk | wijn | wine |
| koffie | coffee | (wit/rood/rosé) | (white/red/rosé) |
| koffie verkeerd | coffee with warm milk | vieux | Dutch brandy |
| kopstoot | beer with a jenever chaser | zoet | sweet |

# Glossary

## Dutch terms

**Abdij** Abbey

**Amsterdammertje** Phallic-shaped bollard placed in rows alongside Amsterdam streets to keep drivers off pavements and out of the canals.

**A.U.B.** *Alstublieft* – "please" (also shown as S.V.P. from French).

**BG** *Begane grond* – "ground floor" ("basement" is K for *kelder*).

**Begijnhof** Similar to a hofje but occupied by Catholic women (*begijns*) who led semi-religious lives without taking full vows.

**Beiaard** Carillon chimes

**Belfort** Belfry

**Beurs** Stock exchange

**Botermarkt** Butter market

**Brug** Bridge

**BTW** *Belasting Toegevoegde Waarde* – VAT (sales tax).

**Burgher** Member of the upper or mercantile classes of a town, usually with certain civic powers.

**Fietspad** Bicycle path

**Gasthuis** Hospice for the sick or infirm

**Geen toegang** No entry

**Gemeente** Municipal, as in *Gemeentehuis* (town hall)

**Gerechtshof** Law Courts

**Gesloten** Closed

**Gevel** Gable: decoration on narrow-fronted canal houses.

**Gezellig** A hard term to translate – something like "cosy", "comfortable" and "inviting" in one – which is often said to lie at the heart of the Dutch psyche. A long, relaxed meal in a favourite restaurant with friends is *gezellig*; grabbing a quick snack is not. The best brown cafés ooze *gezelligheid;* a shopping mall on a Saturday afternoon definitely doesn't.

**Gilde** Guild

**Gracht** Canal

**Groentenmarkt** Vegetable market

**Grote Kerk** Literally "big church" – the main church of a town or village.

**Hal** Hall

**Hijsbalk** Pulley beam, often decorated, fixed to the top of a gable to lift goods, furniture etc. Essential in canal houses whose staircases were narrow and steep, *hijsbalken* are still very much in use today.

**Hof** Courtyard

**Hofje** Almshouse, usually for elderly women who could look after themselves but needed small charities such as food and fuel; usually a number of buildings centred around a small, enclosed courtyard.

**Huis** House

**Ingang** Entrance

**Jeugdherberg** Youth hostel

**Kasteel** Castle

**Kerk** Church

**Koning** King

**Koningin** Queen

**Koninklijk** Royal

**Kunst** Art

**Kursaal** Casino

**Lakenhal** Cloth hall: the building in medieval weaving towns where cloth would be weighed, graded and sold.

**Let Op!** Attention!

**Luchthaven** Airport

**Markt** Central town square and the heart of most Dutch communities, normally still the site of weekly markets.

**Mokum** A Yiddish word meaning "city", originally used by the Jewish community to indicate Amsterdam; now in general usage as a nickname for the city.

**Molen** Windmill

**Nederland** The Netherlands

**Nederlands** Dutch

**Noord** North

**Ommegang** Procession

**Oost** East

**Paleis** Palace

**Plein** A square or open space

Polder An area of land reclaimed from the sea

Poort Gate

Postbus Post office box

Raadhuis Town hall

Randstad Literally "rim-town", this refers to the urban conurbation that makes up much of Noord- and Zuid-Holland, stretching from Amsterdam in the north to Rotterdam and Dordrecht in the south.

Rijk State

Schepenzaal Alderman's Hall

Schone kunsten Fine arts

Schouwburg Theatre

Sierkunst Decorative arts

Spionnetje Small mirror on a canal house enabling the occupant to see who is at the door without descending the stairs.

Spoor Train station platform

Stadhuis The most common word for a town hall.

Stedelijk Civic, municipal

Steeg Alley

Steen Stone

Stichting Institute or foundation.

Straat Street

T/M *Tot en met* – "up to and including".

Toegang Entrance

Toren Tower

Tuin Garden

Uitgang Exit

V.A. *Vanaf* – "from".

V.S. *Verenigde Staten* – "United States".

Vleeshuis Meat market

Volkskunde Folklore

VVV Tourist information office

Waag Old public weighing-house, a common feature of most towns.

Weg Way

West West

Wijk District (of a city)

Z.O.Z. Please turn over (page, leaflet etc)

Zuid South

## Architectural terms

Ambulatory Covered passage around the outer edge of the choir of a church.

Apse Semi-circular protrusion (usually) at the east end of a church.

Art Deco Geometrical style of art and architecture popular in the 1930s.

Art Nouveau Style of art, architecture and design based on highly stylized vegetal forms. Especially popular in the early part of the twentieth century.

Baroque The art and architecture of the Counter-Reformation, dating from around 1600 onwards. Distinguished by extreme ornateness, exuberance and by the complex but harmonious spatial arrangement of interiors.

Carillon A set of tuned church bells, either operated by an automatic mechanism or played by a keyboard.

Carolingian Dynasty founded by Charlemagne; mid-eighth to early tenth century. Also refers to art, etc, of the period.

Caryatid A sculptured (female) figure used as a column.

Chancel The eastern part of a church, often separated from the nave by a screen (see "rood screen" p.392). Contains the choir and ambulatory.

Classical Architectural style incorporating Greek and Roman elements – pillars, domes, colonnades etc – at its height in the seventeenth century and revived, as Neoclassical (see p.392), in the nineteenth century.

Clerestory Upper story of a church, incorporating the windows.

Diptych Carved or painted work on two panels. Often used as an altarpiece – both static and, more occasionally, portable.

Expressionism Artistic style popular at the beginning of the twentieth century, characterized by the exaggeration of shape or colour; often accompanied by the extensive use of symbolism.

Flamboyant Florid form of Gothic (see "Gothic" overleaf).

Fresco Wall painting – durable through application to wet plaster.

**Gable** The triangular upper portion of a wall – decorative or supporting a roof – which is a feature of many Amsterdam canal houses. Initially fairly simple, they became more ostentatious in the late seventeenth century, before turning to a more restrained classicism in the eighteenth and nineteenth centuries.

**Genre painting**. In the seventeenth century the term "genre painting" applied to everything from animal paintings and still lifes through to historical works and landscapes. In the eighteenth century, the term came only to be applied to scenes of everyday life.

**Gothic** Architectural style of the thirteenth to sixteenth centuries, characterized by pointed arches, rib vaulting, flying buttresses and a general emphasis on verticality.

**Merovingian** Dynasty ruling France and parts of the Low Countries from the sixth to the middle of the eighth century. Refers also to art, etc, of the period.

**Misericord** Ledge on choir stall on which occupant can be supported while standing; often carved with secular subjects (bottoms were not thought worthy of religious subjects).

**Nave** Main body of a church.

**Neoclassical** A style of classical architecture (see above) revived in the nineteenth century, popular in the Low Countries during and after French rule in the early nineteenth century.

**Neo-Gothic** Revived Gothic style of architecture popular between the late eighteenth and nineteenth centuries.

**Renaissance** The period of European history marking the end of the medieval period and the rise of the modern world. Defined, amongst many criteria, by an increase in classical scholarship, geographical discovery, the rise of secular values and the growth of individualism. Began in Italy in the fourteenth century. Also refers to the art and architecture of the period.

**Retable** Altarpiece.

**Rococo** Highly florid, light and graceful eighteenth-century style of architecture, painting and interior design, forming the last phase of Baroque.

**Romanesque** Early medieval architecture distinguished by squat forms, rounded arches and naive sculpture.

**Rood screen** Decorative screen separating the nave from the chancel. A rood loft is the gallery (or space) on top of it.

**Stucco** Marble-based plaster used to embellish ceilings, etc.

**Transept** Arms of a cross-shaped church, placed at ninety degrees to nave and chancel.

**Triptych** Carved or painted work on three panels. Often used as an altarpiece.

**Tympanum** Sculpted, usually recessed, panel above a door.

**Vauban** Seventeenth-century military architect, whose fortresses still stand all over Europe - including the Low Countries; hence the adjective Vaubanesque.

**Vault** An arched ceiling or roof.

# Index

## and small print

# Index

Map entries are in colour.

**INDEX**

# Twenty Years of Rough Guides

In the summer of 1981, Mark Ellingham, Rough Guides' founder, knocked out the first guide on a typewriter, with a group of friends. Mark had been travelling in Greece after university, and couldn't find a guidebook that really answered his needs.There were heavyweight cultural guides on the one hand – good on museums and classical sites but not on beaches and tavernas – and on the other hand student manuals that were so caught up with how to save money that they lost sight of the country's significance beyond its role as a place for a cool vacation. None of the guides began to address Greece as a country, with its natural and human environment, its politics and its contemporary life.

Having no urgent reason to return home, Mark decided to write his own guide. It was a guide to Greece that tried to combine some erudition and insight with a thoroughly practical approach to travellers' needs. Scrupulously researched listings of places to stay, eat and drink were matched by careful attention to detail on everything from Homer to Greek music, from classical sites to national parks and from nude beaches to monasteries. Back in London, Mark and his friends got their Rough Guide accepted by a farsighted commissioning editor at the publisher Routledge and it came out in 1982.

The Rough Guide to Greece was a student scheme that became a publishing phenomenon. The immediate success of the book – shortlisted for the Thomas Cook award – spawned a series that rapidly covered dozens of countries. The Rough Guides found a ready market among backpackers and budget travellers, but soon acquired a much broader readership that included older and less impecunious visitors. Readers relished the guides' wit and inquisitiveness as much as the enthusiastic, critical approach that acknowledges everyone wants value for money – but not at any price.

Rough Guides soon began supplementing the "rougher" information – the hostel and low-budget listings – with the kind of detail that independent-minded travellers on any budget might expect. These days, the guides – distributed worldwide by the Penguin group – include recommendations spanning the range from shoestring to luxury, and cover more than 200 destinations around the globe. Our growing team of authors, many of whom come to Rough Guides initially as outstandingly good letter-writers telling us about their travels, are spread all over the world, particularly in Europe, the USA and Australia. As well as the travel guides, Rough Guides publishes a series of dictionary phrasebooks covering two dozen major languages, an acclaimed series of music guides running the gamut from Classical to World Music, a series of music CDs in association with World Music Network, and a range of reference books on topics as diverse as the Internet, Pregnancy and Unexplained Phenomena. Visit **www.roughguides.com** to see what's cooking.

## Rough Guide credits

**Text editor**: Matthew Teller
**Managing Director**: Kevin Fitzgerald
**Series editor**: Mark Ellingham
**Editorial**: Martin Dunford, Jonathan Buckley, Kate Berens, Ann-Marie Shaw, Helena Smith, Olivia Swift, Ruth Blackmore, Geoff Howard, Claire Saunders, Gavin Thomas, Alexander Mark Rogers, Polly Thomas, Joe Staines, Richard Lim, Duncan Clark, Peter Buckley, Lucy Ratcliffe, Clifton Wilkinson, Alison Murchie, Andrew Dickson, Fran Sandham, Sally Schafer, Matthew Milton, Karoline Densley (UK); Andrew Rosenberg, Yuki Takagaki, Richard Koss, Hunter Slaton (US)
**Design & Layout**: Link Hall, Helen Prior, Julia Bovis, Katie Pringle, Rachel Holmes, Andy Turner, Dan May, Tanya Hall, John McKay, Sophie Hewat (UK); Madhulita Mohapatra,

Umesh Aggarwal, Sunil Sharma (India)
**Cartography**: Maxine Repath, Ed Wright, Katie Lloyd-Jones (UK); Manish Chandra, Rajesh Chhibber, Jai Prakash Mishra (India)
**Cover art direction**: Louise Boulton
**Picture research**: Sharon Martins, Mark Thomas
**Online**: Kelly Martinez, Anja Mutic-Blessing, Jennifer Gold, Audra Epstein, Suzanne Welles, Cree Lawson (US); Manik Chauhan, Amarjyoti Dutta, Narender Kumar (India)
**Finance**: Gary Singh
**Marketing & Publicity**: Richard Trillo, Niki Smith, David Wearn, Chloë Roberts, Demelza Dallow, Claire Southern (UK); Geoff Colquitt, David Wechsler, Megan Kennedy (US)
**Administration**: Julie Sanderson
RG India: Punita Singh

## Publishing information

This third edition published August 2003 by **Rough Guides Ltd**,
80 Strand, London WC2R 0RL.
345 Hudson St, 4th Floor,
New York, NY 10014, USA.
**Distributed by the Penguin Group**
Penguin Books Ltd,
80 Strand, London WC2R 0RL
Penguin Putnam, Inc.
375 Hudson Street, NY 10014, USA
Penguin Books Australia Ltd,
487 Maroondah Highway, PO Box 257,
Ringwood, Victoria 3134, Australia
Penguin Books Canada Ltd,
10 Alcorn Avenue, Toronto, Ontario,
Canada M4V 1E4
Penguin Books (NZ) Ltd,
182–190 Wairau Road, Auckland 10, New Zealand
Typeset in Bembo and Helvetica to an original design by Henry Iles.

Printed in Italy by LegoPrint S.p.A

416pp includes index
A catalogue record for this book is available from the British Library

ISBN 1-85828-915-7

The publishers and authors have done their best to ensure the accuracy and currency of all the information in **The Rough Guide to the Netherlands**, however, they can accept no responsibility for any loss, injury, or inconvenience sustained by any traveller as a result of information or advice contained in the guide.

1  3  5  7  9  8  6  4  2

## Help us update

We've gone to a lot of effort to ensure that the third edition of **The Rough Guide to the Netherlands** is accurate and up-to-date. However, things change – places get "discovered", opening hours are notoriously fickle, restaurants and rooms raise prices or lower standards. If you feel we've got it wrong or left something out, we'd like to know, and if you can remember the address, the price, the time, the phone number, so much the better.

We'll credit all contributions, and send a copy of the next edition (or any other Rough Guide if you prefer) for the best letters. Everyone who writes to us and isn't already a subscriber will receive a copy of our full-colour thrice-yearly newsletter. Please mark letters: "**Rough Guide Netherlands Update**" and send to: Rough Guides, 80 Strand, London WC2R 0RL, or Rough Guides, 4th Floor, 345 Hudson St, New York, NY 10014. Or send an email to **mail@roughguides.com**

Have your questions answered and tell others about your trip at
**www.roughguides.atinfopop.com**

## Acknowledgements

**Phil Lee** would like to extend special thanks to Els Wamsteeker of the Amsterdam Tourist Board; Twan van der Heijden of the Den Haag Visitors & Convention Bureau; and Monique de Groot of Rotterdam Marketing. Thanks are also due to Cass Gilbert and Laura Stone for their additions and improvements to this edition, and to my helpful and knowledgeable editor, Matthew Teller.

**Cass Gilbert and Laura Stone** thank Leo, Frank and Jackie of the Roskam family, who made us feel at home for days on end in The Hague and Zutphen – hospitality worthy of the Middle East. Also, all those at Vrienden op de Fiets: thanks for plying us with gargantuan breakfasts to keep our cycling legs going. Laura also thanks her sister Jen, for her two-handed typing in my one-armed days.

**The editor** thanks Madhulita Mohapatra for co-ordinating the pre-press team in Delhi, and for her proofreading; Umesh Aggarwal and Sunil Sharma for typesetting; Maxine Repath and Ed Wright in London, and Manish Chandra, Rajesh Chhibber and Jai Prakash Mishra in Delhi for cartography; Louise Boulton, Sharon Martins and Joe Mee for photo research; Annie Shaw for editing assistance; Karoline Densley for indexing; and Punita Singh, Helena Smith and Katie Pringle for overseeing the whole affair. Also thanks to Stanford's Map & Travel Bookshop, London, for map information.

**SMALL PRINT**

## Readers' letters

Thanks to all those who sent in their comments on the previous edition of this book (apologies if we've misspelled anyone's name):

Tim Adams; Joachim Allgaier; Birgit Arkesteijn; Maarten Bax; A.C. Berridge; Sîan Beusch; Victor Blease; Christel de Boer; David Bradford; Adrian Brown; Craig Bryant; Andy Coates; Alan & Anita Cohen; John Connolly; Adam Cook; Maire Corbett; Kelly Cross; Paul Croy; Steve Doughtery; Peter Dudley; Paul Duggan; Peter Ellis; Bill Fitton; Colin Francis; John Gordon; Carol Hakins; Steven Goldberg; Patricia Griffin; Caroline Harmer; R.E. Havard; Yvonne Jeanneret; Tushar Jiwarajka; Alan Jolly; Peter de Koning; Joep Koperdraat; Jan Lameer; Natali Lekka; Pieter van Litsenburg; Wendy Lloyd; Reinhard Maarleveld; Margot McCarthy; David L. McDonagh; Constance Messer; Abby Miller; P. Moffat; Ronald Moor; Colm Murphy; Janey Napier; Judith Orford; Jill Pearson; Valentina Pennazio; Elizabeth Plummer; Peter da Real; Nick Reeves; Eleanor Renwick; Chris Roberts; Naomi Robinson; G. Rosebery; Bobby Russell; Amy Ryan; Sumitra Sankar; Karin Selter; Ela Serdaroglu; Johanna Sleeswijk; Don & Phyllis Snyder; Jorge Solis; Douglas Smith; Keith Spanner; Dave Sutton; K. Tan; Kiran Thomas; Charles Wass; David Wilson; Andrew White; David Wilson; J. Wood; Alison Wright; James Wright.

# Photo credits

SMALL PRINT

# • TRAVEL • MUSIC • REFERENCE • PHRASEBOOKS •

Rough Guides publishes new books every month

# TRAVEL • MUSIC • REFERENCE • PHRASEBOOKS

Rough Guides music, reference & CDs